"Do you teach second-year New Testament Greek? Here you go. This is your text-book. Or are you returning to the nitty-gritty of Greek grammar, having been away for a couple of decades and hoping for more than just a basic refresher, perhaps like me? Well, Whitacre's textbook is for you too. What a thoughtfully organized, clearly written, and helpful guide to the subject matter. I not only relearned a lot when I read this book, I learned a lot too, especially how to think more intelligently and to write more effectively about the grammar of the New Testament."

— **Steven A. Hunt**
Gordon College

"Some instructors and students of intermediate Greek prefer a concise textbook that avoids complicating matters beyond the basics needed for effectively trans-lating large swaths of the New Testament. Others prefer a very comprehensive text, replete with multiple New Testament examples of every grammatical cat-egory. Whitacre steers a middle course between these two options. He does not illustrate with many biblical passages but has created an ideal reference tool for those who have had two or three semesters of Greek and want both to review what they learned and to understand further why and how things function as they do. Best used in accompaniment with an inductive study of New Testament passages, as Whitacre himself does."

— **Craig L. Blomberg**
Denver Seminary

"Whitacre's volume synthesizes decades of pedagogy and exposition with the leading edge of current Greek scholarship that is unheard of in an introductory grammar. This volume is ideal for those wanting to front-load a general under-standing of Koine Greek before diving into the weeds of morphology, making it the perfect choice for those wanting to refresh and deepen their knowledge. Whitacre achieves a masterful blend of introductory and intermediate descrip-tions designed to dovetail with his *Using and Enjoying Biblical Greek*."

— **Steven E. Runge**
author of *Discourse Grammar of the Greek New Testament*

**EERDMANS
LANGUAGE
RESOURCES**

The Eerdmans Language Resources series is
a collection of textbooks, readers, reference
books, and monographs pertaining to
languages commonly used in biblical and
theological studies. In these volumes,
students and scholars will find indispensable
help in understanding and mastering Hebrew,
Aramaic, Greek, and other languages.

Other ELR Titles

A Grammar of New Testament Greek

Rodney A. Whitacre

WILLIAM B. EERDMANS PUBLISHING COMPANY

GRAND RAPIDS, MICHIGAN

Wm. B. Eerdmans Publishing Co.
4035 Park East Court SE, Grand Rapids, Michigan 49546
www.eerdmans.com

27 26 25 24 23 22 21   1 2 3 4 5 6 7

ISBN 978-0-8028-7927-1

Library of Congress Cataloging-in-Publication Data

A catalog record for this book is available from the Library of Congress.

Greek text taken from Nestle-Aland, *Novum Testamentum Graece*, 28th Revised Edition, edited by Barbara and Kurt Aland, Johannes Karavidopoulos, Carlo M. Martini, and Bruce M. Metzger in cooperation with the Institute for New Testament Textual Research, Münster/Westphalia, © 2012 Deutsche Bibelgesellschaft, Stuttgart. Used by permission.

Contents

Preface

This beginning–intermediate grammar covers the morphological and syntactical material most commonly met when reading texts written in Koine Greek.[1] It is a pedagogical grammar that contains more explanation and repetition than such works often include in order to serve students encountering these topics for the first time.[2] The first two chapters provide an overview of ancient Greek for those learning Greek for the first time or who are coming back to Greek and need a review of the basics. Thus, this grammar is meant for students as they begin to learn Greek, as well as for help in their continued reading afterward. The material is designed not only for occasional reference but also for reading through after completing basic Greek in order to review items already learned and explore further features of the Greek language. While the focus is on the grammar of the New Testament, material is included to aid those also interested in reading more widely.[3]

1. Among books on Greek the word "grammar" sometimes refers only to syntax. I am following the common definition of "grammar" found in English dictionaries which includes both morphology, that is, the forms words take, and syntax, how words form phrases, clauses, and sentences.

2. While this grammar is meant to be useful to all beginning and intermediate students of Greek, it also forms part of an inductive method for learning basic Koine Greek, which I plan to publish, *Learning Koine Greek Passage by Passage.* In this method students begin with an overview of the language using chapters 1 and 2 of this grammar and then learn the language through the study of passages from the New Testament and other writings from the Hellenistic period. As students work through the passages they are referred to sections of this grammar to understand what they are encountering in the texts. See whitacregreek.com for further details.

3. Although there are several significant differences between Koine Greek and Classical Greek, there is a great deal of overlap. For differences on a given topic see BDF and *AGG*, along with the list of differences in *AGG* §§355–56. Michael Boler, *Introduction to Classical and New Testament Greek: A Unified Approach* (Washington, DC: Catholic Education Press, 2020), provides an enjoyable way to fill in basic elements of Classical Greek gram-

The main focus of this grammar is on the information necessary for reading Greek, but it also includes topics that are important for detailed exegesis and valuable in reflection.[4] Some topics are included, such as word formation, that are not usually needed for exegesis but are among the delightful features of ancient Greek. Such deeper engagement with passages through both exegetical study and meditation increases not only one's understanding of a text but also one's experience of the text's power and beauty.

I am grateful for help from students as I have developed and honed various parts of this book over the past several decades. In particular I am thankful to the students who used earlier drafts of this book as part of the inductive method mentioned above.

In the publication of this material the entire team at Eerdmans has been a delight to work with. In particular, I want to thank James Ernest. James played a vital role in my two earlier Greek books, and he has done so once again for this one. For expert help in sorting out the details on the page I greatly appreciate the work of Laurel Draper, the project manager; James Spinti, copyeditor; Lydia Hall, page designer; and Ray Wiersma, proofreader, as well as Meg Schmidt for the beautiful and creative cover design. The love and support of my family is a great blessing: my wife Margaret, our children Seth and Chad, Chad's wife Jessica, and their children Leah, Miriam, Samuel, and Ruth.

In all things, thanks be to God.

χάρις δὲ τῷ θεῷ διὰ Ἰησοῦ Χριστοῦ τοῦ κυρίου ἡμῶν.

Romans 7:25

---

mar while reading a variety of short texts from both the New Testament and classical sources. Similarly, Hans-Friedrich Mueller, *Greek 101: Learning an Ancient Language*, Great Courses (Chantilly, VA: Teaching Company, 2016), teaches basic Greek using Homer and the New Testament simultaneously. Classical Greek grammars cover unfamiliar features encountered in passages written after the New Testament, such as patristic texts, that is, the writings of the ancient Christian teachers.

4. Since the goal is to read ancient texts I will refer to authors rather than speakers, though obviously most of what is said applies to the spoken language as well.

Abbreviations

The abbreviations used in parsing are also gathered together in §2.34.

1D	first declension
2D	second declension
3D	third declension
Abbott-Smith	Abbott-Smith, G. *A Manual Greek Lexicon of the New Testament*. 3rd ed. Edinburgh: T&T Clark, 1937.
acc.	accusative
act.	active
adv.	adverb
Advances	Campbell, Constantine R. *Advances in the Study of Greek: New Insights for Reading the New Testament*. Grand Rapids: Zondervan, 2015.
AGG	Siebenthal, Heinrich von. *Ancient Greek Grammar for the Study of the New Testament*. Oxford: Lang, 2019.
alt.	alternate
aor.	aorist
app.	appendix
BDAG	Danker, Frederick W., Walter Bauer, William F. Arndt, and F. Wilbur Gingrich. *A Greek-English Lexicon of the New Testament and Other Early Christian Literature*. 3rd ed. Chicago: University of Chicago Press, 2000.
BDF	Blass, Friedrich, Albert Debrunner, and Robert W. Funk. *A Greek Grammar of the New Testament and Other Early Christian Literature*. Chicago: University of Chicago Press, 1961.
BNTSyn	Wallace, Daniel B. *The Basics of New Testament Syntax: An Intermediate Greek Grammar*. Grand Rapids: Zondervan, 2000.
CG	Classical Greek, in particular Attic Greek of the fourth and fifth centuries BC.
CGCG	Boas, Evert van Emde, Albert Rijksbaron, Luuk Huitink, and Mathieu de Bakker. *The Cambridge Grammar of Classical Greek*. Cambridge: Cambridge University Press, 2019.

CGEL	Danker, Frederick William, with Kathryn Krug. *The Concise Greek-English Lexicon of the New Testament*. Chicago: University of Chicago Press, 2009.
ch(s).	chapter(s)
conj.	conjunction
CSB	Christian Standard Bible (2017)
d.	died
dat.	dative
Deeper	Köstenberger, Andreas J., Benjamin L. Merkle, and Robert L. Plummer. *Going Deeper with New Testament Greek: An Intermediate Study of the Grammar and Syntax of the New Testament*. Nashville: B&H Academic, 2016.
dir. obj(s).	direct object(s)
DiscGram	Runge, Steven E. *Discourse Grammar of the Greek New Testament: A Practical Introduction for Teaching and Exegesis*. Peabody, MA: Hendrickson, 2010.
esp.	especially
ESV	English Standard Version (2011)
ExSyn	Wallace, Daniel B. *Greek Grammar Beyond the Basics: An Exegetical Syntax of the New Testament*. Grand Rapids: Zondervan, 1997.
fem.	feminine
fr.	from
Funk	Funk, Robert W. *A Beginning-Intermediate Grammar of Hellenistic Greek*. 3rd ed. Salem, OR: Polebridge, 2013.
fut.	future
gen.	genitive
gend.	gender
impf.	imperfect
impv.	imperative
ind.	indicative
indecl.	indeclinable
inf.	infinitive
intran.	intransitive
KG	Koine Greek
Linguistics	Black, David Alan, and Benjamin L. Merkle, eds. *Linguistics and New Testament Greek: Key Issues in the Current Debate*. Grand Rapids: Baker Academic, 2020.
LSJ	Liddell, Henry George, Robert Scott, and Henry Stuart Jones. *A Greek-English Lexicon*. 9th ed. with revised supplement. Oxford: Clarendon, 1996.
LXX	Septuagint, cited from Alfred Rahlfs and Robert Hanhart, *Septuaginta, editio altera* (Stuttgart: Deutsche Bibelgesellschaft, 2006).
masc.	masculine
mid.	middle

Montanari	Montanari, Franco. *The Brill Dictionary of Ancient Greek*. Edited by Madeleine Goh and Chad Schroeder. Leiden: Brill, 2015.
MP	middle/passive
MP1	first middle/passive
MP2	second middle/passive
MT	Masoretic Text
n.	note; footnote
NA²⁸	Aland, Barbara, Kurt Aland, Johannes Karavidopoulos, Carlo M. Martini, and Bruce Metzger, eds. *Novum Testamentum Graece*. 28th ed. Stuttgart: Deutsche Bibelgesellschaft, 2012.
neg.	negative
NET	The NET Bible
neut.	neuter
NIV	New International Version (2011)
nom.	nominative
NRSV	New Revised Standard Version (1989)
num.	number
opt.	optative
pass.	passive
pf.	perfect
pl.	plural
plpf.	pluperfect
prep.	preposition
pres.	present
ptc.	participle
rel.	relative
Revisited	Runge, Steven E., and Christopher J. Fresch, eds. *The Greek Verb Revisited: A Fresh Approach for Biblical Exegesis*. Bellingham, WA: Lexham Press, 2016.
SBLGNT	Holmes, Michael W., ed. *The Greek New Testament: SBL Edition*. Atlanta: Society of Biblical Literature; Bellingham, WA: Logos Bible Software, 2010. http://sblgnt.com. 2nd ed. with apparatus, Logos Bible Software.
sg.	singular
Smyth	Smyth, Herbert Weir. *Greek Grammar*. Revised by Gordon M. Messing. Cambridge: Harvard University Press, 1956. http://www.perseus.tufts.edu/hopper/text?doc=Perseus:text:1999.04.0007.
subj.	subject
subjn.	subjunctive
t-form	tense-form
THGNT	Jongkind, Dirk, Peter J. Williams, Peter M. Head, and Patrick James, eds. *The Greek New Testament*. Cambridge: Cambridge University Press; Wheaton, IL: Crossway, 2018.
tran.	transitive

UBS⁵	Aland, Barbara, Kurt Aland, Johannes Karavidopoulos, Carlo M. Martini, and Bruce Metzger, eds. *The Greek New Testament*. 5th ed. Stuttgart: Deutsche Bibelgesellschaft; United Bible Societies, 2014.
UEBG	Whitacre, Rodney A. *Using and Enjoying Biblical Greek: Reading the New Testament with Fluency and Devotion*. Grand Rapids: Baker Academic, 2015.
voc.	vocative
w.	with
WH	Westcott, B. F., and F. J. A. Hort. *The New Testament in the Original Greek*. London: Macmillan, 1904.

Chapter 1

Introduction to Greek Writing, Pronunciation, and Punctuation

T his chapter begins with material that is important to learn at the outset of a Greek course, followed by several related topics that can be learned as they are met in reading. The final section is included for those who wish to use one of the alternative forms of pronunciation.

ESSENTIAL MATERIAL

1.1. Approaches to Pronunciation

There was no one way to pronounce Greek, any more than there is one way to pronounce English. Some elements of Modern Greek were already present among the dialects in the fifth to fourth centuries BC, including Attic Greek associated with Athens, often referred to as Classical Greek (CG). Other elements of Modern Greek appeared in the Hellenistic period in which Koine Greek (KG) developed, mostly from Attic Greek.[1] Throughout these periods and those that followed there was no uniform way to pronounce Greek.[2]

a. At present there are four main approaches to pronouncing KG. Perhaps most students, at least in the West, are taught a form of pronunciation based on the views of Desiderius Erasmus in the early sixteenth century.[3] He attempted

---

1. The Hellenistic period is roughly 300 BC to AD 300, though some prefer 300 BC to AD 600. The term "koine" is a Greek word meaning "common." The Greek of the Hellenistic period was referred to as ἡ κοινὴ διάλεκτος, "the common dialect," in distinction to the various other dialects.

2. For a brief survey of the development of Greek and the various dialects see *AGG*, 1–8 and *CGCG*, ch. 1, especially §§1.57–97. For a more detailed discussion of this complex material see Geoffrey Horrocks, *Greek: A History of the Language and Its Speakers*, 2nd ed. (Chichester: Wiley, 2014), 110–14, 160–88; and Chrys C. Caragounis, *The Development of Greek and the New Testament: Morphology, Syntax, Phonology, and Textual Transmission* (Grand Rapids: Baker Academic, 2006).

3. Greek was almost unknown in western Europe before Greek speakers fled from

to reconstruct the pronunciation of CG, but most scholars agree that Erasmus's system has flaws. Alternatively, some advocate using Modern Greek pronunciation, while others propose using a reconstruction of how Greek was pronounced around the time of the New Testament.[4] These reconstructions of CG and KG are valuable, but are only approximations; no one has heard any form of ancient Greek pronounced by an ancient Greek! Any of these approaches is fine for reading purposes. As one Greek professor put it, if we are ever able to travel back in time to ancient Greece we will all sound like tourists.[5]

b. The pronunciation offered here draws mostly from CG, and thus is close to the Erasmian pronunciation used in many courses.[6] Since there is increasing interest in moving to a reconstruction of Hellenistic pronunciation or to Modern Greek pronunciation, guidelines to those are included as well (§1.13).

c. The goal in learning ancient Greek is not to be able to speak with native speakers today—they don't exist—but to read the amazing texts that have come down to us from the past.[7] To develop even basic proficiency in reading it is extremely helpful to become comfortable pronouncing Greek, whichever form you choose to use.

1.2. The Alphabet

The upper-case forms are used infrequently and can be learned as you encounter them.

Constantinople at its fall in 1453. When scholars started learning Greek they used the modern pronunciation of these native speakers. Interestingly, Erasmus himself continued to use the modern pronunciation. See W. Sidney Allen, *Vox Graeca: The Pronunciation of Classical Greek*, 3rd ed. (Cambridge: Cambridge University Press, 1987), 143.

4. See Randall Buth at https://www.biblicallanguagecenter.com/; Caragounis, *Development*, ch. 6; and Horrocks, *Greek*, 110–14, 160–88.

5. Hans-Friedrich Mueller, *Greek 101*, disk 1, lecture 1, "The Greek Alphabet and Pronunciation."

6. Drawing especially upon Allen, *Vox Graeca*. For another adaption of Allen see Donald J. Mastronarde, *Introduction to Attic Greek*, 2nd ed. (Berkeley: University of California Press, 2013), and the audio clips provided at http://atticgreek.org.

7. Sound played a fundamental role in communication in ancient Greek culture, influencing both prose and poetry. This topic is covered in many CG grammars since it plays a major role in texts studied in Classics courses, especially in the epic texts, poetry, and drama. For an introduction to this topic with special focus on the Greek New Testament see Caragounis, *Development*, ch. 7, esp. 419–33; John D. Harvey, *Listening to the Text: Oral Patterning in Paul's Letters*, Evangelical Theological Society Studies Series (Grand Rapids: Baker, 1998); and Margaret Ellen Lee and Bernard Brandon Scott, *Sound Mapping the New Testament* (Salem, OR: Polebridge, 2009). For the importance of sound in interpretation as an argument for using a reconstruction of Hellenistic pronunciation see Buth's website (https://www.biblicallanguagecenter.com/), and, more generally, Buth, "The Role of Pronunciation in New Testament Greek Studies," in Black and Merkle, *Linguistics*, 169–94.

The Alphabet

Name	Lower Case	Upper Case	Transliteration	Pronunciation	Example	Meaning
Alpha	α	A	a	f**a**ther	πατήρ	*father*
Beta	β	B	b	**b**og	βασιλεία	*reign*
Gamma	γ	Γ	g	**g**et	γυνή	*woman*
Delta	δ	Δ	d	**d**og	δοῦλος	*slave*
Epsilon	ε	E	e	b**e**t	ἐκκλησία	*church*
Zeta	ζ	Z	z	**z**ip	ζωή	*life*
Eta	η	H	ē	l**a**te	ἡμέρα	*day*
Theta	ϑ	Θ	th	**th**in	ϑεός	*God*
Iota	ι	I	i	k**ee**n or k**i**n	ἵνα, τίς	*that, who?*
Kappa	κ	K	k	**c**og	κύριος	*Lord*
Lambda	λ	Λ	l	**l**og	λαός	*people*
Mu	μ	M	m	**m**ap	μαϑητής	*disciple*
Nu	ν	N	n	**n**ap	ναός	*temple*
Xi	ξ	Ξ	x	ma**x**	νύξ	*night*
Omicron	ο	O	o	**ou**ght	ὄνομα	*name*
Pi	π	Π	p	**p**op	πῦρ	*fire*
Rho	ρ	P	r	**r**un	ῥῆμα	*word*
Sigma	σ, ς	Σ	s	**s**un	σῴζω	*save*
Tau	τ	T	t	**t**on	τέκνον	*child*
Upsilon	υ	Υ	u or y	**ewe**	ὑπομονή	*patience*
Phi	φ	Φ	ph	**ph**ysics	φῶς	*light*
Chi	χ	X	ch	**c**ool or lo**ch**	χάρις	*grace*
Psi	ψ	Ψ	ps	ma**ps**	ψυχή	*soul*
Omega	ω	Ω	ō	t**o**ne	ὥρα	*hour*

a. Editions of ancient Greek texts vary in their use of capital letters. For example, the five main editions of the Greek New Testament use capital letters on proper nouns (Πέτρος, Petros, Peter) and on the first word in a paragraph.[8] In addition, NA[28] also capitalizes the first word in a subsection within a paragraph, while UBS[5], *SBLGNT*, and WH add capitals to the first word in direct speech (since Greek does not have quotation marks).

b. The final form of *sigma* (ς) occurs at the end of a word; the other form (σ) occurs everywhere else.

8. The main editions are NA[28], *SBLGNT*, *THGNT*, UBS[5], and WH. See the list of abbreviations for more about these editions.

c. *Gamma* is always a hard "g" (**g**et, not **g**erm), but when γ occurs before κ, γ, χ, or ξ it is pronounced like ν and is transliterated into English with "n": ἄγγελος, *angelos, angel*. Thus, γγ is pronounced "ng," as in *sing*, γκ is pronounced "nk" as in *ink*, γχ is pronounced "nch" as the "nkh" in *sink-hole*, and γξ is pronounced "nx" as in *lynx*.

d. *Iota* is pronounced short when it is in a syllable ended by a consonant, and it is long when it ends a syllable or is itself a syllable.[9] Thus τινι (τι - νι) = tīnĭ, τισιν (τι - σιν) = tīsĭn, similarly πίστις (πί - στις) = pīstĭs. *Alpha* and *upsilon* also may be short or long, distinguished by how long the sound is drawn out. This distinction is important in CG texts, especially the epics and poetry, but not for most KG texts.

e. The *omicron* is similar to the "o" in "pot" as pronounced in Britain, "a pot of tea," though more lightly, like "awe." Avoid the common practice of pronouncing *omicron* the same as *alpha*. So "awe" not "aah."

f. *Upsilon* is pronounced like the French "u." Pronouncing it like a quick combination of "ee" and "oo" is close enough, somewhat like "puberty." Don't draw it out as if you smelled something foul.

g. It is proper to trill the *rho* like an "r" in Spanish, though a bit more lightly, like in Scottish.

h. *Chi* may be pronounced as "c" in **c**ool or, better, like a heavy guttural "h" sound as in the Scottish lo**ch** or the German Ba**ch**.

i. The line over ē and ō is called a macron, from μακρόν, *long*. It is important to include this line in transliterated texts to distinguish *epsilon* from *eta* and *omicron* from *omega*. For example, ὁδῷ = *hodō*, ἐγκοπή = *enkopē*. Several Unicode fonts include the symbols ē and ō.

j. *Upsilon* is transliterated "y," except when it is in a diphthong. For example, Κύριε, *lord, Lord*, is transliterated *Kyrie* instead of *Kurie: Kyrie eleison, Lord have mercy*. So ὗς, *sow*, is *hys*, but υἱός, *son*, is *huios*. Compare the two *upsilons* in ὑπεραυξάνω, *I increase greatly: hyperauxanō*.

1.3. Diphthongs

When two vowels are pronounced together as one sound they form a diphthong.[10]

Diphthong	Pronunciation	Example
αι	**ai**sle	αἰτία (*cause*)

---

9. This simplified approach to pronouncing *iota* comes from Raphael Kühner, *Grammar of the Greek Language: Principally from the German of Kühner*, trans. William Edward Jelf, 2 vols. (New York: Appleton, 1852), 17, cited in Rodney Decker, *Reading Koine Greek: An Introduction and Integrated Workbook* (Grand Rapids: Baker Academic, 2014), 15 n. 6.

10. Diphthong is from δίφθογγος which is from δύο, *two* and φθόγγος, *voice, sound*.

Diphthong	Pronunciation	Example
αυ	c**ow**	αὐτός (*self*)
ει	**ei**ght	εἰκών (*image*)
ευ	**eu**charist	εὐχαριστέω (*give thanks*)
ηυ	**eu**charist	ηὐχαρίστησα (*I gave thanks*)
οι	**oi**l	οἰκία (*house*)
ου	s**ou**p	οὐδείς (*no one*)
υι	s**ui**te	υἱός (*son*)

At one stage ευ was pronounced as ε followed quickly by υ with a constricted pronunciation. Together the diphthong sounded like the "ell" in the Cockney "bell"; ηυ was pronounced similarly, but with an initial sound more like its η, Beowulf.[11] This pronunciation was a stage on the way to Modern Greek "eff" and "ev" for ευ and "eef" and "eev" for ηυ (§1.13). Often in Koine courses both sounds are given as "eu" in "eucharist" (*AGG* §2b). For reading purposes any of these options is fine.

1.4. Breathing Marks

A vowel at the beginning of a word has a mark over it indicating whether an "h" sound is added (ʽ) or not (ʼ). These marks not only affect pronunciation but also sometimes signal the difference between words. For example, ἕν has the rough breathing so it is pronounced "hen" and it means *one*, while ἐν has a smooth breathing so it is pronounced "en," and means *in*. These breathing marks should always be included when writing Greek.

a. If the vowel is a capital then the breathing mark is in front of it (Ἀβραάμ, *Abraham*). In a diphthong the breathing mark is on the second letter of the diphthong (the *iota* in υἱός, Υἱός, *son*). The *rho* has a rough breathing mark at the beginning of a word since trilling the *rho* causes air to flow around the tongue somewhat like the "h" sound (ῥάβδος, *staff*). This breathing mark on a *rho* is not included in transliteration, Ῥώμη, *Rōmē*, *Rome*.

b. If you are using the reconstructed pronunciation or the modern pronunciation note that the breathing marks are not sounded. So words with a rough breathing mark are pronounced as if they had a smooth breathing mark. Indeed, in Modern Greek the breathing marks are not written, by decree of the Greek government in 1982.

---

11. *CGCG* §§1.21-22, which includes the example of the Cockney "bell." The example of Beowulf is from Juan Coderch, *Classical Greek: A New Grammar; Greek Grammar Taught and Explained, with Examples* (CreateSpace, 2012), 11.

1.5. Iota Subscript

Sometimes an *iota* is placed under an α, η, or ω, thus, ᾳ, ῃ, ῳ. This *iota* subscript does not change the pronunciation and it is not included in transliteration. It is, however, an important part of the word, often signaling the way the word is functioning in a sentence.

1.6. Accents

Three accent marks are used: the acute (´), grave (`), and circumflex (˜). In earlier Greek they denoted changes between lower and higher pitch; rising, falling, rising then falling, respectively. By the second century BC, however, they were increasingly used simply to mark the syllable to be stressed.[12] At that time they began to be written occasionally and by the ninth century AD they appeared on each word.[13]

Words often change their accent when there is a change in a word's form. Such changes in accent are not usually significant for understanding a word, but occasionally they are. For example, ὁ is a definite article, *the*, but ὅ is a relative pronoun, *which*. See appendix 1 for the basic rules of accenting and appendix 2 for a list of the main places where the accent makes a difference.

1.7. Syllabification

Words in Greek have one vowel or diphthong per syllable. Thus Ἰερουσαλήμ (*Jerusalem*) = Ἰ - ε - ρου - σα - λήμ. Notice that vowels which are not part of a diphthong may be a syllable by themselves, and that a single consonant goes with the vowel or diphthong following it. As a rough rule, when two or more consonants are together they stay together if they can be pronounced together easily: ἐπιστρέψας = ἐ - πι - στρέ - ψας; otherwise they are separated.[14]

---

12. Horrocks, *Greek*, 169. Indeed, there have been further changes and now in Modern Greek only a tonos (τόνος, *accent*), that is, an acute acent, is used for indicating the stressed syllable. This practice is by the same decree of the Greek government in 1982 that banned the use of breathing marks.

13. Smyth §161; J. A. L. Lee, *Basics of Greek Accents* (Grand Rapids: Zondervan, 2018), 90, who also includes a series of photos of manuscripts from the first to fifteenth centuries illustrating the development of accenting, along with transcriptions and notes (88–103).

14. A common guideline for consonants that can be pronounced together states that letters that can begin a word are kept together and go with the following vowel. For example, *AGG* §4b. Surveying the words in *CGEL* this would include: βδ, βλ, βρ, γλ, γν, γρ, δρ, ζβ, θλ, θν, θρ, κλ, κν, κρ, κτ, μν, πλ, πν, πρ, πτ, σβ, σθ, σκ, σκλ, σμ, σπ, σπλ, στ, στρ, σφ, σφρ, σχ, τρ, φθ, φλ, φρ, χλ, and χρ. Additionally, when a consonant known as a "stop" (π, β, φ; κ, γ, χ; τ, δ, θ) occurs before μ or ν the two letters stay together. For example,

This guideline can affect pronunciation at times. For example, πίστις (*faith*) is divided πί - στις and thus pronounced pī – stĭs with a long *iota* in the first syllable since it is not closed by a consonant (§1.2d). Doubled consonants are split: θάλασσα = θά - λασ - σα, ἄρρωστοι = ἄρ - ρω - στοι, but this division need not affect pronunciation.

The components of words also guide your pronunciation. For example, ἐπι-στρέψας is a compound verb composed of a verb with the preposition ἐπί added to the front. So when you pronounce the word you will naturally pronounce the preposition as a unit, as the diaeresis (§1.12) in προϋπῆρχεν illustrates.

1.8. Punctuation

Greek uses a period (.) and comma (,) as in English. A Greek question mark looks like an English semicolon (;). A raised dot in Greek (·) is not found in English. It represents a stronger break than a comma, but less than a period. It signals a division in a long sentence. English translations often start a new sentence where there is a raised dot in the Greek. Periods, raised dots, and question marks always signal the completion of a clause; commas do so sometimes, but not always.

FURTHER RELATED DETAILS

1.9. Enclitics and Proclitics

Some words, such as ὁ mentioned in §1.6, do not have an accent because they are pronounced in conjunction with the word either before or after. Sharing an accent does not change the meaning of a word.

a. Enclitics. Enclitics (ἐνκλίνω, *lean on*) share their accent with the word before them. For example, in ὁ θεός ἐστιν ἀγαθός (*God is good*), ἐστιν is pronounced as one word with θεός. Often this sharing will cause a word to have two accents, for example, ἐλέησόν με (*have mercy on me*).

b. Proclitics. Proclitics (προκλίνω, *lean forward*) share their accent with the following word. For example, ἐκ in ἐκ θεοῦ (*from God*) is pronounced with θεοῦ as one word. In ὁ θεός ἐστιν ἀγαθός (*God is good*) ὁ is a proclitic, pronounced with θεός. Since ὁ is a proclitic and ἐστιν is an enclitic the three words are pronounced together with only the one accent on θεός.

c. The main rules for accenting enclitics and proclitics are included in appendix 1. For reading purposes you don't need to learn the rules for accenting enclitics and proclitics. But it is important to know that such accent sharing

---

note the second syllable of αἰχμαλωτίζοντες = αἰ χμα λω τί ζον τες. Since English does not commonly use the sound χμα we would tend to pronounce this word as αἰχ μα λω τί ζον τες, which for most purposes is fine.

happens, otherwise you are likely to wrongly identify a word at times. For example, in ὅ τε Φίλιππος (*and Philip*, Acts 8:38) the enclitic τε has caused the article ὁ, a proclitic, to have an accent and thus look like the relative pronoun ὅ.

1.10. Elision

When a word ending in a short final vowel is followed by a word beginning with a vowel, the short final vowel often is elided, that is, it drops out. Its place is marked by an apostrophe. Elision is especially common in conjunctions and prepositions. For example, ἀλλὰ ὕπαγε becomes ἀλλ᾽ ὕπαγε and ἀπὸ αὐτῶν becomes ἀπ᾽ αὐτῶν. For further details see §4.37 and §5.255b.

1.11. Crasis

Sometimes two words are combined, with the final vowel on the first word melding with the vowel at the front of the second word. The resulting vowel has a mark called a coronis over it, which looks like a smooth breathing mark. For example, καί and ἐγώ become κἀγώ; καί and ἄν become κἄν. Lexicons cite the combined form.

1.12. Diaeresis

Two dots over a letter, like a German umlaut, is called a diaeresis (διαίρεσις, *division*). It is put over the second vowel in a diphthong when the diphthong is pronounced as two separate vowels. So πραῢς is pronounced πρα - ῢς.

1.13. Reconstructed Hellenistic Pronunciation and Modern Pronunciation

Resources vary in their descriptions of some of these sounds.[15] A more detailed description of a reconstructed pronunciation is available on the website for the Biblical Language Center, along with sample recordings.[16] For help with modern pronunciation the web has many resources, and language learning sites such as Duolingo and Mango Languages are very helpful.[17] There are several websites

---

15. Compare the three resources listed in footnote 4 as well as the chart in *AGG* §1b.

16. https://www.biblicallanguagecenter.com/.

17. https://www.duolingo.com/; https://www.mangolanguages.com. Duolingo's course is free, but only available for Modern Greek. Mango's course for Ancient Greek is free, unlike its courses for Koine Greek and Modern Greek. Modern pronunciation is used for the Koine course, but not the Ancient Greek course.

containing the entire Greek New Testament read aloud, many of them using modern pronunciation. Just search "greek audio new testament." There are also free apps for phones.

	Reconstructed	Modern
α	m<u>a</u>ma	<u>a</u>way
β	<u>v</u>oice	<u>v</u>oice
γ	γε, γι – <u>ye</u>s, <u>yi</u>eld γγ, γκ, γχ – si<u>ng</u>, i<u>nk</u>, si<u>nk-h</u>ole	γε, γι – <u>ye</u>s, <u>yi</u>eld before α, ο, ω, ου and consonants: "gh" – a sound not used in English γγ, γκ, γχ – si<u>ng</u>, i<u>nk</u>, si<u>nk-h</u>ole
δ	<u>th</u>is	<u>th</u>is
ε	b<u>e</u>t	b<u>e</u>t
ζ	<u>z</u>oo	ga<u>z</u>e
η[18]	<u>a</u>te	b<u>ee</u>
ϑ	<u>th</u>in	<u>th</u>in
ι	f<u>ee</u>t	b<u>ee</u>
κ	s<u>k</u>ill	s<u>k</u>ill
λ	<u>l</u>ittle	<u>l</u>ittle
μ	<u>m</u>iddle	<u>m</u>iddle
ν	<u>n</u>oodle	<u>n</u>oodle
ξ	a<u>x</u>	a<u>x</u>
ο	n<u>o</u>te	<u>o</u>n
π	s<u>p</u>in	s<u>p</u>in
ρ	th<u>r</u>ill, with slight trill	th<u>r</u>ill, with slight trill
σ, ς	<u>s</u>ue	<u>s</u>ue, except a "z" sound in σμ and σρ
τ	s<u>t</u>ill	s<u>t</u>ill
υ	German ü [somewhat like y<u>ew</u>]	b<u>ee</u>
φ	<u>f</u>in	<u>f</u>in
χ	Ba<u>ch</u>	before e or i sound: <u>h</u>uge before a, o, or u sound: Ba<u>ch</u>
ψ	cu<u>ps</u>	a<u>ps</u>e
ω	n<u>o</u>te	<u>o</u>n

18. The pronunciation of this vowel is the main difference between the reconstructed Greek and Modern Greek. See Randall Buth's discussion of η in "Ἡ Κοινὴ Προφορά Koiné Pronunciation: Notes on the Pronunciation System of Koiné Greek," https://www.biblicallanguagecenter.com/koine-greek-pronunciation/; http://www.biblicallanguagecenter.com/wp-content/uploads/2012/08/Koine-Pronunciation-2012.pdf.

Diphthongs

αι	b<u>e</u>t	b<u>e</u>t
αυ	before ϑ, κ, π, τ, φ, χ: <u>af</u>ter elsewhere: cad<u>av</u>er	before ϑ, κ, ξ, π, ς, τ, φ, χ, ψ: <u>af</u>ter elsewhere: cad<u>av</u>er
ει	f<u>ee</u>t	b<u>ee</u>
ευ,	before ϑ, κ, π, τ, φ, χ: <u>eff</u>ort elsewhere: <u>ev</u>angel	before ϑ, κ, ξ, π, ς, τ, φ, χ, ψ: <u>eff</u>ort elsewhere: <u>ev</u>angel
ηυ	before ϑ, κ, π, τ, φ, χ: str<u>afe</u> elsewhere: br<u>av</u>e	before ϑ, κ, ξ, π, ς, τ, φ, χ, ψ: b<u>eef</u> elsewhere: <u>ev</u>en
οι	German ü [somewhat like y<u>ew</u>]	b<u>ee</u>
ου	s<u>ou</u>p	s<u>oo</u>n or y<u>ou</u>
υι	s<u>ui</u>te	b<u>ee</u>

Chapter 2

Basic Features of Ancient Greek

2.1. Introduction

This chapter provides an introduction to major features of ancient Greek to help orient beginning students as well as provide review for those who want to refresh their Greek from the ground up.[1]

As you read Greek you should focus on a passage sentence by sentence, and move through each sentence clause by clause. Once you understand the basics of clauses and sentences you will be able to read Greek and be prepared for further study of the features of paragraphs and larger sections of discourse.[2]

CORE ELEMENTS IN CLAUSES

2.2. English Clauses

a. A clause is a cluster of words around a verb. The other essential element in a clause is the **subject**, the one acting, being acted upon, or being described.

b. Action Verbs. Some verbs denoting action also require a third element, a **direct object**. Verbs that expect a direct object are called **transitive verbs**. They denote an action that has an object to receive the results or the effect of the action. Those verbs whose action does not transfer to an object are called **intransitive verbs**. Each of the sample clauses in this section can stand on its own as a complete sentence.

---

1. Many grammatical terms will be explained as we meet them. For a quick concise overview of the most essential elements and a list of further resources for grammar help, see appendix 6.

2. For an introduction to discourse analysis, see Robert A. Dooley and Stephen H. Levinsohn, *Analysing Discourse: A Manual of Basic Concepts* (Dallas: SIL International, 2001); *Advances*, chs. 7–8; and *AGG*, ch. 4.

Intransitive	*The light <u>shines</u>.* (John 1:5)
Transitive	*The darkness <u>did not grasp</u> **it**.* (John 1:5)

Some verbs can be either transitive or intransitive.

Intransitive	*Jesus <u>stood</u> on a level place.* (Luke 6:17)
Transitive	*Jesus <u>stood</u> **the child** in their midst.* (Matt 18:2)

Transitive verbs may also have an **indirect object**, that which receives the direct object.

> *The Father has given all judgment <u>to the Son</u>.* (John 5:22)
> › Here "all judgment" is the direct object and "to the Son" is the indirect object.

c. Stative Verbs. Some verbs refer to being in a state or condition. The main difference from action verbs is that no change is taking place (§5.89c[1]).

Sometimes the same verb can be used for either an action or a state. In the sentence, "Jesus stood on a level place" no action takes place, in contrast with "Jesus stood the child in their midst," referring to action by Jesus and change affecting the position of the child.

Even though verbs with a stative sense do not denote action they may take a direct object.

> *And he commanded them strictly that no one know this.* (Mark 5:43)
> › Here the stative verb "know" takes the direct object "this."

d. Equative Verbs. Some verbs, such as "to be" and "to become," make an assertion about the subject rather than refer to an action or state. They affirm that something *is* something, thereby usually identifying or giving a characteristic of the subject. They are called equative or copulative verbs (Latin, *copulo*, *link*). Instead of a direct object, these verbs often take a noun, adjective, or other item, such as a prepositional phrase, called a **subject complement** (Latin, *complere*, *fill up, complete*).

Noun:	*Your word is <u>truth</u>.* (John 17:17)
Adjective:	*This testimony is <u>true</u>.* (Titus 1:13)
Prepositional phrase:	*No one who lies is <u>of the truth</u>.* (1 John 2:21)

2.3. The Core Elements in Greek Clauses

Greek clauses contain the same core elements as English clauses.

a. Within each clause that has a verb denoting action the core elements are the verb and subject, and such clauses also may include a direct object and indirect object.

b. In the case of equative verbs the core elements are verb, subject, and subject complement. The complement is often a noun or adjective (also called a predicate nominative, predicate noun, or predicate adjective), but may take other forms, such as a prepositional phrase.

c. Therefore, you should become familiar with these core elements in a clause:

Subject—Verb—Direct object—Indirect object
Subject—Equative verb—Subject complement

d. Any definite articles or negative particles modifying these elements are also considered part of the core of the clause. Usually οὐ negates verbs in the indicative, and μή the other moods, infinitives, and participles, though there are occasional exceptions in KG.[3]

e. No matter how complex a sentence gets, it is composed of clauses, and each clause has at the most only these elements at its core. Accordingly, the clause provides a primary point of reference when reading a passage.[4] Appendix 7 provides help in how to approach a sentence for those just beginning to read Greek.

---

3. In very general terms, "οὐ is the negative of fact and statement, and *contradicts* or *denies*; μή is the negative of the will and thought, and *rejects* or *deprecates*." Smyth §2688 (emphasis original). So also *CGCG* §56.2, which also notes, "There are, however, several specific uses of μή which do not easily fall under this definition." So this broad distinction can be helpful, but will not always apply, especially in KG where the use of the negatives is simpler than in CG. For the New Testament use of negatives in comparison to their use in CG see BDF §§426–30.

4. This focus on clauses corresponds to the Ancient Greek way of ordering expressions of thought. Ancient Greek authors thought in terms of clusters called κόμμα, κῶλον, and περίοδος, which roughly correspond to a phrase, clause, and period. Among these the κῶλον (*clause*) was the main unit of expression. Each of these three units was closely related to patterns of sounds, especially patterns of long and short syllables. The number of words able to be spoken well within one breath also played a role. Accordingly, the way sounds relate to one another often has an effect on word order and coherence in the expression of thought. Such considerations influenced not only highly trained orators but also the common people more generally, at least to some extent at times. For an introduction to these matters see Margaret Ellen Lee and Bernard Brandon Scott, *Sound Mapping the New Testament* (Salem, OR: Polebridge, 2009), especially chs. 3 and 4, and the articles by Baugh cited below at §5.250b.

2.4. Inflection

Unlike English, inflection plays a major role in Greek. That is, in Greek many nominals and verbals inflect, they change their form, to signal how they are functioning in a sentence, along with various other types of information. Accordingly, a Greek writer has great flexibility in how they convey their thought, which enables a power and beauty of expression that is often not able to be conveyed in English. Any initial frustration with Greek word order eventually becomes delight.

The following sections introduce the basic forms of the Greek verbals and nominals, which chapters 3 and 4 then cover in much greater detail.

KEY FEATURES OF THE VERBALS

2.5. Person and Number

In Greek as in English there are three persons and two numbers, as represented here with personal pronouns.[5]

	Singular	Plural
1st person	I loose.	We loose.
2nd person	You loose.	You loose.
3rd person	He/She/It looses.	They loose.

a. Note that English uses the same pronoun "you" for both singular and plural of the second person, having lost the distinct forms "thee" and "thou" for the second singular and "ye" for the second plural.

b. The English third-person singular has different pronouns for the three genders, but the form of the verb does not change. Indeed, as you see, we use the same form of the verb ("loose") for all persons and numbers except the third singular ("looses").

c. Greek has these same persons and numbers, but each of the six forms has a distinct personal ending on the verb to indicate the person and number. Verbs with personal endings are called **finite verbs**, since they have a subject and thus their reference is limited.[6] Here is an example using a present tense-form.

	Singular		Plural	
1st person	λύω	*I loose.*	λύομεν	*we loose.*
2nd person	λύεις	*You loose.*	λύετε	*you loose.*
3rd person	λύει	*He/She/It looses.*	λύουσι	*They loose.*

---

5. A **pronoun** takes the place of a noun (§5.84; appendix 6).
6. In contrast, infinitives and participles do not signal person in their forms (§§2.10, 21, 34).

Such a layout of the forms of a Greek word is known as a **paradigm**. In this paradigm the **stem** of this verb is λυ- and endings are added to signal the person and number. For example, the **personal ending** μεν signals first person plural, "we." It is added to the stem λυ- with the help of a **linking vowel** ο (also called a variable vowel, connecting vowel, or theme vowel). These verbs are thus composed of stem + linking vowel + personal ending. These individual elements of a word that have grammatical significance are called **morphemes**.

		Stem	Vowel	Ending
1-sg.	λύω	λυ		ω[7]
2-sg.	λύεις	λυ	ει	ς
3-sg.	λύει	λυ	ει	–
1-pl.	λύομεν	λυ	ο	μεν
2-pl.	λύετε	λυ	ε	τε
3-pl.	λύουσι(ν)	λυ		ουσι(ν)

d. Two Main Patterns of Personal Endings. There are two core patterns that cover most of the personal endings.[8] We will explore the tense-forms later, beginning in §2.11. For now just note that one core pattern is for verbs in the **primary tense-forms**, namely, the present, future, and perfect, and the other core pattern is for verbs in the **secondary tense-forms**, the imperfect, aorist, and pluperfect. So the endings here on the present indicative of λύω are among those in the core pattern for primary tense-forms.

e. Personal Endings and Embedded Subjects. Notice that this use of personal endings means that the subject of a verb can be signaled by the form of a verb, without using a separate word for the subject. Thus λύω means "I loose" without needing to add a Greek word meaning "I," even though Greek has a personal pronoun for "I."

2.6. Voice

English has an active voice and a passive voice, but Greek has an active voice and a middle voice, with the passive as a particular use of the middle.[9] The use

---

7. In the 1-sg. and 3-pl. there is no separate linking vowel because the linking vowel and ending have undergone changes. For an explanation see §4.3d.

8. The main exceptions are the personal endings in the imperative. The endings for the imperative are a separate core pattern.

9. The parent language of Greek, Proto-Indo-European, had only these two voices. James Hope Moulton, *A Grammar of New Testament Greek*, vol. 1, *Prolegomena*, 3rd ed. (Edinburgh: T&T Clark, 1908), 151; A. T. Robertson, *A Grammar of the Greek New Testament in the Light of Historical Research*, 4th ed. (Nashville: Broadman, 1934), 803; Carl Conrad, "Active,

of voice in Greek is consistent with other languages that have a middle voice, but it is quite different from English. Greek grammars have tended to understand Greek voice from within an English framework, but it is becoming clear that it is better to understand it on its own terms.[10]

a. Active and Passive in English. In English the active voice signifies that the subject of the sentence is doing the action or is in a particular state or condition, and the passive voice means the subject is being acted upon by someone or something else. A passive sentence would be a transitive sentence in the active, with the direct object of the active sentence serving as the subject of the passive sentence.

Active voice	*Jesus washes the disciples' feet.*
Passive voice	*The disciples' feet are being washed by Jesus.*

b. Active and Middle in Greek. In Greek as in English the active signifies that the subject of the sentence is doing the action or is in a particular state or condition, while the middle signifies that the subject is somehow affected by the action, often as one experiencing or benefitting from the action.[11] The middle always includes subject-affectedness, with a spectrum of particular forms of affectedness that are signaled by the meaning of the verb and the context (§5.93).

The active also may include this subject-affectedness depending on the meaning of the verb and the context. For example, the active form ἀποθνῄσκω,

---

Middle, and Passive: Understanding Ancient Greek Voice," December 16, 2003, https://pages.wustl.edu/files/pages/imce/cwconrad/undancgrkvc.pdf, §4.1; Rachel Aubrey, "Motivated Categories, Middle Voice, and Passive Morphology," in Runge and Fresch, *Revisited*, 577–79. Accordingly, "the middle is older than the passive," and thus "the passive arose out of the middle" (Robertson, *Grammar*, 803).

10. See especially Rutger J. Allan, *The Middle Voice in Ancient Greek: A Study in Polysemy*, Amsterdam Studies in Classical Philology 11 (Amsterdam: Gieben, 2003), and the earlier cross-linguistic study of thirty languages by Suzanne Kemmer, *The Middle Voice*, Typological Studies in Language 23 (Amsterdam: Benjamins, 1993). For a description of recent study within North American biblical studies circles with an introduction to some key issues, see *Advances*, ch. 4, and Jonathan T. Pennington, "The Greek Middle Voice," in Black and Merkle, *Linguistics*, ch. 4. A more detailed introduction is provided by Rachel Aubrey in "Motivated Categories." Among the grammars, *CGCG*, ch. 35 on voice is particularly helpful.

11. Allan, *Middle Voice*, 114; *CGCG* §35.8. This feature of the middle has long been recognized. "The middle voice shows that the action is performed with special reference to the subject." Smyth §1713. It "represents the subject as doing something in which he is interested." Smyth §1714. Indeed, "in the earliest accessible developments of Indo-Germanic speech," the ancient Indian grammarians of Sanskrit used a term for the active that means "a word for another" and a term for the middle that means "a word for oneself." Moulton, *Prolegomena*, 153.

I die, is clearly so! Intransitive verbs in particular include subject-affectedness.[12] So the active voice is "neutral" regarding subject-affectedness.[13]

The middle is a challenging feature of Greek for English speakers. The following uses introduce some of the major features of the middle, with more detailed discussion in §§5.92–94.

c. Passive Use of the Middle. The passive use is the strongest form of subject-affectedness, for the subject is not an agent doing the action in any sense, but the one acted upon by some other agent or force, either explicitly identified or not. As with the English passive, such sentences would be transitive if they were in the active. In English we use helping words (also called auxiliary verbs) to signal the passive; most often the auxiliary verb is a form of "to be."

> ἤγετο ἐν τῷ πνεύματι ἐν τῇ ἐρήμῳ (Luke 4:1)
> *he [Jesus] <u>was led</u> by the Spirit in the wilderness*
> ▸ The active would be, "the Spirit led him [Jesus]."

> ἐπὶ ἡγεμόνας δὲ καὶ βασιλεῖς **ἀχθήσεσθε** ἕνεκεν ἐμοῦ (Matt 10:18)
> *and you <u>will be brought</u> before governors and kings because of me*
> ▸ The active would be, "[they] will bring you."

d. Direct Reflexive Use of the Middle. Occasionally in the middle the action of the subject comes back on the subject directly. This form of subject-affectedness is easy for English speakers to understand, and it is sometimes taken as the main use of the middle, but in fact it is rare. In English we use an active verb with a reflexive pronoun.[14]

> ἀπήγξατο (Matt 27:5)
> *he [Judas] hanged himself*

e. Indirect Reflexive Use of the Middle. In the indirect-reflexive use the verb will have a direct object, like an active verb in an English transitive sentence, but with some form of subject-affectedness as well.[15] When Luke says Herod put Peter in prison (Acts 12:4), the verb for "put," ἔθετο, is a middle, suggesting that Herod is not only the agent doing the action but is also getting something out of it or is involved in some way. The particular way the subject is affected has to be determined from the meaning of the verb and clues in the context, though most often it will involve benefit or experience.

---

12. "It is difficult to think of any intransitive event in which the subject is not, in some way, experiencing the effects of the event." Aubrey, "Motivated Categories," 574.

13. Allan, *Middle Voice*, 19; CGCG §35.1.

14. Greek also has a reflexive pronoun (§§3.53, 5.84b), which is used more often than the direct reflexive middle.

15. More precisely it will have a direct object or a complement (§5.93c). CGCG §§35.3 n. 1, 3.8.

ἐγὼ πολλοῦ κεφαλαίου τὴν πολιτείαν ταύτην **ἐκτησάμην** (Acts 22:28)
I <u>acquired</u> this citizenship with a large sum of money.

In English this sentence has an active verb, *acquired,* and a direct object, *this citizenship.* In both the English and the Greek the direct object is receiving the action of the verb, but in Greek the verb ἐκτησάμην is a middle form, signaling that the action is subject-affected; the subject is a beneficiary of this action.

f. Middle-Only Verbs. Some verbs do not have an active form. This is the case with κτάομαι, *gain, acquire, get* used in Acts 22:28 just cited. The meaning of this verb is inherently subject-affected since the subject of such action is naturally a beneficiary. Or consider κάθημαι, *sit,* which is middle-only. It is subject-affected, since the subject both does the action and experiences it.

Such verbs are often referred to as "deponent," as though they originally had an active form and then put it aside (Latin, *deponere*). But this explanation approaches the Greek middle from the viewpoint of Latin, instead of from a Greek point of view.[16] In languages like Greek the middle is not derived from the active and thus is capable of functioning without it (§5.92b).

g. Analyzing a Middle Verb. Understanding the middle as subject-affected makes sense of the middle in most verbs, even though there are exceptions at times and some verbs are puzzling. When studying a text in detail, attention to the sense of a middle verb is often helpful for understanding that verb, but the use of the middle should not necessarily be emphasized—often the middle is simply how something is said. But when an author has a choice of using an active, there may well be some form of emphasis in choosing to use the middle.[17]

2.7. Signals for Voice in the Paradigms

Voice in Greek is signaled by the personal endings. The pattern in §2.5 illustrates the active voice for each of the persons and numbers. Thus the personal ending μεν signals not only 1-pl., "we," but also the active voice, that is, that "we" are doing or experiencing something or are being described.

a. Traditionally, the paradigms other than the active have been labeled as middle, middle/passive, or passive. However, if the passive is viewed as a particular use of the middle, there are really only active and middle forms. Since the passive use of the middle is common and the identification of certain forms as passive is so established, it seems best to refer to them as middle/passives.

b. For our sample we'll use the middle/passive endings found in the present tense-form. Since English has no distinct translation of the non-passive use of the middle it is translated as an active.

16. Bernard A. Taylor, "Deponency and Greek Lexicography," in *Biblical Greek Language and Lexicography: Essays in Honor of Frederick W. Danker,* ed. Bernard A. Taylor, John A. L. Lee, Peter R. Burton, and Richard E. Whitaker (Grand Rapids: Eerdmans, 2004), 167–76.
17. For possible examples see §5.93c, j.

	Singular	
1st person	λύομαι	*I loose. I am being loosed.*
2nd person	λύῃ	*You (sg.) loose. You are being loosed.*
3rd person	λύεται	*He/She/It looses. He/She/It is being loosed.*
	Plural	
1st person	λυόμεθα	*We loose. We are being loosed.*
2nd person	λύεσθε	*You (pl.) loose. You are being loosed.*
3rd person	λύονται	*They loose. They are being loosed.*

Notice that again the formula is:

stem + linking vowel + personal ending.

		Stem	Vowel	Ending
1-sg.	λύω	λυ	ο	μαι
2-sg.	λύῃ	λυ		η[18]
3-sg.	λύεται	λυ	ε	ται
1-pl.	λυόμεθα	λυ	ο	μεθα
2-pl.	λύεσθε	λυ	ε	σθε
3-pl.	λύονται	λυ	ο	νται

c. Translation of the Middle/Passive. When you come across a middle/passive verb, translate it with an active if the subject of the verb is the agent doing the action. If the subject is not the agent, then translate it with a passive.[19]

καὶ **ἠγέρθη** καὶ διηκόνει αὐτῷ (Matt 8:15)
and she [Peter's mother-in-law] <u>rose</u> and began serving him
> Peter's mother-in-law is the agent of this action, so this middle/passive form is translated with an active.

καὶ πολλὰ σώματα τῶν κεκοιμημένων ἁγίων **ἠγέρθησαν** (Matt 27:52)
and many bodies of the saints who had fallen asleep <u>were raised</u>
> The saints were not the agents raising themselves but were acted upon, so this middle/passive is translated with a passive in English.

18. In the 2-sg. the linking vowel and ending have undergone changes resulting in no separate linking vowel. See further in §4.8c.
19. This helpful guideline is adapted from Pennington, "Greek Middle Voice," 97–98.

2.8. Mood

Along with person, number, and voice, verbs also have moods. This does not mean they are happy or sad! Rather, mood (from the Latin, *modus, mode, manner*) refers to the kind of expression that is being communicated. For example, a sentence might be stating a fact, or giving a command, or raising a possibility, or expressing a wish.

2.9. The Main Ideas of the Moods

In Greek a verb's mood is signaled by its form, which is covered in chapter 4. The following list provides the main ideas and a few simple translations for each of the moods, which are discussed more extensively and illustrated in chapter 5.

a. Indicative. The indicative makes a statement or asks a question.

> ἔνιψεν τοὺς πόδας αὐτῶν (John 13:12)
> *He washed their feet.*

> σύ μου νίπτεις τοὺς πόδας; (John 13:6)
> *Are you washing my feet?*

b. Imperative. The imperative gives a command or makes a request.[20]
  > ▸ The imperative is often used in prayers, so in those contexts it is a request, not a command!

> τὸ πρόσωπόν σου νίψαι. (Matt 6:17)
> *Wash your face.*

> ἄφες ἡμῖν τὰς ἁμαρτίας ἡμῶν. (Luke 11:4)
> *Forgive us our sins.*

c. Subjunctive. The subjunctive expresses that something is contingent, possible, or probable and thus includes a note of uncertainty.

> ἐὰν μὴ πυγμῇ νίψωνται τὰς χεῖρας οὐκ ἐσθίουσιν. (Mark 7:3)
> *If they don't wash their hands with a fist they don't eat.*

d. Optative. The optative expresses a wish or request.

> δώη ἔλεος ὁ κύριος τῷ Ὀνησιφόρου οἴκῳ (2 Tim 1:16)
> *May the Lord grant mercy to the household of Onesiphorus!*

20. At times the imperative expresses permission or a suggestion. See §5.154.

2.10. The Main Ideas of Infinitives and Participles

In contrast to the four moods (§2.9), infinitives and participles are not finite verbs, since they do not specify person and the infinitive lacks number as well. Accordingly, they rarely function as the main verb of a clause or sentence. Rather, they are signals that a verb is functioning like a noun, adjective, adverbial clause, or in one of several other ways. Here are a few examples of common uses as preparation for the detailed discussion in chapter 5.

a. Infinitive. Infinitives usually function as a noun or in conjunction with other verbs in various ways. Since an infinitive is a verb it can have its own modifiers.

> εὐκοπώτερον γάρ ἐστιν κάμηλον διὰ τρήματος βελόνης **εἰσελθεῖν** ἢ πλούσιον εἰς τὴν βασιλείαν τοῦ θεοῦ εἰσελθεῖν. (Luke 18:25)
> *To enter through the eye of a needle is easier for a camel than for a rich person to enter into the kingdom of God.*

In this verse the infinitive **εἰσελθεῖν,** *to enter,* functions as a noun. It is the subject of the verb ἐστιν, *is,* and is modified by διὰ τρήματος βελόνης, *through the eye of a needle.*

> ὑπάγω **ἁλιεύειν.** (John 21:3)
> *I'm leaving to fish.*

Now we see an infinitive, **ἁλιεύειν,** *to fish,* in conjunction with another verb, ὑπάγω, *I am leaving.* In both Greek and English it is common to use an infinitive to express the purpose of the action expressed by the main verb.

b. Participle. Participles usually function as a noun, an adjective, or in conjunction with other verbs in a variety of ways. Since a participle is a verb it can take a direct object, as well as other modifiers such as indirect objects and prepositional phrases.

> μακάριοι οἱ **πενθοῦντες** (Matt 5:4)
> *Those who mourn are blessed.*

The participle **πενθοῦντες,** *those who mourn,* functions as a noun and serves as the subject of the sentence.

> οὗτός ἐστιν ὁ ἄρτος ὁ ἐκ τοῦ οὐρανοῦ **καταβαίνων** (John 6:50)
> *This is the bread which comes down from heaven.*

Now the participle, καταβαίνων, *which comes down,* functions as an adjective to describe ὁ ἄρτος, *the bread.* This participle is modified by the prepositional phrase ἐκ τοῦ οὐρανοῦ, *from heaven.*

ἀκούσας δὲ ὁ βασιλεὺς Ἡρῴδης ἐταράχθη. (Matt 2:3)
And hearing this King Herod was shaken up.

The participle ἀκούσας, *hearing,* forms a subordinate clause that tells us something about the circumstances of the main subject and verb. In this case it tells us when the subject, ὁ βασιλεὺς Ἡρῴδης, *King Herod,* ἐταράχθη, *was shaken up* in response to hearing the report of the birth of Jesus.

Such circumstantial participles can suggest many relations other than time. Participles are one of the most powerful features of Greek grammar and are often of particular significance in exegesis and reflection.

2.11. Tense-Forms, Time, and Aspect

In English a verb's tense is primarily about time. We refer to present tense, past tense, future tense. Verbs in Greek can include reference to time, especially in the indicative mood, but **tense in Greek is not primarily about time** (§5.87). Referring to "tense-form" rather than "tense" helps keep that fact in mind.

Rather than referring to time, Greek tense-forms primarily refer to aspect, that is, they signal the viewpoint the author adopts. Aspect is fundamental to a tense-form and applies in all its moods. There are three aspects. The brief descriptions and illustrations here and in the next section are preparation for the more detailed discussion in §5.87 and sections in chapter 5 for each tense-form.

a. Durative (Imperfective) Aspect. When using the durative aspect an author is adopting a viewpoint from within the action or state, like a reporter embedded on the scene while the action is unfolding.

Θαυμάζω ὅτι οὕτως ταχέως μετατίθεσθε ἀπὸ τοῦ καλέσαντος ὑμᾶς. (Gal 1:6)
I am amazed that you are so quickly deserting the one who called you.

Καὶ πάντες ἐμαρτύρουν αὐτῷ καὶ ἐθαύμαζον ἐπὶ τοῖς λόγοις τῆς χάριτος τοῖς ἐκπορευομένοις ἐκ τοῦ στόματος αὐτου. (Luke 4:22)
And all were speaking approvingly of him and were being amazed at the gracious words that were coming out of his mouth.

b. Aoristic (Perfective) Aspect. This term comes from ἀόριστος, *undefined.*[21] Using the aoristic aspect an author views the action/event/state as though standing apart from it and seeing it as a whole. With the aoristic aspect an author simply refers to the occurrence of an action/event or state.

σὺν ἐμοὶ ἐδούλευσεν εἰς τὸ εὐαγγέλιον. (Phil 2:22)
He served with me in the gospel.
> ▸ Paul is referring to Timothy.

21. "Aorist" in English is pronounced AIR-ist, "aoristic" as air-IS-tic.

c. Resultative (Stative) Aspect. Using this aspect an author's viewpoint is within a current situation, as with the durative aspect, but it is a current action or state that has come about as the result of prior action. This prior action may or may not have ceased, but it is viewed as complete in the sense that it has produced effects that are present in the current situation.

ἡ ἀγάπη τοῦ θεοῦ **ἐκκέχυται** ἐν ταῖς καρδίαις ἡμῶν. (Rom 5:5)
The love of God has been poured out in our hearts.

d. Future. Unlike the other tense-forms, the future does not have aspect. It only has temporal value, referring to action or a state in the future.

ὁδηγήσει ὑμᾶς ἐν τῇ ἀληθείᾳ πάσῃ. (John 16:13)
He will guide you into all truth.
> Jesus is referring to the Spirit of truth.

2.12. The Six Main Tense-Forms

There are six main tense-forms in Greek: the present, the future, the imperfect, the aorist, the perfect, and the pluperfect.[22]

a. Several of these tense-forms are found in all four moods with all the voices, persons, and numbers, and also as infinitives and participles.

b. Here are examples of λούω, *wash*, in each of these six tense-forms, using the first-person singular, active and middle/passive voices.[23] Only the active and passive senses are included since English does not have an equivalent for the middle (§2.6). These general translations reflect how the verb might be translated in the indicative when there is a time reference. The aspect associated with each tense-form is listed; notice how the aspects are reflected in these translations.

Tense-Form	Active	Passive	Aspect
Present	*I am washing*	*I am being washed*	Durative
	λούω	λούομαι	
Future	*I will wash*	*I will be washed*	
	λούσω	λουσθήσομαι	
Imperfect	*I was washing*	*I was being washed*	Durative
	ἔλουον	ἐλουόμην	
Aorist	*I washed*	*I was washed*	Aoristic
	ἔλουσα	ἐλούσθην	

22. Another tense-form, the future perfect, is used very rarely. "I will have washed," "I will have been washed."

23. The verb λούω is used in this case instead of the more common sample word λύω, *loose*, in order to provide a more concrete image.

Tense-Form	Active	Passive	Aspect
Perfect	*I have washed*	*I have been washed*	Resultative
	λέλουκα	λέλουμαι	
Pluperfect	*I had washed*	*I had been washed*	Resultative
	ἐλελούκειν	ἐλελούμην	

2.13. Introduction to the Components Used in Verbs

Given all the elements that go into a Greek verb, perhaps it's not surprising that a particular verb can have well over 150 different forms! Fortunately, with only a few core patterns you have a base for learning the various paradigms (§2.33). In the preceding sections you saw a glimpse of how Greek signals voice, person, and number. Now we look at those signals further, along with the signals of other features like tense-form and mood.

2.14. Parsing a Finite Verb

Identifying the elements in an inflected word is called **parsing**. When a verb is in the indicative, subjunctive, optative, or imperative mood its components will signal which tense-form, mood, voice, person, and number it has. When parsing such a verb these five elements are what you identify. For example, λύομεν, *we loose*, is a present, indicative, active, first person, plural, and λύεται is a present, indicative, middle/passive, third person, singular. You also list the form of the verb in the passage and the form it takes in a lexicon, sometimes referred to as its lexical form or **lemma**. Most verbs are listed by their form in the present, indicative, active or middle/passive, first person, singular. So, using the abbreviations listed below in §2.34, the full parsing of these examples would be:

λύομεν—pres.-ind.-act.-1-pl. < λύω.[24]
λύεται—pres.-ind.-MP-3-sg. < λύω.

The following sections introduce the signals in a verb that convey this information.

---

24. Some prefer to include an English translation for the word being parsed. This translation may be a simple gloss of a basic meaning or meanings of the word, *loose*. This basic word and its range of meanings apart from the nuances of its inflected forms are referred to as a **lexeme**. For verbs some prefer to use the infinitive, *to loose*. Others prefer to give a translation of the inflected lexical form, *I loose*, or of the inflected form being parsed, *we loose*.

2.15. Personal Ending Patterns

As we have seen (§2.5) a finite verb's voice, person, and number are signaled by its personal ending.

2.16. Augment

The secondary tense-forms (imperfect, aorist, and pluperfect) add an augment on the front of the stem, but **only in the indicative**. There are two forms the augment can take.

a. If the verb begins with a consonant then an ε is added to the front. So λυ- becomes ἐλυ-.

b. Verbs that begin with a vowel have that vowel lengthened. The most common lengthenings are

α → η, ε → η, ο → ω.

Thus the verb ἐσθίω, *eat*, has the stem ἐσθι-, so the augmented stem is ἠσθι-.

c. The augment is usually a key signal of past time.[25]

2.17. Reduplication

In the perfect and pluperfect tense-forms the stem is reduplicated.

a. If the stem begins with a consonant then that letter is doubled, with an ε between.[26] The stem of λύω, λυ-, is reduplicated to λελυ-.

b. If the verb begins with a vowel, reduplication lengthens the first vowel, just like an augment. Occasionally reduplication looks like an augment with consonants as well. This potential ambiguity is usually clarified by the presence of other markers such as a tense-form sign.

2.18. Tense-Form Signs

Several of the tense-forms are recognized by signs that are attached to the end of the stem. The main tense-form signs are as follows.

---

25. Some recent studies have disputed this point, but see Peter J. Gentry, "The Function of the Augment in Hellenistic Greek," in *Revisited*, 353–78; Christopher J. Fresch, "Typology, Polysemy, and Prototypes: Situating Nonpast Aorist Indicatives," in *Revisited*, 379–415; and *AGG* §§65, 71a.

26. I have not yet seen an explanation for why this process is called reduplication and not simply duplication.

tense-form sign	+	linking vowel	=	tense-form
σ	+	o or ε	=	Future active and first middle/passive
θησ	+	o or ε	=	Future second middle/passive
σ	+	α or ε	=	Aorist active and first middle/passive
θη			=	Aorist second middle/passive
κ	+	α or ε	=	Perfect active
κ	+	ει	=	Pluperfect active

Thus, the stem plus tense-form sign of λύω in the future active and first middle/passive will be λυσ-, in the future second middle/passive λυθησ-, and so on. In §2.20 you will see a chart for all these forms, but first we have to add one more element.

2.19. Principal Parts

Verbs in Greek, as in English, build their various forms on principal parts.

a. In English there are three principal parts. Some verbs use the same stem for all their forms, some use a modified stem, and others use more than one stem.

	Verb	Principal parts
Same stem	to study:	study, studied, studied.
Modified stem	to sing:	sing, sang, sung.
More than one stem	to go:	go, went, gone.

b. These three principal parts form all the tenses in English with the help of auxiliary verbs such as "will," "have," and "has." For example, the future, "I will sing," the perfect, "I have sung."[27]

c. In Greek there are six principal parts and, as in English, some verbs have the same stem in all their principal parts, others have modified stems, and yet others use more than one stem. Some verbs are not used in all tense-forms so they do not have all six principal parts. Appendix 8 contains a list of the principal parts of verbs used twenty-five times or more in the New Testament.

d. You may need to memorize the principal parts for a few irregular verbs, but for most verbs you will be able to recognize their forms if you have mem-

---

27. For a review of how principal parts work in English search the web for "verb principal parts" to find several helpful sites, such as http://grammar.about.com/.

orized one or two alternate stems. For example, the verb ἐσθίω uses the stem φαγ- in some of its tense-forms. So if you learn ἐσθίω [φαγ-] *eat* you will be prepared to recognize the verb when you come across the future tense-form φάγομαι, *I will eat* or the aorist ἔφαγον, *I ate*.[28]

Notice, however, that the future form φάγομαι prefers the first middle/passive (§2.6f) and doesn't have a future tense-form sign. In this case learning the stem φαγ- lets you know the form is from ἐσθίω, but the future is middle-only and lacks a σ tense-form sign. So occasionally you'll need to decide whether it is easier to note a distinctive feature in a verb's principal parts or simply memorize its parts.

e. The six principal parts are related to the various tense-forms and voices as follows.

1st principal part	Present active and middle/passive
	Imperfect active and middle/passive
2nd principal part	Future active and first middle/passive
3rd principal part	Aorist active and first middle/passive
4th principal part	Perfect active
	Pluperfect active
5th principal part	Perfect middle/passive
	Pluperfect middle/passive
6th principal part	Aorist second middle/passive
	Future second middle/passive

The principal parts are discussed in more detail in §§4.67–75 arranged as in the following chart.

Prin. Part	1	2	3	4	5	6	Stem
Tense-Form	Pres. act./MP Impf. act./MP	Fut. act./ MP1	Aor. act./ MP1	Pf. act. Plpf. act.	Pf. MP Plpf. MP	Aor. MP2 Fut. MP2	

f. In §2.18 we saw that λύω becomes λυσ- when the future tense-form sign is added. A verb stem with modifications that signal its tense-form is called a

---

28. In some resources, such as William D. Mounce, *The Morphology of Biblical Greek* (Grand Rapids: Zondervan, 1994), you will see verb stems designated by an asterisk, for example, *φαγ. I use a hyphen for roots, stems, and tense-aspect stems, though I leave the hyphens out of charts and formulas to avoid unnecessary clutter.

tense-aspect stem.[29] The main modifications that may be present are reduplication, tense-form signs, and changes to the stem. This tense-aspect stem is present in all the forms of the verb in that tense-form. Elements such as augments, linking vowels, and endings are not part of the tense-aspect stem since they are not the same across a verb's moods, infinitives, and participles.[30]

		Stem	Tense-aspect stem	
1. Present act./ MP	πιστεύω	πιστευ-	πιστευ-	Same stem throughout.
2. Future act./ MP1	πιστεύσω	πιστευ-	πιστευσ-	
3. Aorist act./MP1	ἐπίστευσα	πιστευ-	πιστευσ-	
4. Perfect act.	πεπίστευκα	πιστευ-	πεπιστευκ-	
5. Perfect MP	πεπίστευμαι	πιστευ-	πεπιστευ-	
6. Aorist MP2	ἐπιστεύθην	πιστευ-	πιστευθη-	
1. Present act./ MP	βάλλω	βαλ-	βαλλ-	Same stem modified.
2. Future act./ MP1	βαλῶ	βαλ-	βαλ-	
3. Aorist act./MP1	ἔβαλον	βαλ-	βαλ-	
4. Perfect act.	βέβληκα	βαλ-	βεβλη-	
5. Perfect MP	βέβλημαι	βαλ-	βεβλη-	
6. Aorist MP2	ἐβλήθην	βαλ-	βληθη-	
1. Present act./ MP	φέρω	φερ-	φερ-	Three different stems.
2. Future act./ MP1	οἴσω	οἰ-	οἰσ-	
3. Aorist act./MP1	ἤνεγκα	ἐνεκ-	ἐνεγκ-	
4. Perfect act.	ἐνήνοχα	ἐνεκ-	ἐνηνοχ-	
5. Perfect MP				The pf.-MP is not used.
6. Aorist MP2	ἠνέχθην	ἐνεκ-	ἐνεχθη-	

---

29. *CGCG* §11.12.
30. A different approach is taken by Funk, who includes the augment and linking vowel as well, §§3550.1–2.

2.20. Overview of Verbs with Personal Endings: List of Components

The following list illustrates how the elements signaling tense-form, mood, voice, person, and number come together in a sample word. This list gives only the first-person plural (1-pl.) of λύω in the indicative mood. The numbers between dashes represent the principal part used for the stem in a given tense-form. The simple translations represent only one possible sense of a verb's voice per tense-form.

		Aug-ment	+ Redu-plication	+ Stem	+ T-form	+ Vowel	+ Endings	
Present act./MP	λύομεν			-1-		ο/ε	primary	We loose.
Imperfect act./MP	ἐλύομεν	ἐ		-1-		ο/ε	second-ary	We were loosing.
Future act./MP1	λύσομεν			-2-	σ	ο/ε	primary	We will loose.
Aorist act./MP1	ἐλύσαμεν	ἐ		-3-	σ	α/ε	second-ary	We loosed.
Perfect act.	λελύκαμεν		λε	-4-	κ	α/ε	primary	We have loosed.
Pluper-fect act.	ἐλελύκει-μεν	ἐ	λε	-4-	κ	ει	second-ary	We had loosed.
Perfect MP	λελύμεθα		λε	-5-			primary	We have been loosed.
Pluper-fect MP	ἐλελύμεθα	ἐ	λε	-5-			second-ary	We had been loosed.
Aorist MP2	ἐλύθημεν	ἐ		-6-	θη		second-ary	We were loosed.
Future MP2	λυθησό-μεθα			-6-	θησ	ο/ε	primary	We will be loosed.

2.21. Signs of the Four Moods, Infinitives, and Participles

The following are the main signs of the four moods, the infinitives, and the participles.

a. Indicative. The indicative has no distinguishing signs except the augment in the imperfect, aorist, and pluperfect indicative. Only the indicative takes an augment and it does so only in these three secondary tense-forms.

b. Subjunctive. The vowel before the ending is either ω or η. For example, λύο-μεν in the present indicative becomes λύωμεν in the present subjunctive.[31]

---

31. Some forms will be ambiguous. For example, λύω can be either indicative or subjunctive. Usually the context will clarify which mood is being used.

c. Optative. An ι **is added** to the vowel before the ending. For example, λύομεν in the present indicative becomes λύοιμεν in the present optative.

d. Imperative. The imperatives have **their own set of endings** which are one of the twelve core patterns to learn. Fortunately there are not many of these endings, and not all of them are different from the other moods.

e. Infinitive. The infinitives also have their own set of endings, another core pattern. Since infinitives do not have person and number (§2.10) their forms are simple. There are only four infinitive endings, which usually show up as ειν, ναι, or σαι in the active and σθαι in the middle/passive. For example, the present, active, infinitive of λύω is λύειν, and the present, middle/passive, infinitive of λύω is λύεσθαι.

f. Participle. The participles add adjectival endings to the stems of verbs. These adjectival endings are connected to the stem with either ντ, οτ, or μεν. Thus, the distinctive sign of most forms of participles is ντ, οτ, or μεν followed by an adjective ending. Since participles are verbal adjectives their parsing includes both verbal and nominal elements: tense-form, mood (participle), voice, gender, case, number, and lexical form (§2.34). The only feature they lack is person.

KEY FEATURES OF THE NOMINALS

2.22. The Nonverbal Core Elements in Greek Clauses

Having surveyed major features of the verb, we can add the other main components in a clause that were introduced in §§2.2–3.

2.23. Inflection in the Nominal System

Nouns and adjectives inflect in Greek, but thankfully their patterns of forms are less complex than those for the verb.

a. Word order in English plays a major role in signaling how words contribute to the message of a clause or sentence. In the sentence, "The trainer washed the elephant," we know from the word order that the trainer did the washing (he/she is the subject of the sentence and the elephant is the object). If we take the same words and rearrange them we have: "The elephant washed the trainer." Now the elephant is doing the washing—quite a different picture! We have used exactly the same words, merely rearranging their order.

b. In Greek the role that a noun or pronoun plays in a sentence is usually signaled by the form the word takes, not its place in the sentence. In English we have a few examples of words taking different forms for specific uses in a sentence. If we hear someone say, "Her washed the elephant," we realize this is not grammatically correct; it should be "She washed the elephant." In English the form "she" signals a subject and "her" an object.

c. Since the function of a word in Greek is conveyed to a large degree through its form, the word order of a sentence can vary quite a bit. It is not that Greek has no word order and all is chaos. Rather, the variety of word order that is possible means it can be used to convey many shades of emphasis and texture that often cannot be translated. This characteristic is part of the power and beauty of Greek, as already noted regarding verbs (§2.4).

2.24. Introduction to Parsing Nouns

Each noun in Greek has several forms, with each form signaling three points of information: gender, case, and number. When you see a noun you need to be able to parse it by identifying these three features. As with the verb, you also need to identify its lexical form, which is almost always the nominative singular form for a noun.

2.25. Number

In Greek each noun and adjective is either singular or plural, for example, τέκνον, *child* (singular), τέκνα, *children* (plural).[32]

a. Special Uses of the Singular. As in English, occasionally a singular will refer to more than one person or thing. For example, the generic singular is used to refer to a group of people, as in Romans 1:16, Ἰουδαίῳ τε πρῶτον καὶ Ἕλληνι, *to the Jew first and to the Greek*, referring to Jewish and Gentile people. Or the singular may be used distributively, referring to something belonging to each person in a group, as when Paul refers to τὸ σῶμα ὑμῶν, *your [pl.] body [sg.]* (1 Cor 6:19), and the context indicates that he is referring to the bodies of each of them individually.

b. Special Uses of the Plural. In Greek the plural sometimes is used where English uses a singular. For example, the directions "right" and "left" are usually in the plural, and frequently references to festivals and feasts, including the sabbath, are as well. The plural may also be used with abstract nouns like "envy" and "anger," to refer to "kinds, cases, occasions, manifestations of the idea expressed by the abstract substantive."[33] See §5.20b.

---

32. There is also a dual form, for objects that come in pairs. It occurs in Homer, but rarely in CG and even less often in KG. There is no example in the New Testament and in the LXX it only occurs in Job 13:20 and 4 Macc 1:28; 15:2. Here the dual gen. of δύο, *two*, is δυεῖν instead of the usual form δυοῖν. For dual forms see *CGCG*, ch. 10.

33. Smyth §1000. For further details on various uses of singulars and plurals see BDF §§139-42; *AGG* §129; James Hope Moulton and Nigel Turner, *A Grammar of New Testament Greek*, vol. 3, *Syntax* (Edinburgh: T&T Clark, 1963), 22-28.

2.26. Gender

Most nouns in Greek are either masculine, feminine, or neuter. This grammatical gender sometimes corresponds to natural gender. For example, "man" (ἀνήρ) uses a masculine form and "woman" (γυνή) a feminine form. But frequently there is no relation between grammatical gender and natural gender. A few nouns are used as both masculine and feminine. For example, one of the words for "child," παῖς, is used for both a boy, ὁ παῖς, and a girl, ἡ παῖς.

2.27. Case

Case represents the main information we need for how a noun or adjective is functioning in a sentence.
    a. Three of the cases are usually found in the core of a clause.

Nominative	–	the subject
		the subject complement with equative verbs
Accusative	–	the direct object
Dative	–	the indirect object

Thus, in *The Father has given all judgment to the Son* (John 5:22), in Greek "the Father" is in the nominative, "all judgment" is in the accusative, and "to the Son" is in the dative.

	The Father	has given	all judgment	to the Son.
Function:	subject	verb	direct object	indirect object
Greek Case:	**nominative**		**accusative**	**dative**

In *Your word is truth* (John 17:17), "Your word" in Greek is in the nominative and so is "truth," since equative verbs take a nominative for both their subject and their subject complement.

	Your word	is	truth.
Function:	subject	verb	subject complement
Greek Case:	**nominative**		**nominative**

b. There are two further cases in Greek, the vocative and the genitive.
Vocative—an identification of the person or group being spoken to

The former account I made, O Theophilus, concerning all that Jesus began both to do and to teach (Acts 1:1)
Men of Israel, hear these words (Acts 2:22)

Genitive—a description of a noun or other element in a clause

Walk as children of light (Eph 5:8)

Here "of light" is in the genitive in Greek, describing the "children." There are many possible nuances for how a genitive describes another word (known as its **head term**). In this example, among other possibilities, "of light" may be functioning like an adjective (enlightened children), or it may describe the children's source (children from the light), or perhaps it is possessive (children belonging to the light).

c. Notice from these examples that often English uses a prepositional phrase where Greek uses a noun in a particular case. This is especially true in the genitive and dative, with the genitive often translated with "of." There are three main ideas associated with the dative: personal interest, location, and means. So the key prepositions for the dative are "to/for," "in/at/on," and "with/by."

d. Each case can be used in a number of ways. How a case functions depends on the meaning of the word, its role in the clause, and its context in the sentence or paragraph. At times an author may intend only a general sense or even more than one sense. Attention to such details is an important part of exegesis and reflection, but when simply reading a text we might not consider such issues, any more than we dig into the meaning of "of" when we read "children of light."[34]

2.28. Noun Paradigms

Since each noun has a distinct form for each of the five cases in both the singular and plural it will have ten forms, which together form the noun's paradigm.

Singular	Plural
Nominative	Nominative
Genitive	Genitive
Dative	Dative
Accusative	Accusative
Vocative	Vocative

34. Exegesis refers to the careful study of a passage to understand what the author is saying with as much precision as possible. Reflection refers to attention to possible meanings and associations of a passage enriched by the grammatical and lexical details of the Greek. There are many good manuals available for learning how to exegete. For several approaches to reflection and meditation see *UEBG*, ch. 6.

2.29. The Three Declensions

Among the nominals there are three families of patterns known as declensions. These patterns are sets of endings added to the stem of a nominal.

a. The first declension (1D) is characterized by an α or η in most of its endings. Most words that follow this declension are feminine.

b. The second declension (2D) usually has an o in the ending. Most of these words are either masculine or neuter.

c. The third declension (3D) has all three genders and its own set of endings, which often undergo certain changes. In the 3D word below the nominative and vocative singular forms and the dative plural provide examples of such change, with the κ on the stem becoming a ξ.

d. Each declension has more than one paradigm. The following noun paradigms provide one example for each declension. The hyphenated forms help you distinguish the stems and endings.

	First Declension		Second Declension		Third Declension	
	Fem. sg.		Masc. sg.		Fem. sg.	
Nom.	φωνή	φων-ή	θεός	θε-ός	σάρξ	σάρκ-ς
Gen.	φωνῆς	φων-ῆς	θεοῦ	θε-οῦ	σαρκός	σαρκ-ός
Dat.	φωνῇ	φων-ῇ	θεῷ	θε-ῷ	σαρκί	σαρκ-ί
Acc.	φωνήν	φων-ήν	θεόν	θε-όν	σάρκα	σάρκ-α
Voc.	φωνή	φων-ή	θεέ	θε-έ	σάρξ	σάρκ-ς
	Fem. pl		Masc. pl		Fem. pl	
Nom.	φωναί	φων-αί	θεοί	θε-οί	σάρκες	σάρκ-ες
Gen.	φωνῶν	φων-ῶν	θεῶν	θε-ῶν	σαρκῶν	σαρκ-ῶν
Dat.	φωναῖς	φων-αῖς	θεοῖς	θε-οῖς	σάρξι(ν)	σάρκ-σι(ν)
Acc.	φωνάς	φων-άς	θεούς	θε-ούς	σάρκας	σάρκ-ας
Voc.	φωναί	φων-αί	θεοί	θε-οί	σάρκες	σάρκ-ες

2.30. Agreement between Nouns and Adjectives

When an adjective modifies a noun it must match the noun's gender, case, and number. This is called agreement. Since an adjective must be able to match nouns of all three genders, each adjective has to be able to represent thirty different forms. The same is true for the definite article ("the"). Fortunately, many nouns and adjectives, as well as the definite article, share the same patterns as the nouns. Thus, for such words a paradigm will have the following forms.

	Masculine	Feminine	Neuter
Singular	Nominative	Nominative	Nominative
	Genitive	Genitive	Genitive
	Dative	Dative	Dative
	Accusative	Accusative	Accusative
	Vocative	Vocative	Vocative
Plural	Nominative	Nominative	Nominative
	Genitive	Genitive	Genitive
	Dative	Dative	Dative
	Accusative	Accusative	Accusative
	Vocative	Vocative	Vocative

2.31. Apposition

In addition to adjectives agreeing with a noun when they modify it, a noun can also modify another noun when it is in agreement with it in case and number. The second noun explains the first noun.[35] For example, Paul begins many of his letters, Παῦλος ἀπόστολος, *Paul, an apostle*. The second noun, ἀπόστολος, is in apposition to Παῦλος. Both refer to the same person, both have the same syntactical relation to the rest of the clause as nominatives, and they are in agreement in case and number. Nouns in apposition will not necessarily agree in gender since each noun has its own gender.

Apposition takes place when there is such agreement between nouns in any of the cases, not just the nominative. For example, in ἐν Χριστῷ τῷ κυρίῳ *in Christ the Lord*, both nouns are in the dative, with κυρίῳ in apposition to Χριστῷ.

2.32. Guidelines for Parsing Nouns and Adjectives

When writing out the parsing of a noun or adjective use abbreviations such as those in listed in §2.34. For example, a feminine, accusative, plural may be written as: fem.-acc.-pl.

a. Lexical Forms. Usually nouns are listed in lexicons by their nominative singular form and adjectives by their masculine, nominative, singular form. For nouns the lexicon also provides the genitive singular ending and a definite article to indicate the noun's gender.[36] For adjectives the lexicon lists the other nominative singular endings.

35. This structure is also found with words serving as a noun, such as adjectives and participles.
36. Some lexicons, such as Barclay M. Newman, *A Concise Greek-English Dictionary of the*

θεός, οῦ, ὁ, *God*
ἀγαθός, ή, όν, *good*

b. Sometimes the same form can signal more than one parsing. When parsing any word out of context, nominal or verbal, it is best to give all the options for that form, but for a word in a specific context parse its actual form as determined by its function. For example, τέκνον (*child*) is a neuter singular form that can be either nominative or accusative. So out of context it should be parsed neut.-nom./acc.-sg. But in the sentence ὁ θεὸς ἠγάπησεν τὸ τέκνον (*God loved the child*), ὁ θεός (*God*) can only be nominative and thus it is the subject. Accordingly, τέκνον functions as a direct object and so should be parsed neut.-acc.-sg.[37]

c. Many nouns and adjectives use the nominative form for a vocative and should be parsed as vocatives when they have that function in a passage. But when parsing a word out of context the vocative does not need to be cited except when the form is specifically a vocative.

LEARNING AND PARSING VERBALS AND NOMINALS

2.33. Twelve Core Patterns for Verbals and Nominals

The task of learning to recognize the many forms that verbals and nominals can take is one of the main challenges in learning Greek. It is more manageable if you recognize similarities between the specific sets of forms. In this book you will see how these paradigms can be learned efficiently with the help of twelve core patterns.

a. If you learn the twelve core patterns thoroughly you will be able to see the connections between paradigms and be able to recognize more easily the vast majority of forms you encounter in your reading.

b. The main paradigms are described in chapters 3 and 4, but there are further paradigms that are less common, as well as words that are simply irregular. For parsing such words there are many books that offer help in a variety of forms, as well as web resources such as biblehub.com for the New Testament and Perseus for ancient Greek texts in general.[38]

c. The focus in this book is on making this complex material easier to learn.

New Testament, rev. ed. (Stuttgart: Deutsche Bibelgesellschaft, 2010), use a letter instead of the article to indicate gender, for example φωνή, ῆς, f.

37. Since the forms signal function in Greek this sample sentence could be written in a number of ways: τὸ τέκνον ὁ θεὸς ἠγάπησεν; τὸ τέκνον ἠγάπησεν ὁ θεός; ἠγάπησεν τὸ τέκνον ὁ θεός.

38. See *UEBG*, 114–16 for a description of several of these print resources. In addition, Abbott-Smith, appendix B, provides a helpful list of irregular verb forms.

For more precise and detailed discussions that also fill in less common paradigms and features of KG morphology, see Funk and Mounce, *Morphology*, with *AGG* offering help as well. For ancient Greek more generally see Smyth and *CGCG*.

2.34. The Parsing Sequence and Abbreviations Used for Parsing

The following grid is designed for both verbals and nominals.

Word   Tense-Form   Mood+   Voice   Person   Gender   Case   Number   Lex

The first column is for the word as it appears in the passage and the final column is for the word as it appears in a lexicon. The plus (+) in the mood column represents the infinitive and participle, which are not moods but are listed in this column for convenience. The following abbreviations may be shortened due to space limitations.

Verbal Elements:

Tense-Form		Mood+		Voice		Person		Number	
Present	pres.	Indicative	ind.	Active	act.	First	1	Singular	sg.
Future	fut.	Subjunctive	subjn.	Middle	mid.	Second	2	Plural	pl.
Perfect	pf.	Imperative	impv.	Passive	pass.	Third	3		
Imperfect	impf.	Optative	opt.	Middle/ Passive	MP				
Aorist	aor.	Infinitive	inf.						
Pluperfect	plpf.	Participle	ptc.						

Nominal Elements:

Gender		Case		Number	
Masculine	masc.	nominative	nom.	Singular	sg.
Feminine	fem.	genitive	gen.	Plural	pl.
Neuter	neut.	dative	dat.		
		accusative	acc.		
		vocative	voc.		

Items in the general sequence occur with particular verbals and nominals as follows.

	Tense-Form	Mood+	Voice	Person	Gender	Case	Number
Finite verbs:	tense-form	mood+	voice	person			number
Infinitives:	tense-form	mood+	voice				
Participles	tense-form	mood+	voice		gender	case	number
Nouns and Adjectives					gender	case	number

WORD FORMATION AND WORD FAMILIES

This overview of the basic features of ancient Greek concludes with a brief introduction to how new words are formed. We've looked at morphological changes that signal a word's meaning and function and now we look at some of the changes related to the creation of words. For learning to read Greek the details of word formation are not as crucial as knowledge of the morphological changes. But a general idea of a few of the main features will increase your ability to read Greek and will also reveal further enjoyable aspects of the language.

2.35. Etymology

Etymology is the study of a word's history beginning with its derivation from another language or from within the same language. Formerly it was thought that the original form of a word represented the word's true meaning. Indeed, the etymology of "etymology" suggests such a view since the word is from ἔτυμος, ον, *real, true, actual*. But it is often impossible to get to the original form, and scholars instead refer to the earliest recorded use of a word.

More importantly, a word's meaning may shift significantly from its earlier meanings. For example, "envisage" has been used in English since the seventeenth century and its original meaning included, "to meet squarely, to confront." Such uses are in keeping with its derivation from the French *visage*, *face*, thus suggesting the idea of a face-to-face encounter—being in someone's face! It no longer has this sense, but rather is used for viewing, regarding, or picturing something.[39] So to try to find the original idea of confrontation in the current meaning of the word as if that were the true meaning is misguided.

---

39. This information on "envisage" is based on one of Merriam-Webster's daily emails, which describe the meaning of a word and its history.

a. Such inappropriate appeal to etymologies leads some scholars to have a negative view of them. These scholars rightly insist that the meaning of a word must be determined from its use in context, which may or may not be related to its etymology. A **diachronic** study of a word, that is, the study of a word's developing use through time, often illuminates a word. However, **synchronic** study of the word's use around the time the text was written is crucial for understanding the word in a passage.[40] For such information BDAG and *CGEL* are key resources, all the more valuable for their inclusion of actual definitions for words.[41]

Accordingly, etymology is seldom of concern in exegesis since the focus is on the meaning of a word in its passage. However etymology does play an important role when there are only one or two examples of the use of a word and thus few contexts for determining its meaning. For example, the word ἐπιούσιος, ον, usually translated "daily" in the Lord's Prayer (Matt 6:11; Luke 11:3; Didache 8:2), occurs nowhere else before these texts.[42]

b. Nevertheless, for many words we have a significant part of their history and can see the relations between words that together form word families. In English, "words tend not to stand in close relationship to the roots from which they are derived," in contrast to ancient Greek in which "the internal structure of the lexicon is strongly *associative*." In other words, "Much of the basic word-stock falls into families of linked words which share a transparent derivational relationship to each other, whether through formation processes that are active within the language or through patterns of root-based derivation that stretch into prehistory and back to Proto-Indo-European."[43]

The two main ways words are formed are through modification of a root or stem and through joining together two or more words.[44]

---

40. This point is emphasized in books on exegesis and note also C. S. Lewis's comment, "If we read an old poem with insufficient regard for change in the overtones, and even the dictionary meanings, of words since its date—if, in fact, we are content with whatever effect the words accidently produce in our modern minds—then of course we do not read the poem the old writer intended." Lewis, *Studies in Words*, 2nd ed. (Cambridge: Cambridge University Press, 1967), 3.

41. Danker drew upon Johannes E. Louw and Eugene A. Nida, *Greek-English Lexicon of the New Testament: Based on Semantic Domains*, 2 vols., 2nd ed. (New York: United Bible Societies, 1989). John A. L. Lee says that Louw and Nida was "the first New Testament lexicon in five hundred years to apply the definition method in a thoroughgoing way" (Lee, *A History of New Testament Lexicography*, Studies in Biblical Greek 8 [New York: Lang, 2003], 155).

42. BDAG, 376–77 surveys the possible derivations and meanings.

43. Michael Clarke, "Semantics and Vocabulary," in *A Companion to the Ancient Greek Language*, ed. Edgar J. Bakker (Oxford: Blackwell), 131 (emphasis original).

44. *AGG* §358a.

2.36. Word Formation through Modification

In English *baptize, baptizer,* and *baptism* form part of a word family. This family is derived from a Greek word family, with βαπτίζω, ὁ βαπτιστής, and τὸ βάπτισμα representing the respective meanings of the English words.

a. Words within a family share a common **root**. The root is the underlying core of a word that is often modified when forming a particular part of speech such as a verb, noun, adjective, or adverb.[45]

b. Words have **stems**, as we have seen. A stem is a root plus any additional elements that form the word's part of speech, though the stem may be the same as the root.[46] In verbs the stem is often modified and/or a tense-form sign added to signal tense-form, producing a **tense-aspect stem** (§2.19f).

c. Sample Word Family. The root δικ- has the basic sense, "show, point," ultimately derived from the Indo-European root *deik-*, "show."[47] The root δικ- is used in a family of words with the general sense of justice/righteousness, that is, that which is "in accord with the way *pointed* out."[48] To this root are added various suffixes to produce stems for different parts of speech. These suffixes often signal the use of the word, like in English *er* on "baptizer" signals agency and *ism* may signify the result of an action, as in "baptism." Here are a few of the words in this family that occur in the New Testament.[49]

δικαιόω	verb	oω, to make or consider[50]	*show/declare to be righteous, set right*

45. "The fundamental part of a word, which remains after the word has been analyzed into all its component parts, is called a *root.* . . . A root contains the mere idea of a word in the vaguest and most abstract form possible. Thus, the root λεγ, and in another form λογ, contains the idea of *saying* simply." Smyth §193 (italics original). *CGCG* §23.2.

46. This terminology varies among the grammars. For example, Smyth §§191, 367 uses "stem" for the nominals, but "verb stem" or "theme" for verbals. Mounce, *Morphology* §33.3 uses "verbal root" for the verb stem, while Funk §3550 uses "verb base." Others use "root" for what I am calling the "stem," even when the stem is not the same as the root in a particular word.

47. Robert Beekes, *Etymological Dictionary of Greek*, 2 vols., Leiden Indo-European Etymological Dictionary Series 10 (Leiden: Brill, 2010) 1:334. Compare the Greek verb δείκνυμι, *point out, show.*

48. Bruce M. Metzger, *Lexical Aids for Students of New Testament Greek*, 3rd ed. (Grand Rapids: Baker Academic, 1998), 54 (emphasis original).

49. For more extensive lists of the δικ- family see Thomas A. Robinson, *Mastering New Testament Greek: Essential Tools for Students* (Grand Rapids: Baker Academic, 2007), 33–34; Robert Van Voorst, *Building Your New Testament Greek Vocabulary*, 3rd ed., Resources for Biblical Study 40 (Atlanta: Society of Biblical Literature, 1999), 35; Metzger, *Lexical Aids*, 54.

50. Verbs with oω in CG are factitive, that is, they denote making. Smyth §866.3; *CGCG* §23.45. But, "In New Testament, as in LXX, and as usual with verbs in -όω from adjec-

ἡ δικαίωσις	noun	σις, action	*act of pronouncing righteous, acquittal*
τὸ δικαίωμα	noun	μα, result of an action	*decree, legal sentence, a righteous act*
ἡ δικαιοσύνη	noun	συνη, abstract noun	*justice, righteousness, uprightness*
δίκαιος, α, ον	adjective	αιος, belonging to, pertaining to	*just, lawful, righteous, upright*
δικαίως	adverb	ως, adverb	*fairly, justly, uprightly*

2.37. Word Formation through Combination

New words are frequently formed by combining two or more words. The meaning of the new word may or may not be clearly related to its parts. For example, the meaning of "fountainpen" fits with the meaning of the two words from which it is derived. Such a pen has a reservoir of ink in it so the ink can flow out of it, unlike the earlier quill pens that had to be dipped repeatedly in ink. The meaning of "butterfly," on the other hand, has nothing to do with a fly that is partial to butter, let alone an airborne dairy product!

a. Compounds with Prepositions. A very common form of compound is the addition of one or more prepositions (§5.254d). In the following examples the combination is clearly related to the meaning, but at other times the connection is much less clear.[51]

κατά, *against* + κρίσις, *judgment*	→ ἡ κατάκρισις, *condemnation*
διά, *through* + ἡ αὐγή, *ray, beam*	→ διαυγής, ές, *transparent*
ἐκ, *out of* + βαίνω, *go, walk*	→ ἐκβαίνω, *go out of*
διά, *through* + ἐκ *out of* + ἡ ὁδός, *way*	→ ἡ διέξοδος, *a way out through, an outlet*

b. Combinations of Various Parts of Speech. Verbs, nouns, adjectives, adverbs, and particles are often joined together to form new words. Here is a sampling.

---

tives of moral meaning; (1) *to show to be righteous* . . . (2) *to declare, pronounce righteous.*" Abbott-Smith, 116. Danker's first definition is "verify to be in the right," which matches Abbott-Smith's. But Danker then adds the factitive as well, "2. 'put into a condition or state of uprightness', **justify, set right.**" *CGEL*, 97 (emphasis original).

51. Abbott-Smith and LSJ include information on a preposition's use in compounds. Murray J. Harris, *Prepositions and Theology in the Greek New Testament* (Grand Rapids: Zondervan, 2012) provides extensive discussion of prepositions in the New Testament. See further §§5.254, 255.

Adjective + Noun	πολύς, πολλή, πολύ, *much* + ἡ τιμή, *esteem*	→	πολύτιμος, ον, *highly valued*
Adverb + Noun	εὖ, *well* + ὁ καιρός, *time*	→	εὔκαιρος, ον, *well-timed*
Noun + Verb	οἶκος, *house* + νέμω, *manage*	→	ὁ οἰκονόμος, *manager*[52]

Frequently the particle ἀ—or ἀν before a vowel—is added to the front of a word. Most often it is an **alpha privative,** which reverses the sense of the word, like "theist" and "atheist." Occasionally the added ἀ is an **alpha copulative**, which signals union or likeness.

ἀ privative	ἀ + ὁ γάμος, *marriage*	→	ἄγαμος, ον, *unmarried.*
	ἀ + ὅσιος, α, ον, *devout*	→	ἀνόσιος, ον, *irreverent*
ἀ copulative	ἀ + ἡ δελφύς, *womb*	→	ὁ ἀδελφός, *brother* ("of the same womb")[53]

2.38. Applications and Resources

Attention to word formation and word families is not necessary for reading Greek nor usually for exegesis. It is, however, valuable in several ways, besides simply being one of the delightful features of Greek.[54]

a. Vocabulary Building. Learning new words by word family can be an effective way to increase your store of Greek vocabulary. Several books provide lists of words used in the New Testament arranged by word families.[55]

Learning a few suffixes is also very helpful, and several are listed in appendix 3 for a start. Note, however, that the general sense of a suffix is not always followed, especially in KG. So at times a lexicon will indicate that a word's meaning is not what you might have expected from its formation.

At other times lexicons help you see connections between words within a family. For example, in the light of the suffixes in §2.36c notice how Abbott-Smith brings out such connections in his discussion of δικαίωμα, which he describes as "a concrete expression of righteousness, the expression and result of the act of δικαίωσις, 'a declaration that a thing is δίκαιον, or that a person is δίκαιος.'"[56]

---

52. It looks like οἰκονόμος is derived from the noun νόμος, *law*. But νόμος itself is derived from νέμω. Abbott-Smith explains: "νόμος, -ου, ὁ (< νέμω, *to deal out, distribute*) . . . that which is assigned, hence, *usage, custom,* then *law.*" Abbott-Smith, 304.

53. *CGEL,* 6; also Abbott-Smith, 8. On alpha privative and copulative see Smyth §885; *AGG* §367b.

54. See further *UEBG,* 9–19.

55. Robinson, *Mastering,* 11–113, and less extensively Metzger, *Lexical Aids,* 49–72. Van Voorst lists word families by frequency in the New Testament, though without identifying the roots. *Building,* 12–67.

56. Abbott-Smith, 117.

It is also often helpful to examine various senses of a word, "to see, where possible, how they could have radiated out from a central meaning."[57] For example, *CGEL* notes that ἀναιρέω is formed from ἀνά and αἱρέω, and notes, "the polarities of this verb are rooted in the basic signification of 'take up.'"[58] *CGEL* then lists three meanings: 1. in the middle, **"take up (for oneself), claim"**; 2. in the active, "'remove by causing death', **kill**"; and 3. in the active, "'put something aside', **abrogate, annul**."[59] Thus, these various meanings relate to a central meaning, and such connections can help you learn the meanings.

b. Word Pictures. At times attention to word formation provides a memorable word picture. Our translations are accurate but often rob the text of its dynamic liveliness. Recognizing such pictures can help us hear some of that liveliness.[60]

We have just seen that ἀναιρέω is formed from ἀνά, *up* and αἱρέω, *take*, and its various meanings relate to the idea "take up." At Pentecost Peter says, "you killed him," using the aorist indicative of ἀναιρέω (Acts 2:23). While ἀναιρέω can refer to killing, as we have just seen in *CGEL*, there are other more common words that could have been used. Perhaps we should see a more lively sense to "you took him up," as in our expression, "to take someone out."[61]

When Paul says he takes every thought captive to obey Christ (2 Cor 10:5), he uses the verb αἰχμαλωτίζω which is derived from ἡ αἰχμή, *spear* and ἁλίσκομαι, *be taken, captured*. The word means *take prisoner, capture; make captive, enslave*, but it paints the picture of being taken at spear point! Much of our language and thought is related to metaphors, and attention to imagery deepens our engagement with the text.[62] Thus, while Paul is not talking about spears, such images are often delightful and sometimes thought-provoking.

---

57. Lewis, *Studies in Words*, 1.

58. *CGEL* does not give the meanings for those base words listed elsewhere in the lexicon: ἀνά, *up*, αἱρέω, *take*.

59. *CGEL*, 25 (emphasis original).

60. At times metaphors can become dull from usage, but it is not always easy to know when that has happened, and they can flavor a word even when the author is not conscious of the imagery.

61. As always, context is crucial for understanding words and expressions. If we are talking about a couple going on a date, then "to take someone out" has a very different meaning. At times *CGEL* and Maximilian Zerwick and Mary Grosvenor, *An Analysis of the Greek New Testament*, 5th ed., Subsidia Biblica 39 (Rome: Biblical Institute Press, 2010) include more colloquial English expressions. For example, "ἀναθεματίζω [ἀνάθεμα; 'to devote to evil'] 'to invoke consequences if one says what is not true' cp. the colloquial 'I'll be damned, if . . .' **invoke a curse**" (*CGEL*, 24, bold original); "ἀναλόω [. . . 'waste, expend'] . . . *consume* . . . [on Luke 9:54] cp. the imagistic 'waste' used in underworld society" (*CGEL*, 26, bold and italics original). "δεινῶς (< δεινός terrible, powerful) *strongly, exceedingly* (cf Eng. colloq. "terribly"). . . . προσ-έχετε impv -έχω (sc. τὸν νοῦν) *pay attention* (cf Eng. "put one's mind to")" (Zerwick and Grosvenor, *Analysis*, 228, bold and italics original).

62. See George Lakoff and Mark Johnson, *Metaphors We Live By* (Chicago: University of Chicago Press, 2003).

In addition to noting such images from a word's derivation, it is also helpful to note the relation between the basic senses of a word and any metaphorical extensions. For example, θλίβω means *press*, and the "basic idea is one of compression 'squeeze, chafe.'"[63] It is used twice in the New Testament with this meaning, as when Jesus asks for a boat so the crowd won't press him (Mark 3:9).[64] The other NT uses are metaphorical extensions meaning, *oppress, afflict, distress.*[65] When Paul refers in 2 Corinthians 1:6 to being afflicted, he is not referring to a physical pressing as in Mark 3, but the word has that picture. *CGEL's* entry hints at this connection, "3. metaph., *squeeze, oppress, afflict.*"[66]

Similarly, sometimes a New Testament meaning is based on a meaning not used in the New Testament. For example, for νηφάλιος, ον Abbott-Smith notes first that in CG it is used "of drink, *not mixed with wine*," but then in later writers, including all the New Testament passages, it is used "of persons, *sober, temperate.*"[67]

c. Resources. As these examples suggest, a great deal of information on derivations and word families is available in *CGEL* and Abbott-Smith. In addition, Barclay Newman's *Concise Greek-English Dictionary* lists for each word the other words used in the New Testament related to it. For example, for θλίβω he lists ἀπο|θλίβω, θλῖψις, and συν|θλίβω, with lines added to indicate compounds.[68] Maximilian Zerwick and Mary Grosvenor's *Analysis* often includes brief notes on derivation.[69]

John A. L. Lee finds Abbott-Smith the most reliable New Testament lexicon for etymological information. "The information is sound, clearly presented, and carefully limited: questionable or obscure relationships are not entered into."[70]

---

63. *CGEL,* 170.

64. The other text is Matt 7:14 where the "narrow" way, τεθλιμμένη, is "the having been compressed way."

65. Abbott-Smith, 207.

66. *CGEL,* 170.

67. Abbott-Smith, 302. Abbott-Smith in particular includes CG meanings. Consulting a CG lexicon such as James Morwood's and John Taylor's *The Pocket Oxford Classical Greek Dictionary* (Oxford: Oxford University Press, 2002) often sheds light on a word and ways to translate it.

68. Newman, *Concise,* 85. These words mean: ἀποθλίβω, *press against;* θλῖψις, *distress;* συνθλίβω, *crowd around.* *CGEL,* 46, 170, 341. An extensive informal list of word groups for the New Testament is available in Kristopher D. Tripp, *RAW Greek Dictionary: By Root and Prefix* (self-published e-book, 2013). Basic information on the components of a word is available on several websites such as https://biblehub.com.

69. Zerwick and Grosvenor, *Analysis* provides the basic information necessary for reading the New Testament, and includes references to Maximilian Zerwick, *Biblical Greek: Illustrated by Examples* (Rome: Pontifical Institute Press, 1963) for further grammatical discussion. *Analysis* is a delightful resource.

70. John A. L. Lee, "Etymological Follies: Three Recent Lexicons of the New Testament," *Novum Testamentum* 55 (2013): 385.

The most extensive and technical resource in English for Greek etymologies is Robert Beekes's large two-volume *Etymological Dictionary*.

On New Testament word formation in general, Bruce Metzger and Robert van Voorst provide brief introductions, BDF and Heinrich von Siebenthal offer much more extensive information, and Wilbert Howard is the most thorough.[71] On word formation in ancient Greek more generally see Smyth and *CGCG*.[72]

---

71. Metzger, *Lexical Aids*, 41–49; Van Voorst, *Building*, 4–11. BDF §§108–25; *AGG*, appendix 2, including an "Alphabetic list of word-formation elements" at §371. See also the list of prefixes and suffixes in Robinson, *Mastering*, 114–18. James H. Moulton and Wilbert F. Howard, *A Grammar of New Testament Greek*, vol. 2, *Accidence and Word Formation with an Appendix on Semitisms in the New Testament* (Edinburgh: T&T Clark, 1929), 267–410. This book includes detailed discussion of the historical developments of particular words and forms, including special attention to the papyri available at the time.

72. Smyth §§822–99; *CGCG*, ch. 23.

Chapter 3

Morphology of Nominal Forms

THE FIRST AND SECOND DECLENSIONS

3.1. Core Pattern: The Definite Article

The forms of both nouns and adjectives are organized into three major families, called **declensions**. These endings are added to a nominal stem to signal gender, case, and number.

The endings for the first two declensions (1D, 2D) are covered by the first core pattern, the paradigm of the definite article ὁ, ἡ, τό, *the*. This is a **2-1-2 pattern**, meaning the masculine and neuter forms represent the 2D and the feminine represents the 1D. The third declension (3D) follows a different core pattern (§3.16).[1]

	Masc. sg.	Fem. sg.	Neut. sg.
Nom.	ὁ [ος]	ἡ [α]	τό [ον]
Gen.	τοῦ	τῆς	τοῦ
Dat.	τῷ	τῇ	τῷ
Acc.	τόν	τήν	τό [ον]
Voc.	[ε]		

	Masc. pl.	Fem. pl.	Neut. pl.
Nom.	οἱ	αἱ	τά
Gen.	τῶν	τῶν	τῶν
Dat.	τοῖς	ταῖς	τοῖς
Acc.	τούς	τάς	τά

---

1. For lists of nominals in the New Testament organized by their morphology see Mounce, *Morphology*, and Funk, "Appendix II: Nominal System Catalogue." Funk also includes nominals in the Apostolic Fathers and the other literature covered by Walter Bauer, *A Greek-English Lexicon of the New Testament and Other Early Christian Literature*, translated and adapted by William F. Arndt and F. Wilbur Gingrich (Chicago: University of Chicago Press, 1957), an earlier edition of BDAG.

    a. Most of the feminine endings have an α or an η, and most of the masculine and neuter endings have an o or an ω. Accordingly, by alphabetical order the feminine patterns are referred to as the first declension and the masculine and neuter together as the second declension.

    b. The endings on the article match those on nouns and adjectives except in the five places marked by brackets.

1. Thus the masculine, nominative, singular (masc.-nom.-sg.) article is ὁ, but on a noun or adjective the masc.-nom.-sg. ending is -ος, λόγος, *word*, ἀγαθός, *good*. Articles and adjectives have to be in agreement (§2.30), so *the good word* in the nominative would be ὁ ἀγαθὸς λόγος.

2. Likewise the neut.-nom.-sg. article is τό, while τέκνον (*child*) is an example of a neut.-nom.-sg. noun, and ἀγαθόν (*good*) a neut.-nom.-sg. adjective. Putting these together *the good child* in the nominative would be, τὸ ἀγαθὸν τέκνον.

3. The α in brackets in the fem.-nom.-sg. represents the fact that all the fem.-sg. forms can have either an α or an η, which are listed in §§3.6, 7.

    c. The neuter forms of the nominative and accusative, both singular and plural, are the same so you need to pay attention to clues in the context to tell if one of these forms is functioning as a subject or an object. Similarly, notice the overlap in the genitive and dative endings between the masculine and the neuter paradigms. Pay special attention to the places in paradigms where the same ending is used in more than one way.

    d. The article does not have a vocative form, and the same is true for most nouns and adjectives. Almost always a nominative form also serves as the vocative for signaling direct address (§5.28). However, the vocative ending ε for the masc.-sg. is included because this is one vocative ending that should be learned since it is distinct and shows up with some frequency. Other less common forms of the vocative are included in the nominal paradigms below.

3.2. Articles Plus First and Second Declension Endings

If we put the articles together with the endings we get the following pattern. The underline represents the stem of the word. Notice in the feminine singular that the forms are found with either α or η (§§3.1b[3], 3.7).

	Masc. sg.		Fem. sg.		Neut. sg.	
Nom.	ὁ	___ος	ἡ	___η	τὸ	___ον
			ἡ	___α		
Gen	τοῦ	___ου	τῆς	___ης	τοῦ	___ου
			τῆς	___ας		
Dat.	τῷ	___ῳ	τῇ	___ῃ	τῷ	___ῳ
			τῇ	___ᾳ		

	Masc. sg.		Fem. sg.		Neut. sg.	
Acc.	τὸν	___ον	τὴν	___ην	τὸ	___ον
			τὴν	___αν		
Voc.	[ ]	___ε	[ ]	___η	[ ]	___ον
				___α		

	Masc. pl.		Fem. pl.		Neut. pl.	
Nom.	οἱ	___οι	αἱ	___αι	τὰ	___α
Gen.	τῶν	___ων	τῶν	___ων	τῶν	___ων
Dat.	τοῖς	___οις	ταῖς	___αις	τοῖς	___οις
Acc.	τοὺς	___ους	τὰς	___ας	τὰ	___α
Voc.	[ ]	___οι	[ ]	___αι	[ ]	___α

SECOND DECLENSION NOUNS

3.3. Paradigms for the Second Declension

The following paradigms illustrate the core endings on masculine and neuter nouns. We are starting with the 2D since it is less complex than the 1D. The translations are very basic; the cases will not always be translated like this.

	Masc. sg.		Neut. sg.	
Nom.	θεός	*God/god*	ἔργον	*work*
Gen.	θεοῦ	*of God/god*	ἔργου	*of work*
Dat.	θεῷ	*to/for God/god*	ἔργῳ	*to/for work*
Acc.	θεόν	*God/god*	ἔργον	*work*
Voc.	θεέ	*God/god*	ἔργον	*work*

	Masc. pl.		Neut. pl.	
Nom./Voc.	θεοί	*gods*	ἔργα	*works*
Gen.	θεῶν	*of gods*	ἔργων	*of works*
Dat.	θεοῖς	*to/for gods*	ἔργοις	*to/for works*
Acc.	θεούς	*gods*	ἔργα	*works*

3.4. Article and Noun Agreement in the Second Declension

	Masc. sg.		Neut. sg.	
Nom.	ὁ ἀδελφός	*the brother*	τὸ τέκνον	*the child*
Gen.	τοῦ ἀδελφοῦ	*of the brother*	τοῦ τέκνου	*of the child*
Dat.	τῷ ἀδελφῷ	*to/for the brother*	τῷ τέκνῳ	*to/for the child*

	Masc. sg.			**Neut. sg.**	
Acc.	τὸν ἀδελφόν	*the brother*		τὸ τέκνον	*the child*
Voc.	ἀδελφέ	*brother*		τέκνον	*child*
	Masc. pl.			**Neut. pl.**	
Nom.	οἱ ἀδελφοί	*the brothers*		τὰ τέκνα	*the children*
Gen.	τῶν ἀδελφῶν	*of the brothers*		τῶν τέκνων	*of the children*
Dat.	τοῖς ἀδελφοῖς	*to/for the brothers*		τοῖς τέκνοις	*to/for the children*
Acc.	τοὺς ἀδελφούς	*the brothers*		τὰ τέκνα	*the children*
Voc.	ἀδελφοί	*brothers*		τέκνα	*children*

3.5. Feminine Second Declension Nouns

Some nouns follow this masculine paradigm, but are actually feminine in gender. So they will take the feminine definite article and feminine adjectives. In the lexicon they will have the feminine definite article: ὁδός, οῦ, ἡ, *way, road.* Thus in the dat.-sg. "the good way" would be τῇ ἀγαθῇ ὁδῷ.

FIRST DECLENSION NOUNS

3.6. Introduction to the First Declension

The α in brackets with the fem.-nom.-sg. in the core pattern represents the fact that feminine nouns and adjectives in the singular can have either α or η in their endings. The article itself does not change between α and η. Sometimes you will find endings in α and η mixed together in a cluster of words that are in agreement.

> ἡ καλὴ σοφία *(the good wisdom)*
> τὴν καθαρὰν διδαχήν *(the pure teaching)*

3.7. The Three Main Paradigms of the First Declension

Some nouns retain the η in all forms in the singular, others retain α, and yet others mix them.

	Fem. sg.	**Fem. sg.** (ε, ι, ρ)	**Fem. sg.**
Nom./Voc.	φωνή	ἡμέρα	δόξα
Gen.	φωνῆς	ἡμέρας	δόξης
Dat.	φωνῇ	ἡμέρᾳ	δόξῃ
Acc.	φωνήν	ἡμέραν	δόξαν

	Fem. pl.	Fem. pl.	Fem. pl.
Nom./Voc.	φωναί	ἡμέραι	δόξαι
Gen.	φωνῶν	ἡμερῶν	δοξῶν
Dat.	φωναῖς	ἡμέραις	δόξαις
Acc.	φωνάς	ἡμέρας	δόξας

a. Notice that the difference between α and η usually does not affect the parsing of a word. For example, a word ending in either ᾳ or ῃ will be fem.-dat.-sg. Furthermore, while a form ending in η may have a nom.-sg. form ending in either α or η, either form will be in the same place in a lexicon. So there should be no problem as long as you remember to look for a lexical form ending in either α or η.

3.8. Words with Stems Ending in ε, ι, ρ

Usually words that retain the α in the singular have a stem that ends in ε, ι, or ρ. Words with α in the nom.-sg. whose stems do not end in ε, ι, or ρ shift to endings with η in the genitive and dative singular. Those words that retain α in all their forms in the singular will have the same form for both the fem.-gen.-sg. and the fem.-acc.-pl., for example, ἡμέρας in the paradigm above.

a. So if you see the ending ας on a noun or adjective assume it is acc.-pl., unless its stem ends in one of these three letters. In that case the context will have to help you sort out whether it is gen.-sg. or acc.-pl.

b. A lexicon enables you to tell if a word has ας in the gen.-sg. since it lists a noun's genitive ending, along with a definite article to indicate the gender (§2.32a). Thus, most lexicons list our three words as

φωνή, ῆς, ἡ
ἡμέρα, ας, ἡ
δόξα, ης, ἡ

c. Examples of agreement between 1D nouns and the article:

	Fem. sg.		Fem. sg.	
Nom.	ἡ ἀδελφή	*the sister*	ἡ ἡμέρα	*the day*
Gen.	τῆς ἀδελφῆς	*of the sister*	τῆς ἡμέρας	*of the day*
Dat.	τῇ ἀδελφῇ	*to/for the sister*	τῇ ἡμέρᾳ	*to/for the day*
Acc.	τὴν ἀδελφήν	*the sister*	τὴν ἡμέραν	*the day*
Voc.	ἀδελφή	*sister*	ἡμέρα	*day*

	Fem. pl.		**Fem. pl.**	
Nom.	αἱ ἀδελφαί	*the sisters*	αἱ ἡμέραι	*the days*
Gen.	τῶν ἀδελφῶν	*of the sisters*	τῶν ἡμερῶν	*of the days*
Dat.	ταῖς ἀδελφαῖς	*to/for the sisters*	ταῖς ἡμέραις	*to/for the days*
Acc.	τὰς ἀδελφάς	*the sisters*	τὰς ἡμέρας	*the days*
Voc.	ἀδελφαί	*sisters*	ἡμέραι	*days*

3.9. First Declension Masculine Nouns

A few 1D nouns are masculine instead of feminine and some of their forms are unusual. There are two paradigms for these 1D masculine nouns.

a. The more common paradigm is represented by the following two important words, *prophet* and *Messiah*.

	Masc. sg.	**Masc. sg.**
Nom.	προφήτης	μεσσίας
Gen.	προφήτου	μεσσίου
Dat.	προφήτῃ	μεσσίᾳ
Acc.	προφήτην	μεσσίαν
Voc.	προφῆτα	μεσσία
	Masc. pl.	**Masc. pl.**
Nom./Voc.	προφῆται	μεσσίαι
Gen.	προφητῶν	μεσσιῶν
Dat.	προφήταις	μεσσίαις
Acc.	προφήτας	μεσσίας

b. All of these are regular 1D endings except the nom.-sg. and gen.-sg. The gen.-sg. is an unusual feature in these paradigms, but it is actually the easiest to parse since the ending looks masc.-gen.-sg. and that is what it is.

c. The nom.-sg. forms look like gen.-sg. endings. As you learn words from this subpattern you will become familiar with them since you will be memorizing this unusual nom.-sg. form. Usually in a text there will be a definite article to help you out: ὁ προφήτης, ὁ μεσσίας. The lexicon lets you know you are working with a word in this paradigm by listing the nom.-sg. and gen.-sg. endings and the article.

προφήτης, ου, ὁ, *prophet*
μεσσίας, ου, ὁ, *Messiah*

d. Since adjectives have to agree with the noun they modify in gender, case, and number you will see something that looks odd at first, for example,

τοῖς ἀγαθοῖς προφήταις *(to/for the good prophets)*
τὸν ἀγαθὸν μεσσίαν *(the good Messiah)*

e. A second form of this subpattern has the same endings as we just saw in μεσσίας, but now the gen.-sg. is ᾶ. Thirty-five words in the New Testament follow this pattern, most of them proper names. Here is the paradigm for Peter's Aramaic name, Cephas, and the word for Satan.[2]

	Masc. sg.	Masc. sg.
Nom.	Κηφᾶς	σατανᾶς
Gen.	Κηφᾶ	σατανᾶ
Dat.	Κηφᾷ	σατανᾷ
Acc.	Κηφᾶν	σατανᾶν
Voc.	Κηφᾶ	σατανᾶ

FIRST AND SECOND DECLENSION ADJECTIVES

3.10. Three Termination Adjectives (2-1-2) in ος, η, ον

The following paradigm of ἀγαθός *(good)* is characterized by η in all the feminine singular endings. Lexicons list adjectives with their nominative singular endings: ἀγαθός, ή, όν.

	Masc. sg.	Fem. sg.	Neut. sg.
Nom.	ἀγαθός	ἀγαθή	ἀγαθόν
Gen.	ἀγαθοῦ	ἀγαθῆς	ἀγαθοῦ
Dat.	ἀγαθῷ	ἀγαθῇ	ἀγαθῷ
Acc.	ἀγαθόν	ἀγαθήν	ἀγαθόν
Voc.	ἀγαθέ	ἀγαθή	ἀγαθόν

	Masc. pl.	Fem. pl.	Neut. pl.
Nom./Voc.	ἀγαθοί	ἀγαθαί	ἀγαθά
Gen.	ἀγαθῶν	ἀγαθῶν	ἀγαθῶν
Dat.	ἀγαθοῖς	ἀγαθαῖς	ἀγαθοῖς
Acc.	ἀγαθούς	ἀγαθάς	ἀγαθά

2. The plurals of such names occur rarely if ever, but if you see one it will use regular 1D endings.

3.11. Three Termination Adjectives (2-1-2) in ος, α, ον

The paradigm of ἄξιος, α, ον (*worthy*) illustrates adjectives with stems ending in ε, ι, or ρ and thus have α in the feminine singular endings (§3.8).

	Masc. sg.	Fem. sg.	Neut. sg.
Nom.	ἄξιος	ἀξία	ἄξιον
Gen.	ἀξίου	ἀξίας	ἀξίου
Dat.	ἀξίῳ	ἀξίᾳ	ἀξίῳ
Acc.	ἄξιον	ἀξίαν	ἄξιον
Voc.	ἄξιε	ἀξία	ἄξιον

	Masc. pl.	Fem. pl.	Neut. pl.
Nom./Voc.	ἄξιοι	ἄξιαι	ἄξια
Gen.	ἀξίων	ἀξίων	ἀξίων
Dat.	ἀξίοις	ἀξίαις	ἀξίοις
Acc.	ἀξίους	ἀξίας	ἄξια

3.12. Agreement in 2-1-2 Patterns

The following pattern illustrates the agreement between articles, adjectives, and nouns in 2-1-2 patterns.

	Masc. sg.	
Nom.	ὁ ἀγαθὸς ἀδελφός	*the good brother*
Gen.	τοῦ ἀγαθοῦ ἀδελφοῦ	*of the good brother*
Dat.	τῷ ἀγαθῷ ἀδελφῷ	*to/for the good brother*
Acc.	τὸν ἀγαθὸν ἀδελφόν	*the good brother*
Voc.	ἀγαθὲ ἀδελφέ	*good brother*

	Masc. pl.	
Nom.	οἱ ἀγαθοὶ ἀδελφοί	*the good brothers*
Gen.	τῶν ἀγαθῶν ἀδελφῶν	*of the good brothers*
Dat.	τοῖς ἀγαθοῖς ἀδελφοῖς	*to/for the good brothers*
Acc.	τοὺς ἀγαθοὺς ἀδελφούς	*the good brothers*
Voc.	ἀγαθοὶ ἀδελφοί	*good brothers*

	Fem. sg.		Fem. sg.	
Nom.	ἡ ἀγαθὴ ἀδελφή	*the good sister*	ἡ ἀγία ἀδελφή	*the holy sister*
Gen.	τῆς ἀγαθῆς ἀδελφῆς	*of the good sister*	τῆς ἀγίας ἀδελφῆς	*of the holy sister*
Dat.	τῇ ἀγαθῇ ἀδελφῇ	*to/for the good sister*	τῇ ἀγίᾳ ἀδελφῇ	*to/for the holy sister*
Acc.	τὴν ἀγαθὴν ἀδελφήν	*the good sister*	τὴν ἀγίαν ἀδελφήν	*the holy sister*
Voc.	ἀγαθὴ ἀδελφή	*good sister*	ἀγία ἀδελφή	*holy sister*
	Fem. pl.		**Fem. pl.**	
Nom.	αἱ ἀγαθαὶ ἀδελφαί	*the good sisters*	αἱ ἄγιαι ἀδελφαί	*the holy sisters*
Gen.	τῶν ἀγαθῶν ἀδελφῶν	*of the good sisters*	τῶν ἀγίων ἀδελφῶν	*of the holy sisters*
Dat.	ταῖς ἀγαθαῖς ἀδελφαῖς	*to/for the good sisters*	ταῖς ἀγίαις ἀδελφαῖς	*to/for the holy sisters*
Acc.	τὰς ἀγαθὰς ἀδελφάς	*the good sisters*	τὰς ἀγίας ἀδελφάς	*the holy sisters*
Voc.	ἀγαθαὶ ἀδελφαί	*good sisters*	ἄγιαι ἀδελφαί	*holy sisters*

	Neut. sg.	
Nom.	τὸ ἀγαθὸν τέκνον	*the good child*
Gen.	τοῦ ἀγαθοῦ τέκνου	*of the good child*
Dat.	τῷ ἀγαθῷ τέκνῳ	*to/for the good child*
Acc.	τὸ ἀγαθὸν τέκνον	*the good child*
Voc.	ἀγαθὸν τέκνον	*good child*

	Neut. pl.	
Nom.	τὰ ἀγαθὰ τέκνα	*the good children*
Gen.	τῶν ἀγαθῶν τέκνων	*of the good children*
Dat.	τοῖς ἀγαθοῖς τέκνοις	*to/for the good children*
Acc.	τὰ ἀγαθὰ τέκνα	*the good children*
Voc.	ἀγαθὰ τέκνα	*good children*

3.13. ε Contract Adjectives

A few 2-1-2 adjectives have stems ending in ε. When an ending vowel is added to such a stem the vowels contract. For details regarding contraction see §§3.28; 4.11.

In four of the singular forms ε contracts with ο to produce ου. Elsewhere the contraction only changes the accent to a circumflex. The four singular forms in bold highlight the places where contraction produces a distinct form, namely, ε + ος = ους in the masc.-nom.-sg. and ε + ον = ουν in the other three forms. Words following this paradigm will not cause you trouble if when learning such words you memorize all three nom.-sg. forms, for example: χρυσοῦς, ῆ, οῦν, *golden*.

	Masc. sg.	Fem. sg.	Neut. sg.
Nom./Voc.	**χρυσοῦς**	χρυσῆ	**χρυσοῦν**
Gen.	χρυσοῦ	χρυσῆς	χρυσοῦ
Dat.	χρυσῷ	χρυσῇ	χρυσῷ
Acc.	**χρυσοῦν**	χρυσῆν	**χρυσοῦν**
	Masc. pl.	Fem. pl.	Neut. pl.
Nom./Voc.	χρυσοῖ	χρυσαῖ	χρυσᾶ
Gen.	χρυσῶν	χρυσῶν	χρυσῶν
Dat.	χρυσοῖς	χρυσαῖς	χρυσοῖς
Acc.	χρυσοῦς	χρυσᾶς	χρυσᾶ

3.14. Two-Termination Adjectives (2-2)

Two-termination adjectives have only two sets of endings instead of three. The masculine endings are used for both masculine and feminine forms. In the following paradigm there are no new endings if you know the definite article core pattern.

	Masc./fem. sg.	Neut. sg.
Nom.	αἰώνιος	αἰώνιον
Gen.	αἰωνίου	αἰωνίου
Dat.	αἰωνίῳ	αἰωνίῳ
Acc.	αἰώνιον	αἰώνιον
Voc.	αἰώνιε	αἰώνιον
	Masc./fem. pl.	Neut. pl.
Nom./Voc.	αἰώνιοι	αἰώνια
Gen.	αἰωνίων	αἰωνίων
Dat.	αἰωνίοις	αἰωνίοις
Acc.	αἰωνίους	αἰώνια

a. Since adjectives following this pattern use the same form for both the masculine and the feminine, when one of these adjectives modifies a feminine noun its form will look like it is not in agreement.

	Singular	
Nom.	ἡ αἰώνιος βασιλεία	*the eternal kingdom*
Gen.	τῆς αἰωνίου βασιλείας	*of the eternal kingdom*
Dat.	τῇ αἰωνίῳ βασιλείᾳ	*to/for the eternal kingdom*
Acc.	τὴν αἰώνιον βασιλείαν	*the eternal kingdom*
Voc.	αἰώνιε βασιλεία	*eternal kingdom*
	Plural	
Nom.	αἱ αἰώνιοι βασιλεῖαι	*the eternal kingdoms*
Gen.	τῶν αἰωνίων βασιλειῶν	*of the eternal kingdoms*
Dat.	ταῖς αἰωνίοις βασιλείαις	*to/for the eternal kingdoms*
Acc.	τὰς αἰωνίους βασιλείας	*the eternal kingdoms*
Voc.	αἰώνιοι βασιλεῖαι	*eternal kingdoms*

b. The lexicon will help you identify these two-termination adjectives since only the masc.-nom.-sg. form and the ending for the neut.-nom.-sg. will be listed.

αἰώνιος, ον

When memorizing such adjectives it is a good idea to include the neuter ending so you know it is two termination. So memorize "αἰώνιος, ον, *eternal*," not just "αἰώνιος, *eternal*."

THE THIRD DECLENSION

3.15. Basic Endings for the Third Declension

The third declension (3D) has several subpatterns. The core pattern for all of them is the indefinite pronoun τις, τι, *some, someone, something, anyone, any-thing*.[3] You should become thoroughly familiar with this pattern, focusing on the endings section.

---

3. This word does not have an accent when it functions as an indefinite pronoun; it is enclitic (§1.9a). But when it is accented it functions as an interrogative pronoun (*who?, which?, what?, why?*). For uses of the indefinite pronoun see §5.84g, and for uses of the interrogative see §§5.84f, 223.

3.16. Core Pattern: The Indefinite Pronoun

	Indefinite Pronoun		Endings	
	Masc./fem. sg.	Neut. sg.	Masc./fem. sg.	Neut. sg.
Nom.	τις [–]	τι [–]	ς, –	–
Gen.	τινος	τινος	ος	ος
Dat.	τινι	τινι	ι	ι
Acc.	τινα [ν]	τι [–]	α, ν	–
	Masc./fem. pl.	Neut. pl.	Masc./fem. pl.	Neut. pl.
Nom.	τινες	τινα	ες	α
Gen.	τινων	τινων	ων	ων
Dat.	τισι(ν)	τισι(ν)	σι(ν)	σι(ν)
Acc.	τινας [ες]	τινα	ας, ες	α

a. One set of forms covers both the masculine and the feminine nouns and adjectives.

b. This core pattern includes five endings in brackets.

1. The two brackets in the neuter simply clarify that the neut.-nom.-sg. and the neut.-acc.-sg. have a **zero form** ending (a blank ending), as you see in the list of endings on the right.
2. The three brackets in the masc./fem. forms indicate the alternative endings that are used at times.
    - [–]   Some patterns use a ς in the masc./fem.-nom.-sg. and others have a zero form.
    - [ν]   Some patterns use α for the masc./fem.-acc.-sg. and others use ν.
    - [ες] In the plural some patterns use ας in the masc./fem.-acc.-pl. and others use ες.

c. In the dat.-pl. the ν in parentheses means ν is sometimes added. For more details see §4.3e.

d. A vocative form is usually the same as the nominative or else it uses the bare stem.

3.17. Article and Noun Agreement in the Third Declension

Putting the articles together with these 3D endings we get the following pattern. The underline represents the stem.

	Masc./fem. sg.		Neut. sg.	
Nom.	ὁ/ἡ	___ς	τό	___—
	ὁ/ἡ	___—		
Gen.	τοῦ/τῆς	___ος	τοῦ	___ος
Dat.	τῷ/τῇ	___ι	τῷ	___ι
Acc.	τόν	___α	τόν	___—
	τήν	___α		
	τήν	___ν		
	Masc./fem. pl.		**Neut. pl.**	
Nom.	οἱ/αἱ	___ες	τά	___α
Gen.	τῶν	___ων	τῶν	___ων
Dat.	τοῖς/ταῖς	___σι(ν)	τοῖς	___σι(ν)
Acc.	τούς/τάς	___ας	τά	___α

a. The ending ν in the masc./fem.-acc.-sg. is usually found on feminine forms. The ending ες in the masc./fem.-acc.-pl. only appears in a contracted form (§3.31c) so it is not listed here.

b. So if you memorize the paradigm of the indefinite pronoun along with the brackets you will have all the endings, including these variations. Or simply memorize the set of endings.

3.18. Ambiguities Among the Three Declensions

There are ambiguities within the 1D and 2D paradigms, and now in the 3D there are four endings that also show up in the 1D and/or 2D (ος, α, ων, and ας). Compare the two core patterns and learn the various options for such endings.

	First and Second Declension			Third Declension	
	Masc. sg.	Fem. sg.	Neut. sg.	Masc./fem. sg.	Neut. sg.
Nom.	ος	η / α	ον	ς, –	–
Gen.	ου	ης / ας	ου	ος	ος
Dat.	ῳ	ῃ / ᾳ	ῳ	ι	ι
Acc.	ον	ην / αν	ον	α, ν	–
Voc.	ε	η / α	ον		
	Masc. pl.	Fem. pl.	Neut. pl.	Masc./fem. pl.	Neut. pl.
Nom./Voc.	οι	αι	α	ες	α
Gen.	ων	ων	ων	ων	ων
Dat.	οις	αις	οις	σι(ν)	σι(ν)
Acc.	ους	ας	α	ας, ες	α

a. The two signals added by the third declension to pay close attention to are:

ος for a gen.-sg.
α for an acc.-sg.

b. Now as we go through each of the subpatterns watch for how the endings of this core pattern appear, especially those that are modified. We'll see that **the key to each 3D pattern is the ending on the stem.**

3.19. The Square of Stops

Some letters, called "mutes," "stops" or "plosives" (based on how they are sounded), form a pattern known as the square of stops. Changes take place when one of these letters comes in contact with an ending that has a ς.

Two of the basic 3D endings have a ς (ς, masc./fem.-nom.-sg. and σι(ν), masc./fem./neut.-dat.-pl.). The square of stops is one of the twelve core patterns to learn thoroughly. It also plays important roles in the verbal system (§§4.15, 46a).

Type	Voiceless	Voiced	Aspirate	With Sigma			
labials	π	β	φ	+	ς	=	ψ
velars	κ	γ	χ	+	ς	=	ξ
dentals	τ	δ, ζ	ϑ	+	ς	=	ς

a. The names of these letters come from how the letters are formed. The labials are pronounced using the lips, the velars the soft palate (these are also called palatals or gutturals), and the dentals the teeth.[4]

b. This chart indicates that when a stem ends in π and a ς is added, the π and ς combine to produce ψ. Thus the effects of a ς on labials and velars make sense if you think of the sounds of these letters. The dentals are more tricky since they drop out when a ς is added.

---

4. The letters are not arranged alphabetically, but rather from voiceless to voiced to aspirated. Thus, for example, pronouncing π does not involve the vocal cords, but pronouncing β does do so, and φ includes an "h" sound. The ζ is not usually included in the square of stops, but it acts like a dental in several paradigms so it is convenient to learn it as part of this pattern. Historically ζ may have arisen from σδ or from a dz sound. In CG courses it is often pronounced "zd." But the "d" sound was eliminated by the Hellenistic period, and since then it has been pronounced "z." Smyth §26; *CGCG* §1.33.

THIRD DECLENSION NOUNS

3.20. Pattern 1: 3D Stems Ending in a Stop

1. Masculine/Feminine[5]

	Labial	Velar	Dental	Core endings
	Singular			
Nom.	κώνωψ	σάρξ	χάρις	ς, –
Gen.	κώνωπος	σαρκός	χάριτος	ος
Dat.	κώνωπι	σαρκί	χάριτι	ι
Acc.	κώνωπα	σάρκα	χάριτα (χάριν)	α, ν
Voc.	κώνωψ	σάρξ	χάρι	
	Plural			
Nom./Voc.	κώνωπες	σάρκες	χάριτες	ες
Gen.	κωνώπων	σαρκῶν	χαρίτων	ων
Dat.	κώνωψι(ν)	σάρξι(ν)	χάρισι(ν)	σι(ν)
Acc.	κώνωπας	σάρκας	χάριτας	ας, ες

3.21. Pattern 1 Forms Analyzed

The following paradigms show how the endings in the core pattern are present in each of these forms. Note which endings are modified and which are not.

a. Labials

	Singular		Plural	
Nom./Voc.	κώνωψ	(κώνωπ - ς)	κώνωπες	(κώνωπ - ες)
Gen.	κώνωπος	(κώνωπ - ος)	κωνώπων	(κώνωπ - ων)
Dat.	κώνωπι	(κώνωπ - ι)	κώνωψι(ν)	(κώνωπ - σι[ν])
Acc.	κώνωπα	(κώνωπ - α)	κώνωπας	(κώνωπ - ας)

Third declension words that have a stem ending with a labial (π, β, φ) make changes in the nom.-sg. and dat.-pl. according to the square of stops, so pay special attention to these in order to be able to recognize them when they show up in a text. The other endings are clear if you know the endings in the core pattern for 3D words.

5. Some nouns in this pattern are masculine, like κώνωψ, ωπος, ὁ (*gnat*), and some are feminine like σάρξ, σαρκός, ἡ (*flesh*), and χάρις, ιτος, ἡ (*grace*).

b. Velars

	Singular		Plural	
Nom./Voc.	σάρξ	(σαρκ - ς)	σάρκες	(σαρκ - ες)
Gen.	σαρκός	(σαρκ - ος)	σαρκῶν	(σαρκ - ων)
Dat.	σαρκί	(σαρκ - ι)	σάρξι(ν)	(σαρκ - σι[ν])
Acc.	σάρκα	(σαρκ - α)	σάρκας	(σαρκ - ας)

Velars follow the same pattern as the labials, but the stem is a velar, here κ.

c. Dentals

	Singular		Plural	
Nom.	χάρις	(χάριτ - ς)	χάριτες	(χάριτ - ες)
Gen.	χάριτος	(χάριτ - ος)	χαρίτων	(χάριτ - ων)
Dat.	χάριτι	(χάριτ - ι)	χάρισι(ν)	(χάριτ - σι[ν])
Acc.	χάριτα	(χάριτ - α)	χάριτας	(χάριτ - ας)
	(χάριν)	(χάριτ - ν)		
Voc.	χάρι	(χάριτ - -)	χάριτες	(χάριτ - ες)

This third pattern in the square of stops, the dentals (τ, δ, ϑ, ζ), has a feature that makes it look a little different. Here the endings are clear in all the same places as in κώνωψ and σάρξ. But now the endings are also clear in the nom.-sg. and dat.-pl. because **when a ς comes up against a dental, the dental drops out**.

Notice also that for this particular word the options listed in the core pattern for the acc.-sg. ending (α and ν) are both employed. Some words use more than one formation at times.

The vocative singular is the bare stem χάριτ with the τ dropped since τ cannot end a word.

3.22. Lexical Forms for Third Declension Words

In the 1D and 2D you can figure out the form the word will have in the lexicon by simply putting a nom.-sg. ending on the stem. In the 3D the modifications make this more difficult. **Attention to the stem ending is key for the 3D patterns**. As each 3D pattern is discussed the way to find the lexical form will be described. These formulas are gathered together in appendix 4.10 for reference.

Since our first pattern uses the square of stops you can use that pattern to figure out the lexical form. Since the nom.-sg. ending is ς simply add a σ to the stem. Thus:

Stem Ending → Lexical Form Ending

π, β, or φ   ψ

κ, γ, or χ   ξ

τ, δ, ϑ, or ζ   ς (because the dental drops out)

For example, in Acts 27:12 you come across λίβα. Your first thought is probably that this is a fem.-nom.-sg. 1D from λίβα or a neut.-nom./acc.-pl. 2D from λίβον. Finding neither of these forms in a lexicon you remember this could be a 3D form. Since the stem of λίβα ends in a labial you use the guideline and look in the lexicon for λίψ and discover it is the word for *southwest wind*.

Similarly, ἀτμίδα in Acts 2:19 could be 1D or 2D, but is actually 3D. Applying the guideline you look for ἀτμίς and find ἀτμίς, ίδος, ἡ, *vapor*.

Notice that the various options for 1D, 2D, and 3D lexical forms would all be in the same place in the lexicon so such a search of options is not difficult.

3.23. Examples of Third Declension Agreement

The following examples suggest the sort of thing you'll see when 3D words are in agreement with the article and 2-1-2 adjectives. The words used here are: ὁ, ἡ, τό, *the*; ϑνητός, ή, όν, *mortal*; σάρξ, σαρκός, ἡ, *flesh*.

	Singular	
Nom.	ἡ ϑνητὴ σάρξ	*the mortal flesh*
Gen.	τῆς ϑνητῆς σαρκός	*of the mortal flesh*
Dat.	τῇ ϑνητῇ σαρκί	*to/for the mortal flesh*
Acc.	τὴν ϑνητὴν σάρκα	*the mortal flesh*
Voc.	ϑνητὴ σάρξ	*mortal flesh*
	Plural	
Nom.	αἱ ϑνηταὶ σάρκες	*the mortal flesh*[6]
Gen.	τῶν ϑνητῶν σαρκῶν	*of the mortal flesh*
Dat.	ταῖς ϑνηταῖς σαρξίν	*to/for the mortal flesh*
Acc.	τὰς ϑνητὰς σάρκας	*the mortal flesh*
Voc.	ϑνηταὶ σάρκες	*mortal flesh*

6. English uses "flesh" for the singular and the plural, though in a given context something like "pieces of flesh" may be used.

3.24. Pattern 2: 3D Stems Ending in ματ

Notice that ματ ends in a dental, which will drop out as in the first pattern. The distinctive of words in this pattern is μα in the stem.

2. Neuter

	Singular		Plural	
Nom./Voc.	ὄνομα	–	ὀνόματα	α
Gen.	ὀνόματος	ος	ὀνομάτων	ων
Dat.	ὀνόματι	ι	ὀνόμασι(ν)	σι(ν)
Acc.	ὄνομα	–	ὀνόματα	α

   a. The τ drops out in the dat.-pl. when the ending σι(ν) is added since a σ causes a dental to drop.
   b. The τ also drops in the nom.-sg. and acc.-sg. which use the zero form because **τ cannot end a word**.
   c. The lexical form for words following this pattern is easy since they end in μα.
   d. There are, however, eleven neuter nouns used in the New Testament that have a stem ending in τ and follow this pattern, but without μα. Examples include φῶς, φωτός, τό, *light* and ὕδωρ, ὕδατος, τό, *water*. See appendix 4.12.

3.25. Pattern 3: 3D Stems Ending in ρ or ν

In this masc./fem. pattern note that the nom.-sg. uses the zero form.

3. Masculine/Feminine

	Singular		Plural	
Nom.	πατήρ	ς, –	πατέρες	ες
Gen.	πατρός	ος	πατέρων	ων
Dat.	πατρί	ι	πατράσι(ν)	σι(ν)
Acc.	πατέρα	α, ν	πατέρας	ας, ες
Voc.	πάτερ		πατέρες	

	Singular		Plural	
Nom.	εἰκών	ς, –	εἰκόνες	ες
Gen.	εἰκόνος	ος	εἰκόνων	ων
Dat.	εἰκόνι	ι	εἰκόσι(ν)	σι(ν)
Acc.	εἰκόνα	α, ν	εἰκόνας	ας, ες
Voc.	εἰκόν		εἰκόνες	

a. The dat.-pl. σι(ν) ending is clear in both words, though in πατράσι(ν) there is an added α, and in εἰκόσι(ν) the ν drops out. If you remember that the stem sometimes loses a letter in the dat.-pl. then finding the form in the lexicon is usually not a problem.

b. Notice also how the vowel in the middle of some words shifts from long to short to disappearing: πατήρ > πατέρα > πατρός, a feature called **vowel gradation**.[7] Other words in this pattern only shift between long and short, and some don't shift at all. Such vowel gradation is sometimes referred to as **ablaut**.

c. This gradation does not affect the recognition of case and number, and finding the lexical form need not be a problem since it will always have a long vowel. So if the stem ends in ρ look for a lexical form ending in ηρ or ωρ and if it ends in ν look for a stem ending in ην or ων. For example, when you come across γαστρί in Matthew 1:18 and recognize ι as a 3D dat.-sg. ending, then the stem ending ρ leads you to look for either γαστήρ or γαστώρ. You find γαστήρ, γαστρός, ἡ, *belly; womb*.

d. Note that πατήρ uses its bare stem with the ε form of vowel gradation for the vocative singular, πάτερ.

3.26. Pattern 4: 3D Stems Ending in ντ

Since ντ has both a dental like patterns 1 and 2, and a ν as in pattern 3, it will follow the same changes found in those patterns.

4. Masculine

	Singular		Plural	
Nom./Voc.	ἄρχων	ς, –	ἄρχοντες	ες
Gen.	ἄρχοντος	ος	ἀρχόντων	ων
Dat.	ἄρχοντι	ι	ἄρχουσι(ν)	σι(ν)
Acc.	ἄρχοντα	α, ν	ἄρχοντας	ας, ες

a. These endings are all easily recognizable. The τ drops in the nom.-sg. due to the zero ending and dat.-pl. due to the σ ending as in patterns 1 and 2. In the nom.-sg. the vowel before the ν lengthens, as in pattern 3.

b. Adding σι(ν) in the dat.-pl. causes both the ν and the τ to drop, and the

---

7. This shift between long, short, and zero forms is an example of quantitative vowel gradation. Qualitative vowel gradation, on the other hand, refers to shift between vowels not related to each other as long and short, for example, between λέγω and λόγος. See Funk §§907–11; Mounce, *Morphology*, §§3–4, AGG §8.

linking vowel o lengthens to the diphthong ου. This change has to be kept in mind when looking for a lexical form.

Many participles follow this pattern (§4.103) so you will see it often.[8]

3.27. Pattern 5 Introduction

Pattern 5 is the most complex set of 3D patterns. The same endings are used as elsewhere in the 3D, but certain changes will affect how these endings appear. **The distinctive feature in pattern 5 words is a stem that ends in a vowel.**

3.28. Vowel Contraction

When a stem ends in a vowel and that vowel comes in contact with a vowel on an ending the vowels contract and usually produce a new form. The following list contains the most common forms of vowel contraction. This is one of the twelve core patterns to be thoroughly familiar with. It also occurs in the verbal system (see §4.11 for more details).

The first column is arranged as formulas and the second column lists the form you will see in a word and then the vowels that might have produced that form through contraction. Learn the contractions in the way you find most helpful.

α + ε = α	α	<	α + ε
ε + ε = ει	ει	<	ε + ε
ε + α = η	η	<	ε + α
ο + ει = οι	οι	<	ο + ει
ε + ο, ο + ε, ο + ο = ου	ου	<	ε + ο, ο + ε, or ο + ο
ο or ω + any vowel except as above = ω	ω	<	ο or ω + any vowel except as above

3.29. Stem Shift

Another major feature in pattern 5 of the 3D is a stem shift. The stem ending does not remain the same throughout the paradigm! Three forms of stem shift cover the most important paradigms for these 3D words. **In each of the sub-**

---

8. This dat.-pl. has the same form as some act.-3-pl. verbs (§4.1). As usual, such ambiguity must be sorted out by the context.

patterns within pattern 5 the stem is usually an ε, but in the nominative singular and at times in other forms it shifts to a different ending.

As you seek to become familiar with pattern 5, go through the paradigms and note what the endings look like. Correlating them with the basic endings from the core pattern will show you the underlying pattern that you already know and thus help you learn to recognize these new forms.

3.30. Pattern 5a: 3D Stems Ending in ος/ε

The first pattern 5 is neuter, so in both the singular and the plural the same forms are used for both the nominative and accusative.

Neuter

	Singular		Plural	
Nom./Voc.	ἔθνος	(ἔθνος - -)	ἔθνη	(ἔθνε - α)
Gen.	ἔθνους	(ἔθνε - ος)	ἐθνῶν	(ἔθνε - ων)
Dat.	ἔθνει	(ἔθνε - ι)	ἔθνεσι(ν)	(ἔθνε - σι[ν])
Acc.	ἔθνος	(ἔθνος - -)	ἔθνη	(ἔθνε - α)

a. The first pattern uses the neuter endings and the stem shift is between ος in the nominative and accusative singular, and ε elsewhere, shown in parentheses.

b. The zero form in the nom./acc.-sg. means that ος is not modified. So ος will look like the ending and it will be a nom.-sg., as in the 2D, but here we have a neuter pattern so the acc.-sg. also ends with ος.

c. The endings on the dative singular and plural and the genitive plural are recognizable.

d. In the gen.-sg. the ος ending added to the stem ending ε produces **ους**, and in the nom./acc.-pl. the α ending added to the stem ending ε produces **η**.

You can learn this pattern as if it were a new and distinct form of the third 3D. But if you understand how the pattern is formed you can learn to recognize the endings using the rules of vowel contraction and the basic set of endings of the core pattern.

e. Pay special attention to the gen.-sg. **ους** and the nominative and accusative plural **η**, since they look like endings in the 1D and 2D.

3.31. Pattern 5b: 3D Stems Ending in ι/ε

This pattern 5 has two of the most distinctive endings among such paradigms.

Feminine

	Singular		Plural	
Nom.	πόλις	(πολι - ς)	πόλεις	(πολε - ες)
Gen.	πόλεως	(πολε - ος)	πόλεων	(πολε - ων)
Dat.	πόλει	(πολε - ι)	πόλεσι(ν)	(πολε - σι[ν])
Acc.	πόλιν	(πολι - ν)	πόλεις	(πολε - ες)
Voc.	πόλι	(πολι - –)	πόλεις	(πολε - ες)

a. In this pattern we see a shift of stem between ι and ε for these feminine words. The nom.-sg. has the ι stem ending and uses the ς ending from the two options in the core pattern. The acc.-sg. also has ι for the stem ending and now uses the ν ending option, from the options α or ν in the core pattern.

b. The gen.-sg. calls for special attention since the ος ending has been lengthened to ως. It is probably easiest just to learn **εως** as a gen.-sg. 3D ending, but seeing it as a lengthening of the regular ending ος may help you remember it.[9]

c. In the core pattern the acc.-pl. has the options ας or ες, and here we have the ες. This means the nominative and accusative plural forms of these words are identical, which can cause problems at times, especially since **εις** is also a verbal ending (§§4.3, 16)! This ending shows up on verbs far more frequently than on nouns, but if you remember that this pattern has this feature, then when you see a word ending in εις you can be alert for the possibility it is a 3D nominal and watch for clues in the context. **The ες option in the acc.-pl. is only used in paradigms with vowel contraction. So when you see ες uncontracted it will be the nom.-pl.**

d. The vocative singular is the bare stem of the nom.-sg. form, πόλι.

3.32. Pattern 5c: 3D Stems Ending in ευ/ε

This third form of pattern 5 nouns contains features also found in pattern 5b.

Masculine

	Singular		Plural	
Nom.	βασιλεύς	(βασιλευ - ς)	βασιλεῖς	(βασιλε - ες)
Gen.	βασιλέως	(βασιλε - ος)	βασιλέων	(βασιλε - ων)

9. One explanation of this ending is that the stem ending was originally η, as found in Homer. When ος was added the vowels shifted, with the long η becoming a short ε and the short ο becoming a long ω, a change known as quantitative metathesis. See Funk §2001.3; Smyth §270c; *CGCG* §4.76.

	Singular		Plural	
Dat.	βασιλεῖ	(βασιλε - ι)	βασιλεῦσι(ν)	(βασιλευ - σι[ν])
Acc.	βασιλέα	(βασιλε - α)	βασιλεῖς	(βασιλε - ες)
Voc.	βασιλεῦ	(βασιλευ - -)	βασιλεῖς	(βασιλε - ες)

a. This final paradigm for pattern 5 shifts between ευ and ε in the stem. It is similar to pattern 5b, with the two main features for special attention in pattern 5b also appearing in 5c:

εως as a genitive singular ending
εις as both a nominative/vocative and accusative plural ending.

b. The vocative singular is the bare stem of the nom.-sg. form, βασιλεῦ.

3.33. Lexical Form Formulas for Third Declension Pattern 5

For words that follow pattern 5 in the 3D the easiest way to figure out the lexical form is to memorize the nominative singular endings these words can take:

ος, υς, ις, ευς, ης.

a. Two of these endings, υς and ης, are found on 3D adjectives (§§3.36–40). They are included here for completeness so this one list covers both nouns and adjectives in the 3D.
b. When you think you are dealing with a 3D form with a stem shift and vowel contraction you can look in the lexicon under the stem and add each of these endings to find the word.

For example, in Revelation 16:20 you see ὄρη and it has no definite article to guide you (καὶ πᾶσα νῆσος ἔφυγεν καὶ **ὄρη** οὐχ εὑρέθησαν, *and every island fled and mountains were not found*). If you think this is a fem.-nom.-sg. (1D), then ὄρη is itself the lexical form. When you look for it in the lexicon you will not find it. Then you have to remember that η can be a contraction of an α ending with an ε stem ending. **When you suspect a 3D ε stem you expect a stem shift, therefore look in the lexicon for a word with one of these five endings on it.** In this case, you look for ὄρος, ὄρυς, ὄρις, ὄρευς, and ὄρης and in a New Testament lexicon you'll only find ὄρος, ους, τό, *mountain*.[10]

10. Interestingly, in LSJ and Montanari there are listings for ὄρυς, υος, ὁ, a wild animal in Libya mentioned in Herodotus, and ὀρεύς, έως, ὁ, *mule*. When you come across more than one possible match in a lexicon you have to sort out their meanings and usages to see which fits your passage. Our verse probably does not mean "and every island fled and mules were not found."

3.34. Pattern 6: 3D Stems Ending in υ

This final 3D paradigm is the easiest one.

Masculine/Feminine

	Singular		Plural	
Nom.	ἰχθύς	(ἰχθυ - ς)	ἰχθύες	(ἰχθυ - ες)
Gen.	ἰχθύος	(ἰχθυ - ος)	ἰχθύων	(ἰχθυ - ων)
Dat.	ἰχθύϊ	(ἰχθυ - ι)	ἰχθύσι(ν)	(ἰχθυ - σι[ν])
Acc.	ἰχθύν	(ἰχθυ - ν)	ἰχθύας	(ἰχθυ - ας)
Voc.	ἰχθύ	(ἰχθυ - -)	ἰχθύες	(ἰχθυ - ες)

    a. Our final 3D pattern has a stem in υ. The stem does not shift and there are no modifications to the basic endings.[11]

    b. Notice the diaeresis in the dat.-sg. (the two dots over the ι, see §1.12), indicating that the ι ending is a separate vowel and not part of a diphthong.

    c. The vocative singular is the bare stem, ἰχθύ.

3.35. Conspectus of Modified Endings in Third Declension Nouns

In the following conspectus note that out of nineteen endings for the 3D only eight are modified from the core pattern. The modifications in **bold** produce alternate forms and call for special attention (appendix 4.26). If you know the core endings and how 3D patterns work, then by associating these few endings in bold with their core pattern origin you will probably be able to sort out most 3D words without needing to memorize all the paradigms.

Masculine/ feminine							
Nom.	ς	can show up as:	ψ, ξ, ς, ης, ις, ευς, υς	Nom./Voc.	ες	can show up as:	εις
	–	can show up as:	ηρ, ωρ, ην, ων				
Gen.	ος	can show up as:	ους, εως	Gen.	ων		
Dat.	ι			Dat.	σι(ν)		

    11. There is a 3D adjective with υ that does have a υ/ε shift (§3.38), which is why υς is included in the list to learn in §3.33.

Acc.	ν				Acc.	ας		
	α	can show up as:	η			ες	can show up as:	εις

Neuter

Nom./Voc.	–	can show up as:	μα, ος		Nom./Voc.	α	can show up as:	η
Gen.	ος	can show up as:	ους		Gen.	ων		
Dat.	ι				Dat.	σι(ν)		
Acc.	–	can show up as:	μα, ος		Acc.	α	can show up as:	η

THIRD DECLENSION ADJECTIVES

3.36. Introduction to Third Declension Adjectives

Many of the same modifications in the nouns also take place in the adjectives, along with a couple of new ones to pay attention to. With slow and careful study you will be able to see the underlying patterns of what otherwise looks like a mess. As with the 3D nouns, the key to understanding how these paradigms work is found in the ending of the stem.

3.37. Adjectives with ντ Stems (πᾶς)

The first paradigm, πᾶς, πᾶσα, πᾶν, *each, every, all*, has a 3-1-3 pattern.[12] Thus it has 3D forms in the masculine and neuter and 1D forms in the feminine. The only adjectives that follow this pattern in the New Testament are πᾶς and its intensive form ἅπας. But πᾶς occurs more than 1,200 times in the New Testament and this pattern also shows up extensively in the participles (§4.103). So this is one of the twelve core patterns to learn thoroughly.

πᾶς, πᾶσα, πᾶν

	Masc. Sg.	Fem. Sg.	Neut. Sg.
Nom.	πᾶς	πᾶσα	πᾶν
Gen.	παντός	πάσης	παντός
Dat.	παντί	πάσῃ	παντί
Acc.	πάντα	πᾶσαν	πᾶν

12. See §5.8 for ways this word is used.

	Masc. pl.	Fem. pl.	Neut. pl.
Nom.	πάντες	πᾶσαι	πάντα
Gen.	πάντων	πασῶν	πάντων
Dat.	πᾶσι(ν)	πάσαις	πᾶσι(ν)
Acc.	πάντας	πάσας	πάντα

a. Note that the masculine forms use almost the same features as in pattern 4 of the 3D nouns (§3.26). The main difference is the ς in the nom.-sg.

b. The neuters also are similar to pattern 4. The final τ drops out in the neut.-nom./acc.-sg. since adding a zero ending to the stem gives παντ-, and τ cannot end a word.

c. The feminine forms use common 1D endings. The stem is changed because a σ was added which caused the ντ to drop, as in pattern 4 3D nouns (§3.26b).

d. If you memorize for vocabulary all three nominative forms: πᾶς, πᾶσα, πᾶν, then you have built into your memory this change in the stem of the feminine, as well as the masculine and neuter nom.-sg. forms.

3.38. Adjectives with υ/ε Stems

This is a 3-1-3 pattern with stem shifts and vowel contraction like 3D pattern 5 nouns (§§3.27–29).

	Masc. sg.		Fem. sg.	Neut. sg.	
Nom.	εὐθύς	(εὐθυ - ς)	εὐθεῖα	εὐθύ	(εὐθυ - -)
Gen.	εὐθέως	(εὐθε - ος)	εὐθείας	εὐθέως	(εὐθε - ος)
Dat.	εὐθεῖ	(εὐθε - ι)	εὐθείᾳ	εὐθεῖ	(εὐθε - ι)
Acc.	εὐθύν	(εὐθυ - ν)	εὐθεῖαν	εὐθύ	(εὐθυ - -)
Voc.	εὐθύ	(εὐθυ - -)	εὐθεῖα	εὐθύ	(εὐθυ - -)
	Masc. pl.		Fem. pl.	Neut. pl.	
Nom./Voc.	εὐθεῖς	(εὐθε - ες)	εὐθεῖαι	εὐθέα	(εὐθε - α)
Gen.	εὐθέων	(εὐθε - ων)	εὐθειῶν	εὐθέων	(εὐθε - ων)
Dat.	εὐθέσι(ν)	(εὐθε - σι[ν])	εὐθείαις	εὐθέσι(ν)	(εὐθε - σι[ν])
Acc.	εὐθεῖς	(εὐθε - ες)	εὐθείας	εὐθέα	(εὐθε - α)

a. The masculine and neuter represent a form of stem shift not seen in the nouns. Pattern 6 of the 3D nouns has a stem in υ that does not change (§3.34), but here we see a stem shift between υ in the nominative, vocative, and accusative singular, and ε elsewhere.

b. The 3D forms in the masculine use the same endings as the nouns, as you can see by comparing our adjective εὐθύς with the noun πόλις.

	υ/ε stem shift—third declension adjective		ι/ε stem shift—pattern 5b third declension noun	
	Singular		**Singular**	
Nom.	εὐθύς	(εὐθυ - ς)	πόλις	(πολι - ς)
Gen.	εὐθέως	(εὐθε - ος)	πόλεως	(πολε - ος)
Dat.	εὐθεῖ	(εὐθε - ι)	πόλει	(πολε - ι)
Acc.	εὐθύν	(εὐθυ - ν)	πόλιν	(πολι - ν)
Voc.	εὐθύ	(εὐθυ - -)	πόλι	(πολι - -)
	Plural		**Plural**	
Nom./Voc.	εὐθεῖς	(εὐθε - ες)	πόλεις	(πολε - ες)
Gen.	εὐθέων	(εὐθε - ων)	πόλεων	(πολε - ων)
Dat.	εὐθέσι(ν)	(εὐθε - σι[ν])	πόλεσι(ν)	(πολε - σι[ν])
Acc.	εὐθεῖς	(εὐθε - ες)	πόλεις	(πολε - ες)

c. From this comparison you can see that the masculine forms of εὐθύς are the same as 5b nouns, but with an υ instead of an ι in the nom./acc.-sg.

d. The neuter forms also use the same endings as the nouns. The nom./acc.-sg. are regular, with the zero form-ending, but it may look odd. So if you memorize **εὐθύς, εὐθεῖα, εὐθύ**, and not just **εὐθύς**, then you have the odd-looking neuter form in your brain.

e. The feminines use the standard endings, so recognizing their gender, case, and number is not a problem. The stem change in the feminine is unusual, but again, if you memorize adjectives with all three nom.-sg. forms then you will be able to recognize the feminine forms.

f. The vocative singulars in the masculine and neuter use the bare stem εὐθύ.

3.39. Adjectives with εσ/ε Stems

There are sixty-six adjectives used in the New Testament that follow this paradigm, and some are used frequently, like ἀληθής, ἀληθές, *true*.

	Masc./fem. sg.		Neut. sg.	
Nom.	ἀληθής	(ἀληθες - -)	ἀληθές	(ἀληθες - -)
Gen.	ἀληθοῦς	(ἀληθε - ος)	ἀληθοῦς	(ἀληθε - ος)
Dat.	ἀληθεῖ	(ἀληθε - ι)	ἀληθεῖ	(ἀληθε - ι)
Acc.	ἀληθῆ	(ἀληθε - α)	ἀληθές	(ἀληθες - -)
Voc.	ἀληθές	(ἀληθες - -)	ἀληθές	(ἀληθες - -)

	Masc./fem. pl.		Neut. pl.	
Nom./Voc.	ἀληθεῖς	(ἀληθε - ες)	ἀληθῆ	(ἀληθε - α)
Gen.	ἀληθῶν	(ἀληθε - ων)	ἀληθῶν	(ἀληθε - ων)
Dat.	ἀληθέσι(ν)	(ἀληθε - σι[ν])	ἀληθέσι(ν)	(ἀληθε - σι[ν])
Acc.	ἀληθεῖς	(ἀληθε - ες)	ἀληθῆ	(ἀληθε - α)

a. The masc.-nom.-sg. uses the zero form and the ε lengthens to η to distinguish it from the neut.-nom./acc.-sg. In most of the rest of the pattern the ε contracts as in pattern 5 3D nouns (§3.27).

b. The neut.-nom./acc.-sg. forms have a zero ending, which clearly reveal that the stem ending is εσ. This zero form is the standard ending from the core pattern, but because of the εσ stem the resulting form looks like it has an ending in ες, which is the 3D masc./fem.-nom.-pl. ending in the core pattern! Therefore, as you learn these adjectives memorize both nominative forms, **ἀληθής, ἀληθές** so you have that neuter form in your brain. After learning a few adjectives in this pattern you will get used to this option for ες.

c. The vocative singulars use the bare stem ἀληθές.

d. The other tricky feature of this pattern is the α ending that contracts with the ε stem to produce η, so it ends up looking like a 1D fem.-nom.-sg. ending. This ε + α contraction occurs in the neuter of pattern 5a nouns in the neut.-nom./acc.-sg. (§3.30). But now in these adjectives it shows up also in the masc./fem.-acc.-sg. Thus it is in three places in this paradigm:

masc./fem.-acc.-sg.
neut.-nom.-pl.
neut.-acc.-pl.

Accordingly, we have a new possibility for an η ending—a masc./fem.-acc.-sg. adjective. This is the only feature in this pattern not in the nouns and **this paradigm is the only place an η signals an acc.-sg.**

So if you are reading the story of Cornelius in Acts 10 you come across εὐσεβῆ in verse 7:

φωνήσας δύο τῶν οἰκετῶν καὶ στρατιώτην **εὐσεβῆ** τῶν προσκαρτερούντων αὐτῷ
calling two of his servants and a <u>devout</u> soldier from among those attending him (Acts 10:7)

You might take this as a fem.-nom.-sg. (1D) and so this form would be the lexical form. When you search the lexicon you discover this lexical form does not exist, but you see on the page where you are looking: εὐσεβής, ές, *devout*.

In this verse you might possibly have expected this to be an adjective since the fem.-acc.-sg. noun στρατιώτην is right before our word, and, again, this adjective paradigm is the only place we see η as an acc.-sg.

This example illustrates how context and a lexicon enable you to sort out any questions about which form you have in your passage. There are also web resources such as biblehub.com for the New Testament and the Perseus website for other ancient Greek texts that offer help if you come across a word that is simply irregular or you have trouble parsing a word.

3.40. Adjectives with ν Stems

In this paradigm there are no modifications to the endings.

	Masc./fem. sg.	Neut. sg.
Nom.	ἄφρων	ἄφρον
Gen.	ἄφρονος	ἄφρονος
Dat.	ἄφρονι	ἄφρονι
Acc.	ἄφρονα	ἄφρον
Voc.	ἄφρον	ἄφρον
	Masc./fem. pl.	Neut. pl.
Nom./Voc.	ἄφρονες	ἄφρονα
Gen.	ἀφρόνων	ἀφρόνων
Dat.	ἄφροσι(ν)	ἄφροσι(ν)
Acc.	ἄφρονας	ἄφρονα

a. This two-termination 3D adjective follows the pattern 3 3D nouns with a stem ending in ν (§3.25).

b. The neuter forms use the same endings found throughout the 3D. The zero form in the nominative and accusative singular is regular, but may look 2D instead of 3D. Again, memorizing both nominative forms, **ἄφρων, ἄφρον**, is an easy way to plug this neuter form into your head. Note that α shows up in three places: masc./fem.-acc.-sg. and neut.-nom./acc.-pl.

c. The vocative singulars use the bare stem ἄφρον.

3.41. Adjectives with Mixed Patterns

A few common adjectives have paradigms that mix elements of 2-1-2 adjectives and 3D paradigms. Two of the main examples are πολύς, πολλή, πολύ, *many*, and μέγας, μεγάλη, μέγα, *great, large*.

	Masc. sg.	Fem. sg.	Neut. sg.	Masc. sg.	Fem. sg.	Neut. sg.
Nom.	πολύς	πολλή	πολύ	μέγας	μεγάλη	μέγα
Gen.	πολλοῦ	πολλῆς	πολλοῦ	μεγάλου	μεγάλης	μεγάλου
Dat.	πολλῷ	πολλῇ	πολλῷ	μεγάλῳ	μεγάλῃ	μεγάλῳ
Acc.	πολύν	πολλήν	πολύ	μέγαν	μεγάλην	μέγα
Voc.				μεγάλε	μεγάλη	μέγα
	Masc. pl.	Fem. pl.	Neut. pl.	Masc. pl.	Fem. pl.	Neut. pl.
Nom./Voc.	πολλοί	πολλαί	πολλά	μεγάλοι	μεγάλαι	μεγάλα
Gen.	πολλῶν	πολλῶν	πολλῶν	μεγάλων	μεγάλων	μεγάλων
Dat.	πολλοῖς	πολλαῖς	πολλοῖς	μεγάλοις	μεγάλαις	μεγάλοις
Acc.	πολλούς	πολλάς	πολλά	μεγάλους	μεγάλας	μεγάλα

a. For the most part these patterns follow the normal 2-1-2 endings and are formed as if the masculine nominative singular were πολλός and μεγάλος.[13] But in four places in the singular they use 3D endings:

masc.-nom./acc.-sg.
neut.-nom./acc.-sg.

b. An easy way to remember the distinctives of these patterns is to memorize all three nominative forms: πολύς, πολλή, πολύ and μέγας, μεγάλη, μέγα. This approach leaves only the masc.-acc.-sg. form to account for. This accusative uses the familiar ν ending from the core pattern for the 3D (§3.16).

c. The adjective πολύς, πολλή, πολύ is not used in the vocative singular.

COMPARATIVE AND SUPERLATIVE ADJECTIVES

3.42. Introduction to Comparatives and Superlatives

The comparative is properly used when two items are compared, for example, A is better than B. The superlative is properly used when more than two items are involved, for example, A is the best. So we would say, the better of two, the best of three, <u>not</u>, the better of three or the best of two. Such precision is often not followed in either English or Greek. For more details on the use of the comparatives and superlatives see §5.85.

---

13. Smyth §311a.

3.43. Formation of Comparative and Superlative Adjectives

In both English and Greek the forms of comparative and superlative adjectives sometimes follow a common pattern and sometimes they are irregular.

a. Thus, in English the comparative and superlative forms of adjectives are sometimes formed from the positive forms using the endings "er" and "est."

Positive	Comparative	Superlative
big	*bigger*	*biggest*

b. In Greek one common way to form these adjectives uses the following 2-1-2 adjective patterns:

	Comparative ("er")	Superlative ("est")
	– τερος, α, ον	– τατος, η, ον
μακρός (*long*)	μακρότερος (*longer*)	μακρότατος (*longest*)

c. A second common pattern has 3D endings in the comparative and a 2-1-2 pattern in the superlative.

	Comparative ("er")	Superlative ("est")
	– ιων, ιον	– ιστος, η, ον
κακός (*bad*)	κακίων (*worse*)	κάκιστος (*worst*)

This comparative uses a two-termination paradigm and thus the first form serves for both masculine and feminine (§3.40). In these examples the same stem is used for the three forms.

d. Often there are alterations in the stems. For example:

μέγας (*large*) – μείζων (*larger*) – μέγιστος (*largest*)

e. Even in fairly regular patterns the forms can undergo changes, such as contractions. The following paradigm of μείζων, ον is the same as a 3D adjective pattern (§3.40), but with some alternate contracted forms.[14]

---

14. The stems of the contracted forms μείζω and μείζους shift to μειζοσ-. When the endings are added the σ drops out (§4.8c) and the vowels contract; ο(σ)α becomes ω and ο(σ)ες becomes ους. Funk §2351.1.

	Masc./fem. sg.	Neut. sg.
Nom.	μείζων	μεῖζον
Gen.	μείζονος	μείζονος
Dat.	μείζονι	μείζονι
Acc.	μείζονα, μείζω	μεῖζον
Voc.	μεῖζον	μεῖζον

	Masc./fem. pl.	Neut. pl.
Nom./Voc.	μείζονες, μείζους	μείζονα, μείζω
Gen.	μειζόνων	μειζόνων
Dat.	μείζοσι	μείζοσι
Acc.	μείζονας, μείζους	μείζονα, μείζω

f. While many comparative and superlative adjectives are formed from adjectives, others are formed from prepositions. For example:

πρό – *before*
πρότερον, α, ον – *before* (of time, place, or rank)
πρῶτος, η, ον – *first* (of time or place)

g. Along with these patterns that share a common base, sometimes in both English and Greek different words are used to form the positive, comparative, and superlative.

Positive	Comparative	Superlative
good	*better*	*best*
ἀγαθός	βελτίων	βέλτιστος

h. It is helpful to know the two main patterns for comparative and superlative adjectives, indicated in bold in §§3.43b and 3.43c above. But there are a number of irregularities, so the lexicon is frequently needed to sort things out, even if you recognize that a word represents one of the basic patterns.

DIMINUTIVES

3.44. Formation of Diminutives

Greek has several suffixes that can be added to a noun to form a diminutive. For the use of the diminutive see §5.86.

a. Diminutive suffixes found in the New Testament include the following.

-αριον	βίβλος, ου, ἡ, *book, scroll*	→	βιβλάριον, ου, τό, *little book, little scroll*
-ιδιον	κλίνη, ης, ἡ, *bed, couch*	→	κλινίδιον, ου, τό, *little bed, pallet*
-ιον	ἔριφος, ου, ὁ, *goat*	→	ἐρίφιον, ου, τό, *young goat*
-ισκος	νεανίας, ου, ὁ, *young man*	→	νεανίσκος, ου, ὁ, *young man, adolescent*[15]
-ισκη	παῖς, παιδός, ὁ/ἡ, *boy, girl, slave*	→	παιδίσκη, ης, ἡ, *young girl, slave girl*

b. The suffixes αριον and ιδιον usually signal a diminutive, but ιον is used in a variety of ways. Of the 150 words ending in ιον listed in *CGEL*, 22 are identified as diminutives, in addition to those ending in αριον and ιδιον.

ADVERBS

3.45. Formation of Adverbs

Adverbs, like adjectives, have positive, comparative, and superlative forms.[16]

a. Some positive adverbs have a set form, such as ἤδη, *already*, and ἐκεῖ, *there.*[17] Other adverbs, however, are formed from adjectives, often by adding the ending ως to the positive form of an adjective stem.

Adjective: καλός, *good*. Adverb: καλῶς, *well*.

Other positive adverbs use the neuter accusative singular or plural form (§5.80). And some words have both forms of adverb.

> ὀλίγον, *little, a bit* (neut.-acc.-sg. < ὀλίγος, η, ον, *little, few*)
> ὀλίγως, *just, barely*
> ταχύ, *quickly* (neut.-acc.-sg. < ταχύς, εῖα, ύ, *quick*)
> ταχέως, *quickly*

b. Some comparative and superlative adverbs are formed from comparative and superlative adjectives.

A comparative adverb is the same as the acc.-neut.-sg. of the comparative adjective.

---

15. A νεανίας was someone twenty-four to forty years old (BDAG, s.v. "νεανίας," 667), though others say this stage of life begins at twenty-eight (Philo, *De Opificio Mundi* 105, citing Hippocrates). So one use of νεανίσκος could be for someone on the younger end of that range. In later Greek the diminutive νεανίσκος was more common than νεανίας (BDAG, s.v. "νεανίσκος," 667).

16. The neuter accusative may also be used as an adverb (§5.80).

17. "Adverbs, like prepositions and conjunctions, were originally case forms, made from the stems of nouns and pronouns. Some of these nominal and pronominal stems have gone out of common use, so that only petrified forms are left in the adverbs." Smyth §341.

A superlative adverb is the same as the acc.-neut.-pl. of the superlative adjective.

Positive	Comparative	Superlative
καλῶς	κάλλιον	κάλλιστα
well	*very well*	*extremely well*

Ἰουδαίους οὐδὲν ἠδίκησα, ὡς καὶ σὺ **κάλλιον** ἐπιγινώσκεις. (Acts 25:10)
In no way have I wronged the Jews, as in fact you know <u>very well</u>.
> Along with the comparative adverb κάλλιον notice also the use of the neuter singular οὐδέν as an adverb, "in no way" (§5.80).

καὶ ὅσα ἐν Ἐφέσῳ διηκόνησεν, **βέλτιον** σὺ γινώσκεις (2 Tim 1:18)
and how many ways he served in Ephesus, you know <u>very well</u>
> βέλτιον is a comparative adverb, using the accusative neuter singular form of the comparative adjective βελτίων, ον (*better*).

Ἥδιστα οὖν μᾶλλον καυχήσομαι ἐν ταῖς ἀσθενείαις μου (2 Cor 12:9)
Therefore rather <u>most gladly</u> I will boast in my weaknesses
> ἥδιστα is a superlative adverb, using the accusative neuter plural form of the superlative adjective ἥδιστος, η, ον (*gladdest*).

περισσοτέρως ζηλωτὴς ὑπάρχων τῶν πατρικῶν μου παραδόσεων (Gal 1:14)
being <u>very</u> zealous for the traditions of my fathers
> περισσοτέρως is a comparative adverb formed by adding the adverbial ending ως to the stem of the comparative adjective περισσότερος, α, ον (*greater, more*).

c. Correlative Adverbs. Adverbs associated with pronouns or with ὅτε may be correlated with one another in function and frequently in form.

		Interrogative	Indefinite	Demonstrative
Time	ὅτε, *when*	πότε, *when?*	ποτέ, *sometime*	τότε, *then*
			ὁπότε, *whenever*	
Place	οὗ, *where*	ποῦ, *where?*	που, *somewhere*	ἐνθάδε, *here*
			ὅπου, *wherever*	ἐκεῖ, *there*
Manner	ὡς, *how*	πῶς, *how?*	πως, *somehow*	οὕτως, *thus*
			ὅπως, *how*	

d. A lexicon is often needed since some adverbs are not built from adjectives and there are irregularities among some of the adverbs that are built from adjectives.

PRONOUNS

3.46. Personal Pronouns

The first- and second-person pronoun patterns contain some features seen in the nouns, but they also have some distinctive features. Accordingly, their forms are another of the twelve core patterns to learn thoroughly.

3.47. First- and Second-Person Pronouns

	First person		Second person	
	Singular		Singular	
Nom.	ἐγώ	*I*	σύ	*you*
Gen.	ἐμοῦ, μου	*my*	σοῦ, σου	*your*
Dat.	ἐμοί, μοι	*(to) me*	σοί, σοι	*(to) you*
Acc.	ἐμέ, με	*me*	σέ, σε	*you*
	Plural		Plural	
Nom.	ἡμεῖς	*we*	ὑμεῖς	*you*
Gen.	ἡμῶν	*our*	ὑμῶν	*your*
Dat.	ἡμῖν	*(to) us*	ὑμῖν	*(to) you*
Acc.	ἡμᾶς	*us*	ὑμᾶς	*you*

a. These personal pronouns do not have gender.

b. Some of the singular pronouns have alternate forms with no accents. These are enclitics and thus share their accent with the word before them in a passage (§1.9a). There is no difference in meaning between the two forms, though the accented forms can be more emphatic (§5.264a).

3.48. Third-Person Pronouns

	Masc. sg.		Fem. sg.		Neut. sg.	
Nom.	αὐτός	*he*	αὐτή	*she*	αὐτό	*it*
Gen.	αὐτοῦ	*his*	αὐτῆς	*hers*	αὐτοῦ	*its*
Dat.	αὐτῷ	*(to) him*	αὐτῇ	*(to) her*	αὐτῷ	*(to) it*
Acc.	αὐτόν	*him*	αὐτήν	*her*	αὐτό	*it*

	Masc. pl.		Fem. pl.		Neut pl.	
Nom.	αὐτοί	*they*	αὐταί	*they*	αὐτά	*they*
Gen.	αὐτῶν	*their*	αὐτῶν	*their*	αὐτῶν	*their*
Dat.	αὐτοῖς	*(to) them*	αὐταῖς	*(to) them*	αὐτοῖς	*(to) them*
Acc.	αὐτούς	*them*	αὐτάς	*them*	αὐτά	*them*

a. This paradigm is a regular 2-1-2 pattern except in the neut.-nom./acc.-sg., where there is no ν on the ending. So this paradigm is like the article at that point. If you memorize all three nom.-sg. forms (αὐτός, αὐτή, αὐτό) you will have this neuter form. For the uses of this important word see §5.7.

3.49. Demonstrative Pronouns

	Immediate (Near) Demonstratives			Remote (Far) Demonstrative		
	Masc. sg.	Fem. sg.	Neut. sg.	Masc. sg.	Fem. sg.	Neut. sg.
Nom.	οὗτος	αὕτη	τοῦτο	ἐκεῖνος	ἐκείνη	ἐκεῖνο
Gen.	τούτου	ταύτης	τούτου	ἐκείνου	ἐκείνης	ἐκείνου
Dat.	τούτῳ	ταύτῃ	τούτῳ	ἐκείνῳ	ἐκείνῃ	ἐκείνῳ
Acc.	τοῦτον	ταύτην	τοῦτο	ἐκεῖνον	ἐκείνην	ἐκεῖνο
	Masc. pl.	Fem. pl.	Neut. pl.	Masc. pl.	Fem. pl.	Neut. pl.
Nom.	οὗτοι	αὗται	ταῦτα	ἐκεῖνοι	ἐκεῖναι	ἐκεῖνα
Gen.	τούτων	τούτων	τούτων	ἐκείνων	ἐκείνων	ἐκείνων
Dat.	τούτοις	ταύταις	τούτοις	ἐκείνοις	ἐκείναις	ἐκείνοις
Acc.	τούτους	ταύτας	ταῦτα	ἐκείνους	ἐκείνας	ἐκεῖνα

a. As with αὐτός, αὐτή, αὐτό in the previous section, this paradigm is a regular 2-1-2 pattern except in the neut.-nom./acc.-sg., where there is no ν on the ending. So this paradigm is like the article at that point. If you memorize all three nom.-sg. forms of these words you will have this neuter form. For the uses of these words see §§5.6, 84e.

3.50. Indefinite Pronouns

The paradigm of the indefinite pronoun τις, τι is the core pattern for third declension nouns and adjectives (§3.16). This word is enclitic and thus only has an accent when shared with the preceding word. It will only be accented on the last syllable.[18] For the uses of this and other indefinite pronouns see §5.84g.

	Masc./fem. sg.	Neut. sg.
Nom.	τις	τι
Gen.	τινος	τινος
Dat.	τινι	τινι
Acc.	τινα	τι

	Masc./fem. pl.	Neut. pl.
Nom.	τινες	τινα
Gen.	τινων	τινων
Dat.	τισι(ν)	τισι(ν)
Acc.	τινας	τινα

3.51. Relative Pronouns

In Greek the relative pronoun used most often is ὅς, ἥ, ὅ.

	Masc. sg.	Fem. sg.	Neut. sg.	Masc. pl.	Fem. pl.	Neut. pl.
Nom.	ὅς	ἥ	ὅ	οἵ	αἵ	ἅ
Gen.	οὗ	ἧς	οὗ	ὧν	ὧν	ὧν
Dat.	ᾧ	ᾗ	ᾧ	οἷς	αἷς	οἷς
Acc.	ὅν	ἥν	ὅ	οὕς	ἅς	ἅ

a. Most of these words look like forms of the definite article without a τ on the front. For example, instead of τῆς we have ἧς. Indeed, some of the forms look very much like the article:

Relative pronoun:	ὅ, ἥ, οἵ, αἵ
Definite article:	ὁ, ἡ, οἱ, αἱ

b. The key point to remember is that the relative pronoun has an accent and the article does not. Fortunately these forms match each other in gender-case-

---

18. This same paradigm serves for the interrogative pronoun (*who?, which?, what?, why?*), which always has an acute accent. In the two-syllable forms the accent will be on the first syllable, for example, τίνες.

number, except ὅ, which is a **neut.-nom./acc.-sg.** relative pronoun, while ὁ is a **masc.-nom.-sg.** form of the definite article.

c. There is also one more potential confusion:

ἥν fem.-acc.-sg. relative pronoun
ἦν impf.-ind.-act.-3-sg. < εἰμί, *he/she/it was.*

The accent is different, but note especially the difference in breathing marks.

d. You will be able to recognize such differences more easily if you pronounce texts as you read, even just mentally. Also, the structure of the clause will often lead you to expect a verb or a relative clause. For details on the function of relative clauses see §§5.212–19. For a list of duplicates that are distinguished by accent and/or breathing mark see appendix 2.

e. Another form of relative pronoun, οἶος, α, ον, has a qualitative sense, *what sort of, such (as).* For the paradigm see appendix 4.21, and for other correlatives see §3.54.

3.52. Indefinite Relative Pronouns

This word is composed of the relative pronoun, ὅς, ἥ, ὅ and the indefinite pronoun τις τι. Both halves of the word decline in its own usual way! ὅστις, ἥτις, ὅτι, *whoever, whatever.*

	Masc. sg.	Fem. sg.	Neut. sg.	Masc. pl.	Fem. pl.	Neut. pl.
Nom.	ὅστις	ἥτις	ὅτι	οἵτινες	αἵτινες	ἅτινα
Gen.	οὗτινος	ἧστινος	ὅτου	ὧντινων	ὧντινων	ὧντινων
Dat.	ᾧτινι	ᾗτινι	ᾧτινι	οἷστισι(ν)	αἷστισι(ν)	οἷστισι(ν)
Acc.	ὅτινα	ἥτινα	ὅτι	οὕστινας	ἅστινας	ἅτινα

a. The six nominative forms are the only ones used in the New Testament and LXX, apart from one expression that shows up a few times using the neut.-gen.-sg. ὅτου.[19]

b. The most difficult form is ὅτι (*whatever*) since it looks just like the con-

---

19. The neut.-gen.-sg. is found in the phrase ἕως ὅτου, *until, while* (LXX 14×; New Testament 5×). By itself ἕως means *until* and can function as either a preposition or a conjunction. Together with ὅτου it forms a "fixed expression" functioning as a preposition. BDAG, "ὅστις," 6, 730.

junction ὅτι (*that, because*). In *THGNT*, UBS⁵, and NA²⁸ ὅτι the relative pronoun is separated into two words.

[ὅ τι ἂν λέγῃ ὑμῖν] ποιήσατε. (John 2:5)
[Whatever *he says to you*], *do*

For further explanation of indefinite relative clauses see §5.219.

3.53. Reflexive Pronouns

In KG the direct reflexive use of the middle (§2.6d) was used less frequently than in CG, and the use of reflexive pronouns increased.

a. The forms of reflexive pronouns in Greek each combine a personal pronoun with forms of αὐτός, αὐτή, αὐτό.

b. There are no nominative forms, so these words are listed in lexicons by the masc.-gen.-sg. form.

	1st Person: *myself*		2nd Person: *yourself*	
	Masc.	Fem.	Masc.	Fem.
Gen.	ἐμαυτοῦ	ἐμαυτῆς	σεαυτοῦ	σεαυτῆς
Dat.	ἐμαυτῷ	ἐμαυτῇ	σεαυτῷ	σεαυτῇ
Acc.	ἐμαυτόν	ἐμαυτήν	σεαυτόν	σεαυτήν

3rd Person:	*himself*	*herself*	*itself*
	Masc. sg.	Fem. sg.	Neut. sg.
Gen.	ἑαυτοῦ	ἑαυτῆς	ἑαυτοῦ
Dat.	ἑαυτῷ	ἑαυτῇ	ἑαυτῷ
Acc.	ἑαυτόν	ἑαυτήν	ἑαυτό

	themselves (ourselves/yourselves)		
	Masc. pl.	Fem. pl.	Neut. pl.
Gen.	ἑαυτῶν	ἑαυτῶν	ἑαυτῶν
Dat.	ἑαυτοῖς	ἑαυταῖς	ἑαυτοῖς
Acc.	ἑαυτούς	ἑαυτάς	ἑαυτά

c. No forms are listed for the first- and second-person plurals. These forms are supplied by the third-person plural forms. So when you find a third-person plural reflexive pronoun you will need to determine from the verb which person it represents. For the uses of the reflexive pronoun see §5.84b.

3.54. Correlative Pronouns

Many pronouns are correlated with other pronouns in form and function. Thus, ὅσος, *as great/much as*, is correlated with τοσοῦτος, *so great/much*, which is "used to express intensity relative to someth. mentioned in context."[20] Resources vary over whether such words are pronouns or adjectives since often they may have both functions (§5.84).[21]

	Relative	Demonstrative	Interrogative
Quantity	ὅσος *as great/much as*	τοσοῦτος, *so great/much*	πόσος, *how great/much?*
Quality	οἷος, *of what kind, such as*	τοιοῦτος, *of such a kind*	ποῖος, *of what kind?*
Size	ἡλίκος, *how great*	τηλικοῦτος, *so great/large*	πηλίκος, *how large?*

---

20. *CGEL*, 355.

21. Indeed, Smyth entitles section 340 "Correlative Pronouns" and then in that section refers to them as "pronominal adjectives." See Funk §273 and for more complete lists see Smyth §340; *AGG* §61b; and *CGCG* §8.1.

Chapter 4

Morphology of Verbal Forms

THE PRIMARY TENSE-FORMS IN THE INDICATIVE

4.1. The Core Pattern for Primary Personal Endings

Some Greek verbs take well over 150 different forms. Fortunately, you do not need to learn that many forms for each verb! The forms can be arranged in paradigms and there are often similarities between the paradigms. Learning a few core patterns will enable you to recognize the vast majority of forms you meet in reading.

a. The first core pattern is the set of personal endings for what are known as the primary tense-forms, namely, **the present, future, and perfect**. The main information you get from the ending is the verb's voice, person, and number (§§2.5, 7).[1]

	Act. sg.	MP sg.
1.	ω, μι, –	μαι
2.	ς	σαι (= η)
3.	–(ν), σι(ν)	ται
	Act. pl.	**MP pl.**
1.	μεν	μεθα
2.	τε	σθε
3.	ουσι(ν), ασι(ν)	νται

b. This core pattern gathers together all the indicative endings found in the paradigms for primary verbs. Knowledge of this core pattern enables you to learn the specific paradigms more easily and see connections between them.

c. These middle/passive endings are part of the first middle/passive pattern, as are the middle/passive endings for the secondary tense-forms (§4.38).

---

1. In addition, endings that are not shared by the secondary tense-forms may help identify a verb's tense-form. Thus, the MP-3-sg. personal ending ται is used in the present, future, and perfect, while το is used in the imperfect, aorist, and pluperfect (§4.38).

The Present Indicative Tense-Form

4.2. Present Indicative Components

The components found in the present tense-form in the indicative are:

Stem   +   Linking vowel   +   Personal ending.

λυ   +   ο   +   μεν   → λύομεν, *we are loosing.*

The following abstract paradigm highlights the components of this paradigm. The stem is indicated by "–1–," since the 1st principal part is used. For discussion of principal parts see §§2.19; 4.67; and the list in appendix 8.

–1–ω	–1–ομεν
–1–εις	–1–ετε
–1–ει	–1–ουσι(ν)

4.3. Present Indicative Active

Verbs ending in ω in the pres.-ind.-act.-1-sg. are referred to as ω verbs. Compare the abstract pattern in §4.2 with the following paradigm of λύω, *loose.*

		Stem	Vowel	Ending	Simple translation
1-sg.	λύω	λυ		ω	I loose.
2-sg.	λύεις	λυ	ει	ς	You (sg.) loose.
3-sg.	λύει	λυ	ει	–	He/She/It looses.
1-pl.	λύομεν	λυ	ο	μεν	We loose.
2-pl.	λύετε	λυ	ε	τε	You (pl.) loose.
3-pl.	λύουσι(ν)	λυ		ουσι(ν)	They loose.

a. In the core pattern there are three options for the act.-1-sg. ending (ω, μι, –) and this paradigm uses the first option, ω.

b. Omega verbs also take the first options listed for the 3-sg. and 3-pl., namely – and ουσι(ν).

c. Notice the linking vowel o before μεν to connect the personal ending to the stem. **It is common for o to connect endings that begin with a μ or a ν, and for ε to be used elsewhere.** In this particular paradigm the ε has become ει in the singular.[2]

d. The 1-sg. and 3-pl. do not have linking vowels in the paradigm. Actually,

2. Funk calls this change to ει "inexplicable" (§3670.2). For suggested explanations see Mounce, *Morphology* §36.5 nn. 3, 5.

the ω is a lengthening of the linking vowel o with a **zero form** ending, and the ου in ουσι(ν) is also a lengthened form of the o linking vowel.[3] While such information can be helpful at times, in this case it seems easiest to focus on these two endings as you will see them on words.[4]

e. Some forms add a **moveable ν**, signaled in paradigms by (ν). In English we often add an "n" to the word "a" when the following word begins with a vowel, for example, "a car," but "an elephant."[5] Greek uses this optional ν in this way, but also frequently when the following word has a consonant. This moveable ν occurs in a number of nominal and verbal paradigms. But it only occurs with an ε or ι, so a ν after any other vowel is not a moveable ν. Note, however, that a moveable ν is never used with the act.-3-sg. form ει of this core pattern; if you see a word ending in ειν it is not an indicative act.-3-sg.

f. Words with a zero ending (a blank) in the 1-sg. end up with an α and those with a zero form in the 3-sg. end up with ε or ει. So for recognition purposes you could learn ω, μι, α in the 1-sg. and ε/ει in the 3-sg. for these patterns. But you should be aware that these are zero endings, since this will help you recognize connections between various paradigms.

4.4. Present Indicative Active of μι Verbs

The μι verbs use the second options listed in the core pattern (§4.1), namely, μι for the act.-1-sg., σι(ν) for the act.-3-sg., and ασι(ν) for the act.-3-pl. They have stems that end in a vowel, so there is no need for a linking vowel.[6] Another name for the linking vowel is the **thematic vowel**, and such verbs are sometimes called **athematic**. Here is the abstract paradigm.

–1–μι	–1–μεν
–1–ς	–1–τε
–1–σι(ν)	–1–ασι(ν)

τίθημι

		Stem	Vowel	Ending	Simple translation
1-sg.	τίθημι	τίθη		μι	*I put.*
2-sg.	τίθης	τίθη		ς	*You (sg.) put.*
3-sg.	τίθησι(ν)	τίθη		σι(ν)	*He/She/It puts.*

3. Funk §§3180.1, 4; Mounce, *Morphology* §36.5 nn. 1, 8.

4. For additional morphological details see Smyth; Funk; and/or Mounce, *Morphology*.

5. Or even just a vowel sound, as just used in this sentence: an "n." But not all vowels work this way; we do not say "an unicorn."

6. Another distinctive of μι verbs is their reduplicated form in the present and imperfect. See §4.74.

		Stem	Vowel	Ending	Simple translation
1-pl.	τίθεμεν	τίθε		μεν	*We put.*
2-pl.	τίθετε	τίθε		τε	*You (pl.) put.*
3-pl.	τιθέασι(ν)	τίθε		ασι(ν)	*They put.*

a. Note the use of the second options in the core pattern, μι, σι(ν), and ασι(ν).

b. The three endings that have σι(ν) in them are the most confusing. They can be sorted out by the vowels that go with them.[7]

- ουσι(ν) – σι(ν) with **ου** before it = act.-3-pl. from an ω verb
- ασι(ν) – σι(ν) with **α** before it = act.-3-pl. from a μι verb
- σι(ν) – σι(ν) with **some other vowel** before it = act.-3-sg. from a μι verb

c. The vowel at the end of the stem shifts from long (η) in the singular to short (ε) in the plural. Some verbs will have other vowels as stem endings, as you see in the next two words, δίδωμι and ἵστημι. If your focus is on reading rather than writing you do not have to learn all these shifts. Just know they happen. See appendix 4.30 for further sample paradigms.

δίδωμι

		Stem	Vowel	Ending	Simple translation
1-sg.	δίδωμι	δίδω		μι	*I give.*
2-sg.	δίδως	δίδω		ς	*You (sg.) give.*
3-sg.	δίδωσι(ν)	δίδω		σι(ν)	*He/She/It gives.*
1-pl.	δίδομεν	δίδο		μεν	*We give.*
2-pl.	δίδοτε	δίδο		τε	*You (pl.) give.*
3-pl.	διδόασι(ν)	δίδο		ασι(ν)	*They give.*

ἵστημι

		Stem	Vowel	Ending	Simple translation
1-sg.	ἵστημι	ἵστη		μι	*I stand.*
2-sg.	ἵστης	ἵστη		ς	*You (sg.) stand.*
3-sg.	ἵστησι(ν)	ἵστη		σι(ν)	*He/She/It stands.*
1-pl.	ἵσταμεν	ἵστα		μεν	*We stand.*
2-pl.	ἵστατε	ἵστα		τε	*You (pl.) stand.*
3-pl.	ἱστᾶσι(ν)	ἵστα		ασι(ν)	*They stand.*

7. The subjunctives use σι(ν) with yet another vowel, ωσι(ν), in the act.-3-pl., which is a lengthening of ουσι(ν) in keeping with the common sign of a subjunctive (§4.77).

d. Notice that the personal endings in these paradigms are all clear if you've memorized the core pattern. You also see that there is enough of the stem to be able to find the word in a lexicon. There are not many μι verbs, but some of them are used very frequently so you eventually will get used to most of their forms as you read.

e. The common verb ἀφίημι has several irregularities in the present indicative. See the paradigm in appendix 4.30.[8]

4.5. Compound Verbs

Some verbs have a preposition added to them to form a new verb (§2.37a, §4.37).

a. Sometimes the meaning of the new verb is easily recognized from the meaning of its components. For example, εἰς, *into* is added to ἔρχομαι, *come, go* to form εἰσέρχομαι, *come into, go into*. At other times the meaning of the compound is quite distinct from the two original words.[9]

b. If the preposition ends in a vowel then that vowel is usually dropped.

ὑπό + ἀκούω → ὑπ(ο)ακουω → ὑπακούω (*under + hear → obey*)

c. Some prepositions undergo a change if the verb begins with a vowel, for example ἐκ → ἐξ.

ἐκ + ἔρχομαι → ἐξέρχομαι (*out of + come, go → come out of, go out of*)

d. If the verb begins with a rough breathing then some consonants will change to an aspirated form, that is, the one with an "h" sound. For example, π → φ, τ → ϑ.

μετά + ἵστημι → μετ + ἵστημι → μεϑ + ἵστημι → μεϑίστημι
(*behind + stand, cause to stand → move, change*)

4.6. Present Indicative of εἰμί

The following paradigm is one of the twelve core patterns to learn thoroughly. Note that some of the endings correspond to the endings in the core pattern. Technically εἰμί does not have voice, but its present forms are commonly parsed as active.

8. For the various forms of ἀφίημι see Mounce, *Morphology* §96, and more extensively Smyth §777; *CGCG* §§12.34–35, which use its uncompounded form ἵημι, *send*.

9. Abbott-Smith lists meanings for prepositions in compound, as does Harris, *Prepositions*. See also Smyth §§1681–98. *AGG* §184 lists such meanings as well and notes differences between CG and KG in some uses.

Present Indicative of εἰμί

1-sg.	εἰμί	*I am.*
2-sg.	εἶ	*You (sg.) are.*
3-sg.	ἐστί(ν)	*He/She/It is.*
1-pl.	ἐσμέν	*We are.*
2-pl.	ἐστέ	*You (pl.) are.*
3-pl.	εἰσί(ν)	*They are.*

4.7. Present Indicative Middle/Passive Components

The same components are used for the middle/passive as for the active:

Stem	+	Linking vowel	+	Personal ending		
λυ	+	ο	+	μεθα	→ λυόμεθα,	*We loose. We are loosed.*

Singular	Plural
–1– ομαι	–1– ομεθα
–1– η	–1– εσθε
–1– εται	–1– ονται

4.8. Present Indicative Middle/Passive

		Stem	Vowel	Ending	Simple translation
1-sg.	λύω	λυ	ο	μαι	*I am being loosed.*
2-sg.	λύῃ	λυ		ῃ	*You (sg.) are being loosed.*
3-sg.	λύεται	λυ	ε	ται	*He/She/It is being loosed.*
1-pl.	λυόμεθα	λυ	ο	μεθα	*We are being loosed.*
2-pl.	λύεσθε	λυ	ε	σθε	*You (pl.) are being loosed.*
3-pl.	λύονται	λυ	ο	νται	*They are being loosed.*

a. The translation of the middle/passive is discussed in §2.7c. In the paradigms only a simple translation of the passive sense is given since other uses of the middle are translated with an active in English.

b. Note the use of ο for a linking vowel with endings beginning with a μ or a ν, and the ε elsewhere (§4.3c).

c. In the core pattern the 2-sg. ending σαι has a modified form in parentheses, ῃ, which is used here. The ῃ ending is formed by the σ in σαι dropping out—such **dropping of an intervocalic σ is common**. Dropping the σ brings the linking vowel ε into contact with αι. Very often when vowels come into contact like this they contract and produce a different vowel (§4.11). Here the ε contracts with α to produce η and the ι that is left over from αι is subscripted (§1.5) to produce the ending ῃ.

$$ε + σαι → ε(\mathbf{σ})αι → ε + αι = ηι → ῃ$$

Understanding how σαι and ῃ are related may help you remember that both of these are forms for the MP-2-sg.[10]

4.9. Present Indicative Middle/Passive of μι Verbs

Note that the stems of μι verbs have vowels so such verbs can be athematic, that is, they do not use a linking vowel (§4.4).

-1- μαι   -1- μεθα
-1- σαι   -1- σθε
-1- ται   -1- νται

τίθημι

		Stem	Vowel	Ending	Simple translation
1-sg.	τίθεμαι	τίθε		μαι	*I am being put.*
2-sg.	τίθεσαι	τίθε		σαι	*You (sg.) are being put.*
3-sg.	τίθεται	τίθε		ται	*He/She/It is being put.*
1-pl.	τιθέμεθα	τιθέ		μεθα	*We are being put.*
2-pl.	τίθεσθε	τίθε		σθε	*You (pl.) are being put.*
3-pl.	τίθενται	τίθε		νται	*They are being put.*

a. The personal endings all follow the core pattern, with the σαι option in the 2-sg.

b. The final vowel on the stem is short throughout this paradigm, unlike the present indicative active paradigm of μι verbs (§4.4). This is also the case in the two following paradigms.

10. The ending ῃ also shows up in the future (§§4.18, 20–24) and the subjunctive (§4.79d).

δίδωμι

		Stem	Vowel	Ending	Simple translation
1-sg.	δίδομαι	δίδο		μαι	*I am being given.*
2-sg.	δίδοσαι	δίδο		σαι	*You (sg.) are being given.*
3-sg.	δίδοται	δίδο		ται	*He/She/It is being given.*
1-pl.	διδόμεθα	δίδο		μεθα	*We are being given.*
2-pl.	δίδοσθε	δίδο		σθε	*You (pl.) are being given.*
3-pl.	δίδονται	δίδο		νται	*They are being given.*

ἵστημι

		Stem	Vowel	Ending	Simple translation
1-sg.	ἵσταμαι	ἵστα		μαι	*I am being stood.*
2-sg.	ἵστασαι	ἵστα		σαι	*You (sg.) are being stood.*
3-sg.	ἵσταται	ἵστα		ται	*He/She/It is being stood.*
1-pl.	ἱστάμεθα	ἵστα		μεθα	*We are being stood.*
2-pl.	ἵστασθε	ἵστα		σθε	*You (pl.) are being stood.*
3-pl.	ἵστανται	ἵστα		νται	*They are being stood.*

4.10. Present Indicative of Non-μι Verbs without a Linking Vowel

There are a few verbs that are athematic (without a linking vowel, §4.4) but which use the personal endings like verbs with a linking vowel. These endings are usually easy to parse, and a lexicon will let you know you have one of these verbs. They are all middle-only (§2.6f).

δύναμαι

		Stem	Vowel	Ending	Simple translation
1-sg.	δύναμαι	δύνα		μαι	*I am able.*
2-sg.	δύνασαι/η	δύνα		σαι/η	*You (sg.) are able.*
3-sg.	δύναται	δύνα		ται	*He/She/It is able.*
1-pl.	δύναμεθα	δύνα		μεθα	*We are able.*
2-pl.	δύνασθε	δύνα		σθε	*You (pl.) are able.*
3-pl.	δύνανται	δύνα		νται	*They are able.*

a. The 2-sg. of this verb shows up as either δύνασαι or δύνῃ.

4.11. Vowel Contraction

A large number of verbs have stems that end in a vowel, either α, ε, or o.[11] These verbs use the same linking vowels as other verbs, but now the vowel on the end of their stem and the linking vowel come in contact with each other. When this happens the two vowels contract.

The rules of vowel contraction form one of the twelve core patterns to learn thoroughly. The following list contains the most common forms of contraction. In order to learn these forms in such a way that you will be able to recognize them as you parse words in a text, you could either memorize this list or learn each form of contraction as you meet it in reading.

α + ε = α	α < α + ε
ε + ε = ει	ει < ε + ε
ε + α = η	η < ε + α
o + ει = οι	οι < o + ει
ε + o, o + ε, o + o = ου	ου < ε + o, o + ε, or o + o
o or ω + any vowel except as above = ω	ω < o or ω + any vowel except as above

a. If you see an η and suspect it represents a contraction, you expect it to have come from the contraction of an ε and an α.

b. The first item in the list may look strange. It means that when a stem ends in α and an ε is added, it remains an α, though often with a change in accent. In the subjunctive α plus η also remains α (§4.80; app. 4.51).

c. Not all of these forms of contraction occur in the paradigms for the present tense-form, but will be met elsewhere in the verbal system and in some forms of nouns and adjectives (§3.28).

4.12. Present Indicative Active of Contract Verbs

ἀγαπάω – *Present Indicative Active*

		Stem	Vowel	Ending	Simple translation
1-sg.	ἀγαπῶ	ἀγαπα		ω	*I love.*
2-sg.	ἀγαπᾷς	ἀγαπα	ει	ς	*You (sg.) love.*
3-sg.	ἀγαπᾷ	ἀγαπα	ει	–	*He/She/It loves.*
1-pl.	ἀγαπῶμεν	ἀγαπα	o	μεν	*We love.*
2-pl.	ἀγαπᾶτε	ἀγαπα	ε	τε	*You (pl.) love.*
3-pl.	ἀγαπῶσι(ν)	ἀγαπα		ουσι(ν)	*They love.*

11. Most contract verbs are denominatives, that is, they are formed from nouns. Thus, for example, the verb ἀγαπάω, *love*, is related to the noun ἀγάπη, *love*.

a. The ι of the linking vowel in the 2-sg. and 3-sg. gets subscripted in contraction.

	Stem	+	Vowel		Contract			Subscript		Ending	
2-sg.	ἀγαπα	+	ει	→	ἀγαπ(α+ε)ι	=	ἀγαπαι→	ἀγαπᾳ	+	ς →	ἀγαπᾷς
3-sg.	ἀγαπα	+	ει	→	ἀγαπ(α+ε)ι	=	ἀγαπαι→	ἀγαπᾳ	+	- →	ἀγαπᾷ

b. The circumflex accent over the linking vowel is often a sign of a contract verb.

ποιέω – *Present Indicative Active*

		Stem	Vowel	Ending	Simple translation
1-sg.	ποιῶ	ποιε		ω	*I do.*
2-sg.	ποιεῖς	ποιε	ει	ς	*You (sg.) do.*
3-sg.	ποιεῖ	ποιε	ει	-	*He/She/It does.*
1-pl.	ποιοῦμεν	ποιε	ο	μεν	*We do.*
2-pl.	ποιεῖτε	ποιε	ε	τε	*You (pl.) do.*
3-pl.	ποιοῦσι(ν)	ποιε		ουσι(ν)	*They do.*

δικαιόω – *Present Indicative Active*

		Stem	Vowel	Ending	Simple translation
1-sg.	δικαιῶ	δικαιο		ω	*I justify.*
2-sg.	δικαιοῖς	δικαιο	ει	ς	*You (sg.) justify.*
3-sg.	δικαιοῖ	δικαιο	ει	-	*He/She/It justifies.*
1-pl.	δικαιοῦμεν	δικαιο	ο	μεν	*We justify.*
2-pl.	δικαιοῦτε	δικαιο	ε	τε	*You (pl.) justify.*
3-pl.	δικαιοῦσι(ν)	δικαιο		ουσι(ν)	*They justify.*

4.13. Present Indicative Middle/Passive of Contract Verbs

ἀγαπάω – *Present Indicative Middle/Passive*

		Stem	Vowel	Ending	Simple translation
1-sg.	ἀγαπῶμαι	ἀγαπα	ο	μαι	*I am being loved.*
2-sg.	ἀγαπᾷ	ἀγαπα	ε	(σ)αι	*You (sg.) are being loved.*
3-sg.	ἀγαπᾶται	ἀγαπα	ε	ται	*He/She/It is being loved.*

	Stem	Vowel	Ending	Simple translation
1-pl.	ἀγαπώμεθα	ἀγαπα	ο	μεθα	We are being loved.
2-pl.	ἀγαπᾶσθε	ἀγαπα	ε	σθε	You (pl.) are being loved.
3-pl.	ἀγαπῶνται	ἀγαπα	ο	νται	They are being loved.

a. The translation of the middle/passive is discussed in §2.7c. In the paradigms only a simple translation of the passive sense is given since other uses of the middle are translated with an active in English.

b. In the 2-sg. the σ drops out and the ι subscripts. **Note that this form is identical to the act.-3-sg. (§4.12).**

ποιέω – *Present Indicative Middle/Passive*

	Stem	Vowel	Ending	Simple translation
1-sg.	ποιοῦμαι	ποιε	ο	μαι	I am being made.
2-sg.	ποιῇ	ποιε	(ε)	(σ)αι	You (sg.) are being made.
3-sg.	ποιεῖται	ποιε	ε	ται	He/She/It is being made.
1-pl.	ποιούμεθα	ποιε	ο	μεθα	We are being made.
2-pl.	ποιεῖσθε	ποιε	ε	σθε	You (pl.) are being made.
3-pl.	ποιοῦνται	ποιε	ο	νται	They are being made.

c. In the 2-sg. both the linking vowel and the σ on the ending drop out, so the ε stem ending and the α of the personal ending contract (ε+α = η) and the ι subscripts (§§4.8c, 11). The η ending also occurs in the future (§§4.18, 20–24) and the subjunctive (§4.79d).

δικαιόω – *Present Indicative Middle/Passive*

	Stem	Vowel	Ending	Simple translation
1-sg.	δικαιοῦμαι	δικαιο	ο	μαι	I am being justified.
2-sg.	δικαιοῖ	δικαιο	ε	(σα)ι	You (sg.) are being justified.
3-sg.	δικαιοῦται	δικαιο	ε	ται	He/She/It is being justified.
1-pl.	δικαιούμεθα	δικαιο	ο	μεθα	We are being justified.
2-pl.	δικαιοῦσθε	δικαιο	ε	σθε	You (pl.) are being justified.
3-pl.	δικαιοῦνται	δικαιο	ο	νται	They are being justified.

d. In the 2-sg. both the σ and the α on the ending drop out so the ο and ε contract (ο+ει = οι). The ι is not contracted, but note that **this form is identical to the act.-3-sg. (§4.12).**

The Future Indicative Tense-Form

4.14. Future Indicative Components

Verbs in the future tense-form use the 2nd principal part for their active and first middle/passive forms (§4.18), and the 6th principal part for their second middle/passive forms (§4.22). For principal parts see §§2.19; 4.67; and the list in appendix 8.

a. The components for the main paradigm for the future in the active and first middle/passive are similar to those of the present, though now with the 2nd principal part and a σ tense-form sign:

Present: stem (1st prin. part)   +   vowel o/ε   +   primary personal ending

Future: stem (**2nd** prin. part)   +   **σ**   +   vowel o/ε   +   primary personal ending.

–2–	σω	–2–	σομεν
–2–	σεις	–2–	σετε
–2–	σει	–2–	σουσι(ν)

b. A 2nd principal part is needed since it sometimes differs from the 1st principal part used for the present. For example, the future of ἔρχομαι, *come, go,* is ἐλεύσομαι, δίδωμι (*give*) is δώσω, and ἐσθίω (*eat*) is φάγομαι.

4.15. The Square of Stops

The σ tense-form sign causes a change to take place if the stem ends in one of the letters known as a "stop." For details see §3.19. Thus, the stem of πέμπω (*send*) is πεμπ-, so when σ is added it becomes πεμψ-.

	Stem		T-form sign						
πέμπω (*send*) →	πεμπ	+	σ			→	πεμψ	→	πέμψω
ἄγω (*lead*) →	ἀγ	+	σ			→	ἀξ	→	ἄξω
σῴζω (*save*) →	σῳζ	+	σ	=	σῳ(ξ)σ →	σωσ	→	σώσω.

4.16. Future Indicative Active

In the following paradigms note the sign of the future (the σ), and compare the endings with the core pattern for the personal endings to be able to recognize their voice, person, and number. The present tense-form paradigm is included for comparison.

λύω – *Future Indicative Active*

	Present	Future	Stem	T-form sign	Vowel	Ending	Simple translation
1-sg.	λύω	λύσω	λυ	σ		ω	*I will loose.*
2-sg.	λύεις	λύσεις	λυ	σ	ει	ς	*You (sg.) will loose.*
3-sg.	λύει	λύσει	λυ	σ	ει	–	*He/She/It will loose.*
1-pl.	λύομεν	λύσομεν	λυ	σ	ο	μεν	*We will loose.*
2-pl.	λύετε	λύσετε	λυ	σ	ε	τε	*You (pl.) will loose.*
3-pl.	λύουσι(ν)	λύσουσι(ν)	λυ	σ		ουσι(ν)	*They will loose.*

πέμπω – *Future Indicative Active*

	Present	Future	Stem	T-form sign	Vowel	Ending	Simple translation
1-sg.	πέμπω	πέμψω	πεμπ	σ		ω	*I will send.*
2-sg.	πέμπεις	πέμψεις	πεμπ	σ	ει	ς	*You (sg.) will send.*
3-sg.	πέμπει	πέμψει	πεμπ	σ	ει	–	*He/She/It will send.*
1-pl.	πέμπομεν	πέμψομεν	πεμπ	σ	ο	μεν	*We will send.*
2-pl.	πέμπετε	πέμψετε	πεμπ	σ	ε	τε	*You (pl.) will send.*
3-pl.	πέμπουσι(ν)	πέμψουσι(ν)	πεμπ	σ		ουσι(ν)	*They will send.*

4.17. Future Indicative Active of Contract Verbs

The tense-form sign σ prevents vowels from coming into contact with each other in the future tense-form. Instead of contracting, the vowel on the stem ending simply lengthens.

α → η
ε → η
ο → ω

The resulting endings are just like the present indicative endings. For a full paradigm see appendix 4.32.

Lexical form	Present	Future
γεννάω	γεννῶ	γεννήσω
ποιέω	ποιῶ	ποιήσω
φανερόω	φανερῶ	φανερώσω

4.18. Future Indicative First Middle/Passive

-2- σομαι   -2- σομεθα
-2- ση   -2- σεσθε
-2- σεται   -2- σονται

λύω – *Future Indicative First Middle/Passive*

	Present	Future	Stem	T-form sign	Vowel	Ending	Simple translation
1-sg.	λύομαι	λύσομαι	λυ	σ	ο	μαι	*I will loose.*
2-sg.	λύῃ	λύσῃ	λυ	σ		η	*You (sg.) will loose.*
3-sg.	λύεται	λύσεται	λυ	σ	ε	ται	*He/She/It will loose.*
1-pl.	λυόμεθα	λυσόμεθα	λυ	σ	ο	μεθα	*We will loose.*
2-pl.	λύεσθε	λύσεσθε	λυ	σ	ε	σθε	*You (pl.) will loose.*
3-pl.	λύονται	λύσονται	λυ	σ	ο	νται	*They will loose.*

a. While these forms are middle/passive, in the future the first middle/passive is rarely used for the passive sense of the middle (§5.94). These translations are in the active since that is how the middle is translated in English when it is not functioning in a passive sense.

πέμπω – *Future Indicative First Middle/Passive*

	Present	Future	Stem	T-form sign	Vowel	Ending	Simple translation
1-sg.	πέμπομαι	πέμψομαι	πεμπ	σ	ο	μαι	*I will send.*
2-sg.	πέμπῃ	πέμψῃ	πεμπ	σ		η	*You (sg.) will send.*
3-sg.	πέμπεται	πέμψεται	πεμπ	σ	ε	ται	*He/She/It will send.*
1-pl.	πεμπόμεθα	πεμψόμεθα	πεμπ	σ	ο	μεθα	*We will send.*
2-pl.	πέμπεσθε	πέμψεσθε	πεμπ	σ	ε	σθε	*You (pl.) will send.*
3-pl.	πέμπονται	πέμψονται	πεμπ	σ	ο	νται	*They will send.*

4.19. Future Indicative First Middle/Passive of Contract Verbs

As in the future active (§4.17) the tense-form sign prevents vowels from coming into contact with each other and the vowel on the stem ending simply lengthens.

α → η
ε → η
ο → ω

The resulting endings are just like the present indicative endings. For a full paradigm see appendix 4.32.

Lexical form	Present	Future
γεννάω	γεννῶμαι	γεννήσομαι
ποιέω	ποιοῦμαι	ποιήσομαι
φανερόω	φανεροῦμαι	φανερώσομαι

4.20. Liquid Future Verbs

Verbs whose stems end in λ, μ, ν, or ρ are referred to as "liquids." Technically only those ending in λ and ρ are liquids, while μ and ν are nasals.[12]

a. Such verbs use εσ instead of a simple σ for the future tense-form sign. When the linking vowel is added the σ drops, bringing two vowels together (§4.8c) which then contract. Consequently, the endings on the liquid futures are identical with the endings on the present forms of ε contract verbs (§§4.12–13). The forms of ποιέω in the present indicative are included below for comparison.

b. Often minor vowel changes take place within the stem (§4.70).

c. The MP-2-sg. ending η also occurs in the present (§4.8) and the subjunctive (§4.79d).

Liquid Futures

	(μένω)	(αἴρω)	(ποιέω present)
	Act.	Act.	Act.
1-sg.	μενῶ	ἀρῶ	ποιῶ
2-sg.	μενεῖς	ἀρεῖς	ποιεῖς
3-sg.	μενεῖ	ἀρεῖ	ποιεῖ
1-pl.	μενοῦμεν	ἀροῦμεν	ποιοῦμεν
2-pl.	μενεῖτε	ἀρεῖτε	ποιεῖτε
3-pl.	μενοῦσι(ν)	ἀροῦσι(ν)	ποιοῦσι(ν)
	MP1	MP1	MP
1-sg.	μενοῦμαι	ἀροῦμαι	ποιοῦμαι
2-sg.	μενῇ	ἀρῇ	ποιῇ
3-sg.	μενεῖται	ἀρεῖται	ποιεῖται
1-pl.	μενούμεθα	ἀρούμεθα	ποιούμεθα
2-pl.	μενεῖσθε	ἀρεῖσθε	ποιεῖσθε
3-pl.	μενοῦνται	ἀροῦνται	ποιοῦνται

---

12. In forming liquids air flows around the tongue, while formation of nasals incorporates the nose.

When you see such endings with the circumflex check the stem ending. If it is λ, μ, ν, or ρ then the form is probably a future and the lexical form may have a slightly different stem, as here, ἀρ- compared to the lexical form αἰρ-.

4.21. Future Indicative of εἰμί

The paradigm for the future of εἰμί is one of the twelve core patterns to learn thoroughly. The future uses the regular endings from the core pattern, so if you learn that ἐ- is the future stem of εἰμί you will know this paradigm. While technically εἰμί does not have voice these forms are commonly parsed as middle/passive. This is the only paradigm for εἰμί in the future.

1-sg.	ἔσομαι
2-sg.	ἔσῃ
3-sg.	ἔσται
1-pl.	ἐσόμεθα
2-pl.	ἔσεσθε
3-pl.	ἔσονται

4.22. Future Indicative Second Middle/Passive Components

The future second middle/passive is built on the 6th principal part. Its components include the tense-form sign θησ, the linking vowel ο/ε, and the primary middle/passive endings. The presence of θη indicates that this is a second middle/passive pattern. While the future first middle/passive is rarely used for the passive sense of the middle (§4.18a), the future second middle/passive is used almost exclusively for the passive sense (§5.94).

Stem	+	T-form sign	+	Vowel	+	Primary MP endings		
6th part	+	θησ	+	ο/ε	+	μεθα	→	λυθησόμεθα,
								We will be loosed.

a. This pattern is the same as the future first middle/passive but with θη added and using a different principal part. An abstract paradigm highlights the signals:

Future second middle/passive indicative		Future first middle/passive indicative	
–6–θησομαι	–6–θησομεθα	–2–σομαι	–2–σομεθα
–6–θησῃ	–6–θησεσθε	–2–σῃ	–2–σεσθε
–6–θησεται	–6–θησονται	–2–σεται	–2–σονται

b. Since the future second middle/passive uses the 6th principal part, verbs will often have a stem that differs from the lexical form, which is the 1st principal part.

The 6th principal part is also used for the aorist second middle/passive, so it will be listed with an augment (§§2.16; 4.59). This augment is removed for the future second middle/passive, since futures are not augmented. Thus, the 6th principal part of δίδωμι is ἐδόθην. Removing the augment and adding the future second middle/passive's tense-form sign, linking vowel, and endings produces δοθήσομαι, *I will be given*.

c. When a tense-form sign beginning with a ϑ is added to a verb with a stem that ends in one of the square of stops (§3.19) the stem ending is modified. A labial or dental becomes the corresponding aspirated form, while dentals added to ϑ, which is itself a dental, become σ. By far the most common dental verbal ending is ζ.

A labial	(π, β)	becomes φ.	π + ϑ = φϑ	β + ϑ = φϑ
A velar	(κ, γ)	becomes χ.	κ + ϑ = χϑ	γ + ϑ = χϑ
A dental	(τ, δ, ϑ, ζ)	becomes σ.	ζ + ϑ = σϑ	

Labial	πέμπω	→	πεμφθήσομαι
Velar	διώκω	→	διωχθήσομαι
Dental	βαπτίζω	→	βαπτισθήσομαι
	πείθω	→	πεισθήσομαι

So when you see φ, χ, or σ before the tense-form sign ϑησ (or ϑη in the aorist second middle/passive, §4.59) suspect this change may have taken place, or that the stem ends in φ or χ to begin with. For example, the future second middle/passive of δέχομαι, *receive*, is δεχθήσομαι.

A number of verbs add a σ before the ϑησ tense-form sign, so a σ does not always signal a verb with a dental stem.

ἀκούω	→	ἀκουσθήσομαι
κλείω	→	κλεισθήσομαι

d. Some **future second middle/passives** drop the ϑ from the tense-form sign.

	Stem	+	T-form sign	+	Vowel	+	Ending
Fut. MP2	6th	+	ϑησ	+	ο/ε	+	primary
Alt. fut. MP2	6th	+	ησ	+	ο/ε	+	primary

4.23. Future Indicative Second Middle/Passive

λύω – *Future Second Middle/Passive Indicative*

		Stem	T-form sign	Vowel	Ending	Simple translation
1-sg.	λυθήσομαι	λυ	θησ	ο	μαι	*I will be loosed.*
2-sg.	λυθήσῃ	λυ	θησ	ε	(σ)αι	*You (sg.) will be loosed.*
3-sg.	λυθήσεται	λυ	θησ	ε	ται	*He/She/It will be loosed.*
1-pl.	λυθησόμεθα	λυ	θησ	ο	μεθα	*We will be loosed.*
2-pl.	λυθήσεσθε	λυ	θησ	ε	σθε	*You (pl.) will be loosed.*
3-pl.	λυθήσονται	λυ	θησ	ο	νται	*They will be loosed.*

a. The translations are in the passive since the future second middle/passive is used almost exclusively for the passive sense of the middle (§§4.22, 5.94).

b. As in the present and future first middle/passive, the 2-sg. ending σαι is modified by the σ dropping out and the linking vowel ε contracting with α to produce η, and the ι subscripting to produce the ending ῃ.

4.24. Alternate Future Indicative Second Middle/Passive

An alternate form of the future second middle/passive lacks a θ in the tense-form sign. This alternate future second middle/passive is often referred to as the second future passive.

–6-ησομαι	–6-ησομεθα
–6-ησῃ	–6-ησεσθε
–6-ησεται	–6-ησονται

γράφω – *Alternate Future Indicative Second Middle/Passive*

		Stem	T-form sign	Vowel	Ending	Simple translation
1-sg.	γραφήσομαι	γραφ	ησ	ο	μαι	*I will be written.*
2-sg.	γραφήσῃ	γραφ	ησ	ε	(σ)αι	*You (sg.) will be written.*
3-sg.	γραφήσεται	γραφ	ησ	ε	ται	*He/she/it will be written.*
1-pl.	γραφησόμεθα	γραφ	ησ	ο	μεθα	*We will be written.*
2-pl.	γραφήσεσθε	γραφ	ησ	ε	σθε	*You (pl.) will be written.*
3-pl.	γραφήσονται	γραφ	ησ	ο	νται	*They will be written.*

4.25. Future Indicative Second Middle/Passive of Contract Verbs

As with other forms of the future, the tense-form sign prevents vowels from coming into contact with each other and the vowel on the stem ending simply lengthens.

α → η
ε → η
ο → ω

The resulting endings are just like the future indicative first middle/passive endings but with the tense-form sign θη added to form a second middle/passive pattern. For a full paradigm see appendix 4.34.

Lexical form	Future first middle/passive	Future second middle/passive
γεννάω	γεννήσομαι	γεννηθήσομαι
ποιέω	ποιήσομαι	ποιηθήσομαι
φανερόω	φανερώσομαι	φανερωθήσομαι

The Perfect Indicative Tense-Form

4.26. Reduplication

Reduplication is one of the characteristic signs of a perfect. Reduplication can take several forms.

a. When a verb begins with a consonant, that consonant is usually doubled and an ε added.

λύω	>	λέλυκα, *I have loosed.*
πιστεύω	>	πεπίστευκα, *I have believed.*

b. If an aspirated consonant (that is, φ, χ, or θ, forms which include an "h" sound) begins the verb then the doubled letter is the corresponding nonaspirated form (π, κ, τ). These pairs of letters are the labials, velars, and dentals in the square of stops (§3.19).

Labial	–	φ > π	– φανερόω	>	πεφανέρωκα, *I have manifested.*
Velar	–	χ > κ	– χωρέω	>	κεχώρηκα, *I have made room.*
Dental	–	θ > τ	– θνῄσκω	>	τέθνηκα, *I have died.*

c. If the verb begins with a vowel, the vowel is doubled, which produces a corresponding long vowel.

αα	=	η	ἀγαπάω	→	ἠγάπηκα, *I have loved.*
εε	=	η	ἐγγίζω	→	ἤγγικα, *I have approached.*
οο	=	ω.	ὁμολογέω	→	ὡμολόγηκα, *I have confessed.*

d. If the verb begins with σ and another consonant, for example σπ or στ, then reduplication usually shows up as an ε. For example, σπείρω → ἔσπαρκα; σταυρόω → ἐσταύρωκα. The same is true for ἵστημι → ἔστηκα.

e. The combination of a lengthened vowel on the front, the κ tense-form sign, and α or ε as the linking vowel usually distinguishes the perfect active even when the 4th principal part is not distinctive.

f. A compound verb in the perfect reduplicates the verb part, not the preposition. For example, ἀναλύω (*unloose, depart, return*) is composed of the preposition ἀνά (*up, each*) and λύω (*loose*). Since the stem of a compound is reduplicated the perfect is ἀναλέλυκα.

4.27. Perfect Indicative Active Components

The perfect active uses the 4th principal part (§§2.19; 4.67). It has κ as its tense-form sign and uses α and ε as linking vowels.[13] It also adds reduplication to the front of the verb. So the components of the perfect active forms are:

reduplication + stem (4th prin. part) + κ + α/ε + primary personal endings

a. A few verbs lack a κ in the tense-form sign. This alternate form is often referred to as a second perfect (§4.29).

reduplication + stem (4th prin. part) + α/ε + primary personal endings

b. Here are the components of the perfect compared to those of the alternate perfect, using λε to represent any form of reduplication:

	Reduplication +	Stem +	T-form sign +	Vowel +	Ending
Pf. act.	λε	+ 4th	+ κ	+ α/ε	+ primary
Alt. pf. act.	λε	+ 4th		+ α/ε	+ primary

13. There are differing opinions whether κα/ε is the tense-form sign or κ is the tense-form sign with α/ε as linking vowels. Since for reading purposes it comes to the same thing I have used the option that seems easiest for the student to learn in order to recognize the forms when reading. For the issue see Mounce, *Morphology* §34.

Perfect		Alternate perfect	
λε–4–κα	λε–4–καμεν	λε–4–α	λε–4–αμεν
λε–4–κας	λε–4–κατε	λε–4–ας	λε–4–ατε
λε–4–κε(ν)	λε–4–κασι(ν)	λε–4–ε(ν)	λε–4–ασι(ν)

c. Some verbs use a 4th principal part that differs from their 1st principal part. For example, δίδωμι (*give*) is δέδωκα, λέγω (*say*) is εἴρηκα. Fortunately, the changes between principal parts are often less drastic. For more on principal parts see §§2.19; 4.67; and the list in appendix 8.

4.28. Perfect Indicative Active

λύω – *Perfect Indicative Active*

		Redupli-cation	Stem	T-form sign	Vowel	Ending	Simple translation
1-sg.	λελύκα	λε	λυ	κ	α	–	*I have loosed.*
2-sg.	λελύκας	λε	λυ	κ	α	ς	*You (sg.) have loosed.*
3-sg.	λελύκε(ν)	λε	λυ	κ	ε	-(ν)	*He/She/It has loosed.*
1-pl.	λελύκαμεν	λε	λυ	κ	α	μεν	*We have loosed.*
2-pl.	λελύκατε	λε	λυ	κ	α	τε	*You (pl.) have loosed.*
3-pl.	λελύκασι(ν)	λε	λυ	κ	α	σι(ν)	*They have loosed.*

a. The 1-sg. takes the zero form option from the core pattern.

b. The linking vowel ε only shows up in the 3-sg., and this distinguishes it from the 1-sg. since they both have a zero form ending.

c. The 3-pl. takes a simple σι(ν) ending, but with the α linking vowel it looks like the ασι(ν) ending in the core pattern. When you see κασι(ν) expect it to be this perfect tense-form.

ἐγγίζω – *Perfect Indicative Active*

		Redupli-cation	Stem	T-form sign	Vowel	Ending	Simple translation
1-sg.	ἤγγικα	ε	ἐγγι	κ	α	–	*I have drawn near.*
2-sg.	ἤγγικας	ε	ἐγγι	κ	α	ς	*You (sg.) have drawn near.*
3-sg.	ἤγγικε(ν)	ε	ἐγγι	κ	ε	-(ν)	*He/She/It has drawn near.*
1-pl.	ἠγγίκαμεν	ε	ἐγγι	κ	α	μεν	*We have drawn near.*
2-pl.	ἠγγίκατε	ε	ἐγγι	κ	α	τε	*You (pl.) have drawn near.*
3-pl.	ἠγγίκασι(ν)	ε	ἐγγι	κ	α	σι(ν)	*They have drawn near.*

4.29. Alternate Perfect Indicative Active

ἔρχομαι – *Perfect Indicative Active*

	Perfect t-form	Reduplication	Stem	Vowel	Ending	Simple translation
1-sg.	ἐλήλυθα	ε	ληλυθ	α	–	I have come.
2-sg.	ἐλήλυθας	ε	ληλυθ	α	ς	You (sg.) have come.
3-sg.	ἐλήλυθε(ν)	ε	ληλυθ	ε	–(ν)	He/She/It has come.
1-pl.	ἐληλύθαμεν	ε	ληλυθ	α	μεν	We have come.
2-pl.	ἐληλύθατε	ε	ληλυθ	α	τε	You (pl.) have come.
3-pl.	ἐληλύθασι(ν)	ε	ληλυθ	α	σι(ν)	They have come.

a. This verb is middle-only in the present and future, but has an active form in the perfect.

b. Notice that the κ tense-form sign is missing, so this verb is an alternate form of the perfect, often referred to as a second perfect.

οἶδα

1-sg.	οἶδα	I know	1-pl.	οἴδαμεν	we know
2-sg.	οἶδας	you (sg.) know	2-pl.	οἴδατε	you (pl.) know
3-sg.	οἶδε(ν)	he/she/it knows	3-pl.	οἴδασιν	they know

a. This common verb is a perfect in form, but functions as a present. See §4.75c.

4.30. Perfect Indicative Active of Contract Verbs

	ἀγαπάω	ποιέω	πληρόω
1-sg.	ἠγάπηκα	πεποίηκα	πεπλήρωκα
2-sg.	ἠγάπηκας	πεποίηκας	πεπλήρωκας
3-sg.	ἠγάπηκε(ν)	πεποίηκε(ν)	πεπλήρωκε(ν)
1-pl.	ἠγαπήκαμεν	πεποιήκαμεν	πεπληρώκαμεν
2-pl.	ἠγαπήκατε	πεποιήκατε	πεπληρώκατε
3-pl.	ἠγαπήκασι(ν)	πεποιήκασι(ν)	πεπληρώκασι(ν)

a. The standard lengthening of the vowels on the end of the stem is the only distinctive feature to note.

4.31. Perfect Indicative Middle/Passive Components

The perfect uses the same first middle/passive pattern of endings as in the present tense-form. The middle/passive has reduplication like the perfect active, but it is built on the 5th principal part and it has no tense-form sign or linking vowel. The 2-sg. form now uses σαι instead of η. Thus the components of the perfect middle/passive are as follows:

	reduplication	+	stem	+	ending
Pf. MP	λε	+	5th	+	μαι

λε-5-μαι	λε-5-μεθα
λε-5-σαι	λε-5-σθε
λε-5-ται	λε-5-νται

4.32. Stem Changes in the Perfect Middle/Passive

The lack of a linking vowel and tense-form sign means the endings are added directly to the stem. When consonants are added to consonants changes occur. You do not necessarily need to memorize the following sets of changes. Look them over and then examine the sample paradigms to see which of these changes are minor enough that you can still recognize the endings, and which are not and need to be learned.

a. Before μαι (1-sg.) and μεθα (1-pl.)

π, β, φ	+	μ	>	μ	γεγραφ	+	μαι	>	γέγραμμαι
κ, γ, χ	+	μ	>	γ	δεδεχ	+	μαι	>	δέδεγμαι
τ, δ, θ, ζ	+	μ	>	σ	πεπειθ	+	μαι	>	πέπεισμαι

b. The σαι ending (2-sg.) will follow the square of stops.

π, β, φ	+	σ	>	ψ	γεγραφ	+	σαι	>	γέγραψαι
κ, γ, χ	+	σ	>	ξ	δεδεχ	+	σαι	>	δέδεξαι
τ, δ, θ, ζ	+	σ	>	σ	πεπειθ	+	σαι	>	πέπεισαι

c. Before ται (3-sg.)

π, β, φ	+	τ	>	π	γεγραφ	+	ται	>	γέγραπται
κ, γ, χ	+	τ	>	κ	δεδεχ	+	ται	>	δέδεκται
τ, δ, θ, ζ	+	τ	>	σ	πεπειθ	+	ται	>	πέπεισται

d. Before ϑε (2-pl. σϑε with the σ dropped out)

π, β, φ	+	ϑ	>	φ	γεγραφ	+	(σ)ϑε >	γέγραφϑε
κ, γ, χ	+	ϑ	>	χ	δεδεχ	+	(σ)ϑε >	δέδεχϑε
τ, δ, ϑ, ζ	+	ϑ	>	σ	πεπειϑ	+	(σ)ϑε >	πέπεισϑε

4.33. Perfect Indicative Middle/Passive

The following paradigms offer examples of verbs with vowel stems as well as stems ending in a labial (γράφω, *write*), a velar (δέχομαι, *take, receive*), and a dental (πείϑω, *persuade*).

	λύω	γράφω	δέχομαι	πείϑω
1-sg.	λέλυμαι	γέγραμμαι	δέδεγμαι	πέπεισμαι
2-sg.	λέλυσαι	γέγραψαι	δέδεξαι	πέπεισαι
3-sg.	λέλυται	γέγραπται	δέδεκται	πέπεισται
1-pl.	λελύμεϑα	γεγράμμεϑα	δεδέγμεϑα	πεπείσμεϑα
2-pl.	λέλυσϑε	γέγραφϑε	δέδεχϑε	πέπεισϑε
3-pl.	λέλυνται	γεγραμμένοι εἰσί(ν)	δεδεγμένοι εἰσί(ν)	πεπεισμένοι εἰσί(ν)

a. If you have a general understanding of these changes you will probably be able to recognize the forms while reading without learning these changes in detail.

b. Verbs whose stem ends in a consonant usually use a periphrastic participle for the 3-pl. See §5.188.

4.34. Perfect Indicative Middle/Passive of Contract Verbs

	ἀγαπάω	ποιέω	πληρόω
1-sg.	ἠγάπημαι	πεποίημαι	πεπλήρωμαι
2-sg.	ἠγάπησαι	πεποίησαι	πεπλήρωσαι
3-sg.	ἠγάπηται	πεποίηται	πεπλήρωται
1-pl.	ἠγαπήμεϑα	πεποιήμεϑα	πεπληρώμεϑα
2-pl.	ἠγάπησϑε	πεποίησϑε	πεπλήρωσϑε
3-pl.	ἠγάπηνται	πεποίηνται	πεπλήρωνται

a. As with the perfect active paradigm of contract verbs (§4.30), the standard lengthening of the vowels on the end of the stem is the only distinctive feature to watch.

THE SECONDARY TENSE-FORMS IN THE INDICATIVE

4.35. Introduction to the Secondary Tense-Forms

The secondary tense-forms—the imperfect, aorist, and pluperfect—take an augment in the indicative. Only the secondary tense-forms have an augment, and they only have it in the indicative mood. All other moods drop the augment.

4.36. Augments

The augment is an addition to the front of the stem. It can take a couple of forms.

a. If the verb begins with a consonant then an ε is added for the augment. This is called a **syllabic augment** since it adds a syllable to the word. The stem of λύω is λυ-. When it is augmented it becomes ἐλυ-.

b. If the verb begins with a vowel then the vowel is lengthened, called a **temporal augment**. The most common forms of lengthening are:

α	→	η	αι	→	ῃ
ε	→	η	ει	→	ῃ
ο	→	ω.	οι	→	ῳ

The stem of ἀγαπάω (*love*) is ἀγαπα-. When augmented it becomes ἠγαπα-.
The stem of αἰτέω (*ask*) is αἰτε-. When augmented it becomes ᾐτε-.

When a short ι or υ is augmented the initial letter is lengthened but looks the same.

ἰάομαι (*heal*) → ἰασάμην
ὑμνέω (*sing*) → ὕμνησα

When the long vowels η and ω are augmented they remain the same.

ἡγέομαι (*lead*) → ἡγησάμην
ὠφελέω (*help*) → ὠφέλησα

4.37. Compound Verbs

Some verbs have a preposition added to the front of their stem. When such a verb is augmented the augment is added to the stem, not to the preposition on the front. Thus περιπατέω is composed of περί and πατέω so the augment comes between these two elements:

περι | ε-πατησα → περιεπάτησα.

a. Often adding the augment will cause changes to the preposition. The final vowel of the preposition might drop (§1.10). For example, ἀποστέλλω is composed of ἀπό and στέλλω. To form the aorist of this verb the ο on ἀπό drops and στέλλω is augmented with an ε. In this case, the stem changes slightly from στελλ- to στειλ-. So

ἀπ + ε + στειλ- → ἀπεστειλ-, to which the personal endings are added.

b. Sometimes prepositions ending in a consonant can change. It is normal for ἐκ to change to ἐξ when followed by a word beginning with a vowel, and this same thing happens when it is in a compound. ἐκβάλλω becomes ἐξέβαλον, again with a slight stem change.

c. Sometimes a preposition drops a letter and also changes the letter that is left. When ἐπί is followed by a word beginning with a vowel the ι drops and an apostrophe is added: ἐπ'. But when the word following has a rough breathing the π shifts to a φ to match the "h" sound of the rough breathing:

ἐπί + ἵστημι = ἐπ → ἐπ' → ἐφ' → ἐφίστημι.

4.38. Core Pattern for Secondary Personal Endings

The core pattern for the personal endings of the secondary tense-forms in the indicative should be learned well since it gathers together the endings in the specific paradigms. The main information you get from the ending is the verb's voice, person, and number (§§2.5, 7).[14] These middle/passive endings are part of the first middle/passive pattern, as are the middle/passive endings for the primary tense-forms (§4.1).

---

14. In addition, endings that are not shared by the primary tense-forms may help identify a verb's tense-form. Thus, the personal ending το is used in the imperfect, aorist, and pluperfect while ται is used in the present, future, and perfect (§4.1).

	Act. sg.	MP sg.
1.	ν, –	μην
2.	ς	σο (= ου, ω)
3.	–(ν)	το
	Act. pl.	**MP pl.**
1.	μεν	μεθα
2.	τε	σθε
3.	ν, σαν	ντο

The Imperfect Indicative Tense-Form

4.39. Imperfect Indicative Components

The imperfect only occurs in the indicative. It is formed using the 1st principal part, so a verb will normally have the same stem for both the present and the imperfect tense-forms. The imperfect has an augment on the front and uses the linking vowels ο/ε. So the components are:

	augment	+	stem	+	linking vowel	+	personal ending
impf. act./ MP	ε	+	1st	+	ο/ε	+	secondary

ε–1–ον	ε–1–ομεν
ε–1–ες	ε–1–ετε
ε–1–ε(ν)	ε–1–ον

4.40. Imperfect Indicative Active

λύω – *Imperfect Indicative Active*

		Augment	Stem	Linking vowel	Ending	Simple translation
1-sg.	ἔλυον	ε	λυ	ο	ν	*I was loosing.*
2-sg.	ἔλυες	ε	λυ	ε	ς	*You (sg.) were loosing.*
3-sg.	ἔλυε(ν)	ε	λυ	ε	–(ν)	*He/She/It was loosing.*
1-pl.	ἐλύομεν	ε	λυ	ο	μεν	*We were loosing.*
2-pl.	ἐλύετε	ε	λυ	ε	τε	*You (pl.) were loosing.*
3-pl.	ἔλυον	ε	λυ	ο	ν	*They were loosing.*

a. The 1-sg. and 3-pl. share the same form, so context will have to indicate which is being used.

4.41. Imperfect Indicative Middle/Passive

The same elements are used, now with the first middle/passive endings.

ε-1-ομην   ε-1-ομεθα
ε-1-ου   ε-1-εσθε
ε-1-ετο   ε-1-οντο

λύω – *Imperfect Indicative Middle/Passive*

		Augment	Stem	Linking vowel	Ending	Simple translation
1-sg.	ἐλυόμην	ε	λυ	ο	μην	*I was being loosed.*
2-sg.	ἐλύου	ε	λυ	ε	(σ)ο	*You (sg.) were being loosed.*
3-sg.	ἐλύετο	ε	λυ	ε	το	*He/She/It was being loosed.*
1-pl.	ἐλυόμεθα	ε	λυ	ο	μεθα	*We were being loosed.*
2-pl.	ἐλύεσθε	ε	λυ	ε	σθε	*You (pl.) were being loosed.*
3-pl.	ἐλύοντο	ε	λυ	ο	ντο	*They were being loosed.*

a. The middle is translated with the active in English, so the translations are only given for the passive use of the middle.

b. When the ending σο is added to the ε linking vowel in the MP-2-sg. the σ drops out and the vowels ε and ο contract to produce ου. The MP-2-sg. is the most difficult form in the imperfect indicatives, but it is rare, without any instances in the New Testament or LXX.

4.42. Imperfect Indicative of Contract Verbs

When a verb has a stem ending in a vowel, that vowel contracts with the linking vowel in keeping with the core pattern for vowel contraction (§4.11).

α + ε = α	α < α + ε
ε + ε = ει	ει < ε + ε
ε + α = η	η < ε + α
ο + ει = οι	οι < ο + ει
ε + ο, ο + ε, ο + ο = ου	ου < ε + ο, ο + ε, or ο + ο
ο or ω + any vowel except as above = ω	ω < ο or ω + any vowel except as above

In the following paradigms note how the core patterns for secondary personal endings and for vowel contraction help make sense out of these forms. Some of the forms will be easy to recognize, but others less so. Watch especially for forms that may be confused with other forms.

ἀγαπάω –*Imperfect Indicative Active*

		Augment	Stem	Vowel	Ending	Simple translation
1-sg.	ἠγάπων	ε	ἀγαπα	ο	ν	*I was loving.*
2-sg.	ἠγάπας	ε	ἀγαπα	ε	ς	*You (sg.) were loving.*
3-sg.	ἠγάπα	ε	ἀγαπα	ε	–	*He/She/It was loving.*
1-pl.	ἠγαπῶμεν	ε	ἀγαπα	ο	μεν	*We were loving.*
2-pl.	ἠγαπᾶτε	ε	ἀγαπα	ε	τε	*You (pl.) were loving.*
3-pl.	ἠγάπων	ε	ἀγαπα	ο	ν	*They were loving.*

ποιέω – *Imperfect Indicative Active*

		Augment	Stem	Vowel	Ending	Simple translation
1-sg.	ἐποίουν	ε	ποιε	ο	ν	*I was making.*
2-sg.	ἐποίεις	ε	ποιε	ε	ς	*You (sg.) were making.*
3-sg.	ἐποίει	ε	ποιε	ε	–	*He/She/It was making.*
1-pl.	ἐποιοῦμεν	ε	ποιε	ο	μεν	*We were making.*
2-pl.	ἐποιεῖτε	ε	ποιε	ε	τε	*You (pl.) were making.*
3-pl.	ἐποίουν	ε	ποιε	ο	ν	*They were making.*

δικαιόω – *Imperfect Indicative Active*

		Augment	Stem	Vowel	Ending	Simple translation
1-sg.	ἐδικαίουν	ε	δικαιο	ο	ν	*I was justifying.*
2-sg.	ἐδικαίους	ε	δικαιο	ε	ς	*You (sg.) were justifying.*
3-sg.	ἐδικαίου	ε	δικαιο	ε	–	*He/She/It was justifying.*
1-pl.	ἐδικαιοῦμεν	ε	δικαιο	ο	μεν	*We were justifying.*
2-pl.	ἐδικαιοῦτε	ε	δικαιο	ε	τε	*You (pl.) were justifying.*
3-pl.	ἐδικαίουν	ε	δικαιο	ο	ν	*They were justifying.*

ἀγαπάω – *Imperfect Indicative Middle/Passive*

		Augment	Stem	Vowel	Ending	Simple Translation
1-sg.	ἠγαπώμην	ε	ἀγαπα	ο	μην	*I was being loved.*
2-sg.	ἠγαπῶ	ε	ἀγαπα	(ε)	(σ)ο	*You (sg.) were being loved.*
3-sg.	ἠγαπᾶτο	ε	ἀγαπα	ε	το	*He/She/It was being loved.*

		Augment	Stem	Vowel	Ending	Simple Translation
1-pl.	ἠγαπῶμεθα	ε	ἀγαπα	ο	μεθα	*We were being loved.*
2-pl.	ἠγαπᾶσθε	ε	ἀγαπα	ε	σθε	*You (pl.) were being loved.*
3-pl.	ἠγαπῶντο	ε	ἀγαπα	ο	ντο	*They were being loved.*

a. In the 2-sg. the linking vowel drops, as does the σ of the ending, so the α and the o contract. This form would be a very confusing form, but recall that it is rare, with no instances in the New Testament or LXX.

ποιέω – *Imperfect Indicative Middle/Passive*

		Augment	Stem	Vowel	Ending	Simple translation
1-sg.	ἐποιούμην	ε	ποιε	ο	μην	*I was being made.*
2-sg.	ἐποιοῦ	ε	ποιε	(ε)	(σ)ο	*You (sg.) were being made.*
3-sg.	ἐποιεῖτο	ε	ποιε	ε	το	*He/She/It was being made.*
1-pl.	ἐποιούμεθα	ε	ποιε	ο	μεθα	*We were being made.*
2-pl.	ἐποιεῖσθε	ε	ποιε	ε	σθε	*You (pl.) were being made.*
3-pl.	ἐποιοῦντο	ε	ποιε	ο	ντο	*They were being made.*

b. In the 2-sg. the linking vowel drops, as does the σ of the ending, so the ε and the o contract.

δικαιόω – *Imperfect Indicative Middle/Passive*

		Augment	Stem	Vowel	Ending	Simple translation
1-sg.	ἐδικαιούμην	ε	δικαιο	ο	μην	*I was being justified.*
2-sg.	ἐδικαιοῦ	ε	δικαιο	(ε)	(σ)ο	*You (sg.) were being justified.*
3-sg.	ἐδικαιοῦτο	ε	δικαιο	ε	το	*He/She/It was being justified.*
1-pl.	ἐδικαιούμεθα	ε	δικαιο	ο	μεθα	*We were being justified.*
2-pl.	ἐδικαιοῦσθε	ε	δικαιο	ε	σθε	*You (pl.) were being justified.*
3-pl.	ἐδικαιοῦντο	ε	δικαιο	ο	ντο	*They were being justified.*

c. In the 2-sg. the linking vowel drops, as does the σ of the ending, so the o and the o contract.

4.43. Imperfect Indicative of μι Verbs

a. Imperfect Indicative Active. These forms use secondary endings for the most part, but some verbs switch to non-μι forms in a few places in the singular. In the paradigms note the 2-sg. and 3-sg. of τίθημι which behave like an ω verb, and the 1/2/3-sg. of δίδωμι which have endings like an ο contract verb. The pattern of ἵστημι is mercifully regular.

τίθημι – *Imperfect Indicative Active*

		Augment	Stem	Vowel	Ending	Simple Translation
1-sg.	ἐτίθην	ε	τιθη		ν	*I was putting.*
2-sg.	ἐτίθεις	ε	τιθ	ει	ς	*You (sg.) were putting.*
3-sg.	ἐτίθει	ε	τιθ	ει	–	*He/She/It was putting.*
1-pl.	ἐτίθεμεν	ε	τιθε		μεν	*We were putting.*
2-pl.	ἐτίθετε	ε	τιθε		τε	*You (pl.) were putting.*
3-pl.	ἐτίθεσαν	ε	τιθε		σαν	*They were putting.*

δίδωμι – *Imperfect Indicative Active*

		Augment	Stem	Vowel	Ending	Simple translation
1-sg.	ἐδίδουν	ε	διδο	ο	ν	*I was giving.*
2-sg.	ἐδίδους	ε	διδο	ε	ς	*You (sg.) were giving.*
3-sg.	ἐδίδου	ε	διδο	ε	–	*He/She/It was giving.*
1-pl.	ἐδίδομεν	ε	διδο		μεν	*We were giving.*
2-pl.	ἐδίδοτε	ε	διδο		τε	*You (pl.) were giving.*
3-pl.	ἐδίδοσαν	ε	διδο		σαν	*They were giving.*

> ➤ ο + ο and ο + ε contract to ου (§4.11).

ἵστημι – *Imperfect Indicative Active*

		Augment	Stem	Vowel	Ending	Simple translation
1-sg.	ἵστην	ε	ἱστη		ν	*I was placing.*
2-sg.	ἵστης	ε	ἱστη		ς	*You (sg.) were placing.*
3-sg.	ἵστη	ε	ἱστη		–	*He/She/It was placing.*
1-pl.	ἵσταμεν	ε	ἱστα		μεν	*We were placing.*
2-pl.	ἵστατε	ε	ἱστα		τε	*You (pl.) were placing.*
3-pl.	ἵστασαν	ε	ἱστα		σαν	*They were placing.*

> ➤ When an initial ι is augmented it is lengthened but a long ι looks the same as a short ι (§4.36b).

b. Imperfect Indicative Middle/Passive. These paradigms use secondary endings with none of the irregularities found in the active of some verbs noted in the previous section.

τίθημι – *Imperfect Indicative Middle/Passive*

		Augment	Stem	Vowel	Ending	Simple translation
1-sg.	ἐτιθέμην	ε	τιθε		μην	*I was being put.*
2-sg.	ἐτίθεσο	ε	τιθε		σο	*You (sg.) were being put.*
3-sg.	ἐτίθετο	ε	τιθε		το	*He/She/It was being put.*
1-pl.	ἐτιθέμεθα	ε	τιθε		μεθα	*We were being put.*
2-pl.	ἐτίθεσθε	ε	τιθε		σθε	*You (pl.) were being put.*
3-pl.	ἐτίθεντο	ε	τιθε		ντο	*They were being put.*

δίδωμι – *Imperfect Indicative Middle/Passive*

		Augment	Stem	Vowel	Ending	Simple translation
1-sg.	ἐδιδόμην	ε	διδο		μην	*I was being given.*
2-sg.	ἐδίδοσο	ε	διδο		σο	*You (sg.) were being given.*
3-sg.	ἐδίδοτο	ε	διδο		το	*He/She/It was being given.*
1-pl.	ἐδιδόμεθα	ε	διδο		μεθα	*We were being given.*
2-pl.	ἐδίδοσθε	ε	διδο		σθε	*You (pl.) were being given.*
3-pl.	ἐδίδοντο	ε	διδο		ντο	*They were being given.*

ἵστημι – *Imperfect Indicative Middle/Passive*

		Augment	Stem	Vowel	Ending	Simple translation
1-sg.	ἱστάμην	ε	ἱστα		μην	*I was being placed.*
2-sg.	ἵστασο	ε	ἱστα		σο	*You (sg.) were being placed.*
3-sg.	ἵστατο	ε	ἱστα		το	*He/She/It was being placed.*
1-pl.	ἱστάμεθα	ε	ἱστα		μεθα	*We were being placed.*
2-pl.	ἵστασθε	ε	ἱστα		σθε	*You (pl.) were being placed.*
3-pl.	ἵσταντο	ε	ἱστα		ντο	*They were being placed.*

> ➤ When an initial ι is augmented it is lengthened but a long ι looks the same as a short ι (§4.36b).

4.44. Imperfect Indicative of εἰμί

The imperfect indicative of εἰμί has some distinct forms, so it is one of the twelve core patterns to learn. While εἰμί does not actually have voice it is commonly parsed as active, except ἤμην and ἤμεθα as middle/passive in keeping with the usual use of their endings as middle/passive.[15]

ἤμην	ἦμεν, ἤμεθα
ἦς, ἦσθα	ἦτε
ἦν	ἦσαν

The Aorist Indicative Tense-Form

4.45. Introduction to the Aorists

The aorist occurs in four patterns with no difference in meaning between them. The most common pattern uses σ as a tense-form sign plus α/ε linking vowels. This sigmatic aorist is often referred to as the first aorist, or weak aorist. The second most common pattern, often called the second or strong aorist, has no tense-form sign and is recognized by a distinctive stem. The remaining patterns are much less common, but occur in verbs that are used frequently. The third form is known as a root aorist since the personal ending is added directly to the stem without a linking vowel. The fourth form, the κ aorist, has a κ tense-form sign.

All aorists use the 3rd principal part for the active and first middle/passive forms and the 6th principal part for the second middle/passive.

4.46. First Aorist Indicative Active and First Middle/Passive Components

Like the other secondary tenses, the aorist has an augment in the indicative, but not in the other moods. For details regarding augments see §§2.16; 4.36. The tense-form sign for the first aorist active and first middle/passive is σ and its linking vowels are α/ε, that is, it is ε in the 3-sg. and α elsewhere.[16] The components are as follows:

---

15. The alternate form ἦσθα occurs twice in the New Testament and ἤμεθα five times.

16. There are differing opinions whether σα/ε is the tense-form sign or whether σ is the tense-form sign with α/ε as linking vowels. Since for reading purposes it comes to the same thing I have used the option that seems easiest for the student to learn in order to recognize the forms when reading. For the issue see Mounce, *Morphology* §34.

Augment +	Stem +	Sign +	Linking + vowel	Secondary endings		
ε	+ λυ	+ σ	+ α/ε	+ μεν	→	ἐλύσαμεν, *We loosed.*

ε–3–σα   ε–3–σαμεν
ε–3–σας   ε–3–σατε
ε–3–σε   ε–3–σαν

a. The Square of Stops. Since the tense-form sign is σ the changes associated with the square of stops occur here. For details see §3.19. Thus, for example:

	Stem	Augment	Sign		Vowel		Ending
πέμπω (send)	πεμπ →	ἐπεμπ	+σ	[π+σ = ψ] +	α +	μεν →	ἐπέμψαμεν
ἀνοίγω (open)	ἀνοιγ →	ἠνοιγ	+σ	[γ+σ = ξ] +	α +	μεν →	ἠνοίξαμεν
σῴζω (save)	σῳζ →	ἐσῳζ	+σ	[(ζ)σ] +	α +	μεν →	ἐσῴσαμεν

4.47. First Aorist Indicative Active

λύω – *First Aorist Indicative Active*

		Augment	Stem	T-form sign	Vowel	Ending	Simple translation
1-sg.	ἔλυσα	ε	λυ	σ	α	–	*I loosed.*
2-sg.	ἔλυσας	ε	λυ	σ	α	ς	*You (sg.) loosed.*
3-sg.	ἔλυσε(ν)	ε	λυ	σ	ε	-(ν)	*He/She/It loosed.*
1-pl.	ἐλύσαμεν	ε	λυ	σ	α	μεν	*We loosed.*
2-pl.	ἐλύσατε	ε	λυ	σ	α	τε	*You (pl.) loosed.*
3-pl.	ἔλυσαν	ε	λυ	σ	α	ν	*They loosed.*

a. The 1-sg. takes the zero form option from the core pattern.

b. The linking vowel ε only shows up in the 3-sg. When two forms take the zero ending, the 1-sg. will have an α and the 3-sg. an ε.

πέμπω – *First Aorist Indicative Active*

		Augment	Stem	T-form sign	Vowel	Ending	Simple translation
1-sg.	ἔπεμψα	ε	πεμπ	σ	α	–	*I sent.*
2-sg.	ἔπεμψας	ε	πεμπ	σ	α	ς	*You (sg.) sent.*
3-sg.	ἔπεμψε(ν)	ε	πεμπ	σ	ε	-(ν)	*He/She/It sent.*
1-pl.	ἐπέμψαμεν	ε	πεμπ	σ	α	μεν	*We sent.*
2-pl.	ἐπέμψατε	ε	πεμπ	σ	α	τε	*You (pl.) sent.*
3-pl.	ἔπεμψαν	ε	πεμπ	σ	α	ν	*They sent.*

4.48. First Aorist Indicative Active of Contract Verbs

In the aorist the tense-form sign separates the vowel on the stem ending from the linking vowel. The vowel on the stem ending lengthens.

α → η
ε → η
ο → ω

a. Thus the endings will look the same as on noncontract verbs. The only thing to note is the presence of an η or ω before the tense-form sign. An η leads you to expect a lexical form ending in α or ε, and an ω points to a lexical form ending in an ο.

b. So, for example, when you see ἐποίησας note the ς on the end as the sign of an act.-2-sg., the σ+α pointing to a first aorist, and the ε augment for the indicative. The η before the tense-form sign points you to a lexical form of either ποιαω or ποιεω since η is a lengthening of either α or ε. When you check the lexicon you find ποιέω.

	γεννάω	ποιέω	φανερόω	Ending
1-sg.	ἐγέννησα	ἐποίησα	ἐφανέρωσα	–
2-sg.	ἐγέννησας	ἐποίησας	ἐφανέρωσας	ς
3-sg.	ἐγέννησε(ν)	ἐποίησε(ν)	ἐφανέρωσε(ν)	-(ν)
1-pl.	ἐγεννήσαμεν	ἐποιήσαμεν	ἐφανερώσαμεν	μεν
2-pl.	ἐγεννήσατε	ἐποιήσατε	ἐφανερώσατε	τε
3-pl.	ἐγέννησαν	ἐποίησαν	ἐφανέρωσαν	ν

c. A few contract verbs do not lengthen their stem ending. If your interest is in learning to read Greek, not write or speak it, you do not need to learn which verbs are involved. If you simply know that such verbs exist you won't have trouble parsing them. For example, καλέω takes the forms:

ἐκάλεσα	ἐκαλέσαμεν
ἐκάλεσας	ἐκαλέσατε
ἐκάλεσε(ν)	ἐκάλεσαν

4.49. Root Aorists

There are a few verbs that form the aorist by adding the usual secondary personal endings directly to the root (stem) of the 3rd principal part. These verbs do not use the middle/passive voice so only active forms are involved. These paradigms represent the most common of these verbs, and each of them is also found in compounds.

(ἵστημι)	(ἀναβαίνω)	(γίνωσκω)
ἔστην	ἀνέβην	ἔγνων
ἔστης	ἀνέβης	ἔγνως
ἔστη	ἀνέβη	ἔγνω
ἔστημεν	ἀνέβημεν	ἔγνωμεν
ἔστητε	ἀνέβητε	ἔγνωτε
ἔστησαν	ἀνέβησαν	ἔγνωσαν

a. Occasionally verbs will appear as both a root aorist and a regular first aorist. For example, ἵστημι appears as ἔστησα as well as the root form listed here. Fortunately, both forms have the same stem, στη-, so you can identify them if you know that one stem. The following examples illustrate these two forms and also the fact that this verb can be used transitively (*cause someone/something to stand*) or intransitively (*stand*).

> ἐπιλαβόμενος παιδίον **ἔστησεν** αὐτὸ παρ' ἑαυτῷ (Luke 9:47)
> *taking a child, he <u>stood/placed/set</u> him by his side*

> καὶ ἰδοὺ ἀνὴρ **ἔστη** ἐνώπιόν μου ἐν ἐσθῆτι λαμπρᾷ (Acts 10:30)
> *and behold, a man <u>stood</u> before me in shining clothing*

4.50. First Aorist Indicative First Middle/Passive Components

The first aorist middle has the same components as the active:

Augment	+	Stem	+	Sign	+	Linking vowel	+	Secondary endings		
ε	+	λυ	+	σ	+	α/ε	+	μεθα	→	ἐλυσάμεθα, *I loosed.*

ε–3–σαμην	ε–3–σαμεθα
ε–3–σω	ε–3–σασθε
ε–3–σατο	ε–3–σαντο

4.51. First Aorist Indicative First Middle/Passive

λύω – *First Aorist Indicative First Middle/Passive*

		Augment	Stem		Ending	Simple translation
1-sg.	ἐλυσάμην	ε	λυ	σα	μην	*I loosed.*
2-sg.	ἐλύσω	ε	λυ	σα	(σ)ο	*You (sg.) loosed.*
3-sg.	ἐλύσατο	ε	λυ	σα	το	*He/she/It loosed.*
1-pl.	ἐλυσάμεθα	ε	λυ	σα	μεθα	*We loosed.*
2-pl.	ἐλύσασθε	ε	λυ	σα	σθε	*You (pl.) loosed.*
3-pl.	ἐλύσαντο	ε	λυ	σα	ντο	*They loosed.*

a. While this form is middle/passive, in the aorist the first middle/passive is rarely used for the passive sense of the middle (§5.94). These translations are in the active since that is how the middle is translated in English.

b. The MP.-2-sg. drops the σ of σο and then the vowels α and ο contract to produce ω (§§4.8c, 11):

	Stem	Augment	T-sign	Vowel	Ending	
πιστεύω (believe)	πιστευ →	ἐπιστευ	+ σ	+ α = ἐπιστευσα +	(σ)ο →	ἐπιστεύσω
πέμπω (send)	πεμπ →	ἐπεμπ	+ σ	+ α = ἐπέμψα +	(σ)ο →	ἐπέμψω
ἀνοίγω (open)	ἀνοιγ →	ἠνοιγ	+ σ	+ α = ἠνοίξα +	(σ)ο →	ἠνοίξω
σῴζω (save)	σῳζ →	ἐσῳζ	+ σ	+ α = ἐσῳ(ζ)σα +	(σ)ο →	ἐσώσω.

c. This ω ending on the MP.-2-sg. might be confused with the act.-1-sg. in the present, but the present will not have an augment nor the σ tense-form sign. In any case, the aor.-ind.-MP-2-sg. only shows up eight times in the New Testament.

πέμπω – *First Aorist Indicative First Middle/Passive*

		Augment	Stem	T-form sign	Vowel	Ending	Simple translation
1-sg.	ἐπεμψάμην	ε	πεμπ	σ	α	μην	*I sent.*
2-sg.	ἐπέμψω	ε	πεμπ	σ	α	(σ)ο	*You (sg.) sent.*
3-sg.	ἐπέμψατο	ε	πεμπ	σ	α	το	*He/She/It sent.*
1-pl.	ἐπεμψάμεθα	ε	πεμπ	σ	α	μεθα	*We sent.*
2-pl.	ἐπέμψασθε	ε	πεμπ	σ	α	σθε	*You (pl.) sent.*
3-pl.	ἐπέμψαντο	ε	πεμπ	σ	α	ντο	*They sent.*

4.52. First Aorist Indicative First Middle/Passive of Contract Verbs

The stem vowel lengthens before the tense-form sign.

	γεννάω	ποιέω	φανερόω	Ending
1-sg.	ἐγεννησάμην	ἐποιησάμην	ἐφανερωσάμην	μην
2-sg.	ἐγεννήσω	ἐποιήσω	ἐφανερώσω	(σ)ο
3-sg.	ἐγεννήσατο	ἐποιήσατο	ἐφανερώσατο	το
1-pl.	ἐγεννησάμεθα	ἐποιησάμεθα	ἐφανερωσάμεθα	μεθα
2-pl.	ἐγεννήσασθε	ἐποιήσασθε	ἐφανερώσασθε	σθε
3-pl.	ἐγεννήσαντο	ἐποιήσαντο	ἐφανερώσαντο	ντο

4.53. Liquid Aorists

Some verbs whose stems end in λ, μ, ν, or ρ drop the σ tense-form sign and often have minor vowel changes within the stem (§4.70). In the following paradigms notice the presence of the basic personal endings along with the minor vowel changes in the stem and the lack of a σ.

	(ἀποστέλλω)	(μένω)	(αἴρω)
	Active	Active	Active
1-sg.	ἀπέστειλα	ἔμεινα	ἦρα
2-sg.	ἀπέστειλας	ἔμεινας	ἦρας
3-sg.	ἀπέστειλε(ν)	ἔμεινε(ν)	ἦρε(ν)

1-pl.	ἀπεστείλαμεν	ἐμείναμεν	ἤραμεν
2-pl.	ἀπεστείλατε	ἐμείνατε	ἤρατε
3-pl.	ἀπέστειλαν	ἔμειναν	ἦραν
	Middle/Passive	Middle/Passive	Middle/Passive
1-sg.	ἀπεστειλάμην	ἐμεινάμην	ἠράμην
2-sg.	ἀπεστείλω	ἐμείνω	ἤρω
3-sg.	ἀπεστείλατο	ἐμείνατο	ἤρατο
1-pl.	ἀπεστειλάμεθα	ἐμεινάμεθα	ἠράμεθα
2-pl.	ἀπεστείλασθε	ἐμείνασθε	ἤρασθε
3-pl.	ἀπεστείλαντο	ἐμείναντο	ἤραντο

a. Note these examples of slight changes in the stem compared to the lexical form (§4.70).

Lexical form stem	στελλ-[17]	μέν-	αἰρ-
3rd principal part stem	στειλ-	μειν-	ἀρ-

b. The liquid aorist endings are exactly the same as the first aorist endings, but without a σ.

4.54. κ Aorists

Several verbs have a κ instead of a σ in their aorist active forms.

a. The endings are regular so they cause no difficulty if you learn their principal parts and know the core patterns.

b. These same verbs are root aorists (§4.49) in their middle/passive aorist forms. So again the endings are clear; these middle/passive forms simply lack a linking vowel.

c. The confusing thing is to see a κ in a tense-form outside the perfect active where it is a normal part of the form (§4.27).

d. The aorist active of φέρω, ἤνεγκα, follows this same pattern, but unlike κ aorists it is not a μι verb and it retains the κ in the middle/passive. It is a second aorist using first aorist endings without the σ.

---

17. The stem of ἀποστέλλω is στελλ- since it is a compound verb with the preposition ἀπό added to the front.

	(τίθημι)	(δίδωμι)	(ἀφίημι)
	Active	Active	Active
1-sg.	ἔθηκα	ἔδωκα	ἀφῆκα
2-sg.	ἔθηκας	ἔδωκας	ἀφῆκας
3-sg.	ἔθηκε(ν)	ἔδωκε(ν)	ἀφῆκε(ν)
1-pl.	ἐθήκαμεν	ἐδώκαμεν	ἀφήκαμεν
2-pl.	ἐθήκατε	ἐδώκατε	ἀφήκατε
3-pl.	ἔθηκαν	ἔδωκαν	ἀφῆκαν
	Middle/Passive	Middle/Passive	Middle/Passive
1-sg.	ἐθέμην	ἐδόμην	ἀφείμην
2-sg.	ἔθου	ἔδου	ἀφεῖσο
3-sg.	ἔθετο	ἔδοτο	ἀφεῖτο
1-pl.	ἐθέμεθα	ἐδόμεθα	ἀφείμεθα
2-pl.	ἔθεσθε	ἔδοσθε	ἀφεῖσθε
3-pl.	ἔθεντο	ἔδοντο	ἀφεῖντο

4.55. Second Aorist Indicative Active and First Middle/Passive Components

Verbs that use the second aorist form do not have the σ tense-form sign and α/ε linking vowels. Instead they use ο/ε for linking vowels. The components of the second aorist active and middle/passive forms are:

Augment + Stem (3rd prin. part) + ο/ε + Secondary personal endings

The following abstract paradigm is identical to that for the imperfect (§4.39), except for the stem.

ε–3–ον ε–3–ομεν
ε–3–ες ε–3–ετε
ε–3–ε(ν) ε–3–ον

4.56. Second Aorist Stems

The components of the second aorist are the same as the imperfect, except the imperfect uses the stem of the 1st principal part and the second aorist uses the stem of the 3rd principal part. **The distinctive sign of the second aorist is its stem**, which is always different from the 1st principal part.

In the chart below notice that the second aorists for ἔχω (*have*), βάλλω (*throw, put*), and λαμβάνω (*take, receive*) have modified stems, but a different stem is used for the aorist of λέγω (*say, speak*) and ἔρχομαι (*come, go*).[18]

Principal part	1st	3rd	Stem(s)
Tense-Form	Present act./MP	Aorist act./ MP	
Same stem	λύω	ἔλυσα	λυ
	πιστεύω	ἐπίστευσα	πιστευ
Modified stem	ἔχω	ἔσχον	σεχ
	βάλλω	ἔβαλον	βαλ
	λαμβάνω	ἔλαβον	λαβ
Different stem	λέγω	εἶπον	λεγ, εἰπ[19]
	ἔρχομαι	ἦλθον	ἐρχ, ἐλθ

a. The stem of ἔχω undergoes a variety of changes in its various principal parts, though signs are present to help you identify each tense-form, as here in the second aorist.

b. The stem of βάλλω, βαλ-, adds a λ in the present (§4.70b[2]).

c. The stem of λαμβάνω, λαβ-, adds a μ in the present (§4.73a).

4.57. Second Aorist Indicative Active

As seen in the previous section, the 3rd principal part for λαμβάνω (*take, receive*) is ἔλαβον, so the second aorist stem is λαβ-.

λαμβάνω – *Second Aorist Indicative Active*

		Augment	Stem	Vowel	Ending	Simple translation
1-sg.	ἔλαβον	ε	λαβ	ο	ν	I received.
2-sg.	ἔλαβες	ε	λαβ	ε	ς	You (sg.) received.
3-sg.	ἔλαβε(ν)	ε	λαβ	ε	-(ν)	He/She/It received.
1-pl.	ἐλάβομεν	ε	λαβ	ο	μεν	We received.
2-pl.	ἐλάβετε	ε	λαβ	ε	τε	You (pl.) received.
3-pl.	ἔλαβον	ε	λαβ	ο	ν	They received.

18. See Mounce, *Morphology*, for more precise information about stems, which he refers to as verbal roots. On such terminology see §2.36b n. 46.

19. More precisely, εἰπ- is a different verb, which provides the aorist form for the same meaning as λέγω. See appendix 8, n. f.

a. Some second aorists in the Hellenistic period were occasionally given first aorist endings. In the New Testament this is especially common in forms of εἶδον and εἶπον.[20]

Singular	Plural	Singular	Plural
εἶδον	εἴδομεν	εἶδα	εἴδαμεν
εἶδες	εἴδετε	εἶδας	εἴδατε
εἶδεν	εἶδον	εἶδεν	εἶδαν and εἴδοσαν

4.58. Second Aorist Indicative First Middle/Passive

The following abstract paradigm is identical to the one for the imperfect (§4.39), except for the stem.

ε–3–ομην   ε–3–ομεθα
ε–3–ου   ε–3–εσθε
ε–3–ετο   ε–3–οντο

λαμβάνω – Second Aorist Indicative First Middle/Passive

		Augment	Stem	Vowel	Ending	Simple translation
1-sg.	ἐλαβόμην	ε	λαβ	ο	μην	I received.
2-sg.	ἐλάβου	ε	λαβ	ο	(σ)ο	You (sg.) received.
3-sg.	ἐλάβετο	ε	λαβ	ε	το	He/She/It received.
1-pl.	ἐλαβόμεθα	ε	λαβ	ο	μεθα	We received.
2-pl.	ἐλάβεσθε	ε	λαβ	ε	σθε	You (pl.) received.
3-pl.	ἐλάβοντο	ε	λαβ	ο	ντο	They received.

a. While this form is middle/passive, in the aorist the first middle/passive is rarely used for the passive sense of the middle (§5.94). These translations are in the active since that is how the middle is translated in English when not used with a passive sense.

20. See Funk §4122. He notes that one advantage of this use of first aorist endings is the ability to distinguish the 3-pl. form from the 1-sg. ending, which are ambiguous in the second aorist. *CGEL* and BDAG offer help identifying such forms by listing the alternate form and referring to the regular form. For example, they list εἶπα and refer to εἶπον. BDAG also discusses the alternate forms in the articles on words that have such a mixture of forms.

b. The MP-2-sg. drops the σ of σο and then the vowels ο and ο contract to produce ου (§§4.8c, 11).

c. The stem is the only difference between the imperfect and the second aorist of λαμβάνω.

λαμβάνω – *Imperfect and Second Aorist Indicative*

	Imperfect active	2 Aorist active	Imperfect middle/passive	2 Aorist middle/passive
1-sg.	ἐλάμβανον	ἔλαβον	ἐλαμβανόμην	ἐλαβόμην
2-sg.	ἐλάμβανες	ἔλαβες	ἐλαμβάνου	ἐλάβου
3-sg.	ἐλάμβανε(ν)	ἔλαβε(ν)	ἐλαμβάνετο	ἐλάβετο
1-pl.	ἐλαμβάνομεν	ἐλάβομεν	ἐλαμβανόμεθα	ἐλαβόμεθα
2-pl.	ἐλαμβάνετε	ἐλάβετε	ἐλαμβάνεσθε	ἐλάβεσθε
3-pl.	ἐλάμβανον	ἔλαβον	ἐλαμβάνοντο	ἐλάβοντο

4.59. Aorist Indicative Second Middle/Passive Components

The aorist second middle/passive is built on the 6th principal part. Its components include an augment, the tense-form sign θη, and the secondary **active** (!) endings (§4.38):

	MP2 sg.
1.	ν, –
2.	ς
3.	–(ν)
	MP2 pl.
1.	μεν
2.	τε
3.	σαν

a. Since the tense-form sign ends in a vowel no linking vowel is used. The basic components are:

Augment + Stem	+ T-form sign	+ Secondary active endings
ε + 6th part	+ θη	+ μεν → ἐλύθημεν, *We were loosed.*

ε–6–θην	ε–6–θημεν
ε–6–θης	ε–6–θητε
ε–6–θη	ε–6–θησαν

b. When a tense-form sign beginning with a ϑ is added to a verb with a stem that ends in one of the square of stops (§3.19) the stem ending is modified. A labial or dental becomes the corresponding aspirated form, while dentals added to ϑ, which is itself a dental, become σ. By far the most common dental verbal ending is ζ.

A labial	(π, β)	becomes φ.	π + ϑ = φϑ	β + ϑ = φϑ
A velar	(κ, γ)	becomes χ.	κ + ϑ = χϑ	γ + ϑ = χϑ
A dental	(τ, δ, ϑ, ζ)	becomes σ.	ζ + ϑ = σϑ	

So when you see φ, χ, or σ before the tense-form sign ϑη (or ϑησ in the future second middle/passive, §4.22) suspect this change may have taken place, or that the stem ends in φ or χ to begin with. For example, the aorist second middle/passive of δέχομαι, *take, receive*, is ἐδέχϑην.

Labial	πέμπω	→	ἐπέμφϑην
Velar	διώκω	→	ἐδιώχϑην
Dental	βαπτίζω	→	ἐβαπτίσϑην
	πείϑω	→	ἐπείσϑην

c. At times a σ is added before the ϑη tense-form sign in verbs without a dental stem.

ἀκούω → ἠκούσϑην
κλείω → ἐκλείσϑην

d. A 6th principal part may be a modification of the 1st principal part, as in βάλλω (*throw*), ἐβλήϑην (*I was thrown*), and λαμβάνω (*receive*), ἐλήμφϑην (*I was received*), or use a different stem, as in λέγω (*say*), ἐρρέϑην (*I was said*). For more about principal parts see §§2.19; 4.67; and the list in appendix 8.

4.60. Aorist Indicative Second Middle/Passive

λύω – *Aorist Indicative Second Middle/Passive*

		Augment	Stem	T-form sign	Ending	Simple translation
1-sg.	ἐλύϑην	ε	λυ	ϑη	ν	*I loosed. I was loosed.*
2-sg.	ἐλύϑης	ε	λυ	ϑη	ς	*You (sg.) loosed. You were loosed.*
3-sg.	ἐλύϑη	ε	λυ	ϑη	–	*He/She/It loosed. He/She/It was loosed.*

		Augment	Stem	T-form sign	Ending	Simple translation
1-pl.	ἐλύθημεν	ε	λυ	θη	μεν	*We loosed. We were loosed.*
2-pl.	ἐλύθητε	ε	λυ	θη	τε	*You (pl.) loosed. You (pl.) were loosed.*
3-pl.	ἐλύθησαν	ε	λυ	θη	σαν	*They loosed. They were loosed.*

a. The second middle/passive forms of the aorist are most often used with the passive sense of the middle, but not infrequently with other middle senses as well (§5.94). In these translations the active represents the non-passive uses of the middle, since that is how the middle is translated in English.

b. Most contract verbs in the aorist passive lengthen their vowel stem when the tense-form sign is added.

ἀγαπάω → ἠγαπήθην
ποιέω → ἐποιήθην
πληρόω → ἐπληρώθην

c. When a tense-form sign beginning with a θ is added to a verb with a stem that ends in one of the square of stops (§3.19) the stem ending is modified. See §4.59b.

4.61. Alternate Aorist Indicative Second Middle/Passive

Some aorist second middle/passives lack the θ in the tense-form sign. This pattern is sometimes referred to as a second aorist passive, but this is confusing since this form is not related to the second aorist, which always has a distinctive stem (§4.56).

ε–6–ην   ε–6–ημεν
ε–6–ης   ε–6–ητε
ε–6–η   ε–6–ησαν

γράφω – Alternate Aorist Indicative Second Middle/Passive

		Augment	Stem	T-form sign	Ending	Simple translation
1-sg.	ἐγράφην	ε	γραφ	η	ν	*I wrote. I was written.*
2-sg.	ἐγράφης	ε	γραφ	η	ς	*You (sg.) wrote. You (sg.) were written.*
3-sg.	ἐγράφη	ε	γραφ	η	–	*He/She/It wrote. He/She/It was written.*

		Augment	Stem	T-form sign	Ending	Simple translation
1-pl.	ἐγράφημεν	ε	γραφ	η	μεν	*We wrote. We were written.*
2-pl.	ἐγράφητε	ε	γραφ	η	τε	*You (pl.) wrote. You (pl.) were written.*
3-pl.	ἐγράφησαν	ε	γραφ	η	σαν	*They wrote. They were written.*

a. The second middle/passive forms of the aorist are most often used with the passive sense of the middle, but not infrequently they are used with other middle senses as well (§5.94). In these translations the active represents the non-passive uses of the middle, since that is how the middle is translated in English.

The Pluperfect Indicative Tense-Form

4.62. Pluperfect Indicative Components

The pluperfect is based on the same stem as the perfect, and thus the pluperfect active uses the 4th principal part. The pluperfect has reduplication like the perfect, but usually also adds an augment before the reduplication. Its tense-form sign is κ and it uses ει as its linking vowels throughout.[21] So the components of the pluperfect active are:

Augment	+	Redupli-cation	+	Stem	+	Sign	+	Vowels	+	Secondary endings		
(ε)[22]	+	λε	+	4th part	+	κ	+	ει	+	μεν	→	ἐλελύκειμεν, *We had loosed.*

ελε–4–κειν	ελε–4–κειμεν
ελε–4–κεις	ελε–4–κειτε
ελε–4–κει(ν)	ελε–4–κεισαν

21. There are differing opinions whether κει is the tense-form sign or whether κ is the tense-form sign with ει as linking vowels. Since for reading purposes it comes to the same thing I have used the option that seems easiest for the student to learn in order to recognize the forms when reading. For the issue see Mounce, *Morphology* §34.

22. This augment is in parentheses since it is not always included.

4.63. Pluperfect Indicative Active

λύω – *Pluperfect Indicative Active*

		Aug-ment	Redupli-cation	Stem	T-form sign	Vowel	Ending	Simple translation
1-sg.	ἐλελύκειν	ε	λε	λυ	κ	ει	ν	*I had loosed.*
2-sg.	ἐλελύκεις	ε	λε	λυ	κ	ει	ς	*You (sg.) had loosed.*
3-sg.	ἐλελύκει(ν)	ε	λε	λυ	κ	ει		*He/She/It had loosed.*
1-pl.	ἐλελύκειμεν	ε	λε	λυ	κ	ει	μεν	*We had loosed.*
2-pl.	ἐλελύκειτε	ε	λε	λυ	κ	ει	τε	*You (pl.) had loosed.*
3-pl.	ἐλελύκεισαν	ε	λε	λυ	κ	ει	σαν	*They had loosed.*

a. The 3-pl. uses the second option in the core pattern for secondary personal endings.

b. The act.-1-sg. ειν only shows up in one verb in the New Testament (ᾔδειν, §4.64b) and rarely outside the New Testament, so you do not need to worry about confusing it with an infinitive (§4.93). The moveable ν is not used with ει (§4.3e), so it will not appear on this act.-3-sg.

4.64. Alternate Pluperfect Indicative Active

Some pluperfects lack the κ tense-form sign. This alternate paradigm is often called the second pluperfect.

      ελε–4–ειν   ελε–4–ειμεν
      ελε–4–εις   ελε–4–ειτε
      ελε–4–ει(ν)   ελε–4–εισαν

γράφω – *Alternate Pluperfect Indicative Active*

		Aug-ment	Redupli-cation	Stem	Vowel	Ending	Simple translation
1-sg.	ἐγεγράφειν	ε	γε	γραφ	ει	ν	*I had written.*
2-sg.	ἐγεγράφεις	ε	γε	γραφ	ει	ς	*You (sg.) had written.*
3-sg.	ἐγεγράφει(ν)	ε	γε	γραφ	ει		*He/She/It had written.*

		Aug-ment	Redupli-cation	Stem	Vowel	Ending	Simple translation
1-pl.	ἐγεγράφειμεν	ε	γε	γραφ	ει	μεν	*We had written.*
2-pl.	ἐγεγράφειτε	ε	γε	γραφ	ει	τε	*You (pl.) had written.*
3-pl.	ἐγεγράφεισαν	ε	γε	γραφ	ει	σαν	*They had written.*

a. The 3-pl. uses the second option in the core pattern for secondary personal endings.

b. The act.-1-sg. ειν only shows up in one verb in the New Testament, ᾔδειν, an alternate pluperfect from οἶδα, and rarely outside the New Testament, so you do not need to worry about confusing it with an infinitive (§4.93). The moveable ν is not used with ει (§4.3e) so it will not appear on this act.-3-sg.

4.65. Pluperfect Indicative Middle/Passive Components

The pluperfect middle/passive uses the same stem as the perfect middle/passive, and thus uses the 5th principal part. As with the pluperfect active, the middle/passive usually has an augment before the reduplication. The first middle/passive personal endings are added directly to the stem. So the components and abstract paradigm are:

Augment +	Reduplication +	Stem +	Secondary endings		
ε	+ λε	+ 5th part	+ μεθα	→	ἐλελύμεθα, *We had loosed. We had been loosed.*

ελε–5–μην	ελε–5–μεθα
ελε–5–σο	ελε–5–σθε
ελε–5–το	ελε–5–ντο

4.66. Pluperfect Indicative Middle/Passive

λύω – *Pluperfect Indicative Middle/Passive*

		Augment	Reduplication	Stem	Ending	Simple translation
1-sg.	ἐλελύμην	ε	λε	λυ	μην	*I had loosed. I had been loosed.*
2-sg.	ἐλέλυσο	ε	λε	λυ	σο	*You (sg.) had loosed. You (sg.) had been loosed.*
3-sg.	ἐλέλυτο	ε	λε	λυ	το	*He/She/It had loosed. He/She/It had been loosed.*

		Augment	Reduplication	Stem	Ending	Simple translation
1-pl.	ἐλελύμεθα	ε	λε	λυ	μεθα	*We had loosed.*
						We had been loosed.
2-pl.	ἐλέλυσθε	ε	λε	λυ	σθε	*You (pl.) had loosed.*
						You (pl.) had been loosed.
3-pl.	ἐλέλυντο	ε	λε	λυ	ντο	*They had loosed.*
						They had been loosed.

a. In these translations the active represents the middle, since that is how the middle is translated in English when not used with a passive sense.

PRINCIPAL PARTS

4.67. Introduction to Principal Parts

Verbs in Greek, as in English, build their various forms on principal parts. See the basic introduction to principal parts in §2.19.

a. In Greek there are six principal parts. The list in §2.19e indicates how these six principal parts are related to the various tense-forms. As noted in §2.19c, some verbs have the same stem in all six principal parts, some have a modified stem, and some use more than one stem. A list of principal parts provides the tense-aspect stems for a verb, that is, the stem with any additions or changes which signal each of the verb's tense-forms (§2.19f).

b. Lexicons list verbs by their present tense-form. Although we learn vocabulary using the present tense-form, the main stem is found in the aorist. "The present tense is, in fact, the most 'irregular' of all the tenses and the second aorist is one of the most 'regular.'"[23]

c. Thus, when you learn a new verb, look at its principal parts. If different stems are used then learn them. **For many verbs, if you know the present and any alternate stems you can recognize the other forms from their various tense-form indicators such as augments, reduplication, and tense-form signs.** Often any changes in a stem will be minor and come in the vowels. Only a few sets of principal parts will probably need to be memorized by rote (§4.75). The list of principal parts in appendix 8 provides alternate stems for those verbs that have notable changes.

d. The principal parts of most verbs follow one of several patterns. These patterns may be identified by the way the present tense-form modifies the stem.[24]

---

23. Mounce, *Morphology* §33.2.

24. This is the approach followed, for example, by Funk §356, ch. 31; and Mounce, *Morphology*, §33.3.

The collection of patterns listed below covers eight of the major patterns.[25] Appendix 8 contains a list of the principal parts for verbs occurring twenty-five times or more in the New Testament.

e. When learning a new verb it is helpful to look over the list of principal parts, along with the alternate stems listed, to see which forms will be difficult to recognize. Note in particular any verbs that are middle-only or lack tense-form signs (§2.19d).

The explanations given below are not important in themselves for learning to read Greek, but they may help you understand the changes and thus be better able to recognize forms.

4.68. Type 1: The Same Stem in All the Parts

Prin. Part	1st	2nd	3rd	4th	5th	6th	Stem(s)
	Pres. act./ MP	Fut. act./ MP1	Aor. act./ MP1	Pf. act.	Pf. MP	Aor. MP2	
	λύω	λύσω	ἔλυσα	λέλυκα	λέλυμαι	ἐλύθην	λυ
	πιστεύω	πιστεύσω	ἐπίστευσα	πεπίστευκα	πεπίστευ-μαι	ἐπι-στεύθην	πιστευ
	ἀγαπῶ	ἀγαπήσω	ἠγάπησα	ἠγάπηκα	ἠγάπημαι	ἠγαπήθην	ἀγαπα
	δικαιῶ	δικαιώσω	ἐδικαίωσα	δεδικαίωκα	δεδικαίω-μαι	ἐδικαι-ώθην	δικαιο
	εὐλογῶ	εὐλογήσω	εὐλόγησα	εὐλόγηκα	εὐλόγημαι	εὐλο-γήθην	εὐλογε
	πληρῶ	πληρώσω	ἐπλήρωσα	πεπλήρωκα	πεπλήρω-μαι	ἐπλη-ρώθην	πληρο
	ποιῶ	ποιήσω	ἐποίησα	πεποίηκα	πεποίημαι	ἐποιήθην	ποιε

25. The same selection of patterns is used in *UEBG*, 68–73, while more complete lists of principal parts, as well as explanations of particular forms and patterns of verbs used in the New Testament, are available in Mounce, *Morphology*; and Funk, "Appendix III: Verbal System Catalogue." For forms outside the New Testament see Smyth §§496–598; *CGCG*, ch. 22; and "Classified List of Verbs" in James Hadley and Frederic Forest De Allen, *A Greek Grammar for Schools and Colleges* (New York: D. Appleton and Company, 1885), 153–87. The verbs used to illustrate these eight major patterns are common in the New Testament. However, some of the principal parts listed are not used in the New Testament and thus are not included in lexicons focused on the New Testament. These additional principal parts are based on Montanari.

a. Most contract verbs have the same stem throughout, but lengthen the stem ending when tense-signs are added.

b. Some verbs, however, whose stems end in α or ε do not lengthen their stem ending. For example, the aorist of γελάω is ἐγέλασα (not ἐγέλησα), the aorist of κοπιάω is ἐκοπίασα (not ἐκοπίησα), the aorist of τελέω is ἐτέλεσα (not ἐτέλησα).

c. In the New Testament εὐλογέω does not usually augment to ηὐλογε-.

4.69. Type 2: Stems Ending in One of the Consonants in the Square of Stops

a. Minor Stem Changes.

Prin. Part	1st	2nd	3rd	4th	5th	6th	Stem(s)
	Pres. act./ MP	Fut. act./ MP1	Aor. act./ MP1	Pf. act.	Pf. MP	Aor. MP2	
	ἔχω	ἕξω	ἔσχον	ἔσχηκα	ἔσχημαι	ἐσχέθην	σεχ
	γράφω	γράψω	ἔγραψα	γέγραφα	γέγραμμαι	ἐγράφην	γραφ
	στρέφω	στρέψω	ἔστρεψα	ἔστροφα	ἔστραμμαι	ἐστράφην	στρεφ

1. While the stem is σεχ- the σ of this stem drops out in the present (ἔχω) and the ε of the stem drops out in the aorist and perfect active to leave σχ-: ἔσχον, ἔσχηκα. The future has a ξ, in keeping with the square of stops when a σ is added to a χ, but notice that the breathing is changed to a rough breathing on the future, ἕξω.

2. γράφω has no unusual changes—they all follow the square of stops (§3.19). Notice that it uses the alternate form of the perfect active (without the κ, §4.29) and the alternate form of the aorist second middle/passive (without the ϑ, §4.61).

3. στρέφω illustrates vowel changes in the stem. Notice also the alternate form of the aorist second middle/passive, though outside the New Testament the usual form is also found, ἐστρέφϑην.

b. Minor Stem Changes and the Present Augmented to -ζω, -πτω, or -σσω.

Principal part	1st	2nd	3rd	4th	5th	6th	Stem(s)
	Pres. act./ MP	Fut. act./ MP1	Aor. act./ MP1	Pf. act.	Pf. MP	Aor. MP2	
	ἁγιάζω	ἁγιάσω	ἡγίασα	ἡγίακα	ἡγίασμαι	ἡγιάσϑην	ἁγιαδ
	σῴζω	σώσω	ἔσωσα	σέσωκα	σέσωσμαι	ἐσώϑην	σωδ
	κρύπτω	κρύψω	ἔκρυψα	κέκρυφα	κέκρυμμαι	ἐκρύβην	κρυφ
	κηρύσσω	κηρύξω	ἐκήρυξα	κεκήρυχα	κεκήρυγμαι	ἐκηρύχϑην	κηρυκ

1. Very early Greek had a semivowel called a consonantal iota (ι), which had a "y" sound. When it was added to the present stem of a verb with a stem ending in one of the square of stops (§4.15) it caused the augmentation of a dental to ζ, a labial to πτ, and a velar to σσ.[26]
2. Thus, for the most part all these stem changes apart from the present follow the square of stops. So when you learn a word that ends in ζω, πτω, or σσω expect its forms to follow the square of stops outside the present tense-form.
3. The main exception among the words in this list is the form ἐκρύβην, which is an alternate form of the aorist second middle/passive with the tense-form sign η instead of θη (§4.61). The unusual stem ending β is due to the influence of an earlier form of this verb. Outside the New Testament the more normal ἐκρύφην is also found.

4.70. Type 3: Stems Ending in a Liquid (λ, ρ) or a Nasal (μ, ν)

a. Minor Stem Changes.

Prin. part	1st	2nd	3rd	4th	5th	6th	Stem(s)
	Pres. act./ MP	Fut. act./ MP1	Aor. act./ MP1	Pf. act.	Pf. MP	Aor. MP2	
	θέλω	θελήσω	ἠθέλησα	τεθέληκα	τεθέλημαι	ἐθελήθην	θελ
	κρίνω	κρινῶ	ἔκρινα	κέκρικα	κέκριμαι	ἐκρίθην	κριν
	μένω	μενῶ	ἔμεινα	μεμένηκα			μεν

1. κρίνω and μένω lack a σ in the future and aorist, following the pattern of the liquid future and liquid aorist (§§4.20, 53).[27] In the perfect and aorist second middle/passive of κρίνω the ν simply drops out. The aorist stem of μένω adds an ι, while an η is added to the end of its stem in the perfect.
2. The stem of θέλω was originally ἐθελε-, which explains the augment in the aorist active and the η before the tense-form signs. Similarly, the imperfect, built off the present, is ἤθελον. The aorist second middle/passive, however, has ε as the augment instead of an η. None of these peculiarities obscures the stem θελ-, and the tense-form signs are clear.

26. For details see Funk §§905, 932; Mounce, *Morphology* §§26.1–10.

27. These are called liquids even though some of these verbs are actually nasals since their stems end in μ or ν (§4.20).

b. Minor Stem Changes and the Present Augmented by Doubling λ or Adding ι.

Prin. Part	1st	2nd	3rd	4th	5th	6th	Stem(s)
	Pres. act./MP	Fut. act./MP1	Aor. act./MP1	Pf. act.	Pf. MP	Aor. MP2	
	βάλλω	βαλῶ	ἔβαλον	βέβληκα	βέβλημαι	ἐβλήθην	βαλ
	αἴρω	ἀρῶ	ἦρα	ἦρκα	ἦρμαι	ἤρθην	ἀρ

1. Both of these verbs have liquid futures (§4.20) and αἴρω also has a liquid aorist (§4.53).
2. The stem βαλ- not only adds a λ in the present, but in the last three principal parts it reduces its vowel (§3.25b) and adds an η.

4.71. Type 4: Minor Stem Changes and the Present Stem Augmented by Adding -σκ or -ισκ

Prin. part	1st	2nd	3rd	4th	5th	6th	Stem(s)
	Pres. act./MP	Fut. act./MP1	Aor. act./MP1	Pf. act.	Pf. MP	Aor. MP2	
	γινώσκω	γνώσομαι	ἔγνων	ἔγνωκα	ἔγνωσμαι	ἐγνώσθην	γνο
	εὑρίσκω	εὑρήσω	εὗρον	εὕρηκα	εὕρημαι	εὑρέθην	εὑρ

a. In the case of γινώσκω not only is σκ added to the end of the present stem, but the beginning of the present tense-form has also been modified. The form of γινώσκω was originally γιγνώσκω, and is listed this way in CG lexicons.[28] In later Greek the second γ dropped to give us γινώσκω. The stem is actually γνο- but since it lengthens to γνω- in all its principal parts, as you can see, you could learn that form for reading purposes.

4.72. Type 5: Minor Stem Changes and the Present Augmented by Adding νυ

Prin. part	1st	2nd	3rd	4th	5th	6th	Stem(s)
	Pres. act./MP	Fut. act./MP1	Aor. act./MP1	Pf. act.	Pf. MP	Aor. MP2	
	δείκνυμι	δείξω	ἔδειξα	δέδειχα	δέδειγμαι	ἐδείχθην	δεικ

28. Such reduplication is itself a common feature. See principal parts pattern 7 (§4.74).

4.73. Type 6: Stem Changes and the Present Augmented by Adding αν

Prin. part	1st	2nd	3rd	4th	5th	6th	Stem(s)
	Pres. act./ MP	Fut. act./ MP1	Aor. act./ MP1	Pf. act.	Pf. MP	Aor. MP2	
	λαμβάνω	λήμψομαι	ἔλαβον	εἴληφα	εἴλημμαι	ἐλήμφθην	λαβ
	μανθάνω	μαθήσω	ἔμαθον	μεμάθηκα			μαθ

a. The stem λαβ- undergoes quite a few changes in the various principal parts. When the vowel in the stem is short, as in λαβ-, a nasal is inserted after this vowel, here giving λαμβ- in the first principal part.[29] While λημφ- is not a distinct stem, it may be worth learning along with λαβ- to aid in recognizing forms of λαμβάνω.

4.74. Type 7: The Present Stem Reduplicates

Prin. part	1st	2nd	3rd	4th	5th	6th	Stem(s)
	Pres. act./MP	Fut. act./ MP1	Aor. act./ MP1	Pf. act.	Pf. MP	Aor. MP2	
	γίνομαι	γενήσομαι	ἐγενόμην	γέγονα	γεγένημαι	ἐγενήθην	γεν
	δίδωμι	δώσω	ἔδωκα	δέδωκα	δέδομαι	ἐδόθην	δο
	ἵστημι	στήσω	ἔστησα	ἔστηκα	ἔσταμαι	ἐστάθην	στα
	τίθημι	θήσω	ἔθηκα	τέθεικα	τέθειμαι	ἐτέθην	θε

a. γίνομαι was originally γίγνομαι and is listed under this form in CG lexicons. So the present tense-form was reduplicated, but then lost the second γ.

b. ἵστημι is the reduplicated form σιστα- with the initial σ dropped and replaced by a rough breathing in the present and perfect tense-forms. The reduplicated present tense-form was not actually used and is not listed in CG lexicons.

c. The vowels in the stems δο-, στα-, and θε- are often lengthened, so think of these verbs as having both long and short vowels in their stems, δω-, στη-, and θη-. In some forms it looks like there is only the consonant left, δ-, στ-, θ- (§4.81)!

4.75. Type 8: More than One Stem

This is a complete list of the verbs used in the New Testament that use more than one stem.

---

29. Funk §485.20. For two possible explanations for the formation of the stem λημφ- see Mounce, *Morphology*, 306.

Prin. part	1st Pres. act./MP	2nd Fut. act./ MP1	3rd Aor. act./ MP1	4th Pf. act.	5th Pf. MP	6th Aor. MP2	Stem(s)
	αἱρέω	αἱρήσομαι	εἱλόμην		ἥρημαι	ἡρέθην	αἱρε, ϝελ
	ἔρχομαι	ἐλεύσομαι	ἦλθον	ἐλήλυθα			ἐρχ, ἐλθ
	ἐσθίω	φάγομαι	ἔφαγον				ἐσθ, φαγ
	λέγω	ἐρῶ	εἶπον	εἴρηκα	εἴρημαι	ἐρρέθην	εἰπ, ϝερ, ϝεπ
	οἶδα	εἰδήσω	ᾔδειν				οἰδ, ϝιδ
	ὁράω	ὄψομαι	εἶδον	ἑώρακα		ὤφθην	ϝορα, ὀπ, ϝιδ
	πάσχω		ἔπαθον	πέπονθα			παθ, πονθ
	πίνω	πίομαι	ἔπιον	πέπωκα	πέπομαι	ἐπόθην	πι, πο, πω
	τρέχω		ἔδραμον				τρεχ, δραμ
	φέρω	οἴσω	ἤνεγκα	ἐνήνοχα		ἠνέχθην	φερ, οἰ, ἐνεκ

a. Several stems have a letter called a digamma (ϝ) on their front, representing a "w" sound. It dropped from use, but it accounts for the formation of a number of words. For practical purposes the simplified stems listed should help you recognize the forms.

b. The explanation of the patterns for several of these words is fairly complex so it is probably easiest just to learn their principal parts. But for an explanation of a particular form or pattern see Funk or Mounce, *Morphology*. The digamma in particular is discussed in Funk, §§905, 933, and Mounce, *Morphology* §27. When reading outside the New Testament consult Smyth or *CGCG* for help with forms, with Smyth being the more detailed.

c. The relation between οἶδα and ὁράω, however, is worth sorting out since their forms show up hundreds of times and are easily confused.[30] Both of these verbs are actually forms of an underlying verb εἴδω, *see*, which is not used in the New Testament. In the aorist its form is εἶδον and it means *see*, while in the perfect its form is οἶδα and means *know*.[31] LSJ suggests there is a connection: "οἶδα *I see with the mind's eye, i.e. I know.*"[32]

New Testament lexicons cause confusion by listing οἶδα as a lexical form, unlike CG lexicons such as LSJ and Montanari, which at their listings for οἶδα refer you to εἴδω.[33] Similarly, some New Testament lexicons discuss εἶδον under ὁράω, while others, like *CGEL* and BDAG, list εἶδον as a separate lexical form.

30. See also appendix 8, nn. b and h.

31. LSJ, 483; Montanari, 597. For the paradigm of οἶδα see §4.29b.

32. LSJ, s.v. "εἴδω B.," 483. Whether or not this association is correct, it can help you remember the relation between these words.

33. *CGEL* lists οἶδα and refers to εἶδον for the "root" (247), and BDAG says οἶδα is "really the perf. of the stem εἰδ-" (693).

Adding further confusion, some Greek teachers associate εἶδον with βλέπω, as in Modern Greek where εἶδα serves as the aorist of βλέπω.[34]

The forms of these two verbs are also easily confused. The signals may be summarized as follows.

When you see:			It is:
εἰδ-	in the indicative	=	the aorist indicative of εἶδον, *see* (often associated with ὁράω or βλέπω)
εἰδ-	in the nonindicative	=	a form of οἶδα, *know*
ἰδ-	in the nonindicative	=	a form of εἶδον, *see*

Thus if a beginning student learns εἶδον [ἰδ-], *see* and οἶδα [εἰδ-], *know* then the stems of these verbs can be easily remembered:

εἶδον [ἰδ-], *see*	εἰδ- in the indicative	=	the aorist indicative of εἶδον (ὁράω)
	ἰδ- in the nonindicative	=	a nonindicative form of εἶδον (ὁράω)
οἶδα [εἰδ-], *know*	οἰδ- in the indicative	=	a form of οἶδα
	εἰδ- in the nonindicative	=	a form of οἶδα

A LIST OF BASIC GREEK TENSE-FORM COMPONENTS

4.76. A Core Pattern for Identifying Tense-Forms

This chart is one of the twelve core patterns to become familiar with. The nine forms in italics are those used most frequently. You should either memorize this chart, beginning with those in italics, or build your knowledge of these key signs as you encounter the various tense-forms.

	Augment	+ Redu- plication	+ Stem	+ T-form sign	+ Vowel	+ Personal ending
Pres. act./MP			1st		o/ε	primary
Impf. act./MP	ε		1st		o/ε	secondary
Fut. act./MP1			2nd	σ	o/ε	primary

34. Note the similar alternation of these words in Luke 10:24, πολλοὶ προφῆται καὶ βασιλεῖς ἠθέλησαν **ἰδεῖν** ἃ ὑμεῖς **βλέπετε** καὶ οὐκ **εἶδαν**. *Many prophets and kings wanted to see what you see and they did not see.* On the form of εἶδαν see §4.57a.

	Augment	+ Redu-plication	+ Stem	+ T-form sign	+ Vowel	+ Personal ending
Liq. Fut. act./ MP1			2nd (λ,μ,ν,ρ)	(σ̵)	o/ε	primary
1 Aor. act./MP1	ε		3rd	σ	α/ε	secondary
Liq. Aor. act./ MP1	ε		3rd (λ,μ,ν,ρ)	(σ̵)	α/ε	secondary
κ Aor. act./ MP1	ε		3rd (κ)		α/ε	secondary
2 Aor. act./MP1	ε		3rd (?)		o/ε	secondary
Pf. act.		λε	4th	κ	α/ε	primary
Alt. Pf. act.		λε	4th		α/ε	primary
Plpf. act.	(ε)	λε	4th	κ	ει	secondary
Alt. Plpf. act.	(ε)	λε	4th		ει	secondary
Pf. MP		λε	5th			primary
Fut. Pf. MP		λε	5th	σ		primary
Plpf. MP	(ε)	λε	5th			secondary
Aor. MP2	ε		6th	θη		secondary **act.**
Alt. Aor. MP2	ε		6th		η	secondary **act.**
Fut. MP2			6th	θησ	o/ε	primary
Alt. Fut. MP2			6th	ησ	o/ε	primary

THE SUBJUNCTIVE MOOD

4.77. Subjunctive Components

A verb uses the same principal parts for all its moods.

a. The characteristic of the subjunctive is a lengthened linking vowel; watch for η and ω before the personal ending.

b. The subjunctive uses the same personal endings as the indicative. In the first two paradigms below the present indicative forms are given for comparison. The vast majority of subjunctives are in the present and aorist, so you should focus on these forms.[35] As always, the present uses the stem of the 1st principal part and the aorist uses the stems of the 3rd and 6th principal parts.

35. There is no imperfect or future subjunctive. There is a perfect subjunctive, but it appears only ten times in the New Testament in the active, all of them forms of οἶδα, *know*. The perfect middle/passive is also rare. It is formed with the subjunctive of εἰμί plus a participle.

c. Exactly the same endings are used for both the present and the aorist. This means that in the aorist subjunctive the primary endings are used instead of the secondary as elsewhere in the aorist.

d. The aorist drops the augment since only the indicative has an augment. The first aorist retains the σ as the tense-form sign, which will be a key to identifying the first aorist subjunctive. The second aorist is recognized by its stem from the 3rd principal part, which is always different from the 1st principal part (§4.56).

4.78. Subjunctive Active

Present, 1 Aorist and 2 Aorist Subjunctives: Active

	Pres. (λύω)	1 Aor. (λύω)	2 Aor. (λαμβάνω)	Pres. ind. (λύω)
1-sg.	λύω	λύσω	λάβω	λύω
2-sg.	λύῃς	λύσῃς	λάβῃς	λύεις
3-sg.	λύῃ	λύσῃ	λάβῃ	λύει
1-pl.	λύωμεν	λύσωμεν	λάβωμεν	λύομεν
2-pl.	λύητε	λύσητε	λάβητε	λύετε
3-pl.	λύωσι(ν)	λύσωσι(ν)	λάβωσι(ν)	λύουσι(ν)

4.79. Subjunctive Middle/Passive

Present, 1 and 2 Aorist Subjunctives: Middle/Passive

	Pres. MP (λύω)	1 Aor. MP1 (λύω)	2 Aor. MP1 (λαμβάνω)	1 Aor. MP2 (λύω)	Alt. 1 Aor. MP2 (γράφω)	2 Aor. MP2 (λαμβάνω)	Pres. ind. (λύω)
1-sg.	λύωμαι	λύσωμαι	λάβωμαι	λυθῶ	γραφῶ	λαβῶ	λύομαι
2-sg.	λύῃ	λύσῃ	λάβῃ	λυθῇς	γραφῇς	λαβῇς	λύῃ
3-sg.	λύηται	λύσηται	λάβηται	λυθῇ	γραφῇ	λαβῇ	λύεται
1-pl.	λυώμεθα	λυσώμεθα	λαβώμεθα	λυθῶμεν	γραφῶμεν	λαβῶμεν	λυόμεθα
2-pl.	λύησθε	λύσησθε	λάβησθε	λυθῆτε	γραφῆτε	λαβῆτε	λύεσθε
3-pl.	λύωνται	λύσωνται	λάβωνται	λυθῶσι(ν)	γραφῶσι(ν)	λαβῶσι(ν)	λύονται

a. As in the indicative (§4.59), the **aorist second middle/passive** subjunctive uses **active endings.**[36]

b. The accent on aorist second middle/passive subjunctives is always a circumflex, which distinguishes the second aorist active subjunctive (§4.78) from the second aorist second middle/passive. Such differences can be learned as you encounter examples in reading.[37]

c. Some verbs have η instead of θη, as illustrated by γράφω. These alternate forms are often referred to as second aorist even though such verbs do not use alternate second aorist stems (§4.61).

d. The main difficulties in these paradigms are the ambiguities. First, the η ending can be either act.-3-sg. or MP-2-sg. subjunctive, but also a present indicative MP-2-sg. (§§4.8c, 13b) or a future indicative (§§4.18, 20–24). Second, the ω of the act.-1-sg. is now either an indicative (§4.3d) or a subjunctive.[38]

4.80. Subjunctive of Contract Verbs

Contract verbs in the present tense-form with η or ω in the indicative occasionally result in the same form as the subjunctive. For example, ἀγαπῶμεν is a pres.-act.-1-pl., but may be either indicative or subjunctive; ποιῇ is pres.-act.-3-sg., either indicative or subjunctive, but it also can be pres.-ind.-MP-2-sg. The aorist forms are more easily distinguished. The paradigms for the contract forms of the subjunctive are included in appendix 4.51.

4.81. Subjunctive of μι Verbs

The subjunctive endings show up clearly in the μι verbs, though δίδωμι uses an ω before the personal ending throughout. Notice that some verbs have a first aorist, and some have an alternate aorist, while the active of δίδωμι uses both of them![39] These alternate forms are often referred to as second aorists, but this is

36. Here the second middle/passive uses θε/ε instead of θη/η. This ε contracts with the lengthened linking vowels η and ω, which produces the circumflex accent. See Funk §4431.2. This θε/ε is also evident in the second middle/passive optative (§4.90e).

37. For example, note Luke 12:5. ὑποδείξω δὲ ὑμῖν τίνα **φοβηθῆτε· φοβήθητε** τὸν μετὰ τὸ ἀποκτεῖναι ἔχοντα ἐξουσίαν ἐμβαλεῖν εἰς τὴν γέενναν, *But I will point out to you whom you should fear. Fear the one who, after killing, has authority to throw into Gehenna.* Here the aorist second middle/passive subjunctive φοβηθῆτε is immediately followed by the aorist second middle/passive imperative φοβήθητε, distinguished only by their accents.

38. For example, in Heb 11:32 the form λέγω is subjunctive not indicative: *And what more might I say?* (or, *can I say?, shall I say?*). This is an example of the deliberative use of the subjunctive (§5.141).

39. Indeed, the aor.-subjn.-act.-3-sg. of δίδωμι shows up in the form listed above, δῷ,

confusing since they do not have alternate stems as in the second aorist (§4.56). If you are not learning to write or speak Greek you do not need to remember which form of aorist shows up in which paradigm.

δίδωμι – *Subjunctive*

	Pres. act.	1 Aor. act.	Alt. Aor. act.	Pres. MP	1 Aor. MP1	Alt. Aor. MP1	Aor. MP2
1-sg.	διδῶ	δώσω	δῶ	διδῶμαι	δώσωμαι	δῶμαι	δοθῶ
2-sg.	διδῷς	δώσῃς	δῷς	διδῷ	δώσῃ	δῷ	δοθῇς
3-sg.	διδῷ	δώσῃ	δῷ	διδῶται	δώσηται	δῶται	δοθῇ
1-pl.	διδῶμεν	δώσωμεν	δῶμεν	διδώμεθα	δωσώμεθα	δώμεθα	δοθῶμεν
2-pl.	διδῶτε	δώσητε	δῶτε	διδῶσθε	δώσησθε	δῶσθε	δοθῆτε
3-pl.	διδῶσι(ν)	δώσωσι(ν)	δῶσι(ν)	διδῶνται	δώσωνται	δῶνται	δοθῶσι(ν)

a. In the alternate non-sigmatic aorists the stem δο looks like it is just a δ-.

ἵστημι – *Subjunctive*

	Pres. act.	1 Aor. act.	Alt. Aor. act.	Pres. MP	1 Aor. MP1	Alt. Aor. MP1	Aor. MP2
1-sg.	ἱστῶ	στήσω	στῶ	ἱστῶμαι	στήσωμαι	στῶμαι	σταθῶ
2-sg.	ἱστῇς	στήσῃς	στῇς	ἱστῇ	στήσῃ	στῇ	σταθῇς
3-sg.	ἱστῇ	στήσῃ	στῇ	ἱστῆται	στήσηται	στῆται	σταθῇ
1-pl.	ἱστῶμεν	στήσωμεν	στῶμεν	ἱστώμεθα	στησώμεθα	στώμεθα	σταθῶμεν
2-pl.	ἱστῆτε	στήσητε	στῆτε	ἱστῆσθε	στήσησθε	στῆσθε	σταθῆτε
3-pl.	ἱστῶσι(ν)	στήσωσι(ν)	στῶσι(ν)	ἱστῶνται	στήσωνται	στῶνται	σταθῶσι(ν)

b. In the alternate non-sigmatic aorists the stem στα- looks like it is just a στ-.

τίθημι – *Subjunctive*

	Pres. act.	1 Aor. act.	Alt. Aor. act.	Pres. MP	1 Aor. MP1	Alt. Aor. MP1	Aor. MP2
1-sg.	τιθῶ	θήσω	θῶ	τιθῶμαι	θήσωμαι	θῶμαι	τεθῶ
2-sg.	τιθῇς	θήσῃς	θῇς	τιθῇ	θήσῃ	θῇ	τεθῇς
3-sg.	τιθῇ	θήσῃ	θῇ	τιθῆται	θήσηται	θῆται	τεθῇ

but also as δώῃ and even as δοῖ! Appendix B in Abbott-Smith lists unusual verb forms, and BDAG discusses them as well under each verb.

	Pres. act.	1 Aor. act.	Alt. Aor. act.	Pres. MP	1 Aor. MP1	Alt. Aor. MP1	Aor. MP2
1-pl.	τιθῶμεν	θήσωμεν	θῶμεν	τιθώμεθα	θησώμεθα	θώμεθα	τεθῶμεν
2-pl.	τιθῆτε	θήσητε	θῆτε	τιθῆσθε	θήσησθε	θῆσθε	τεθῆτε
3-pl.	τιθῶ-σι(ν)	θήσω-σι(ν)	θῶσι(ν)	τιθῶνται	θήσωνται	θῶνται	τεθῶσι(ν)

c. In the alternate non-sigmatic aorist the stem θε- looks like it is just a θ-.

4.82. Present Subjunctive of εἰμί

The paradigm of the subjunctive of εἰμί is the same as the subjunctive active endings. The subjunctive of εἰμί only occurs with active endings.[40] It is parsed as active, though εἰμί does not actually have voice.

ὦ	ὦμεν
ᾖς	ἦτε
ᾖ	ὦσι

THE IMPERATIVE MOOD

4.83. The Core Pattern for the Imperative

The imperative is recognized by its endings, so they are a core pattern to be familiar with. The vast majority of imperatives occur in the present and aorist tense-forms, so you should focus on these.[41]

		Active	Middle/Passive
Singular	2nd pers.	-, ε, ς, θι, σον	σο (= ου), σαι
	3rd pers.	τω	σθω
Plural	2nd pers.	τε	σθε
	3rd pers.	τωσαν	σθωσαν

---

40. The subjunctive of εἰμί is not one of the twelve core patterns since there is nothing unusual about it, but it is an important paradigm to know.

41. The imperfect and future do not occur in the imperative. The perfect imperative is used four or five times in the New Testament: Mark 4:39, Acts 15:29, Eph 5:5, and Jas 1:19. The forms used in these verses are clear, but ἴστε (< οἶδα) in Heb 12:17 may be indicative or imperative. Funk §462; Mounce, *Morphology*, 146–47.

4.84. Imperative Components

As you go through these endings and the following paradigms notice the following points.

a. The 2-pl. endings are the same as those for the indicative. This means that **in the present the 2-pl. indicative and imperative have the same form.** Context will have to indicate which is being used, and sometimes it is not clear.

λύετε   pres.-**ind./impv.**-act.-2-pl.

λύεσθε   pres.-**ind./impv.**-MP-2-pl.

b. The 3-sg. and 3-pl. endings show up clearly in the paradigms so once you learn the core pattern they should be no problem. Notice, however, that you have to distinguish a simple 1-sg. ω ending on a verb from these third person endings, τω and σθω.[42]

c. The 2-sg. endings are the ones to watch in particular.

➤ With a zero form ending you usually see the linking vowel ε (λυ + ε + – : λῦε).

➤ ε as an actual ending is used with some μι verbs and it contracts with the stem (τιθε + ε: τίθει).

➤ σ is used on the aorist of some μι verbs (θές).

➤ θι is an active ending, though you will also see it in the aorist second middle/passive, since the aor.-MP2-impv. uses active endings.

➤ σο sometimes drops the σ and vowels contract, usually to ου (§§4.8c, 11).

➤ σον and σαι[43] are irregular (see n. 45).

➤ Both σο and σαι appear in the MP-2-sg. of the indicative, so they may already be familiar (§§4.1, 38).

d. In the aorist the lack of augment is a further sign of the imperative.

e. The paradigms for the contract verbs are included since they cause problems in some forms of the present. Their forms are clear in the aorist, but are included for comparison.

---

42. In CG the 3-pl. endings are ντων and σθων. So instead of seeing λυέτωσαν you will see λυόντων (the same form as a pres.-ptc.-act.-masc./neut.-gen.-pl., §4.107), and instead of λυέσθωσαν you will see λυέσθων. Smyth §466.3; *CGCG* §11.29; *AGG* §70; Mounce, *Morphology*, §§70–72.

43. Note that σαι is also an ending on the aor.-opt.-act.-3-sg. (§4.90) and the aor.-inf.-act. (§4.97).

4.85. Present Imperative

	(λύω)	(γεννάω)	(ποιέω)	(φανερόω)
	Active	Active	Active	Active
2-sg.	λῦε	γέννα	ποίει	φανέρου
3-sg.	λυέτω	γεννάτω	ποιείτω	φανερούτω
2-pl.	λύετε	γεννᾶτε	ποιεῖτε	φανεροῦτε
3-pl.	λυέτωσαν	γεννάτωσαν	ποιείτωσαν	φανερούτωσαν
	MP	MP	MP	MP
2-sg.	λύου	γεννῶ	ποιοῦ	φανεροῦ
3-sg.	λυέσθω	γεννάσθω	ποιείσθω	φανερούσθω
2-pl.	λύεσθε	γεννᾶσθε	ποιεῖσθε	φανεροῦσθε
3-pl.	λυέσθωσαν	γεννάσθωσαν	ποιείσθωσαν	φανερούσθωσαν

4.86. Present Imperative of μι Verbs

	(ἵστημι)	(τίθημι)	(δίδωμι)	(ἀφίημι)
	Active	Active	Active	Active
2-sg.	ἵστη[44]	τίθει	δίδου	ἀφίει
3-sg.	ἱστάτω	τιθέτω	διδότω	ἀφιέτω
2-pl.	ἵστατε	τίθετε	δίδοτε	ἀφίετε
3-pl.	ἱστάτωσαν	τιθέτωσαν	διδότωσαν	ἀφιέτωσαν
	MP	MP	MP	MP
2-sg.	ἵστασο	τίθεσο	δίδοσο	ἀφίεσο
3-sg.	ἱστάσθω	τιθέσθω	διδόσθω	ἀφιέσθω
2-pl.	ἵστασθε	τίθεσθε	δίδοσθε	ἀφίεσθε
3-pl.	ἱστάσθωσαν	τιθέσθωσαν	διδόσθωσαν	ἀφιέσθωσαν

4.87. Aorist and Perfect Imperatives

	(λύω)	(γεννάω)	(ποιέω)	(φανερόω)
	Active	Active	Active	Active
2-sg.	λῦσον[45]	γέννησον	ποίησον	φανέρωσον
3-sg.	λυσάτω	γεννησάτω	ποιησάτω	φανερωσάτω

44. ἵστη has no ending. The η is a lengthened stem ending. Mounce, *Morphology* §71.3 n. 2.

45. According to Mounce, "there is no obvious reason" for the act.-2-sg. σον and the MP-2-sg. σαι endings, *Morphology* §72.1 n. 1; they are "irregular (origin unknown)," Funk §4600.3.

	(λύω)	(γεννάω)	(ποιέω)	(φανερόω)
	Active	Active	Active	Active
2-pl.	λύσατε	γεννήσατε	ποιήσατε	φανερώσατε
3-pl.	λυσάτωσαν	γεννησάτωσαν	ποιησάτωσαν	φανερωσάτωσαν
	MP	MP	MP	MP
2-sg.	λῦσαι	γέννησαι	ποίησαι	φανέρωσαι
3-sg.	λυσάσθω	γεννησάσθω	ποιησάσθω	φανερωσάσθω
2-pl.	λύσασθε	γεννήσασθε	ποιήσασθε	φανερώσασθε
3-pl.	λυσάσθωσαν	γεννησάσθωσαν	ποιησάσθωσαν	φανερωσάσθωσαν

	2 Aor. act. (βάλλω)	1 Aor. MP2 (λύω)	1 Aor. MP2 (γράφω)	Pf. act. (λύω)
2-sg.	βάλε	λύθητι[46]	γράφηθι	λέλυκε
3-sg.	βαλέτω	λυθήτω	γραφήτω	λελυκέτω
2-pl.	βάλετε	λύθητε	γράφητε	λελύκετε
3-pl.	βαλέτωσαν	λυθήτωσαν	γραφήτωσαν	λελυκέτωσαν

	2 aor. MP1			Pf. MP
2-sg.	βαλοῦ			λέλυσο
3-sg.	βαλέσθω			λελύσθω
2-pl.	βάλεσθε			λέλυσθε
3-pl.	βαλέσθωσαν			λελύσθωσαν

4.88. Aorist Imperative of μι Verbs

	(ἵστημι)	(τίθημι)	(δίδωμι)	(ἀφίημι)
	Active	Active	Active	Active
2-sg.	στῆθι	θές[47]	δός	ἄφες
3-sg.	στήτω	θέτω	δότω	ἀφέτω
2-pl.	στῆτε	θέτε	δότε	ἄφετε
3-pl.	στήτωσαν	θέτωσαν	δότωσαν	ἀφέτωσαν
	Middle/Passive	Middle/Passive	Middle/Passive	Middle/Passive
2-sg.	στῶ	θοῦ	δοῦ	ἀφοῦ
3-sg.	στάσθω	θέσθω	δόσθω	ἀφέσθω
2-pl.	στάσθε	θέσθε	δόσθε	ἀφέσθε
3-pl.	στάσθωσαν	θέσθωσαν	δόσθωσαν	ἀφέσθωσαν

46. The imperative ending θι is deaspirated to τι when added to θη.
47. Notice that three of these verbs use ς for the ending in the 2-sg.

4.89. Present Imperative of εἰμί

2-sg.   ἴσθι

3-sg.   ἔστω

2-pl.   ἔστε

3-pl.   ἔστωσαν

THE OPTATIVE MOOD

4.90. Optative Components

The optative occurs primarily in the present and aorist tense-forms.[48]

a. There are no new endings for the optative, though some show up in distinctive ways. For example, the secondary endings are used throughout, even in the present, except for the ending μι, which is used for the act.-1-sg. throughout. Furthermore, the act.-3-pl. ending uses ν as in the secondary endings, but with an ε added before it.

b. The key sign of the optative is an ι added to the linking vowel or tense-sign.

c. The linking vowel throughout the present is o combined with the ι: οι.

d. In the aorist active and first middle/passive the tense-sign σ and linking vowel α have an ι added: σαι.[49]

e. In the aorist second middle/passive the tense-sign θη takes the form θε with ιη added to it: θειη.[50]

f. The aorist of the optative does not have an augment, since only the indicative has an augment.

g. You will probably be able to recognize most of these forms if you know the core patterns for the secondary endings and the distinctive signs of the optative:

οι	in the **present** and **second aorist**
σαι	in the **first aorist**
θειη	in the **aorist second middle/passive**

48. In the LXX the future optative occurs six times and the perfect optative once; neither occurs in the New Testament.

49. Note that σαι is also an ending on the aor.-impv.-MP-2-sg. (§4.87) and the aor.-inf.-act. (§4.97). In CG the aor.-opt.-act.-3-sg. has σειε and the 2-sg. has σειας, while the 3-pl. has σειαν, which shows up in Acts 17:27. *CGCG* §13.12; Mounce, *Morphology* §63.1 nn. 1, 2.

50. The form θε shows up primarily here and in the subjunctive (§4.79a n. 36). See Funk §§4431.2; 449; Mounce, *Morphology* §§34.4

4.91. Present and Aorist Optatives

	Present (λύω) Active	1 Aorist (λύω) Active	2 Aorist (βάλλω) Active
1-sg.	λύοιμι	λύσαιμι	βάλοιμι
2-sg.	λύοις	λύσαις	βάλοις
3-sg.	λύοι	λύσαι	βάλοι
1-pl.	λύοιμεν	λύσαιμεν	βάλοιμεν
2-pl.	λύοιτε	λύσαιτε	βάλοιτε
3-pl.	λύοιεν	λύσαιεν	βάλοιεν
	MP	MP1	MP1
1-sg.	λυοίμην	λυσαίμην	βαλοίμην
2-sg.	λύοιο[51]	λύσαιο	βάλοιο
3-sg.	λύοιτο	λύσαιτο	βάλοιτο
1-pl.	λυοίμεθα	λυσαίμεθα	βαλοίμεθα
2-pl.	λύοισθε	λύσαισθε	βάλοισθε
3-pl.	λύοιντο	λύσαιντο	βάλοιντο
		MP2	MP2
		λυθείην	βαλείην
		λυθείης	βαλείης
		λυθείη	βαλείη
		λυθείημεν	βαλείημεν
		λυθείητε	βαλείητε
		λυθείησαν	βαλείησαν

a. The μι verbs use ιη in some forms of the optative instead of a simple ι. Only εἴη (pres.-opt.-act.-3-sg. < εἰμί) occurs with any frequency in the New Testament (12×). Lexicons like *CGEL* will help you sort out these forms when you meet them.[52]

---

51. The MP-2-sg. ending σο loses its σ when it is added to the οι in the present and second aorist, and to the σαι in the first aorist.

52. For a more detailed discussion of the optative paradigms see Mounce, *Morphology* §§60–69.

THE INFINITIVE

4.92. Infinitive Components

The infinitive has the easiest set of endings to learn since there are only four of them. The infinitive does not take personal endings, so each tense-form only has two or three forms for the infinitive, depending on whether it uses only first middle/passive endings, as in the present and perfect, or both first and second middle/passive endings as in the aorist and future.

4.93. The Core Pattern for the Infinitive

An infinitive is recognized by its ending. The following endings form a core pattern to be familiar with. The bracketed forms are the endings as they usually appear.

εν [ειν], ι [σαι], ναι, σθαι

a. ειν is the linking vowel ε contracted with the infinitive ending εν in the present and second aorist.

$$λυ \quad + \quad ε \quad + \quad εν \quad = \quad λύειν$$
$$βαλ \quad + \quad ε \quad + \quad εν \quad = \quad βαλεῖν$$

b. σαι is the tense-form suffix σ and the linking vowel α of the first aorist active with the infinitive ending ι.[53]

c. The ending εν contracts with the stem endings in contract verbs, as you see in the paradigms below.

> an α contract verb will contract with εν to form ᾶν: γεννα + εν = γεννᾶν
> an ε contract verb will contract with εν to form εῖν: ποιε + εν = ποιεῖν
> an ο contract verb will contract with εν to form οῦν: φανερο + εν = φανεροῦν

d. The other two endings, ναι for the active and σθαι for the middle/passive, behave themselves and are easy to recognize, though ναι shows up frequently on the aorist MP2, which uses active endings (§4.59).

4.94. The Infinitive of εἰμί

The present occurs 129 times in the New Testament, the future much less often.

---

53. Note that σαι is also an ending on the aor.-impv.-MP-2-sg. (§4.87) and the aor.-opt.-act.-3-sg. (§4.90).

Present εἶναι
Future ἔσεσθαι

4.95. Present Infinitive

Present

	(λύω)	(γεννάω)	(ποιέω)	(φανερόω)
Active	λύειν	γεννᾶν	ποιεῖν	φανεροῦν
MP	λύεσθαι	γεννᾶσθαι	ποιεῖσθαι	φανεροῦσθαι

Present Infinitives of Some μι Verbs

	(ἵστημι)	(τίθημι)	(δίδωμι)	(δείκνυμι)
Active	ἱστάναι	τιθέναι	διδόναι	δεικνύναι
MP	ἵστασθαι	τίθεσθαι	δίδοσθαι	δείκνυσθαι

4.96. Future Infinitive

The future is formed quite regularly and there are only two verbs that use a future infinitive in the New Testament.

ἔσεσθαι < εἰμί
εἰσελευσεσθαι < εἰσέρχομαι

Examples from the LXX include

ἄξειν < ἄγω
ποιήσειν < ποιέω
δώσειν < δίδωμι

4.97. Aorist Infinitive

1 Aorist

	(λύω)	(γεννάω)	(ποιέω)	(φανερόω)
Active	λῦσαι	γέννησαι	ποίησαι	φανέρωσαι
MP1	λύσασθαι	γεννήσασθαι	ποιήσασθαι	φανερώσασθαι
MP2	λυθῆναι	γεννηθῆναι	ποιηθῆναι	φανερωθῆναι

2 Aorist

	(βάλλω)
Active	βαλεῖν
MP1	βαλέσθαι
MP2	βαλῆναι

a. In liquid aorist infinitives the σ drops out since the stem ends in λ, μ, ν, or ρ (§4.53).

αἴρω	→	ἆραι
ἀποστέλλω	→	ἀποστεῖλαι
μένω	→	μεῖναι

4.98. Aorist Active and Middle/Passive Infinitives of Some μι Verbs

	(ἵστημι)	(τίθημι)	(δίδωμι)	(ἀφίημι)
Active	στῆσαι[54]	θεῖναι	δοῦναι	ἀφεῖναι
MP1	στήσασθαι	θέσθαι	δόσθαι	ἀφέσθαι
MP2	σταθῆναι	τεθῆναι	δοθῆναι	ἀφεθῆναι

a. Note that these infinitives are root aorist forms since the ending is added directly to the stem (§4.49).

   b. There are also non-μι verbs that have root aorist forms, for example

γινώσκω	→	γνῶναι
ἀναβαίνω	→	ἀναβῆναι

4.99. Perfect Infinitive

	(λύω)	(γεννάω)	(ποιέω)	(φανερόω)
Active	λελυκέναι	γεγεννηκέναι	πεποιηκέναι	πεφανερωκέναι
MP	λελῦσθαι	γεγεννῆσθαι	πεποιῆσθαι	πεφανερῶσθαι

54. This word also uses στῆναι for an aorist active infinitive.

THE PARTICIPLE

4.100. Participle Components

a. **The key signs of the participle are the stem formatives ντ, οτ, and μεν,** to which are added adjective endings.

ντ	=	active participle or aorist middle/passive participle
οτ	=	perfect active participle
μεν	=	middle/passive participle

b. **Endings.** Participles are verbs with adjectival endings.

ντ	3-1-3 pattern of endings like πᾶς, πᾶσα, πᾶν (§3.37, app. 4.13)
οτ	3-1-3 pattern of endings like πᾶς, πᾶσα, πᾶν (§3.37, app. 4.13)
μεν	2-1-2 pattern of endings like ἀγαθός, ἀγαθή, ἀγαθόν (§3.10)

c. **Base.** The base of the participle is formed from the appropriate principal part. Note especially that the aorist does not have an augment, as is true of all nonindicative forms.

d. **Reduplication.** The perfect includes reduplication, as in other moods. Sometimes reduplication looks like an augment. Since participles do not take augments, if you see any change on the front of a participle it will be a perfect.[55] So the formula for a perfect participle is:

redupli-cation	base from the principal part	+	tense-form sign	+	linking vowel	+	participle sign: ντ, οτ, or μεν	+	adjectival ending

4.101. Participle Formulas

In the following list the tense-form sign, linking vowel, and participle sign are collected together. For example: **οντ** instead of ο + ντ, **σοντ** instead of σ + ο + ντ, and **σαντ** instead of σ + α + ντ. The question mark in the second aorist formula represents its distinctive stem (§4.56).

---

55. I owe this way of expressing this point to Rob Plummer from his "Daily Dose of Greek" videos.

ντ

Present active	λυ	+	οντ	+	3-1-3 adjective endings
2 Aorist active	?	+	οντ	+	3-1-3 adjective endings
Future active	λυ	+	σοντ	+	3-1-3 adjective endings
1 Aorist active	λυ	+	σαντ	+	3-1-3 adjective endings
Aorist second middle/passive	λυ	+	θεντ	+	3-1-3 adjective endings

μεν

Present middle/passive		λυ	+	ομεν	+	2-1-2 adjective endings
Future first middle/passive		λυ	+	σομεν	+	2-1-2 adjective endings
Future second middle/passive		λυ	+	θησομεν	+	2-1-2 adjective endings
Aorist first middle/passive		λυ	+	σαμεν	+	2-1-2 adjective endings
Perfect middle/passive	λε	+ λυ	+	μεν	+	2-1-2 adjective endings

οτ

perfect active	λε	+	λυ	+	κοτ	+	3-1-3 adjective ending

4.102. The Participle Box

	Masc. sing.	Fem. sing.	Neut. sing.	Sign		Sign
Pres./2 aor. act.	ων	ουσα	ον	οντ	**MP**	ομεν
1 Aor. act.	σας	σασα	σαν	σαντ	**MP1**	σαμεν
Aor. MP2	θεις	θεισα	θεν	θεντ		
Pf. act.	κως	κυια	κος	κοτ	**MP**	μεν

a. The participle is formed using common adjective endings and tense-form signs. There are only a few distinctive items to learn in order to parse participles. Learning the participle box will enable you to sort out participle forms, including the distinctive bits.

b. The first three items in each row of the box are the nom.-sg. endings (masc.-sg., fem.-sg., neut.-sg.), followed by the key sign for the participles. The future is not included because its paradigm is usually the same as the present with the σ tense-form sign added, as you see in the formula above in §4.101.

c. On the right side of the participle box are the signs for the middle/passive forms.

d. If you memorize this box you will have what you need to recognize all the forms. The following three sections describe features related to this participle box that are especially important to understand, assuming you know the basic 2-1-2 and 3-1-3 adjectival endings (§3.18).

4.103. Nominative Singulars in ντ and οτ

The three nom.-sg. forms include two of the difficult forms to watch for in the paradigms below. Specifically, the masc.-sg. and neut.-sg. forms require special attention because they use a zero form, which means the τ on οντ is the ending. But τ cannot end a word (§3.24b), and also it drops out when σ is added (§3.19b).

a. The **neut.-sg.** uses the zero form of the 3D (§3.16):

λυ + οντ + – → λυοντ → λυον(τ̶) → λύον

b. The **masc.-sg.** also uses the zero form option in the 3D (§3.16), but with the vowel lengthened to distinguish this form from the neut.-sg:

λυ + οντ + – → λυοντ → λυον(τ̶) → λύον → λύ(ο→ω)ν → λύων

This pattern also shows up in some 3D nouns (§3.26).

c. In the **perfect masc.-sg.** a ς ending is used which causes the τ to drop and then the vowel lengthens:

λε + λυ + κοτ + ς → λελυκο(τ̶)ς → λελυκος → λελυκ(ο→ω)ς → λελυκώς

d. The **perfect neut.-sg.**, λελυκός, is irregular, but learning it as part of the pattern "κως, κυια, **κος**, κοτ" will enable you to recognize it.

4.104. Feminine Stem Formative with ντ and οτ

A σ was added before the stem formatives in the feminine forms, which caused the ντ and the οτ to drop out, and the vowel to lengthen.[56] Here is how this works in the fem.-nom.-sg. for the pres.-ptc.-act of λύω:

λυ + οντ + σ + α → λυο(ν̶τ̶)σα → λύουσα

As you will see in the paradigms below, this pattern occurs throughout the feminine active participle as well as the aorist second middle/passive. So, by memorizing the participle box you will have in your brain the four fem.-nom.-sg. forms, which will enable you to remember this distinctive characteristic of the feminine.

56. For a more precise explanation see Funk §2471.3; Mounce, *Morphology* §91.1 n. 2.

4.105. Dative Plurals in 3-1-3 Patterns

In 3-1-3 patterns the dat.-pl. ending is σι(ν) (§3.16). The σ on σι(ν) causes the ντ to drop and the vowel to lengthen, as in the feminine forms (§4.104). The fem.-sg. form in the participle box can remind you of this characteristic of the dat.-pl.

$$\lambda\upsilon + o\nu\tau + \sigma\iota(\nu) \rightarrow \lambda\upsilon o(\text{ντ})\sigma\iota(\nu) \rightarrow \lambda\upsilon(o\rightarrow o\upsilon)\sigma\iota(\nu) \rightarrow \lambda\upsilon o\tilde{\upsilon}\sigma\iota(\nu)$$

a. Note that these dat.-pl. forms can look like indicative verbs in the 3 pl. (§4.1), so you have to watch for signs in the context to see which you are dealing with in a passage.

λυοῦσιν: pres.-ind.-act.-3-pl. **or** pres.-ptc.-act.-masc./neut.-dat.-pl. < λύω, *loose.*

4.106. Introduction to Participle Paradigms

As you go through the following paradigms note (1) how the features discussed in the previous sections work in each paradigm, (2) how the participle box helps sort out the difficulties in the nom.-sg. and dat.-pl., and (3) how the rest of the forms have a clear sign of the participle and follow the normal adjectival endings.

Present Participles

4.107. Present Active Participle

	Masc. sg.	Fem. sg.	Neut. sg.
Nom.	λύων	λύουσα	λῦον
Gen.	λύοντος	λυούσης	λύοντος
Dat.	λύοντι	λυούσῃ	λύοντι
Acc.	λύοντα	λύουσαν	λῦον
	Masc. pl.	Fem. pl.	Neut. pl.
Nom.	λύοντες	λύουσαι	λύοντα
Gen.	λυόντων	λυουσῶν	λυόντων
Dat.	λύουσι(ν)	λυούσαις	λύουσι(ν)
Acc.	λύοντας	λυούσας	λύοντα

4.108. Present Participle of εἰμί

The present participle of εἰμί is the same as the endings on the present active participle given above. For example:

Nom.-sg.	ὤν	οὖσα	ὄν
Gen.-sg.	ὄντος	οὔσης	ὄντος
Dat.-pl.	οὖσι(ν)	οὔσαις	οὖσι(ν)

For the full paradigm see appendix 4.69.

4.109. Present Active Participle of Contract Verbs

Contract verbs in the present active will have the usual changes when the o on οντ is added: α + ο = ω; ε + ο = ου; ο + ο = ου (§4.11).

α contract	nom.-sg.	ἀγαπῶν	ἀγαπῶσα	ἀγαπῶν
ἀγαπάω	gen.-sg.	ἀγαπῶντος	ἀγαπώσης	ἀγαπῶντος
	dat.-pl.	ἀγαπῶσιν	ἀγαπώσαις	ἀγαπῶσιν
ε contract	nom.-sg.	ποιῶν	ποιοῦσα	ποιοῦν
ποιέω	gen.-sg.	ποιοῦντος	ποιούσης	ποιοῦντος
	dat.-pl.	ποιοῦσιν	ποιούσαις	ποιοῦσιν
ο contract	nom.-sg.	δικαιῶν	δικαιοῦσα	δικαιοῦν
δικαιόω	gen.-sg.	δικαιοῦντος	δικαιούσης	δικαιοῦντος
	dat.-pl.	δικαιοῦσιν	δικαιούσαις	δικαιοῦσιν

4.110. Present Active Participle of μι Verbs

The μι verbs have a short stem vowel before the sign of the participle, so the stem of ἵστημι, ἵστη-, is ἵστα-, and so forth. Otherwise, these forms follow the normal pattern.

ἵστημι	nom.-sg.	ἱστάς	ἱστᾶσα	ἱστάν
	gen.-sg.	ἱστάντος	ἱστάσης	ἱστάντος
	dat.-pl.	ἱστᾶσι(ν)	ἱστάσαις	ἱστᾶσι(ν)
τίθημι	nom.-sg.	τιθείς	τιθεῖσα	τιθέν
	gen.-sg.	τιθέντος	τιθείσης	τιθέντος
	dat.-pl.	τιθεῖσι(ν)	τιθείσαις	τιθεῖσι(ν)

δίδωμι	nom.-sg.	διδούς	διδοῦσα	διδόν
	gen.-sg.	διδόντος	διδούσης	διδόντος
	dat.-pl.	διδοῦσι(ν)	διδούσαις	διδοῦσι(ν)
δείκνυμι	nom.-sg.	δεικνύς	δεικνῦσα	δεικνύν
	gen.-sg.	δεικνύντος	δεικνύσης	δεικνύντος
	dat.-pl.	δεικνῦσι(ν)	δεικνύσαις	δεικνῦσι(ν)

4.111. Present Middle/Passive Participle

	Masc. sg.	Fem. sg.	Neut. sg.
Nom.	λυόμενος	λυομένη	λυόμενον
Gen.	λυομένου	λυομένης	λυομένου
Dat.	λυομένῳ	λυομένῃ	λυομένῳ
Acc.	λυόμενον	λυομένην	λυόμενον

	Masc. pl.	Fem. pl.	Neut. pl.
Nom.	λυόμενοι	λυόμεναι	λυόμενα
Gen.	λυομένων	λυομένων	λυομένων
Dat.	λυομένοις	λυομέναις	λυομένοις
Acc.	λυομένους	λυομένας	λυόμενα

4.112. Present Middle/Passive Participle of Contract Verbs

Contract verbs in the present middle/passive will have the usual changes when the linking vowel o is added: α + o = ω; ε + o = ου; o + o = ου (§4.11).

α contract	nom.-sg.	ἀγαπώμενος	ἀγαπωμένη	ἀγαπώμενον
ἀγαπάω	gen.-sg.	ἀγαπωμένου	ἀγαπωμένης	ἀγαπωμένου
	dat.-pl.	ἀγαπωμένοις	ἀγαπωμέναις	ἀγαπωμένοις
ε contract	nom.-sg.	ποιούμενος	ποιουμένη	ποιούμενον
ποιέω	gen.-sg.	ποιουμένου	ποιουμένης	ποιουμένου
	dat.-pl.	ποιουμένοις	ποιουμέναις	ποιουμένοις
o contract	nom.-sg.	δικαιούμενος	δικαιουμένη	δικαιούμενον
δικαιόω	gen.-sg.	δικαιουμένου	δικαιουμένης	δικαιουμένου
	dat.-pl.	δικαιουμένοις	δικαιουμέναις	δικαιουμένοις

4.113. Present Middle/Passive Participle of μι Verbs

ἵστημι	nom.-sg.	ἱστάμενος	ἱσταμένη	ἱστάμενον
	gen.-sg.	ἱσταμένου	ἱσταμένης	ἱσταμένου
	dat.-pl.	ἱσταμένοις	ἱσταμέναις	ἱσταμένοις
τίθημι	nom.-sg.	τιθέμενος	τιθεμένη	τιθέμενον
	gen.-sg.	τιθεμένου	τιθεμένης	τιθεμένου
	dat.-pl.	τιθεμένοις	τιθεμέναις	τιθεμένοις
δίδωμι	nom.-sg.	διδόμενος	διδομένη	διδόμενον
	gen.-sg.	διδομένου	διδομένης	διδομένου
	dat.-pl.	διδομένοις	διδομέναις	διδομένοις
δείκνυμι	nom.-sg.	δεικνύμενος	δεικνυμένη	δεικνύμενον
	gen.-sg.	δεικνυμένου	δεικνυμένης	δεικνυμένου
	dat.-pl.	δεικνυμένοις	δεικνυμέναις	δεικνυμένοις

Future Participles

4.114. Future Participle

Future participles follow the paradigms of the present participles with the addition of the tense-form signs σ in the active and first middle/passive and θησ in the second middle/passive. For full paradigms see appendix 4.76–78.

Act.	nom.-sg.	λύσων	λύσουσα	λῦσον
	gen.-sg.	λύσοντος	λυσούσης	λύσοντος
	dat.-pl.	λύσουσι(ν)	λυσούσαις	λύσουσι(ν)
MP1	nom.-sg.	λυσόμενος	λυσομένη	λυσόμενον
	gen.-sg.	λυσομένου	λυσομένης	λυσομένου
	dat.-pl.	λυσομένοις	λυσομέναις	λυσομένοις
MP2	nom.-sg.	λυθησόμενος	λυθησομένη	λυθησόμενον
	gen.-sg.	λυθησομένου	λυθησομένης	λυθησομένου
	dat.-pl.	λυθησομένοις	λυθησομέναις	λυθησομένοις

Aorist Participles

4.115. First Aorist Active Participle

	Masc. sg.	Fem. sg.	Neut. sg.
Nom.	λύσας	λύσασα	λῦσαν
Gen.	λύσαντος	λυσάσης	λύσαντος
Dat.	λύσαντι	λυσάσῃ	λύσαντι
Acc.	λύσαντα	λύσασαν	λῦσαν
	Masc. pl.	Fem. pl.	Neut. pl.
Nom.	λύσαντες	λύσασαι	λύσαντα
Gen.	λυσάντων	λυσασῶν	λυσάντων
Dat.	λύσασι(ν)	λυσάσαις	λύσασι(ν)
Acc.	λύσαντας	λυσάσας	λύσαντα

4.116. First Aorist Active Participle of Contract Verbs

a. Most contract verbs lengthen their stem ending when a tense-form sign is added, so there is no change in the tense-form sign or the endings (§4.48).

ἀγαπάω	→	ἀγαπήσας, ἀγαπήσαντος
τηρέω	→	τηρήσας, τηρήσαντος
πληρόω	→	πληρώσας, πληρώσαντος

b. A few contract verbs retain their original vowel (§4.48c).

καλέω → καλέσας, καλέσαντος

4.117. First Aorist Active Participle of μι Verbs

ἵστημι	nom.-sg.	στήσας	στήσασα	στῆσαν
	gen.-sg.	στήσαντος	στησάσης	στήσαντος
	dat.-pl.	στησᾶσι(ν)	στησάσαις	στησᾶσι(ν)

4.118. First Aorist First Middle/Passive Participle

	Masc. sg.	Fem. sg.	Neut. sg.
Nom.	λυσάμενος	λυσαμένη	λυσάμενον
Gen.	λυσαμένου	λυσαμένης	λυσαμένου
Dat.	λυσαμένῳ	λυσαμένῃ	λυσαμένῳ
Acc.	λυσάμενον	λυσαμένην	λυσάμενον

	Masc. pl.	Fem. pl.	Neut. pl.
Nom.	λυσάμενοι	λυσάμεναι	λυσάμενα
Gen.	λυσαμένων	λυσαμένων	λυσαμένων
Dat.	λυσαμένοις	λυσαμέναις	λυσαμένοις
Acc.	λυσαμένους	λυσαμένας	λυσάμενα

4.119. First Aorist First Middle/Passive Participle of μι Verbs

ἵστημι	nom.-sg.	στησάμενος	στησαμένη	στησάμενον
	gen.-sg.	στησαμένου	στησαμένης	στησαμένου
	dat.-pl.	στησαμένοις	στησαμέναις	στησαμένοις

4.120. First Aorist Second Middle/Passive Participle

	Masc. sg.	Fem. sg.	Neut. sg.
Nom.	λυθείς	λυθεῖσα	λυθέν
Gen.	λυθέντος	λυθείσης	λυθέντος
Dat.	λυθέντι	λυθείσῃ	λυθέντι
Acc.	λυθέντα	λυθεῖσαν	λυθέν

	Masc. pl.	Fem. pl.	Neut. pl.
Nom.	λυθέντες	λυθεῖσαι	λυθέντα
Gen.	λυθέντων	λυθεισῶν	λυθέντων
Dat.	λυθεῖσι(ν)	λυθείσαις	λυθεῖσι(ν)
Acc.	λυθέντας	λυθείσας	λυθέντα

4.121. Alternate First Aorist Second Middle/Passive Participle

The alternate first aorist second middle/passive participle is the same as the first aorist second middle/passive (§4.120), but without the ϑ (§4.61).

	Masc. sg.	Fem. sg.	Neut. sg.
Nom.	γραφείς	γραφεῖσα	γραφέν
Gen.	γραφέντος	γραφείσης	γραφέντος
Dat.	γραφέντι	γραφείσῃ	γραφέντι
Acc.	γραφέντα	γραφεῖσαν	γραφέν
	Masc. pl.	Fem. pl.	Neut. pl.
Nom.	γραφέντες	γραφεῖσαι	γραφέντα
Gen.	γραφέντων	γραφεισῶν	γραφέντων
Dat.	γραφεῖσι(ν)	γραφείσαις	γραφεῖσι(ν)
Acc.	γραφέντας	γραφείσας	γραφέντα

4.122. First Aorist Second Middle/Passive Participle of Contract Verbs

Contract verbs simply lengthen their final vowel before the tense-form sign, as in the active (§4.116).

ἀγαπάω → ἀγαπηθείς, ἀγαπηθέντος
τηρέω → τηρηθείς, τηρηθέντος
πληρόω → πληρωθείς, πληρωθέντος

4.123. Alternate First Aorist Active Participle of μι Verbs

ἵστημι	nom.-sg.	στάς	στᾶσα	στάν
	gen.-sg.	στάντος	στάσης	στάντος
	dat.-pl.	στᾶσι(ν)	στάσαις	στᾶσι(ν)
τίθημι	nom.-sg.	θείς	θεῖσα	θέν
	gen.-sg.	θέντος	θείσης	θέντος
	dat.-pl.	θεῖσι(ν)	θείσαις	θεῖσι(ν)
δίδωμι	nom.-sg.	δούς	δοῦσα	δόν
	gen.-sg.	δόντος	δούσης	δόντος
	dat.-pl.	δοῦσι(ν)	δούσαις	δοῦσι(ν)

4.124. Alternate First Aorist First Middle/Passive Participle of μι Verbs

ἵστημι	nom.-sg.	στάμενος	σταμένη	στάμενον
	gen.-sg.	σταμένου	σταμένης	σταμένου
	dat.-pl.	σταμένοις	σταμέναις	σταμένοις

τίθημι	nom.-sg.	θέμενος	θεμένη	θέμενον
	gen.-sg.	θεμένου	θεμένης	θεμένου
	dat.-pl.	θεμένοις	θεμέναις	θεμένοις
δίδωμι	nom.-sg.	δόμενος	δομένη	δόμενον
	gen.-sg.	δομένου	δομένης	δομένου
	dat.-pl.	δομένοις	δομέναις	δομένοις

4.125. Alternate First Aorist Second Middle/Passive Participle of μι Verbs

ἵστημι	nom.-sg.	σταθείς	σταθεῖσα	σταθέν
	gen.-sg.	σταθέντος	σταθείσης	σταθέντος
	dat.-pl.	σταθεῖσι(ν)	σταθείσαις	σταθεῖσι(ν)
τίθημι	nom.-sg.	τεθείς	τεθεῖσα	τεθέν
	gen.-sg.	τεθέντος	τεθείσης	τεθέντος
	dat.-pl.	τεθεῖσι(ν)	τεθείσαις	τεθεῖσι(ν)
δίδωμι	nom.-sg.	δοθείς	δοθεῖσα	δοθέν
	gen.-sg.	δοθέντος	δοθείσης	δοθέντος
	dat.-pl.	δοθεῖσι(ν)	δοθείσαις	δοθεῖσι(ν)
δείκνυμι	nom.-sg.	δειχθείς	δειχθεῖσα	δειχθέν
	gen.-sg.	δειχθέντος	δειχθείσης	δειχθέντος
	dat.-pl.	δειχθεῖσι(ν)	δειχθείσαις	δειχθεῖσι(ν)

4.126. Second Aorist Active Participle

	Masc. sg.	Fem. sg.	Neut. sg.
Nom.	γενών	γενοῦσα	γενόν
Gen.	γενόντος	γενούσης	γενόντος
Dat.	γενόντι	γενούσῃ	γενόντι
Acc.	γενόντα	γενοῦσαν	γενόν

	Masc. pl.	Fem. pl.	Neut. pl.
Nom.	γενόντες	γενοῦσαι	γενόντα
Gen.	γενόντων	γενουσῶν	γενόντων
Dat.	γενοῦσι(ν)	γενούσαις	γενοῦσι(ν)
Acc.	γενόντας	γενούσας	γενόντα

4.127. Second Aorist First Middle/Passive Participle

	Masc. sg.	Fem. sg.	Neut. sg.
Nom.	γενόμενος	γενομένη	γενόμενον
Gen.	γενομένου	γενομένης	γενομένου
Dat.	γενομένῳ	γενομένῃ	γενομένῳ
Acc.	γενόμενον	γενομένην	γενόμενον

	Masc. pl.	Fem. pl.	Neut. pl.
Nom.	γενόμενοι	γενόμεναι	γενόμενα
Gen.	γενομένων	γενομένων	γενομένων
Dat.	γενομένοις	γενομέναις	γενομένοις
Acc.	γενομένους	γενομένας	γενόμενα

4.128. Second Aorist Second Middle/Passive Participle

	Masc. sg.	Fem. sg.	Neut. sg.
Nom.	γενηθείς	γενηθεῖσα	γενηθέν
Gen.	γενηθέντος	γενηθείσης	γενηθέντος
Dat.	γενηθέντι	γενηθείσῃ	γενηθέντι
Acc.	γενηθέντα	γενηθεῖσαν	γενηθέν

	Masc. pl.	Fem. pl.	Neut. pl.
Nom.	γενηθέντες	γενηθεῖσαι	γενηθέντα
Gen.	γενηθέντων	γενηθεισῶν	γενηθέντων
Dat.	γενηθεῖσι(ν)	γενηθείσαις	γενηθεῖσι(ν)
Acc.	γενηθέντας	γενηθείσας	γενηθέντα

Perfect Participles

4.129. Perfect Active Participle

	Masc. sg.	Fem. sg.	Neut. sg.
Nom.	λελυκώς	λελυκυῖα	λελυκός
Gen.	λελυκότος	λελυκυίας	λελυκότος
Dat.	λελυκότι	λελυκυίᾳ	λελυκότι
Acc.	λελυκότα	λελυκυῖαν	λελυκός

	Masc. pl.	Fem. pl.	Neut. pl.
Nom.	λελυκότες	λελυκυῖαι	λελυκότα
Gen.	λελυκότων	λελυκυιῶν	λελυκότων
Dat.	λελυκόσι(ν)	λελυκυίαις	λελυκόσι(ν)
Acc.	λελυκότας	λελυκυίας	λελυκότα

4.130. Perfect Active Participle of μι Verbs

ἵστημι	Nom.-sg.	ἑστηκώς	ἑστηκυῖα	ἑστηκός
	Gen.-sg.	ἑστηκότος	ἑστηκυίας	ἑστηκότος
	Dat.-pl.	ἑστηκόσι(ν)	ἑστηκυίαις	ἑστηκόσι(ν)
τίθημι	Nom.-sg.	τεθεικώς	τεθεικυῖα	τεθεικός
	Gen.-sg.	τεθεικότος	τεθεικυίας	τεθεικότος
	Dat.-pl.	τεθεικόσι(ν)	τεθεικυίαις	τεθεικόσι(ν)
δίδωμι	Nom.-sg.	δεδωκώς	δεδωκυῖα	δεδωκός
	Gen.-sg.	δεδωκότος	δεδωκυίας	δεδωκότος
	Dat.-pl.	δεδωκόσι(ν)	δεδωκυίαις	δεδωκόσι(ν)

4.131. Alternate Perfect Active Participle

ἵστημι	Nom.-sg.	ἑστώς	ἑστῶσα	ἑστός
	Gen.-sg.	ἑστότος	ἑστώσης	ἑστότος
	Dat.-pl.	ἑστόσι(ν)	ἑστώσαις	ἑστόσι(ν)
οἶδα	Nom.-sg.	εἰδώς	εἰδυῖα	εἰδός
	Gen.-sg.	εἰδότος	εἰδυίας	εἰδότος
	Dat.-pl.	εἰδόσι(ν)	εἰδυίαις	εἰδόσι(ν)

4.132. Perfect Middle/Passive Participle

	Masc. sg.	Fem. sg.	Neut. sg.
Nom.	λελυμένος	λελυμένη	λελυμένον
Gen.	λελυμένου	λελυμένης	λελυμένου
Dat.	λελυμένῳ	λελυμένη	λελυμένῳ
Acc.	λελυμένον	λελυμένην	λελυμένον

	Masc. pl.	Fem. pl.	Neut. pl.
Nom.	λελυμένοι	λελυμέναι	λελυμένα
Gen.	λελυμένων	λελυμένων	λελυμένων
Dat.	λελυμένοις	λελυμέναις	λελυμένοις
Acc.	λελυμένους	λελυμένας	λελυμένα

4.133. Perfect Middle/Passive Participle of μι Verbs

ἵστημι	Nom.-sg.	ἑστημένος	ἑστημένη	ἑστημένον
	Gen.-sg.	ἑστημένου	ἑστημένης	ἑστημένου
	Dat.-pl.	ἑστημένοις	ἑστημέναις	ἑστημένοις
τίθημι	Nom.-sg.	τεθειμένος	τεθειμένη	τεθειμένον
	Gen.-sg.	τεθειμένου	τεθειμένης	τεθειμένου
	Dat.-pl.	τεθειμένοις	τεθειμέναις	τεθειμένοις
δίδωμι	Nom.-sg.	δεδομένος	δεδομένη	δεδομένον
	Gen.-sg.	δεδομένου	δεδομένης	δεδομένου
	Dat.-pl.	δεδομένοις	δεδομέναις	δεδομένοις

Greek Syntax

5.1. Introduction to This Chapter on Syntax

In this chapter we see how words function and fit together in phrases, clauses, and sentences. As with the morphological material in chapters 3 and 4, this survey of the basic elements of Greek syntax is presented in such a way that it can be read through as well as consulted for reference. The discussion of a few points is given in more than one section for ease of use, especially for those using this book to learn beginning Greek.

Many of the topics in chapter 5 are summarized in appendix 5, "Summary of Selected Syntax Topics." The topics in appendix 5 are numbered to correspond to the topics in this chapter. You may find it helpful when studying a new topic to check this summary for its key points. This summary may also be useful for a quick review of the options when you are analyzing a word or construction in a passage, though at times you will need to review the fuller discussion. The indexes and the table of contents can provide help locating topics.

THE DEFINITE ARTICLE

5.2. Introduction to the Definite Article

Daniel Wallace makes a startling claim for the Greek article: "One of the greatest gifts bequeathed by the Greeks to Western civilization was the article."[1] Later he notes, "In short, there is no more important aspect of Greek grammar than the article to help shape our understanding of the thought and theology of the NT writers."[2]

---

1. *ExSyn*, 207.
2. *ExSyn*, 208. Compare Robertson's statement, "The development of the Greek article is one of the most interesting things in human speech. . . . The article is never meaningless in Greek, though it often fails to correspond with the English idiom." A. T. Robertson,

The great significance of the article is matched by its complexity. The follow-ing sections cover the major features you will meet most often.[3]

a. In English the definite article, "the," often indicates that something is specific and definite, while the indefinite article, "a, an," indicates something belongs to a general class. Thus, "the child is reading the book" refers to some specific book, but "a child is reading a book" refers to a nonspecified book, though "a book" indicates that it is a book rather than something else, like a magazine or a text message. So also with "the child" compared to "a child."

b. In Greek there is no indefinite article. Thus the Greek article should some-times be translated with "the," and the lack of an article translated with "a, an," but often this is not the case. A word that has an article in agreement with it in gender, case and number is said to be **arthrous** or **articular**. When there is no article the construction is called **anarthrous**.

The Article as a Structure Signal[4]

5.3. Attributive and Predicate Positions

The article may signal that an adjective or other modifier is modifying a noun or other substantive, or it may signal that something is being predicated, that is, asserted to be a quality or characteristic of someone or something.[5]

5.4. Attributive Positions

If there is an article in front of the adjective or modifier then it is usually modifying the noun or substantive. This attributive position is found in three patterns in Greek, but each is translated the same way in English. In these examples three kinds of modifiers are illustrated, an adjective, a prepositional phrase, and a participle with its own prepositional phrase.

a. *1st Position*: article—adjective/modifier—noun/substantive (common)

[art-adj-substantive: TAS][6]

A Grammar of the Greek New Testament in the Light of Historical Research, 4th ed. (Nashville: Broadman, 1934), 754, 756.

3. For a more thorough discussion see *ExSyn*, 206–90; and the more streamlined dis-cussion in *BNTSyn*, 114–28; as well as *CGCG*, ch. 28.

4. For fuller discussion of the article as a structure signal see Funk §§125–129.5.

5. A substantive is any word or cluster that functions like a noun.

6. T represents the article since it most often begins with a τ. For this convention see Funk §6840.2; and note Daniel Wallace's use of TSKS for Granville Sharp's rule (*ExSyn*, 270–90; *BNTSyn*, 120–28; *Granville Sharp's Canon and Its Kin: Semantics and Significance*,

ὁ ἀγαθὸς ἀνήρ	*the good man*
ἡ ἐν τῇ ἀγορᾷ γυνή	*the woman in the marketplace*
τὰ διὰ τῆς ἀγορᾶς τρέχοντα τέκνα	*the children running through the marketplace*

b. *2nd Position:* article—noun/substantive—article—adjective/modifier (less common)

[art-substantive-art-adj: TSTA]

ὁ ἀνὴρ ὁ ἀγαθός	*the good man*
ἡ γυνὴ ἡ ἐν τῇ ἀγορᾷ	*the woman in the marketplace*
τὰ τέκνα τὰ διὰ τῆς ἀγορᾶς τρέχοντα	*the children running through the marketplace*

c. *3rd Position:* noun/substantive—article—adjective/modifier (rare)

[substantive-art-adj: STA]

ἀνὴρ ὁ ἀγαθός	*the good man*
γυνὴ ἡ ἐν τῇ ἀγορᾷ	*the woman in the market*
τέκνα τὰ διὰ τῆς ἀγορᾶς τρέχοντα	*the children running through the market*

d. While all three positions are translated the same way in English there is a difference in emphasis in Greek between the first attributive position and the other two positions in which the adjective/modifier comes last. In most contexts the emphasis falls on the modifier when it comes last. For example, in Jesus's parable of the soils, after describing the various unfavorable conditions into which some of the seed fell we come to the climax:

καὶ ἄλλα ἔπεσεν εἰς **τὴν γῆν τὴν καλήν** (Mark 4:8)
and other (seed) fell into <u>the good earth</u>

The context indicates that the emphasis is on the condition of this soil, that it is good. The second attributive position helps convey that emphasis.

ὁ πατήρ μου δίδωσιν ὑμῖν **τὸν ἄρτον** ἐκ τοῦ οὐρανοῦ **τὸν ἀληθινόν** (John 6:32)
my Father gives you the <u>true bread</u> from heaven

Studies in Biblical Greek 14 [New York: Lang, 2009]; §5.11). The characteristic of the attributive position is thus TA, article-adjective.

In the context Jesus is making a contrast with the bread Moses gave in the wilderness. The second attributive position emphasizes the adjective, and the fact that the adjective comes after the prepositional phrase further increases that emphasis (§5.263b).

Similarly, consider the emphasis on the modifier in the following example of the rare third attributive position.

Εἰρήνην ἀφίημι ὑμῖν, **εἰρήνην τὴν ἐμὴν** δίδωμι ὑμῖν (John 14:27)
Peace I leave with you, <u>my peace</u> I give to you

Here clearly the repetition of εἰρήνην with the addition of τὴν ἐμήν emphasizes the modifier.

e. An attributive relation also occurs with no articles present. In such cases the noun may come before the adjective or vice versa.[7] Such a lack of articles is also found at times for a predicate construction (§5.5b), so ultimately context must guide whether we have attribution or predication.

Ἐν μεγάλῃ δὲ οἰκίᾳ οὐκ ἔστιν μόνον **σκεύη χρυσᾶ καὶ ἀργυρᾶ** (2 Tim 2:20)
In a great house there are not only <u>gold and silver vessels</u>

τυφλοί εἰσιν **ὁδηγοί** (Matt 15:14)
they are blind guides

5.5. Predicate Position

When a noun or other substantive has an article and the adjective or other modifier lacks an article then a statement is being made. The adjective or modifier is being predicated of the noun/substantive. "This (noun) <u>is</u> this (modifier)." As in §5.4, the article is represented by "T" in the following formulas.

ἀγαθὸς ὁ ἀνήρ	*The man is good.*	adjective + [article + substantive] (ATS)
ὁ ἀνὴρ ἀγαθός	*The man is good.*	[article + substantive] + adjective (TSA)

a. The verb "to be" is often omitted, that is, it is signaled by this structure rather than expressed with a verb form. In English such omission is also possible at times, though often the verb needs to be supplied in a translation. For help sorting out which noun/substantive is the subject, especially if both words have an article or both lack an article see §5.26c.

7. Wallace refers to the noun-adjective order as the fourth attributive position, and the adjective-noun order as an "(anarthrous) first attributive position." *ExSyn*, 309–10; *BNTSyn*, 138. But the lack of articles means neither order is really an attributive position, especially since a predicate construction can also lack articles (§5.5b).

εἰ ὅλον **τὸ σῶμα ὀφθαλμός** (1 Cor 12:17)
if the whole body <u>were</u> an eye
> Notice that ὅλον (neut.-nom.-sg. < ὅλος, η, ον, *whole*) is also in predicate position even though it is attributive, as is common for this word and several others (§5.6).

ἀληθιναὶ καὶ δίκαιαι αἱ κρίσεις σου (Rev 16:7)
true and just <u>are</u> your judgments
> αἱ κρίσεις is the subject so we could translate, "Your judgments are true and just." But the order in the Greek also works in English in this case, and so some of the focus on ἀληθιναὶ καὶ δίκαιαι can be preserved.

b. A predicate construction may lack an article. The adjective may either precede or follow the noun.[8] Since such anarthrous constructions can also be used for an attributive (§5.4e), context must guide whether there is predication or attribution.

μακάριος ἀνὴρ οὗ οὐ μὴ λογίσηται κύριος ἁμαρτίαν. (Rom 4:8)
<u>*Blessed is the man*</u> *whose sin the Lord will most certainly not reckon.*
> Paul is quoting Psalm 32:2 (31:2 in the LXX). μακάριος ἀνήρ occurs twelve other times in the LXX and also in James 1:12. On οὐ μή with the subjunctive see §5.139.

χωρὶς γὰρ νόμου **ἁμαρτία νεκρά** (Rom 7:8)
for apart from the law <u>sin is dead</u>

5.6. Attributive and Predicate Positions with οὗτος and ἐκεῖνος

Some words appear in predicate position (no article before them), even though they are attributive. The most common words that take this construction are οὗτος, αὕτη, τοῦτο, *this*, and ἐκεῖνος, ἐκείνη, ἐκεῖνο, *that*, and note also the example of ὅλος, η, ον in §5.5a.

ὁ μαθητὴς **ἐκεῖνος** ὃν ἠγάπα ὁ Ἰησοῦς (John 21:7)
<u>*that*</u> *disciple whom Jesus loved*
> ὁ μαθητὴς ἐκεῖνος is a predicate position, but with ἐκεῖνος it is not "that is the disciple."

---

8. Wallace refers to the adjective-noun order as the "(anarthrous) first predicate position," and the noun-adjective order as the "(anarthrous) second predicate position." *ExSyn*, 310–11; *BNTSyn*, 138–39. But the lack of articles means neither order is really a predicate position, especially since an attributive construction can also lack articles (§5.4e).

ὁ ἄνθρωπος **οὗτος** δίκαιος καὶ εὐλαβής (Luke 2:25)
this man was righteous and devout
> οὗτος is in the predicate position, but it simply modifies its head term, "this man," not "this is the man." The other two adjectives, δίκαιος καὶ εὐλαβής, are also in predicate position, but unlike οὗτος they do not normally take a predicate position when they are attributive. So here they form the predicate and function as subject complements. In this case the verb "to be" is understood rather than expressed with a verb form in the Greek, but has to be supplied in an English translation, "was." It is in the past due to the context.

5.7. Attributive and Predicate Positions with αὐτός

Some words have different meanings, nuances, or usages depending on whether they are in attributive or predicate position. One very common example is αὐτός, αὐτή, αὐτό (*-self, same, he/she/it*). This word functions most often as the third-person pronoun, but may also signal an intensive or identity.

a. Third-Person Pronoun. The third-person pronoun matches the gender of the noun it represents.

λέγει πρὸς **αὐτὸν** ἡ γυνή (John 4:15)
the woman said to him
> αὐτόν is in the masculine because the reference is to Jesus.

λέγω γὰρ ὑμῖν ὅτι οὐ μὴ φάγω **αὐτὸ** ἕως ὅτου πληρωθῇ ἐν τῇ βασιλείᾳ τοῦ θεοῦ (Luke 22:16)
for I say to you that I will not eat it until it is fulfilled in the kingdom of God
> In the previous verse Jesus said, "I have greatly desired to eat this Passover with you." The Greek word for Passover is neuter, τὸ πάσχα,[9] hence this use of the neuter pronoun αὐτό.

ἠπίστουν **αὐταῖς** (Luke 24:11)
they did not believe them
> After the resurrection Mary Magdalene, Joanna, Mary the mother of James, and other women with them told the apostles that Jesus had been raised (Luke 24:10). When Luke refers to these women here in the next verse he uses the feminine αὐταῖς.[10] The pronoun in "they did

---

9. τὸ πάσχα comes from the Hebrew and is indeclinable, that is, it uses the same form for all the cases.

10. Note that αὐταῖς is the complement since ἀπιστέω uses the dative for its complement (§5.72).

not believe" is not a separate word in the Greek, but rather is signaled by the personal ending on the verb ἠπίστουν.[11]

εἰσερχόμενοι δὲ εἰς τὴν οἰκίαν ἀσπάσασθε **αὐτήν** (Matt 10:12)
And as you enter the house greet <u>it</u>
> αὐτήν is accusative as the direct object of the verb "greet." It is feminine because it is referring to "house," which is feminine in Greek, οἰκία, ας, ἡ.

Καὶ ἀφεὶς **αὐτοὺς** πάλιν ἀπελθὼν προσηύξατο ἐκ τρίτου (Matt 26:44)
And leaving <u>them</u> again and going away he prayed a third time
> αὐτούς refers to Jesus's disciples.

b. Intensive. As an intensive adjective αὐτός, αὐτή, αὐτό emphasizes the word it agrees with in gender, case, and number. In English it is often translated with a pronoun ending in "-self," like himself, herself, itself, yourself, ourselves, themselves.

αὐτὸς δὲ ὁ Ἰωάννης εἶχεν τὸ ἔνδυμα αὐτοῦ ἀπὸ τριχῶν καμήλου (Matt 3:4)
Now John <u>himself</u> had his clothing from camel's hair

αὐτὸς γὰρ ἐγίνωσκεν τί ἦν ἐν τῷ ἀνθρώπῳ (John 2:25)
for he <u>himself</u> knew what was in the person

In this second example the subject of the verb, "he," is not a separate word in Greek, but rather it is signaled by the ending on the verb. The nominative αὐτός intensifies this understood subject. Whenever αὐτός, αὐτή, αὐτό is in the nominative and does not have an article it will be intensive since it will be in agreement with the subject of the verb, whether the subject is given explicitly or only implied in the verb.

Ἐν **αὐτῇ** τῇ ὥρᾳ ἠγαλλιάσατο [ἐν] τῷ πνεύματι τῷ ἁγίῳ (Luke 10:21)
In the hour <u>itself</u> he rejoiced in the Holy Spirit
> More smoothly in English: "In that very hour," or "At that very time/moment."

καὶ **αὐτὸς** ὁ θεὸς μετ᾽ αὐτῶν ἔσται (Rev 21:3)
and God <u>himself</u> will be with them

c. Identity. When a form of αὐτός, αὐτή, αὐτό has an article it functions as an adjective of identity and will be translated "same."

---

11. ἠπίστουν – impf.-ind.-act.-3-pl. < ἀπιστέω, *not believe*. For the pattern of this contract verb see §4.42.

καὶ διαιρέσεις διακονιῶν εἰσιν, καὶ **ὁ αὐτὸς** κύριος (1 Cor 12:5)
and there are a variety of services, and the same Lord

οὐχὶ καὶ οἱ τελῶναι **τὸ αὐτὸ** ποιοῦσιν; (Matt 5:46)
Don't the tax collectors do the same thing?

μετὰ Ἰσαὰκ καὶ Ἰακὼβ τῶν συγκληρονόμων τῆς ἐπαγγελίας **τῆς αὐτῆς**
(Heb 11:9)
with Isaac and Jacob, fellow heirs of the same promise

d. Summary of the Uses of αὐτός, αὐτή, αὐτό. The uses are listed in order of the clarity of their signs, with the presence of an article being the clearest sign.

Function	Sign	Translation
1. Identity	Has an article before it	*same*
2. Intensive	In the nominative or in agreement	*himself, herself, itself, themselves, etc.*
3. Third-person pronoun	Not in the nominative and not in agreement	*he, she, it, they, them, etc.*

Thus αὐτός, αὐτή, αὐτό serves as a personal pronoun only when (1) it does not have a definite article with it and thus signals identity, and (2) it is not in the nominative or in agreement with another word and thus is intensive.

5.8. Attributive and Predicate Positions with πᾶς

The adjective πᾶς, πᾶσα, πᾶν (*each, every, all, the whole*) is normally in the predicate position (anarthrous) even though it functions attributively. When it is in the plural a group is viewed collectively, *all*, though with abstract nouns the focus is usually on individual expressions of the idea of the noun (§5.20b). In the singular the focus is on the individual members of a whole group, *each, every*, or on a group, either without restriction, *all*, or without exception, *everyone/everything*.[12] In the attributive position (arthrous) in both the singular and plural a group is being viewed collectively with more emphasis on it as a whole, *all, the whole*.

---

12. For the paradigm of πᾶς, πᾶσα, πᾶν see §3.37, appendix 4.13. Wallace affirms that even when πᾶς is anarthrous it has a form of definiteness since it points to something specific. *ExSyn*, 253; *BNTSyn*, 113.

πᾶς, πᾶσα, πᾶν	predicate (anarthrous)	attributive (articular)
sg.	each, every, any; all, everyone/ everything	(the) whole, all
pl.	all	all

The same number of people/items are involved either way, but the focus is different. These distinctions are consistent in CG, but less so in KG, so context must be taken into consideration, as usual.[13] The lexicons give guidance for the multiple constructions and nuances of this word.[14] Here are some examples.

a. Adjective

πᾶν οὖν **δένδρον** μὴ ποιοῦν καρπὸν καλὸν ἐκκόπτεται καὶ εἰς πῦρ βάλλεται (Matt 3:10)
therefore <u>every tree</u> that does not bring forth good fruit is cut down
> ➤ This is an anarthrous construction referring to the individual members of the group.

καὶ ἰδοὺ ὥρμησεν **πᾶσα ἡ ἀγέλη** κατὰ τοῦ κρημνοῦ εἰς τὴν θάλασσαν (Matt 8:32)
<u>the whole herd</u> rushed down the hill into the sea
> ➤ Notice the definite article before the noun signaling a focus on the group as a whole.

τῇ ἐκκλησίᾳ τοῦ θεοῦ τῇ οὔσῃ ἐν Κορίνθῳ σὺν **τοῖς ἁγίοις πᾶσιν** τοῖς οὖσιν ἐν ὅλῃ τῇ Ἀχαΐᾳ (2 Cor 1:1)
to the church of God that is at Corinth, with <u>all the saints</u> who are in the whole of Achaia
> ➤ Here πᾶς follows the article and noun, but it still focuses on the group as a whole.

ἵνα **πᾶν στόμα** φραγῇ καὶ ὑπόδικος γένηται **πᾶς ὁ κόσμος** τῷ θεῷ (Rom 3:19)
that <u>every mouth</u> may be stopped, and <u>all the world</u> may be brought under the judgment of God
> ➤ Notice the lack of article (anarthrous) with the first πᾶς, focusing on each individual, and the article (arthrous) with the second, viewing humanity as a whole.

---

13. For CG see Smyth §1174; *CGCG* §29.45.
14. See also Funk, ch. 51, for the various constructions found in the New Testament.

πᾶσα σὰρξ ὡς χόρτος (1 Pet 1:24)
All flesh is as grass
> Here the singular focuses on a group without restriction.

b. Noun or Pronoun

ἀλλ᾽ ἡμῖν εἷς θεὸς ὁ πατὴρ ἐξ οὗ **τὰ πάντα** (1 Cor 8:6)
yet for us there is one God, the Father, from whom are all things
> τὰ πάντα, the sum total, the universe viewed as a whole.

συνέκλεισεν γὰρ ὁ θεὸς **τοὺς πάντας** εἰς ἀπείθειαν, ἵνα **τοὺς πάντας** ἐλεήσῃ (Rom 11:32)
For God enclosed all in disobedience, that he might have mercy upon all
> These articles suggest the reference is to humanity viewed as a composite whole.

κατ᾽ ἰδίαν δὲ τοῖς ἰδίοις μαθηταῖς ἐπέλυεν **πάντα** (Mark 4:34)
privately to his own disciples he expounded everything
> "Everything" in the sense of all the individual parables (see Mark 4:33), taking πάντα as a neut.-acc.-pl.

πάντα δὲ δοκιμάζετε, τὸ καλὸν κατέχετε (1 Thess 5:21)
put everything to the test; retain that which is good
> If πάντα is a masc.-acc.-sg. then this is "everything" in the sense of each thing, here perhaps referring specifically to each prophecy that is given (see 1 Thess 5:20). Alternatively, if πάντα is a neut.-acc.-pl., the reference would be more broadly to all things.

c. Sometimes in Greek, as in English, "all" or "the whole" is used imprecisely, for effect.

καὶ ἰδοὺ **πᾶσα** ἡ πόλις ἐξῆλθεν εἰς ὑπάντησιν τῷ Ἰησοῦ (Matt 8:34)
And behold, all the city came out to meet Jesus
> The article indicates that the city is being viewed as a whole. Perhaps every individual is included, but the reference may just as well be more imprecise.

Other Uses of the Article

5.9. Bracketing Force of the Article

An article and its noun or other substantive may be separated from one another by one or more words that modify the noun. In this way Greek enables an author to use a compact grammatical structure to paint a complex picture.

τὸν τῆς παροικίας ὑμῶν **χρόνον** (1 Pet 1:17)
the time of your sojourn

> Whenever you see two articles together like τὸν τῆς suspect there is such bracketing present.

ὁ μετὰ τετρακόσια καὶ τριάκοντα ἔτη γεγονὼς **νόμος** (Gal 3:17)
the law, which came after 430 years

> This string of modifiers is sandwiched between the article and its noun. This forms a compact description: the-having-come-after-430-years-law.

καὶ λέγει τῷ ἀνθρώπῳ **τῷ** τὴν ξηρὰν χεῖρα **ἔχοντι** (Mark 3:3)
and he said to the man who had the withered hand

> Here the first article, τῷ, is in agreement with the participle ἔχοντι which is functioning as an adjective to modify τῷ ἀνθρώπῳ (§5.184).

5.10. Apollonius's Canon

Apollonius Dyscolus was a Greek grammarian in Alexandria, Egypt, in the second century AD.[15] He noted that when a noun is modified by a genitive, both the head term and the genitive usually will have an article, or they will both lack an article.

ἐν **τῷ** λόγῳ **τῆς** ἀληθείας (Col 1:5)
in the word of truth

ἐν λόγῳ ἀληθείας (2 Cor 6:7)
in truthful speech

> This translation takes ἀληθείας as an attributive genitive, that is, one functioning as an adjective (§5.44). This expression could be translated "in the word of truth" (§5.20d), but it occurs in a long string of expressions describing Paul's hardships in verses 6:4-10, all of which are anarthrous. They are probably anarthrous to highlight the quality of these hardships (§5.22), that is, these were the sort of things that Paul had endured.

a. Exceptions can occur for a number of reasons.[16] For example, the genitive may be a proper noun, and thus be definite without an article (§5.20a).

---

15. Ἀπολλώνιος ὁ Δύσκολος. δύσκολος, ον means *hard, difficult*. When used of persons δύσκολος refers to someone who is "difficult to please, always discontented, morose, bad humored, irritable." Montanari, 566. Ceslaus Spicq, *Theological Lexicon of the New Testament* (Peabody, MA: Hendrickson, 1994), 1:388 cites several interesting references from the Hellenistic period to such people.

16. For a more extensive set of exceptions see Wesley Perschbacher, *New Testament Greek Syntax: An Illustrated Manual* (Chicago: Moody Press, 1995), 45-47.

ἐν τῇ βίβλῳ Μωϋσέως (Mark 12:26)
in the book of Moses

b. Similarly, the object of a preposition is often considered definite without the article (§5.20d) and so may lack the article while its object has an article.

εἰς κοινωνίαν τοῦ υἱοῦ αὐτοῦ (1 Cor 1:9)
into the fellowship of his son

c. Another exception follows a feature of Hebrew grammar called a construct chain, formed by two or more nouns. The first noun or nouns lack an article, but the whole chain is definite or indefinite depending on whether the final noun in the chain is definite or indefinite. These chains often are conveyed by the genitive in Greek, with indefinite noun(s) followed by a definite noun in the genitive.

εἰς ἔπαινον δόξης τῆς χάριτος αὐτοῦ (Eph 1:6)
to the praise of the glory of his grace
> ▸ δόξης lacks the article contrary to Apollonius's Canon, but it follows the Hebrew construct model and may therefore be taken as definite.

5.11. Granville Sharp's Rule (TSKS)

In 1798 Granville Sharp published a book on a particular grammatical construction that Wallace summarizes in this way: "When two nouns are connected by καί and the article precedes only the first noun, there is a close connection between the two."[17] Wallace helpfully refers to this construction as TSKS: T = article, S = substantive, K = καί.[18] It applies not only to nouns but also to participles and adjectives serving as substantives.

a. A TSKS construction always signifies some sort of connection between the two substantives, at times connoting equality or even identity. But note that **if one or both of the substantives are impersonal, plural, or a proper name then Granville Sharp's rule does not apply.[19] Both substantives, however, may still refer to the same person or thing**.

b. The following are examples of this construction signaling identity, that is, an article joining two substantives that refer to the same person. The second and third examples are highly significant statements regarding the divinity of Christ.[20]

---

17. *ExSyn*, 270. On this topic see *ExSyn*, 270–90; *BNTSyn*, 120–28, and more extensively, Wallace, *Granville Sharp's Canon and Its Kin.*

18. Funk also uses this convention; §6840.2.

19. *ExSyn*, 270–72; *BNTSyn*, 120–21.

20. See the discussion of these passages in *ExSyn*, 276–77; *BNTSyn*, 122–23.

τὸν ἀπόστολον καὶ ἀρχιερέα τῆς ὁμολογίας ἡμῶν Ἰησοῦν (Heb 3:1)
the apostle and high priest of our confession, Jesus

τοῦ μεγάλου θεοῦ καὶ σωτῆρος ἡμῶν Ἰησοῦ Χριστοῦ (Titus 2:13)
our great God and Savior, Jesus Christ

τοῦ θεοῦ ἡμῶν καὶ σωτῆρος Ἰησοῦ Χριστοῦ (2 Pet 1:1)
our God and Savior, Jesus Christ

c. The following examples show distinct groups that are connected in some sense. Granville Sharp's rule is not itself present, but the meanings of the words and the context indicate a connection.

Ἰδὼν δὲ πολλοὺς τῶν Φαρισαίων καὶ Σαδδουκαίων (Matt 3:7)
And seeing many of the Pharisees and Sadducees
> The single article binds these nouns together, but since they are in the plural this construction does not come under Granville Sharp's rule. In this case the meaning of the words points to two distinct sets of people, though here they are being viewed as forming one group that is present at this scene.

Καὶ αὐτὸς ἔδωκεν τοὺς μὲν ἀποστόλους . . . , τοὺς δὲ ποιμένας καὶ διδασ-κάλους (Eph 4:11)
He gave some as apostles . . . and others as pastors and teachers
> These two groups are somehow related to each other, but again the nouns are in the plural so Granville Sharp's rule does not apply. There is much discussion over whether these two words refer to a single group of people, "pastor-teachers," or to two distinct groups that have something in common, like the Pharisees and Sadducees in the previous example.

5.12. The Article Used for Identification

This use is similar to the English definite article, pointing to something as specific and definite. There are a number of reasons why something might be definite. Here are a few examples, with a label for each.[21]

a. **Monadic.** The article is often used with words that signify something of which there is only one, for example, "the sun," "the moon."

ὁ ἥλιος σκοτισθήσεται, καὶ ἡ σελήνη οὐ δώσει τὸ φέγγος αὐτῆς (Matt 24:29)
the sun will be darkened and the moon will not give its light

21. For further forms of identification and their labels see *ExSyn*, 216–31; *BNTSyn*, 97–103.

b. Anaphoric. At times an article signals a reference back to the same noun/ substantive earlier in the passage.[22] Often this earlier instance does not have an article. The article thus helps make connections within a passage.

Καὶ τῇ ἡμέρᾳ τῇ τρίτῃ **γάμος** ἐγένετο ἐν Κανὰ τῆς Γαλιλαίας, καὶ ἦν ἡ μήτηρ τοῦ Ἰησοῦ ἐκεῖ· ἐκλήθη δὲ καὶ ὁ Ἰησοῦς καὶ οἱ μαθηταὶ αὐτοῦ εἰς **τὸν γάμον**. (John 2:1-2)
And the third day there was <u>a wedding</u> in Cana of Galilee, and the mother of Jesus was there. And Jesus also was invited and his disciples to <u>the wedding</u>.

καὶ στὰς **ὁ Ἰησοῦς** ἐφώνησεν αὐτούς (Matt 20:32)
and <u>Jesus</u> stopped and called them
> The first reference to Jesus in this story is anarthrous (Matt 20:30) and now this articular reference is anaphoric, referring back to that first reference. The next reference to Jesus in this story is also articular (20:34), helping to tie the story together. Then a new story starts with a reference to Jesus that is anarthrous (Matt 21:1), followed by an articular use (Matt 21:6). Yet another story follows the same pattern of anarthrous (Matt 21:12) and articular (Matt 21:16) references to Jesus.

c. Well-Known. The article is sometimes used when the person or thing is well-known or familiar.

καὶ πτύξας **τὸ** βιβλίον ἀποδοὺς **τῷ** ὑπηρέτῃ ἐκάθισεν (Luke 4:20)
And he rolled up <u>the</u> scroll, gave it back to <u>the</u> attendant, and sat down
> The first article, τὸ βιβλίον (*the scroll*), is anaphoric, referring back to the scroll mentioned earlier in verse 17. In that first reference there is no article with βιβλίον,[23] but thereafter in this passage this noun has the article as a way of pointing back to the item we've already met in the story. The second article, τῷ ὑπηρέτῃ (*the attendant*), points to the well-known official commonly found in a synagogue service.

d. Par Excellence. The article can be used when someone or something is the best of its kind.

ὁ προφήτης εἶ σύ; καὶ ἀπεκρίθη· οὔ. (John 1:21)
"Are you <u>the</u> prophet?" And he answered, "No."
> The officials questioning John are not asking if he is a prophet, but

22. Compare ἀναφέρω, *bring back, refer, recall to mind*.
23. καὶ ἐπεδόθη αὐτῷ **βιβλίον** τοῦ προφήτου Ἠσαΐου, *and a scroll of the prophet Isaiah was given to him* (Luke 4:17). Words can be definite even if they lack an article (§5.20), and most English translations have "the scroll" here in 4:17, though an indefinite sense may also work well.

rather whether he is "the prophet." This article could point to one who is well-known, the prophet they have all been hearing about who has come on the scene. Or they may be referring to the prophet like Moses who was expected in the last days, based on Deuteronomy 18:15. In this case this article points to the prophet par excellence, the prophet above other prophets. Compare the use of "the Prophet" in Islam. Similarly, when you see the term "the apostle" in the writings of the church fathers this is a reference to Paul, who is viewed as the apostle par excellence.

e. Deictic. The article can be used to point to a person or thing present either to the senses or in one's mind.[24]

καὶ λέγει αὐτοῖς· ἰδοὺ ὁ ἄνθρωπος. (John 19:5)
and he [Pilate] said to them, "Behold <u>the</u> man."
> This article can be a pointer to Jesus who is standing there before them. Some commentators make more of this article, suggesting, for example, par excellence, Jesus as the ultimate human being. This example illustrates how a text can work on more than one level. Pilate's statement is likely to be deictic, but John the gospel writer could be seeing more significance in the expression.[25]

Ἐνορκίζω ὑμᾶς τὸν κύριον ἀναγνωσθῆναι **τὴν** ἐπιστολὴν πᾶσιν τοῖς ἀδελφοῖς. (1 Thess 5:27)
I adjure you by the Lord that <u>this</u> letter be read to all the brothers and sisters.
> If deictic, this article points to the letter that they have in hand, the one they have just read. Alternatively, this article could function as a possessive pronoun, "my letter" (§5.18), which, of course, would also refer to the letter they are currently reading.

5.13. The Generic Article

The article can indicate the group or class to which something or someone belongs. It is often left untranslated or translated with an indefinite article in English.

αἱ ἀλώπεκες φωλεοὺς ἔχουσιν καὶ **τὰ** πετεινὰ τοῦ οὐρανοῦ κατασκηνώσεις (Luke 9:58)
<u>foxes</u> *have dens and* <u>birds</u> *of the sky (have) nests*
> Here the second example, τὰ πετεινά, is usually translated "the birds" because of the additional modifier, though it is still generic, referring to a class of beings rather than particular members of that class.

24. "Deictic" comes from δεικτός, ή, όν, *demonstrable* (note δείκνυμι, *point out, show*).
25. See John 11:51 for an explicit example of this double level.

ὁ θεός, ἱλάσθητί μοι τῷ ἁμαρτωλῷ. (Luke 18:13)
God, be merciful to me, a sinner.

> ➤ If this is a generic article then the tax official is highlighting the class of people he belongs to, which also says something about the kind of person he is. Alternatively, perhaps he views himself as the chief of sinners, the sinner par excellence (§5.12d).

5.14. The Article with Abstract Nouns

Abstract nouns refer to concepts, experiences, ideas, qualities, and feelings that are not experienced by means of our five senses. Examples include "faith," "hope," "love," "law," "salvation," "grace." We don't encounter love as an object that we can see, hear, taste, touch, or smell, though we may experience love for a person or an object or from a person that we encounter through one or more of these senses.[26]

The article can be used with such a noun to highlight its particular quality. This use is similar to the generic use of the article, which often also includes some focus on the quality of the category to which something belongs, as seen just above in Luke 18:13. English does not use a definite article with abstract nouns.

Ἡ ἀγάπη μακροθυμεῖ, χρηστεύεται ἡ ἀγάπη (1 Cor 13:4)
Love is patient, love is kind

> ➤ The use of the article focuses attention on love, highlighting its particular quality.

ὅτι ὁ νόμος διὰ Μωϋσέως ἐδόθη, ἡ χάρις καὶ ἡ ἀλήθεια διὰ Ἰησοῦ Χριστοῦ ἐγένετο (John 1:17)
for the law was given through Moses, grace and truth came through Jesus Christ

> ➤ Here the articles with the abstract nouns "grace" and "truth" highlight their quality; these are the kinds of things that have come through Jesus. Notice that νόμος (law) also is articular. In some contexts "law" can have an article focusing on its particular quality, but here ὁ νόμος refers to the Mosaic law, so this article is individualizing, pointing to that which is the example par excellence of law.

---

26. Sometimes the line between abstract nouns and concrete nouns is unclear. Furthermore, some nouns can be used as either abstract or concrete, which is usually the case, for example, with adjectives that can be used substantively. For example, ἅγιος, α, ον refers to a quality, *holy*, but as a noun it refers to a person or thing that can be encountered by our senses. We cannot encounter the holiness of a saint by our five senses, but we can encounter ὁ ἅγιος/ἡ ἁγία, the saint, and what we see in them or hear from them conveys the quality of holiness.

πᾶς ὁ ποιῶν **τὴν** ἁμαρτίαν δοῦλός ἐστιν **τῆς** ἁμαρτίας (John 8:34)
everyone who practices <u>sin</u> is a slave of <u>sin</u>

> ▸ ἁμαρτία can either be a concrete noun referring to a particular action or an abstract noun referring to a quality. Nothing in the context points to a particular sinful act, so these articles do not seem to be individualizing. Rather, they highlight sin as a particular type of activity. This fits with the context, which is a discussion of a particular type of freedom in contrast to the opponents' claim not to have been enslaved by anyone (8:33).

5.15. The Article as Noun Signal (Substantizer)

The article can substantize virtually any part of speech, that is, it can turn it into a noun substitute. This use is also found in English, but it is more extensive in Greek.

τοὺς πτωχοὺς γὰρ πάντοτε ἔχετε μεθ᾽ ἑαυτῶν (John 12:8)
for <u>the</u> poor you always have with you

> ▸ "Poor" is an adjective (πτωχός, ή, όν), and here the article signals that it is functioning as a noun. This use of the article to substantize adjectives is particularly common in both Greek and English.

οὐ φρονεῖς **τὰ** τοῦ θεοῦ ἀλλὰ **τὰ** τῶν ἀνθρώπων (Matt 16:23)
you are not thinking <u>the things</u> of God but <u>the things</u> of humans

> ▸ Here the article is substantizing genitives, a very common feature in Greek. In English we have to add a noun or pronoun. The neuter plural article is reflected in this literal translation, but more smoothly it could be rendered, "you do not have in mind the concerns of God, but merely human concerns." (NIV).

οἱ δὲ τοῦ Χριστοῦ [᾽Ιησοῦ] τὴν σάρκα ἐσταύρωσαν (Gal 5:24)
and <u>those who are</u> of Christ Jesus have crucified the flesh

> ▸ This is another example of the article substantizing a genitive, and we need to add a noun or pronoun in English.

ἀφώριζεν ἑαυτὸν φοβούμενος **τοὺς** ἐκ περιτομῆς (Gal 2:12)
he [Cephas/Peter] separated himself, fearing <u>those</u> (people who are) of the circumcision (party)

> ▸ Here the article is used with a prepositional phrase, another very common construction in Greek. Prepositions with an article serve as a noun or an adjective (§§5.15–16). In this case, the noun "circumcision" is used as a metonymy for those whom Paul is opposing who are teaching that the gentiles must be circumcised.

Λέγει αὐτῷ· ποίας; ὁ δὲ Ἰησοῦς εἶπεν· **τὸ** οὐ φονεύσεις οὐ μοιχεύσεις, οὐ κλέ-ψεις (Matt 19:18)

And he [a scribe] said to him, "Which (commandments)?" And Jesus said, "You shall not murder, you shall not commit adultery, you shall not steal"

> ⊳ The article is here used with a statement, in this case a quotation, packaging it, as it were.

ἵνα ᾖ παρ᾽ ἐμοὶ **τὸ** ναὶ ναὶ καὶ **τὸ** οὒ οὔ; (2 Cor 1:17)

so that there should be with me "Yes, yes," and "No, no"?

> ⊳ Here is another example of the article packaging and pointing to a statement.

τὰ ἄνω ζητεῖτε, οὗ ὁ Χριστός ἐστιν ἐν δεξιᾷ τοῦ θεοῦ καθήμενος (Col 3:1)

seek <u>the things</u> above, where Christ is sitting at the right hand of God

> ⊳ In this case the article is substantizing the adverb ἄνω, *above*. We need to add a noun in English, and since the article is a neuter plural we supply "things."

5.16. The Article as Adjective Signal

When an article modifies a prepositional phrase and it is in agreement with a noun/substantive it usually modifies that noun/substantive adjectivally.

ὁ λέων **ὁ ἐκ τῆς φυλῆς Ἰούδα** (Rev 5:5)

the Lion <u>of the tribe of Judah</u>

πῶς δύνασθε ὑμεῖς πιστεῦσαι δόξαν παρὰ ἀλλήλων λαμβάνοντες, καὶ τὴν δό-ξαν **τὴν παρὰ τοῦ μόνου θεοῦ** οὐ ζητεῖτε; (John 5:44)

How are you able to believe while receiving glory from one another, and you do not seek the glory <u>that is from the only God</u>?

> ⊳ In παρὰ ἀλλήλων there is no article and it modifies the participle λαμ-βάνοντες. So δόξαν παρὰ ἀλλήλων is not a certain type of glory, but rather they are receiving from one another glory. In **τὴν παρά**, on the other hand, the presence of the article τήν signals this prepositional phrase is modifying τὴν δόξαν, describing a certain kind of glory.

5.17. The Article for a Pronoun

When followed by μέν or δέ the article serves as a pronoun, whether in a μέν … δέ construction or with δέ by itself. This use occurs in narratives when there is a change of subject or speaker.[27]

27. Relative clauses can also function in this way (§5.217b). For further uses of μέν … δέ see §5.246d.

οἱ μὲν ἐχλεύαζον, οἱ δὲ εἶπαν (Acts 17:32)
some began scoffing, but others said

ὁ δὲ ἀποκριθεὶς εἶπεν . . . ἡ δὲ εἶπεν (Matt 15:26–27)
But he, answering, said . . . but she said

5.18. The Article for a Possessive Pronoun

The context may signal that an article implies possession and thus serves like a possessive pronoun.[28]

ἐκτείνας **τὴν** χεῖρα (Matt 8:3)
stretching out his hand

λέγει αὐτῷ Σίμων Πέτρος· κύριε, μὴ τοὺς πόδας μου μόνον ἀλλὰ καὶ **τὰς** χεῖρας καὶ **τὴν** κεφαλήν. (John 13:9)
Simon Peter said to him, "Lord, not only my feet but also my hands and my head."

The Absence of the Definite Article

5.19. Anarthrous Words

A word that does not have an article is said to be anarthrous. Such a word may be definite, indefinite or qualitative.

5.20. Definite

A word can lack an article and still be definite.[29]

a. Monadic Nouns and Proper Names. A word is definite without an article when referring to something that is unique, such as the sun, or a particular person. Such words, however, often do have an article with them. So, for example, you will see both Ἰησοῦς and ὁ Ἰησοῦς, and both are translated simply "Jesus" in English.[30] Names that come into Greek from another language may not have

---

28. This usage may actually be more common than most translations and commentaries suggest. The older commentaries by H. C. G. Moule note possible occurrences of this construction frequently in the New Testament.

29. In addition to the cases discussed here in §5.20 others include pronominal adjectives like πᾶς (§5.8), words following Apollonius's corollary (§5.23), subject complements following Colwell's rule (§5.24), and complements in a double accusative of object and complement (§5.77a). See *ExSyn*, 245–54; *BNTSyn*, 108–13.

30. For the paradigm of Ἰησοῦς see app. 4.12.

inflectional endings, in which case the article is sometimes used to clarify the case of the noun.

ἀκούσαντες ὅτι **Ἰησοῦς** παράγει (Matt 20:30)
hearing that <u>Jesus</u> was passing by

καὶ στὰς **ὁ Ἰησοῦς** ἐφώνησεν αὐτούς (Matt 20:32)
and <u>Jesus</u> came to a standstill and called them
  > This article is anaphoric. See the discussion of this text in §5.12b.

Καὶ ἔσονται σημεῖα ἐν **ἡλίῳ** καὶ **σελήνῃ** καὶ ἄστροις (Luke 21:25)
And there will be signs in <u>the sun</u> and <u>moon</u> and stars
  > Here English idiom has only one article before the first word in the series.

καὶ **ὁ ἥλιος** ἐγένετο μέλας ὡς σάκκος τρίχινος καὶ **ἡ σελήνη** ὅλη ἐγένετο ὡς αἷμα (Rev 6:12)
and <u>the sun</u> became black as sackcloth made of hair and <u>the</u> full <u>moon</u> became as blood

Ἀβραὰμ ἐγέννησεν **τὸν** Ἰσαάκ, Ἰσαὰκ δὲ ἐγέννησεν **τὸν** Ἰακώβ (Matt 1:2)
Abraham fathered <u>Isaac</u>, and Isaac fathered <u>Jacob</u>
  > All three of these names are based on the Hebrew and are indeclinable in Greek. Here the nouns Ἀβραάμ and Ἰσαάκ do not have articles when they are the subjects of the verbs, but Ἰσαάκ does have an article, as does Ἰακώβ when the article is needed to clarify that these proper nouns are functioning as direct objects.

b. Abstract Nouns. Nouns such as "faith, hope, love, grace" often lack an article in Greek, in keeping with their natural focus on a particular quality (§5.14). In the plural they can refer to particular kinds or occurrences of the idea (§2.25b). They can be definite if, for example, the focus in the context is not on faith in general but on the faith of a particular person or faith with a particular focus, such as faith in Christ. The article also may be present with an abstract noun for other reasons, such as anaphora (§5.12b). When abstract nouns have the article in Greek they are still translated without an article in English, unless the context suggests otherwise.

ἀλλὰ **πίστις** δι' ἀγάπης ἐνεργουμένη (Gal 5:6)
but <u>faith</u> working through love

Τί τὸ ὄφελος, ἀδελφοί μου, ἐὰν **πίστιν** λέγῃ τις ἔχειν, ἔργα δὲ μὴ ἔχῃ; μὴ δύναται **ἡ πίστις** σῶσαι αὐτόν; (Jas 2:14)
What is the difference, my brothers and sisters, if someone say that they have <u>faith</u>, but they do not have works? <u>Faith</u> is not able to save him/her, is it?

> ‣ The first reference to faith introduces the subject and then the second reference has an article due to anaphora, as do further references to faith in the verses that follow.

πολύς τε ὄχλος τῶν ἱερέων ὑπήκουον **τῇ πίστει** (Acts 6:7)
a large crowd of priests became obedient to <u>the faith</u>
> ‣ Here a specific faith is in view.

ἡ πίστις σου σέσωκέν σε (Matt 9:22)
your <u>faith</u> has saved you
> ‣ The article corresponds to the genitive σου, both pointing to the faith of this specific person.

Ἀποθέμενοι οὖν πᾶσαν **κακίαν** καὶ πάντα **δόλον** καὶ **ὑποκρίσεις** καὶ **φθόνους** καὶ πάσας **καταλαλιάς** (1 Pet 2:1)
So put away all <u>wickedness</u> and all <u>deceit</u> and <u>occurrences of hypocrisy</u> and <u>envy</u> and all <u>occurrences of slander</u>.
> ‣ The first two abstract nouns are singular and the remaining three are in the plural. English translations often use the singular for all five nouns. But these plurals for *hypocrisy*, *envy*, and *slander* probably refer to particular kinds or occurrences of these qualities. It is possible that the two singulars, *wickedness* and *deceit*, may do so as well, since the anarthrous singular with πᾶς can refer to individual members of a group (§5.8). "So put away every act [or, kind] of wickedness and every act [or, kind] of deceit."

c. Generic Nouns. The article can signal that a word is used generically, to refer to a class of people or things (§5.13). But some words can function in this way without an article. Similarly, sometimes in English idiom a generic noun may have a definite article, but at other times it has an indefinite article or no article at all.

ποῦ **σοφός**; ποῦ **γραμματεύς**; ποῦ **συζητητὴς** τοῦ αἰῶνος τούτου; (1 Cor 1:20)
Where is <u>the wise person</u>? Where is <u>the scribe</u>? Where is <u>the debater</u> of this age?

πᾶς **ἄνθρωπος** πρῶτον τὸν καλὸν οἶνον τίθησιν (John 2:10)
every <u>person</u> serves the good wine first
> ‣ This example is also related to the structures with πᾶς (§5.8).

d. Objects of Prepositions. The object of a preposition may be definite without an article, though just because a noun/substantive is in a prepositional phrase does not mean it is necessarily definite. If the object of a preposition has an article it is definite, and if it is anarthrous it may or may not be definite.

ἐπέπεσεν τὸ πνεῦμα τὸ ἅγιον ἐπ᾽ αὐτοὺς ὥσπερ καὶ ἐφ᾽ ἡμᾶς **ἐν ἀρχῇ** (Acts 11:15)
the Holy Spirit fell upon them just as also upon us at <u>the beginning</u>
> ἀρχή is monadic and thus definite.

ἠκούσθη ὅτι **ἐν οἴκῳ** ἐστίν (Mark 2:1)
it was heard that he was <u>at home</u>
> ἐν οἴκῳ is an idiom for "at home." So this idiom indicates that this is a reference to a specific home/house and *not* an indefinite one, "a house." Lexicons will help you identify such idioms.

τὸν ἥλιον αὐτοῦ ἀνατέλλει ἐπὶ **πονηροὺς** καὶ **ἀγαθοὺς** καὶ βρέχει ἐπὶ **δικαίους** καὶ **ἀδίκους** (Matt 5:45)
he causes his sun to rise on <u>the evil</u> and <u>the good</u>, and he causes it to rain on <u>the righteous</u> and <u>the unrighteous</u>
> These nouns are definite though generic, that is, not focused on specific individuals. They are also qualitative, focusing on these types of people.

ἀλλὰ ῥῦσαι ἡμᾶς **ἀπὸ τοῦ πονηροῦ** (Matt 6:13)
but deliver us from the Evil One
> The presence of the article with the object of a preposition sends a clear signal that the object is definite. This could be a reference to "the evil" meaning some great, well-known form of evil, but the primary reference is to the Evil One, since Jesus often refers to the devil.[31]

e. Ordinal Numbers. When a noun/substantive is modified by an ordinal number it is made definite and usually is anarthrous.[32]

ἐχθὲς ὥραν **ἑβδόμην** ἀφῆκεν αὐτὸν ὁ πυρετός (John 4:52)
Yesterday at <u>the seventh</u> hour the fever left him

---

31. If a great evil is in view then a good candidate would be apostasy like the provocation in the wilderness, Ps 95:8 (LXX 94:8), as suggested by Jeffrey Gibson, *The Disciples' Prayer: The Prayer Jesus Taught in Its Historical Setting* (Minneapolis: Fortress, 2015), 148-60. Many of the church fathers and modern scholars have taken it as a reference to the Evil One, as have modern Greek translations and the NIV. According to Harris, *Prepositions*, 41, the choice of ἀπό may further suggest a personal enemy is in view.

32. An ordinal number indicates order, for example, "second, third, fourth."

5.21. Indefinite

An anarthrous noun/substantive may be indefinite, referring to a person or thing as a member of a category, but without identifying them as a specific individual. This is the difference between "the book" and "a book," "the child" and "a child" (§5.2a).

οὐ δύναται **πόλις** κρυβῆναι ἐπάνω ὄρους κειμένη (Matt 5:14)
a city set on a hill is not able to be hidden

ὥστε αὐτὸν εἰς **πλοῖον** ἐμβάντα καθῆσθαι ἐν τῇ θαλάσσῃ (Mark 4:1)
so he got into a boat and sat on the sea

   a. The indefinite pronoun τις, τι (§5.84g) and the number "one," εἷς, μία, ἕν (app. 4.24) may also function in this way.

καί **τις** ἀνὴρ χωλὸς ἐκ κοιλίας μητρὸς αὐτοῦ ὑπάρχων ἐβαστάζετο (Acts 3:2)
And a man who was lame from his mother's womb was being carried

Καὶ ἦρεν **εἷς** ἄγγελος ἰσχυρὸς λίθον ὡς μύλινον μέγαν (Rev 18:21)
And a mighty angel took up a stone like a great millstone

5.22. Qualitative

An anarthrous noun/substantive may be used qualitatively, that is, with a focus on the kind of person or thing it is. Abstract nouns normally include a qualitative sense (§5.20b), but concrete nouns may do so as well. James H. Moulton commented: "For exegesis, there are few of the finer points of Greek which need more constant attention than this omission of the article when the writer would lay stress on the quality or character of the object."[33]

τίς γὰρ **υἱὸς** ὃν οὐ παιδεύει **πατήρ**; (Heb 12:7)
For what <u>son</u> is there whom <u>a father</u> does not discipline?
   ▸ Both nouns are anarthrous, focusing on the character or quality of being a son and a father.

δόξαν ὡς μονογενοῦς παρὰ **πατρός**, πλήρης **χάριτος** καὶ **ἀληθείας** (John 1:14)
<u>glory</u> as a unique son from <u>a father</u>, full of <u>grace</u> and <u>truth</u>
   ▸ Here we have three abstract nouns and one concrete one (πατήρ). All

---

33. James H. Moulton, *A Grammar of New Testament Greek*, vol. 1, *Prolegomena*, 3rd ed. (Edinburgh: T&T Clark, 1908), 83. Several of my examples are from his discussion.

four should be seen as qualitative, focusing on their quality, the sort of character they have. English translations take πατρός as definite, "the father," which is possible grammatically as the object of a preposition and also as monadic if this is a reference to God as father. But here it is part of a comparison (ὡς, *as*) and thus does not seem to be a reference to God directly. Taking πατρός as qualitative focuses attention on the character or quality of being a father. Using the indefinite form ("a father") does not really capture the qualitative sense of the Greek, but translating it "from father," doesn't work either.

κύριε, πρὸς τίνα ἀπελευσόμεθα; **ῥήματα** ζωῆς αἰωνίου ἔχεις (John 6:68)
Lord, to whom shall we go? You have <u>words</u> *of eternal life*
> Most English translations have "the words of eternal life," presumably seeing ζωῆς αἰωνίου as definite and thus the ῥήματα as definite (§5.23). But perhaps instead there is a qualitative nuance in this expression. The translation given here may not convey this nuance in English very well either—perhaps, as with the previous example, you simply need to read the Greek to see it!

ἐπ᾽ ἐσχάτου τῶν ἡμερῶν τούτων ἐλάλησεν ἡμῖν **ἐν υἱῷ** (Heb 1:2)
in these last days he has spoken to us in/by <u>a son</u>
> Many English translations treat this noun as definite, "in/by his son." An anarthrous noun/substantive can be definite within a prepositional phrase (§5.20d). But here the context is a contrast between God speaking in/by his son with his speaking earlier by prophets (1:1). The focus is on a new form of communication, so υἱῷ seems best understood as qualitative.

5.23. Apollonius's Corollary

According to Apollonius's Canon, a noun/substantive (head term) and its genitive modifier usually either both have an article or both lack it (§5.10). As a follow-up, both of the nouns/substantives (the head term and the genitive) will often have the same nuance. That is, they will often both be definite, indefinite, or qualitative. So if one of them is itself definite without an article, then the expression can be definite even without any articles.[34]

εἶδεν [τὸ] πνεῦμα [τοῦ] θεοῦ καταβαῖνον ὡσεὶ περιστεράν (Matt 3:16)
he saw the Spirit of God coming down like a dove
> Notice from the brackets that some manuscripts have πνεῦμα θεοῦ and some have τὸ πνεῦμα τοῦ θεοῦ. Both forms refer to the Spirit of God, not a spirit of a god, since θεός in this context is specific and definite. One could translate this "a spirit from God," since there are times when

---

34. See *ExSyn*, 250–52; *BNTSyn*, 112

the head term and the genitive do not share the same nuance. But the combination "indefinite + definite" is "the *least* likely possibility for this construction."[35] So there would have to be clear grounds from the context to support this interpretation.

5.24. Colwell's Rule

In 1933 E. C. Colwell published an article on a particular construction found in some sentences that contain an equative verb such as εἰμί, or γίνομαι. He suggested that when a subject complement comes before an equative verb it usually lacks an article even if it is definite.

After further research Colwell's rule has been fine-tuned to say that an anarthrous subject complement which precedes an equative verb is "normally qualitative, sometimes definite, and only rarely indefinite."[36] Context, as usual, must clarify the nuance.

If it is **qualitative** then it points to the noun as representing a certain kind of thing, if **definite** then the noun points to a particular instance of something, and if **indefinite** the noun points to an instance of something, but not a particular instance, "a book" vs. "the book" (§§5.2a, 12, 20c).

ῥαββί, σὺ εἶ ὁ υἱὸς τοῦ θεοῦ, σὺ **βασιλεὺς** εἶ τοῦ Ἰσραήλ. (John 1:49)
Rabbi, you are the Son of God, you are the king of Israel.
> Since there is no article before βασιλεύς perhaps Nathanael is saying Jesus is "a king of Israel." If so then βασιλεύς would be indefinite, which is the least likely option. Here, however, the subject complement is definite in keeping with John's Gospel as a whole. Note also the first clause in this sentence in which the subject complement ὁ υἱός is definite, coming after the equative verb and articular.

κύριε, θεωρῶ ὅτι **προφήτης** εἶ σύ. (John 4:19)
Sir, I see that you are a prophet.
> Since a noun in this structure can be definite this could be a reference to "the prophet," perhaps the prophet like Moses as in John 1:21.[37] The Samaritans did not recognize a succession of prophets, but looked for the coming of the prophet like Moses. But this woman does not think of Jesus as this eschatological figure (see John 4:25), so this is probably an example of the indefinite nuance, as translated here.

Καὶ ὁ λόγος **σὰρξ** ἐγένετο (John 1:14)
And the Word became flesh

35. *ExSyn*, 251, discussing this example (emphasis original).
36. *ExSyn*, 262, with the identical quotation in *BNTSyn*, 117.
37. Discussed in §5.12d.

> ➤ The subject complement σάρξ is likely qualitative. The reference is not to "the flesh," nor to "a flesh," but to a certain kind of thing, "flesh."

καὶ **θεὸς** ἦν ὁ λόγος (John 1:1)
and the Word was <u>God</u>

> ➤ If the subject complement θεός is taken as definite, it would be saying the Son is the Father, since θεός here refers to the Father. Elsewhere John does not say the Son is the Father, but rather speaks of them as distinct, as he does here, "the Word was with God" (John 1:1–2). If θεός is indefinite, "a god," then the Logos is one god among others. The Gospels, however, clearly put Jesus in a category beyond anything else that can be called a "god." Finally, if this subject complement is qualitative then it would refer to the kind of being this Word is, that is, he shares the nature of God. In this way John would be saying Jesus is God, without confusing the Father and the Son, the view that corresponds to what we see in the rest of John's Gospel.[38]

CASES

5.25. The Most Common Case Uses

The cases can have a great many specific uses. When simply reading we may not tend to notice particular uses of cases, but they are important in careful exegesis and are often suggestive for reflection. The following chart lists the most common uses.

Case	Use	Simple English Signal[39]
Nominative	Subject	**Nom.** verbs obj.
	Subject complement	Subj. is/becomes **nom.**
Vocative	Direct address	O **Voc.**, you verb.
Genitive	Description	**of**
Dative	Indirect object	**to/for**
	Means/instrument/agent	**with/by**
	Location	**in/at/on**
Accusative	Direct object	Subj. verbs **acc.**

38. This discussion is based on the more extensive treatment in *ExSyn*, 266–69, see also *BNTSyn*, 119–20.
39. The generic formulas in this column represent simple English expressions. For example, "nom. verbs obj." stands for a sentence such as, "Peter (nom.) follows (verbs) Jesus (obj.)."

a. While the following discussion focuses on the use of the cases by themselves, usually in Greek a prepositional phrase is used to express a nuance found in the genitive, dative, or accusative. For example, the dative by itself can express location (§5.64), but in KG it frequently does so in conjunction with the preposition ἐν. Similarly, the simple case uses in Greek will often have to be translated in English with prepositional phrases since English has such a limited system of cases.

b. Many of the less common uses listed below make sense when you pay attention to the meaning of the words used with them. For example, the genitive, dative, and accusative of time will be used with words referring to time, though each of the cases has a different nuance when used for time, as discussed below.

c. The labels given for the various case uses, as with other grammatical labels, are simply a convenient way to remember them and discuss them with others.

Nominative

5.26. Subject

Most frequently the nominative designates the subject of the clause (§2.27a).

> ὁ πατὴρ ἀγαπᾷ τὸν υἱόν (John 3:35)
> _The Father_ loves the Son

a. Neuter Plural Subject with a Singular Verb. In CG when the subject is in the neuter plural it takes a verb in the third-person singular. In KG this norm is also often followed, but at times you will find a plural verb used with a neuter plural subject.

> τὰ δὲ ἱμάτια αὐτοῦ ἐγένετο λευκὰ ὡς τὸ φῶς (Matt 17:2)
> and his _clothes became_ white as the light

> τὰ πρόβατα τῆς φωνῆς αὐτοῦ ἀκούει (John 10:3)
> and _the sheep hear_ his voice

> τὰ δὲ ζιζάνιά εἰσιν οἱ υἱοὶ τοῦ πονηροῦ (Matt 13:38)
> and _the weeds are_ the sons of the evil one
> ‣ Here we see a plural verb used with a neuter plural subject.

b. Singular Verb with a Compound Subject. A verb with a compound subject will normally be plural, but may be singular. We need to use a plural in English.

Μετὰ ταῦτα ἦλθεν ὁ Ἰησοῦς καὶ οἱ μαθηταὶ αὐτοῦ εἰς τὴν Ἰουδαίαν γῆν (John 3:22)

After these things <u>Jesus and his disciples came</u> into the Judean region

ὧν ἐστιν Φύγελος καὶ Ἑρμογένης (2 Tim 1:15)[40]

among whom <u>are Phygelus and Hermogenes</u>

c. Subject of an Equative Verb. Equative verbs usually have two nominatives (§2.27a). **Usually the word that is a pronoun, or articular, or a proper noun will be the subject.**[41] When both words are a proper noun or both have an article or both lack an article, then the word that comes first in the clause is usually the subject. If one word is a noun and the other an adjective, the noun will be the subject. These guidelines apply whether the verb is expressed or omitted (§5.5).

1. Noun

    Εὐλογητὸς ὁ θεός (2 Cor 1:3)
    Blessed be <u>God</u>

    › ὁ θεός is the subject, though in English it is smoother to put the subject complement first especially when the subject is further modified in the sentence.

    Μακάριος ἀνήρ (Jas 1:12)
    Blessed is <u>the man</u>

    › An example of the same construction as in 2 Corinthians 1:3 but with the verb omitted.

2. Pronoun

    σὺ εἶ Πέτρος (Matt 16:18)
    <u>you</u> are Peter

    ὑμεῖς μάρτυρες (1 Thess 2:10)
    <u>you</u> are witnesses

40. There is dispute about the significance of using a singular verb with a compound subject. Wallace thinks an author uses the singular when they want "to *highlight* one of the subjects." *ExSyn*, 401; *BNTSyn*, 178 (emphasis original). Similarly, Smyth says "the verb may be singular if it refers to the nearer or more important or more emphatic subject." Smyth §968. BDF, however, claims that sometimes both subjects are viewed equally. BDF §135. Wallace disagrees (*ExSyn*, 401 n. 17), but this example from 2 Timothy is an example of equality, as far as we can tell; though perhaps Phygelus was the ringleader! See also 2 Thess 2:16–17. So such emphasis may be present, but, as usual, context must play a part in expressing the nuance.

41. *ExSyn*, 42–45; *BNTSyn*, 31–32.

3. Proper noun

  Ἰησοῦς ἐστιν ὁ χριστός (John 20:31)
  Jesus is the Christ

4. Both with articles

  ὁ δὲ **ἀγρός** ἐστιν ὁ κόσμος (Matt 13:38)
  and the field is the world
  > The context confirms ὁ ἀγρός as the subject since Jesus is explaining
    several features of the parable.

  τὸ δὲ **κέντρον** τοῦ θανάτου ἡ ἁμαρτία (1 Cor 15:56)
  and the sting of death is sin
  > Here either noun makes sense as the subject, but τὸ κέντρον is men-
    tioned in the previous verse so it is the topic that is being further de-
    scribed and thus is the subject.

5. Neither with articles

  Ἔστιν δὲ **πίστις** ἐλπιζομένων ὑπόστασις (Heb 11:1)
  Now faith is the realization of things hoped for
  > The theme in the context is faith, which confirms πίστις as the subject.

  πᾶσα **γραφὴ** θεόπνευστος καὶ ὠφέλιμος πρὸς διδασκαλίαν (2 Tim 3:16)
  every scripture is inspired and useful for teaching
  > Here the verb is omitted. Since γραφή is a noun while θεόπνευστος and
    ὠφέλιμος are adjectives, γραφή as the subject.[42]

  καὶ ματαία **σωτηρία** ἀνθρώπου (Ps 59:13 [MT 60:11])
  and human rescue is empty
  > Since σωτηρία is a noun and ματαία an adjective σωτηρία is the subject.

5.27. Subject Complement with Equative Verbs (εἰμί, γίνομαι, ὑπάρχω)

The subject complement (Latin, *complere, fill up, complete*) renames, labels, or
describes the subject of the verb.
  a. Most often the subject complement will be in the nominative (§2.27a).

---

42. For the relation between the translations *every scripture* and *all scripture* see §5.8.
See *ExSyn*, 313–14 for reasons not to break up the two adjectives and instead translate,
"every inspired scripture is also profitable for teaching."

ὑμεῖς γάρ ἐστε **ἡ δόξα** ἡμῶν (1 Thess 2:20)
For you are our glory
> For ὑμεῖς as the subject rather than δόξα see §5.26c.

οὗτος **ἄρχων τῆς συναγωγῆς** ὑπῆρχεν (Luke 8:41)
this one was a leader of the synagogue
> ἄρχων is a masc.-nom.-sg. noun (§3.26).

b. Other cases and constructions can also serve as a subject complement.

αὐτῶν ἐστιν ἡ βασιλεία τῶν οὐρανῶν (Matt 5:3)
theirs is the kingdom of heaven
> This genitive, αὐτῶν, serves as the subject complement.

ὁ ὢν ἐκ τῆς γῆς **ἐκ τῆς γῆς** ἐστιν (John 3:31)
the one who is of the earth is of the earth
> The subject of this sentence is ὁ ὢν, "the one who is," "the one being," which is modified by the prepositional phrase ἐκ τῆς γῆς. Then that same prepositional phrase is repeated as the subject complement of ἐστιν.

λίθον ὃν ἀπεδοκίμασαν οἱ οἰκοδομοῦντες, οὗτος ἐγενήθη **εἰς κεφαλὴν γωνίας** (Mark 12:10)
the stone that the builders rejected, this one became the head of the corner
> Often a prepositional phrase with εἰς is used for a subject complement with an equative verb. This construction follows a Hebrew idiom and is often found in quotes from the LXX.

c. Occasionally nonequative verbs take a nominative complement.

μένει **ἱερεὺς** εἰς τὸ διηνεκές (Heb 7:3)
he remains a priest forever
> When μένω signifies that "a pers. or thing continues in the same state" it may take a nominative complement.[43]

5.28. Direct Address

The nominative is used often to indicate the person or group that is being addressed.
a. In the singular the vocative case plays this role, but there are no vocative forms for the plural, and many words lack a distinct form for the singular as well.

43. BDAG, s.v. "μένω," 1.b., 631, "Occasionally even μένω can be used as an equative verb." *ExSyn*, 40 n. 11.

τέκνα, πῶς δύσκολόν ἐστιν εἰς τὴν βασιλείαν τοῦ θεοῦ εἰσελθεῖν (Mark 10:24)
Children, how difficult it is to enter the kingdom of God

Οὐαὶ δὲ ὑμῖν, **γραμματεῖς** καὶ **Φαρισαῖοι ὑποκριταί**, ὅτι . . . (Matt 23:13)
Woe to you, <u>scribes</u> and <u>Pharisees</u>, <u>hypocrites</u>, because . . .

τὸ **ἄλαλον καὶ κωφὸν πνεῦμα**, ἐγὼ ἐπιτάσσω σοι, ἔξελθε ἐξ αὐτοῦ (Mark 9:25)
<u>Mute and deaf spirit</u>, I command you, come out of him

Μὴ φοβοῦ, τὸ **μικρὸν ποίμνιον** (Luke 12:32)
Fear not, <u>little flock</u>

b. Sometimes a nominative form is used for direct address even when there is a vocative form available.

ὁ **θεός**, ἱλάσθητί μοι τῷ ἁμαρτωλῷ. (Luke 18:13)[44]
<u>God</u>, be merciful to me, a sinner.

Ναί, κύριε, ὁ **θεός**, ὁ **παντοκράτωρ**, ἀληθιναὶ καὶ δίκαιαι αἱ κρίσεις σου (Rev 16:7)
Yes, Lord, <u>God</u>, <u>the Almighty</u>, true and just are your judgments
> Here the vocative form κύριε occurs together with nominatives of direct address. Note also the example of the predicate position (§5.5).

ἐξομολογοῦμαί σοι, **πάτερ**, κύριε τοῦ οὐρανοῦ καὶ τῆς γῆς, ὅτι ἀπέκρυψας ταῦτα ἀπὸ σοφῶν καὶ συνετῶν καὶ ἀπεκάλυψας αὐτὰ νηπίοις· ναὶ ὁ **πατήρ**, ὅτι οὕτως εὐδοκία ἐγένετο ἔμπροσθέν σου. (Luke 10:21)
I thank you, <u>Father</u>, Lord of heaven and earth, that you have hidden these things from the wise and intelligent and have revealed them to infants; yes <u>Father</u>, for so it was well-pleasing before you.
> This one sentence has both a nominative used as a vocative and an actual vocative of the same noun.

5.29. Independent Nominative

There are several ways in which a nominative may be grammatically independent from the rest of the sentence and yet contribute to its content.

a. Nominative Absolute. The nominative is used for titles, headings, and greetings. This use is called "absolute" since the nominative stands on its own, apart from the other grammatical structures.

---

44. This use of ὁ θεός as a vocative is very common in the LXX.

Βίβλος γενέσεως Ἰησοῦ Χριστοῦ (Matt 1:1)
The book of the generation of Jesus Christ

Παῦλος δοῦλος Χριστοῦ Ἰησοῦ (Rom 1:1)
Paul, a slave of Christ Jesus
> The second nominative, δοῦλος, is in apposition to the nominative absolute, Παῦλος (§2.31).

χάρις ὑμῖν καὶ εἰρήνη ἀπὸ θεοῦ πατρὸς ἡμῶν καὶ κυρίου Ἰησοῦ Χριστοῦ (Phlm 3)
grace to you and peace from God our Father and the Lord Jesus Christ

b. Hanging Nominative (Pendent). A nominative may announce a topic at the beginning of a sentence which is then picked up by a pronoun later in the sentence. Since this nominative is related to the following pronoun it is independent, but not absolute.

Ὁ νικῶν ποιήσω αὐτὸν στῦλον (Rev. 3:12)
The one who is victorous I will make him a pillar

c. Parenthetic Nominative. The nominative may add a parenthetical comment within a sentence.

Ἐγένετο ἄνθρωπος ἀπεσταλμένος παρὰ θεοῦ, ὄνομα αὐτῷ Ἰωάννης (John 1:6)
A man was sent from God, a name for him (was) John/his name (was) John

5.30. Nominative as Complement with Verbs Used as a Passive

Some verbs that take a double accusative of object and complement in the active (§5.77) end up with two nominatives when used as a passive! The word that would be the accusative of object in the active becomes the subject in the passive, and the accusative of complement is in the nominative case, like a complement. Compare the first example below with the second.

καὶ καλέσεις τὸ ὄνομα αὐτοῦ Ἰωάννην (Luke 1:13)
and you will call his name John
> The verb takes the double accusative of object, τὸ ὄνομα αὐτοῦ, and complement, Ἰωάννην. Although the neuter form τὸ ὄνομα could be nominative or accusative, here it is accusative along with Ἰωάννην since καλέω expects the double accusative.[45]

ἐκλήθη τὸ ὄνομα αὐτοῦ Ἰησοῦς (Luke 2:21)
his name was called Jesus

---

45. BDAG, s.v. "καλέω," 1.b–c, 502–3.

> Now with καλέω in the second middle/passive the neuter form τὸ ὄνομα is the subject so it is nominative, and Ἰησοῦς is also nominative.

ὥσπερ γὰρ διὰ τῆς παρακοῆς τοῦ ἑνὸς ἀνθρώπου **ἁμαρτωλοὶ** κατεστάθησαν **οἱ πολλοί**, οὕτως καὶ διὰ τῆς ὑπακοῆς τοῦ ἑνὸς **δίκαιοι** κατασταθήσονται **οἱ πολλοί** (Rom 5:19)
For as through the disobedience of one man <u>the many</u> were caused to become <u>sinners</u>, so also through the obedience of one man <u>the many</u> were caused to become <u>righteous ones</u>

5.31. Nominative for Time

On rare occasions a nominative may function adverbially to express time.

σπλαγχνίζομαι ἐπὶ τὸν ὄχλον, ὅτι ἤδη **ἡμέραι τρεῖς** προσμένουσίν μοι (Matt 15:32)
I have compassion on the crowd, for they now have remained with me <u>three days</u>
> Normally an accusative of time would be expected (§5.82).[46]

Vocative

5.32. Vocative of Direct Address

The vocative is used to indicate the one(s) being addressed (§2.27b).

διδάσκαλε, τί ποιήσας ζωὴν αἰώνιον κληρονομήσω; (Luke 10:25)
<u>*Teacher*</u>, *what shall I do so I may inherit eternal life?*

Τὸν μὲν πρῶτον λόγον ἐποιησάμην περὶ πάντων, **ὦ Θεόφιλε**, ὧν ἤρξατο ὁ Ἰησοῦς ποιεῖν τε καὶ διδάσκειν (Acts 1:1)
The first word, <u>O Theophilus</u>, I produced concerning all that Jesus began to do and teach

Genitive

5.33. Introduction to the Genitive

Some books refer to over fifty uses of the genitive! Analyzing the particular use of a genitive is often unnecessary when reading, but is important in exegesis and valuable also in meditation on a passage. Note that more than one use is

---

46. See *ExSyn*, 64; BDF §144; and Robertson, *Grammar*, 460. BDAG, s.v. "ἡμέρα." 2.c, 437, "It is striking to find the nom. denoting time."

a viable option at times. In general, the *"genitive is the limiting* [or] *specifying case* and is used to circumscribe the meaning of noun/substantive, adjectives, adverbs, and less often verbs."[47]

5.34. Description

All genitives that modify a word describe that word, their **head term**. So this category fits many genitives (§2.27b), and further uses refer to specific forms of description. But sometimes the description is very general and there is nothing more specific to be said about it. This is sometimes called the generic genitive.[48]

> ἐγένετο Ἰωάννης . . . κηρύσσων βάπτισμα **μετανοίας** (Mark 1:4)
> *John came . . . preaching a baptism of repentance*

5.35. Possession

A genitive may indicate the owner of the head term, either in the sense of property owned or more generally. The first example below is possession of property, while the other two are broader senses of possession.

> ἓν τῶν πλοίων, ὃ ἦν **Σίμωνος** (Luke 5:3)
> *one of the boats, which was Simon's*

> καὶ ἥψατο τῆς χειρὸς **αὐτῆς** (Matt 8:15)
> *and he touched her hand*

> καὶ καλέσεις τὸ ὄνομα **αὐτοῦ** Ἰησοῦν (Luke 1:31)
> *and you will call his name Jesus*

5.36. Complement

When a word in the genitive completes the information conveyed by the verb it serves as a complement (Latin, *complere, fill up, complete*) and is part of the core of the clause.[49] At times verbs taking genitive complements have meanings related to the uses of the genitive, but not always. One grammar lists such verbs

---

47. Funk §0888 (emphasis original).
48. Or more dramatically, "This is the 'catch-all' genitive, the 'drip pan' genitive, the 'black hole' of genitive categories that tries to suck many a genitive into its grasp!" *ExSyn*, 79; *BNTSyn*, 45.
49. Some resources refer to this usage as an object or direct object.

as those "meaning 'begin' or 'end' . . . many verbs expressing sensorial or mental processes . . . many verbs expressing leading, difference or superiority" and "many verbs meaning 'take part in', 'meet', 'strive for', and their opposites."[50]

a. You'll also find that some verbs can take more than one case and may have distinct nuances depending on the case used. For example, ἄρχω (*rule*) takes the genitive (verb of ruling) and ἀκούω (*hear*) can take either an accusative or a genitive (verb of perception). Abbott-Smith and BDAG offer help sorting out which cases particular verbs take, but unfortunately *CGEL* does not do so consistently.

> οὐκ ἀφίστατο **τοῦ ἱεροῦ** (Luke 2:37)
> *she did not leave <u>the temple</u>*
> > ▸ This example is related to the genitive of separation (§5.50).

> ἠγοράσθητε γὰρ **τιμῆς** (1 Cor 6:20)
> *for you were bought <u>at a price</u>*
> > ▸ This verb is related to the genitive of price/value (§5.52).

> καὶ ἐμνήσθησαν **τῶν ῥημάτων** αὐτοῦ (Luke 24:8)
> *and they remembered his <u>words</u>*
> > ▸ While the genitive is often used with verbs of remembering and forgetting, a connection between such verbs and the various uses of the genitive is not clear.

5.37. Subject of a Genitive Absolute

The genitive absolute is discussed in more detail in §5.200.

> [Καταβάντος δὲ **αὐτοῦ** ἀπὸ τοῦ ὄρους] ἠκολούθησαν αὐτῷ ὄχλοι πολλοί. (Matt 8:1)
> *[And after <u>he</u> came down from the mountain] a great crowd followed him*

5.38. Subjectival/Objectival

The terms subjectival and objectival do not refer to psychological states! Rather, the genitive can function like a subject or an object when the head term is a verbal noun. This use is one of the more important uses of the genitive to understand,

---

50. *CGCG* §30.21. Compare Richard Young, *Intermediate New Testament Greek: A Linguistic and Exegetical Approach* (Nashville: Broadman & Holman, 1994), 40–41 who cites verbs of (1) ruling, surpassing, (2) perception, (3) desiring, lacking, obtaining, (4) remembering, forgetting, (5) caring, neglecting, (6) accusing, (7) separation, (8) conveying a partitive idea, and (9) touching." See also Smyth §§1343–71; BDF §§169–78; Funk §§594–97; *AGG* §167.

and fortunately we have a similar construction in English. A noun like "love" is a verbal noun, but a noun like "aardvark" is not; there is no verb "to aardvark." So in the phrase ἡ ἀγάπη τοῦ θεοῦ (*the love of God*, Rom 5:5) the head term ἡ ἀγάπη, *love*, is a verbal noun. The modifier, τοῦ θεοῦ, *of God*, can indicate the one doing the loving (a subjective genitive), or the one being loved (an objective genitive). Thus in English and Greek this expression may refer to God's love for us (God as subject) or our love for God (God as object). When analyzing a genitive the first thing to observe is whether or not the head term is a verbal noun.

> τὸ κήρυγμα Ἰησοῦ Χριστοῦ (Rom 16:25)
> *the preaching of Jesus Christ*
>> ▸ Is this phrase referring to the preaching which Jesus himself did (subjectival) or Paul's preaching about Jesus (objectival)?

> τίς ἡμᾶς χωρίσει ἀπὸ τῆς ἀγάπης τοῦ Χριστοῦ; (Rom 8:35)
> *Who will separate us from the love of Christ?*
>> ▸ This example is more clearly subjectival since it more likely refers to Christ's love for us rather than our love for him, though it is worth reflecting on both options.

> ἡ δὲ τοῦ πνεύματος βλασφημία οὐκ ἀφεθήσεται (Matt 12:31)
> *but the blasphemy of the Spirit will not be forgiven*
>> ▸ Now we have a genitive that is clearly objectival—the Spirit is not blaspheming (subjectival), but is being blasphemed (objectival)!

a. At times both options fit the context and both may be present, as in Romans 5:5. Wallace refers to this use as a "plenary genitive" and Zerwick calls it a "general" genitive.[51] As Zerwick notes, "In interpreting the sacred text . . . we must beware lest we sacrifice to clarity of meaning part of the fulness of the meaning."[52]

5.39. Relationship

The genitive can refer to the person someone is related to as a family member or in some other form of relationship. The head term is often omitted and has to be determined from the context.

> Δαυὶδ τὸν τοῦ Ἰεσσαί (Acts 13:22)
> *David, the (son) of Jesse*

> τὸν δοῦλον τοῦ ἀρχιερέως (Matt 26:51)
> *the slave/servant of the high priest*

---

51. *ExSyn*, 119–21; *BNTSyn*, 59. Zerwick, *Biblical Greek* §§36–39.
52. Zerwick, *Biblical Greek* §36.

> ‣ Depending on how we understand this relationship it is possible that this genitive is more possession than relationship.

δοῦλος **Χριστοῦ Ἰησοῦ** (Rom 1:1)
servant/slave of Christ Jesus
> ‣ We can read and translate this expression easily, but what sort of genitive is this? Paul frequently uses this expression of himself, and both relationship and possession are viable.

5.40. Association

The genitive can be used to express some form of bond or connection, similar to a prepositional phrase using σύν. Indeed, most examples of this genitive are with nouns that are compounds with σύν on the front. With verbs association is usually expressed with the dative (§5.69 n. 50).

ἐστὲ συμπολῖται **τῶν ἁγίων** (Eph 2:19)
you are fellow-citizens with the saints

5.41. Subordination

That which is in the genitive is under the authority of the head term. This use corresponds to the genitive with verbs of ruling (§5.36).[53]

κύριός ἐστιν ὁ υἱὸς τοῦ ἀνθρώπου καὶ **τοῦ σαββάτου** (Mark 2:28)
the Son of Man is lord even of the sabbath

ὁ βασιλεὺς **τῶν ἐθνῶν** (Rev 15:3)
King of the nations

τοῦ ἀγγέλου **τῶν ὑδάτων** (Rev 16:5)
the angel with authority over the waters

5.42. Epexegetical (Explanation)

The genitive restates the head term. Often the head term is a general term and the genitive is a specific case. This relation can be expressed using "namely," or "that is."

---

53. See §5.253 for another example in 2 Cor 4:4.

σημεῖον ἔλαβεν **περιτομῆς** (Rom 4:11)
he received a sign of circumcision
he received a sign, namely, circumcision

5.43. Reference (Respect)

The genitive can modify a noun or adjective to indicate that with reference to which something is said to be true. It can be translated "with reference to," but often a smoother less precise translation is possible, such as "of" or "about." The dative (§5.68) and accusative (§5.81) may also function in this way.

καρδία πονηρὰ **ἀπιστίας** (Heb 3:12)
an evil heart with reference to unbelief

τὸ γνωστὸν **τοῦ θεοῦ** (Rom 1:19)
that which is known with reference to God

5.44. Attributive/Attributed

a. An attributive genitive functions like an adjective to describe an attribute of the head term. This is sometimes called a **Hebrew genitive** since it corresponds to a construction in Hebrew, a fact that probably accounts for its relatively frequent use in the New Testament. It is also called a **qualitative genitive** since the genitive describes the kind of thing the noun represents.

τὸν οἰκονόμον **τῆς ἀδικίας** (Luke 16:8)
the unjust steward

b. In an attributed genitive the head term is the attribute which is attributed to the word in the genitive.

ἐν καινότητι **ζωῆς** (Rom 6:4)
in newness of life
> Here the genitive ζωῆς, *life*, is described as "new" by the head term καινότητι. This option is more likely than an attributive genitive, "in living newness."

5.45. Content

The genitive gives the content that fills the head term. This includes not only physical content but also, for example, the content or topic of a form of communication.[54]

---

54. Young, *Intermediate*, 27.

τὸ δίκτυον **τῶν ἰχθύων** (John 21:8)
the net (full) of fish

Ὑμεῖς οὖν ἀκούσατε τὴν παραβολὴν **τοῦ σπείραντος**. (Matt 13:18)
Hear then the parable of the sower.

ἀλλ᾽ αὐτοὶ ἐν ἑαυτοῖς τὸ ἀπόκριμα **τοῦ θανάτου** ἐσχήκαμεν (2 Cor 1:9)
indeed, we ourselves have had the sentence of death within ourselves

5.46. Material

The genitive indicates what the head term is composed of.

ἀγέλη **χοίρων πολλῶν** (Matt 8:30)
a herd of many swine

5.47. Partitive

The genitive is the whole of which the head term is a part. Sometimes this use is called "the genitive of the whole" since the word in the genitive is the whole.

πολλοὶ ἐπίστευσαν εἰς αὐτὸν **τῶν Σαμαριτῶν** (John 4:39)
many of the Samaritans believed in him

τινὰς **τῶν μαθητῶν** αὐτου (Mark 7:2)
some of his disciples

5.48. Source/Producer

The genitive indicates the source or producer of the head term. The other side of the relationship is covered in the next category, genitive of product.

διὰ δικαιοσύνης **πίστεως** (Rom 4:13)
righteousness sourced in/produced by faith

τὴν ἑνότητα **τοῦ πνεύματος** (Eph 4:3)
the unity of the Spirit
> The Spirit is the one who produces the unity.[55]

---

55. Wallace includes a separate category for such a use, the genitive of production/producer, in *ExSyn* (104), but omits it in *BNTSyn*.

ἡ εἰρήνη **τοῦ θεοῦ** (Phil 4:7)
the peace of God
> The sort of peace that is sourced in or produced by God.

5.49. Product

The genitive is that which is sourced in or produced by the head term, the opposite side of the relation with genitive of source/producer (§5.48).

ὁ δὲ θεὸς **τῆς εἰρήνης** (Rom 16:20)
And the God of peace
> God is described as one who produces peace. Alternatively, this could be a simple genitive of description (§5.34) or an attributive genitive (§5.44), saying God is characterized by peace.

5.50. Separation

The genitive indicates that from which someone or something is separated or distinguished.

ἐκτινάξατε τὸν κονιορτὸν **τῶν ποδῶν** ὑμῶν (Matt 10:14)
shake the dust from your feet

5.51. Comparison

This genitive is used with a comparative adjective.

μείζω **τούτων** ὄψῃ. (John 1:50)
You will see greater things than these.
> μείζω looks like a verb, but it is a neut.-acc.-pl. from the comparative adjective of μέγας, μεγάλη, μέγα (*great*). The neut.-acc.-pl. is normally μείζονα, but sometimes it has this contracted form. See §3.43e.

5.52. Price/Value

The price or value of the head term is in the genitive.

οὐχὶ δύο στρουθία **ἀσσαρίου** πωλεῖται; (Matt 10:29)
Are not two sparrows sold for an assarion?

5.53. Time during Which

When a word in the genitive refers to time it will often indicate the general time within which something takes place.[56]

> προσεύχεσθε δὲ ἵνα μὴ γένηται **χειμῶνος** (Mark 13:18)
> *And pray that it not be <u>during winter</u>*

> **νυκτὸς** καὶ **ἡμέρας** ἐργαζόμενοι (2 Thess 3:8)
> *working <u>night</u> and <u>day</u>*
> > ➤ Using these genitives Paul is saying he worked in both of these time periods. Some manuscripts have the accusatives νυκτὰ καὶ ἡμέραν, suggesting he worked all day long and all night long (§5.82)!

5.54. Place

The genitive indicates the place in which or from which something is done.

> ἵνα βάψῃ τὸ ἄκρον τοῦ δακτύλου αὐτοῦ **ὕδατος** (Luke 16:24)
> *that he [Lazarus] might dip the end of his finger <u>in water</u>*

5.55. Means/Agent

The genitive indicates that by which or by whom something is done. It is found both with verbs and with verbal nouns and adjectives.

> ὁ γὰρ θεὸς ἀπείραστός ἐστιν **κακῶν** (Jas 1:13)
> *For God is not tempted <u>by evil</u>*

> ἔσονται πάντες διδακτοὶ **θεοῦ** (John 6:45)
> *they shall all be taught <u>by God</u>*

5.56. Cause/Reason

The genitive can indicate the cause or reason something happens. This use is common in CG but rare in KG.[57]

---

56. The dative is used for the point in time at which something happens (§5.66) and the accusative for the length of time (§5.82), though such distinctions are not always followed in KG.

57. Smyth §§1405–9; CGCG §§30.30, 38.50; BDF §178; AGG §167i.

ἐν τοῖς δεσμοῖς **τοῦ εὐαγγελίου** (Phlm 13)
in bonds <u>because of the gospel</u>

κινδυνεύομεν ἐγκαλεῖσθαι **στάσεως** (Acts 19:40)
we are in danger of being charged <u>with rioting</u>

5.57. Purpose/Goal

The genitive can indicate the goal or purpose of an action.

ἵνα ὁ θεὸς ἀνοίξῃ ἡμῖν θύραν **τοῦ λόγου** (Col 4:3)
that God would open for us a door <u>for the word</u>

Dative

5.58. Three Main Categories of the Dative

The dative has three main categories of usage (1) personal interest, (2) location, and (3) instrument. There are also a few more uses beyond these categories.

Personal Interest

5.59. Indirect Object

The indirect object indicates the one less directly involved than the direct object—it receives the direct object (§2.27a). English usually expresses the indirect object either with a prepositional phrase using "to" or by word order.

καὶ πάντα ἀποδώσω **σοι** (Matt 18:26)
and I will give all things <u>to you</u>
and I will give <u>you</u> all things

ὁ δὲ Ἰησοῦς λέγει **αὐτοῖς·** ναί. (Matt 21:16)
And Jesus said <u>to them</u>, "Yes."
  ‣ Here the object that is received is the content of the statement.

5.60. Advantage/Disadvantage

The dative can be used to indicate the one for or against whose benefit or advantage something is done.

Μὴ θησαυρίζετε ὑμῖν θησαυροὺς ἐπὶ τῆς γῆς (Matt 6:19)
Do not store up for yourselves treasures upon earth

τὰ βρώματα τῇ κοιλίᾳ (1 Cor 6:13)
food (is) for the stomach

μαρτυρεῖτε ἑαυτοῖς ὅτι υἱοί ἐστε τῶν φονευσάντων τοὺς προφήτας (Matt 23:31)
you testify against yourselves that you are sons of those who murdered the prophets

5.61. Possession

Sometimes the notion of advantage (§5.60) extends further to the idea of posses-sion. This usage often occurs with εἰμί or γίνομαι, either stated or implied. Often that which is possessed is not physical, so this is ownership in a more general sense.

καὶ ἔσται χαρά σοι (Luke 1:14)
and there will be joy for you
and joy will be yours
and you will have joy

εἰς πόλιν τῆς Γαλιλαίας ᾗ ὄνομα Ναζαρέθ (Luke 1:26)
to a town of Galilee for which a name (was) Nazareth
whose name (was) Nazareth
> This dative could also be viewed as reference (respect), "with reference to which a name was Nazareth." See §5.68.

5.62. Relationship

The dative can indicate personal interest to the point of some form of familial or social relationship.

ἐμοὶ μαθηταί ἐστε (John 13:35)
you are my disciples

5.63. Feeling (Ethical)

The dative can indicate the personal interest of the one involved through an expression of emotion or personal opinion. It often has the sense, "as far as [someone] is concerned," "from the perspective of."

Ἐμοὶ γὰρ τὸ ζῆν Χριστὸς καὶ τὸ ἀποθανεῖν κέρδος. (Phil 1:21)
For as far as I'm concerned to live is Christ and to die is gain.

ὁ δὲ Πιλᾶτος βουλόμενος **τῷ ὄχλῳ** τὸ ἱκανὸν ποιῆσαι ἀπέλυσεν αὐτοῖς τὸν Βαραββᾶν (Mark 15:15)
And Pilate, wanting to satisfy <u>the crowd</u>, released for them Barabbas

> The crowd has demanded that Pilate crucify Jesus and release Barabbas, so Pilate is satisfying their emotion/opinion. τὸ ἱκανὸν ποιῆσαι may mean, "do someone a favor."[58]

Location

5.64. Place/Sphere

The dative can indicate the place something happens or is located, either a physical place or some other sort of location, often metaphorical.

ἐπέθηκαν αὐτοῦ **τῇ κεφαλῇ** (John 19:2)
they placed (it) <u>on his head</u>

μακάριοι οἱ καθαροὶ **τῇ καρδίᾳ** (Matt 5:8)
Blessed (are) the pure <u>in heart</u>

> Since "heart" can refer to one's inner being this dative can be understood as expressing the sphere/place in which this purity is found. Alternatively, this could be taken as a dative of reference (§5.68).

θανατωθεὶς μὲν **σαρκί**, ζῳοποιηθεὶς δὲ **πνεύματι** (1 Pet 3:18)
having been put to death <u>in the flesh</u>, but having been made alive <u>in the spirit</u>

> If σαρκί and πνεύματι refer to Christ's human nature then these datives may be either sphere or reference (§§5.64, 68). But πνεύματι could refer instead to the Holy Spirit, in which case πνεύματι could be a dative of means/instrument/agent, "having been made alive by the Spirit" (§5.67).

5.65. Destination

The dative can indicate where the subject is going. It is used with intransitive verbs, so while it often can be translated with "to" it is not an indirect object.

ἰδοὺ ὁ βασιλεύς σου ἔρχεταί **σοι** (Matt 21:5)
Behold, your king is coming <u>to you</u>

καὶ ὡς ἐρχόμενος ἤγγισεν **τῇ οἰκίᾳ** (Luke 15:25)
and when he came and drew near <u>the house</u>

---

58. BDAG, s.v. "ἱκανός," 1, 472.

5.66. Time When

The dative is often used for the time at which something takes place or for a period of time viewed as a whole.[59]

καὶ τῇ τρίτῃ ἡμέρᾳ ἐγερθήσεται (Matt 20:19)
and on the third day he will be raised

τεσσεράκοντα καὶ ἓξ ἔτεσιν οἰκοδομήθη ὁ ναὸς οὗτος (John 2:20)
This temple was built in forty-six years
> Here we see a dative for a period of time viewed as a whole. Since the temple was still under construction in Jesus's day the reference is to the state of the temple at the time of this encounter.[60]

Instrument

5.67. Means/Instrument/Agent

The dative often indicates that by which or with which something is done. The dative usually refers to an impersonal means or instrument, and a personal agent is most often signaled by ὑπό with a genitive. But at times the dative is also used for personal agency, especially with a passive use of a middle/passive verb.

ἀνεῖλεν δὲ Ἰάκωβον τὸν ἀδελφὸν Ἰωάννου μαχαίρῃ (Acts 12:2)
and he killed Jacob, John's brother, with a sword

καὶ ἐξέβαλεν τὰ πνεύματα λόγῳ (Matt 8:16)
he cast out the spirits with a word

πρὸς τὸ θεαθῆναι αὐτοῖς (Matt 6:1)
in order to be seen by them
> Here we see the dative for personal agency with a passive use of the middle/passive.

59. Smyth §1447. The genitive of time is used for a general reference to the time during which something takes place (§5.53), and the accusative for the length of time (§5.82), though such distinctions are not always followed in KG.

60. Wallace in *ExSyn*, 560–61 argues that ναός has its proper sense of *sanctuary*, referring to the inner part of the temple in contrast to ἱερόν, the entire temple complex. But his translation, "this temple was built forty-six years ago," does not make sense in the context, since the point is not when but how long. The switch from ἱερόν in 2:14 and 2:15 to ναός in 2:19 focuses on the essential part of the temple, perhaps still referring to the temple as a whole through synecdoche, the part for the whole. A sensitivity to the temple proper in contrast to its outer parts occurs again in John 10:23. See Rodney A. Whitacre, *John*, IVP New Testament Commentary 4 (Downers Grove, IL: InterVarsity Press, 1999), 268.

Other Uses of the Dative

5.68. Reference (Respect)

The dative may indicate that with reference to which something is said to be true. It can be translated "with reference to," but a smoother translation is usually possible. The genitive (§5.43) and accusative (§5.81) also function in this way.

> οἵτινες ἀπεθάνομεν **τῇ ἁμαρτίᾳ**, πῶς ἔτι ζήσομεν ἐν αὐτῇ; (Rom 6:2)
> *We who died <u>with reference to sin</u>, how shall we yet live in it?*
> *We who died <u>to sin</u>, how shall we yet live in it?*

> νωθροὶ γεγόνατε **ταῖς ἀκοαῖς** (Heb 5:11)
> *you have become sluggish <u>in hearing</u>*

> ἐνεδυναμώθη **τῇ πίστει** (Rom 4:20)
> *he was made strong <u>in faith</u>*
> ▸ These last two examples use the translation "in," but here the idea is not a dative of sphere/place since "sluggish" and "strong" are not places, either literally or metaphorically.

5.69. Association

The dative indicates the person or thing with which the subject associates or is accompanied by. Usually the preposition σύν is used, but not always. With verbs the dative is normally used for association, but with nouns the genitive occasionally is used (§5.40).

> συνεζωοποίησεν **τῷ Χριστῷ** (Eph 2:5)
> *He made us alive together <u>with Christ</u>*
> ▸ Notice that this dative is not in a prepositional phrase with σύν, but the verb is a compound with σύν.

5.70. Manner (Adverbial)

This dative functions like an adverb and can sometimes be translated with an adverb, though often with "with" or "in."

> ἐγὼ **χάριτι** μετέχω (1 Cor 10:30)
> *I partake <u>with thanks</u>*
> ▸ "Thanks" is not an instrument by which Paul partakes, but the manner in which he does so, "thankfully."

ἐγὼ **παρρησίᾳ** λελάληκα τῷ κόσμῳ (John 18:20)
I have spoken <u>openly</u> to the world

5.71. Cause

The dative can give the reason for the action of the verb, usually an unintended reason. At times "because" in English includes the idea of intention, so this will not always be a good choice. When "because" does not work try "on the basis of."

τῇ **ἀπιστίᾳ** ἐξεκλάσθησαν (Rom 11:20)
they were broken off <u>because of their unbelief</u>
> This example works with either "because" or "on the basis of." But note that some interpret this dative as a dative of means/instrument/agent (§5.67): they were broken off by means of their unbelief, that is, it was their unbelief that broke them off.

5.72. Complement

When a word in the dative completes the information conveyed by the verb it serves as a complement (Latin, *complere, fill up, complete*) and is part of the core of a clause.[61] At times verbs taking complements have meanings related to the uses of the dative, but not always. Richard Young lists verbs referring to (1) worship, (2) service, (3) thanksgiving, (4) obedience and disobedience, (5) belief and unbelief, (6) rebuking, (7) helping, (8) pleasing, and (9) following or meeting, to which could be added verbs of likeness.[62]

πιστεύω, κύριε· καὶ προσεκύνησεν **αὐτῷ**. (John 9:38)
I believe, Lord. And he worshiped <u>him</u>.

ἀκολούθει **μοι**. καὶ ἀναστὰς ἠκολούθησεν **αὐτῷ**. (Matt 9:9)
Follow <u>me</u>. And getting up he followed <u>him</u>.
> The meaning of this verb fits with the dative, especially the dative of association (§5.69).

Οὐδεὶς δύναται **δυσὶ κυρίοις** δουλεύειν (Matt 6:24)
No one is able to serve <u>two masters</u>

---

61. Some resources refer to this usage as an object or direct object.
62. Young, *Intermediate*, 44–45. See also the list of such verbs in Smyth §§1461–66; *CGCG* §30.39; Funk §§591–93.3; *AGG* §174.

ἐπίστευσεν δὲ Ἀβραὰμ **τῷ θεῷ** καὶ ἐλογίσθη αὐτῷ εἰς δικαιοσύνην (Rom 4:3)
And Abraham believed <u>God</u> and it was counted to him as righteousness

5.73. Degree/Measure

The dative is used with comparative adjectives and adverbs to indicate nature or degree of difference indicated by the comparative.

ὁ δὲ **πολλῷ** μᾶλλον ἔκραζεν (Mark 10:48)
But he cried out <u>all</u> the more
> In the common expression πολλῷ μᾶλλον the accusative μᾶλλον (*more*) is modified by the dative πολλῷ (*much*). So woodenly it is "more by much," the dative telling the degree of difference, namely, a lot. It is usually translated "how much more," or "much more."

5.74. Recipient

The dative is used for the recipients of a letter or other form of communication. This is like an indirect object, but it occurs with no verb in the clause, such as in titles and greetings.

ταῖς δώδεκα **φυλαῖς** ταῖς ἐν τῇ διασπορᾷ (Jas 1:1)
<u>to the</u> twelve <u>tribes</u> that are in the dispersion

Accusative

5.75. Direct Object

When the action of a verb transfers to an object, this direct object receives the results or the effect of the action (§§2.2b, 27a).

ἔλαβεν **τοὺς ἑπτὰ ἄρτους** (Matt 15:36)
he took <u>the seven loaves</u>

5.76. Double Accusative of Person and Thing

A few verbs take two accusatives, one giving the person affected and the other the thing involved.

ἐκεῖνος **ὑμᾶς** διδάξει **πάντα** (John 14:26)
He will teach <u>you all things</u>

5.77. Double Accusative of Object and Complement

In this form of double accusative both accusatives refer to the same person or thing, unlike the double accusative of person and thing.

a. This construction occurs with verbs for such activities as naming, appointing, electing, choosing, making, calling, and considering.[63] One of the accusatives gives the direct object and the other a predicate complement to that object indicating that which the direct object has been named, made, called, and so forth. When the complement comes before the object it can be definite even if it is anarthrous.[64]

> οὐκέτι λέγω **ὑμᾶς δούλους** (John 15:15)
> *I no longer call you servants*
> > "You" is the direct object and "servants" is what they are called.

> πατέρα ἴδιον ἔλεγε **τὸν θεόν ἴσον ἑαυτὸν** ποιῶν τῷ θεῷ (John 5:18)
> *he was calling God his own Father making himself equal to God*
> > We have two examples of this form of double accusative back to back. πατέρα is an example of a complement that is anarthrous but definite, here made clear by ἴδιον.

> ποιήσω **ὑμᾶς ἁλιεῖς** ἀνθρώπων (Matt 4:19)
> *I will make you fishers of men/people*
> > The object is "you" and "fishers" is what they will be made. The predicate nature of this construction can be seen by comparing the parallel passage in Mark, cited in the next section (§5.78), which uses an infinitive of γίνομαι to connect the two objects.

b. When a verb that takes a double accusative of object and complement is used with the passive sense of the middle voice the verb ends up with two nominatives (§5.30) like a Type 2 sentence (§5.207).

5.78. Predicate

a. An accusative direct object with a main verb may be described using an infinitive or participle of an equative verb, in particular εἰμί or γίνομαι. The predicate complement will also be in the accusative.

> ποιήσω ὑμᾶς γενέσθαι **ἁλιεῖς** ἀνθρώπων (Mark 1:17)
> *I will make you to become fishers of men/people*

---

63. According to Funk, §522, the most common verbs in the New Testament that use this construction include ἐπικαλέω, ἔχω, καλέω, λέγω, ὀνομάζω, ποιέω, and τίθημι. For a more complete list see *ExSyn*, 183 n. 24; not included in *BNTSyn*.

64. *ExSyn*, 248; *BNTSyn*, 85.

> ➤ This is like the double accusative of object and complement in the previous section, but now with the infinitive expressed. ὑμᾶς is the object of ποιήσω which is described by the predicate accusative ἁλιεῖς as indicated by the infinitive γενέσθαι.

ὡς δὲ ἐγεύσατο ὁ ἀρχιτρίκλινος τὸ ὕδωρ **οἶνον** γεγενημένον (John 2:9)
And when the head waiter tasted the water that had become <u>wine</u>
> ➤ τὸ ὕδωρ is the object of ἐγεύσατο and it is further described with the perfect participle from γίνομαι and the predicate accusative οἶνον.

b. Another common construction using a predicate accusative is the infinitive for a content clause (indirect discourse). An accusative is used not only for the predicate after the infinitive of an equative verb but also for the subject of the infinitive (§5.79).

ᾔδεισαν **τὸν χριστὸν** αὐτὸν εἶναι (Luke 4:41)
they knew that he was <u>the Christ</u>
> ➤ The infinitive is used for the content of what they knew (§5.169). The subject of the infinitive is the accusative αὐτόν, and τόν χριστόν is the predicate accusative.

c. Such infinitives occur frequently in prepositional phrases (§§5.174–80).

ἐπίστευσεν εἰς τὸ γενέσθαι αὐτὸν **πατέρα** πολλῶν ἐθνῶν (Rom 4:18)
he believed with the result that he became <u>the father</u> of many nations
> ➤ εἰς τό with the infinitive is used for a purpose or result clause (§§5.177, 178). The accusative of reference αὐτόν serves as the subject of the infinitive, and πατέρα is the predicate accusative.

5.79. Subject of an Infinitive

If the subject of an infinitive is the same as the main verb it is not expressed but simply assumed. When, however, the subject of an infinitive is not the same as that of the main verb it is in the accusative. Technically this is an accusative of reference (§5.81). For more detail on such constructions see §§5.167b, 169, 174–80, 236.

ἄφετε **τὰ παιδία** ἔρχεσθαι πρός με (Mark 10:14)
Allow <u>the children</u> to come to me
> ➤ In form παιδία can be nominative or accusative, but here it is the accusative subject of the infinitive ἔρχεσθαι. Grammatically, this infinitive functions as the object of the verb ἄφετε. Thus the coming is what is to

be allowed, and this coming is with reference to the children. English requires us to translate using children as the subject of the infinitive.

καὶ ἐν τῷ σπείρειν **αὐτὸν** ὃ μὲν ἔπεσεν παρὰ τὴν ὁδόν (Luke 8:5)
And while he sowed some fell by the road
> ▸ Very woodenly this would be "And in the sowing with reference to him some fell by the road."

5.80. Manner (Adverbial)

The accusatives of a few nouns and several adjectives serve as adverbs, qualifying the verbal action, indicating the way in which something happens. Adjectives with this function are often in the neuter singular and plural. Lexicons often list such words as separate items.

ἐὰν **μόνον** ἅψωμαι τοῦ ἱματίου αὐτοῦ σωθήσομαι (Matt 9:21)
If only I touch his garment I will be saved/healed
> ▸ Here the neut.-acc.-sg. of the adjective μόνος, η, ον serves as an adverb. *CGEL* lists this accusative as a separate entry, and directs you to the article on μόνος. In that article the second meaning listed is "nt. [neuter] μόνον as adv. marking narrow limitation ***merely, just, only.***"[65]

δικαιούμενοι **δωρεὰν** τῇ αὐτοῦ χάριτι (Rom 3:24)
being justified freely by his grace
> ▸ Here the accusative of the noun δωρεά, ᾶς, ἡ (*gift*) is an adverbial accusative. Again lexicons often list this accusative as a separate word. For example, *CGEL* has: "**δωρεάν** [adv. acc. of δωρεά] adv.—1. 'being freely given/without charge', ***freely*** = the positive aspect *for nothing.* . . . 2. 'being without purpose', ***in vain*** = the neg. aspect *for nothing.* . . . 3. 'being undeserved', ***without cause.***"[66]

5.81. Reference (Respect)

Like the genitive (§5.43) and dative (§5.68), the accusative may limit an adjective or the verbal action by indicating that with respect to which the statement is being made. It can be translated "with respect/reference to," but a smoother translation is usually possible.

65. *CGEL*, 237.
66. *CGEL*, 103–4.

πᾶς δὲ ὁ ἀγωνιζόμενος **πάντα** ἐγκρατεύεται (1 Cor 9:25)
And everyone who competes exercises self-control <u>with reference to everything/in everything</u>

5.82. Extent of Time/Space

The accusative can indicate length of time or distance in space. It can also express the place to which something moves.[67]

ἔμειναν οὐ **πολλὰς ἡμέρας** (John 2:12)
They remained not <u>many days</u>.

καὶ αὐτὸς ἀπεσπάσθη ἀπ᾽ αὐτῶν ὡσεὶ λίθου **βολήν** (Luke 22:41)
And he withdrew from them about a stone's <u>throw</u>.

5.83. Oaths

That by which or on the basis of which one swears an oath is put in the accusative.

ὁρκίζω σε **τὸν θεόν**, μή με βασανίσῃς. (Mark 5:7)
I adjure you <u>by God</u>, do not torment me.

μὴ ὀμνύετε μήτε **τὸν οὐρανὸν** μήτε **τὴν γῆν** (Jas 5:12)
do not swear, either <u>by heaven</u> or <u>by earth</u>

PRONOUNS

5.84. Pronouns

A pronoun is used in place of a noun. *He went into the city* instead of *Jesus went into the city*. The personal, reflexive, and reciprocal pronouns are only used as noun substitutes. Other pronouns, however, are also used to modify nouns, including the relative, demonstrative, interrogative, indefinite, and possessive pronouns. Indeed, some resources refer to many of these words as pronominal adjectives rather than speak of the adjectival use of pronouns.[68] In KG, "The

---

67. The genitive often indicates the general time within which something takes place (§5.53) and the dative is used for the point in time at which something happens (§5.66), though such distinctions are not always followed in KG.

68. Smyth even labels a section "Correlative Pronouns" and then discusses them in that section as "pronominal adjectives." Smyth §340. For correlative pronouns see §3.54. Their use follows the same options discussed here in §5.84.

distinctions between different kinds of pronouns and even between pronouns and adjectives are often blurred."[69]

Each of the following words have meanings and uses in addition to these basic ones. The lexicon will sort out most issues for these words and other pronouns not mentioned.

a. Personal Pronouns.[70] Because Greek verbs have personal endings the nominative personal pronoun is not used as frequently as the other cases. When a nominative personal pronoun is used it may add a bit of emphasis (§5.264a[4]).

1. In addition to the common uses of the personal pronoun (§2.5; appendix 7), it occasionally is used reflexively.

    Μὴ θησαυρίζετε **ὑμῖν** θησαυροὺς ἐπὶ τῆς γῆς (Matt 6:19)
    Do not store up treasures <u>for yourselves</u> on earth

2. The article may serve as a personal pronoun in a μέν . . . δέ construction. See §5.17.

b. Reflexive Pronouns. A reflexive pronoun signals that the action of the verb occurs with respect to the verb's subject. In KG the use of reflexive pronouns increased as the use of the direct reflexive middle/passive (§2.6d) became less frequent than in CG.[71]

> πᾶσιν **ἐμαυτὸν** ἐδούλωσα (1 Cor 9:19)
> *I have made <u>myself</u> a slave to all*

1. The third-person plural forms are also used for first- and second-person plurals. So when you find a third-person plural reflexive pronoun you will need to determine from the verb which person it represents.

    Καὶ ἰδού τινες τῶν γραμματέων εἶπαν ἐν **ἑαυτοῖς**· οὗτος βλασφημεῖ. (Matt 9:3)
    And behold, some of the scribes said among <u>themselves</u>, "This person is blaspheming."
    > This reflexive pronoun is 3-pl. since the subject is 3-pl., as seen by the 3-pl. verb εἶπαν and the expressed subject, τινες.

    καὶ μὴ δόξητε λέγειν ἐν **ἑαυτοῖς**· πατέρα ἔχομεν τὸν Ἀβραάμ. (Matt 3:9)
    And do not think to say among <u>yourselves</u>, "We have Abraham as father."
    > Here we have the same form as in the previous verse, now functioning as a 2-pl. reflexive pronoun since the subject is 2-pl., as seen by the 2-pl. verb, δόξητε.

69. Young, *Intermediate*, 71.
70. For paradigms see §§3.46–48.
71. For paradigms see §3.53.

2.   Occasionally a reflexive pronoun is used as a reciprocal pronoun, "one another, each other" (§5.84c).[72]

χαριζόμενοι **ἑαυτοῖς** (Eph 4:32)
forgiving <u>one another</u>

3.   The reflexive pronoun is also used sometimes as a simple possessive.[73]

ἄφες τοὺς νεκροὺς θάψαι τοὺς **ἑαυτῶν** νεκρούς (Matt 8:22)
leave the dead to bury <u>their own</u> dead

c. The Reciprocal Pronoun. The reciprocal pronoun ἀλλήλων, ἀλλήλοις, ἀλλήλους, *one another, each other*, is used with a plural subject and indicates the action is carried out among those involved.

Ἀλλήλων τὰ βάρη βαστάζετε (Gal 6:2)
Carry the burdens <u>of one another</u>

d. Relative Pronouns. Relative pronouns, including indefinite relative pronouns, initiate clauses.[74] They are discussed in §§5.212–19.

e. Demonstrative Pronouns. The demonstrative pronouns point out something near by or far away, either physically or in some other sense. They often function as a personal pronoun. These pronouns include οὗτος, *this*, ἐκεῖνος, *that*, ὅδε, *this*, along with the correlatives τοσοῦτος, *so great/much*, τοιοῦτος, *of such a kind*, and τηλικοῦτος, *so great/large* (§3.54). Both οὗτος and ἐκεῖνος take the predicate position (§5.6).[75]

οὐχ **οὗτός** ἐστιν ὁ τέκτων (Mark 6:3)
Is not <u>this</u> the carpenter

οὗτος ἦν ἐν ἀρχῇ πρὸς τὸν θεόν. (John 1:2)
<u>*This one*</u> *was in the beginning with God.*
   ▸ Most translations have, "He was in the beginning with God."

καὶ ὁ ἄνθρωπος **οὗτος** δίκαιος (Luke 2:25)
and <u>this</u> man was righteous
   ▸ The demonstrative here is used adjectively. Note the predicate position.

---

72. BDAG, s.v. "ἑαυτοῦ," 2, 269.
73. BDAG, s.v. "ἑαυτοῦ," 3, 269.
74. For paradigms see §§3.51–52.
75. For paradigms of οὗτος and ἐκεῖνος see §3.49, app. 4.20. The forms of ὅδε, ἥδε, τόδε are simply the definite article with δέ added. The only forms used in the New Testament are the fem.-dat.-sg. and fem.-acc.-sg., τῇδε and τήνδε, and the neut.-acc.-pl. τάδε.

κατέβη **οὗτος** δεδικαιωμένος εἰς τὸν οἶκον αὐτοῦ παρ᾽ **ἐκεῖνον** (Luke 18:14)
This one went down to his house justified rather than that one

τάδε λέγει τὸ πνεῦμα τὸ ἅγιον (Acts 21:11)
Thus says the Holy Spirit
> This neut.-acc.-pl. of ὅδε to introduce a prophetic statement is the most common use of this pronoun in the New Testament. More literally, "The Holy Spirit is saying these things."

ὅτι μιᾷ ὥρᾳ ἠρημώθη ὁ **τοσοῦτος** πλοῦτος (Rev 18:17)
because in one hour such great wealth has been devastated
> In this example the correlative demonstrative (§3.54) serves as an adjective.

f. Interrogative Pronouns. Several pronouns are used when asking questions, including ποῖος, α, ον, *of what sort?*; πόσος, η, ον, *how much?, how great?, how many?*; and ποταπός, ή, όν, *of what sort?* However, the interrogative used most often is τίς, τί, both in direct and indirect questions. See §5.223.

τίς, τί may also function as an adjective and an adverb.
τί σημεῖον δεικνύεις ἡμῖν (John 2:18)
What sign do you show us
> Here the interrogative is used as an adjective.

τί με ἐρωτᾷς περὶ τοῦ ἀγαθοῦ; (Matt 19:17)
Why are you asking me about the good?
> τί is often used as an interrogative adverb.

g. Indefinite Pronouns. A number of indefinite words may function as both pronouns and adjectives.[76]

ἄλλος, ἄλλη, ἄλλο, *other, another*
ἕκαστος, η, ον, *each, every*
ἕτερος, α, ον, *other, another*
μηδείς, μηδεμία, μηδέν, *no one, nothing*
μόνος, η, ον, *only, alone*
οὐδείς, οὐδεμία, οὐδέν, *no one, nothing*
πᾶς, πᾶσα, πᾶν, *each, every, any, all; (the) whole*

Such words refer to a person or thing in a general way, without being specific. One of the most common of these indefinites is τις, τι, *some, someone, something, anyone, anything*. In addition to its use as a pronoun and an adjective

---

76. For paradigms see §3.16 for τις, §3.37 for πᾶς, app. 4.24 for οὐδείς and μηδείς.

it also often functions like the English indefinite article "a" (§5.21a). Perhaps ironically, when we say "a certain one" we mean an uncertain one!

1. **Pronoun.**

   εἶπέν **τις** πρὸς αὐτόν (Luke 9:57)
   someone said to him

   ἀνατρέπουσιν τήν **τινων** πίστιν (2 Tim 2:18)
   they are upsetting the faith of some

   Πάντα μοι παρεδόθη ὑπὸ τοῦ πατρός μου (Matt 11:27)
   All things have been handed over to me by my Father

   Οὐδεὶς δύναται δυσὶ κυρίοις δουλεύειν (Matt 6:24)
   No one is able to serve two masters

2. **Adjective.**

   Καὶ ἦν **τις βασιλικὸς** οὗ ὁ υἱὸς ἠσθένει ἐν Καφαρναούμ. (John 4:46)
   And there was a certain royal official whose son was sick in Capernaum

   εἶδον ὅτι **πλοιάριον ἄλλο** οὐκ ἦν ἐκεῖ (John 6:22)
   they saw that another small boat was not there

   Ἀσπάσασθε **πάντα ἅγιον** ἐν Χριστῷ Ἰησοῦ. (Phil 4:21)
   Greet every saint in Christ Jesus.

   τοῦτο μόνον θέλω μαθεῖν ἀφ᾽ ὑμῶν (Gal 3:2)
   I want to learn from you this only

h. Possessive Pronouns. Among the various ways of signaling possession in Greek is the use of ἐμός, ἐμή, ἐμόν, *my, mine*; σός, σή, σόν, *your, yours* (sg.); ἡμέτερος, α, ον, *our, ours*; ὑμέτερος, α, ον, *your, yours* (pl.), and ἴδιος, α, ον, *one's own*, often used adjectivally.[77]

   κύριε κύριε, οὐ τῷ **σῷ** ὀνόματι ἐπροφητεύσαμεν (Matt 7:22)
   Lord, Lord, did we not prophesy in your name

   ἕκαστος γὰρ τὸ **ἴδιον** φορτίον βαστάσει (Gal 6:5)
   For each one will carry his/her own burden

---

77. Along with these possessive pronouns the genitive (§5.35), dative (§5.61), and article (§5.18) can signal possession.

ὅσα γὰρ προεγράφη, εἰς τὴν **ἡμετέραν** διδασκαλίαν ἐγράφη (Rom 15:4)
for as much as was written previously was written for <u>our</u> instruction

COMPARATIVES AND SUPERLATIVES

5.85. Comparatives, Superlatives, Elatives

The superlative is dropping out of use in KG. Sometimes the comparative is used for the superlative and sometimes the superlative is used for the comparative. Furthermore, sometimes a superlative has an **elative** sense, that is, it means "very." A lexicon is often needed for sorting out comparatives and superlatives.[78]

ἄνθρωπος εἶχεν τέκνα δύο. καὶ προσελθὼν **τῷ πρώτῳ** εἶπεν (Matt 21:28)
A man had two children. And going to <u>the first</u> he said
> πρώτῳ is a superlative (§3.42). Since only two children are involved here a comparative would have been more proper.

τίς ἄρα **μείζων** ἐστὶν ἐν τῇ βασιλείᾳ τῶν οὐρανῶν; (Matt 18:1)
Who is the <u>greatest</u> in the kingdom of heaven?
> μείζων, ον, *greater*, is the comparative of μέγας, *great* (§3.43e), but here it functions as the superlative.

τὰς πόλεις ἐν αἷς ἐγένοντο αἱ **πλεῖσται** δυνάμεις αὐτοῦ (Matt 11:20)
the cities in which <u>very many</u> of his miracles occurred
> πλεῖστος, η, ον, *most*, is the superlative of πολύς, *much, many*. Here it could have its superlative sense ("most of his miracles"), but it may be the **elative** sense, "very many."

Τὸν μὲν **πρῶτον** λόγον ἐποιησάμην περὶ πάντων, ὦ Θεόφιλε, ὧν ἤρξατο ὁ Ἰησοῦς ποιεῖν τε καὶ διδάσκειν (Acts 1:1)
The <u>first/former</u> account, Theophilos, I composed concerning all that Jesus began to do and to teach
> Here is another example of the superlative πρῶτος, which properly means *first*. But since such superlatives often are used for comparatives in KG πρῶτος can mean *former*. If Luke is using it in this sense then he is simply referring to this as the second of two volumes. But if he is using it as a true superlative then it would imply that he intends to write at least three volumes.

---

78. For the forms of comparatives and superlatives see §3.43.

ὡς κόκκῳ σινάπεως, ὃς ὅταν σπαρῇ ἐπὶ τῆς γῆς, **μικρότερον** ὂν πάντων τῶν σπερμάτων τῶν ἐπὶ τῆς γῆς (Mark 4:31)
like a mustard seed that when sown on the ground, though it is the smallest of all the seeds on the ground/on earth

> μικρότερον is a comparative, following the -τερος, α, ον pattern (§3.43b). This is another example of a comparative used as a superlative since the reference is to all the seeds sown, of which there are more than two!

DIMINUTIVES

5.86. Function of Diminutives

A diminutive conveys the idea that something is little, young, dear, or some similar idea. For example a βίβλος is a book or scroll, and a βιβλάριον is a little book or scroll. A word may have a diminutive form but not signal such a nuance in actual usage, so check a lexicon to be sure. See §3.44 for the formation of diminutives as well as other examples.

VERBS

Aspect and Aktionsart

5.87. Verbal Aspect

The primary referent in Greek verbs is not time (§2.11) but rather **aspect**, that is, **the viewpoint the author is adopting**. Aspect is part of the verb's "semantics," meaning it is hardwired into the verb's form and thus plays a role in all forms of a verb.[79] Verbal aspect is a complex topic that is the subject of much discussion and debate at present.[80] This section touches on a few high points outlining the approach followed in this book.

79. There is debate over whether or not there are exceptions, when a verb's aspect can be overridden by its meaning and the context.

80. There is even a great variety of terms used for aspect. "These terms do not always overlap entirely, and there is some disagreement (and much confusion) in scholarly views concerning the precise values of the Greek aspect stems." *CGCG* §33.6. For a helpful introduction see Bruce A. McMenomy, *Syntactical Mechanics: A New Approach to English, Latin, and Greek*, new ed., Oklahoma Studies in Classical Culture 51 (Norman: University of Oklahoma Press, 2014), 91–102. In biblical studies two major works have provided the context for much of the discussion: Stanley E. Porter, *Verbal Aspect in the Greek of the New Testament, with Reference to Tense and Mood*, Studies in Biblical Greek 1 (New York: Lang, 1989); and Buist M. Fanning, *Verbal Aspect in New Testament Greek*, Oxford Theological Monographs (Oxford: Clarendon, 1990). For a brief introduction to the current discussion

a. Durative (Imperfective). When using the durative aspect an author is adopting a viewpoint from within the action or state, like a reporter embedded on the scene while it is unfolding. The action, event, or state may be incomplete, in process, on-going, or repeated (§5.88), but the verb's aspect does not itself say so; it is simply a matter of viewpoint. Durative aspect in Greek is expressed by the present and imperfect tense-forms.

For example, Joseph heard that Archelaus βασιλεύει τῆς Ἰουδαίας ἀντὶ τοῦ πατρὸς αὐτοῦ Ἡρῴδου ("<u>was reigning</u> over Judea in place of his father Herod") (Matt 2:22). The historical present βασιλεύει with its durative aspect views the action from within, as it was unfolding.

b. Aoristic (Perfective). This term comes from ἀόριστος, *undefined*.[81] While the durative aspect adopts a viewpoint from within the action/event/state as it is unfolding or on-going, the aoristic aspect views the action/event/state as though standing apart from it and seeing it as a whole.[82] The aoristic aspect does not define whether the action/event/state is simple or complex, nor whether it is completed or ongoing. Aoristic aspect is expressed by the aorist tense-form.

An example often cited is Paul's statement, ἐβασίλευσεν ὁ θάνατος ἀπὸ Ἀδὰμ μέχρι Μωϋσέως ("*death reigned from Adam to Moses*") (Rom 5:14). Here the prepositional phrase "from Adam to Moses" tells us that this action lasted a long time, but Paul's use of an aorist (ἐβασίλευσεν) indicates he is viewing this lengthy reign as a whole. If Paul had used an imperfect tense-form he would have been viewing the action from an internal perspective as it is in progress, "death was reigning from Adam to Moses."

c. Resultative (Stative). While most scholars are in general agreement regarding the aoristic and durative aspects, there is much debate regarding the aspect of the perfect and pluperfect tense-forms.

Some scholars think these two tense-forms have no aspect, while most scholars think they express a third aspect. There are a number of diverse views, however, regarding what it is and how it should be labeled.[83] Nevertheless, they generally

---

see appendix 5 in *UEBG*, and the resources mentioned there. See also *Advances*, ch. 5; and especially the essays in *Revisited*; and Constantine R. Campbell, "Aspect and Tense in New Testament Greek," in Black and Merkle, *Linguistics*, 37–53.

81. The aoristic aspect "is generally to be regarded as the default aspect, as the inconspicuous, unmarked one, as unspecified." *AGG* §194e. This aspect is also called "perfective," but that is unnecessarily confusing with the perfect tense-form. Moulton complained about this confusion back in 1908! Moulton, *Prolegomena*, 111 n. 2.

82. A seminal statement of the distinction between these first two aspects is provided by Fanning, *Verbal Aspect*, 27: "The action can be viewed from a reference-point *within* the action, without reference to the beginning or end-point of the action, but with focus instead on its internal structure or make-up. Or the action can be viewed from a vantage-point *outside* the action, with focus on the whole action from beginning to end, but without reference to its internal structure."

83. Essays in *Revisited* offer a convenient discussion of many of these views, with resources cited that provide further detail.

agree that the basic idea of this third aspect is a reference to what has come about as the result of prior action.[84] Thus, when using this aspect an author's viewpoint is within a situation in which an action or state has come about as the result of prior action. This prior action may or may not have ceased, but it is viewed as complete in the sense that it has produced effects that are present in the situation in view, whether that situation is the present time in view in the text, or, in the case of the pluperfect, a time prior to the text's point of reference.[85]

Continuing the example from Romans 5:14, if Paul had said, "death has reigned from Adam to Moses," he would have been adopting the viewpoint of his current time in the light of this prior action. Thus he would be viewing the reign of death as continuing right up to the present though complete in some sense. If Paul had used a pluperfect this viewpoint would be shifted to the past: "death had reigned from Adam to Moses." In this case he would be viewing death's reign as having occurred in the past and then come to completion in the past, at least in the light of some other event that then took place or in some other sense relevant to his discussion.

d. The Future and Aspect. Unlike the other tense-forms, the future has temporal value, referring to action or a state in the future. There is currently no general agreement about its aspect. It seems best to view the future as neutral in aspect and thus as having only temporal value and no aspectual value.[86] When the angel Gabriel tells Mary that her son βασιλεύσει ἐπὶ τὸν οἶκον Ἰακὼβ εἰς τοὺς αἰῶνας (*"will reign over the house of Jacob forever"*) (Luke 1:33), this future predicts a future event without a specifically future aspectual point of view.

e. Aspect and Tense-Form List. From the perspective just outlined five of the six major tense-forms each expresses one of three aspects. The aspects are discussed further in the sections on each of the tense-forms.

Present	–	durative	Aorist	–	aoristic	Perfect	–	resultative
Imperfect	–	durative				Pluperfect	–	resultative

f. Aspect and Time. Aspect does not signal time. The main morphological signal of past time is the augment on the indicative of secondary tense-forms—

---

84. The main debate is whether aspect plays a part in conveying this general function of the perfect and pluperfect tense-forms or whether there is no aspect and the sense is conveyed instead by pragmatics, that is, the meaning of the verb and signals in the context (§5.88c). So the disagreement is not on the nuance of these tense-forms, but rather at the level of theory, namely, the role of semantics (aspect) and pragmatics in signaling this nuance.

85. H. P. V. Nunn, *A Short Syntax of New Testament Greek*, 5th ed. (Cambridge: Cambridge University Press, 1938), §96.

86. Fanning, *Verbal Aspect*, 122–24, noting that this is the "most widely held view in NT grammars" (122). Thus it may reflect either durative or aoristic aspect. CGCG §33.43n2.

the imperfect, aorist, and pluperfect.[87] The following translations are examples of how the various aspects may be represented in English with a temporal reference (see further §5.90).

	Present	Past	Future
Aoristic:	*I wash.*	*I washed.*	*I will wash.*
Durative:	*I am washing.*	*I was washing.*	*I will be washing.*
Resultative:	*I have washed.*	*I had washed.*	*I will have washed.*

g. Aspect and Nonindicative Verbs. Outside the indicative the verb forms retain their aspect value, but do not signal time. Only the present and the aorist occur with frequency in nonindicative forms. In such nonindicative forms the aorist will often be translated in English with a present or a perfect, depending on the meaning of the verb, the type of construction, and the context. So it is best to associate the aorist primarily with the aoristic aspect rather than past time, even though the aorist indicative for past time is very common.

h. Aspect and the Event. It is very important to note that aspect concerns the viewpoint adopted by the author and does not in itself indicate anything about the nature of the actual event.[88] For example, in John 2:20 the Jews say to Jesus, τεσσεράκοντα καὶ ἓξ ἔτεσιν **οἰκοδομήθη** ὁ ναὸς οὗτος, καὶ σὺ ἐν τρισὶν ἡμέραις ἐγερεῖς αὐτόν (*"This temple was built in forty-six years, and will you raise it up in three days?"*). The verb "was built" (οἰκοδομήθη) is in the aorist, so its aoristic aspect means the event is being viewed as a whole, just saying it happened. But obviously the event itself was not simple—it took forty-six years.[89] Even good commentaries and grammars sometimes err by saying the verb is in the aorist and *therefore* it is an action that happened at a single point in time.[90]

5.88. Verbal *Aktionsart*

Verbs communicate not only the viewpoint of the author through their aspect, but also what the author is saying about the actual nature of the action, event,

87. The temporal reference of the augment is a point of dispute. The view that verb forms do not signal temporal reference is especially associated with Stanley Porter; see *Verbal Aspect*, 76–83; or, more briefly and accessibly, Porter, *Idioms of the Greek New Testament*, Biblical Languages: Greek 2 (Sheffield: Sheffield Academic, 1992), 25–26. For the view taken here, which is the most common view, see Fresch, "Typology, Polysemy, and Prototypes" in *Revisited*, 379–415; and *AGG* §193a.

88. The way verbs refer to characteristics of an action, event, or state is discussed in the next section.

89. Choice of tense-form may also be affected by a verb's role in a narrative. See §5.135.

90. This problem was examined in a classic article by Frank Stagg, "The Abused Aorist," *Journal of Biblical Literature* 91 (1972): 222–31.

or situation. This nuance is often referred to as a verb's *Aktionsart* (German for "kind of action," plural, *Aktionsarten*).[91]

a. Signals of *Aktionsart*. *Aktionsart* is signaled by:[92]

the verbal aspect of the tense-form + the meaning of the verb + the context.

b. Role of the Meaning of the Verb. The meaning of the verb is important since some verbs themselves point to an on-going activity, others to a singular/momentary event, and yet others to a state. Many verbs can function in any of these ways.

c. Pragmatics: The Role of Context. The features in a context are often referred to as **pragmatics**, in distinction to semantics, which are hardwired in the verb itself, as with aspect.

So, for example, the aspect of the aorist verb translated "was built" in John 2:20, cited in §5.87h, views a complex event as a single whole. Since the meaning of the verb and the context ("forty-six years") also indicate that this statement lumps a complex event together as a whole, in this case the aspect and the *Aktionsart* match. This is an example of the *Aktionsart* labeled "global" (§5.125) since it describes the action as a complete whole. This is the most common *Aktionsart* for the aorist.

Sometimes, however, an aorist can be used to say that an event did happen at a single point of time. Although the aoristic aspect by itself does not send this signal, that aspect in combination with the meaning of the particular verb and elements in the context can do so. For example, when Jesus healed Peter's mother-in-law Matthew says, καὶ **ἥψατο** τῆς χειρὸς αὐτῆς, καὶ ἀφῆκεν αὐτὴν ὁ πυρετός, καὶ ἠγέρθη καὶ διηκόνει αὐτῷ (*"And he touched her hand, and the fever left her, and she rose, and served him"*) (Matt 8:15). The word touched (ἥψατο) is in the aorist and here it refers to a single action at a point in time, as the meaning of the word and the context make clear. The label for this *Aktionsart* is "punctiliar" (§5.126). The same word for "touch" is used in John 20:17 in the present imperative (ἅπτου) when Jesus meets Mary Magdalene after his resurrection and says, μή μου ἅπτου (*"Do not touch me"*). Now the durative aspect of the present tense-form in connection with the verb and the context suggest a "progressive" *Aktionsart* (§5.98), and a translation such as "Don't cling to me" (CSB) or "Do not hold on to me" (NIV).

---

91. *CGCG* §33.8 prefers the term "lexical aspect" instead of *Aktionsart* to refer to the role of the meaning of the verb for signaling "the objective properties of an action, rather than with subjective ways of presenting that action" as in aspect, which *CGCG* refers to as grammatical aspect. The role of "the context/construction in which that verb is used" for signaling lexical aspect is mentioned in §33.9.

92. Constantine R. Campbell, *Basics of Verbal Aspect in Biblical Greek* (Grand Rapids: Zondervan, 2008), provides many helpful examples of working with this formula.

5.89. Assessing the Nuances of a Tense-Form

The aspect and *Aktionsart* of verbs are among the most rewarding and enjoyable features of Greek to pay attention to when reading, studying, or reflecting on a passage. But the application of these insights is not always simple and straightforward. It has well been said, "Be wise and humble, and don't overstate opinions about the impact of any particular verb form," for languages "are replete with exceptions, subtleties, frozen forms, and inexplicable and mysterious habits."[93]

Several of the main *Aktionsarten* are discussed below and the bibliography lists a few resources for learning further about aspect, *Aktionsart*, and other features of the Greek verb.[94] In these further resources you will discover that there are a number of factors that affect which tense-form is used. Here are some of the key points made in these resources.

a. Some verbs are found in only a limited number of tense-forms, which obviously affects which tense-form is used. Don't read too much into the fact that an imperfect is used instead of an aorist if the verb has no aorist form![95]

b. A verb's mood plays an important role in which tense-form is used.[96]

c. The basic meaning of the verb often influences the choice and significance of aspect and tense-form.

1. The most fundamental distinction is between verbs that refer to a **state** and those that refer to **action** (§§2.2b–c). Action verbs refer to change and stative verbs do not. "Thus, for example, verbs like *to be, to have,* and *to know* are normally *states*, while *to become, to get,* and *to discover* are *actions* (along with other more clearly 'active' ideas: *go, build, take, hit*)."[97] So, to illustrate, when stative verbs are used with durative verbs the idea may be the duration of that state.

2. Among action verbs, some are **telic**, that is, they refer to an action that implies completion, such as ἀνοίγω, *open* and ἀγοράζω, *buy.* Other verbs are **atelic** and do not imply completion, such as ζάω, *live* and ἐσθίω, *eat.* Some verbs may be used in either way.

93. Jonathan T. Pennington, "Greek Middle Voice," in Black and Merkle, *Linguistics,* 98.

94. See *CGCG,* ch. 33; *AGG* §§192–95; Fanning, *Verbal Aspect; ExSyn; BNTSyn; Deeper;* Porter, *Idioms,* ch. 1; David L. Mathewson and Elodie Ballantine Emig, *Intermediate Greek Grammar: Syntax for Students of the New Testament* (Grand Rapids: Baker Academic, 2016), ch. 11; Campbell, *Basics of Verbal Aspect; Advances,* ch. 5; and the essays in *Revisited.* These resources represent more than one approach to these topics.

95. Though, on a different level, it might be worth exploring why that particular verb is not used in the aorist. Perhaps its meaning was viewed by ancient Greeks as inherently durative.

96. See the very helpful discussion in Steven M. Baugh, *Introduction to Greek Tense Form Choice in the Non-Indicative Moods* (Self-published, 2009).

97. Fanning, *Verbal Aspect,* 130 (emphasis original). Chapter 3 in Fanning offers an extended discussion of verb types, with six subcategories under "action."

Whether a verb refers to a state or an action, and whether it is telic or atelic, is part of its meaning and so plays an important role in signaling *Aktionsart*. For example,

καὶ αὐτὸς **ἦν διανεύων** αὐτοῖς καὶ **διέμενεν** κωφός (Luke 1:22)
and he <u>kept making signs</u> to them and he <u>remained</u> mute

> διανεύω, *make a sign*, is an action verb that is telic. So this periphrastic imperfect (§§5.187–88) signals a completed action that is done repeatedly (§5.120). διαμένω, *remain, stay*, is a stative verb and atelic. So here in the imperfect it refers to a state that is ongoing, at least at this point in the story (§5.119).

Outside the indicative fewer tense-forms are used and, as you might expect, telic verbs prefer the aorist tense-form and atelic verbs the present.[98]

d. Sometimes a particular tense-form is used because of the verb's role in a discourse (§5.135).

e. Conjunctions and sentence connectors may affect the nuance of a verb. For example, a clause beginning with γάρ (*for*) usually plays a supporting role in a narrative and is not used for the main line of the story. Often the aorist is used for the main line of a narrative (§5.135), but if an aorist is in a γάρ clause it is usually not part of the main line.[99]

f. A tense-form may be used because it is part of an idiom. There is no decision to use one tense-form rather than another; it's simply how something is said.[100] For example, in the New Testament ἄρχομαι, *begin*, is always followed by a present tense-form of the complementary infinitive (§5.166). So the author is not conveying something in particular by the use of the present; it is just how that construction is expressed.[101]

But then the further question can be asked of why the present is the default tense-form of the complementary infinitive with ἄρχομαι. Perhaps it seemed natural to view ἄρχομαι with a complementary infinitive as referring to the outset of an unfolding event or activity. If the action is beginning then it is obviously incomplete and thus durative.

So when there is a default tense-form in a particular construction you may be able to see why this is so from the verb's aspect, but you should not expect

98. See *CGCG* §33.8; Baugh, *Tense Form Choice*, 10–13. For a much more developed analysis see Fanning, *Verbal Aspect*, ch. 3.

99. See Stephen H. Levinsohn, "Verb Forms and Grounding in Narrative," in Runge and Fresch, *Revisited*, 171; *DiscGram*, 51–54. *Advances*, ch. 8 provides a helpful brief introduction to the work of Levinsohn and Runge.

100. While the author may not choose the tense-form it could be asked why the idiom uses the particular tense-form. Perhaps there is something about the aspect of the tense-form that contributes to its use in the idiom.

101. Baugh, *Tense Form Choice*, 19–20.

a particular *Aktionsart* to be present.[102] Indeed, for a number of such particular constructions there is "no obvious reason" for the use of one tense-form or another.[103]

5.90. Translation of the Major Tense-Forms in the Indicative

The following translations are a very basic starting point for beginning students and do not represent the way to translate these forms in every context. The translations of the non-passive uses of the middle are actives, since that is how they are usually translated in English (§2.7c). Furthermore, outside the indicative the translations vary quite a bit depending on the particular type of construction, as discussed later in this chapter.

a. Present. Usually the present indicative in Greek is translated with either the simple present or the present progressive in English.

Active	λύω	*I loose. I am loosing.*
Middle	λύομαι	*I loose. I am loosing.*
Passive	λύομαι	*I am loosed. I am being loosed.*

b. Imperfect. The past progressive in English matches the aspect of the imperfect, though there are times when a simple past tense fits the verb or the context better.

Active	ἔλυον	*I was loosing. I loosed.*
Middle	ἐλυόμην	*I was loosing. I loosed.*
Passive	ἐλυόμην	*I was being loosed. I was loosed.*

c. Future.

Active	λύσω	*I will loose.*
Middle	λύσομαι	*I will loose.*
Passive	λυθήσομαι	*I will be loosed.*

d. Aorist. The aorist indicative is often translated with a simple past tense in English, but sometimes with a perfect tense.

---

102. In such complementary infinitives, "the difference between the stems is purely **aspectual**." *CGCG* §51.15 (emphasis original).

103. Fanning, *Verbal Aspect*, 399.

Active	ἔλυσα	*I loosed. I have loosed.*
Middle	ἐλύσαμην	*I loosed. I have loosed.*
Passive	ἐλύθην	*I was loosed. I have been loosed.*

e. Perfect. The perfect indicative is translated with an English perfect or a present, since the resultative aspect of the Greek perfect tense-form views the current situation as having come about due to a previous action.

Active	λέλυκα	*I have loosed. I loose.*
Middle	λέλυμαι	*I have loosed. I loose.*
Passive	λέλυμαι	*I have been loosed. I am loosed.*

f. Pluperfect. The pluperfect views the situation in the past as having come about due to a previous action. So it is like the perfect, but moved back a stage.

Active	ἐλελύκειν	*I had loosed.*
Middle	ἐλελύμην	*I had loosed.*
Passive	ἐλελύμην	*I had been loosed.*

Further General Verbal Details

5.91. Causative/Permissive

In Greek, as in English, a verb may refer to an action that the subject permits or causes to take place, rather than one that the subject does. The form of the verb does not signal this usage, but rather the meaning of the verb and the context. Since this usage occurs in English it should not cause a problem when reading, though attention to it may be fruitful in exegesis and reflection.

> ἔλαβεν ὁ Πιλᾶτος τὸν Ἰησοῦν καὶ **ἐμαστίγωσεν** (John 19:1)
> *Pilate took Jesus and <u>had him scourged</u>*
> > ‣ ἐμαστίγωσεν – aor.-ind.-act.-3-sg. < μαστιγόω. Pilate himself would not have done the scourging; rather, he caused it to take place.

> **βαπτισθήτω** ἕκαστος ὑμῶν (Acts 2:38)
> *each of you <u>be baptized</u>*
> > ‣ βαπτισθήτω – aor.-impv.-MP-3-sg. < βαπτίζω. Presumably the people would not do the baptizing, but rather cause it to happen by going to those who were baptizing the new believers. This nuance fits the pas-

sive use easily since a passive is used for action of an agent other than the subject. But βαπτισθήτω could be a different use of the middle than the passive and be translated, "get yourself baptized."[104]

Ἀνέβη δὲ καὶ Ἰωσὴφ . . . **ἀπογράψασθαι** (Luke 2:4–5)
So Joseph also went up . . . to register himself

> ἀπογράψασθαι – aor.-inf.-MP < ἀπογράφω. Some English translations have "to be registered" since Joseph would not have done the registration. He was seeking to have the proper official register him. He went up "to get himself registered."[105]

5.92. Voice

The following sections on voice build on the introduction in §2.6. This discussion represents an overview of key themes in a current approach to this topic.[106] As research continues on the middle we can expect additions and modifications.

a. Variation in Voice between Tense-Forms. The active and middle-passive forms show up in a variety of combinations among the verbs. Since the active can include subject-affectedness (§2.6b) there is often apparently no change in meaning.[107]

104. Carl Conrad, "Active, Middle, and Passive: Understanding Ancient Greek Voice," December 16, 2003, https://pages.wustl.edu/files/pages/imce/cwconrad/undancgrkvc .pdf, §3.b. So also Nunn, *Short Syntax* §81(3), referring to the first middle/passive form ἐβαπτίσαντο in 1 Cor 10:2.

105. Nunn, *Short Syntax* §81(3).

106. The major resources include Rutger J. Allan, *The Middle Voice in Ancient Greek: A Study in Polysemy*, Amsterdam Studies in Classical Philology 11 (Amsterdam: Gieben, 2003); Rachel Aubrey, "Motivated Categories, Middle Voice, and Passive Morphology," in Runge and Fresch, *Revisited*, ch. 18; *CGCG*, ch. 35; Jonathan T. Pennington, "The Greek Middle Voice," in Black and Merkle, *Linguistics*, ch. 4; *Advances*, ch. 4; Suzanne Kemmer, *The Middle Voice*, Typological Studies in Language 23 (Amsterdam: Benjamins, 1993). Carl Conrad's several important unpublished articles are available at https://sites.wustl.edu /cwconrad/ancient-greek-voice/. On the homepage of this site is an untitled summary from 2005 and a link to "a terse, very compact formulation of a very complex issue" from 2011. The series of commentaries in the *Baylor Handbook on the Greek New Testament* (Waco, TX: Baylor University Press, 2003–present) uses this recent approach to voice.

107. A common example is the shift from the present active to the future middle. "From the earliest times in Greek the Future has a large proportion of Middle forms, there being whole categories of verbs in which a present active took a future middle without any ascertainable reason." James Hope Moulton and Wilbert Francis Howard, *A Grammar of New Testament Greek*, vol. 2, *Accidence and Word-formation with an Appendix on Semitisms in the New Testament* (Edinburgh: T&T Clark, 1929), 218, capitalization original.

An example of a verb that varies in voice with no change in meaning is ἀνα-βαίνω, *go up*, which becomes ἀναβήσομαι in the future and back to the active in the aorist, ἀνέβην. Several verbs vary not only in voice but also in root, with no apparent change in meaning. For example ἔρχομαι, *come, go*, is middle-only in the present and future, ἐλεύσομαι, but not in the aorist, ἦλθον, and similarly ἐσθίω has φάγομαι in the future and ἔφαγον in the aorist with no change in meaning.

The lexicons give some help in sorting out such variations in particular verbs, though naturally their explanations will often be out of sync with this more recent approach to voice.[108] Indeed, more research is needed concerning how voice relates to the meanings of verbs and their use in context.[109]

b. Variation in Meaning between Voices. The meanings of some verbs vary between the voices. For example, ἄρχω in the active means *rule*, but in the middle it means *begin*; similarly, ἅπτω, *kindle*, and ἅπτομαι, *touch*. In most verbs there is a relation between the meanings found in the voices, but as verbs like these two indicate, as well as middle-only verbs, the middle is not dependent on the active.[110] In languages like Greek the active and the middle are both basic; one is not derived from the other.

c. Variation in Usage between Voices. Some verbs that are transitive in the active lack an external object in the middle. In English such verbs are intransitive, but this term is not appropriate for Greek since in the middle the verb's action transfers to the subject, in different ways and to varying degrees as evident in the several forms of subject-affectedness (§5.93).[111] Thus παύω, *stop*, is transitive in the active, with a "focus on an obj. that is kept from carrying on an action," while in the middle the focus is "on oneself discontinuing an activity."[112]

πανσάτω τὴν γλῶσσαν ἀπὸ κακοῦ (1 Pet 3:10)
he/she must <u>stop</u> their tongue from evil

καὶ **ἐπαύσαντο** καὶ ἐγένετο γαλήνη. (Luke 8:24)
And they [the wind and waves] <u>stopped</u> and it became calm.

---

108. For example, BDAG often refers to a θη/η form functioning as a non-passive use of the middle as "passive with active meaning." From the more recent point of view such a verb is neither passive nor does it have an active meaning, even if it must be translated into English with an active verb (§2.7c, §5.94).

109. See Allan, *Middle Voice*, ch. 5 for an attempt to account for (near) synonyms between active and middle verbs in CG.

110. Aubrey, "Motivated Categories," 583–84.

111. Allan, *Middle Voice*, 6–19; Aubrey, "Motivated Categories," 568–75; Pennington, "Greek Middle Voice," 93–97; CGCG §35.3.

112. *CGEL*, 276.

5.93. Types of Subject-Affectedness in the Middle

The list of forms of subject-affectedness in §2.6 is here repeated and expanded, with more extensive explanation.[113] While this material is often helpful in understanding particular words, as always the meaning of a verb and its context play important roles. Furthermore, not every middle verb will correspond to these general patterns of use.[114] As research continues on the middle we should have more clarity, but, as with language in general, there will always be "exceptions, subtleties, frozen forms, and inexplicable and mysterious habits."[115]

a. The Agent-Patient Spectrum. To understand the various uses of the middle it is helpful to think of a spectrum representing the ways a subject is related to the action of the verb. On one end of the spectrum the subject is purely the agent of the action, while at the other end the subject is not an agent at all, but purely acted upon by someone or something else, referred to as the patient. The agent end of the spectrum is represented by an active verb used transitively, as in "Jesus washes the disciples' feet." The patient end is represented by a verb used passively in which the action transfers entirely to the subject, "The disciples' feet are being washed by Jesus." The active form, with the subject as agent and a verb used transitively, may be thought of as the prototypical transitive form of a clause.[116] Other forms of voice then represent views both of the subject and of the verb in relation to transitivity that differ from those of the prototypical form.[117]

---

113. This list is based primarily on Allan, *Middle Voice*, ch. 2, the similar categories in Aubrey, "Motivated Categories," 594–616, and material in *CGCG* ch. 35. Kemmer, *Middle Voice*, 267–70 provides a detailed "Checklist for Middle Semantics." For a brief introductory list of categories focused on middle-only verbs see Neva F. Miller, "Appendix 2: A Theory of Deponent Verbs," in *Analytical Lexicon of the Greek New Testament*, ed. Barbara Friberg, Timothy Friberg, and Neva F. Miller (Grand Rapids: Baker, 2000), 423–30.

114. For example, the middle-only verb ἰάομαι, *heal*, "is somewhat problematic since it is not clear how the meaning 'heal' relates to middle semantics," that is, how it represents subject-affectedness, since the subject does not seem to be involved as beneficiary or experiencer. Allan, *Middle Voice*, 113 n. 200. Miller, "A Theory of Deponent Verbs," 427, lists this verb as an example of reciprocity, which she describes as, "Some verbs involve situations where two parties are involved and where the removal of one party would render the verb meaningless and no action possible." Reciprocity is not understood this way in the resources cited above in footnote 106, as we will see in §5.93i. But perhaps in the light of verbs like ἰάομαι further research on the middle will expand the category of reciprocity or develop a new category. Or perhaps ἰάομαι is simply an exception.

115. Pennington, "Greek Middle Voice," 98.

116. More specifically, this construction is the prototype for a two-participant event, with agent and patient. Allan, *Middle Voice*, 6–19; Aubrey, "Motivated Categories," 587–94; Kemmer, *Middle Voice*, 50–52.

117. The issue of transitivity is discussed extensively in Allan, *Middle Voice*, and Aubrey, "Motivated Categories."

Accordingly, the middle is not used when the subject is an agent of an action that simply transfers to an object, as in the active. Rather, in all uses of the middle the action affects the subject in some way, usually as the beneficiary or the experiencer of the event. In some of the particular uses of the middle the subject is more agent-like, that is, involved volitionally, initiating, and performing the action, while in others the subject is more patient-like, the one being acted upon.[118] Thus, some of the agent-like uses are closer to the transitive prototype in the active, while patient-like uses are further from that prototype and closer to the passive end of the spectrum.[119] The following sections provide an introduction to the ways the middle functions in these various uses, including an indication of how each is related to this agent-patient spectrum.[120]

b. Direct Reflexive. On rare occasions the action of the verb in the middle comes back on the subject directly. In this use the subject is more agent-like, initiating and performing the action. This is an emphatic way of indicating that the subject is the beneficiary.[121] Often verbs referring to activity such as washing, dressing, and grooming use the direct reflexive. The direct reflexive is translated in English with an active verb and a reflexive pronoun (§2.6d).

ἐνίψατο (John 9:7)
he [the man born blind] *washed himself*

c. Indirect Reflexive. In the indirect reflexive, like the direct reflexive, the subject is more agent-like. But now the verb has a direct object or complement that is affected by the action, as with verbs in the active.[122] Unlike the active, though, in the middle the subject is also affected, usually in the sense of being a beneficiary (§2.6e).[123] For example, αἱρέω in the active voice means *take*, while its middle includes a focus on the subject, *choose, prefer*. The active ἀποδίδωμι means *give back*, while in the middle it means *sell*, which includes the idea of the subject as beneficiary.

118. Allan, *Middle Voice*, ch. 2. Aubrey, "Motivated Categories," 594–612 organizes the various uses of the middle by those in which the subject is more agent-like and those in which the subject is more patient-like.

119. Aubrey, "Motivated Categories," 620.

120. For more detailed analysis see Allan, *Middle Voice*, Aubrey, "Motivated Categories," and the literature they cite.

121. Allan, *Middle Voice*, 114.

122. Some verbs have a direct object in the accusative, while other verbs have a genitive or dative complement, often referred to as a direct object. See §§5.36, 72. Matthew 8:3 provides an example of an indirect reflexive middle with a genitive complement, ἥψατο **αὐτοῦ**, *he touched him*, and Matthew 4:25 has a dative complement, ἠκολούθησαν **αὐτῷ** ὄχλοι πολλοί, *great crowds followed him*.

123. In contrast to the direct reflexive, "the indirect reflexive is an *unemphatic* way of expressing that the subject is the beneficiary." Allan, *Middle Voice*, 114, emphasis original.

When Mark says the daughter of Herodias asked King Herod for the head of John the Baptizer (Mark 6:25), the word "asked" is in the middle, ἠτήσατο, even though this verb is usually in the active and is used in the active twice by Herod in this scene (6:22, 23). While some scholars think there is no difference in nuance between the active and middle forms of this verb, the subject-affectedness of the middle fits well with the focus in this story on the interests of this daughter and her mother.[124] Similarly in Matthew 27:58 this same verb is used in the middle for Joseph of Arimathea's asking Pilate for Jesus's body.

d. Physical Change of Position or Location. Often the middle is used for verbs referring to the subject changing physical posture or location. The subject is agent-like, as the initiator and actor, but also patient-like, as the experiencer of the change.[125] The active of such verbs is often causative. Examples of change of posture include στρέφω, *turn*, which in the active means to turn something, while in the middle it means to turn oneself. The active καθίζω means *set down*, and in the middle it means *sit down*. An example of change of location is πορεύω, *bring, carry, convey*, which in the middle means *go, travel*, focusing on the subject as experiencer. Several middle-only verbs (§2.6f) refer to change of location, including ἀφικνέομαι, *arrive*, and ἔρχομαι, *come, go*. As is often the case, a reference to the physical may be used metaphorically, for example, ἔρχεται ὥρα, *an hour is coming* (John 4:21).

124. BDAG, for example, thinks there is no difference, "αἰτέω," 30. Allan, *Middle Voice*, 108 n. 192, doubts that the middle of αἰτέω has a "distinct meaning" but says it "may however emphasize that the subject profits or hopes to profit as a result of the request." BDF §316(2) says the middle of αἰτέω is often used in commercial settings, citing both of these passages and noting that the use in the passage in Mark "is quite subtle, since the daughter of Herodias, after the King's pronouncement, stands in a sort of business relationship to him." Similarly, Zerwick says this passage "makes a quite classical distinction between αἰτῶ (simply 'ask') and αἰτοῦμαι (avail oneself of one's right to ask)." Maximilian Zerwick, SJ, *Biblical Greek: Illustrated by Examples* (Rome: Biblical Institute Press, 1963), §234. In this case the middle would include benefit associated with a particular kind of context. This interpretation of this passage may be correct, but it would not fit other texts in which the active and middle of αἰτέω alternate, such as James 4:2–3 and 1 John 5:14–15. BDF says the alternation in these texts is arbitrary, but Moulton, *Prolegomena*, 160, questions this assessment for the passage in James. He notes that Joseph Mayor cites ancient grammarians who say the middle of αἰτέω means *ask* μεθ᾽ ἱκεσίας, *with supplication*, or μετὰ παρακλήσεως, *with imploring*. Joseph B. Mayor, *The Epistle of St. James: The Greek Text with Introduction, Notes, and Comments*, 2nd ed. (1897; repr. Grand Rapids: Baker, 1978), 133. This interpretation is attractive since it represents a form of benefit/experience that seems appropriate in all of these passages. The commentaries discuss yet further possible explanations for the alternation of voice in these texts.

125. Allan, *Middle Voice*, 76; Aubrey, "Motivated Categories," 598, who includes this use in her section on more agent-like uses. Allan notes that such a verb may on occasion also be used of an inanimate subject, "something moving spontaneously," and thus in a more patient-like way. Allan, *Middle Voice*, 80.

When used of a group the subject is less agent-like than when used of an individual, "since the actions of the individual participants in a collective motion event are not conceived of as separate actions."[126]

e. Physical Process. The middle may be used when the subject undergoes some sort of internal process that is spontaneous; that is, it is not initiated by the subject. Accordingly, in this use the subject is more patient-like. Such verbs are often causative in their active forms. Examples include αὐξάνω and φύω, *grow*, which in the active mean to cause something to grow, and in the middle they refer to the subject itself growing; ξηραίνω in the active means cause something to *dry up*, and in the middle, *become dry*; φθείρω in the active means *destroy*, and in the middle, *perish*. First Peter 2:2 provides an example of a metaphorical use, ἵνα ἐν αὐτῷ αὐξηθῆτε εἰς σωτηρίαν, *that by it* [appropriate uncontaminated milk] *you may grow unto salvation*.

f. Mental/Emotional Process. The subject may be affected as the experiencer or beneficiary of an internal process in thought or emotion. For example, μιμνήσκω, *remind*, in the middle means *remember*; πείθω, *persuade*, in the middle means *believe, obey*.

Such activity may be intentional on the part of the subject and thus the subject is agent-like, for example, λογίζομαι, *reckon*, and πυνθάνομαι, *inquire*. Or it may be unintentional, caused by something outside the subject, and the subject is more patient-like. For example, φοβέω in the active means *cause alarm*, but in the middle it means *fear*, which includes the subject as experiencer and more patient-like.[127]

g. Perception. A particular form of mental process involves perception through the senses. Examples include αἰσθάνομαι, *perceive, notice*; γεύομαι, *taste*; θεάομαι, *look at*; and ἅπτομαι, *touch*. Perception can be either intentional or unintentional, and thus the subject more agent-like or more patient-like. But generally perception tends to be more agent-like, since "the perceiving subject is typically actively involved in the perception."[128]

h. Speech. When verbs referring to forms of speech are in the middle the subject is initiating the action, and thus agent-like, but the subject is also included within the focus of the action as experiencer or beneficiary.[129] Many

---

126. Allan, *Middle Voice*, 83; see also Aubrey, "Motivated Categories," 599–600.

127. "Simple emotion events involve a high degree of affectedness of the Experiencer." Kemmer, *Middle Voice*, 130. She is referring to words like "fear" that include emotion as part of their meaning, noting that they are "low in volitionality," thus more patient-like. See also Allan, *Middle Voice*, 64–65.

128. Allan, *Middle Voice*, 95. See further Allan, *Middle Voice*, 95–101; Aubrey, "Motivated Categories," 610–12.

129. Both Allan, *Middle Voice*, 105–07, and Aubrey, "Motivated Categories," 609–10, label this category "speech act." They are referring simply to the expression of something with words, not Speech Act Theory, which concerns speech that not only gives information but performs an action. For example, when Jesus says καθαρίσθητι, *Be cleansed!* his statement

such verbs for speech are middle-only, such as ἀρνέομαι, *deny*, προσεύχομαι, *pray*, and ἐντέλλομαι, *command*. These actions may be understood as benefiting the subject, while including emotional or at least mental involvement of the subject as experiencer.[130]

i. Reciprocal Action. Many of these types of subject-affectedness involve action that includes one or more participants along with the subject. Reciprocal action refers to events in which the focus is on both participants equally and their interaction with one another.[131] In this use the subject is more agent-like. Examples include διαλέγομαι, *converse, discuss*, and μάχομαι, *fight*. In such verbs both parties are engaged in the same form of action.

j. Passive. The passive in Greek is not a separate voice, but one of the uses of the middle (§2.6c). Even MP2 forms with ϑη/η, which are frequently used in a passive sense, are not infrequently used in other senses of the middle as well (§5.94).

Along the spectrum from agent-like to patient-like events, the passive use of the middle is on the far end of the patient-like uses. Indeed, the subject is not just patient-like, but simply is the patient, the one acted upon by some other agent or force, either explicitly identified or not. The following examples illustrate the three voices, using προσάγω, *bring*.

> Active: ἵνα ὑμᾶς **προσαγάγη** τῷ ϑεῷ (1 Pet 3:18)
> *that he* [Christ] *might* <u>bring</u> *you to God*

This aorist subjunctive is an active verb used transitively, with the direct object ὑμᾶς, *you*.

> Middle: **προσηγαγόμην** ὑμᾶς πρὸς ἐμαυτόν (Exod 19:4)
> *I* <u>brought</u> *you to myself*
>
> ➤ This aorist indicative is a first middle/passive, a form that is only rarely used as a passive (§5.94) and would make no sense as a passive here given the rest of the clause. The middle indicates that the subject, God, is included as affected by the exodus, presumably as experiencer, though perhaps in some other sense. Since this verb occurs frequently in the active, it is possible that this use of the middle highlights God's involvement (§2.6g).

---

effects what it signifies, καὶ εὐθέως ἐκαθαρίσθη αὐτοῦ ἡ λέπρα, *and immediately his leprosy was cleansed* (Matt 8:3).

130. Allan, *Middle Voice*, 107. Kemmer, *Middle Voice*, 133–34, discusses "speech action that involves emotion as part of their lexical meaning."

131. Allan, *Middle Voice*, 84–88; Aubrey, "Motivated Categories," 605–6; Kemmer, *Middle Voice*, 95–127. Miller, "A Theory of Deponent Verbs," 427, understands this category differently. See §5.93 n. 114.

Passive: θυμίαμα **προσάγεται** τῷ ὀνόματί μου (Mal 1:11)
incense is brought to my name

> ➤ Both the context and the inanimate subject, θυμίαμα, *incense*, signal that προσάγεται is functioning as a passive. The subject is not the agent bringing something, but the patient that is acted upon. The agent who is doing the action is not stated explicitly.

5.94. Voice in the Aorist and Future Tense-Forms

The aorist and future have two forms for the middle/passive, a sigmatic form (§§4.18, 50) and a form using θη or η (§§4.22–24, 59–61).[132] Although according to recent research both paradigms are middle/passive, grammars have traditionally labeled the sigmatic forms as middles and the θη/η forms as passives. Instead, they should both be labeled middle/passive, and the sigmatic forms may be labeled first middle/passive (MP1) and the θη/η forms in the aorist and future labeled second middle/passive (MP2).[133]

Within the spectrum of uses of the middle (5.93a), the first middle/passive forms are generally more agent-like and the second middle/passive forms more patient-like.[134] Thus the traditional distinctions do reflect accurately the way these forms most often are used, with one important exception. While the θη/η forms in the future are almost always used in a passive sense, the θη/η forms of the aorist are often used for other kinds of subject-affectedness as well.[135] From their original more patient-like uses the θη/η forms were increasingly used for more agent-like forms of subject-affectedness. This increased use for agent-like events is sporadic in the Hellenistic period but not infrequent. Eventually the θη/η forms became the preferred form of middle, and the use of the sigmatic middle decreased to the point that in Modern Greek it has disappeared.[136]

The labels and most common uses can be summarized as follows. While the examples are indicatives, these uses are found in the other moods as well, along with the infinitives and participles.

132. For discussion of the form and function of verbs using θη/η see Aubrey, "Motivated Categories," and the more detailed study of CG in Allan, *Middle Voice*, chs. 3 and 4.

133. For this approach see Carl Conrad, "Active, Middle, and Passive," §4.3, which is adopted also by Pennington, "Greek Middle Voice," 93.

134. Allan, *Middle Voice*, 174–77; Aubrey, "Motivated Categories," 573, 620.

135. Allan, *Middle Voice*, 200–202. Aubrey, "Motivated Categories," 602, mentions the increased use of θη/η for "events with more agency in their conception, such as reflexives, reciprocals, and mental activities, which involve a more prototypical agent as the primary figure." For the types of subject-affectedness see §5.93. For a more detailed comparison between the uses of the sigmatic middle and the θη/η forms of the aorist in CG see Allan, *Middle Voice*, 157–77.

136. Allan, *Middle Voice*, 148; Aubrey, "Motivated Categories," 573, 602. For the historical development of the θη/η forms see Moulton, *Prolegomena*, ch. 7; Aubrey, "Motivated Categories," 571–73, 577–81, 594.

Label	Example	Use
Aorist: first middle/passive	ἐλυσάμην	Almost always middle, more agent-like.
Aorist: second middle/ passive	ἐλύθην	Very often passive, but not infrequently middle.
Future: first middle/ passive	λύσομαι	Almost always middle, more agent-like.
Future: second middle/ passive	λυθήσομαι	Almost always passive, more patient-like.

The meaning of the particular word and the way it is functioning in the context will indicate whether it is used as a middle or a passive in a given instance, as with other middles (§2.7c).

> ὃν ἐγὼ ἀπεκεφάλισα Ἰωάννην, οὗτος **ἠγέρθη** (Mark 6:16)
> *John, whom I beheaded, he <u>has been raised</u>*

> **ἠγέρθη** ταχὺ καὶ ἤρχετο πρὸς αὐτόν (John 11:29)
> *she <u>got up</u> quickly and went to him*

5.95. εἰμί, γίνομαι, and ὑπάρχω

The verbs εἰμί, γίνομαι, and ὑπάρχω are equative, that is, they do not refer to action, but rather they link a subject to its subject complement (§§2.27a; 5.26c, 27). They affirm that something *is* something, thereby usually identifying or giving a characteristic of the subject. Each of these three equative verbs have their own distinctive use and feel.

a. Such verbs take a subject complement instead of a direct object. This subject complement is in the same case as the subject, which is usually nominative.[137] You can think of an equative verb as an equal sign; "this *is* that" is similar to "this = that." The subject complement is also referred to as a predicate noun or predicate adjective, or more generally as a predicate nominative.

b. εἰμί. This verb only appears in the present, future, and imperfect. In all three of its tense-forms εἰμί is usually used to make an assertion, either saying the subject *is* something, or affirming that something about the subject is true.

Present

> θεοῦ γάρ **ἐσμεν** συνεργοί (1 Cor 3:9)
> *For we <u>are</u> God's fellow workers*

---

137. Other cases are used at times with certain constructions involving the infinitive (§§5.167b[1] n. 203; 5.169) and the participle (§§5.200b n. 226; 5.203).

οἶδα ὅτι ἀληθής **ἐστιν** ἡ μαρτυρία ἣν μαρτυρεῖ περὶ ἐμοῦ (John 5:32)
I know that the testimony which he testifies about me <u>is</u> true

μακάριοί **ἐστε** ἐὰν ποιῆτε αὐτά (John 13:17)
blessed <u>are</u> you if you do them

Future

ἔσονται σεισμοὶ κατὰ τόπους (Mark 13:8)
there <u>will be</u> earthquakes in various places

καὶ μακάριος **ἔσῃ** (Luke 14:14)
and you <u>will be</u> blessed

καὶ ὅπου εἰμὶ ἐγὼ ἐκεῖ καὶ ὁ διάκονος ὁ ἐμὸς **ἔσται** (John 12:26)
and where I am there also <u>will</u> my servant <u>be</u>

Imperfect

The imperfect of εἰμί is translated as a simple past, *was, were*, not a progressive.

ὅτε γὰρ **ἦμεν** ἐν τῇ σαρκί (Rom 7:5)
For when we <u>were</u> in the flesh

καὶ σὺ **ἦσθα** μετὰ Ἰησοῦ τοῦ Γαλιλαίου (Matt 26:69)
you also <u>were</u> with Jesus the Galilean

ἄχρι γὰρ νόμου ἁμαρτία **ἦν** ἐν κόσμῳ (Rom 5:13)
for until the law sin <u>was</u> in the world

c. γίνομαι. This equative verb is generally less static than εἰμί, with "the central mng. [meaning] 'transfer from one state or condition to another.'"[138] It can be used in a variety of ways that require several different translations in English. Here are a few examples.

φανερὸν γὰρ **ἐγένετο** τὸ ὄνομα αὐτοῦ (Mark 6:14)
for his name <u>became</u> [aorist] known

καὶ **γίνεται** λαῖλαψ μεγάλη ἀνέμου (Mark 4:37)
and a great wind storm <u>arose</u> [present]

---

138. BDAG, s.v. "γίνομαι," introduction, 196. Definition from *CGEL*, s.v. "γίνομαι," introduction, 79.

Καὶ ὅτε **ἐγένετο** κατὰ μόνας (Mark 4:10)
and when he <u>was</u> [aorist] alone

κύριε, **γέγονεν** ὃ ἐπέταξας (Luke 14:22)
Sir, what you ordered <u>has been done</u> [perfect]

1. **καὶ ἐγένετο**: This expression, also in the form ἐγένετο δέ, is based on a Hebrew idiom that occurs frequently in the LXX.[139] In the New Testament it occurs most often in Luke and Acts. It can be translated "And it came to pass," "and it happened," "and it came about." Modern translations usually leave it out, representing the view of some grammarians that it is redundant or "meaningless."[140] Other scholars, however, point to the discourse function of this construction, noting that "it picks out from the general background the *specific circumstance* for the foreground events that are to follow."[141]
2. Καὶ ἐγένετο/ἐγένετο δέ is usually followed by a clause that sets the scene for the event that follows. This clause is occasionally a genitive absolute or an infinitive construction, but most often a finite verb, often with conjunctions such as ὅτε or ὡς.[142] Such clauses are placed in brackets in the following examples.

139. This construction is one of a number of Semitisms in the New Testament, that is, elements of Greek that represent influence from the LXX, or more directly from Hebrew or Aramaic. For a brief introduction to this complex and debated issue see *AGG*, 6–7; Coulter H. George, "Jewish and Christian Greek," in *A Companion to the Ancient Greek Language*, ed. Edgar J. Bakker (Oxford: Blackwell), 267–80; Geoffrey Horrocks, *Greek: A History of the Language and Its Speakers*, 2nd ed. (Chichester: Wiley, 2014), 147–52; and Chrys C. Caragounis, *The Development of Greek and the New Testament: Morphology, Syntax, Phonology, and Textual Transmission* (Grand Rapids: Baker Academic, 2006), 40–42, 44, who criticizes Horrocks for not recognizing the extent of Semitic influence. Also note the earlier, more extensive discussion in Moulton and Howard, *Accidence and Word-formation*, 411–85.

140. BDF §472(3), see further §442(5), where this use of ἐγένετο is called "purely pleonastic."

141. Stephen H. Levinsohn, *Discourse Features of New Testament Greek: A Coursebook on the Information Structure of New Testament Greek*, 2nd ed. (Dallas: SIL International, 2000), 177 (emphasis original).

142. The form with καὶ ἐγένετο/ἐγένετο δέ and καί with a finite verb is a literal rendering of the Hebrew. The LXX is often a little less literal, leaving out καί before the finite verb at the end. The use of an infinitive construction is a more Greek form, found occasionally outside the Bible. According to Zerwick, in Acts only the Greek form is found, while in Luke's Gospel the more literal Hebrew form is found eleven times and the LXX form twenty-two times, but the Greek form only five times. Zerwick, *Biblical Greek* §389. The Gospel of Luke often has a Jewish accent! Indeed, there are a number of Semitisms in the first half of Acts as well. For its occurrence with conjunctions, see BDAG, s.v. "γίνομαι," 4.f, 198.

The foregrounded event that follows is usually an independent clause with a finite verb. This clause is the subject of ἐγένετο, it is what happened.

Καὶ ἐγένετο [ὅτε ἐτέλεσεν ὁ Ἰησοῦς τὰς παραβολὰς ταύτας], μετῆρεν ἐκεῖθεν. (Matt 13:53)
And it came about [when Jesus finished these parables] he moved on from there.
> The ὅτε clause sets the scene. The independent clause μετῆρεν ἐκεῖθεν is the foregrounded event; it is what happened. Grammatically, μετῆρεν ἐκεῖθεν is the subject of ἐγένετο.

καὶ ἐγένετο [ἐν τῷ εὐλογεῖν αὐτὸν αὐτοὺς] διέστη ἀπ᾽ αὐτῶν (Luke 24:51)
And it happened [while he was blessing them] he departed from them
> For this use of the infinitive in a prepositional phrase see §5.175.

ἐγένετο δὲ [τοῦ δαιμονίου ἐξελθόντος] ἐλάλησεν ὁ κωφός (Luke 11:14)
And it happened [after the demon came out] the mute man spoke
> The clause in brackets is a genitive absolute. See §5.200.

Ἐγένετο δὲ [ἐν τῷ βαπτισθῆναι ἅπαντα τὸν λαὸν] καὶ Ἰησοῦ βαπτισθέντος καὶ προσευχομένου [ἀνεῳχθῆναι τὸν οὐρανὸν] καὶ [καταβῆναι τὸ πνεῦμα τὸ ἅγιον σωματικῷ εἴδει ὡς περιστερὰν ἐπ᾽ αὐτόν], καὶ [φωνὴν ἐξ οὐρανοῦ γενέσθαι]· σὺ εἶ ὁ υἱός μου ὁ ἀγαπητός, ἐν σοὶ εὐδόκησα.[143] (Luke 3:21-22)
And it came about [while all the people were being baptized] and Jesus having been baptized and while he was praying, [heaven having been opened] and [the Holy Spirit having decended in bodily form like a dove upon him], and [a voice having come from heaven], "You are my beloved son, in you I am well pleased."
> Four infinitives are used to set the scene, with a genitive absolute included as well![144] Instead of a finite verb spelling out the foreground event, here the event is a direct quote of the voice from heaven, identifying Jesus. So the quote is the subject of ἐγένετο and thus the focus. The extensive setting of the scene and the unusual construction for the foreground event point to the significance of this witness by the Father to the Son.[145]

---

143. On the aorist εὐδόκησα see §5.125b on Mark 1:11.
144. The genitive absolute is, καὶ Ἰησοῦ βαπτισθέντος καὶ προσευχομένου. For genitive absolutes see §5.200.
145. Alternatively, Levinsohn takes the first infinitive as setting the temporal scene and then the remaining infinitives as subjects of ἐγένετο, giving the specific circumstance. "The implication is that the coming of the Spirit upon Jesus is but the specific circumstance for the following foreground events, viz., his temptation by the devil and subsequent ministry." *Discourse*, 178. The coming of the Spirit upon Jesus is certainly

Ἐγένετο δὲ [ἐν μιᾷ τῶν ἡμερῶν] καὶ αὐτὸς ἐνέβη εἰς πλοῖον (Luke 8:22)
And it came about [on one of the days] he got into a boat
> In this example the scene is set with a simple prepositional phrase instead of a clause. καί is included with the finite verb ἐνέβη as part of the Hebrew idiom, but it is not included in a translation.

d. ὑπάρχω. This verb has a variety of senses, including, *initiate; be ready; exist, be there; be real; be (a quality or characteristic of); be at one's disposal, belong to,* among others.[146] When used as the equivalent of εἰμί it may have "the sense 'be inherently (so)' or 'be really,'" or it may mean "to function or be in a state as determined by circumstance."[147] The particular nuance, when there is one, is not always clear.

οὗτος ἄρχων τῆς συναγωγῆς **ὑπῆρχεν** (Luke 8:41)
he was a leader of the synagogue
> Using this verb may add a bit of focus on Jairus's identity as the leader. The placing of both the subject and the subject complement before the verb also point to such a focus (§5.260).

ἐὰν ἀδελφὸς ἢ ἀδελφὴ γυμνοὶ **ὑπάρχωσιν** (Jas 2:15)
if a brother or sister is naked
> This is an example of ὑπάρχω used of being in a state determined by circumstance.

ἡμῶν γὰρ τὸ πολίτευμα ἐν οὐρανοῖς **ὑπάρχει** (Phil 3:20)
for our commonwealth is in heaven
> Perhaps using the verb adds the sense of this really being so.

Ἤκουον δὲ ταῦτα πάντα οἱ Φαρισαῖοι φιλάργυροι **ὑπάρχοντες** (Luke 16:14)
And the Pharisees, being lovers of money, were listening to all these things
> Here the verb is used for the existence of a quality or characteristic, with perhaps some stress on this really being so.[148]

---

foundational for all that follows, but it seems better to take the Father's witness as the foreground event within the story of Jesus's baptism. In this way the unusual grammar puts an emphasis on the Father's identification of Jesus as the beloved Son, a relation and identity that is at the heart of all that follows, including the account of the temptation, "If you are God's son" (Luke 4:3, 9).

146. Montanari, 2188–89; BDAG, 1029–30.

147. The first definition is from BDAG, s.v. "ὑπάρχω," 2, 1029. BDAG says, "the basic idea: come into being fr. [from] an originating point and so take place; gener. [generally] 'inhere, be there.'" The second definition is from *CGEL*, 361.

148. Of the sixty uses of ὑπάρχω in the New Testament, forty-two are participles, including the common expression τὰ ὑπάρχοντα, *possessions*.

ὑπάρχων ἐν βασάνοις (Luke 16:23)
being in torment
> › Another participle, this time referring to a state determined by circum-
> stances.

5.96. Preparatory *There/It*

a. In English we often use a preparatory "there" with the verb "to be." In Mark
13:8 we could translate ἔσονται σεισμοὶ κατὰ τόπους as *earthquakes will be in
various places*, but using "there" is smoother English, "there will be earthquakes
in various places." The next clause in that verse illustrates this point even more
clearly. We translate ἔσονται λιμοί as "there will be famines," not "famines
will be."
  b. A preparatory "it" is often used in English when in Greek an infinitive is the
subject of a sentence (§5.167), but occasionally with forms of εἰμί as well.[149]

καὶ ἀκούσας ὅτι Ἰησοῦς ὁ Ναζαρηνός **ἐστιν** ἤρξατο κράζειν (Mark 10:47)
And hearing that it was Jesus the Nazarene he began to cry out
> › Although ἐστιν is in the present tense-form we translate it in the past
> when the context is set in the past (§5.104).

Present Tense-Form: Aspect and Aktionsarten

5.97. Aspect of the Present

The aspect found in the present tense-form is durative (§5.87a), viewing the
action or state from within, as something in process. Often English idiom will
use the simple present, but the durative aspect is still present in the Greek.
  The following are some common *Aktionsarten* found in the present tense-form.

5.98. Progressive: Action That Is Ongoing

This is an action that is in process, usually a form of continuous action in the
given context.

ἐὰν [γὰρ] προσεύχωμαι γλώσσῃ, τὸ πνεῦμά μου **προσεύχεται** (1 Cor 14:14)
For if I am praying in a tongue, my spirit is praying
> › προσεύχεται – pres.-ind.-MP-3-sg. < προσεύχομαι.

149. See further Nunn, *Short Syntax* §12.

ἡμῖν τί **ἀτενίζετε** (Acts 3:12)

why are you <u>staring</u> at us?

> ἀτενίζετε – pres.-ind.-act.-2-pl. < ἀτενίζω.

5.99. Iterative: Action That Occurs Repeatedly

This action is not continuous, but rather starts and stops on an irregular but ongoing basis.

πολλάκις γὰρ **πίπτει** εἰς τὸ πῦρ (Matt 17:15)

For he often <u>falls</u> into the fire

> πίπτει – pres.-ind.-act.-3-sg. < πίπτω. πολλάκις, *often*, indicates that this action happens repeatedly. πίπτω is a telic verb so tense-forms with durative aspect often will point to iterative action.

Αἰτεῖτε . . . ζητεῖτε . . . κρούετε (Matt 7:7)

Ask . . . seek . . . knock

> αἰτεῖτε, ζητεῖτε, κρούετε are each pres.-impv.-act.-2-pl. These present imperatives probably have the sense of doing these things repeatedly. The forms could be indicative (§4.84a), but the context indicates they are imperative.

5.100. Customary: Action That Occurs Regularly, or an Ongoing State

In contrast to the iterative, customary action happens on a regular basis. This label is also used with verbs that do not signify action, but rather a state or condition.[150]

νηστεύω δὶς τοῦ σαββάτου (Luke 18:12)

I <u>fast</u> twice a week

> νηστεύω – pres.-ind.-act.-1-sg. < νηστεύω. This is his regular custom, as indicated in the context by *twice a week*.

παρ᾽ ὑμῖν **μένει** καὶ ἐν ὑμῖν ἔσται (John 14:17)

he [the Paraklete] <u>remains</u> with you and will be in you

> μένει – pres.-ind.-act.-3-sg. < μένω. The meaning of the atelic verb μένω, *remain*, and the second statement (*will be in you*) suggest that

---

150. This idea is similar to that of the resultative aspect, but the resultative aspect usually includes some level of reference to the action that produces the current situation (§§5.87c, 114).

Jesus is saying that having the Holy Spirit remaining with them will be the ongoing state for believers.

5.101. Continuative: Action That Began in the Past and Is Continuing on in the Present

When a present refers to past action continuing to the present there will usually be an adverb or prepositional phrase to clarify the sense.[151] This use is similar to the intensive perfect (§5.115a), but speaks of continuing action, while the perfect has in view the results of the past action, which may or may not continue on further.[152]

ἀπ᾽ ἀρχῆς ὁ διάβολος **ἁμαρτάνει** (1 John 3:8)
the devil has been sinning from the beginning
> ἁμαρτάνει – pres.-ind.-act.-3-sg. < ἁμαρτάνω. The prepositional phrase *from the beginning* points to continuous activity from a point in the past, in this case, the beginning.

5.102. Instantaneous: Action That Takes Place at a Single Point in Time

In this case the meaning of the verb and the clues in the context indicate a single action in the present. The viewpoint of the durative aspect is "compressed and any durative sense is thus reduced."[153] Buist Fanning notes that this use occurs with two types of actions. First, a performative action, that is, "one which is 'done' in the very act of speaking," and second, with "acts of *speaking* narrowly focused on the present moment."[154]

Καίσαρα **ἐπικαλοῦμαι.** (Acts 25:11)
I appeal to Caesar!
> ἐπικαλοῦμαι – pres.-ind.-MP-1-sg. < ἐπικαλέω. This verb usually means *call; name*, but in the middle it can be used as a technical term for appealing the ruling of a lower court.[155] Accordingly, here it functions as a performative.

---

151. Ernest De Witt Burton, *Syntax of the Moods and Tenses in New Testament Greek*, 3rd ed. (Edinburgh: T&T Clark, 1898), §17; Fanning, *Verbal Aspect*, 217–19. Wallace notes that some take this as a broader category and do not think such explicit signals are necessary. *ExSyn*, 519; *BNTSyn*, 222–23. But Fanning thinks such examples of a broader sense are better seen as customary or gnomic uses. *Verbal Aspect*, 217 n. 30.

152. *ExSyn*, 519; *BNTSyn*, 222–23.

153. Fanning, *Verbal Aspect*, 202.

154. Fanning, *Verbal Aspect*, 202 (emphasis original).

155. BDAG, s.v. "ἐπικαλέω," 3, 373.

καὶ τὰ νῦν λέγω ὑμῖν, ἀπόστητε ἀπὸ τῶν ἀνθρώπων τούτων (Acts 5:38)
And now I tell you, stay away from these men
> This verb of speaking is focused on the present moment, as τὰ νῦν makes clear.[156]

5.103. Gnomic: A General Truth

The term "gnomic" comes from γνώμη, *thought, judgment, opinion, intention, maxim*. A gnomic saying refers to a wisdom saying, or a statement of what generally happens without reference to a particular occasion. The future (§5.112) and aorist (§5.129) may also be used in this way.

ἱλαρὸν γὰρ δότην **ἀγαπᾷ** ὁ θεός (2 Cor 9:7)
for God loves a cheerful giver
> ἀγαπᾷ – pres.-ind.-act.-3-sg. < ἀγαπάω.

τὸ πνεῦμα ὅπου θέλει **πνεῖ** (John 3:8)
the wind blows where it wants to
> πνεῖ – pres.-ind.-act.-3-sg. < πνέω.

These passages are not about what God or the wind is doing at a given time and place, but rather what is true in general.

5.104. Historical (Narrative): Action That Occurs in the Past

This use of the present indicative occurs mostly in narrative. In KG it frequently occurs with verbs of speech or motion.[157] Some scholars think it functions as in English to add a sense of immediacy and vividness in telling a story.[158] Others affirm, rather, that it calls attention to a transition in the story and the importance of the speech or action that follows, highlighting "which themes are of intrinsic interest to the author himself."[159] These discourse functions, however,

---

156. BDAG, s.v. "νῦν," 2.b., 681: "with art.: neut. pl. τὰ ν. . . . *as far as the present situation is concerned* = *now*."

157. "Virtually all historical presents are used either to introduce reported discourse or as verbs of propulsion." *Advances*, 140.

158. Fanning, *Verbal Aspect*, 226; Wallace in *ExSyn*, 527; Funk §783; BDF §321; but denied by Runge in *DiscGram*, 125–28.

159. Elizabeth Robar, "The Historical Present in NT Greek: An Exercise in Interpreting Matthew," in *Revisited*, 350. "The HP [Historical Present] does not create a boundary; it simply attracts extra attention to it, often because of the significance of the speech or event that follows." *DiscGram*, 134. See further §5.135.

do not exclude a sense of vividness;[160] both are worth considering as you study and reflect on texts. But note that "in some writers or with some verbs the historical present is dulled to a *standard narrative tense which loses its original vivid force*," for example, in verbs of speaking.[161]

> Καὶ **ἔρχεται** πρὸς αὐτὸν λεπρός (Mark 1:40)
> *And a leper <u>came</u> to him*
> > ➤ ἔρχεται – pres.-ind.-MP-3-sg. < ἔρχομαι. This is an example of a verb of motion and also a transition point in a story.

> ἥψατο καὶ **λέγει** αὐτῷ (Mark 1:41)
> *he touched him and <u>said</u> to him*
> > ➤ λέγει – pres.-ind.-act.-3-sg. < λέγω. The historical present with a verb of speech calls the reader's attention to the importance of Jesus's statement that follows, but perhaps without a sense of vividness included.

> Τῇ ἐπαύριον **βλέπει** τὸν Ἰησοῦν ἐρχόμενον πρὸς αὐτόν (John 1:29)
> *The next day he <u>saw</u> Jesus coming toward him*
> > ➤ βλέπει – pres.-ind.-act.-3-sg. < βλέπω. The change in time and action is clear, while the use of the historical present also helps call attention to the shift. Here the historical present is with a verb other than of speech or motion.

5.105. Futuristic: Action That Occurs in the Future

We have this usage in English. The nuance in Greek may include a sense of immediacy or certainty.

> ναί, **ἔρχομαι** ταχύ. (Rev 22:20)
> *Yes <u>I am coming</u> soon.*
> > ➤ ἔρχομαι – pres.-ind.-MP-1-sg. < ἔρχομαι. This example could express immediacy, certainty, or perhaps both.

> Λέγει αὐτῷ ἡ γυνή· οἶδα ὅτι Μεσσίας **ἔρχεται** (John 4:25)
> *And the woman said, "I know that Messiah <u>is coming</u>"*

---

160. Fanning, *Verbal Aspect*, 231–32. So also *CGCG* §33.54: "The **present indicative** is used occasionally to highlight **decisive or crucial events** in a narrative, often those that definitively change the situation in the narrated world; in effect, this so-called **historic(al) present** (or 'narrative present') makes it seem as if an action that occurred in the past occurs in the present and is, there, all the more urgent" (emphasis original). See also Smyth §1883.

161. Fanning, *Verbal Aspect*, 233–34 (emphasis original).

> ἔρχεται – pres.-ind.-MP-3-sg. < ἔρχομαι. In the context this example is probably expressing certainty.

5.106. Conative (Tendential): What One Attempts or Desires to Do

Εἰδότες οὖν τὸν φόβον τοῦ κυρίου ἀνθρώπους **πείθομεν** (2 Cor 5:11)
Knowing therefore the fear of the Lord, we <u>are trying to persuade</u> people
> πείθομεν – pres.-ind.-act.-1-pl. < πείθω. Or perhaps Paul is referring to what is actually taking place. As often, more than one *Aktionsart* may be a viable candidate within a context.

Future Tense-Form: Aspect and Aktionsarten

5.107. Aspect and *Aktionsarten* of the Future

While there is much debate about the future, it seems best to view it as neutral in aspect, able to reflect either a durative or aoristic aspect (§5.87d n. 86). Accordingly, various *Aktionsarten* of the present and aorist tense-forms may be represented depending on the meaning of the verb, whether it is telic or atelic (§5.89c), and the context.

5.108. Predictive, Global: Action Viewed as a Whole

τέξεται δὲ υἱόν, καὶ καλέσεις τὸ ὄνομα αὐτοῦ Ἰησοῦν· αὐτὸς γὰρ **σώσει** τὸν λαὸν αὐτοῦ ἀπὸ τῶν ἁμαρτιῶν αὐτῶν. (Matt 1:21)
She will give birth to a son, and you will call his name Jesus, for he <u>will save</u> his people from their sins.
> σώσει – fut.-ind.-act.-3-sg. < σῴζω. The saving of his people refers to a complex event, but here it is simply viewed as a whole and predicted as a future event.

5.109. Predictive, Punctiliar: Action That Takes Place at a Single Point in Time

τέξεται δὲ υἱόν, καὶ καλέσεις τὸ ὄνομα αὐτοῦ Ἰησοῦν· αὐτὸς γὰρ σώσει τὸν λαὸν αὐτοῦ ἀπὸ τῶν ἁμαρτιῶν αὐτῶν. (Matt 1:21)
She <u>will give birth</u> to a son, and you will call his name Jesus, for he will save his people from their sins.
> τέξεται – fut.-ind.-MP-3-sg. < τίκτω. A future event is viewed as a whole, but the nature of the event is something that takes place at a

single point in time, though a woman in labor may not see it as a simple event in a point of time while she is going through it!

5.110. Deliberative

The deliberative future occurs when the writer is reflecting on what should be done. This usage is usually found in questions in the first person.

ὦ γενεὰ ἄπιστος καὶ διεστραμμένη, ἕως πότε μεθ᾽ ὑμῶν **ἔσομαι**; (Matt 17:17)
O faithless and twisted generation, how long <u>shall</u> I <u>be</u> with you?

> ἔσομαι – fut.-ind.-MP-1-sg. < εἰμί.

οὐ πολὺ [δὲ] μᾶλλον **ὑποταγησόμεθα** τῷ πατρὶ τῶν πνευμάτων καὶ **ζήσομεν**; (Heb 12:9)
and shall we not much more <u>submit ourselves</u> to the Father of spirits and <u>live</u>?

> ὑποταγησόμεθα – fut.-ind.-MP-1-pl. < ὑποτάσσω. ζήσομεν – fut.-ind.-act.-1-pl. < ζάω/ζῶ.[162]

5.111. Imperatival

The future can be used for the giving of a command.

ἀγαπήσεις κύριον τὸν θεόν σου (Matt 22:37)
You <u>shall love</u> the Lord your God

> ἀγαπήσει – fut.-ind.-act.-3-sg. < ἀγαπάω.

τέξεται δὲ υἱόν, καὶ **καλέσεις** τὸ ὄνομα αὐτοῦ Ἰησοῦν· αὐτὸς γὰρ σώσει τὸν λαὸν αὐτοῦ ἀπὸ τῶν ἁμαρτιῶν αὐτῶν. (Matt 1:21)
She will give birth to a son, and you <u>will call</u> his name Jesus, for he will save his people from their sins.

> καλέσεις – fut.-ind.-act.-2-sg. < καλέω. Here is yet a third verb in the future in this one verse. This verb, like the other two we have looked at above, may be a predictive future, but the context may suggest this is a command, not a prediction—the angel is not predicting what Joseph will do, but telling him what to do.

---

162. Most lexicons give the lexical form as ζάω, but *CGEL* notes this is not accurate and lists it under ζῶ (161).

5.112. Gnomic: A General Truth

Occasionally the future is used for a proverb, wisdom saying, or a statement of what generally happens, without reference to a particular occasion. This use is also found in the present (§5.103) and aorist (§5.129).

μόλις γὰρ ὑπὲρ δικαίου τις **ἀποθανεῖται** (Rom 5:7)
For scarcely <u>will</u> *someone* <u>die</u> *for a righteous person*
> ἀποθανεῖται – fut.-ind.-MP-3-sg. < ἀποθνῄσκω.

5.113. A Note on the Future Second Middle/Passive

The future second middle/passive is normally predictive, expressing an expectation. The context can add a note of certainty or promise. The future second middle/passive is rarely, if ever, imperatival, expressing a command.

μακάριοι οἱ πεινῶντες καὶ διψῶντες τὴν δικαιοσύνην, ὅτι αὐτοὶ **χορτασθήσ-ονται.** (Matt 5:6)
Blessed are those who hunger and thirst for righteousness, for they themselves <u>will be filled</u>.
> χορτασθήσονται – fut.-ind.-MP-3-pl. < χορτάζω. The *Aktionsart* is global. Jesus is making a prediction which in this context is a promise.

ὁ δὲ ὑπομείνας εἰς τέλος οὗτος **σωθήσεται** (Matt 10:22)
The one who endures to the end, this is the one who <u>will be saved</u>
> σωθήσεται – fut.-ind.-MP-3-sg. < σῴζω. *Aktionsart*: global. Prediction/promise.

Perfect Tense-Form: Aspect and Aktionsarten

5.114. Aspect of the Perfect

The perfect has a resultative aspect, that is, the author adopts a viewpoint within a current situation that has come about from a prior action (§5.87c). Thus the perfect occurs most often with action verbs that refer to a change in the subject or object.[163] This prior action may or may not have ceased, but it is

---

163. Michael G. Aubrey, "The Greek Perfect Tense-Form: Understanding Its Usage and Meaning," in Black and Merkle, *Linguistics*, 55–82, calls attention to the significance of whether the verb refers to an action or state, in what way, if any, it is transitive, and how many participants are in view. He suggests that when stative verbs are used in the perfect

viewed as complete in the sense that it has reached a point at which something has occurred in the current situation.[164] Thus this aspect signals that the action is being viewed neither from within (durative) nor as a whole from without (aoristic), but from within the situation that has come about from a prior action. In a sense, then, the resultative aspect combines the aoristic aspect and the durative by including a past event viewed as complete in some sense and the present situation viewed from within a continuing process or state.[165]

5.115. Two Emphases

Occasionally there is more emphasis on either the past action (extensive) or the current situation (intensive), though usually both are in view to some extent; otherwise, presumably, another tense-form would have been used.[166] Such emphasis is not due to the aspect, but rather to the meaning of the verb and signals in the context. So these emphases are signaled the same way as *Aktionsarten*, but they are not kinds of action. Rather, they are points of focus, though not infrequently there is no particular emphasis.

a. Intensive Emphasis. The intensive emphasis has a greater focus on the present situation than the prior action that led to it.

> πεπληρώκατε τὴν Ἰερουσαλὴμ τῆς διδαχῆς ὑμῶν (Acts 5:28)
> *You have filled Jerusalem with your teaching*
> > ➤ πεπληρώκατε – pf.-ind.-act.-2-pl. < πληρόω. The authorities are describing the current situation that has come about because of the disciples' teaching.

b. Extensive Emphasis. This emphasis is more extensive in that it includes not only attention to the present situation, but also some level of focus on the past action/event that led up to it.

> εἰ καὶ ἐγνώκαμεν κατὰ σάρκα Χριστόν, ἀλλὰ νῦν οὐκέτι γινώσκομεν (2 Cor 5:16)
> *even though we have known Christ according to the flesh, yet now we know [him in this way] no longer*

---

they may extend "the semantics of the stative verb to adapt to the perfect," for example, πεπίστευκα, *have come to believe*. Or they may extend "the perfect to adapt to the semantics of the stative verb," for example, μεμέθυσμαι, *be completely drunk* (*Linguistics*, 81).

164. Nunn, *Short Syntax* §96.

165. Nicholas J. Ellis, "Aspect-Prominence, Morpho-Syntax, and a Cognitive-Linguistic Framework for the Greek Verb," in Runge and Fresch, *Revisited*, 122–60. Ellis refers to the resultative aspect as "combinative," and relates this to the morphological form of the perfect, which includes both durative and aoristic elements. See also *Deeper*, 230, 297; and BDF §340.

166. Sometimes, however, a tense-form is used as a set expression, with little of the nuance of the form included. For example, οἶδα, *know*, is a perfect form but apparently has become a simple present in function without any resultative sense.

> ἐγνώκαμεν – pf.-ind.-act.-1-pl. < γινώσκω. This perfect clearly focuses on the past action since it is contrasted to the present action expressed by the adverb νῦν, *now*, and the present tense-form γινώσκομεν in the second clause.

c. Examples of Both Emphases Together. The following examples include verbs with intensive and extensive emphases in the same sentence.

καὶ ἡμεῖς **πεπιστεύκαμεν** καὶ **ἐγνώκαμεν** ὅτι σὺ εἶ ὁ ἅγιος τοῦ θεοῦ (John 6:69)
And we have believed and know that you are the Holy One of God
> πεπιστεύκαμεν – pf.-ind.-act.-1-pl. < πιστεύω. ἐγνώκαμεν – pf.-ind.-act.-1-pl. < γινώσκω. While both verbs probably focus on the present state of believing and knowing, perhaps πεπιστεύκαμεν includes an extensive sense, referring to the disciples' coming to faith.

νῦν **ἔγνωκαν** ὅτι πάντα ὅσα **δέδωκάς** μοι παρὰ σοῦ εἰσιν (John 17:7)
Now they know that all things that you have given me are from you
> ἔγνωκαν – pf.-ind.-act.-3-pl. < γινώσκω. δέδωκας – pf.-ind.-act.-2-sg. < δίδωμι. ἔγνωκαν appears to be intensive, focused on their present state of knowing. δέδωκας seems extensive, including reference to the past activity of the Father giving to the Son.

καὶ γὰρ οὐ **δεδόξασται** τὸ **δεδοξασμένον** ἐν τούτῳ τῷ μέρει εἵνεκεν τῆς ὑπερ-βαλλούσης δόξης. (2 Cor 3:10)
For indeed that which has been clothed in glory in this context has not been clothed in glory because of the glory that surpasses it.
> δεδόξασται – pf.-ind.-MP-3-sg. < δοξάζω. δεδοξασμένον – pf.-ptc.-MP-neut.-nom.-sg. < δοξάζω. The participle is extensive, referring either to the former glory under Moses or to the glory on Moses's face that Paul has referred to in 3:7. The indicative perfect is intensive, referring to the glory that has come in Christ. "For indeed that which had been clothed in glory (in the past), (now) in this context is not clothed in glory because of the glory that surpasses it."

5.116. Two Roles

A perfect often plays one of two roles in a context. It may refer to a **state/ condition** that provides a detail that is simply part of the context that is being described. Or it may refer to a result that is **currently relevant** and plays a more direct role in the unfolding action or argument.[167] These two nuances are

---

167. Regarding the perfect indicative, *CGCG* §33.11 says, "The perfect indicative expresses a state, located at the present, that is the result of a completed action; or it

signaled, like an *Aktionsart*, by the aspect, the meaning of the verb, and signals in the context (§5.88a).

a. Present State. Some verbs in the perfect tense-form refer entirely to the present, such as ἕστηκα, *I stand* and τέθνηκα, *I am dead*.[168] Other verbs may refer to a present state depending on the context. In such cases, the verb may provide a detail present in the context that does not itself effect what follows.

> κύριε, ὁ παῖς μου **βέβληται** ἐν τῇ οἰκίᾳ παραλυτικός (Matt 8:6)
> *Lord, my servant lies at home paralyzed*
>
> ▸ βέβληται – pf.-ind.-MP-3-sg. < βάλλω. The perfect refers to the present state/condition of the servant. This detail is part of the context, but does not itself effect what follows. Note that this also is an example of the intensive emphasis.

> ναὶ κύριε, ἐγὼ **πεπίστευκα** ὅτι σὺ εἶ ὁ χριστὸς ὁ υἱὸς τοῦ θεοῦ ὁ εἰς τὸν κόσμον ἐρχόμενος (John 11:27)
> *Yes Lord, I believe that you are the Christ, the Son of God who is coming into the world*
>
> ▸ πεπίστευκα – pf.-ind.-act.-1-sg. < πιστεύω. This statement of faith is not followed by further action or discussion related to it, nor is there attention to the past events that have led up to it. So the emphasis seems to be intensive, and the reference is to a present state that provides an important detail, but does not play a role in what follows. Notice that the English present is the best translation since translating it "I have believed" would point too much to the past (§5.90e).

Although at times English idiom requires a simple past tense, the perfect is rarely if ever simply the equivalent of an aorist in the New Testament.[169]

> ῥαββί, πότε ὧδε **γέγονας**; (John 6:25)
> *Rabbi, when did you get here?*
>
> ▸ γέγονας – pf.-ind.-act.-2-sg. < γίνομαι. English idiom prefers the simple past in the light of πότε, *when*, but the sense in Greek is not just the past arrival; it includes the state of being present.

---

expresses that the effects of the completed action are still in some way relevant at the present."

168. BDF §341.

169. In the Hellenistic period the perfect was beginning to be used like the aorist in narrative texts, and eventually the perfect dropped away apart from a few frozen forms. In Modern Greek the perfect aspect is conveyed through periphrastic constructions. Horrocks, *Greek*, 176–78; Zerwick, *Biblical Greek* §289 n. 9. For proposed examples of the perfect for the aorist in the New Testament see BDF §343, though according to AGG §200f, "it is not entirely clear whether there are early traces of this development in the NT." See also Zerwick, *Biblical Greek* §289.

b. Relevant Effects. A result of prior action that is relevant to the unfolding action or argument in the current context.

ὕπαγε, σατανᾶ· **γέγραπται** γάρ· κύριον τὸν θεόν σου προσκυνήσεις καὶ αὐτῷ μόνῳ λατρεύσεις. (Matt 4:10)
Depart, Satan, for it <u>has been written</u>, "You shall worship the Lord your God and you shall serve him alone."

> γέγραπται – pf.-ind.-MP-3-sg. < γράφω. Jesus's use of this text that has been written makes clear its relevance to the present discussion. The perfect of γράφω is used sixty-nine times in the New Testament, almost always with this sense, including Pilate's famous statement ὃ γέγραφα, γέγραφα, *What I have written, I have written* (John 19:22). This example in Matthew 4 seems neither intensive nor extensive in emphasis.[170]

[ὁ] Ἰησοῦς εἶπεν· **τετέλεσται** (John 19:30)
Jesus said, "It <u>is finished</u>"

> τετέλεσται – pf.-ind.-MP-3-sg. < τελέω. There is much discussion about what exactly Jesus is referring to here. Whatever it is, he is clearly referring to having accomplished something and in the larger context we see that it enables the next stage of the activity to begin. Note that "is finished" is a form of perfect in English, not a present.

παρέλαβον, ὅτι Χριστὸς ἀπέθανεν ὑπὲρ τῶν ἁμαρτιῶν ἡμῶν κατὰ τὰς γραφὰς καὶ ὅτι ἐτάφη καὶ ὅτι **ἐγήγερται** τῇ ἡμέρᾳ τῇ τρίτῃ κατὰ τὰς γραφάς (1 Cor 15:3–4)
I received that Christ died for our sins according to the scriptures and that he was buried and that he <u>was raised </u>on the third day according to the scriptures

> ἐγήγερται – pf.-ind.-MP-3-sg. < ἐγείρω. Paul's statement about Christ begins with two aorist indicatives, ἀπέθανεν, *he died*, and ἐτάφη, *he was buried*. Then comes ἐγήγερται, a perfect for which almost all English translations use a simple past. But the Greek perfect signals that the current situation is being viewed in the light of this past event that has enormous consequences, as Paul goes on to spell out.[171]

5.117. Analysis of the Perfect

The perfect is particularly interesting to analyze since it has options for both emphasis and role. Consider, for example, the perfect κεκάθικεν (< καθίζω, *sit*) that occurs at the end of Hebrews 12:2.

---

170. This verb could be translated "it is written," a form of the perfect in English that is fading from use. Note "It is finished" in the next example.
171. On this example see *AGG* §§200d–e.

ἀφορῶντες εἰς τὸν τῆς πίστεως ἀρχηγὸν καὶ τελειωτὴν Ἰησοῦν, ὃς ἀντὶ τῆς προκειμένης αὐτῷ χαρᾶς ὑπέμεινεν σταυρὸν αἰσχύνης καταφρονήσας ἐν δεξιᾷ τε τοῦ θρόνου τοῦ θεοῦ **κεκάθικεν**.

Notice how the following translations interpret the nuance of κεκάθικεν.

ESV: looking to Jesus, the founder and perfecter of our faith, who for the joy that was set before him endured the cross, despising the shame, and *is seated* at the right hand of the throne of God.

NET: keeping our eyes fixed on Jesus, the pioneer and perfecter of our faith. For the joy set out for him he endured the cross, disregarding its shame, and *has taken his seat* at the right hand of the throne of God.

NIV: fixing our eyes on Jesus, the pioneer and perfecter of faith. For the joy set before him he endured the cross, scorning its shame, and *sat down* at the right hand of the throne of God.

The ESV conveys an emphasis on the present state (intensive perfect), the NET includes more of the past action (extensive), and the NIV focuses solely on the past event, leaving out the nuance of either a current state or relevant effect. The NET translation seems to work best, since the context mentions what led up to Jesus taking his seat as part of the author's encouragement to his readers who are facing trials.

This perfect is best seen as intensive, since the current situation with Jesus seated in heaven is the focus, not the prior taking of his seat, though that is in the background as just noted. It contributes a relevant effect, since the author sees the fact that Jesus has taken his seat to be relevant to his readers' situation; it is part of his encouragement of his readers.

Imperfect Tense-Form: Aspect and Aktionsarten

5.118. Aspect of the Imperfect

The imperfect tense-form has the durative aspect. Consequently, its view-point is similar to the present tense-form, a viewpoint from within the action as it is progressing. The imperfect only occurs in the indicative and thus it usually refers to action in the past. In English this sense is conveyed with the past progressive "was/were –ing." The simple past would be "Jesus came into the city," and the past progressive would be "Jesus was coming into the city."

Note, however, that the Greek imperfect is not always translated with a past progressive in English; sometimes a simple past fits English style better, but the Greek verb will still have the durative aspect.

Since the imperfect and the present both have durative aspect they share several *Aktionsarten* in common.

5.119. Progressive: Action That Is Ongoing

This is the *Aktionsart* closest to the main sense of the imperfect. It depicts an action that is in the process of unfolding, usually a form of continuous action in the given context.

καὶ πολλοὶ πλούσιοι **ἔβαλλον** πολλά (Mark 12:41)
and many rich people <u>were putting</u> in much
> ἔβαλλον – impf.-ind.-act.-3-pl. < βάλλω.

5.120. Iterative: Action That Occurs Repeatedly

καὶ **ἠρώτα** αὐτὸν ἵνα τὸ δαιμόνιον ἐκβάλῃ ἐκ τῆς θυγατρὸς αὐτῆς (Mark 7:26)
and she <u>kept asking</u> him to cast out the demon from her daughter
> ἠρώτα – impf.-ind.-act.-3-sg. < ἐρωτάω. One of the striking features of this story is this woman's persistence, and the iterative sense fits with that motif. The *Aktionsart* of this tense-form paints a very poignant picture.

5.121. Ingressive: Focus on the Beginning of an Action or the Entrance into a State

καὶ ἀνοίξας τὸ στόμα αὐτοῦ **ἐδίδασκεν** αὐτοὺς λέγων (Matt 5:2)
and opening his mouth he <u>began teaching</u> them
> ἐδίδασκεν – impf.-ind.-act.-3-sg. < διδάσκω. This *Aktionsart* fits here since this is the beginning of the Sermon on the Mount.

διερρήσσετο δὲ τὰ δίκτυα αὐτῶν (Luke 5:6)
and their nets <u>were beginning to break</u>
> διερρήσσετο – impf.-ind.-act.-3-sg. < διαρήσσω. The progressive *Aktionsart* is also possible here; the nets were in the process of breaking.

5.122. Customary: Action That Occurs Regularly, or an Ongoing State

In contrast to the iterative, customary action happens on a regular basis. This label is also used with verbs that do not signify action, but rather a state or condition.[172]

---

172. This idea is similar to that of the resultative aspect, but the resultative includes reference to the action that produces the state or condition.

καθ᾽ ἡμέραν ἐν τῷ ἱερῷ **ἐκαθεζόμην** διδάσκων (Matt 26:55)
day after day I <u>used to sit</u> in the temple teaching

> ἐκαθεζόμην – impf.-ind.-MP-1-sg. < καθέζομαι. This was his regular custom, as indicated in the context by *day after day*.

αὐτὸς γὰρ **ἐγίνωσκεν** τί ἦν ἐν τῷ ἀνθρώπῳ (John 2:25)
for he himself <u>knew</u> what was in a person

> ἐγίνωσκεν – impf.-ind.-act.-3-sg. < γινώσκω. The prior verse says Jesus knew all persons (πάντας), so now in 2:25 his knowing what was "in a man/person" (ἐν τῷ ἀνθρώπῳ) is not merely referring to knowledge Jesus had in this particular setting (progressive). Nor is this a knowledge he had every now and then (iterative), or that he began to have at this point (ingressive). Rather, the context suggests that having such knowledge was Jesus's ongoing condition. We see this same knowledge in the next story, and the Greek text links this bit of 2:25 with that story: *For he himself knew what was in man* [ἐν τῷ ἀνθρώπῳ]. *Now there was a man* [ἄνθρωπος] *of the Pharisees.*

5.123. Conative (Tendential): What a Person Attempts or Desires to Do

καθ᾽ ὑπερβολὴν ἐδίωκον τὴν ἐκκλησίαν τοῦ θεοῦ καὶ **ἐπόρθουν** αὐτήν (Gal 1:13)
I used to persecute the church of God to an extraordinary degree and <u>was trying to annihilate it</u>

> ἐπόρθουν – impf.-ind.-act.-1-sg. < πορθέω. Since Paul did not actually annihilate the church this verb is probably conative. Notice also that the first imperfect, ἐδίωκον, may be taken as customary (*I used to persecute*), since Paul seems to have been persecuting the church on a regular basis.

ἤθελον δὲ παρεῖναι πρὸς ὑμᾶς ἄρτι (Gal 4:20)
and I <u>would like</u> to be with you now

> ἤθελον – impf.-ind.-act.-1-sg. < θέλω. Paul could have used a present to simply say, "I wish I could be with you now," but the imperfect is a little less direct.

Aorist Tense-Form: Aspect and Aktionsarten

5.124. Aspect of the Aorist

The aorist, since it is aoristic in aspect, views the action or state as a simple, undefined whole (§§2.11b, 5.87b).

ὁ **λαβὼν** αὐτοῦ τὴν μαρτυρίαν ἐσφράγισεν (John 3:33)
the one who <u>receives</u> his testimony set his seal
the one who <u>has received</u> his testimony set his seal

> λαβών – aor.-ptc.-act.-masc.-nom.-sg. < λαμβάνω. This second aorist participle views the reception as a whole, not from within the process. If the participle were in the present tense-form then we might translate, "the one who is receiving his testimony."

> English translations of this verse are divided between using a present and a perfect, in part because the main verb, ἐσφράγισεν, is an aorist indicative, which itself may refer to a past event or one that continues up to the present (§5.125b).

5.125. Global (Constative): Action Viewed as a Whole

This *Aktionsart* is closest to the aoristic aspect. It is global, "in the sense of considering all the parts of a 'situation' together."[173]

a. Since this is the basic idea of the aorist in general this is the default *Aktionsart* for an aorist unless the meaning of the verb and/or the context suggests a more particular nuance. Outside the indicative it is sometimes translated with a present.

τρὶς **ἐναυάγησα** (2 Cor 11:25)
three times I <u>was shipwrecked</u>

> ἐναυάγησα – aor.-ind.-act.-1-sg. < ναυαγέω. Paul's repeated experience is viewed as a whole, as a particular sort of experience among many that he is listing in this passage.

ὃς ἂν **σκανδαλίσῃ** ἕνα τῶν μικρῶν τούτων (Mark 9:42)
whoever <u>causes</u> one of these little ones <u>to stumble</u>

> σκανδαλίσῃ - aor.-subjn.-act.-3-sg. < σκανδαλίζω.

b. **Sometimes the global aorist is used for events viewed as a whole that continue up to the present, and the English perfect or present is used.**[174] This use differs from the perfect tense-form in that it does not include the idea of having reached a stage of completion in some sense as in the perfect (§§5.87c, 114).

οἱ πέντε **ἔπεσαν**, ὁ εἷς ἔστιν, ὁ ἄλλος οὔπω **ἦλθεν** (Rev 17:10)
The five [kings] fell, the one is, and the other <u>has</u> not yet <u>come</u>

> ἦλθεν – aor.-ind.-act.-3-sg. < ἔρχομαι. The presence of οὔπω, *not yet*,

---

173. AGG §194f.
174. Burton, *Moods and Tenses* §§18, 46; Smyth §1940.

indicates the action continues to the present, that is, the current situation envisioned by the author.

εὑρήσετε πῶλον δεδεμένον ἐφ᾽ ὃν οὐδεὶς οὔπω ἀνθρώπων **ἐκάθισεν** (Mark 11:2)
you will find a colt tied, upon which no one among men <u>has</u> yet <u>sat</u>

> ἐκάθισεν – aor.-ind.-act.-3-sg. < καθίζω. οὔπω, *not yet*, again shows us that this action continues up to the present so the English perfect is used. In Greek two negatives don't make a positive, but rather reinforce the negative idea (§5.265), so this clause would not be translated "no one has not yet sat."

Καὶ αὐτὸς **ἔδωκεν** τοὺς μὲν ἀποστόλους, τοὺς δὲ προφήτας, τοὺς δὲ εὐαγγελιστάς, τοὺς δὲ ποιμένας καὶ διδασκάλους (Eph 4:11)
And he himself <u>gave</u> some to be apostles, some prophets, some evangelists, and some pastors and teachers

> ἔδωκεν – aor.-ind.-act.-3-sg. < δίδωμι. This complex action of God is being viewed as a whole. God was continuing this activity in Paul's time and in our own, so we could translate, "He has given," but that does not appear to be Paul's focus in this passage.

Ἐφανέρωσά σου τὸ ὄνομα τοῖς ἀνθρώποις οὓς **ἔδωκάς** μοι ἐκ τοῦ κόσμου. (John 17:6)
I <u>manifested</u> your name to the persons whom you <u>gave</u> me out of the world.

> ἐφανέρωσα – aor.-ind.-act.-1-sg. < φανερόω. ἔδωκας – aor.-ind.-act.-2-sg. < δίδωμι. The whole tone and perspective of Jesus's final prayer in John 17 suggest he is stepping back and viewing the course of his ministry as a whole. So these aorists may have a global *Aktionsart*. Since the global aorist can refer to events viewed as a whole that continue up to the present we could translate, "I have manifested your name" and "whom you have given to me." These aorists would not be culminative (§5.128), unless we thought the context suggests that Jesus has now ceased manifesting and the Father has ceased giving.

σὺ εἶ ὁ υἱός μου ὁ ἀγαπητός, ἐν σοὶ **εὐδόκησα**. (Mark 1:11)
You are my beloved Son, in whom I <u>am well-pleased</u>.

> The aorist is viewing the Father's pleasure in the Son as a whole. Both the identification of Jesus as the beloved son and the context of Jesus's baptism point to this aorist as not simply a statement about an attitude in the past, but one that continues to the present that grounds the launch of Jesus's ministry.[175]

---

175. Fanning says this is an example of the aorist used for a present stative idea, due to Semitic influence. *Verbal Aspect*, 276. Alternatively, *AGG* §191l takes the use here as analogous to a gnomic aorist (§5.129). See Luke 1:47 for a similar example.

5.126. Punctiliar: Action That Takes Place at a Single Point in Time

While it is important to understand that the aorist in itself (its aspect) does not refer to action at a single point in time, the aorist can be used for this idea. The meaning of the verb and features in the context can point us in this direction.

καὶ ἐκτείνας τὴν χεῖρα **ἥψατο** αὐτοῦ λέγων· θέλω, καθαρίσθητι· καὶ εὐθέως ἡ λέπρα **ἀπῆλθεν** ἀπ᾽ αὐτοῦ. (Luke 5:13)
And stretching out his hand he <u>touched</u> him, saying, "I will. Be clean." And immediately the leprosy <u>departed</u> from him.

> ἥψατο – aor.-ind.-MP-3-sg. < ἅπτομαι. ἀπῆλθεν – aor.-ind.-act.-3-sg. < ἀπέρχομαι. Both the meaning of ἅπτομαι (*touched*), a telic verb (§5.89c[2]), and the context point to a punctiliar action. The nuance of ἀπέρχομαι (*departed*) is more ambiguous, but the fact that Luke says it happened εὐθέως, *immediately*, clarifies that the action was punctiliar.

ὅσοι γὰρ εἰς Χριστὸν **ἐβαπτίσθητε**, Χριστὸν **ἐνεδύσασθε** (Gal 3:27)
for as many of you as <u>were baptized</u> into Christ <u>put on</u> Christ

> ἐβαπτίσθητε – aor.-ind.-MP-2-pl. < βαπτίζω. ἐνεδύσασθε – aor.-ind.-MP-2-pl. < ἐνδύω. ἐβαπτίσθητε, *you were baptized*, points to a past event viewed as a whole (aoristic aspect). The simple past is used in English since this is something that occurred at a particular point in time and thus punctiliar in *Aktionsart*.

> ἐνεδύσασθε, *you put on*, speaks of that same event, spelling out what took place in their baptism. So a simple past tense in English can be used. Most English translations, however, use a perfect, "you have put on Christ," since being clothed with Christ continues up to the present. Thus ἐνεδύσασθε has a global *Aktionsart*.

αὐτῶν δὲ **διηνοίχθησαν** οἱ ὀφθαλμοὶ καὶ ἐπέγνωσαν αὐτόν (Luke 24:31)
and their eyes <u>were opened</u> and they recognized him

> διηνοίχθησαν – aor.-ind.-MP-3-pl. < διανοίγω. This seems to be an example of the punctiliar *Aktionsart*.

5.127. Ingressive: Focus on the Beginning of an Action or the Entrance into a State

δι᾽ ὑμᾶς **ἐπτώχευσεν** πλούσιος ὤν, ἵνα ὑμεῖς τῇ ἐκείνου πτωχείᾳ **πλουτήσητε** (2 Cor 8:9)
for you he <u>became poor</u>, although being rich, so that you by his poverty <u>might become rich</u>

> ἐπτώχευσεν – aor.-ind.-act.-3-sg. < πτωχεύω. πλουτήσητε – aor.-subjn.-act.-2-pl. < πλουτέω. The point of this passage is Christ's entrance into our condition that we might enter into his. Notice that πλουτήσητε is

in the subjunctive—a verb's aspect and *Aktionsarten* apply in all the moods, not just the indicative.

Διὰ τοῦτο ὥσπερ δι᾽ ἑνὸς ἀνθρώπου ἡ ἁμαρτία εἰς τὸν κόσμον **εἰσῆλθεν** καὶ διὰ τῆς ἁμαρτίας ὁ θάνατος, καὶ οὕτως εἰς πάντας ἀνθρώπους ὁ θάνατος **διῆλθεν**, ἐφ᾽ ᾧ πάντες **ἥμαρτον** (Rom 5:12)
Because of this, just as through one man sin <u>entered</u> into the world and through sin, death (entered into the world), so also death <u>spread</u> to all persons, because all <u>have sinned</u>

> εἰσῆλθεν – aor.-ind.-act.-3-sg. < εἰσέρχομαι. διῆλθεν – aor.-ind.-act.-3-sg. < διέρχομαι. ἥμαρτον – aor.-ind.-act.-3-pl. < ἁμαρτάνω. These three aorists may function in three different ways, given the meanings of the verbs and the context. εἰσῆλθεν, *entered*, seems punctiliar, referring to the fall in the garden. διῆλθεν, *spread*, may be either global, viewing the complex event of the spread of sin as a whole, or ingressive, with the idea that death began to spread to everyone. ἥμαρτον, *have sinned*, seems to be global, speaking of all human sin up to the present, so the English perfect is used. But some take ἥμαρτον as punctiliar, *because all sinned*, referring to all having sinned when Adam sinned, since we are all in Adam as the head of the human race.

καὶ ὁμολογουμένως μέγα ἐστὶν τὸ τῆς εὐσεβείας μυστήριον· ὃς **ἐφανερώθη** ἐν σαρκί, **ἐδικαιώθη** ἐν πνεύματι, **ὤφθη** ἀγγέλοις, **ἐκηρύχθη** ἐν ἔθνεσιν, **ἐπιστεύθη** ἐν κόσμῳ, **ἀνελήμφθη** ἐν δόξῃ (1 Tim 3:16)
And beyond dispute great is the mystery of godliness: he who <u>was manifested</u> in the flesh, <u>was justified</u> in the spirit, <u>was seen</u> by angels, <u>was preached</u> among the nations, <u>was believed</u> on in the world, <u>was taken up</u> in glory

> ἐφανερώθη – aor.-ind.-MP-3-sg. < φανερόω. ἐδικαιώθη – aor.-ind.-MP-3-sg. < δικαιόω. ὤφθη – aor.-ind.-MP-3-sg. < ὁράω. ἐκηρύχθη – aor.-ind.-MP-3-sg. < κηρύσσω. ἐπιστεύθη – aor.-ind.-MP-3-sg. < πιστεύω. ἀνελήμφθη – aor.-ind.-MP-3-sg. < ἀναλαμβάνω. Some of these aorists may be punctiliar in their *Aktionsart*, such as the final one, ἀνελήμφθη (*was taken up*). Others may be ingressive, such as ἐκηρύχθη (*was preached*) and ἐπιστεύθη (*was believed*), since the preaching and the believing began and are continuing. The rest seem to be global in their *Aktionsart*. But since this passage is poetic perhaps they are all global. See the commentaries for the interpretation of this complex verse.

5.128. Culminative: Focus on an Action Now Ceased in the Present

Often this nuance is found in the aorist of verbs that refer to a process or an effort. Such verbs are sometimes translated into English like a perfect with the helping words "have" and "has." The global aorist can also be translated with an English perfect, but without the idea that the action has now ceased (§5.125b).

ἰδοὺ **ἐνίκησεν** ὁ λέων ὁ ἐκ τῆς φυλῆς Ἰούδα (Rev 5:5)
Behold, the Lion of the tribe of Judah <u>has won</u>

> ἐνίκησεν – aor.-ind.-act.-3-sg. < νικάω. This verb means *conquer, prevail*. His activity has now ceased; it has been completed, as the context emphasizes.

ἐγὼ γὰρ **ἔμαθον** ἐν οἷς εἰμι αὐτάρκης εἶναι (Phil 4:11)
For I <u>have learned</u> to be content in whatever circumstances I am

> ἔμαθον – aor.-ind.-act.-1-sg. < μανθάνω. Alternatively, if Paul does not think the learning has come to an end, then this would be a global aorist for activity continuing to the time of writing (§5.125b).

5.129. Gnomic: A General Truth

The aorist can be used in proverbial and wisdom sayings, or statements of what generally happens, without reference to a particular occasion. The present (§5.103) and future (§5.112) may also be used as a gnomic.

ἐξηράνθη ὁ χόρτος καὶ τὸ ἄνθος **ἐξέπεσεν** (1 Pet 1:24)
The grass <u>withers</u> and the flower <u>falls</u>

> ἐξηράνθη – aor.-ind.-MP-3-sg. < ξηραίνω. ἐξέπεσεν – aor.-ind.-act.-3-sg. < ἐκπίπτω. Note that English uses the present, not the past, for the gnomic idea.

ἐπὶ τῆς Μωϋσέως καθέδρας **ἐκάθισαν** οἱ γραμματεῖς καὶ οἱ Φαρισαῖοι. (Matt 23:2)
The legal scholars and the Pharisees <u>sit</u> on Moses's seat.

> ἐκάθισαν – aor.-ind.-act.-3-pl. < καθίζω. Jesus is not referring to what the legal scholars and Pharisees are doing at a particular time and place, but rather he is using imagery to refer to a general truth about their role and authority.

5.130. Proleptic: A Future Action Viewed as Already Completed

"The aorist may be substituted for the future when a future event is vividly represented as having actually occurred."[176] The aorist "underscores . . . the *certainty* and *immediacy* (or *imminence*) of the action contemplated."[177] The proposed examples in the New Testament are not always clear.

ἐὰν μή τις μένῃ ἐν ἐμοί, **ἐβλήθη** ἔξω ὡς τὸ κλῆμα καὶ **ἐξηράνθη** (John 15:6)
If anyone does not remain in me, he or she <u>is thrown out</u> like a branch and <u>withers</u>

---

176. Smyth §1934, similarly *BNTSyn*, 242.
177. Caragounis, *Development*, 268 (emphasis original). Wallace says it is used "to stress the certainty of the event." *ExSyn*, 564.

> ἐβλήθη – aor.-ind.-MP-3-sg. < βάλλω. ἐξηράνθη – aor.-ind.-MP-3-sg. < ξηραίνω. This example is clear since the context refers to what will happen in the future. These aorists could also be translated as futures, but the present fits better with the conditional construction.

ἀλλ' ἐν ταῖς ἡμέραις τῆς φωνῆς τοῦ ἑβδόμου ἀγγέλου, ὅταν μέλλῃ σαλπίζειν, καὶ **ἐτελέσθη** τὸ μυστήριον τοῦ θεοῦ (Rev 10:7)
but in the days of the sound of the seventh angel, when he is about to blow his trumpet, the mystery of God is indeed completed
> ἐτελέσθη – aor.-ind.-MP-3-sg. < τελέω. This is another clear example due to the future context. Again a future could be used in English. Most English translations do not translate the καί, but it works well as an ascensive use adding emphasis to this climactic moment, "indeed" (§5.264b[2]).

οὓς δὲ ἐδικαίωσεν, τούτους καὶ **ἐδόξασεν** (Rom 8:30)
and those whom he justified he also glorified
> ἐδόξασεν – aor.-ind.-act.-3-sg. < δοξάζω. A number of scholars take this as a proleptic reference to future glorification, but it may well refer to the entry into God's glory in this life (2 Cor 3:18). On this second interpretation this aorist would be constative or perhaps better, in the light of 2 Corinthians 3:18, ingressive, "he has begun to glorify."

λέγει Ἰησοῦς· νῦν **ἐδοξάσθη** ὁ υἱὸς τοῦ ἀνθρώπου καὶ ὁ θεὸς **ἐδοξάσθη** ἐν αὐτῷ (John 13:31)
Jesus said, "Now the Son of Man is glorified and God is glorified in him"
> ἐδοξάσθη – aor.-ind.-MP-3-sg. < δοξάζω. If proleptic then these verbs point to the crucifixion which is about to take place, often referred to in John as Jesus's glorification. But some scholars take these aorists as reflecting the heavenly Christ bearing witness through the earthly Jesus to what took place, and thus with global *Aktionsart*.

5.131. Epistolary

When writing a letter an author sometimes uses the aorist to refer to his or her present act of writing since it will be in the past when the recipients read the document.

Ἴδετε πηλίκοις ὑμῖν γράμμασιν **ἔγραψα** τῇ ἐμῇ χειρί. (Gal 6:11)
See with what large letters I wrote to you with my own hand.
> Most English translations appropriately have "I am writing" or "I have written."

Pluperfect Tense-Form: Aspect and Aktionsarten

5.132. Aspect of the Pluperfect

The pluperfect occurs only eighty-six times in the New Testament, and is used mostly in narrative passages. As with the perfect tense-form, the aspect is resultative, with two emphases and two roles (§§5.114–17).

The pluperfect views the action as having occurred in the past and come to completion in the past. So it is like the perfect, but moved back a stage. For example, the perfect "I have studied" suggests activity that began in the past and comes up to the present in some way. The pluperfect, "I had studied," implies activity that occurred and then was completed in the past.

5.133. Two Emphases

a. Intensive Emphasis. The pluperfect may refer to action having gone on in the past and then come to completion in the past, with some emphasis on the past situation that followed from the action.

ἤγαγον αὐτὸν ἕως ὀφρύος τοῦ ὄρους ἐφ᾽ οὗ ἡ πόλις **ᾠκοδόμητο** αὐτῶν (Luke 4:29)
they led him to the brow of the hill on which their city <u>had been built</u>

> ᾠκοδόμητο – plpf.-ind.-MP-3-sg. < οἰκοδομέω. Since the focus is on the completed action in the past most English translations use a simple past, "was built."

ἐδεῖτο δὲ αὐτοῦ ὁ ἀνὴρ ἀφ᾽ οὗ **ἐξεληλύθει** τὰ δαιμόνια εἶναι σὺν αὐτω (Luke 8:38)
The man from whom the demons <u>had gone out</u> pleaded to be with him

> ἐξεληλύθει – plpf.-ind.-act.-3-sg. < ἐξέρχομαι. The focus is on the man's present desire to be with Jesus.

b. Extensive Emphasis. The pluperfect may refer to action having gone on in the past and then come to completion in the past, with some emphasis on that past action.

ταῦτα εἶπαν οἱ γονεῖς αὐτοῦ ὅτι ἐφοβοῦντο τοὺς Ἰουδαίους· ἤδη γὰρ **συνε-τέθειντο** οἱ Ἰουδαῖοι ἵνα ἐάν τις αὐτὸν ὁμολογήσῃ χριστόν, ἀποσυνάγωγος γένηται. (John 9:22)
His parents said these things because they feared the Jews. For the Jews already <u>had agreed</u> that if anyone confessed him to be Christ, that person would be put out of the synagogue.

> συνετέθειντο – plpf.-ind.-MP-3-pl. < συντίθημι. The focus seems to be on what took place in the past.

5.134. Two Roles

The verses just cited in §5.133 also illustrate the two roles (§5.116).

a. Present State. A state or condition in the past resulting from a prior action that provides a detail in the past context that does not itself effect what followed.

> ἤγαγον αὐτὸν ἕως ὀφρύος τοῦ ὄρους ἐφ᾽ οὗ ἡ πόλις **ᾠκοδόμητο** αὐτῶν (Luke 4:29)
> *they led him to the brow of the hill on which their city had been built*
> ‣ ᾠκοδόμητο – plpf.-ind.-MP-3-sg. < οἰκοδομέω. The completed state of the building of the city is a detail in the context, but does not play a role in the action/discussion that follows.

b. Relevant Effects. A result of prior action that was relevant to the unfolding action or argument in the past context.

> ταῦτα εἶπαν οἱ γονεῖς αὐτοῦ ὅτι ἐφοβοῦντο τοὺς Ἰουδαίους· ἤδη γὰρ **συνε-τέθειντο** οἱ Ἰουδαῖοι ἵνα ἐάν τις αὐτὸν ὁμολογήσῃ χριστόν, ἀποσυνάγωγος γένηται. (John 9:22)
> *His parents said these things because they feared the Jews. For the Jews already had agreed that if anyone confessed him to be Christ, that person would be put out of the synagogue.*
> ‣ συνετέθειντο – plpf.-ind.-MP-3-pl. < συντίθημι. This agreement of the Jewish opponents is relevant to the action that has taken place.

5.135. The Function of Indicative Tense-Forms in Narratives

In narratives the aorist indicative is often used to move the story along, providing the framework, the mainline of the story. The imperfect, perfect, and pluperfect indicatives as well as periphrastic participles (§5.187) often fill in details.[178] The historical present may also provide background information, often calling attention to transitions in the narrative and highlighting the importance of the speech or action that follows (§5.104).[179]

In the following translation of Mark 2:13–14 bold is used for aorists, underlining for nonaorists, and italics for historical presents.[180] The wooden translation highlights the forms.

---

178. See Smyth §1909; and more recently, *CGCG* §33.13; Levinsohn, "Verb Forms and Grounding," 166–72.

179. See Levinsohn, "Verb Forms and Grounding," 171; Robar, "Historical Present in NT Greek," 329–52; and *DiscGram*, ch. 6.

180. The nonaorists are all imperfects since there are no perfects, pluperfects, or

Καὶ **ἐξῆλθεν** πάλιν παρὰ τὴν θάλασσαν· καὶ πᾶς ὁ ὄχλος <u>ἤρχετο</u> πρὸς αὐτόν, καὶ <u>ἐδίδασκεν</u> αὐτούς. 14 Καὶ παράγων **εἶδεν** Λευὶν τὸν τοῦ Ἀλφαίου καθήμενον ἐπὶ τὸ τελώνιον, καὶ λέγει αὐτῷ· ἀκολούθει μοι. καὶ ἀναστὰς **ἠκολούθησεν** αὐτῷ.

[13]*And he **went out** again by the sea, and all the crowd <u>was coming</u> to him, and he <u>was teaching</u> them.* [14]*And passing by he **saw** Levi the son of Alphaeus sitting at the tax collection station, and he says to him, "Follow me." And getting up he **followed** him.*

The aorists are used for the main events of the story line: Jesus going out, seeing Levi, and Levi's following Jesus. Background details are supplied by imperfects, including the crowd coming to Jesus and his teaching them. The historical present is common with verbs of speech, as here with *says*, which highlights the importance of what follows, namely, Jesus's call to follow, and adds vividness (§5.104).

Next, consider this example from John 6:16–21 which includes other nonaorist forms.

Ὡς δὲ ὀψία **ἐγένετο κατέβησαν** οἱ μαθηταὶ αὐτοῦ ἐπὶ τὴν θάλασσαν [17]καὶ ἐμβάντες εἰς πλοῖον <u>ἤρχοντο</u> πέραν τῆς θαλάσσης εἰς Καφαρναούμ. καὶ σκοτία ἤδη <u>ἐγεγόνει</u> καὶ οὔπω <u>ἐληλύθει</u> πρὸς αὐτοὺς ὁ Ἰησοῦς, [18]ἥ τε θάλασσα ἀνέμου μεγάλου πνέοντος <u>διεγείρετο</u>. [19]ἐληλακότες οὖν ὡς σταδίους εἴκοσι πέντε ἢ τριάκοντα θεωροῦσιν τὸν Ἰησοῦν περιπατοῦντα ἐπὶ τῆς θαλάσσης καὶ ἐγγὺς τοῦ πλοίου γινόμενον, καὶ **ἐφοβήθησαν**. [20]ὁ δὲ λέγει αὐτοῖς· ἐγώ εἰμι· μὴ φοβεῖσθε. [21]<u>ἤθελον</u> οὖν λαβεῖν αὐτὸν εἰς τὸ πλοῖον, καὶ εὐθέως **ἐγένετο** τὸ πλοῖον ἐπὶ τῆς γῆς εἰς ἣν <u>ὑπῆγον</u>.

*And when evening **came**, his disciples **went down** to the sea;* [17]*and getting into a boat, they <u>were going</u> [impf.] over the sea to Capernaum. And it already <u>had become</u> [plpf.] dark, and Jesus <u>had</u> not yet <u>come</u> [plpf.] to them.* [18]*And, a great wind blowing, the sea <u>was becoming aroused</u> [impf.].* [19]*Therefore, having rowed about 25 or 30 stadia, they see Jesus walking on the sea and coming near the boat, and they **were afraid**.* [20]*But he says to them, It is I! Don't be afraid!* [21]*Then they <u>were willing</u> [impf.] to take him into the boat, and immediately the boat **was** at the land toward which they <u>were going</u> [impf.].*

In this passage the main events of the story are the coming of evening, the disciples going down to the sea, and their fear when they encountered Jesus. Various details of the story are filled in with nonaorist forms, and then the historical present *see* highlights Jesus walking on the water and *says* highlights Jesus's statement, both verbs also adding a sense of vividness.

This example illustrates that the main events of the story are not necessarily the most significant details. The supplementary details may convey key points,

---

periphrasitics in this passage. I have not marked the circumstantial participles since there are other guidelines for their functions in narratives (§5.189b).

as we see here, since Jesus's walking on the sea and his statement are of great significance in this story.

While these tense-forms do not always have such functions in a narrative, it is useful to consider whether a tense-form is used as much for a narrative purpose as for a particular aspect and *Aktionsart*. Keep in mind, however, that words often have more than one usage or nuance at the same time.

The Subjunctive

5.136. Introduction to the Subjunctive

The indicative mood is used for making statements and asking questions, but the subjunctive cannot be summed up as easily. It is often described as having the sense of something as possible, probable, or uncertain rather than definite. Thus it is used for action that is viewed as potential rather than actual. This general idea is applied in a variety of ways and each of these uses has a particular signal that indicates how it is functioning. **It is important to keep in mind that the tense-forms of verbs in the subjunctive refer only to aspect, not time.** Consequently, the aorist subjunctive is often translated with an English present, since the aorist refers to the past primarily in the indicative.

5.137. Purpose (Final)

The conjunctions ἵνα and ὅπως usually introduce a subordinate clause that contains a subjunctive, though occasionally a ἵνα clause uses a future indicative (§5.232). Both conjunctions can introduce a purpose clause, while ἵνα may also introduce other sorts of clauses as well, depending on the context. Purpose clauses indicate the intended outcome of the action in the main clause, whether or not it actually happens.

> Τεκνία μου, ταῦτα γράφω ὑμῖν **ἵνα μὴ ἁμάρτητε**. (1 John 2:1)
> *My little children, these things write I to you, <u>that you may not sin</u>.*
> > ‣ ἁμάρτητε – aor.-subjn.-act.-2-pl. < ἁμαρτάνω. John intends that his message prevent his readers from sinning.

5.138. Result (Consecutive)

A result clause introduced by ἵνα simply says what happened as a result of the action of the main clause whether it was intended or not, in contrast to a purpose clause, which gives the intended result. For result clauses with ὥστε see §5.236.

ῥαββί, τίς ἥμαρτεν, οὗτος ἢ οἱ γονεῖς αὐτοῦ, **ἵνα** τυφλὸς **γεννηθῇ**; (John 9:2)
Rabbi, who sinned, this man, or his parents, <u>that he should be born</u> blind?

> γεννηθῇ – aor.-subjn.-MP-3-sg. < γεννάω. This ἵνα clause clearly expresses result, since the parents would not have intended that their son be born blind.

a. It is sometimes difficult to say whether a ἵνα clause expresses purpose or result, and indeed, in some cases it includes both, especially when God is the subject of the verb.[181]

οὕτως γὰρ ἠγάπησεν ὁ θεὸς τὸν κόσμον, ὥστε τὸν υἱὸν τὸν μονογενῆ ἔδωκεν, **ἵνα** πᾶς ὁ πιστεύων εἰς αὐτὸν μὴ **ἀπόληται** ἀλλ᾽ **ἔχῃ** ζωὴν αἰώνιον. (John 3:16)
For God loved the world so much, with the result <u>that</u> he gave his only begotten Son, that whoever believes in him <u>might not perish</u>, but <u>might have</u> eternal life.

> ἀπόληται – aor.-subjn.-MP-3-sg. < ἀπόλλυμι. ἔχῃ – pres.-subjn.-act.-3-sg. < ἔχω. The subordinate ἵνα clause (*that ... might not perish*) could spell out the purpose of God's giving of his Son or what has actually happened as a consequence of God's giving his Son. Since God is the subject it would be common for both to be in view.[182]

5.139. Strong Negation

The negative particles οὐ and μή can be used together to express a strong negative, stating emphatically that something will not take place. In the New Testament this construction always uses the aorist subjunctive.[183]

Many occurrences of this construction are in quotations from the Old Testament or in sayings of Jesus, so perhaps the authors thought, "inspired language was fitly rendered by words of a peculiarly decisive tone."[184] Accordingly, translations often do not include this nuance since either there does not seem to be any special emphasis or because the emphasis is more subtle than English can convey.

For other forms of double negatives see §5.265.

---

181. "In many cases purpose and result cannot be clearly differentiated, and hence ἵνα is used for the result that follows according to the purpose of the subj. or of God. As in Semitic and Gr-Rom. thought purpose and result are identical in declarations of the divine will." BDAG, s.v. "ἵνα," 3, 477.

182. On taking οὕτως as an intensive see §5.246b n. 266.

183. In CG the aorist and the future are often used and occasionally the present. See Smyth §2755.

184. Moulton, *Prolegomena*, 192.

Ὁ οὐρανὸς καὶ ἡ γῆ παρελεύσεται, οἱ δὲ λόγοι μου **οὐ μὴ παρέλθωσιν.**
(Matt 24:35)
Heaven and earth will pass away, but my words <u>will certainly not pass away</u>.

> ▸ παρέλθωσιν – aor.-subjn.-act.-3-pl. < παρέρχομαι.

τὸν ἐρχόμενον πρὸς ἐμὲ **οὐ μὴ ἐκβάλω** ἔξω (John 6:37)
the one that comes to me <u>I will certainly not reject</u>

> ▸ ἐκβάλω – aor.-subjn.-act.-1-sg. < ἐκβάλλω.

πνεύματι περιπατεῖτε καὶ ἐπιθυμίαν σαρκὸς **οὐ μὴ τελέσητε** (Gal 5:16)
walk by the Spirit and <u>you will certainly not carry out</u> the desire of the flesh

> ▸ τελέσητε – aor.-subjn.-act.-2-pl. < τελέω.

5.140. Hortatory

When the subjunctive occurs in the first person, either singular or plural, it can
express an exhortation or encouragement to join in some activity. A first-person
subjunctive verb is hortatory only if there is no signal for one of the other uses. For
example, in John 6:37 (discussed in §5.139) the presence of οὐ μή signals that the
1-sg. subjunctive ἐκβάλω is not hortatory, but rather part of a strong negation.

> **ἄγωμεν** καὶ ἡμεῖς ἵνα ἀποθάνωμεν μετ᾽ αὐτοῦ (John 11:16)
> <u>*Let us* also *go*</u> with him that we may die with him
>
> > ▸ ἄγωμεν – pres.-subjn.-act.-1-pl. < ἄγω. The apostles have objected to
> > going back to Judea, but Jesus says that is where he is going. So Thomas
> > encourages the band of disciples to go with Jesus and die with him.
> > Thomas is a model of discipleship in John's Gospel, despite today often
> > being referred to as Doubting Thomas! Note also the example of ἵνα
> > with the subjunctive for purpose (§5.137).

> **ἀποθώμεθα** οὖν τὰ ἔργα τοῦ σκότους, **ἐνδυσώμεθα** [δὲ] τὰ ὅπλα τοῦ φωτός.
> (Rom 13:12)
> <u>*Let us put off*</u> the works of darkness, and <u>*let us clothe ourselves with*</u> the armor of light.
>
> > ▸ ἀποθώμεθα – aor.-subjn.-MP-1-pl. < ἀποτίθημι. ἐνδυσώμεθα – aor.-
> > subjn.-MP-1-pl. < ἐνδύω.

5.141. Deliberative

The subjunctive is used in questions that ask for guidance, as one is deliberating
about what to do. It can also be used in rhetorical questions, in which one is
debating with oneself over the right course of action. A variety of translations
are used to express this idea.

ἀπελθόντες **ἀγοράσωμεν** δηναρίων διακοσίων ἄρτους καὶ δώσομεν αὐτοῖς φαγεῖν; (Mark 6:37)
are we to go and buy two hundred denarii worth of bread, and give it to them to eat?

> ἀγοράσωμεν – aor.-subjn.-act.-1-pl. < ἀγοράζω. The question mark at the end of the sentence points us to a deliberative use of the subjunctive. Sometimes, as here, a deliberative question includes the idea of how something is possible.

ἐπιμένωμεν τῇ ἁμαρτίᾳ, ἵνα ἡ χάρις πλεονάσῃ; (Rom 6:1)
Should we continue in sin, that grace may increase?

> ἐπιμένωμεν – pres.-subjn.-act.-1-pl. < ἐπιμένω. This is an example of a rhetorical question concerning what one ought to do. Such questions are not looking for a response, but rather they are a rhetorical device to engage the reader/hearer in a line of thought being developed.

5.142. Indefinite Relative Clauses

Some relative clauses do not refer to a particular person or thing, but to a general class. In English it is the difference between saying "he who" or "she who" and "whoever." The indicative can also be used in indefinite clauses (§5.219).

a. A relative clause can be clearly marked as indefinite by using the subjunctive mood and adding the particle ἄν, or less frequently ἐάν.

[**ὃς** γὰρ **ἐὰν** θέλῃ τὴν ψυχὴν αὐτοῦ σῶσαι] ἀπολέσει αὐτήν (Mark 8:35)
[for whoever wants to save their [his] life] will lose it

> θέλῃ - pres.-subjn.-act.-3-sg. < θέλω.

[Εἰς **ἣν** δ᾽ **ἂν** πόλιν ἢ κώμην εἰσέλθητε] (Matt 10:11)
And into whichever city or village you enter

> Here ἄν is added to ἥν to make the expression indefinite. This relative pronoun ἥν is in the accusative since it is the object of εἰς, which takes an accusative. It is fem.-sg. in agreement with πόλιν and κώμην (*city, village*). We also have a subjunctive verb, εἰσέλθητε – aor.-subjn.-act.-2-pl. < εἰσέρχομαι.

b. Another indefinite relative pronoun, ὅστις, ἥτις, ὅτι (§3.52), usually is used with the indicative, but it can also take the subjunctive.

[**ὅστις** οὖν ταπεινώσει ἑαυτὸν ὡς τὸ παιδίον τοῦτο], οὗτός ἐστιν ὁ μείζων ἐν τῇ βασιλείᾳ τῶν οὐρανῶν. (Matt 18:4)
[Whoever therefore will humble himself as this little child], this one is the greatest in the kingdom of heaven.

[ὅστις δ᾽ ἂν ἀρνήσηταί με ἔμπροσθεν τῶν ἀνθρώπων], ἀρνήσομαι κἀγὼ αὐτὸν ἔμπροσθεν τοῦ πατρός μου τοῦ ἐν [τοῖς] οὐρανοῖς. (Matt 10:33)
[But underline*whoever* denies me before people], I also will deny before my Father who is in heaven.*

> ἀρνήσηται – aor.-subjn.-MP-3-sg. < ἀρνέομαι.

5.143. Indefinite Local and Temporal Clauses

As with the indefinite relative clauses (§5.219) so also in indefinite local and temporal clauses, both the indicative and the subjunctive can be used.

a. The most common form of such clauses is an indefinite temporal clause with a subjunctive and introduced by ὅταν, *whenever*, a combination of ὅτε and ἄν. It can refer to "an action that is conditional, possible, and, in many instances, repeated."[185]

Καὶ **ὅταν προσεύχησθε**, οὐκ ἔσεσθε ὡς οἱ ὑποκριταί (Matt 6:5)
And underline*whenever you pray*, *you shall not be like the hypocrites*

> προσεύχησθε – pres.-subjn.-MP-2-pl. < προσεύχομαι.

b. This construction can also be used for a definite future event. This construction does not mean that the event is indefinite, but that the time it will occur is unknown. "Whenever" doesn't work well for this nuance so it can't always be conveyed in English.

ἐλεύσονται δὲ ἡμέραι, καὶ **ὅταν ἀπαρθῇ** ἀπ᾽ αὐτῶν ὁ νυμφίος, τότε νηστεύσουσιν (Luke 5:35)
but days will come, and underline*when* *the bridegroom* underline*is taken* *from them, then they will fast*

> ἀπαρθῇ- aor.-subjn.-MP-3-sg. < ἀπαίρω.

Ὅταν δὲ **ἔλθῃ** ὁ υἱὸς τοῦ ἀνθρώπου ἐν τῇ δόξῃ αὐτοῦ (Matt 25:31)
But underline*when* *the Son of Man* underline*comes* *in his glory*

> ἔλθῃ - aor.-subjn.-act.-3-sg. < ἔρχομαι.

c. The following verse has both an indefinite local and an indefinite temporal clause. These clauses use local and temporal conjunctions followed by the subjunctive, one with ἄν and the other with ἐάν.

ὅπου ἐὰν εἰσέλθητε εἰς οἰκίαν, ἐκεῖ μένετε **ἕως ἂν ἐξέλθητε** ἐκεῖθεν (Mark 6:10)
underline*wherever you enter* *a house, remain there* underline*until such time as you leave* *from there*

> εἰσέλθητε – aor.-subjn.-act.-2-pl. < εἰσέρχομαι. ἐξέλθητε – aor.-subjn.-act.-2-pl. < ἐξέρχομαι. ὅπου can mean "where" but here in Mark 6:10 with

185. BDAG, s.v. "ὅταν," 1, 730.

ἐάν and the subjunctive it is indefinite. In the second clause most English translations simply have "until" for a smoother translation. While ἕως, "until," usually introduces a simple temporal clause, it also occurs with ἄν when there is uncertainty about when the time will come.

διδάσκαλε, ἀκολουθήσω σοι [**ὅπου ἐὰν** ἀπέρχῃ]. (Matt 8:19)
Teacher, I will follow you [underline]wherever[/underline] you go].
> ἀπέρχῃ - pres.-subjn.-MP-2-sg. < ἀπέρχομαι.

d. As with ὅπου and ἕως, οὖ, *where*, is usually definite, but not always.[186] In the following example the presence of ἐάν and the subjunctive tells us the idea is indefinite.

ἵνα ὑμεῖς με προπέμψητε [**οὖ ἐὰν** πορεύωμαι] (1 Cor 16:6)
so you can send me on my journey, [underline]wherever[/underline] I go]
> πορεύωμαι - pres.-subjn.-MP-1-sg. < πορεύομαι.

5.144. Prohibition

Prohibition is a command or request that an action not be done. It can be expressed by μή with the present imperative (§5.160) or by μή with the aorist subjunctive.

a. A prohibition with an aorist subjunctive is for an action viewed as a whole, with some contexts suggesting the sense of a categorical command.

τὰς ἐντολὰς οἶδας· **μὴ φονεύσῃς, μὴ μοιχεύσῃς, μὴ κλέψῃς, μὴ ψευδομαρτυρήσῃς, μὴ ἀποστερήσῃς** (Mark 10:19)
You know the commandments: [underline]You shall not murder, you shall not commit adultery, you shall not steal, you shall not give false testimony, you shall not defraud[/underline]
> The verbs are aor.-subjn.-act.-2-sg. < φονεύω, μοιχεύω, κλέπτω, ψευδομαρτυρέω, ἀποστερέω. These are examples of categorical commands.

μὴ φοβηθῇς παραλαβεῖν Μαρίαν τὴν γυναῖκά σου (Matt 1:20)
[underline]do not fear[/underline] to take Mary as your wife
> φοβηθῇς - aor.-subjn.-MP-2-sg. < φοβέω.

b. While μή with the present imperative can sometimes have the nuance, "stop" (§5.160), μή with the aorist subjunctive, when the context warrants it, can mean "don't begin."[187] In the example just given from Matthew 1:20 it seems

---

186. This is the gen.-sg. form of the relative pronoun ὅς, ἥ, ὅ, which can function as a relative pronoun, but also as an adverb of place, *where*. This adverbial use of οὖ is usually treated as a distinct word in lexicons.

187. Earlier grammarians sometimes suggested this sense is always present, while

Joseph already has such fear, so this nuance would not fit this context. Most English translations include this nuance in the following example, as brought out in the second translation.

> μὴ ἐγκακήσητε καλοποιοῦντες (2 Thess 3:13)
> *do not be weary* in doing good
> *do not become/grow weary* in doing good
> > ▸ ἐγκακήσητε – aor.-subjn.-act.-2-pl. < ἐγκακέω.

The following verses are also clear examples of prohibiting activity that has not yet begun.

> μὴ ἀδικήσητε τὴν γῆν (Rev 7:3)
> *Do not harm* the earth
> > ▸ ἀδικήσητε – aor.-subjn.-act.-2-pl. < ἀδικέω.

> μηδὲν πράξῃς σεαυτῷ κακόν (Acts 16:28)
> *Do nothing* harmful to yourself
> > ▸ πράξῃς – aor.-subjn.-act.-2-sg. < πράσσω. This aorist subjunctive for prohibition illustrates the use of a different form of μή than the simple form.

5.145. Noun Clause with ἵνα

Along with purpose and result clauses (§§5.137, 138), ἵνα with the subjunctive can also be used for a noun clause, similar to the use of an infinitive for a noun (§§5.167, 168). This construction is often best translated with an infinitive in English.

> ἐμὸν βρῶμά ἐστιν [ἵνα ποιήσω τὸ θέλημα τοῦ πέμψαντός με] (John 4:34)
> *my food is [that I do the will of the one who sent me]*
> *my food is [to do the will of the one who sent me]*
> > ▸ ποιήσω – aor.-subjn.-act.-1-sg. < ποιέω. In this example the ἵνα clause is the subject of ἐστιν.

5.146. Epexegetical (Explanation) Clause with ἵνα

Sometimes a ἵνα clause adds an explanation to a noun, adjective, or verb. An infinitive can also be used this way (§5.170), and in English it is often best to use an infinitive for this sort of ἵνα clause.

---

more recent grammarians rightly note the role of context in conveying such a sense, not just the construction itself. For a nuanced affirmation of this sense see Michael G. Aubrey, "Greek Prohibitions," in *Revisited*, 486–538.

οὐκ εἰμὶ [ἐγὼ] ἄξιος [**ἵνα λύσω** αὐτοῦ τὸν ἱμάντα τοῦ ὑποδήματος] (John 1:27)
I am not worthy to unloose the strap of his sandal
> λύσω – aor.-subjn.-act.-1-sg. < λύω. This ἵνα clause explains the adjective "worthy," though some take it as result.

Ἀβραὰμ ὁ πατὴρ ὑμῶν ἠγαλλιάσατο [**ἵνα ἴδῃ** τὴν ἡμέραν τὴν ἐμήν] (John 8:56)
Abraham your father rejoiced to see my day
> ἴδῃ - aor.-subjn.-act.-3-sg. < ὁράω/εἶδον.[188] This ἵνα clause explains the verb "rejoiced," giving its content or grounds.

5.147. Appositional Clause with οὗτος

A ἵνα clause is sometimes in apposition to a form of οὗτος, αὕτη, τοῦτο earlier in the sentence. Since the ἵνα clause explains the οὗτος, αὕτη, τοῦτο this construction is sometimes labeled epexegetical, but grammatically the ἵνα clause is like a noun in apposition (§2.31). For further discussion of this construction see §5.228.

αὕτη δέ ἐστιν ἡ αἰώνιος ζωὴ **ἵνα** γινώσκωσιν σὲ τὸν μόνον ἀληθινὸν θεὸν καὶ ὃν ἀπέστειλας Ἰησοῦν Χριστόν. (John 17:3)
And this is eternal life, that they may know you, the only true God, and Jesus Christ whom you sent.
> γινώσκωσιν – pres.-subjn.-act.-3-pl. < γινώσκω.

5.148. Content Clause (Indirect Discourse)

A ἵνα clause can provide the content of what is said, felt, thought, intended, and so forth (§5.222). Most indirect commands are expressed with a ἵνα clause or an infinitive (§5.169).

εἰ υἱὸς εἶ τοῦ θεοῦ, εἰπὲ [**ἵνα** οἱ λίθοι οὗτοι ἄρτοι **γένωνται**] (Matt 4:3)
If you are God's son, command these stones that they become loaves of bread
> γένωνται – aor.-subjn.-MP-3-pl. < γίνομαι. ἵνα may give us the content of what he is to say. We could translate more smoothly, *tell these stones to become loaves of bread.*

ὧδε λοιπὸν ζητεῖται ἐν τοῖς οἰκονόμοις, [**ἵνα** πιστός τις **εὑρεθῇ**]. (1 Cor 4:2)
Now, moreover, it is sought in stewards that one be found faithful
> εὑρεθῇ - aor.-subjn.-MP-3-sg. < εὑρίσκω. ἵνα introduces the clause that gives the content of what is sought.

---

188. Lexicons vary over whether the lexical form should be ὁράω or εἶδον. See §§4.75c and appendix 8, nn. b and h.

5.149. Future-More-Likely Condition

This form of condition is discussed in more detail in §5.240.

ἐὰν οὖν ὁ υἱὸς ὑμᾶς **ἐλευθερώσῃ**, ὄντως ἐλεύθεροι ἔσεσθε. (John 8:36)
If then the Son sets you free, you will be really free.

> ἐλευθερώσῃ - aor.-subjn.-act.-3-sg. < ἐλευθερόω. If the Son does this, and it's likely or at least possible that he will, then this is what will happen.

5.150. General Condition

For a more detailed discussion of this condition see §5.242.

ἐὰν **εἴπωμεν** ὅτι οὐχ ἡμαρτήκαμεν, ψεύστην ποιοῦμεν αὐτόν (1 John 1:10)
If we say that we have not sinned, we make him a liar

> εἴπωμεν – aor.-subjn.-act.-1-pl. < λέγω/εἶπον.[189] If we say this, then this is what always happens.

The Optative

5.151. Introduction to the Optative

In CG the optative is used frequently in a variety of ways, but in the Hellenistic period it was being absorbed by the subjunctive. The optative is used 68 times in the New Testament and 638 times in the LXX. In the New Testament it only occurs in the present and aorist, usually in the 3-sg. (§4.90).

a. The basic sense of the optative is often said to be "wish," and that use is actually where this mood gets its name (Latin, *opto, I wish*). But as with the subjunctive, the general sense is not always clear in some of the actual uses. So you should focus on the uses and not worry whether the idea of wish is clear or not. In addition to the two uses listed below, the optative can also occur in a conditional clause (§5.241).

b. As with the subjunctive and the imperative, optative verbs do not refer to time. The present has the durative aspect, viewing the action from within, as in process, and the aorist, with its aoristic aspect, views the action as a whole, whether the action itself is complex or simple.

---

189. Lexicons vary over whether the lexical form should be λέγω or εἶπον. See appendix 8, n. f.

5.152. Wish

The most common use of the optative is to express a wish.

> εἶπεν δὲ Μαριάμ· ἰδοὺ ἡ δούλη κυρίου· **γένοιτό** μοι κατὰ τὸ ῥῆμά σου. (Luke 1:38)
> *And Mary said, "Behold, the servant of the Lord; may it be to me according to your word."*
> ➤ γένοιτο – aor.-opt.-MP-3-sg. < γίνομαι.

> Τί οὖν; ἁμαρτήσωμεν, ὅτι οὐκ ἐσμὲν ὑπὸ νόμον ἀλλ᾽ ὑπὸ χάριν; **μὴ γένοιτο.** (Rom 6:15)
> *What then? Shall we sin because we are not under law but under grace? May it not be!*
> ➤ γένοιτο – aor.-opt.-MP-3-sg. < γίνομαι. The expression μὴ γένοιτο appears fifteen times in the New Testament, all in Paul except Luke 20:16. In Paul it almost always expresses a strong rejection of an idea just stated in a rhetorical question.[190] As such, it could be translated, "No way!" "Absolutely not!"

> ἔλεος ὑμῖν καὶ εἰρήνη καὶ ἀγάπη **πληθυνθείη** (Jude 2)
> *may mercy, peace, and love be multiplied to you*
> ➤ πληθυνθείη – aor.-opt.-MP-3-sg. < πληθύνω. Use of the optative is common in greetings in ancient Greek, though rare in the New Testament.

5.153. Potential

The second most common use of the optative in the New Testament is for what could or might happen or be true. It is frequently found in deliberative questions in which the writer is pondering the meaning of something, the identity of someone, what should be done, and so forth. These are usually indirect questions, but occasionally direct questions (§5.223).

> ἡ δὲ ἐπὶ τῷ λόγῳ διεταράχθη καὶ διελογίζετο ποταπὸς **εἴη** ὁ ἀσπασμὸς οὗτος. (Luke 1:29)
> *But she was greatly troubled at the saying, and was considering what kind of greeting this might be.*
> ➤ εἴη – pres.-opt.-act.-3-sg. < εἰμί. The direct form of Mary's question would be, "What kind of greeting is this?"

---

190. The one exception is Gal 6:14 where Ἐμοὶ δὲ μὴ γένοιτο καυχᾶσθαι can be translated, "May I never boast."

νεύει οὖν τούτῳ Σίμων Πέτρος πυθέσθαι τίς ἂν **εἴη** περὶ οὗ λέγει. (John 13:24)
So Simon Peter gestured to this one to ask Jesus who it <u>might be</u> that he was referring to.

> ▸ εἴη – pres.-opt.-act.-3-sg. < εἰμί. The direct question would be, "To whom are you referring?" Of the twelve uses of εἴη in the New Testament this is the only one outside Luke and Acts.

ὁ δὲ εἶπεν· πῶς γὰρ ἂν **δυναίμην** ἐὰν μή τις ὁδηγήσει με; (Acts 8:31)
And he said, "How in the world <u>can</u> I, unless someone will guide me?"

> ▸ δυναίμην – pres.-opt.-MP-1-sg. < δύναμαι. The translation "how in the world" is a less common use of γάρ.[191]

The Imperative

5.154. Introduction to the Imperative

The imperative is often used for giving a command, but it is also used to express a request, including when addressing God or one who is a superior in some sense. At times it expresses permission or suggestion rather than command.[192] Such nuances must be determined from context, which is not always clear. The imperative shows up primarily in the present and aorist tense-forms (§4.83). Imperatives do not refer to time and the tense-forms have their normal aspectual values (§§2.11, 5.87).

5.155. Two Types of Commands/Requests

An imperative may be used for either a general or a specific command, principle, or request. Both tense-forms can function in these two ways, though the present is used more often for general precepts and requests while the aorist is more often used for specific commands and requests when a particular situation is in view.

a. Present. At times the present includes the idea that the action is to take place on an ongoing basis, but note that this is an *Aktionsart* of the verb, not a part of its aspect, which concerns viewpoint and not the action itself (§§2.11, 5.87–88).

---

191. BDAG, s.v. "γάρ," 1.f, 189: "oft. in questions, where the English idiom leaves the word untransl., adds *then, pray,* or prefixes *what!* or *why!* to the question . . . πῶς γὰρ ἂν δυναίμην; *how in the world can I?* Ac 8:31."

192. "The imperative can express a variety of nuances: peremptory commands, polite requests, suggestions, etc. . . . The Greek imperative is thus not inherently impolite." *CGCG* §34.20. So also *AGG* §212a.

b. Aorist. Similarly, the aorist is often used when commanding or request-ing that an action be started, as opposed to the continuation of an action, as is often the case in the present. As usual, the context must clarify whether this nuance is present.

5.156. Translating the Imperative

The imperative can be translated a number of ways. The following simple trans-lations for the present and the aorist, in the active, the middle, and the passive use of the middle, give a starting point for beginning students.

2-sg.-act./mid.	Loose!	**2-pl.-act./mid.**	Loose!
3-sg.-act./mid.	He/she/it must/should loose!	**3-pl.-act./mid.**	They must/should loose!
2-sg.-pass.	Be loosed!	**2-pl.-pass.**	Be loosed!
3-sg.-pass.	He/she/it must/should be loosed!	**3-pl.-pass.**	They must/should be loosed!

5.157. First-Person and Third-Person Imperatives

a. There are no first-person forms for the imperative in English or in Greek. In Greek the hortatory subjunctive is used for the idea of exhorting oneself or one's group to a certain action, which is similar to a first-person imperative (§5.140).

b. The imperative in English only occurs in the second person, but in Greek it also occurs in the third person (§4.83). This use is often difficult for English speakers to understand. The author is telling one person what another person must or should do. Often the third-person imperative is translated using the word "let."

> *Let him take up his cross.*
> *Let them help the poor.*

At times "let" may sound like one is giving permission or a suggestion, which are possible nuances of an imperative (§5.154). When a particular imperative does not have one of these nuances then sometimes using "must" or "is to/are to" may express the idea better.

> *He must take up his cross. He is to take up his cross.*
> *They must help the poor. They are to help the poor.*

Other translations are possible. For example, the first three petitions in the Lord's Prayer (Matt 6:9–10) are third-person imperatives, "hallowed be [ἁγιασθήτω] your name, your kingdom come [ἐλθέτω], your will be done [γενηθήτω]."

Major Uses of the Imperative

5.158. Command

Most commonly the imperative will express a command.

ἐγὼ δὲ λέγω ὑμῖν· **ἀγαπᾶτε** τοὺς ἐχθροὺς ὑμῶν καὶ **προσεύχεσθε** ὑπὲρ τῶν διωκόντων ὑμᾶς (Matt 5:44)
But I say to you, "Love your enemies, and pray for those who persecute you
> ἀγαπᾶτε – pres.-impv.-act.-2-pl. < ἀγαπάω. προσεύχεσθε – pres.-impv.-MP-2-pl. < προσεύχομαι. Both of these present imperatives express general commands. These 2-pl. forms could be indicatives (§4.84a), but the context points to the imperative mood.

ἐγείρεσθε ἄγωμεν· ἰδοὺ ὁ παραδιδούς με ἤγγικεν. (Mark 14:42)
Rise, let us be going; see, my betrayer is at hand.
> ἐγείρεσθε – pres.-impv.-MP-2-pl. < ἐγείρω. Here we see a present imperative used for a specific command in a particular situation. Again we have a form that could be indicative instead of imperative, but the context clarifies which is intended.

παραστήσατε ἑαυτοὺς τῷ θεῷ ὡσεὶ ἐκ νεκρῶν ζῶντας (Rom 6:13)
present yourselves to God as those who have been brought from death to life
> παραστήσατε – aor.-impv.-act.-2-pl. < παρίστημι. Now we see an aorist imperative used for a general command.

ἐπανάγαγε εἰς τὸ βάθος καὶ **χαλάσατε** τὰ δίκτυα ὑμῶν εἰς ἄγραν (Luke 5:4)
Go out into the deep and let down your nets for a catch
> ἐπανάγαγε – aor.-impv.-act.-2-sg. < ἐπανάγω. χαλάσατε – aor.-impv.-act.-2-pl. < χαλάω. These aorists speak of specific commands in a specific situation. Notice the shift from singular to plural. Jesus addresses Peter as the leader, and then shifts to include Peter's companions as well.

μείνατε ὧδε καὶ **γρηγορεῖτε** (Mark 14:34)
remain here and watch
> μείνατε – aor.-impv.-act.-2-pl. < μένω. γρηγορεῖτε – pres.-impv.-act.-2-pl. < γρηγορέω. The first command in the aorist gives a specific

command for a particular situation and then the second command in the present spells out the on-going activity they are to do as they remain there.

5.159. Request

When addressed to God or to one considered to be a superior the imperative conveys a request. The aorist "is by far the predominant tense form used in prayers to God (or to the gods by pagan Greeks)."[193]

εἴ τι δύνῃ, **βοήθησον** ἡμῖν σπλαγχνισθεὶς ἐφ' ἡμᾶς (Mark 9:22)
if you are able, have compassion on us and <u>help</u> us
> βοήθησον – aor.-impv.-act.-2-sg. < βοηθέω. The participle σπλαγχνισ-θείς is attendant circumstance (§5.201) and thus is also translated as an imperative, "have compassion."

ἁγιασθήτω τὸ ὄνομά σου· **ἐλθέτω** ἡ βασιλεία σου· **γενηθήτω** τὸ θέλημά σου . . . τὸν ἄρτον ἡμῶν τὸν ἐπιούσιον **δὸς** ἡμῖν σήμερον (Matt 6:9–11)
<u>*Hallowed be*</u> *your name; your kingdom <u>come</u>; your will <u>be done</u> . . . <u>give</u> us today our nourishment for life in the kingdom of God*[194]
> ἁγιασθήτω – aor.-impv.-MP-3-sg. < ἁγιάζω. ἐλθέτω – aor.-impv.-act.-3-sg. < ἔρχομαι. γενηθήτω – aor.-impv.-MP-3-sg. < γίνομαι. δός – aor.-impv.-act.-2-sg. < δίδωμι. We have a string of aorist imperatives.

τὸν ἄρτον ἡμῶν τὸν ἐπιούσιον **δίδου** ἡμῖν τὸ καθ' ἡμέραν (Luke 11:3)
<u>*give*</u> *us day by day our nourishment for life in the kingdom of God*
> δίδου – pres.-impv.-act.-2-sg. < δίδωμι. Although the aorist is the preferred tense-form in prayers, Luke's version uses the present, thereby emphasizing that this is something disciples need on an on-going basis. The context clarifies this nuance through the expression *day by day* (τὸ καθ' ἡμέραν).

5.160. Prohibition (Negative Command)

Prohibition is a command that an action not be done.
a. It can be expressed by μή with the aorist subjunctive (§5.144) or by μή with the present imperative. When μή negates a present imperative it often has the

---

193. Baugh, *Tense Form Choice*, 41.
194. This translation takes ἐπιούσιος as meaning "necessary for existence" (BDAG, 376), which refers in this context to life in the kingdom of God.

sense of "do not continue," or "stop." This nuance is not always present, so you need to consider the context.[195]

καὶ **μὴ συσχηματίζεσθε** τῷ αἰῶνι τούτῳ, ἀλλὰ **μεταμορφοῦσθε** τῇ ἀνακαινώσει τοῦ νοός (Rom 12:2)
Do not be conformed to this world, but be transformed by the renewal of your mind

> συσχηματίζεσθε – pres.-impv.-MP-2-pl. < συσχηματίζω. μεταμορφοῦσθε – pres.-impv.-MP-2-pl. < μεταμορφόω. The first clause is a negative command (a prohibition) with μή and the second clause is a positive command. It is possible that the sense is "stop conforming," and instead "be in the process of being transformed."

μὴ κλαίετε, οὐ γὰρ ἀπέθανεν ἀλλὰ καθεύδει (Luke 8:52)
Stop crying, for she is not dead but is sleeping

> μὴ κλαίετε – pres.-impv.-act.-2-pl. < κλαίω. Most English translations have "stop crying" or "stop wailing."

καὶ ἰδὼν αὐτὴν ὁ κύριος ἐσπλαγχνίσθη ἐπ' αὐτῇ καὶ εἶπεν αὐτῇ· **μὴ κλαῖε**. (Luke 7:13)
And when the Lord saw her, he had compassion on her and said to her, "Do not cry."

> μὴ κλαῖε – pres.-impv.-act.-2-sg. < κλαίω. The context suggests the nuance, "do not continue crying."

b. μή occurs in a variety of compounded forms, which can also be used for prohibition.

Μὴ οὖν **βασιλευέτω** ἡ ἁμαρτία ἐν τῷ θνητῷ ὑμῶν σώματι εἰς τὸ ὑπακούειν ταῖς ἐπιθυμίαις αὐτοῦ, **μηδὲ παριστάνετε** τὰ μέλη ὑμῶν ὅπλα ἀδικίας τῇ ἁμαρτίᾳ (Rom 6:12–13)
So do not let sin reign in your moral body so that you obey its desires, and do not present your members to sin as instruments for unrighteousness

> βασιλευέτω – pres.-impv.-act.-3-sg. < βασιλεύω. παριστάνετε – pres.-impv.-act.-2-pl. < παριστάνω. The first verb has the simple μή and the second uses the negative particle μηδέ (*and not, nor*), formed from μή and δέ. Again, the nuance of "do not continue" seems appropriate here.

Τοῦ λοιποῦ κόπους μοι μηδεὶς **παρεχέτω** (Gal 6:17)
From now on let no one inflict troubles on me

---

195. Earlier grammarians sometimes suggested this sense is always present, while more recent grammarians rightly note the role of context in conveying such a sense, not just the construction itself. For a nuanced affirmation of this sense see M. Aubrey, "Greek Prohibitions," 486–538.

> παρεχέτω – pres.-impv.-act.-3-sg. < παρέχω. Instead of a simple μή we have the negative μηδείς (*no one*) functioning as a subject. This word is formed from μή and εἷς, μιά, ἕν (*one*) (app. 4.24).

5.161. Permission

a. Occasionally the meaning of the verb and the context suggest the imperative is expressing permission or consent rather than command.

ὃ θέλει **ποιείτω**, οὐχ ἁμαρτάνει, **γαμείτωσαν** (1 Cor 7:36)
let him do what he wants, he does not sin, let them marry
> ποιείτω – pres.-impv.-act.-3-sg. < ποιέω. γαμείτωσαν – pres.-impv.-act.-3-pl. γαμέω. Paul may say that the person is permitted to get married. A different interpretation is seen in the NIV's, "They should get married." This translation is stronger than permission, but less than an outright command.

b. When an imperative has a passive sense it can have this idea of permission.

σώθητε ἀπὸ τῆς γενεᾶς τῆς σκολιᾶς ταύτης. (Acts 2:40)
Save yourselves from this crooked generation.
> σώθητε – aor.-impv.-MP-2-pl. < σῴζω. We cannot save ourselves, but we can permit it to happen by appeal to the one who can save (§5.91). We could put this more colloquially, "You need to get saved." The imperative is saying what must/should happen.

5.162. Greetings

In greetings the imperative is simply an exclamation. It may be used either at the beginning or the conclusion of the communication.

χαῖρε ὁ βασιλεὺς τῶν Ἰουδαίων (John 19:3)
Hail, king of the Jews!
> χαῖρε – pres.-impv.-act.-2-sg. < χαίρω, *to rejoice*. The soldiers are not commanding Jesus to rejoice! This imperative was commonly used as a simple greeting.

χαῖρε, κεχαριτωμένη, ὁ κύριος μετὰ σοῦ. (Luke 1:28)
Greetings, favored woman, the Lord is with you.
> Here is the same verb we just saw in John 19:3, but now there is division among the translations over whether it is the stereotyped greeting, or an actual encouragement to rejoice.

ἐξ ὧν διατηροῦντες ἑαυτοὺς εὖ πράξετε."Ἑρρωσθε. (Acts 15:29)
from which, guarding yourselves, you will do well. Farewell.

> ἔρρωσθε – pf.-impv.-MP-2-pl. < ῥώννυμι. This greeting is the conclusion of the letter from the Jerusalem council to the gentiles. ῥώννυμι means *be strong*. BDAG explains: "Gr-Rom. [Greco-Roman] letters gener[ally] included at the beginning inquiries about a recipient's health and at the conclusion a wish for the recipient's well-being. The latter formulation was freq[uently] expressed w[ith] the verb ῥ. in the perf. pass. impv. **be in good health, farewell, goodbye.**"[196]

The Infinitive

5.163. Introduction to the Infinitive

The infinitive in both English and Greek is a verbal noun. It shows up primarily in the present, aorist, and perfect, and has the usual verbal aspect for these tense-forms: present is durative, aorist is aoristic, perfect is resultative (§§5.87a–c).[197] At times the article τοῦ is used with the infinitive with no change in meaning.[198]

5.164. Purpose (Final)

The infinitive can signal purpose, that is, the intended outcome of the action in the main clause, whether or not it actually happens.[199] Infinitives have this same adverbial function in English, so these infinitives are relatively easy to understand and translate.

καὶ γὰρ ὁ υἱὸς τοῦ ἀνθρώπου οὐκ ἦλθεν **διακονηθῆναι** ἀλλὰ **διακονῆσαι** καὶ **δοῦναι** τὴν ψυχὴν αὐτοῦ λύτρον ἀντὶ πολλῶν (Mark 10:45)
for even the Son of Man did not come to be served but to serve, and to give his life as a ransom for many

> διακονηθῆναι – aor.-inf.-MP < διακονέω. διακονῆσαι – aor.-inf.-act. < διακονέω. δοῦναι – aor.-inf.-act. < δίδωμι.

---

196. BDAG, s.v., "ῥώννυμι," 908–09. This word occurs only here in the New Testament, though also in some manuscripts at Acts 23:30. Ignatius of Antioch, one of the apostolic fathers writing in the early second century, uses it in his letters.

197. The future ἔσεσθαι (fut.-inf.-MP < εἰμί) shows up four times in the New Testament and εἰσελεύσεσθαι (fut.-inf.-MP < εἰσέρχομαι) once.

198. Infinitives with τοῦ are found primarily for the purpose, result, and epexegetical senses, and with verbs that use a genitive for a complement. *AGG* §225.

199. ἵνα with the subjunctive also serves in this way (§5.137).

Τότε παραγίνεται ὁ Ἰησοῦς ἀπὸ τῆς Γαλιλαίας ἐπὶ τὸν Ἰορδάνην πρὸς τὸν Ἰωάννην **τοῦ βαπτισθῆναι** ὑπ᾽ αὐτοῦ. (Matt 3:13)
Then Jesus came from Galilee to the Jordan to John, to be baptized by him.
> βαπτισθῆναι – aor.-inf.-MP < βαπτίζω. Note the presence of τοῦ.

ἰδοὺ ἐξῆλθεν ὁ σπείρων **τοῦ σπείρειν**. (Matt 13:3)
Check it out! A sower went out to sow.
> σπείρειν – pres.-inf.-act. < σπείρω. In Mark's account a simple infinitive
> is used (Mark 4:3), illustrating the lack of difference in meaning be-
> tween an infinitive with τοῦ and a simple infinitive. For the translation
> "Check it out!" see §5.185 n. 213.

5.165. Result (Consecutive)

The infinitive can signal result, that is, an actual outcome whether intended
or not.[200]

καὶ εἷς ἐκ τῶν πρεσβυτέρων λέγει μοι· μὴ κλαῖε, ἰδοὺ ἐνίκησεν ὁ λέων ὁ ἐκ
τῆς φυλῆς Ἰούδα, ἡ ῥίζα Δαυίδ, **ἀνοῖξαι** τὸ βιβλίον καὶ τὰς ἑπτὰ σφραγῖδας
αὐτοῦ. (Rev 5:5)
*And one of the elders said to me, "Stop weeping! Look, the lion of the tribe of Judah,
the root of David, has conquered and so he can open the scroll and its seven seals."*
> ἀνοῖξαι – aor.-inf.-act. < ἀνοίγω. This is a case where the English infinitive "to
> open" does not work. If we think this infinitive is giving the result of Christ's
> conquering then we have to use an English idiom for result. It is often dif-
> ficult to determine whether an infinitive expresses purpose or result.[201]

ὑμεῖς δὲ ἰδόντες οὐδὲ μετεμελήθητε ὕστερον **τοῦ πιστεῦσαι** αὐτῷ (Matt 21:32)
and having seen it, you did not later repent so as to believe him
> πιστεῦσαι – aor.-inf.-act. < πιστεύω. Purpose is also possible. Note the
> presence of τοῦ.

καὶ ἐθεράπευσεν αὐτόν, ὥστε τὸν κωφὸν **λαλεῖν** καὶ **βλέπειν** (Matt 12:22)
and he healed him, so that the mute person spoke and saw
> Result clauses are often introduced with ὥστε which takes either the
> indicative or infinitive. The construction with an infinitive is a bit com-
> plicated. The accusative τὸν κωφόν serves as the subject of the two
> infinitives, λαλεῖν and βλέπειν. These infinitives are translated with
> finite verbs in English. Since the context is a past event, English idiom
> shifts these infinitives to the past. For more detailed explanation of
> such constructions with an infinitive see §§5.79, 167b, 174.

200. ἵνα with the subjunctive also serves in this way (§5.138).
201. *ExSyn*, 590. See §5.138a for ἵνα clauses that may be purpose, result, or both.

5.166. Complementary

Some verbs need another verb to complete their meaning (Latin, *complere, fill up, complete*). For example, if you hear "they began," you cannot picture this since you don't know what it is they began to do. The complementary use of the infinitive supplies the missing content: "they began to study Greek." This use of the infinitive is very common in both English and Greek.[202]

Ἀπὸ τότε **ἤρξατο** ὁ Ἰησοῦς **κηρύσσειν** καὶ **λέγειν**· μετανοεῖτε (Matt 4:17)
From that time began Jesus to preach and to say, "Repent."
> ἤρξατο – aor.-ind.-MP-3-sg. < ἄρχω. κηρύσσειν – pres.-inf.-act. < κηρύσσω. λέγειν – pres.-inf.-act. < λέγω.

5.167. Subject

a. In English we can use an infinitive as the subject of a sentence, "To study Greek is enjoyable," although the use of a preparatory "it" (§5.96) is smoother: "It is enjoyable to study Greek." In this second sentence "to study" is still the subject of "is." The "it" is a placeholder for the subject so the normal English order can be preserved: subject–verb.

οὐ γάρ ἐστιν καλὸν **λαβεῖν** τὸν ἄρτον τῶν τέκνων καὶ τοῖς κυναρίοις **βαλεῖν** (Mark 7:27)
for it is not right to take the children's bread and to throw it to the dogs
> λαβεῖν – aor.-inf.-act. < λαμβάνω. βαλεῖν – aor.-inf.-act. < βάλλω. Note the use of the preparatory "it." A more wooden translation would be: "To take the children's bread and to throw it to the dogs is not right."

b. δεῖ and ἔξεστιν. Two verbs in particular often have an infinitive for their subject, δεῖ (*it is necessary, one must; it is appropriate, one ought/should*) and ἔξεστιν (*it is permitted/lawful*). These are 3-sg. forms from δέω and ἔξειμι. In the 3-sg. they function as impersonal verbs, that is, they take impersonal subjects, almost always using an infinitive for their subject.

ὁ δὲ εἶπεν πρὸς αὐτοὺς ὅτι καὶ ταῖς ἑτέραις πόλεσιν **εὐαγγελίσασθαί** με **δεῖ** τὴν βασιλείαν τοῦ θεοῦ (Luke 4:43)
But he said to them, "To preach the good news of the kingdom of God in the other towns is necessary with respect to/for me"
> εὐαγγελίσασθαι – aor.-MP-inf. < εὐαγγελίζομαι. This translation is obvi-

202. For detailed discussion of such verb chains with infinitives and participles see Funk, chs. 37–38.

ously very wooden—not what an English speaker would say. We would use the preparatory "it": "It is necessary for me to preach the good news . . ." Here is the core of the Greek clause:

εὐαγγελίσασθαί με δεῖ τὴν βασιλείαν τοῦ θεοῦ

1. This infinitive serves as the subject of the impersonal verb: to preach the good news is necessary. The first accusative, με (*me*) serves as the subject of the infinitive and τὴν βασιλείαν (*the kingdom*) is the direct object of the infinitive, which might be clearer if English had a verb "to gospel." So we would have "to gospel the kingdom of God."[203]

2. For a Greek author the με functions as an "accusative of reference." That is, the accusative can tell us that with reference to which something is true (§5.81). The wooden translation above is in keeping with this idiom, but in English we need to turn this accusative of reference into the subject of the infinitive. Such accusatives are often referred to simply as the subject of the infinitive (§5.79). So if με is the subject we translate it "I" and come up with:

but he said to them, "I must preach the good news of the kingdom of God in the other towns."

δεῖ τὸν υἱὸν τοῦ ἀνθρώπου πολλὰ **παθεῖν** καὶ **ἀποδοκιμασθῆναι** ἀπὸ τῶν πρεσβυτέρων καὶ ἀρχιερέων καὶ γραμματέων καὶ **ἀποκτανθῆναι** καὶ τῇ τρίτῃ ἡμέρᾳ **ἐγερθῆναι**. (Luke 9:22)
It is necessary for the Son of Man <u>to suffer</u> many things and <u>to be rejected</u> by the elders and chief priests and legal scholars and <u>to be killed</u> and on the third day <u>to be raised</u>.

> παθεῖν - aor.-inf.-act. < πάσχω. ἀποδοκιμασθῆναι - aor.-inf.-MP < ἀποδοκιμάζω. ἀποκτανθῆναι - aor.-inf.-MP < ἀποκτείνω. ἐγερθῆναι - aor.-inf.-MP < ἐγείρω. The first accusative, τὸν υἱὸν τοῦ ἀνθρώπου, is the subject of the infinitives, with the second accusative, πολλά, as the object of the first infinitive. We could also translate: "The Son of Man must suffer many things."

μελλήσετε δὲ ἀκούειν πολέμους καὶ ἀκοὰς πολέμων· ὁρᾶτε μὴ θροεῖσθε **δεῖ** γὰρ **γενέσθαι** (Matt 24:6)
And you are about to hear of wars and rumors of wars. See that you are not alarmed, for <u>it is necessary</u> for [these things] <u>to happen</u>

203. Five times in the New Testament the infinitive with δεῖ is εἶναι from the equative verb εἰμί, which takes a subject complement rather than a direct object (§§2.27a; 5.27). When the infinitive is an equative verb one of the accusatives will serve as the subject of the infinitive and the other accusatives its subject complement. For examples, see Luke 2:49, 1 Cor 11:19, 1 Tim 3:2, 2 Tim 2:24, and Titus 1:7.

> γενέσθαι – aor.-inf.-MP < γίνομαι. In this case the accusative of reference is implied in the context. We could render it, "these things must take place."

οὐκ ἔδει καὶ σὲ ἐλεῆσαι τὸν σύνδουλόν σου, ὡς κἀγὼ σὲ ἠλέησα; (Matt 18:33)
Was it not appropriate for you also to have mercy on your fellow servant, as I in fact had mercy on you?

> ἔδει – impf.-ind.-act.-3-sg. < δεῖ. ἐλεῆσαι – aor.-inf.-act. < ἐλεέω. We probably have an example of appropriateness rather than necessity.

ἔξεστιν ἡμᾶς Καίσαρι φόρον δοῦναι ἢ οὔ; (Luke 20:22)
Is it lawful for us to give taxes to Caesar or not?

> δοῦναι – aor.-inf.-act. < δίδωμι. The accusative ἡμᾶς is the subject of the infinitive and the accusative, φόρον, is its object.

5.168. Nominal Uses Other Than as a Subject

As a nominal an infinitive can serve as a direct object, modifier, or object of a preposition (§§5.174–80). In prepositional phrases the infinitive always has an article. In other constructions it may have an article to indicate the case, especially for the genitive and accusative, but otherwise the article makes no apparent difference.

a. Direct Object. The infinitive can serve as a simple direct object. The English infinitive also functions in this same way, so the translation is often easy.

θεὸς γάρ ἐστιν ὁ ἐνεργῶν ἐν ὑμῖν καὶ τὸ θέλειν καὶ τὸ ἐνεργεῖν ὑπὲρ τῆς εὐδοκίας (Phil 2:13)
for God is the one working in you both to will and to work for his good pleasure

> θέλειν – pres.-inf.-act. < θέλω. ἐνεργεῖν – pres.-inf.-act. < ἐνεργέω. These infinitives are the direct object of the working.

b. Epexegetical Genitive. The genitive articular infinitive may be used as an epexegetical genitive to provide an explanation (§§5.42, 146, 170).

c. Dative of Cause. The dative articular infinitive is very rare, with only one example in the New Testament.

οὐκ ἔσχηκα ἄνεσιν τῷ πνεύματί μου τῷ μὴ εὑρεῖν με Τίτον τὸν ἀδελφόν μου (2 Cor 2:13)
I did not have rest in my spirit because I did not find Titus my brother

> εὑρεῖν – aor.-inf.-act. < εὑρίσκω. This infinitive functions as a dative of cause (§5.71). The subject of the infinitive is the accusative με.

5.169. Content Clause (Indirect Discourse)

An infinitive can be used with verbs of speaking, writing, thinking, feeling, and other such activities to provide the content, just like a ὅτι clause (§5.222a). Since this construction is not limited to verbs of communication, the label "indirect discourse" can be confusing. We find, "He <u>said</u> that he would study Greek," but also, for example, "she <u>thought</u> that she would study Greek," "they <u>believed</u> that they should study Greek."

a. Grammatically, such an infinitive is the direct object of the verb.[204] While sometimes we can use an infinitive in English for this construction, often that does not work. So we must translate with an English idiom, using "that" and changing the infinitive to a finite verb, though including a "that" is often unnecessary.

When the subject of the infinitive is not the same as that of the main verb it will be in the accusative (§5.79). A few verbs in English can take such a construction. For example, instead of saying "I think (that) **he** <u>is</u> fortunate," we could say, "I consider **him** <u>to be</u> fortunate." This construction is rare in English, but very common in Greek.

> ἐγὼ ἐμαυτὸν οὐ λογίζομαι **κατειληφέναι** (Phil 3:13)
> *I do not consider myself <u>to have secured</u> this*
> > ▸ κατειληφέναι – pf.-inf.-act. < καταλαμβάνω. The infinitive gives us the content of what Paul did not consider. As just noted, with the verb "consider" we can use an infinitive for the Greek infinitive, and note how "myself" corresponds to the accusative ἐμαυτόν. Another way to translate this would be, "I do not consider that I myself have secured this."

> ὁ οὖν ὄχλος ὁ ἑστὼς καὶ ἀκούσας ἔλεγεν **βροντὴν γεγονέναι** (John 12:29)
> *So the crowd that stood there and heard it was saying <u>that it thundered</u>*
> > ▸ γεγονέναι – pf.-inf.-act. < γίνομαι. The verb ἔλεγεν (*he/she was saying*) indicates we have reported speech. The content clause is βροντὴν γεγονέναι, very woodenly, "to have happened with respect to thunder." In this example an infinitive does not work in English. We can use "that" to introduce this indirect discourse, though in this case it is optional. Since the accusative βροντὴν functions like the subject of the infinitive we could translate, "that thunder happened," but this is still not good English. Using the preparatory "it" (§5.96) gives us a smooth translation in English, such as that given above.

> Τί τὸ ὄφελος, ἀδελφοί μου, ἐὰν **πίστιν** λέγῃ τις **ἔχειν** (Jas 2:14)
> *What is the profit, my brothers and sisters, if someone says <u>that they have faith</u>*

---

204. Accordingly, this use could be included as a subsection of the previous section on the substantival use of the infinitive (§5.168). See *Deeper*, 371–72.

> ἔχειν – pres.-inf.-act. < ἔχω. The verb of communication λέγῃ is followed by an infinitive. In this case the subject of the infinitive is the same as the main verb, and the accusative, πίστιν, is the direct object of the infinitive.

Εἶπεν δὲ πρὸς αὐτούς· πῶς λέγουσιν **τὸν χριστὸν εἶναι Δαυὶδ υἱόν;** (Luke 20:41)
And he said to them, "How are they saying that the Christ is David's Son?"
> εἶναι – pres.-inf.-act. < εἰμί. Since εἰμί is an equative verb it takes a nominative for its subject and its complement. So in this construction there is an accusative for both the subject (χριστόν) and the complement (υἱόν). When translating we add "that" and change the infinitive into a finite form of the same verb, "is."

ἀναστὰς δὲ εἷς ἐξ αὐτῶν ὀνόματι Ἄγαβος ἐσήμανεν διὰ τοῦ πνεύματος λιμὸν μεγάλην **μέλλειν ἔσεσθαι** ἐφ᾽ ὅλην τὴν οἰκουμένην, ἥτις ἐγένετο ἐπὶ Κλαυδίου. (Acts 11:28)
And standing up, one of them, named Agabus, signified through the Spirit that there is going to be a great famine over all the world, which took place in the days of Claudius.
> ἐσήμανεν – aor.-ind.-act.-3-sg. < σημαίνω. μέλλειν – pres.-inf.-act. < μέλλω. ἔσεσθαι – fut.-inf.-MP < εἰμί. The first infinitive, μέλλειν, signals the content of the main verb, ἐσήμανεν, which refers to communication. μέλλω, *be about to*, often takes a complementary infinitive to refer to the future. In CG the future infinitive was usually used as here, but in KG the present and aorist infinitives are much more common.

b. Indirect commands are often expressed by the infinitive after verbs of command, exhortation, request, and so forth.[205]

Παρακαλῶ οὖν ὑμᾶς . . . **παραστῆσαι** τὰ σώματα ὑμῶν θυσίαν ζῶσαν (Rom 12:1)
So I encourage you . . . to offer your bodies as a living sacrifice
> παραστῆσαι – aor.-inf.-act. < παρίστημι. Offering is what Paul is encouraging them to do; that is the content of his encouragement. This is another example in which the infinitive works in English. The accusative τὰ σώματα is the direct object of the infinitive.

5.170. Epexegetical (Explanation)

Like a ἵνα clause (§5.146), an infinitive can add material that explains or unpacks a noun, pronoun, adjective, or verb.

---

205. The other common form for indirect command/request is with a ἵνα clause (§§5.148, 225).

a. Noun.

ἔδωκεν αὐτοῖς <u>ἐξουσίαν</u> [τέκνα θεοῦ **γενέσθαι**] (John 1:12)
*he gave to them <u>power</u> [**to become** children of God]*

> ▸ γενέσθαι – aor.-inf.-MP< γίνομαι. The infinitive explains what sort of ἐξουσία (*power, authority*) John has in mind.

ἐπλήσθη ὁ χρόνος **τοῦ τεκεῖν** αὐτήν (Luke 1:57)
the time <u>of her giving birth</u> was fulfilled

> ▸ τεκεῖν – aor.-inf.-act. < τίκτω. The infinitive explains which time is referred to. The accusative αὐτήν gives us the subject of the infinitive. Woodenly, "the time of the giving birth with reference to her." Note the presence of τοῦ, which does not affect the meaning (§5.163).

βραδεῖς τῇ καρδίᾳ **τοῦ πιστεύειν** (Luke 24:25)
slow of heart <u>to believe</u>

> ▸ πιστεύειν – pres.-inf.-act. < πιστεύω. The infinitive describes the nature of the slowness of heart. We have another example of the presence of τοῦ.

b. Pronoun.

Σίμων, ἔχω σοί <u>τι</u> **εἰπεῖν**. (Luke 7:40)
*Simon, I have <u>something</u> [**to say** to you].*

> ▸ εἰπεῖν – aor.-inf.-act. < λέγω/εἶπον.[206] The infinitive develops the pronoun τι, *something*.

c. Adjective.

οὐκ εἰμὶ <u>ἱκανός</u> . . . [**λῦσαι** τὸν ἱμάντα τῶν ὑποδημάτων αὐτοῦ] (Mark 1:7)
*I am not <u>fit</u> [**to unloosen** the strap of his sandals]*

> ▸ λῦσαι – aor.-inf.-act. < λύω. The infinitive unpacks the adjective ἱκανός (*sufficient, fit*). In John's version of this story a ἵνα clause is used instead of the infinitive (John 1:27).

d. Verb.

τί <u>πειράζετε</u> τὸν θεὸν [**ἐπιθεῖναι** ζυγὸν ἐπὶ τὸν τράχηλον τῶν μαθητῶν] (Acts 15:10)
*why <u>are you testing</u> God [**by placing** a yoke upon the neck of the disciples]*

> ▸ ἐπιθεῖναι – aor.-inf.-act. < ἐπιτίθημι. The infinitive explains the testing that Peter has in mind.

---

206. Lexicons vary over whether the lexical form should be λέγω or εἶπον. See appendix 8, n. f.

5.171. Appositional Clause with οὗτος

An infinitive is sometimes in apposition to a form of οὗτος, αὕτη, τοῦτο earlier in the sentence. Since the infinitive explains the οὗτος, αὕτη, τοῦτο this construction is sometimes labeled epexegetical, but grammatically it is like a noun in apposition (§2.31). For further discussion of this construction see §5.228.

> θρησκεία καθαρὰ καὶ ἀμίαντος παρὰ τῷ θεῷ καὶ πατρὶ **αὕτη** ἐστίν, **ἐπισκέ-πτεσθαι** ὀρφανοὺς καὶ χήρας ἐν τῇ θλίψει αὐτῶν, ἄσπιλον ἑαυτὸν **τηρεῖν** ἀπὸ τοῦ κόσμου. (Jas 1:27)
> *Pure religion and undefiled before our God and Father is <u>this</u>, <u>to visit</u> orphans and widows in their affliction, and <u>to keep</u> oneself unspotted by the world.*
> > ▸ ἐπισκέπτεσθαι – pres.-inf.-MP < ἐπισκέπτομαι. τηρεῖν – pres.-inf.-act. < τηρέω.

5.172. Imperatival

Occasionally the infinitive can be used as an imperative, serving as the main verb in the clause.

> **χαίρειν** μετὰ χαιρόντων, **κλαίειν** μετὰ κλαιόντων. (Rom 12:15)
> <u>*Rejoice*</u> *with those rejoicing,* <u>*weep*</u> *with those weeping.*
> > ▸ χαίρειν – pres.-inf.-act. < χαίρω. κλαίειν – pres.-inf.-act. < κλαίω.

5.173. Absolute

The infinitive can be "absolute," that is, used without syntactical connections to the rest of the sentence. It occurs this way in stereotyped greetings.

> Κλαύδιος Λυσίας τῷ κρατίστῳ ἡγεμόνι Φήλικι **χαίρειν**. (Acts 23:26)
> *Claudius Lysias to the most excellent governor Felix,* <u>*greetings*</u>.
> > ▸ χαίρειν – pres.-inf.-act. < χαίρω.

5.174. Prepositional Phrases

The infinitive is frequently used as the object of a preposition. This construction is a challenge for English speakers since infinitives do not work this way in English. Instead of translating with a prepositional phrase we have to translate the construction as a clause with a subject, a finite verb, and perhaps other modifiers.

a. From a Greek point of view, what we take as the subject (§5.79) is simply an accusative of reference (§5.81). If the subject is the same as that of the main verb, it is left unstated.

b. Since the meaning of a preposition is related to the case used with it, the infinitive has a definite article to indicate its case.

c. So the infinitive is translated as a finite verb and the accusative of reference is translated as its subject. Here is an example from Luke's version of the parable of the sower.

καὶ ἐν τῷ σπείρειν αὐτὸν ὃ μὲν ἔπεσεν παρὰ τὴν ὁδόν (Luke 8:5)
And <u>as he was sowing</u> some fell along the path

> σπείρειν – pres.-inf.-act. < σπείρω. ἔπεσεν – aor.-ind.-act.-3-sg. < πίπτω.

The infinitive τῷ σπείρειν, *sow*, is a verbal noun, but we wouldn't say "the to sow." Instead we could translate it "the sowing." To see how this construction works in Greek we could say, "in the sowing with reference to him." To translate in smoother English we change the infinitive to a finite verb and the accusative to its subject, "he was sowing." In such constructions ἐν means "in" in the sense of time contemporaneous with the main verb, so we can add "while" or "as." We end up with, "while/as he was sowing." The past progressive is used because the main verb in this sentence, ἔπεσεν, is in the past, which sets the time frame. The infinitive is in the present tense-form, which has a durative aspect (§§5.87a, 97), and, in this case, the progressive *Aktionsart* (§5.98).[207]

d. As you first work with this challenging construction simply learn that a prepositional phrase with an articular infinitive will have to be translated with a finite verb and will have an accusative for its subject. As you become more familiar with Greek you won't have to mentally change this construction to fit English, but simply pick up the meaning as it is conveyed in the Greek of these very interesting forms of prepositional phrases.

5.175. Prepositional Phrases for Time: πρίν, πρὸ τοῦ; ἐν τῷ; μετὰ τό

The preposition points to a time either before, during, or after the action of the main verb. The preposition ἐν points to the present situation in the text, but with two possible nuances. With a present infinitive it will have a progressive sense, "while," and with the aorist a global sense, "when" or "at."[208]

before	–	πρίν, πρὸ τοῦ
while, when	–	ἐν τῷ
after	–	μετὰ τό

---

207. Outside the indicative tense-forms do not usually have time significance, only aspect (§§2.11; 5.87).

208. Von Siebenthal suggests the aorist can even have the sense "after," but his example from Luke 11:37 is not clear, as he himself notes. *AGG* §226.

κύριε, κατάβηθι [**πρὶν ἀποθανεῖν** τὸ παιδίον μου]. (John 4:49)
Lord, come down [before my child dies].
> ἀποθανεῖν – aor.-inf.-act. < ἀποθνήσκω.

ἐπιθυμίᾳ ἐπεθύμησα τοῦτο τὸ πάσχα φαγεῖν μεθ᾽ ὑμῶν [**πρὸ τοῦ με παθεῖν**]
(Luke 22:15)
with desire I have desired to eat this Passover with you [before I suffer]
> παθεῖν – aor.-inf.-act. < πάσχω.

[**ἐν** δὲ **τῷ καθεύδειν** τοὺς ἀνθρώπους] ἦλθεν αὐτοῦ ὁ ἐχθρός (Matt 13:25)
but [while folks were sleeping] his enemy came
> καθεύδειν – pres.-inf.-act. < καθεύδω.

καὶ [**ἐν τῷ εἰσαγαγεῖν** τοὺς γονεῖς τὸ παιδίον Ἰησοῦν] . . . αὐτὸς ἐδέξατο αὐτὸ
εἰς τὰς ἀγκάλας (Luke 2:27–28)
*and [when the parents brought in the child Jesus] . . . he [Symeon] took him into
his arms*
> εἰσαγαγεῖν – aor.-inf.-act. < εἰσάγω. The aorist points to the present sit-
> uation, but not to unfolding action, as the present would. Here the aor-
> ist with ἐν has the sense, "at the bringing in of the child by the parents."

[**Μετὰ** δὲ **τὸ παραδοθῆναι** τὸν Ἰωάννην] ἦλθεν ὁ Ἰησοῦς εἰς τὴν Γαλιλαίαν
(Mark 1:14)
And [after John was arrested] Jesus came into Galilee
παραδοθῆναι – aor.-inf.-MP < παραδίδωμι.

5.176. Prepositional Phrase for Cause: διὰ τό

οὐκ ἔχετε [**διὰ τὸ μὴ αἰτεῖσθαι** ὑμᾶς] (Jas 4:2)
you do not have [because you do not ask]
> αἰτεῖσθαι – pres.-inf.-MP< αἰτέω.

εἶπεν παραβολὴν [**διὰ τὸ** ἐγγὺς **εἶναι** Ἰερουσαλὴμ αὐτὸν καὶ **δοκεῖν** αὐτοὺς] ὅτι
παραχρῆμα μέλλει ἡ βασιλεία τοῦ θεοῦ ἀναφαίνεσθαι. (Luke 19:11)
*He told a parable because he was near Jerusalem and they supposed that the kingdom
of God was going to appear immediately.*
> εἶναι – pres.-inf.-act. < εἰμί. δοκεῖν – pres.-inf.-act. < δοκέω. Both of
> these infinitives are part of the prepositional phrase with διά. The final
> infinitive, ἀναφαίνεσθαι, is complementary to μέλλει (§5.166).

5.177. Prepositional Phrases for Purpose: πρὸς τό, εἰς τό

ἐνδύσασθε τὴν πανοπλίαν τοῦ θεοῦ [**πρὸς τὸ δύνασθαι** ὑμᾶς **στῆναι**] (Eph 6:11)
put on the whole armor of God [so that you may be able to stand]

> δύνασθαι – pres.-inf.-MP< δύναμαι. στῆναι – aor.-inf.-act. < ἵστημι. Note that the second infinitive, στῆναι (*stand*), is complementary (§5.166) to δύνασθαι (*be able*).

καὶ ὁ υἱὸς τοῦ ἀνθρώπου παραδίδοται [**εἰς τὸ σταυρωθῆναι**] (Matt 26:2)
and the Son of Man is handed over [to be crucified]

> σταυρωθῆναι – aor.-inf.-MP < σταυρόω. The accusative subject of the infinitive ("he") is not given. It is not unusual to have to supply the subject from the context, though in this case using a simple infinitive works. A translation that brings out this Greek construction would include the subject: "and the Son of Man is handed over in order that he be crucified."

5.178. Prepositional Phrases for Result: πρὸς τό, εἰς τό

οὐχὶ ἡ συνείδησις αὐτοῦ ἀσθενοῦς ὄντος οἰκοδομηθήσεται [**εἰς τὸ** τὰ εἰδω-λόθυτα **ἐσθίειν**]; (1 Cor 8:10)
will not his conscience, being weak, be strengthened [so that he eats things sacrificed to idols]?

> ἐσθίειν – pres.-inf.-act. < ἐσθίω. We have another example of the accusative subject of the infinitive ("he") being left out. Most English translations use a simple infinitive, something like "will not his conscience, being weak, be strengthened to eat things sacrificed to idols?"

5.179. Prepositional Phrase for Content: εἰς τό

Ἐρωτῶμεν δὲ ὑμᾶς ... [**εἰς τὸ μὴ** ταχέως **σαλευθῆναι** ὑμᾶς] (2 Thess 2:1–2)
And I ask you ... [that you not be quickly shaken]

> σαλευθῆναι – aor.-inf.-MP < σαλεύω. The prepositional phrase indicates what Paul asks.

5.180. Prepositional Phrase for Explanation (Epexegetical): εἰς τό

ἔστω δὲ πᾶς ἄνθρωπος ταχὺς [**εἰς τὸ ἀκοῦσαι**] (Jas 1:19)
Let every person be quick [to listen]

> ἀκοῦσαι – aor.-inf.-act. < ἀκούω. The prepositional phrase explains what James means by "quick."

The Participle

5.181. Introduction to the Participle

The participle occurs frequently in Greek texts (6658× in the New Testament), and it has superpowers! Here is a brief overview of its various uses, compared to English.

a. A participle in English is a **verbal adjective**, and this is one of its usages in Greek as well. (*The singing bird flew away*.)

b. In English another "ing" form, called a gerund, functions as a **noun**. (*Singing is fun*.) The Greek participle can also serve in this way, known as the **substantival** use. Even when a participle functions as an adjective or a noun it is still a verbal form, which means it has verbal aspect and it can take a direct object and various modifiers like any other verb.

c. Third, English uses an "ing" word along with a form of "to be" for expressions such as progressives: *"we are singing," "we were singing."* In such expressions the form of "to be" functions as an auxiliary verb. Greek has a similar use of εἰμί and the participle, called a **periphrastic** construction.

d. Fourth, some verbs in English and Greek use a participle to **complete their meaning**, for example the verb "to begin." (*They began singing*.)[209]

e. And finally, the most frequent use of the participle is the **circumstantial** participle (also called an **adverbial** participle). Here it functions like an adverbial clause, that is, a subordinate clause to supply additional information about the main clause. *"After singing for an hour we took a break."* In this English sentence "singing" is a gerund (a verbal noun) functioning as the object of the preposition "after." But in Greek "after singing" can be expressed with a circumstantial participle, without a preposition. This example also shows us a participle taking a modifier, since "singing" is modified by the prepositional phrase, "for an hour." Such participles tell us more about the circumstances of the main clause, in this case, when we took a break. In Greek, participles can indicate not only when something happens, but also why or how it happens.

5.182. Aspect and Time in Participles

a. The participle shows up primarily in the present, aorist, and perfect, and has the usual verbal aspect for these tense-forms (§5.87): the present is durative (action or a state viewed from within, as in process), the aorist is aoristic (action or a state undefined, viewed as a whole), and the perfect is resultative (a present state/condition or set of currently relevant effects resulting from completed action).[210] It is often impossible to convey the nuance of the participle's aspect in English.

---

209. The infinitive has this same use (*"They began to sing,"* §5.166).
210. There is also a future participle, which occurs thirteen times in the New Testament (§4.114; app. 4.76–78).

b. As with other nonindicatives, the tense-forms of participles do not in themselves express time. Nevertheless, they often situate the action or state described by the participle in relation to that of the main verb. The following are the general patterns that usually occur.

The **present** – action/event/state at the same time as that of the main verb
The **future** – action/ event/state in the future relative to that of the main verb
The **aorist** – action/ event/state prior to that of the main verb
The **perfect** – action/ event/state completed at the time of the main verb

So, for example, if the main verb is in the past, then a present participle can refer to past time contemporaneous with the main verb ("while ___ing"), and an aorist participle to action or a state prior to the main verb ("after ___ing"). Thus, if we have a simple clause like "Jesus came into the city," we can add a circumstantial participle, "teaching." In Greek, if this participle is in the present it will normally refer to action or a state at the same time as the action of the main verb (§5.191),

Present participle – <u>While teaching</u>, *Jesus came into the city*.
Aorist participle – <u>After teaching</u>, *Jesus came into the city*.

Note, however, that the meaning of the verb and the context are key signals of time, not the tense-form of the participle by itself. Pay special attention to how this tricky issue is handled in the examples in the following sections.[211]

5.183. Participles Used as Adjectives and Nouns

When a participle has an article it will function as an adjective or noun. If it does not have an article it can still function in this way, or it may function in one of the other ways discussed below.

5.184. Adjectival

When a participle is used adjectivally it will most often agree in gender, case, and number with a noun in the same clause. It may be used as either an attributive or a predicate (§§5.3–5).

a. Attributive. When the participle describes an attribute of a noun it will usually be translated with a relative clause.

---

211. See Baugh, *Tense Form Choice*, ch. 5.

Σαῦλος δὲ μᾶλλον ἐνεδυναμοῦτο καὶ συνέχυννεν [τοὺς] Ἰουδαίους **τοὺς κατ-οικοῦντας** ἐν Δαμασκῷ συμβιβάζων ὅτι οὗτός ἐστιν ὁ χριστός. (Acts 9:22)
But Saul increased all the more in strength, and confounded the Jews <u>who were dwell-ing</u> in Damascus by proving that Jesus was the Christ.

> ▸ συνέχυννεν – impf.-ind.-act.-3-sg. < συγχύννω/συγχέω.[212] κατοικοῦν-τας – pres.-ptc.-act.-masc.-acc.-pl. < κατοικέω. This participle is in the same gender, case, and number as the noun τοὺς Ἰουδαίους (*the Jews*) and so this participle is used as an adjective to describe this noun. Note that this participle is itself modified by the prepositional phrase ἐν Δαμασκῷ (*in Damascus*). κατοικοῦντας is in the present tense-form but translated in the past since the context, including the impf.-ind. συν-έχυννεν (*he confounded*), sets the time frame in the past.

οὐδεὶς δύναται ἐλθεῖν πρός με ἐὰν μὴ ὁ πατὴρ **ὁ πέμψας** με ἑλκύσῃ αὐτόν (John 6:44)
No one can come to me unless the Father <u>who sent</u> me draws that person

> ▸ πέμψας – aor.-ptc.-act.-masc.-nom.-sg. < πέμπω, *to send*. This participle is in the same gender, case, and number as the noun ὁ πατήρ (*the Fa-ther*) and so this participle is used as an adjective to modify this noun. Note that ὁ πέμψας has a direct object, με (*me*). Because πέμψας is in the aorist the aspect is aoristic, the action is viewed as a whole. The meaning of this verb and the context indicate the sending was in the past, so a past translation is appropriate.

οἱ δὲ διάκονοι ᾔδεισαν **οἱ ἠντληκότες** τὸ ὕδωρ (John 2:9)
though the servants <u>who had drawn </u>the water knew

> ▸ ἠντληκότες – pf.-ptc.-act.-masc.-nom.-pl. < ἀντλέω. ἠντληκότες is in the same gender, case, and number as the noun οἱ διάκονοι (*the servants*), and so this participle is used as an adjective to modify this noun. Note that this participle has a direct object, τὸ ὕδωρ (*the water*). The participle by itself has the resultative aspect so it refers to servants "who are in a state of having drawn" the water. Since the context points to past time the participle should be translated with an appropriate form of past tense.

b. Predicate. The predicate use of the participle may function as a predicate adjective in a subject complement, or it may modify a noun by making an as-sertion about it as a complement.

τεθλιμμένη ἡ ὁδὸς ἡ ἀπάγουσα εἰς τὴν ζωήν (Matt 7:14)
<u>*Compressed*</u> *is the way that leads to life*

> ▸ τεθλιμμένη – pf.-ptc.-MP-fem.-nom.-sg. < θλίβω. This participle is the subject complement in a predicate position with the equative verb

212. This verb shows up in two forms.

elided (§5.5). This clause also includes a participle used as an attributive adjective, ἡ ὁδὸς **ἡ ἀπάγουσα**, *the way* <u>that leads</u>.

Οὐδὲν δὲ **συγκεκαλυμμένον** ἐστὶν ὃ οὐκ ἀποκαλυφθήσεται καὶ κρυπτὸν ὃ οὐ γνωσθήσεται. (Luke 12:2)
And nothing is <u>concealed</u> that will not be revealed and hidden that will not be known.
> συγκεκαλυμμένον – pf.-ptc.-MP-neut.-nom.-sg. < συγκαλύπτω. Here the participle is a predicate adjective, forming the subject complement, with ἐστίν present. It is parallel with the predicate adjective κρυπτόν in the next clause. Alternatively, συγκεκαλυμμένον ἐστίν may form a perfect periphrastic (§5.188), *nothing has been concealed*.

θεωροῦσιν τὸν Ἰησοῦν **περιπατοῦντα** ἐπὶ τῆς θαλάσσης (John 6:19)
They saw Jesus <u>walking</u> upon the lake
> περιπατοῦντα – pres.-ptc.-act.-masc.-acc.-sg. < περιπατέω. This participle is not attributive, "the walking Jesus," but rather as a complement it makes an assertion about Jesus, that he was walking. Often it is difficult to distinguish this predicate use of the participle from the circumstantial use. In this case the participle is probably not circumstantial, since the focus seems to be more on the simple fact that he was walking (§5.189g).

5.185. Substantival (Noun)

When a participle is used substantively, that is, as a noun substitute, it will usually be translated with a noun or with a relative clause beginning "he who," "she who," "the one who," "they who," "those which" and so forth. Many grammars view this as a particular use of the adjectival participle, since all adjectives can be used as nouns as well.

ἰδοὺ[213] ἐξῆλθεν **ὁ σπείρων** σπεῖραι. (Mark 4:3)
Check it out! A <u>sower</u> went out to sow.
> σπείρων – pres.-ptc.-act.-masc.-nom.-sg. < σπείρω. The article with the participle σπείρων indicates it functions as a noun or adjective. Since there is no noun in agreement with it, it is the noun. It is nominative since it is the subject of ἐξῆλθεν (*he went out*). The durative aspect of the

---

213. This word is an imperative, but it became a set form for an exclamation, with an acute accent instead of the normal circumflex. Danker comments: "In communities accustomed to oral communication, ἰδού would serve to nuance a narrative reduced to writing, especially to focus on exceptional moments in the narrative. Translators and typographers use a variety of devices, apart from a one-word gloss, to capture the signifying versatility of this particle." *CGEL*, 173–74. Often it seems similar to our colloquial "check it out" or "get this."

present tense-form means the action is viewed from within as it is in process, like the word "sower," which refers to one engaged in an activity.

ἔφερον πρὸς αὐτὸν πάντας **τοὺς** κακῶς **ἔχοντας** καὶ **τοὺς δαιμονιζομένους** (Mark 1:32)
they brought to him all who were sick and those possessed by demons

> ἔφερον – impf.-ind.-act.-3-pl. < φέρω. ἔχοντας – pres.-ptc.-act.-masc.-acc.-pl. < ἔχω. δαιμονιζομένους – pres.-ptc.-MP-masc.-acc.-pl. < δαιμονίζομαι. The phrase τοὺς κακῶς ἔχοντας is literally, "those who have (it) badly/ill," a common idiom for being sick. Both of these substantival participles are direct objects of the main verb ἔφερον (*they brought*). The adjective πάντας modifies both participles. Notice that both participles are translated in the past, taking their time reference from the impf.-ind. ἔφερον.

καὶ προσεύχεσθε ὑπὲρ **τῶν διωκόντων** ὑμᾶς (Matt 5:44)
pray for those who persecute you

> διωκόντων – pres.-ptc.-act.-masc.-gen.-pl. < διώκω. This substantival participle is the object of the preposition ὑπέρ (*for, on behalf of*). The present tense-form views the action as in process—the context must determine whether or not it is going on at the present time.

αὐτοὶ γὰρ ἀγρυπνοῦσιν ὑπὲρ τῶν ψυχῶν ὑμῶν ὡς λόγον **ἀποδώσοντες** (Heb 13:17)
for they are keeping watch over your souls as those who will give an account

> ἀποδώσοντες – fut.-ptc.-act.-masc.-nom.-pl. < ἀποδίδωμι. There is no article but the context clarifies the usage as a noun.

5.186. Complementary Participles

Some verbs in both English and Greek use a participle to complete their meaning (Latin, *complere, fill up, complete*), similar to the complementary infinitive (§5.166).[214] Such participles, sometimes referred to as **supplementary** participles, are essential to the sentence as a part of the verb.

Complementary infinitive   – *They began to sing.*
Complementary participle   – *They began singing.*

Notice in the following examples that the participle is always in the nominative, and it will be either singular or plural to match the main verb. Such participles never have a definite article with them.

214. For detailed discussion of such verb chains with infinitives and participles see Funk, chs. 37–38.

Ὡς δὲ **ἐπαύσατο λαλῶν**, εἶπεν πρὸς τὸν Σίμωνα (Luke 5:4)
And when he <u>finished speaking</u>, he said to Simon
  > ἐπαύσατο – aor.-ind.-MP-3-sg. < παύω. λαλῶν – pres.-ptc.-act.-masc.-nom.-sg. < λαλέω.

καὶ **ἐπαύσαντο οἰκοδομοῦντες** τὴν πόλιν καὶ τὸν πύργον (Gen 11:8)
and they <u>stopped building</u> the city and the tower
  > ἐπαύσαντο – aor.-ind.-MP-3-pl. < παύω. οἰκοδομοῦντες – pres.-ptc.-act.-masc.-nom.-pl. < οἰκοδομέω.

ὡς δὲ **ἐπέμενον ἐρωτῶντες** αὐτόν, ἀνέκυψεν καὶ εἶπεν αὐτοῖς· ὁ ἀναμάρτητος ὑμῶν πρῶτος ἐπ᾽ αὐτὴν βαλέτω λίθον. (John 8:7)
And when they <u>continued asking</u> him, he straightened up and said to them, "The sinless one among you is to cast the first stone at her."
  > ἐπέμενον – impf.-ind.-act.-3-pl. < ἐπιμένω. ἐρωτῶντες – pres.-ptc.-act.-masc.-nom.-pl. < ἐρωτάω.

5.187. Periphrastic Use of the Participle

In this construction an auxiliary verb and a participle combine to form a verb tense.[215] This construction is common in Greek and even more so in English, since English has fewer verb forms to work with.[216] For example, the Greek imperfect indicative tense-form refers to past progressive action and English has to use the auxiliary verb "to be" with a participle for this tense. So for the Greek imperfect ἔλυον English has "they were loosing." Such periphrastic participles usually serve as the main verb of a clause and are thus part of the core of the clause.

5.188. List of Periphrastic Constructions

The common auxiliary in Greek is εἰμί. In the following list notice how the tense-forms of εἰμί and the participle work together to form the tense-form of the periphrastic construction.

εἰμί +	Participle =	Tense-Form	Example	Translation
present	present	present	ἐστὶν λύων	*he/she/it is loosing*
			εἰσὶν λύοντες	*they are loosing*

215. An auxiliary verb contributes to the grammar of the verb, for example, its tense-form, not to its lexical content. Such verbs are also referred to as helping words.
216. "To be" is the most common auxiliary verb in English, but many others are employed to indicate not only tense but also mood and voice. Among the most common are: have, do, shall, will, should, would, can, could, might, may, and must.

εἰμί +	Participle =	Tense-Form	Example	Translation
present	perfect	perfect	ἐστὶν λελύκως	*he/she/it has loosed*
			εἰσὶν λελυκότες	*they have loosed*
imperfect	present	imperfect	ἦν λύων	*he/she/it was loosing*
			ἦσαν λύοντες	*they were loosing*
imperfect	perfect	pluperfect	ἦν λελύκως	*he/she/it had loosed*
			ἦσαν λελυκότες	*they had loosed*
future	present	future	ἔσται λύων	*he/she/it will loose*
			ἔσονται λύοντες	*they will loose*
future	perfect	future perfect	ἔσται λελύκως	*he/she/it will have loosed*
			ἔσονται λελυκότες	*they will have loosed*

a. The participle is always in the nominative, and it will be singular or plural to match the form of εἰμί. Such participles never have a definite article with them.

b. These examples are all in the third-person, but periphrastics can occur in any person.

c. The auxiliary εἰμί is sometimes separated from the participle by one or more words.

d. Use of a periphrastic for the present, future, and future perfect is rare.[217]

e. The use of a periphrastic construction for a nonindicative mood is possible, but rare.

ἦν γὰρ **διδάσκων** αὐτοὺς ὡς ἐξουσίαν ἔχων καὶ οὐχ ὡς οἱ γραμματεῖς (Mark 1:22)
for he <u>was teaching</u> them as having authority and not as the scribes
> διδάσκων – pres.-ptc.-act.-masc.-nom.-sg. < διδάσκω.
> ἦν ... διδάσκων = impf. of εἰμί + pres. ptc. = imperfect.

ἔσεσθε γὰρ εἰς ἀέρα **λαλοῦντες**. (1 Cor 14:9)
for you <u>will be speaking</u> into the air.
> λαλοῦντες – pres.-ptc.-act.-masc.-nom.-pl. < λαλέω.
> ἔσεσθε ... λαλοῦντες = fut. of εἰμί + pres. ptc. = future.

Καὶ ἦλθεν εἰς Ναζαρά, οὗ **ἦν τεθραμμένος** (Luke 4:16)
And he came to Nazareth, where he <u>had been brought up</u>
> τεθραμμένος – pf.-ptc.-MP-masc.-nom.-sg. < τρέφω.
> ἦν τεθραμμένος = impf. of εἰμί + pf. ptc. = pluperfect.

217. All but once in the New Testament the future perfect is a periphrastic (Matt 16:19; 18:18; Luke 12:52; Heb 2:13). Apart from a variant reading in Luke 19:40, the only other instance occurs in Heb 8:11: εἰδήσουσιν < οἶδα. Since οἶδα itself is a perfect tense-form that always functions as a present, εἰδήσουσιν is usually parsed as a future.

5.189. Circumstantial (Adverbial) Use of the Participle

a. The circumstantial is the most frequent use of the participle. It forms an adverbial clause that supplies additional information about the action or point of discussion in a main clause. Using circumstantial participles clarifies what is primary and what is secondary. The fact that the information in the main verb is primary does not mean that the action/point made by the participle is unimportant.[218]

b. Circumstantial participles that come before the main verb usually provide context for the action/point conveyed by the main verb, while participles that come after the main verb usually add elaboration by explaining or developing the main action/point.[219] Thus, whereas participles coming before the main verb simply add background information, those that come after modify the main verbal action/point.[220]

c. Unlike the complementary and periphrastic participles, the circumstantials are not grammatically essential to the sentence. "The circumstantial participle may be removed and the sentence will not bleed."[221]

d. The clause modified by the circumstantial is usually the main clause of a sentence, but at times it is a subordinate clause.

e. The participle must agree with its subject in gender, case, and number and will most often be in the nominative since the additional information is usually about the action of the subject of the main clause. Occasionally, however, the gender, number, and case will indicate the participle refers to someone or something other than the subject.

f. A circumstantial participle never has a definite article with it.

g. To illustrate, we could say "Jesus spoke to the people." If we wanted to add more information about the circumstances of his teaching we could add a subordinate clause to mention when he taught, "while he was coming into the city." In Greek this subordinate clause could be expressed with a conjunction and a finite verb, just as here in English, or it could be expressed several other ways, including with a circumstantial participle:

> ὁ Ἰησοῦς εἶπεν τοῖς ἀνθρώποις **ἐρχόμενος** εἰς τὴν πόλιν.
> *Jesus spoke to the people <u>coming</u> into the city.*

In this literal English translation it looks like the participle is saying that the people are entering the city. But in Greek the nom.-sg. ending on ἐρχόμε<u>νος</u> shows us that the participle is telling us more about Jesus's activity, not that of the people. If we change the participle to agree with τοῖς ἀνθρώποις we would have:

---

218. *DiscGram*, 253, and throughout ch. 12 on these participles.

219. For placement before the main verb, see *DiscGram*, 208–10, 243–62; for placement after the main verb, see Levinsohn, *Discourse*, 183–86; *DiscGram*, 262–68.

220. *DiscGram*, 262.

221. Robertson, *Grammar*, 1124.

ὁ Ἰησοῦς εἶπεν τοῖς ἀνθρώποις **ἐρχομένοις** εἰς τὴν πόλιν.

Now the participle is telling us about the people. It could be used adjectivally, describing the people (§5.184a):

Jesus spoke to the people <u>who were coming</u> into the city.

Or it could be used as a predicate for a simple assertion about the people (§5.184b):

Jesus spoke to the people <u>coming</u> into the city.

Or it could be circumstantial:

Jesus spoke to the people <u>while they were coming</u> into the city.

h. It is very common for the present tense-form to refer to action at the same time as the main verb, as in the example just examined, and the aorist to action prior to the action of the main verb (§5.182). For some circumstantial participles the temporal is the primary nuance, while for others the temporal may be present, but secondary.

5.190. Eight Possible Nuances of the Circumstantial Participle

There are eight adverbial relations a circumstantial participle may imply, though note carefully that the participle in itself is not conveying these nuances.

a. The most important clues for identifying the type of information conveyed are, as usual, the meaning of the verb and the context.

b. To express one of these eight uses of a circumstantial participle we can translate it as a finite verb in a subordinate clause. Usually there are several ways of conveying the idea in English. Some of the translations I give below are overly literal to help you see the function of the participle. **Note, however, that a simple "___-ing" form is closer to the sense of the participle, and often provides a good translation.** After all, there are clear and unambiguous ways of expressing each of these eight types of clauses that the author could have used. Using participles makes the communication more streamlined and easier to follow, but it also means "the relationship between the clauses is no longer specified."[222]

c. Frequently more than one nuance is possible. Indeed, at times more than one nuance may be present or no particular nuance.

---

222. Randall Buth, "Participles as Pragmatic Choice: Where Semantics Meets Pragmatics," in Runge and Fresch, *Revisited*, 289.

5.191. Time

In our example above we saw a present participle telling us what went on at the same time as Jesus spoke to the people, namely, he was entering the city. This is an example of the participle taking its time reference from the main verb. As noted above (§5.182), if a participle expresses time it is usually time relative to the time of the main verb.

The **present**	–	action at the same time as that of the main verb
The **future**	–	action in the future relative to that of the main verb
The **aorist**	–	action prior to that of the main verb
The **perfect**	–	action completed at the time of the main verb

While these nuances are common, there are exceptions, so we need to pay attention to the meaning of the verb and the context. The present and aorist are the most common forms of participles, so you should focus on them at the outset.

a. Present.

Προσευχόμενοι δὲ μὴ βατταλογήσητε ὥσπερ οἱ ἐθνικοί (Matt 6:7)
And when/while you are praying do not babble on like the gentiles
> Προσευχόμενοι – pres.-ptc.-MP-masc.-nom.-pl. < προσεύχομαι.

b. Aorist.

καὶ **νηστεύσας** ἡμέρας τεσσεράκοντα καὶ νύκτας τεσσεράκοντα ὕστερον ἐπείνασεν. (Matt 4:2)
And after fasting forty days and forty nights afterward he was hungry.
> νηστεύσας – aor.-ptc.-act.-masc.-nom.-sg. < νηστεύω.

c. Future.

ὃς ἐληλύθει **προσκυνήσων** εἰς Ἰερουσαλήμ (Acts 8:27)
who had come to Jerusalem to worship
> προσκυνήσων – fut.-ptc.-act.-masc.-nom.-sg. < προσκυνέω. A future circumstantial participle may convey purpose.[223]

d. Perfect.

ἠγαλλιάσατο πανοικεὶ **πεπιστευκὼς** τῷ θεῷ (Acts 16:34)
he rejoiced with his whole household, having believed in God

---

223. In CG the future participle is often used to signal purpose. Of the thirteen uses of the future participle in the New Testament, only four signify purpose (Acts 8:27; 22:5; 24:11, 17).

> ‣ πεπιστευκώς – pf.-ptc.-act.-masc.-nom.-sg. < πιστεύω. The translation "having" is often also used for an aorist circumstantial participle. The perfect, however, usually includes the sense not only of a prior action, like the aorist, but of a prior action that has produced a certain state.

Note this further example from John 20:6–7:

Then Simon Peter came, following him, and went into the tomb. He saw the linen wrappings lying there, and the cloth that had been on Jesus' head, not lying with the linen wrappings but rolled up in a place by itself (NRSV).

ἀλλὰ χωρὶς **ἐντετυλιγμένον** εἰς ἕνα τόπον
but _rolled up_ in a place by itself

This perfect middle/passive participle ἐντετυλιγμένον is usually translated "rolled up," pointing to its present state, not "having been rolled up," which is more of a reference to the past action. These two senses of the perfect participle correspond to its two emphases in general (§5.115).

e. Sometimes the meaning of the verb and context suggest a temporal nuance but the nuance is not tied to the main verb in the usual way. As always, the meaning of the verb and the context must be taken into account.

οὐ γὰρ ἄδικος ὁ θεὸς ἐπιλαθέσθαι τοῦ ἔργου ὑμῶν καὶ τῆς ἀγάπης ἧς ἐνεδείξασθε εἰς τὸ ὄνομα αὐτοῦ, **διακονήσαντες** τοῖς ἁγίοις καὶ **διακονοῦντες**. (Heb 6:10)
For God is not unjust to forget your work and the love that you showed toward his name, _having served_ the saints and _continuing to serve_ them.

> ‣ διακονήσαντες – aor.-ptc.-act.-masc.-nom.-pl. < διακονέω. διακονοῦντες – pres.-ptc.-act.-masc.-nom.-pl. < διακονέω. The aorist participle, διακονήσαντες (*having served*), has its common reference to action prior to the main verb ἐνεδείξασθε (*you showed*). But here the present participle, διακονοῦντες, is not action which is contemporaneous with the main verb in the past, but rather continuing action in the present.

5.192. Cause

ἐχάρησαν οὖν οἱ μαθηταὶ **ἰδόντες** τὸν κύριον. (John 20:20)
So the disciples rejoiced _because they saw_ the Lord.

> ‣ ἰδόντες – aor.-ptc.-act.-masc.-nom.-pl. < ὁράω. Notice the common nuance of antecedent action in this aorist participle. First they see and then they rejoice. Indeed, the most common translation is, "when they saw the Lord." This is an example of more than one nuance being possible, or even present (§5.190c).

5.193. Condition

πῶς ἡμεῖς ἐκφευξόμεθα τηλικαύτης **ἀμελήσαντες** σωτηρίας (Heb 2:3)
how shall we escape if we neglect so great a salvation

> ἀμελήσαντες – aor.-ptc.-act.-masc.-nom.-pl. < ἀμελέω.

5.194. Concession

ἓν οἶδα ὅτι τυφλὸς **ὢν** ἄρτι βλέπω (John 9:25)
one thing I know, that although I was blind, now I see

> ὢν – pres.-ptc.-act.-masc.-nom.-sg. < εἰμί. Concession indicates some-
> thing despite which something else happens or is true.

5.195. Means/Instrument

τίς δὲ ἐξ ὑμῶν **μεριμνῶν** δύναται προσθεῖναι ἐπὶ τὴν ἡλικίαν αὐτοῦ πῆχυν
ἕνα; (Matt 6:27)
and which of you by worrying is able to add to his stature a single cubit?

> μεριμνῶν – pres.-ptc.-act.-masc.-nom.-sg. < μεριμνάω.

5.196. Manner

καὶ ἕτερα πολλὰ **βλασφημοῦντες** ἔλεγον εἰς αὐτόν. (Luke 22:65)
And they were saying many other things against him slanderously.

> βλασφημοῦντες – pres.-ptc.-act.-masc.-nom.-pl. < βλασφημέω. A par-
> ticiple for manner often functions like an adverb, though here "blas-
> phemingly" would be awkward.

5.197. Purpose

αἵτινες ἠκολούθησαν τῷ Ἰησοῦ ἀπὸ τῆς Γαλιλαίας **διακονοῦσαι** αὐτῷ
(Matt 27:55)
who followed Jesus from Galilee in order to serve him

> διακονοῦσαι – pres.-ptc.-act.-fem.-nom.-pl. < διακονέω. The reference
> is to the women who followed Jesus so the participle is in the feminine,
> since participles agree in number and gender with the subject. The
> subject is the pronoun αἵτινες – fem.-nom.-pl. < ὅστις, ἥτις, ὅτι, *whoever,*
> *whatever; who, which* (§3.52).

ἀπέστειλεν αὐτὸν **εὐλογοῦντα** ὑμᾶς (Acts 3:26)
he sent him to bless you

> εὐλογοῦντα – pres.-ptc.-act.-masc.-acc.-sg. < εὐλογέω. This example illustrates a circumstantial participle whose subject is not the subject of the main verb. The accusative direct object of ἀπέστειλεν, αὐτόν, is the subject of this accusative circumstantial participle.

5.198. Result

ἵνα μὴ κάμητε ταῖς ψυχαῖς ὑμῶν **ἐκλυόμενοι** (Heb 12:3)
so that you not grow weary in your souls <u>with the result that you give up</u>

> ἐκλυόμενοι – pres.-ptc.-MP-masc.-nom.-pl. < ἐκλύω.

5.199. Determining the Nuance of a Circumstantial Participle

It is often hard to determine which nuance a participle conveys, if any. Several of the examples just given could be under a different category.

a. To sort out the possible nuances of a circumstantial participle simply try out each of the eight possibilities to see which of them make sense given the meaning of the verb and the context. The following example refers to the coming of ὁ παράκλητος, the Paraclete, as John at times refers to the Holy Spirit.

Καὶ **ἐλθὼν** ἐκεῖνος ἐλέγξει τὸν κόσμον (John 16:8)

Temporal	–	*after coming that one will convict the world*[224]
Cause	–	*because he comes that one will convict the world*
Condition	–	*if he comes that one will convict the world*
Concession	–	*although coming that one will convict the world*
Means	–	*by coming he will convict the world*
Manner	–	*in a coming sort of way that one will convict the world*
Purpose	–	*in order to come that one will convict the world*
Result	–	*as a result of coming that one will convict the world*

b. This exercise provides a set of possible nuances. To determine which is likely you need to study the passage for clues. At times more than one viable option fits the context and the author's thought in general.

c. While exegesis attempts to find the one correct nuance, when meditating on a passage you may find it helpful to work with any or all of the viable options. Thus, when reflecting on a circumstantial participle you might try to eliminate

---

224. If the participle had been in the present it would be: *while coming that one will convict the world.*

the interpretations that would not fit with the thought of the document and with Scripture as a whole, and then reflect on the nuances of all the options that are left (§2.27d).[225]

5.200. Genitive Absolute

a. The genitive absolute is a special form of the circumstantial participle. It adds information about the circumstances of the action of the main verb as a circumstantial participle does, but now the additional information is not something further done by or affirmed about the subject of the main verb. The subject of this additional action or state is put in the genitive and the action or state is expressed with a genitive participle. Let's unpack this intriguing construction in slow motion.

Compare these two sentences.

> ὁ Ἰησοῦς εἶπεν τοῖς ἀνθρώποις **ἐρχόμενος** εἰς τὴν πόλιν.
> *Jesus spoke to the people while he was coming into the city.*

Here we have a simple main clause telling us what Jesus did, which is modified by a circumstantial participle telling us what else Jesus did.

> *Jesus entered the city while the people were coming to him.*

In this second sentence the participle does not add more information about what the subject of the main verb, Jesus, was doing, but what someone else did. In other words, this sentence includes the action of two different characters, Jesus and the people. "Jesus entered" is our main clause, and "while the people were coming to Him" is a subordinate temporal clause. The genitive absolute is a common way to say this second clause in Greek.

> ὁ Ἰησοῦς εἰσῆλθεν εἰς τὴν πόλιν [ἐρχομένων τῶν ἀνθρώπων πρὸς αὐτόν].
> *Jesus entered the city [while the people were coming to him].*

In this genitive absolute the participle is in the genitive (ἐρχομένων) and so is the noun that functions as the subject of the genitive participle (τῶν ἀνθρώπων).

b. A participle in a genitive absolute never has an article with it, but it may have modifiers, as here with the prepositional phrase πρὸς αὐτόν.[226] Usually the gen-

---

225. On meditation/reflection see further *UEBG*, ch. 6.
226. When the participle is an equative verb both the subject and the subject complement are in the genitive. ὀψίας ἤδη **οὔσης** τῆς ὥρας, *the hour already being late* (Mark 11:11).

itive noun/pronoun and participle are grammatically unconnected to the other clauses of the sentence, which is why this construction is called "absolute."

c. So the signs of the genitive absolute are:

a genitive noun or pronoun + a genitive participle – unconnected to other clauses.

d. There are times in KG, however, when the subject of the genitive absolute is in fact referred to in the main clause. For example:

> Ταῦτα **αὐτοῦ** λαλοῦντος πολλοὶ ἐπίστευσαν εἰς <u>αὐτόν</u>. (John 8:30)
> *While <u>he</u> was saying these things, many believed in **him**.*

Genitive absolute	–	Ταῦτα	<u>αὐτοῦ</u>	λαλοῦντος
		dir. obj.	subj.	gen. ptc.
Main clause	–	πολλοὶ	ἐπίστευσαν	εἰς <u>αὐτόν</u>
		subj.	main verb	prep. phrase

The subject of the genitive absolute (αὐτοῦ) is a person that is also referred to in the main clause (αὐτόν), in this case as the object of the preposition. This is still a genitive absolute, even though it is improper in form since it is connected to the main clause.

e. Genitive absolutes are frequently temporal, as in this translation, but they can have any of the eight nuances possible in a circumstantial participle.[227]

Temporal	–	*While he was saying these things, many believed in Him.*[228]
Cause	–	*Because he was saying these things, many believed in Him.*
Condition	–	*If he was saying these things, many believed in Him.*
Concession	–	*Although he was saying these things, many believed in Him.*
Means	–	*By his saying these things, many believed in Him.*
Manner	–	*In a saying these things sort of way, many believed in Him.*
Purpose	–	*In order for him to be saying these things, many believed in Him.*
Result	–	*As a result of his saying these things, many believed in Him.*

In this case the temporal, causal, and result interpretations sound like good

---

227. Wallace says genitive absolutes are temporal "about 90% of the time," and then regarding the other nuances he cites Robertson, *Grammar*, 1130: "All the varieties of the circumstantial participle can appear in the absolute participle." *ExSyn*, 655. *BNTSyn*, 284 includes these points but without the quotation from Robertson.

228. If the participle had been in the aorist it would be: *After he said these things, many believed in him.*

possibilities, while several do not, and some, like manner, make no sense at all. In exegesis we would then see which of these viable options are supported by the context.

f. These examples illustrate the fact that the genitive absolute is translated into English as a subordinate clause, with the genitive noun/pronoun as the subject and the participle as a finite verb.

Here are a few more examples, with brackets around the genitive absolutes.

> ἤδη δὲ [**αὐτοῦ καταβαίνοντος**] οἱ δοῦλοι αὐτοῦ ὑπήντησαν αὐτῷ (John 4:51)
> *And now, <u>while he was going down,</u> his servants met him*
> ‣ καταβαίνοντος – pres.-ptc.-act.-masc.-gen.-sg. < καταβαίνω. This is another example of an element in the genitive absolute (in this case, the subject) also showing up in the main clause: αὐτοῦ ... αὐτοῦ ... αὐτῷ (*he ... his ... him*) all refer to the same person.

> [**Συνηγμένων** δὲ **τῶν Φαρισαίων**] ἐπηρώτησεν αὐτοὺς ὁ Ἰησοῦς (Matt 22:41)
> *Now <u>since the Pharisees were gathered together,</u> Jesus asked them*
> ‣ συνηγμένων – pf.-ptc.-MP-masc.-gen.-pl. < συνάγω. Most translations take this as temporal (*while*), but it could perhaps also make sense in context as causal.

> ἐγὼ δὲ ἔζων χωρὶς νόμου ποτέ, [**ἐλθούσης** δὲ **τῆς ἐντολῆς**] ἡ ἁμαρτία ἀνέζησεν (Rom 7:9)
> *And I was alive apart from the law at one time, but <u>when the commandment came</u> sin came to life again*
> ‣ ἐλθούσης – aor.-ptc.-act.-fem.-gen.-sg. < ἔρχομαι. The genitive noun (ἐντολῆς, *commandment*) is a feminine so the participle will also be in the feminine genitive. Causal also makes sense, but the context focuses on a sequence of events, so temporal is probably a better choice.

5.201. Attendant Circumstance

a. In this use the participle refers to an action that is parallel to the main verb. It shares in the mood of the main verb and is translated as such, with "and" added. For example, if the main verb is an imperative then the participle will also serve as an imperative and be translated that way. When the main verb is in the indicative a simple "-ing" form sometimes works fine.

> [**ἐγερθεὶς**] παράλαβε τὸ παιδίον (Matt 2:20)
> <u>*Get up and*</u> *take the child*
> ‣ ἐγερθείς – aor.-ptc.-MP-masc.-nom.-sg. < ἐγείρω. παράλαβε – aor.-impv.-act.-2-sg. < παραλαμβάνω.

καὶ αὐτὸς ἐδίδασκεν ἐν ταῖς συναγωγαῖς αὐτῶν

And he was teaching in their synagogues

[δοξαζόμενος ὑπὸ πάντων].
(Luke 4:15)

and was glorified by all.

being glorified by all.

> ἐδίδασκεν – impf.-ind.-act.-3-sg. < διδάσκω. δοξαζόμενος – pres.-ptc.-MP-masc.-nom.-sg. < δοξάζω.

b. Translating the participle as a finite verb gives the impression in English that the participle conveys information of equal importance to that of the main verb, but this is not the case.[229] The string of participles at the end of Matthew's Gospel illustrates this point.

[**πορευθέντες**] οὖν   μαθητεύσατε πάντα τὰ ἔθνη,

Therefore go and

Therefore going,   make disciples of all nations

> πορευθέντες – aor.-ptc.-MP-masc.-nom.-pl. < πορεύω.

[**βαπτίζοντες**   αὐτοὺς εἰς τὸ ὄνομα τοῦ πατρὸς καὶ τοῦ υἱοῦ καὶ τοῦ ἁγίου πνεύματος],

and baptize

baptizing   them in the name of the Father and the Son and the Holy Spirit,

> βαπτίζοντες – pres.-ptc.-act.-masc.-nom.-pl. < βαπτίζω.

[**διδάσκοντες**   αὐτοὺς τηρεῖν πάντα ὅσα ἐνετειλάμην ὑμῖν] (Matt 28:19–20a)

and teach

teaching   them to observe everything that I have commanded you

> διδάσκοντες – pres.-ptc.-act.-masc.-nom.-pl. < διδάσκω.

Most English translations take πορευθέντες, *going*, as an attendant circumstance participle sharing the imperative mood of the main verb, μαθητεύσατε, *disciple, make a disciple*. This makes both ideas of equal importance, but by using the participle the text indicates the main focus is on μαθητεύσατε. "The participle backgrounds the action of going, relegating it to a supportive role and thereby keeping attention focused on the main action of the sentence."[230]

229. Young, *Intermediate*, 158; *Deeper*, 336; especially *DiscGram*, 263–68.
230. *DiscGram*, 251.

Note, however, that such grammatically subordinate material may refer to key points in the passage (§5.135). The two participles that follow μαθητεύσατε could also be taken as attendant circumstance and thus translated as imperatives. But only a few translations do so, and, indeed, these participles seem to function like regular circumstantial participles, elaborating what the main verb means. Thus, "These clauses practically describe what is meant by 'make disciples.'"[231]

c. Since an attendant circumstance participle has the same elements as a circumstantial participle, it is a matter of interpretation whether a given participle is attendant circumstance or circumstantial. As usual, the meaning of the verb and context are the main clues, and not all cases will be clear.

5.202. Pleonastic

Pleonastic means "unnecessary" (πλείων, *more*). Most often this construction involves the verb ἀποκρίνω, *answer, respond*, in the aorist second middle/passive indicative or participle. Here is a typical example:

> **ἀποκριθεὶς** δὲ ὁ Ἰησοῦς εἶπεν (Matt 3:15)
> *And <u>answering</u> Jesus said*
> > ▸ ἀποκριθείς – aor.-ptc.-MP-masc.-nom.-sg. < ἀποκρίνω.

a. Here Jesus is answering a question by John the Baptist. But often this construction shows up when there was no question asked nor even an earlier statement. For example, here is part of the story of the transfiguration:

> ⁴καὶ ὤφθη αὐτοῖς Ἠλίας σὺν Μωϋσεῖ καὶ ἦσαν συλλαλοῦντες τῷ Ἰησοῦ. ⁵καὶ **ἀποκριθεὶς** ὁ Πέτρος λέγει τῷ Ἰησοῦ· ῥαββί, καλόν ἐστιν ἡμᾶς ὧδε εἶναι, καὶ ποιήσωμεν τρεῖς σκηνάς, σοὶ μίαν καὶ Μωϋσεῖ μίαν καὶ Ἠλίᾳ μίαν. ⁶οὐ γὰρ ᾔδει τί **ἀποκριθῇ**, ἔκφοβοι γὰρ ἐγένοντο. (Mark 9:4–6)

> ⁴*And Elijah appeared to them with Moses, and they were talking with Jesus.* ⁵*And <u>answering</u> [ἀποκριθείς], Peter said to Jesus, "Rabbi, it is good that we are here and we should make three tents, one for you and one for Moses and one for Elijah."* ⁶*For he did not know what <u>to answer</u> [ἀποκριθῇ], for they were terrified.*

Neither use of ἀποκρίνω in this passage, the participle in 9:5 nor the subjunctive in 9:6, mean "answer." Here it is closer to "respond." Most English translations leave out ἀποκριθείς in 9:5, viewing it as redundant, and translate 9:6, "he did not know what to say."

b. So why did authors use ἀποκριθείς in this way? Basically, it signals that what follows is a response to what has proceeded. The translation "answering" thus can give the wrong impression in English, as if there had been a question.

---

231. *DiscGram*, 252.

The main function of the pleonastic participle is to call attention to a statement that follows, often signaling that direct discourse is coming. This construction is often used when there is a change in speaker or a speaker to about to make "an authoritative pronouncement."[232]

5.203. Content (Indirect Discourse)

After verbs referring to communication, thought, feeling, and perception the content of what is said, heard, felt, and so forth can be expressed several ways (§5.222), including by a participle. In such expressions the participle will be in the accusative case and its subject will be a noun or pronoun in the accusative as well. It is translated as a subordinate clause, usually beginning with "that," and the participle translated as a finite verb.

> ἀκούω [τὰ ἐμὰ τέκνα ἐν ἀληθείᾳ περιπατοῦντα] (3 John 4)
> *I hear that my children are walking in truth*
> > ▸ περιπατοῦντα – pres.-ptc.-act.-neut.-acc.-pl. < περιπατέω. The accusative τὰ τέκνα is the subject of this content clause expressed by the participle.

> ὃς οὐ γινώσκει [τὴν Ἐφεσίων πόλιν νεωκόρον οὖσαν τῆς μεγάλης Ἀρτέμιδος] (Acts 19:35)
> *who does not know that the city of the Ephesians is the temple guardian of the great Artemis*
> > ▸ οὖσαν – pres.-ptc.-act.-fem.-acc.-sg. < εἰμί, *to be*. The accusative τὴν πόλιν (*the city*) is the subject. Normally a form of εἰμί will have a nominative subject and a nominative for the complement (§§2.27a; 5.26c, 27). But in this participle construction the subject is in the accusative, so the complement is also in the accusative, νεωκόρον (*temple guardian*).

5.204. Independent Participle

Occasionally the participle can function as a finite verb, serving as the main verb of a clause.
a. Indicative.

> οὐ μόνον δέ, ἀλλὰ καὶ **καυχώμενοι** ἐν τῷ θεῷ (Rom 5:11)
> *Not only this, but also we boast in God*
> > ▸ καυχώμενοι – pres.-ptc.-MP-masc.-nom.-pl. < καυχάομαι.

---

232. Levinsohn, *Discourse*, 231, cited in *DiscGram*, 150. This use of ἀποκριθείς is frequent in the LXX.

b. Imperative.

Οἱ οἰκέται **ὑποτασσόμενοι** ἐν παντὶ φόβῳ τοῖς δεσπόταις (1 Pet 2:18)
Servants, <u>submit yourselves</u> in all reverence to your masters
> ὑποτασσόμενοι – pres.-ptc.-MP-masc.-nom.-pl. < ὑποτάσσω. If we take
> this form as having a passive sense we would translate: "Servants, be
> submitted."

5.205. Identifying Participle Use

Work down this section to identify how a participle is functioning.
1. Does the participle have a definite article?

YES The participle is used either substantively (like a noun) or adjectivally.
Is there a noun near the participle in agreement with the participle?

    YES The participle is functioning as an adjective modifying that noun.

    NO The participle is functioning as a noun, so determine its case and
use in the sentence (e.g., nominative, subject; genitive, possession;
dative, indirect object; accusative, direct object; and so forth).

NO If the participle is anarthrous it still could be functioning as an adjective or
noun, though usually in one of the following ways.

**2. Is the participle in the nominative case and with a verb that takes a
complementary participle like ἄρχομαι (*begin*) or παύομαι (*stop*)?**

YES The participle is almost certainly a complementary (supplementary)
participle.

**3. Is the participle in the nominative and with a form of εἰμί, γίνομαι or
ὑπάρχω?**

YES The participle is probably part of a periphrastic construction.

4. Is the participle in the genitive with a genitive noun or pronoun?

YES It is probably a genitive absolute. Try translating it as a circumstantial
participle (esp. temporal).

5. Is the participle in the accusative and near an accusative noun or pronoun and after a verb of perception or communication?

YES   The participle may be giving the content (indirect discourse) of the verb.

6. Is there a noun near the participle in agreement with it?

YES   The participle is probably modifying the noun adjectively, predicatively as a complement, or perhaps as a noun in apposition.

7. Is the participle in the nominative and not functioning in any of the ways above?

YES   The participle is probably used circumstantially or for attendant circumstance or, rarely, pleonastically. Try these various options to see which of them fit in the context (§5.199).

When you see a participle in the nominative and it does not have a definite article, it is usually circumstantial or attendant circumstance. But as the first point in the flow chart notes, even without the article it can still function as a noun or adjective.

> ἡμεῖς δὲ κηρύσσομεν Χριστὸν **ἐσταυρωμένον** (1 Cor 1:23)
> *But we preach Christ <u>crucified</u>*
>> ➤ ἐσταυρωμένον – pf.-ptc.-MP-masc.-acc.-sg. < σταυρόω. This participle agrees in gender, case, and number with Χριστόν and may function as an adjective, even though it does not have an article, "Christ who was crucified," or as a complement, "Christ as crucified." Or it may be taken as a noun in apposition to Χριστόν, "Christ, the one having been crucified," "Christ, the (one) crucified."

SENTENCES AND CLAUSES

5.206. Introduction to Clauses and Sentences

An overview of the core elements in clauses was provided in chapter 2. Now we examine the various types of clauses in more detail, along with the major ways in which they are combined to form sentences.[233]

---

233. For a much more detailed discussion of sentences and clauses see *CGCG*, chs. 39–51; *AGG* §§253–90.

5.207. Four Basic Clause Core Types

The following core elements can vary in order, but most clauses contain one of these four sets of elements.[234] The subject may be either stated or embedded in the verb.

Type 1: subject – intransitive verb

> ἔρχομαι – *I am coming* (Rev 22:20)
> ἔρχεται ὥρα – *a time is coming* (John 4:23)

Type 2: subject – equative verb – subject complement[235]

> σὺ εἶ ὁ χριστός – *You are the Anointed One* (Matt 16:16)
> φάντασμά ἐστιν – *It is an apparition* (Matt 14:26)
> τὰ δὲ ἱμάτια αὐτοῦ ἐγένετο λευκά – *and his clothes became white* (Matt 17:2)

Type 3: subject – transitive verb – direct object/complement

> ἐξουσίαν ἔχει ὁ υἱὸς τοῦ ἀνθρώπου – *the Son of Man has authority* (Matt 9:6)
> ὑμεῖς ἐμὲ πεφιλήκατε – *you have loved me* (John 16:27)

Direct objects are in the accusative. Some verbs, however, take a genitive or dative to complete their meaning. Such words are referred to as complements.[236]

> τὰ πρόβατα τῆς φωνῆς αὐτοῦ ἀκούει – *the sheep hear his voice* (John 10:3)
> ἐπίστευσαν τῇ γραφῇ – *they believed the scripture* (John 2:22)

Type 4: subject – transitive verb – direct object – indirect object

> κἀγὼ δίδωμι αὐτοῖς ζωὴν αἰώνιον – *and I give eternal life to them* (John 10:28)
> φέρουσιν αὐτῷ τυφλόν – *they brought a blind man to him* (Mark 8:22)

5.208. Independent and Dependent Clauses

a. The English and Greek examples just examined in §5.207 are **independent clauses**, that is, they can stand on their own as complete sentences.

---

234. Funk, in chs. 32 and 33, lists six types, adding as distinct types of sentences the two forms of double accusative (§§5.76, 77).

235. A subject complement is also referred to as a predicate complement, predicate noun, or predicate adjective.

236. *CGCG* §26.3. See further §§5.36, 72.

b. A clause can become **dependent** on another clause in the larger sentence in order to tell us more about that other clause. Since such a clause depends on the other clause to complete its function it is subordinate to that other clause.

5.209. Introduction to Coordinate and Subordinate Clauses

a. A long sentence in Greek is like a train with many cars. Each clause is like a train car, and conjunctions and sentence connectors are like the couplers between the cars.[237] They help us follow the flow of thought from one clause to the next and from one sentence to the next. There are two major types of connections, coordinate and subordinate.

b. Coordinate Clauses. Independent clauses can be connected together to form a set of **coordinate clauses** composing a larger sentence, known as a **compound sentence**.

c. Subordinate Clauses. Often the signal that a clause is subordinate is a conjunction that signals the clause is contributing to the thought of another clause. For example, "They came to the city" is an independent clause and can stand as a complete sentence. But if we add a subordinating conjunction we indicate that it is now subordinate to another clause. Thus if we add "because" to "they came into the city" this conjunction signals that this clause is giving the cause or reason of something in another clause. "Jesus spoke to the people because they came into the city." A sentence that contains a main clause and one or more subordinate clauses is referred to as a **complex sentence**.

5.210. Coordinate Clauses

When two independent clauses are connected as coordinate clauses either they usually signal addition, using a conjunction such as *and*, or they signal contrast, often using a conjunction such as *but* or *or*. The most common coordinating conjunctions in Greek are **καί, ἀλλά**, and **ἤ**.[238]

> τούτῳ ὁ θυρωρὸς ἀνοίγει **καὶ** τὰ πρόβατα τῆς φωνῆς αὐτοῦ ἀκούει **καὶ** τὰ ἴδια πρόβατα φωνεῖ κατ᾽ ὄνομα **καὶ** ἐξάγει αὐτά. (John 10:3)
> *To him the doorkeeper opens <u>and</u> the sheep hear his voice <u>and</u> he calls his own sheep by name <u>and</u> leads them out.*
>   ▸ Four clauses that could each stand as a complete sentence are linked together in a compound sentence.

---

237. Punctuation often signals breaks between clauses (§1.8).

238. In addition to connecting clauses within a sentence these words can also connect whole sentences (§5.246).

ἐγὼ δαιμόνιον **οὐκ** ἔχω, **ἀλλὰ** τιμῶ τὸν πατέρα μου, **καὶ** ὑμεῖς ἀτιμάζετέ με.
(John 8:49)
I do not have a demon, but I honor my Father, and you dishonor me.

> ➤ This sentence has three clauses, each with a finite verb and separated by commas. The first clause is contrasted with the second, as signaled by ἀλλά. The οὐ . . . ἀλλά pattern between the first two clauses is very common (§5.246c). The third is grammatically coordinate to the second through καί, but the change from "honor" to "dishonor" signals a contrast.

Subordinate Clauses

5.211. List of Subordinate Clauses

Subordinate clauses may function like a noun, adjective, or adverb. This list is an outline of the sections that follow, with references given on the right. Some clauses are very simple, but others are complex, requiring extended explanation. The most common signals are listed; for a more extensive list see §5.247.

Like a Noun or Adjective:

There are three main categories of such clauses, relative clauses (§§5.212–19), discourse clauses (§§5.220–26), and explanatory clauses (§§5.227–28).

Relative clauses	ὅς, ἥ, ὅ; ὅστις, ἥτις, ὅτι; ὅσος, η, ον; οἷος, η, ον; ἄν, ἐάν; participle	§§5.212–19
Direct statements, questions, and commands/requests	change in person and number, and sometimes introduced by ὅτι	§§5.220–26
Indirect statements and questions	statements: ὅτι, ὡς, infinitive, participle	§§5.220–26
	questions: εἰ, interrogatives like τίς, τί	
Explanation clauses	ἵνα, infinitive	§§5.227, 146, 170
Appositional clauses with οὗτος, αὕτη, τοῦτο	ὅτι, ἵνα, infinitive	§§5.228, 147, 171

Like an Adverb:

Temporal	ὅτε, ἐπεί, ἕως, πρίν, ὡς, participle	§§5.229, 231
Local	οὗ, ὅθεν, ὅπου, participle	§§5.230, 231
Purpose (Final)	ἵνα, ὅπως, participle	§5.232
Causal	ὅτι, ἐπεί, participle	§5.233
Comparative	ὡς, ὥσπερ, καθώς, participle	§5.234

Concessive	καίπερ, participle	§5.235
Result (Consecutive)	ὥστε, ἵνα, participle	§5.236
Conditional	εἰ, ἐάν, εἰ μή, participle	§§5.237–45

Subordinate Clauses Functioning Like a Noun or Adjective

Relative Clauses

5.212. Introduction to Relative Clauses

Relative clauses frequently function like adjectives, providing information about nouns, but they may also function as nouns themselves. Participles can function in these ways as well (§§5.183–85).

5.213. Basic Components of Relative Clauses

A relative clause begins with a relative pronoun. In English the main relative pronouns are "who," "whom," "which," "that," and "whose."

> the kingdom of heaven is like a_king [**who** wanted to settle accounts with his servants] (Matt 18:23)

> Behold, my servant [**whom** I have chosen] (Matt 12:18)

> And behold, the star [**which** they had seen in the east] went before them (Matt 2:9)

> And they did not understand the saying [**that** he spoke to them]. (Luke 2:50)

> the one coming after me is mightier than I, [**whose** sandals I am not worthy to carry] (Matt 3:11)

In each example the relative pronoun in bold is referring back to something in the main clause in italics, describing it like a fancy adjective. This word or phrase in the main clause in italics is called the **antecedent**.

5.214. Relative Clause as Adjective

As in the English examples above, a relative clause in Greek can be used adjectivally to modify a noun.

a. The noun in the main clause can be the subject, direct object, indirect object, a genitive modifier, or the object of a preposition. Indeed, any noun can be modified by a relative clause, just as any noun can be modified by an adjective.

καὶ ἐπίστευσαν τῇ γραφῇ καὶ τῷ λόγῳ [ὃν εἶπεν ὁ Ἰησοῦς]
and they believed the scripture and the word [that Jesus spoke] (John 2:22)

The relative clause is telling us more about τῷ λόγῳ (*the word*), so it is functioning like an adjective.

b. In English the relative pronoun does not change form for the most part, but relative pronouns in Greek take different gender-case-number forms (§3.51).[239] So in this example notice that the relative pronoun ὅν is in the masc.-acc.-sg. **The relative pronoun usually takes its gender and number from the word it is describing**, that is, its **antecedent**. Since λόγῳ is masc.-sg. so is the relative pronoun.

c. Next notice that λόγῳ is in the dative since the verb πιστεύω takes a dative for its complement (§5.72). But ὅν is in the accusative. **The relative pronoun usually gets its case from how it is functioning within the relative clause.** Here the relative pronoun ὅν is the direct object of εἶπεν (*he spoke*).

This function of the relative pronoun within its own clause is perhaps the main difficulty in understanding Greek relative clauses. The following example illustrates how two sentences can be joined, with one of them being changed to a relative clause.

1. *Two sentences, each with "the word" as a direct object:*

   And they believed the scripture and the word. Jesus spoke the word.
   καὶ ἐπίστευσαν τῇ γραφῇ καὶ **τῷ λόγῳ**. ὁ Ἰησοῦς εἶπεν **τὸν λόγον**.

2. *The direct objects lined up with each other:*

And they believed the scripture and	*the word.*	
	The word	*Jesus spoke.*
καὶ ἐπίστευσαν τῇ γραφῇ καὶ	**τῷ λόγῳ**.	
	τὸν λόγον	εἶπεν ὁ Ἰησοῦς.

239. Actually, relative pronouns are one of the few places in English where we have different forms for different functions. *Who* is used for a subject like a nominative in Greek, *whom* for an object like an accusative in Greek, and *whose* for a possessive like a genitive in Greek. The English examples above illustrate these three functions. There is no separate form for the indirect object in English; instead we use a prepositional phrase with *to whom* or *for whom*.

3. *The direct object in the second sentence replaced with a relative pronoun:*

And they believed the scripture and	the word.	
	that	Jesus spoke.
καὶ ἐπίστευσαν τῇ γραφῇ καὶ	τῷ λόγῳ.	
	ὃν	εἶπεν ὁ Ἰησοῦς

4. *The relative clause added to the main clause:*

And they believed the scripture and <u>the word that</u> Jesus spoke.
καὶ ἐπίστευσαν τῇ γραφῇ καὶ **τῷ λόγῳ ὃν** εἶπεν ὁ Ἰησοῦς.

Here are further examples.

> ἀλλ' ἔστιν ἀληθινὸς ὁ πέμψας με, [**ὃν** ὑμεῖς οὐκ οἴδατε] (John 7:28)
> but the one who sent me is true, [<u>whom</u> you do not know]

This ὃν is telling us more about ὁ πέμψας με (*the one who sent me*), a substantival participle serving as the subject of the verb ἔστιν in the main clause. Since ὁ πέμψας με is masc.-sg. so is the relative pronoun. But the pronoun is accusative since it serves as the direct object of οὐκ οἴδατε (*you do not know*) within its own clause.

> πᾶσα φυτεία [**ἣν** οὐκ ἐφύτευσεν ὁ πατήρ μου ὁ οὐράνιος] ἐκριζωθήσεται. (Matt 15:13)
> Every plant [<u>that</u> my heavenly Father did not plant] will be rooted up.

This relative clause is telling us more about the noun "plant." The pronoun ἣν is fem.-sg. to match the gender and number of the antecedent φυτεία, but ἣν is in the accusative since it is the direct object of the verb within the relative clause, ἐφύτευσεν (*he planted*).

5.215. Attraction of the Relative Pronoun

At times the case of the relative pronoun is changed to match that of the antecedent.

> πάτερ ἅγιε, τήρησον αὐτοὺς ἐν τῷ ὀνόματί σου [**ᾧ** δέδωκάς μοι] (John 17:11)
> Holy Father, keep them in <u>your name</u> [**that** you have given me]

In this example notice that the relative pronoun ᾧ is in the dative even though it is the direct object of δέδωκας (*you have given*) and thus should be accusative. It has the gender and number of the antecedent (neut.-sg.), but it has been conformed to the case of the antecedent as well. This attraction of the relative pronoun to the case of its antecedent is fairly common. It does not change the function or meaning of the relative.

> καὶ νῦν δόξασόν με . . . τῇ δόξῃ [ᾗ εἶχον πρὸ τοῦ τὸν κόσμον εἶναι παρὰ σοί]
> (John 17:5)
> *and now glorify me <u>with the glory</u> [**that** I had with you before the world began]*

Here the relative is fem.-sg., as we would expect, but we would expect it to be in the accusative (ἥν), since it is the direct object of εἶχον (*I had*). It has been attracted into the dative, the case of the antecedent.

5.216. Reverse Attraction of the Relative Pronoun

Occasionally the antecedent matches the relative pronoun instead of having the case one expects it to have from its function in its clause.

> λίθον [ὃν ἀπεδοκίμασαν οἱ οἰκοδομοῦντες], οὗτος ἐγενήθη εἰς κεφαλὴν γωνίας
> (Mark 12:10)
> <u>*The stone*</u> *[**that** the builders rejected], this was made the head of the corner*

In this verse ὅν is in the accusative as the direct object of ἀπεδοκίμασαν (*they rejected*) within the relative clause. Its antecedent, λίθον, is in apposition to οὗτος and thus should be nominative (§2.31), but it has been conformed to the case of the relative pronoun.

5.217. Relative Clause as Noun or Pronoun

a. Relative clauses can function as nouns, just as adjectives often have this function. An adjective is functioning as a noun when there is no noun for it to modify.[240] Similarly, **if there is no antecedent for a relative clause to modify then it will function as a noun.**

> [ὃς οὐκ ἔστιν ἐκ τοῦ θεοῦ] οὐκ ἀκούει ἡμῶν (1 John 4:6)
> *[<u>the one who</u> is not of God] does not hear us*

In this verse there is no antecedent for this relative clause to modify so it functions as a noun. The relative pronoun ὅς is in the nominative since this clause serves as the subject of the main clause. Notice that in English we have

240. The adjective agrees with the noun it modifies in gender-case-number (§2.30).

to add a noun or pronoun. We would not say "Who is not of God does not hear us." So we add something like "the one who," "he who," "she who," "that which," or in the plural, "the ones who," "they who," and so forth.[241]

καὶ ἔλεγεν· [ὃς ἔχει ὦτα ἀκούειν] ἀκουέτω. (Mark 4:9)
And he was saying, ["The one who has ears to hear] must hear."

ὃς is not modifying a noun so it is the noun. As a nominative it functions as the subject of the main verb ἀκουέτω. Since it is masc.-sg. we translate it "he who," or generically, "the one who."

[ῸΟ ἦν ἀπ᾽ ἀρχῆς], [ὃ ἀκηκόαμεν], [ὃ ἑωράκαμεν τοῖς ὀφθαλμοῖς ἡμῶν], [ὃ ἐθε-ασάμεθα καὶ αἱ χεῖρες ἡμῶν ἐψηλάφησαν] περὶ τοῦ λόγου τῆς ζωῆς (1 John 1:1)
[That which was from the beginning], [which we have heard], [which we have seen with our eyes], [which we beheld and our hands handled], concerning the word of life

Again notice that in English we need to supply a nominal, in this case "that," not "who" since these relative clauses are neuter. Here we have four relative clauses describing something. Since these relative clauses are functioning like nouns they give us four descriptions of this reality that John is talking about, which is then clarified through the final prepositional phrase—it has to do with the word of life.

ὅσα γὰρ προεγράφη, εἰς τὴν ἡμετέραν διδασκαλίαν ἐγράφη (Rom 15:4)
for as much as was written previously was written for our instruction
> The correlative relative pronoun (§3.54) is the subject of its relative clause, and that relative clause is the subject of ἐγράφη in the main clause. Here ὅσα has the sense, "everything."

b. A relative pronoun can be used as a pronoun with μέν constructions similar to the article (§5.17), with or without a following δέ. See further §5.246d.

οἱ δὲ ἀμελήσαντες ἀπῆλθον, **ὃς μὲν** εἰς τὸν ἴδιον ἀγρόν, **ὃς δὲ** ἐπὶ τὴν ἐμπορίαν αὐτοῦ (Matt 22:5)
But they didn't care and went away, one to his own field, another to his business

5.218. Relative Clause as Object of a Preposition

Ἰακὼβ δὲ ἐγέννησεν τὸν Ἰωσὴφ τὸν ἄνδρα Μαρίας, [ἐξ ἧς ἐγεννήθη Ἰησοῦς] (Matt 1:16)
and Jacob begat Joseph, the husband of Mary, [of whom Jesus was born]

241. In this verse the relative may function as an indefinite, "whoever" (§5.219a).

ἧς is fem.-sg. in agreement with the antecedent Μαρίας, and it is genitive because the preposition ἐκ takes a genitive.

> οὗτός ἐστιν ὁ υἱός μου ὁ ἀγαπητός, [ἐν ᾧ εὐδόκησα]. (Matt 3:17)
> *This is my beloved* <u>Son</u>, *[in **whom** I am well pleased]*.

The preposition ἐν takes a dative so the relative pronoun ᾧ is in that case, and it is masc.-sg. to agree with its antecedent, ὁ υἱός.

5.219. Indefinite Relative Clauses

Some relative clauses do not refer to a particular person or thing, but to a general class. In English it is the difference between saying "the one who" and "whoever."

a. In KG a simple relative clause can have this indefinite nuance. Both the indicative and the subjunctive can be used in indefinite relative clauses.

> [ὃς οὐκ ἔστιν ἐκ τοῦ θεοῦ] οὐκ ἀκούει ἡμῶν (1 John 4:6)
> *[the one who is not of God] does not hear us*
> *[whoever is not of God] does not hear us*
> ➤ This simple relative clause with an indicative can be understood as either definite or indefinite.

b. A relative clause can be clearly marked as indefinite by adding the particle ἄν or less frequently ἐάν to the clause and using the subjunctive mood in the verb.

> [ὃς γὰρ ἐὰν θέλῃ τὴν ψυχὴν αὐτοῦ σῶσαι] ἀπολέσει αὐτήν (Mark 8:35)
> *[for whoever wants to save their/his life] will lose it*

> [Εἰς ἣν δ' ἄν πόλιν ἢ κώμην εἰσέλθητε] (Matt 10:11)
> *[And into whichever city or village you enter]*
> ➤ ἄν is added to ἣν to make the expression indefinite. This relative pronoun ἣν is in the accusative since it is the object of εἰς, which takes an accusative. It is fem.-sg. in agreement with πόλιν and κώμην (*city, village*). We also have a subjunctive verb, εἰσέλθητε: aor.-subjn.-act.-2-pl. < εἰσέρχομαι.

c. Another indefinite relative pronoun, ὅστις, ἥτις, ὅτι (§3.52), usually is used with the indicative, but it can also take the subjunctive.

> [ὅστις οὖν ταπεινώσει ἑαυτὸν ὡς τὸ παιδίον τοῦτο], οὗτός ἐστιν ὁ μείζων ἐν τῇ βασιλείᾳ τῶν οὐρανῶν. (Matt 18:4)
> *[Whoever therefore will humble himself as this little child], this one is the greatest in the kingdom of heaven.*

[ὅστις δ' ἂν ἀρνήσηταί με ἔμπροσθεν τῶν ἀνθρώπων], ἀρνήσομαι κἀγὼ αὐτὸν
ἔμπροσθεν τοῦ πατρός μου τοῦ ἐν [τοῖς] οὐρανοῖς (Matt 10:33)
*[But <u>whoever</u> denies me before people], I also will deny before my Father who is in
heaven*

d. Just as the simple relative pronoun can sometimes signal an indefinite
clause, so also this indefinite pronoun can be used as a simple relative. Indeed,
in KG texts this is usually the case. As you might expect, context is our indication of what is going on.

μὴ σὺ μείζων εἶ τοῦ πατρὸς ἡμῶν Ἀβραάμ, [**ὅστις** ἀπέθανεν]; (John 8:53)
*You are not greater[242] than our father <u>Abraham</u>, [**who** died], are you?*

> ▸ The reference is clearly to a particular, definite person. Questions that
> begin with μή usually expect a negative answer, something like, "no, of
> course not" (§5.224). The translation shows one way English can signal
> this nuance.

Discourse Clauses

5.220. Direct and Indirect Discourse

Direct discourse reports the actual words a person said. Indirect discourse reports the content of what a person said. Both direct and indirect discourse
may be used for a statement, question, or command/request/suggestion/
permission.

5.221. Signs of Direct and Indirect Discourse

Quotation marks signal direct discourse in English and the word "that" signals
indirect discourse.

Direct discourse	Jesus said, "I am the light of the world."
Indirect discourse	Jesus said that he was the light of the world.

a. Greek does not use quotation marks so it is sometimes unclear whether
a statement is direct or indirect. The clearest indication occurs when there
is a change in pronoun and/or tense-form, as in the example just given. The
shift from the 1-sg. "I" with a present tense to the 3-sg. "he" with a past tense
clearly signals which clause is direct and which indirect. However, this shift in

---

242. Notice that now μείζων is a comparative, *greater*, in contrast to its use above in
Matt 18:4. See §5.85.

person and/or tense-form after verbs of speech does not necessarily indicate indirect discourse.

ἀπεκρίθη ἡ γυνὴ καὶ εἶπεν αὐτῷ· [οὐκ ἔχω ἄνδρα]. (John 4:17)
The woman answered and said to him, ["I do not have a husband."]
> The shift from the 3-sg. aorist εἶπεν (*she said*) to the 1-sg. present ἔχω (*I have*) does not signal indirect discourse as the content makes clear.

This sequence of tenses is discussed further in §5.226.

b. Some editions of the Greek New Testament, including UBS[5], *SBLGNT* and Westcott-Hort, provide help by capitalizing the first letter of what is a direct quote in the editors' estimation. NA and *THGNT*, on the other hand, do not do so.[243]

NA[28]	Λέγει πρὸς αὐτὸν ἡ γυνή· κύριε, δός μοι τοῦτο τὸ ὕδωρ
UBS[5]	λέγει πρὸς αὐτὸν ἡ γυνή, Κύριε, δός μοι τοῦτο τὸ ὕδωρ
SBLGNT	λέγει πρὸς αὐτὸν ἡ γυνή· Κύριε, δός μοι τοῦτο τὸ ὕδωρ
THGNT	Λέγει πρὸς αὐτὸν ἡ γυνή· κύριε, δός μοι τοῦτο τὸ ὕδωρ
WH	λέγει πρὸς αὐτὸν ἡ γυνή Κύριε, δός μοι τοῦτο τὸ ὕδωρ
	The woman said to him, "Sir, give me this water" (John 4:15)

c. A common signal of indirect discourse in Greek is ὅτι, *that*, though ὅτι can also introduce direct discourse.

εἶπον οὖν ὑμῖν [**ὅτι** ἀποθανεῖσθε ἐν ταῖς ἁμαρτίαις ὑμῶν] (John 8:24)
Therefore I said to you [that you would die in your sins]
> We have a shift in person and tense-form from the aorist εἶπον (*I said*) to the future ἀποθανεῖσθε (*you will die*), but also the presence of ὅτι. So these signals could signal indirect discourse as in the translation, or direct discourse: "Therefore I said to you, 'You will die in your sins.'"

ὡμολόγησεν [**ὅτι** ἐγὼ οὐκ εἰμὶ ὁ χριστός] (John 1:20)
he confessed, ["I am not the Christ"]
> ὅτι introduces this quote, but the shift of person and tense from ὡμολόγησεν to εἰμί and the context signal it is direct discourse.

d. Often it is not clear whether a statement is reported directly or indirectly. For example, did Jesus say John 3:16? He is clearly speaking in verses 10–12, and most interpreters and translations think the direct quote continues through

---

243. This selection also illustrates the differences in punctuation between these editions (here seen after γυνή). Furthermore, NA[28] signals minor breaks within paragraphs by a capital on the first word of the new section, as here on Λέγει, and a short space before that first word. In *THGNT* this word is capitalized because it begins a new paragraph.

verse 15. But the remainder of the section, verses 16–21, may continue the quote or they may be John the Gospel writer's comment. Several English translations have footnotes indicating that it is unclear where the quote ends.[244]

5.222. Indirect Discourse for Various Forms of Content

Both direct and indirect discourse are used for reported speech, but indirect discourse is also used more broadly for what is thought, felt, sensed, perceived, and so forth. Indirect "discourse" is thus a confusing term, since often it is not referring to discourse as such. Accordingly, it is clearer to call such clauses "content clauses," since they give the content of what is said, thought, felt, and so forth.

a. While ὅτι often is used to signal a content clause there are several other signals used as well, including ἵνα (§5.148), an infinitive (§5.169), and a participle (§5.203).[245]

> λέγω δὲ ὑμῖν **ὅτι** τοῦ ἱεροῦ μεῖζόν ἐστιν ὧδε. (Matt 12:6)
> *But I tell you that something greater than the temple is here.*
> > ▸ This ὅτι clause is used for reported speech.

> νῦν οἴδαμεν **ὅτι** οἶδας πάντα . . . πιστεύομεν **ὅτι** ἀπὸ θεοῦ ἐξῆλθες. (John 16:30)
> *Now we know that you know all things . . . we believe that you have come from God.*
> > ▸ Now ὅτι clauses give the content of what is known and believed.

> εἰ υἱὸς εἶ τοῦ θεοῦ, εἰπὲ τῷ λίθῳ τούτῳ [**ἵνα** γένηται ἄρτος]. (Luke 4:3)
> *If you are God's son, command this stone [that it become bread].*
> > ▸ The ἵνα clause gives us the content of the command.

> Πάντα οὖν ὅσα ἐὰν θέλητε [**ἵνα** ποιῶσιν ὑμῖν οἱ ἄνθρωποι] (Matt 7:12)
> *Therefore whatever you want [that people should do to you]*
> > ▸ ἵνα introduces the clause giving the content of what it is desired (*you want*).

> καὶ ὃς ἂν μὴ ἔχῃ, καὶ ὃ δοκεῖ [**ἔχειν**] ἀρθήσεται ἀπ᾽ αὐτοῦ (Luke 8:18)
> *and whoever does not have, even what he or she thinks [that they have] will be taken from them*
> > ▸ The "having" is what this person is thinking. The expression δοκεῖ ἔχειν would be woodenly, "he/she thinks to have." Since δοκέω (*think*) sig-

---

244. I think verses 16–21 are John's comment based on larger discourse features in the context, especially the similar comment at John 3:31–36. See Whitacre, *John*, 91–92.

245. ὡς is also used to introduce a content clause, although there are no examples in the New Testament.

nals that content is expected we can use an English idiom instead of an infinitive. In this case we can use "that they have," or simply "he or she thinks they have."

Ἀκούομεν γάρ [τινας **περιπατοῦντας** ἐν ὑμῖν ἀτάκτως] (2 Thess 3:11)
For we hear [that some among you are living in an undisciplined fashion]
> ‣ The content of what is heard is given by the participial clause. The accusative τινας is the subject of the participle περιπατοῦντας which is also in the accusative.

5.223. Direct and Indirect Questions

Both direct and indirect questions can be introduced by

- conjunctive particle   –   εἰ
- interrogative adverb   –   ποῦ, *where?*
- interrogative pronouns/   –   τίς, τί, *who?, what?, why?*[246]
  adjectives[247]   ποῖος, α, ον, *of what sort?,*
                                πόσος, η, ον, *how much?, how great?, how many?*
                                ποταπός, ή, όν, *of what sort?*

Ἐξορκίζω σε κατὰ τοῦ θεοῦ τοῦ ζῶντος ἵνα ἡμῖν εἴπῃς [εἰ σὺ εἶ ὁ χριστὸς ὁ υἱὸς τοῦ θεοῦ]. (Matt 26:63)
I solemnly command you by the living God that you tell us [whether you are the Christ of God].
> ‣ Here εἰ does not signal a conditional clause, but rather an indirect question. The direct question would be, "Are you the Christ of God?" We also see ἵνα introducing the content of the solemn command: ἵνα ἡμῖν εἴπῃς, *that you tell us* (§5.148).

λοιπὸν οὐκ οἶδα [εἴ τινα ἄλλον ἐβάπτισα] (1 Cor 1:16)
Otherwise, I do not know [whether I baptized someone else]
> ‣ The direct question would be, "Did I baptize someone else?" For the accent on εἰ see §1.9a.

246. This word has the same paradigm as the indefinite pronoun, τις, τι, which is used for the core pattern for third declension nouns and adjectives (§3.16). The indefinite pronoun is enclitic and so does not have an accent of its own (§1.9a), while the interrogative always has an acute accent.
247. Resources differ over whether these words should be considered adjectives that can be used pronominally, or pronouns that can be used adjectively. See §5.84.

Ἰδόντες δὲ οἱ περὶ αὐτὸν τὸ ἐσόμενον εἶπαν· κύριε, [εἰ πατάξομεν ἐν μαχαίρῃ]; (Luke 22:49)

And those around him, seeing what was about to happen, said, ["Lord, shall we strike with the sword?"]

> ➤ Now εἰ introduces a direct question, which is confirmed by the question mark at the end of the clause. Such questions expect a yes or no answer. In CG εἰ is not used for direct questions, but this use is common in the LXX and occurs a number of times in the New Testament.[248]

καὶ ἠρώτησαν αὐτὸν καὶ εἶπαν αὐτῷ· [τί οὖν βαπτίζεις εἰ σὺ οὐκ εἶ ὁ χριστὸς οὐδὲ Ἠλίας οὐδὲ ὁ προφήτης;] (John 1:25)

And they asked him and said to him, ["Why then are you baptizing if you are not the Christ nor Elijah nor the Prophet?"]

> ➤ τί is the neuter form of the interrogative pronoun, τίς, τί. Here it introduces a direct question, indicated by the question mark at the end. Also we see εἰ introducing a conditional clause, its more common use.

οὗτος εἰ ἦν προφήτης, ἐγίνωσκεν ἄν [τίς καὶ **ποταπὴ** ἡ γυνὴ ἥτις ἅπτεται αὐτοῦ]. (Luke 7:39)

If this man were a prophet, he would know [who and what sort of woman this is who is touching him].

> ➤ We have both an interrogative pronoun and interrogative adjective in an indirect question, giving the content of what he would have known.

ἴδε **πόσα** σου κατηγοροῦσιν. (Mark 15:4)

See how many things they are accusing you of.

> ➤ Here πόσος is in an indirect question, but it may also be used in direct questions.

5.224. The Use of οὐ/μή in Questions

When οὐ (οὐκ, οὐχ, οὐχί) is used in a question the writer expects a positive answer. When a form of μή is used a negative answer is expected.

μήτι δύναται τυφλὸς τυφλὸν ὁδηγεῖν; οὐχὶ ἀμφότεροι εἰς βόθυνον ἐμπεσοῦνται; (Luke 6:39)

A blind person is not able to lead a blind person, is he/she? Will they not both fall into a hole?

> ➤ The "is he/she?" at the end of the first question is a common way in English to signal the expectation of a negative response. To the second question Jesus is expecting everyone to say, "yes of course."

---

248. For possible influence from Hebrew see BDF §440(3); Zerwick, *Biblical Greek* §401; and T. Muraoka, *A Syntax of Septuagint Greek* (Leuven: Peeters, 2016), 756.

5.225. Direct and Indirect Commands/Requests

Direct commands or requests are most often expressed by the imperative mood, while the most common ways to express indirect commands or requests is with an infinitive (§5.169) or a ἵνα clause (§5.148) after verbs meaning to request, to exhort, to command, and so forth.

> παρήγγειλεν αὐτοῖς [ἀπὸ Ἱεροσολύμων **μὴ χωρίζεσθαι**] (Acts 1:4)
> *He instructed them [not to leave Jerusalem]*
> > ➤ χωρίζεσθαι – pres.-inf.-MP < χωρίζω. The main verb, παρήγγειλεν, could also be translated "he ordered" or "he commanded."

> διδάσκαλε, δέομαί σου [**ἐπιβλέψαι** ἐπὶ τὸν υἱόν μου] (Luke 9:38)
> *Teacher, I beg you [to look at my son]*
> > ➤ ἐπιβλέψαι – aor.-inf.-act. < ἐπιβλέπω.

> ἠρώτα [**ἵνα καταβῇ** καὶ **ἰάσηται** αὐτοῦ τὸν υἱόν] (John 4:47)
> *he asked [that he come down and heal his son]*
> > ➤ καταβῇ – aor.-subjn.-act.-3-sg. < καταβαίνω. ἰάσηται – aor.-subjn.-MP1-3-sg. < ἰάομαι.

> δεήθητε οὖν τοῦ κυρίου τοῦ θερισμοῦ [**ὅπως** ἐργάτας **ἐκβάλῃ** εἰς τὸν θερισμὸν αὐτοῦ] (Luke 10:2)
> *therefore entreat the Lord of the harvest [that he send out workers in his harvest]*
> > ➤ ἐκβάλῃ – aor.-subjn.-act.-3-sg. < ἐκβάλλω. While ἵνα is the most common conjunction used in such constructions, as you read you will find others as well, such as ὅπως.

5.226. Sequence of Tenses in Indirect Discourse

When an indirect statement is introduced by a verb for past time such as, "she said," "he heard," "they saw," Greek retains the tense-form of the original statement, but English usually changes the form. Compare the following direct quotes with their form in indirect discourse.

a. Present.

> ὁ ἀπόστολος **ἔρχεται** εἰς τὴν πόλιν.
> *"The apostle comes into the city."*

εἶπον ὅτι ὁ ἀπόστολος **ἔρχεται** εἰς τὴν πόλιν.   Greek retains the present tense-form.
They said that the apostle was coming into the city.   English changes the form.

335

b. Future.

ὁ ἀπόστολος **ἐλεύσεται** εἰς τὴν πόλιν.
"The apostle <u>will come</u> into the city."

εἶπον ὅτι ὁ ἀπόστολος **ἐλεύσεται** εἰς τὴν πόλιν.   Greek retains the future tense-form.
They said that the apostle <u>would come</u> into the city.   English changes the form.

c. Past.

ὁ ἀπόστολος **ἦλθεν** εἰς τὴν πόλιν.
"The apostle <u>came</u> into the city."

εἶπον ὅτι ὁ ἀπόστολος **ἦλθεν** εἰς τὴν πόλιν.   Greek retains the aorist tense-form.
They said that the apostle <u>had come</u> into the city.   For reporting something in the past
They said that the apostle <u>came</u> into the city.   English can retain the form or change it.

The exact form of the English can vary depending on the peculiarities of particular words in English.

ἀλλ᾽ ὅτε εἶδον ὅτι οὐκ **ὀρθοποδοῦσιν** πρὸς τὴν ἀλήθειαν τοῦ εὐαγγελίου (Gal 2:14)
but when I saw that they <u>were not behaving in line</u> with the truth of the gospel
> This Greek present can become a past progressive in English.

ἠκούσθη ὅτι ἐν οἴκῳ **ἐστίν** (Mark 2:1)
it was heard that he <u>was</u> at home
> Here the Greek present becomes a past in English.

Ἠκούσατε ὅτι **ἐρρέθη** τοῖς ἀρχαίοις (Matt 5:21)
You heard that it <u>was said</u> to the ancients
> The Greek aorist tense-form can be a simple past in English "that it was said," or it can be shifted back: "that it had been said."

Καὶ ὅτε εἶδεν ὁ δράκων ὅτι **ἐβλήθη** εἰς τὴν γῆν (Rev 12:13)
And when the dragon saw that he <u>had been cast</u> onto the earth
> Again the aorist could be rendered with a simple past: "that he was cast."

Explanatory Clauses

5.227. Epexegetical (Explanation) Clauses

Clauses adding explanation usually use an infinitive or a ἵνα clause.

> οὐ χρείαν εἶχεν [ἵνα τις μαρτυρήσῃ περὶ τοῦ ἀνθρώπου] (John 2:25)
> *He did not have need [that anyone bear witness concerning man]*
> ▸ The ἵνα clause explains what sort of need (χρείαν) is in view.

For more detail on such ἵνα clauses see §5.146 and for infinitives see §5.170.

5.228. Appositional Clauses after οὗτος

Occasionally οὗτος, αὕτη, τοῦτο, *this*, comes early in a sentence and is then explained by means of an infinitive, a ὅτι clause, or a ἵνα clause. The explanatory material functions like a noun in apposition (§2.31) to the form of οὗτος, αὕτη, τοῦτο. Since it offers an explanation it is sometimes referred to as epexegetical. Because οὗτος, αὕτη, τοῦτο is explained by something coming later it is called cataphoric, that is, further "down" (κατά) the text. Cataphoric is the opposite of anaphoric, which refers to material earlier in the context (ἀνά, up, §5.12b).

> ἐν **τούτῳ** ἐγνώκαμεν τὴν ἀγάπην, **ὅτι** ἐκεῖνος ὑπὲρ ἡμῶν τὴν ψυχὴν αὐτοῦ ἔθηκεν (1 John 3:16)
> *By this we have known love, that that one laid down his life for us*

For an example with the infinitive see §5.171 and for ἵνα see §5.147.

Subordinate Clauses Functioning Like an Adverb

5.229. Temporal Clauses

Such clauses indicate when something takes place.

> [ὅτε ἤμην νήπιος], ἐλάλουν ὡς νήπιος (1 Cor 13:11)
> *[When I was a child], I used to speak as a child*

> [ὡς γὰρ ὑπάγεις μετὰ τοῦ ἀντιδίκου σου ἐπ᾽ ἄρχοντα] (Luke 12:58)
> *[For while you are going with your accuser to the magistrate]*

For participles with a temporal nuance see §5.191.

5.230. Local Clauses

Such clauses indicate where something takes place.

> Μὴ θησαυρίζετε ὑμῖν θησαυροὺς ἐπὶ τῆς γῆς, [**ὅπου** σὴς καὶ βρῶσις ἀφανίζει]
> καὶ [**ὅπου** κλέπται διορύσσουσιν καὶ κλέπτουσιν] (Matt 6:19)
> *Do not lay not up for yourselves treasures upon the earth, [<u>where</u> moth and rust*
> *consume], and [<u>where</u> thieves break through and steal]*

5.231. Indefinite Local and Temporal Clauses

Both the indicative and the subjunctive can be used in indefinite local and temporal clauses.

a. The most common form of such clauses is an indefinite temporal clause
with a subjunctive and introduced by ὅταν, *whenever*, a combination of ὅτε
and ἄν. It can refer to "an action that is conditional, possible, and, in many
instances, repeated."[249]

> Καὶ [**ὅταν προσεύχησθε**], οὐκ ἔσεσθε ὡς οἱ ὑποκριταί (Matt 6:5)
> *And [<u>whenever</u> you pray], you shall not be like the hypocrites*

b. This construction can also be used for a definite future event when the
event itself is definite, but the time it will occur is unknown. "Whenever"
doesn't work well for this nuance so it can't always be conveyed in English.

> ἐλεύσονται δὲ ἡμέραι, καὶ [**ὅταν ἀπαρθῇ** ἀπ᾽ αὐτῶν ὁ νυμφίος] (Luke 5:35)
> *but days are coming, and [<u>when</u> the bridegroom <u>is taken</u> from them]*

> [Ὅταν δὲ ἔλθῃ ὁ υἱὸς τοῦ ἀνθρώπου ἐν τῇ δόξῃ αὐτοῦ] (Matt 25:31)
> *[But <u>when</u> the Son of Man <u>comes</u> in his glory]*

c. The following verse has both an indefinite local and an indefinite temporal clause. These clauses use local and temporal conjunctions followed by the
subjunctive, one with ἄν and the other with ἐάν.

> [**ὅπου ἐὰν εἰσέλθητε** εἰς οἰκίαν], ἐκεῖ μένετε [**ἕως ἂν ἐξέλθητε** ἐκεῖθεν]
> (Mark 6:10)
> *[<u>wherever you enter</u> a house], remain there [<u>until such time as you leave</u> from there]*

ὅπου can mean "where" but here in Mark 6:10 with ἐάν and the subjunctive
it is indefinite. In the second clause most English translations simply have "until" for a smoother translation. While ἕως, "until," usually introduces a simple

---

249. BDAG, s.v. "ὅταν," 1, 730.

temporal clause, it also occurs, as here, with ἄν when there is uncertainty about when the time will come. Here is another example:

> διδάσκαλε, ἀκολουθήσω σοι [ὅπου ἐὰν ἀπέρχῃ]. (Matt 8:19)
> *Teacher, I will follow you [wherever you go].*

The final example of ὅπου ἐάν is with an indicative for an indefinite local clause. The use of the indicative for an indefinite clause is much less common than the subjunctive, but not rare.

> καὶ [ὅπου ἄν εἰσεπορεύετο εἰς κώμας ἢ εἰς πόλεις ἢ εἰς ἀγρούς] (Mark 6:56)
> *and [wherever he entered, into villages or into towns or into rural areas]*

d. As with ὅπου and ἕως, οὗ, *where*, is usually definite, but not always.[250] In the following example the presence of ἐάν and the subjunctive indicates the idea is indefinite.

> ἵνα ὑμεῖς με προπέμψητε [οὗ ἐὰν πορεύωμαι] (1 Cor 16:6)
> *so you can send me on my journey, [wherever I may go]*

5.232. Purpose (Final) Clauses

Purpose clauses indicate the intended outcome of the action in the main clause, whether or not it actually happens. Both ὅπως and ἵνα can introduce a purpose clause (§5.137), as can a participle (§5.197). Occasionally ἵνα uses a future indicative instead of the more common subjunctive.

> [ὅπως μὴ καυχήσηται πᾶσα σὰρξ ἐνώπιον τοῦ θεοῦ] (1 Cor 1:29)
> *[that all flesh might not boast before God]*
> > ▸ ὅπως takes a subjunctive. In such expressions with πᾶς Greek negates the verb but English idiom negates the noun so we would say, "that no flesh may boast." Here σάρξ is usually translated "one" or "human being."[251]

> Μακάριοι οἱ πλύνοντες τὰς στολὰς αὐτῶν, [ἵνα ἔσται ἡ ἐξουσία αὐτῶν ἐπὶ τὸ ξύλον τῆς ζωῆς καὶ τοῖς πυλῶσιν εἰσέλθωσιν εἰς τὴν πόλιν]. (Rev 22:14)
> *Blessed are those who wash their robes, [that their right may be to the tree of life and by the gates they may enter into the city].*

---

250. This is the gen.-sg. form of the relative pronoun ὅς, ἥ, ὅ. This genitive form can function as a relative pronoun, but also as an adverb of place, *where*. The adverbial use of οὗ is treated as a distinct word in lexicons.

251. BDAG, s.v. "σάρξ," 3.a, 915; *CGEL*, s.v. "σάρξ," 1.c, 318; Abbott-Smith, s.v. "σάρξ," 2. (a), 403.

> ➤ Here ἵνα is used with both a future indicative, ἔσται, and an aorist subjunctive, εἰσέλθωσιν. This ἵνα clause could also be understood as signaling result.

5.233. Causal Clauses

Such clauses indicate the cause or reason something takes place.

> μακάριοι οἱ πενθοῦντες, [ὅτι αὐτοὶ παρακληθήσονται]. (Matt 5:4)
> *Blessed are those who mourn, [because they will be comforted].*

For participles suggesting a causal sense see §5.192.

5.234. Comparative Clauses

Such clauses indicate what something or some action is like.

> οὐκ ἔδει καὶ σὲ ἐλεῆσαι τὸν σύνδουλόν σου, [ὡς κἀγὼ σὲ ἠλέησα]; (Matt 18:33)
> *Should you not also have had mercy on your fellow servant [as I had mercy on you]?*

5.235. Concessive Clauses

Such clauses refer to something despite which something else happens or is true.

> [καίπερ ὢν υἱός], ἔμαθεν ἀφ᾽ ὧν ἔπαθεν τὴν ὑπακοήν (Heb 5:8)
> *[Although being a son], he learned obedience by the things which he suffered*

For participles used with a concessive sense see §5.194.

5.236. Result (Consecutive) Clauses

ὥστε, *so that, with the result that,* introduces a result clause. A result clause says what happened as a result of the action of the main clause. This result may be what actually happened, whether it was intended or not, or it may refer to an intended result.[252] Such an intended result is very close to a purpose clause with

---

252. In CG when ὥστε is followed by an indicative it refers to an actual result, but when followed by an infinitive it refers to a result that naturally or inevitably would

ἵνα (§5.137).²⁵³ ἵνα can also introduce a result clause (§5.138), as can a participle (§5.198).

> καὶ ἰδοὺ σεισμὸς μέγας ἐγένετο ἐν τῇ θαλάσσῃ, [ὥστε τὸ πλοῖον καλύπτεσθαι ὑπὸ τῶν κυμάτων]. (Matt 8:24)
> *And behold, there arose a great storm on the lake, [with the result that the boat was covered with the waves].*
>
> ➤ Here we see ὥστε with an infinitive for an actual result. Note that the infinitive, καλύπτεσθαι, is translated like a finite verb, "was covered." The accusative τὸ πλοῖον is translated as the subject of the infinitive, "the boat was covered." For more detailed explanation of such constructions with an infinitive see §§5.79, 167b, 174.

> ἔδωκεν αὐτοῖς ἐξουσίαν πνευμάτων ἀκαθάρτων [ὥστε ἐκβάλλειν αὐτά] (Matt 10:1)
> *he gave them authority over unclean spirits that they may cast them out*
>
> ➤ In this example ὥστε with an infinitive is used for an intended result, illustrating how similar this construction is to a purpose clause with ἵνα.

5.237. Conditional Sentences

A conditional statement has two sections: "If this/then that." The "if" part is known as the **protasis**, and the "then" part as the **apodosis**. Structurally, the apodosis is the main clause and the protasis is a subordinate clause. The word "then" is not always used in English. For example, "If we study well/we will learn this material."

In Greek there are several ways to form conditional statements, each with its own signals and each expressing "a different attitude of the speaker towards the likelihood of the condition in the protasis being fulfilled."²⁵⁴ Some forms use εἰ for "if" and others use ἐάν (which is a combination of εἰ and ἄν).²⁵⁵ Tense-form and mood are also signs indicating a particular type of conditional statement.

---

follow, without indicating whether or not it actually occurred. Smyth §§2257–58; CGCG §§46.4, 7. In KG the use of ὥστε with an indicative is rare and ὥστε with an infinitive is used for both actual and intended results. *AGG* §279.

253. BDAG, s.v. "ὥστε," 2, 1107.

254. *CGCG* §49.1.

255. Both ἐάν and ἄν are also signals for indefinite relative clauses (§5.219b).

5.238. Type 1: Indefinite Conditions

This form of condition simply states the condition without any indication that it is viewed as fulfilled or not.[256]

a. An indefinite condition is composed of

Protasis (if)	Apodosis (then)
εἰ + any indicative	any finite verb
εἰ ἐμὲ ἐδίωξαν,	καὶ ὑμᾶς **διώξουσιν** (John 15:20)
If *they* persecuted *me*	*they will also* persecute *you*

b. In this form of conditional statement the person is saying that if something is true then something else is going to be true. Since this is the form of condition used when someone does think the condition is fulfilled, the context will have to indicate whether they believe the condition to be true or whether they are either noncommittal or simply making an argument. In this example Jesus views the condition as true, since he has indeed been persecuted. At times it will be unclear what the author thinks about the condition.

c. Some grammars suggest that in Type 1 conditions εἰ can be translated "since": "since they persecuted me, they will also persecute you." But the construction itself does not say this, and there are clear ways to say "since" if that is the form of statement the author wants to make. So it is best to stick with "if," and look for signs in the context that indicate how the author views the truthfulness/reality of the condition.

> εἰ δὲ Χριστὸς **οὐκ ἐγήγερται**,/ματαία ἡ πίστις ὑμῶν (1 Cor 15:17)
> *And if Christ has not been raised/your faith is worthless*

In this case Paul clearly does not believe the truthfulness of the condition, and to translate with "since" here would be a grave misreading (as it were). By using this form of conditional statement Paul is simply saying, if Christ has not been raised then here's what follows as logically necessary, your faith is worthless. Note that the verb is missing in the apodosis in keeping with the predicate position (§5.5).

5.239. Type 2: Contrary-to-Fact Conditions

The condition is viewed as unfulfilled.[257]

---

256. Type 1 conditions are also called simple, open, or neutral conditions.

257. Type 2 are also called counterfactual, unfulfilled, unreal, or hypothetical conditions.

a. A contrary-to-fact condition is composed of

Protasis (if)	Apodosis (then)
εἰ + any indicative in a secondary tense, usually imperfect or aorist[258]	any indicative in a secondary tense, usually + ἄν

b. The protasis is assumed to be unreal/untrue/unfulfilled, and the apodosis states what would have been the case if the protasis were true.

> εἰ ἔτι ἀνθρώποις **ἤρεσκον**, Χριστοῦ δοῦλος οὐκ **ἂν ἤμην**. (Gal 1:10)
> *If I were still pleasing people I would not be Christ's slave.*[259]

> κύριε, εἰ **ἦς** ὧδε/**οὐκ ἂν** μου **ἀπέθανεν** ὁ ἀδελφός. (John 11:32)
> *Lord, if you were here/my brother would not have died.*

Using this form of conditional statement Mary of Bethany is saying, "if you had been here (and you weren't), then my brother would not have died."

5.240. Type 3: Future-More-Likely Conditions

Fulfillment of the condition is viewed as possible or probable, or occasionally as only a hypothetical possibility of an imaginary case that will not occur.[260]

a. The signals for a future-more-likely condition include

Protasis (if)	Apodosis (then)
ἐάν + subjunctive	any finite verb, usually a future, an imperative, or a subjunctive

b. The supposition of the protasis is yet to be fulfilled, with the subjunctive of the protasis adding a note of uncertainty, though not necessarily doubt.

c. Generally the aorist in the protasis anticipates a single future event or an event viewed as a whole, and a present anticipates a repeated or generalized situation. As always, however, watch the meaning of the verb and clues in the context for such nuances.

Aorist	ἐὰν μόνον **ἅψωμαι** τοῦ ἱματίου αὐτοῦ	**σωθήσομαι**. (Matt 9:21)
	If only I touch his garment	*I will be healed.*

258. The secondary tenses are the imperfect, aorist, and pluperfect (§4.35).
259. ἤρεσκον is probably a conative use of the imperfect (§5.123), "trying to please."
260. *ExSyn*, 696; *BNTSyn*, 313; Smyth §2322. Type 3 conditions are also called future more vivid, prospective, or future open conditions.

We have ἐάν + aorist subjunctive in the protasis and a future indicative in the apodosis. The meaning of the verb "touch" and the context suggest a single event in the future. Using this form of conditional statement the woman is expressing some uncertainty over whether she will be able to touch Jesus's garment. Note that the uncertainty is about the protasis, not the apodosis. She is not uncertain about the healing; she expects the healing to take place if only she can fulfill the condition, namely, that she touch his garment.

Present   Καὶ **ἐὰν** ὁ πούς σου **σκανδαλίζῃ** σε,   **ἀπόκοψον** αὐτόν (Mark 9:45)
           And if your foot <u>causes</u> you <u>to stumble</u>,   *<u>cut</u> it off*

In this example we have ἐάν + present subjunctive in the protasis and an imperative in the apodosis. This form of condition is saying, "if your foot causes you to stumble, and that's a possibility or even a probability, then cut it off." In this case we are dealing with hyperbole and imagery—cutting off a foot will not prevent one from sinning! Jesus is saying, if you find sources of sin in your life, and that might happen or it is even probable, then take strong measures to get rid of them.

ἐὰν εἴπωμεν· ἐξ οὐρανοῦ,/**ἐρεῖ·** διὰ τί οὐκ ἐπιστεύσατε αὐτῷ; (Luke 20:5)
If we <u>say</u>, "From heaven,"/he <u>will say</u>, "Why did you not believe him?"

Here the condition is not suggesting it is possible or probable that the chief priests and experts in the law would say this. This condition is merely hypothetical; they are deliberating over their possible courses of action in this confrontation with Jesus.

εἰ ταῦτα **οἴδατε,**/μακάριοί **ἐστε**/**ἐὰν ποιῆτε** αὐτά. (John 13:17)
If you <u>know</u> these things,/you <u>are</u> blessed/if you <u>do</u> them.

This is an interesting example since there are two conditions, a Type 1 and a Type 3. Does Jesus believe they know these things? The construction does not tell us, though either way the conclusion follows logically. Does Jesus believe they will do these things? The construction leaves it up in the air.

5.241. Type 4: Future-Less-Likely Conditions

The Type 4 condition is used for a condition oriented to the future, something that potentially will occur or is a hypothetical possibility.[261] Often these are like Type 3 conditions, but with less expectation that the protasis will be fulfilled.

---

261. Type 4 are also called future-less-vivid or future-remote conditions.

The context must clarify whether or not the author expects the condition in the protasis to be fulfilled, and sometimes it is not clear.

a. A future-less-likely condition is composed of

Protasis (if)	Apodosis (then)
εἰ + optative	various

b. The protasis uses the potential optative (§5.153). In CG the apodosis also used an optative and ἄν, while in KG other moods are used as well, and often ἄν is not included.

c. This type of conditional statement was very common in CG, but was fading from use during the Hellenistic period. There is no complete example of this form of condition in the New Testament in which an optative is used in the apodosis. The closest example to a future-less-likely condition in the New Testament is in 1 Peter.

> ἀλλ᾽ εἰ καὶ **πάσχοιτε** διὰ δικαιοσύνην,/μακάριοι. (1 Pet 3:14)
> *But if indeed you suffer because of righteousness,/you are blessed.*

This protasis has εἰ with an optative, but the apodosis does not have an optative. Since the verb is missing from the apodosis we could supply an optative, but in KG it is just as likely to be a future indicative.

This form of conditional statement could signal that Peter does not have any strong expectation that his readers will be suffering for righteousness' sake. There are, however, numerous references in the letter to the readers' experience of suffering (for example, 1:6–7; 2:12, 15; 3:9, 16; 4:12, 14). So perhaps the "harm" or "hurt" that he is referring to in the context (κακόω, 3:13) is more severe than the insults and social shunning they have experienced to this point, and he is not expecting it to get worse.

Alternatively, Peter may be simply saying that, hypothetically speaking, if they experience such suffering this is what follows, namely, they are blessed.

5.242. Type 5: General Conditions

A general condition states what always happens given the conditions referred to in the protasis.[262]

a. A general condition is composed of

Protasis (if)	Apodosis (then)
ἐάν + subjunctive	present indicative

---

262. Type 5 are also called present general, generic, or habitual conditions.

b. This form is sometimes listed as a subset of Type 3 since both have the same signals in the protasis. In the apodosis, however, a general condition can only have a present indicative, and it is not future-oriented the way Type 3 conditions are.

c. The reference is often timeless, like a proverb or a wisdom saying. "A stitch in time **saves** nine." "A penny saved **is** a penny earned." Maybe we should call this the Ben Franklin Condition!

> ἐάν τις **περιπατῇ** ἐν τῇ ἡμέρᾳ,/**οὐ προσκόπτει** (John 11:9)
> *If anyone <u>walks</u> in the day/he or she <u>does not stumble</u>*

> καὶ ἐὰν βασιλεία ἐφ᾿ ἑαυτὴν **μερισθῇ**,/**οὐ δύναται** σταθῆναι ἡ βασιλεία ἐκείνη (Mark 3:24)
> *And <u>if</u> a kingdom <u>is divided</u> against itself,/that kingdom <u>is not able</u> to stand*

> ἐὰν μή τις **γεννηθῇ** ἄνωθεν, οὐ **δύναται** ἰδεῖν τὴν βασιλείαν τοῦ θεοῦ (John 3:3)
> *<u>if</u> someone <u>is</u> not <u>born</u> from above/he or she <u>is</u> not <u>able</u> to see the kingdom of God*

5.243. Summary of Conditions

Type	Signs	Nuance
1. Indefinite	If – εἰ + any ind. Then – any finite vb.	If this is true, and the context will have to indicate whether or not I think it is true.
2. Contrary-to-Fact	If – εἰ + secondary ind. Then – secondary ind. + ἄν	If this is true, and I don't believe that it is.
3. Future-More-Likely	If – ἐάν + subjunctive Then – any finite vb.	If this is true, and I think it's possible, probable, or hypothetical.
4. Future-Less-Likely	If – εἰ + optative Then – various	If this is true, and I think it's unlikely to be true, or I'm just raising a hypothetical possibility.
5. General	If – ἐάν + subjunctive Then – present ind.	If this is true, then this is what I think always happens.

This numbering system is frequently used in resource material so you should be aware of it. However, the following layout and the summary that follows may help you learn the patterns more easily.

5.244. Conditions Arranged by Key Signs

This is the same chart as above, but with types using εἰ listed first and then those using ἐάν.

Type	Signs	Nuance
1. Indefinite	If – εἰ + any ind. Then – any finite vb.	If this is true and the context will have to indicate whether or not I think it is true.
2. Contrary-to-Fact	If – εἰ + secondary ind. Then – secondary ind. + ἄν	If this is true and I don't believe that it is.
4. Future-Less-Likely	If – εἰ + optative Then – various	If this is true and I think it's unlikely to be true, or I'm just raising a hypothetical possibility.
3. Future-More-Likely	If – ἐάν + subjunctive Then – any finite vb.	If this is true and I think it's possible, probable, or hypothetical.
5. General	If – ἐάν + subjunctive Then – present ind.	If this is true then this is what I think always happens.

Summary of the Key Signs to Watch For

εἰ   =   1, 2, or 4

- 2 must have imperfects or aorists and usually has ἄν in the apodosis.
- 4 must have an optative in the protasis.

ἐάν   =   3 or 5

- 5 must have a present indicative in the apodosis.

5.245. Future-Most-Likely Conditions

Yet another form of condition is not usually included in the list with the other five types.[263] Occasionally a future condition will be expressed with εἰ and a future indicative, rather than ἐάν and a subjunctive as in Type 3. It conveys a sense of strong emotion. "The protasis commonly suggests something undesired, or feared, or intended independently of the speaker's will; the apodosis commonly conveys a threat, a warning, or an earnest appeal to the feelings."[264] In English a present tense is used in the protasis.

> εἰ πάντες **σκανδαλισθήσονται** ἐν σοί,/ἐγὼ οὐδέποτε **σκανδαλισθήσομαι** (Matt 26:33)
> *If they all fall away because of you,/I (myself) will never fall away!*

---

263. This form of condition is also called the emotional future condition.

264. Smyth §2328; see also *CGCG* §49.5. Funk discusses this form of condition in the context of a future more vivid condition but regards it as "a special form of first class condition." Funk §858.4.

Sentence Connectors and Conjunctions

5.246. Major Sentence Connectors and Conjunctions

While conjunctions connect elements of various sorts (§5.247a), certain words connect primarily sentences and clauses, and occasionally also paragraphs.

    a. Three of the most common sentence connectors are also conjunctions, καί, ἤ, and ἀλλά.

    b. Among the other sentence connectors the most common are γάρ, οὖν, and δέ, including ὁ δέ and μέν . . . δέ. The various uses of connectors can be sorted out with the help of a lexicon.[265]

    For example, in John 3:16 we find the connector γάρ.

> οὕτως **γὰρ** ἠγάπησεν ὁ θεὸς τὸν κόσμον, ὥστε τὸν υἱὸν τὸν μονογενῆ ἔδωκεν (John 3:16)
> *For God loved the world so much that as a result he gave his unique Son*[266]

The four common connectors γάρ, οὖν, δέ, and μέν are **postpositive**, that is, they do not stand first in their clause, which means that γάρ is not the first word in this sentence. In this case, γάρ signals that we are now going to be given the grounds or an explanation for what has been said (§5.247d), in this case in verses 3:14–15: "And as Moses lifted up the serpent in the wilderness, even so must the Son of Man be lifted up, that whoever believes may in him have eternal life" (John 3:14–15). In this case γάρ connects not only sentences but also a paragraph, since a new paragraph begins at 3:16.

    c. Often conjunctions and sentence connectors work in pairs with each other or other words, especially negative particles.[267] For example, καί . . . καί, *both . . . and*; ἤ . . . ἤ, *either . . . or*; οὐ . . . ἀλλά, *not . . . but*; τέ . . . τέ, *not only . . . but*.

> Διαμαρτύρομαι . . . **καὶ** τὴν ἐπιφάνειαν αὐτοῦ **καὶ** τὴν βασιλείαν αὐτοῦ (2 Tim 4:1)
> *I solemnly attest to . . . both his manifestation and his kingdom*

> **ἢ** γὰρ τὸν ἕνα μισήσει καὶ τὸν ἕτερον ἀγαπήσει **ἢ** ἑνὸς ἀνθέξεται καὶ τοῦ ἑτέρου καταφρονήσει. (Matt 6:24)
> *For either he/she will hate the one and love the other, or he/she will respect the one and despise the other.*

---

265. See also Funk, ch. 43.

266. BDAG takes οὕτως as a reference to what follows, *in this way*. BDAG, s.v. "οὕτω/οὕτως," 2, 742. But the ὥστε clause suggests we have the intensive use here (mng. 3), *so much*.

267. For a more extensive discussion, see Funk, chs. 41 and 42. When sentence connectors and conjunctions work in pairs they are sometimes referred to as correlatives.

μὴ κλαίετε, **οὐ** γὰρ ἀπέθανεν **ἀλλὰ** καθεύδει. (Luke 8:52)
Stop crying, for she is <u>not</u> dead <u>but</u> is sleeping.

Most of these pairs are easily sorted out with a lexicon, but one such pair, μέν . . . δέ is subtle enough that we should discuss it.

d. μέν . . . δέ. The postpositive particle μέν distinguishes "the word or clause with which it stands from that which follows."[268] In other words, it highlights a word or clause as something distinct. It packages a word or clause in the context of one or more other items. The context must indicate the nature of the relation between the units in the text.

μέν may be used alone or paired with a following δέ. If there is a contrast then sometimes a μέν . . . δέ construction can be translated "on the one hand . . . on the other," but often μέν is left untranslated and δέ is rendered as "but." Or μέν can be translated "while" and the δέ left untranslated.

If the elements are not contrasted but simply distinguished from one another, as in a list, the nuance is hard to convey in English. The δέ can be rendered "and," though this translation loses the nuance of the μέν . . . δέ construction. See further §§5.17, 217b.

Ἐγὼ **μὲν** ὑμᾶς βαπτίζω ἐν ὕδατι εἰς μετάνοιαν,
ὁ **δὲ** ὀπίσω μου ἐρχόμενος ἰσχυρότερός μού ἐστιν (Matt 3:11)
I am baptizing you with water for repentance,
<u>but</u> the one coming after me is mightier than I

Ἰωάννης **μὲν** σημεῖον ἐποίησεν οὐδέν,
πάντα **δὲ** ὅσα εἶπεν Ἰωάννης περὶ τούτου ἀληθῆ ἦν. (John 10:41)
<u>While</u> John did no sign, everything John said about this person was true.

ἡ δὲ ἄνωθεν σοφία πρῶτον **μὲν** ἁγνή ἐστιν, ἔπειτα εἰρηνική, ἐπιεικής (Jas 3:17)
But the wisdom that is from above is first pure, then peaceable, courteous
> Here μέν introduces a list of characteristics of wisdom. This is an example of μέν used without δέ.

Καὶ αὐτὸς ἔδωκεν τοὺς **μὲν** ἀποστόλους, τοὺς **δὲ** προφήτας, τοὺς **δὲ** εὐαγγελιστάς, τοὺς **δὲ** ποιμένας καὶ διδασκάλους (Eph 4:11)
And he himself gave some to be apostles, some prophets, some evangelists, and some pastors and teachers
> And here we see μέν followed by δέ repeated in a list.

---

268. Abbott-Smith, s.v. "μέν," 283.

5.247. A List of Major Sentence Connectors and Conjunctions

Sections 5.206-46 illustrated many of the major ways of relating clauses and sentences.

a. In general, conjunctions connect two items that are of the same grammatical type, such as two nouns, two adverbs, two prepositional phrases, two verbs, two clauses, two sentences—virtually any type of expression.

b. There are other connectors that are limited to connecting sentences (§5.246b).

c. Greek abounds in both of these forms of connectors, thereby offering detailed guidance for following the flow of thought. Some words serve as both a sentence connector and a conjunction, including the very common words καί, ἤ, and ἀλλά (§5.246a).

d. The following list of major sentence connectors and conjunctions gives a few of the most common uses for reference. Most of these words have multiple uses and nuances, so consult the lexicons to fill out the information offered here.[269] Such words are very important not only for seeing the flow of thought within clauses, between clauses, and between sentences, but also within paragraphs and larger discourses.[270]

Major Sentence Connectors and Conjunctions

Connector/ Conjunction	Possible Use	Translation
ἀλλά	contrast	*but, yet*
ἄρα	conclusion (inference)	*so, then, consequently*
γάρ	cause (reason) - direct cause/effect relation	*for, because, since*
	grounds (basis)	*for, because, since*
	explanation	*for, that is, for example*
δέ	addition	*and*
	sequence, transition[271]	*then, now*
	contrast	*but*
διό	conclusion (inference)	*therefore*
ἐάν	condition	*if*

---

269. See also Funk, chs. 41–46.

270. For a list of connections and uses see *UEBG*, appendix 2, and the resources listed on page 220.

271. "Although δέ and καί . . . may be translated with *and*, these particles operate on different levels: whereas δέ serves to indicate shifts from one text segment/topic to another . . . , καί connects several things said about a topic, linking several elements *within* a larger text segment." *CGCG* §59.21. See further *DiscGram*, 23–36. At times the shift indicated by δέ signals emphasis or climax. See, for example, Luke 10:20; 1 Pet 1:7–8.

Connector/ Conjunction	Possible Use	Translation
εἰ	condition	*if*
	indirect question	*whether*
ἐπεί	time	*when*
	grounds (basis)	*for, because, since*
ἕως	time	*until*
ἤ	alternative	*or*
ἵνα	purpose	*in order that, so, so that*
	result	*so that*
	content (noun clause)	*that*
καθώς	comparison	*just as*
καί	addition, sequence, series, simultaneity	*and*
καίπερ	concession	*although*
μέν	distinction	(often untranslatable, see §5.246d)
μή	negative purpose	*lest, in order that … not*
ὅθεν	place	*from where*
ὅπου	place	*where*
ὅπως	purpose	*in order that*
ὅς, ἥ, ὅ	identification	*who, which*
ὅτε	time	*when*
ὅτι	cause (reason)—direct cause/effect relation	*for, because, since*
	grounds (basis)	*for, because, since*
	content (indirect statement)	*that*
	content (direct statement)	*"…"*
οὗ	place	*where*
οὖν	conclusion (inference)	*so, therefore*
	(transitional or resumptive—see BDAG)	*now, then*
πρίν	time	*before*
τέ	addition[272]	*and*
ὡς	comparison	*as*
	time	*when*
	purpose	*in order that*
	content (indirect statement)	*that*
ὥσπερ	comparison	*just as*
ὥστε	conclusion (inference)	*therefore, so*
	result	*so that*

272. *CGEL* (348): "enclitic particle used to connect an idea closely to another in a manner that is tighter than with καί."

5.248. Asyndeton

While most clauses and sentences are connected by conjunctions and connectors, occasionally they are simply placed next to one another.[273] "The absence of connectives in a language so rich in means of coordination as is Greek is more striking than in other languages."[274] Thus when there is no explicit connection the effect is often powerful, being used "for emphasis, solemnity, or rhetorical value (staccato effect), or when there is an abrupt change in topic."[275] When there is "a distinct advance in the thought," then asyndeton "generally expresses emotion of some sort, and is the mark of liveliness, rapidity, passion, or impressiveness, of thought, each idea being set forth separately and distinctly."[276]

WORD CLUSTERS WITHIN CLAUSES

5.249. Introduction to Clusters within Clauses

As you read along in a passage you should look for word clusters. The largest clusters within a sentence are the clauses discussed in the previous sections (§§5.206–45). Within the clauses there are several ways in which words are joined together, among which the following are common.

5.250. Agreement in Gender, Case, and Number

The use of agreement to connect nouns/substantives with their modifiers is discussed in §2.30.

a. Often in the New Testament the words are next to one another, but occasionally they are separated.

φῶς εἰμι τοῦ κόσμου (John 9:5)
I am the light of the world

ἐὰν δὲ ἄλλῳ ἀποκαλυφθῇ καθημένῳ, ὁ πρῶτος σιγάτω (1 Cor 14:30)
but if a revelation is given to another person who is sitting, the first person should be silent

---

273. Asyndeton means "not bound together," from σύν, *with, together* and δέω, *bind*, with an alpha privative on the front (§2.37b).
274. Smyth §2165a.
275. *ExSyn*, 658.
276. Smyth §2165a. See Smyth §§2165–2167 for further details.

b. A particular type of separation called **hyperbaton** occurs frequently in CG and occasionally in the New Testament, especially in books with a higher style such as Hebrews.[277] "Such displacement usually gives prominence to the first of two words thus separated, but sometimes to the second also."[278] Hyperbaton takes several forms; the following examples illustrate a specific form that makes use of agreement.

καὶ **καλὸν** γευσαμένους θεοῦ **ῥῆμα** (Heb 6:5)
and having tasted <u>the good word</u> of God

καὶ **τὰς αὐτὰς** πολλάκις προσφέρων **θυσίας** (Heb 10:11)
and offering <u>the same sacrifices</u> many times

ἵνα καὶ αὐτοὶ **σωτηρίας** τύχωσιν **τῆς ἐν Χριστῷ Ἰησοῦ** (2 Tim 2:10)
that they also might meet with <u>the salvation which is in Christ Jesus</u>

5.251. Attributive and Predicate Positions

The following examples illustrate the use of the article to signal these two positions which were introduced in §§5.3-5.

εἶπεν δὲ **τῷ ἀνδρὶ τῷ** ξηρὰν **ἔχοντι** τὴν χεῖρα· ἔγειρε καὶ στῆθι εἰς τὸ μέσον (Luke 6:8)
he said <u>to the man who had</u> the withered hand, "Rise and stand in the middle"
> In this example of the second attributive position the first article goes with the noun ἀνδρί, *man*, and the second article with the participle ἔχοντι, *having* which is modifying ἀνδρί. Notice also the example of hyperbaton, with an adjective, ξηράν, *withered*, separated from the noun it modifies, χεῖρα, *hand*.

ὅτι **τὸ** ἐν ἀνθρώποις **ὑψηλὸν** βδέλυγμα ἐνώπιον τοῦ θεοῦ (Luke 16:15)
for <u>that which is highly valued</u> among people is <u>something detestable</u> before God
> The subject is τὸ ὑψηλόν, *that which is highly valued*, and the subject complement in predicate position is βδέλυγμα, *something detestable*.

---

277. See Steven M. Baugh, "Hyperbaton and Greek Literary Style in Hebrews," *Novum Testamentum* 59 (2017): 194-213. His article on another aspect of ancient rhetoric is also very stimulating, "Greek Periods in the Book of Hebrews," *Novum Testamentum* 60 (2018): 24-44. For a quick introduction see Baugh, *Ephesians*, Evangelical Exegetical Commentary (Bellingham, WA: Lexham Press, 2016), 8-25.
278. Smyth §3028. *CGCG* §60.18 notes, "Hyperbaton with the **modifier preceding the head** . . . involves strong emphasis on the modifier" (emphasis original).

5.252. Bracketing Article

The bracketing of the article was introduced in §5.9. The verse just examined includes an example of bracketing,

τὸ ἐν ἀνθρώποις **ὑψηλόν** (Luke 16:15)
that which is highly valued among people
> ▸ The article brackets, or nests, the prepositional phrase.

αἰτείτω παρὰ **τοῦ διδόντος** θεοῦ πᾶσιν ἁπλῶς καὶ μὴ **ὀνειδίζοντος**, καὶ δοθή-σεται αὐτῷ (Jas 1:5)
he/she should ask from God who gives to all simply and does not criticize and it will be given to him/her
> ▸ This example is similar to Granville Sharp's rule (§5.11) with two nouns/substantives connected by καί and initiated by a single article. Here, however, the participles are not functioning as nouns but as adjectives modifying θεοῦ, *God*, which is the object of the preposition παρά, *from*. So this article connects the two participles and also brackets the indirect object πᾶσιν, *to all* and the adverb ἁπλῶς, *simply*.

5.253. Genitive Modifiers

A very common cluster within a clause is the combination of a word and its genitive modifier. These clusters are usually easy to recognize, with the genitive normally coming after the word it modifies. When the genitive precedes the word it modifies there is a bit of emphasis on the genitive. It is usually next to the word it modifies or fairly close.

Sometimes a large string of genitives is used. In such cases usually each genitive modifies the one that precedes it.

ἐν οἷς ὁ θεὸς **τοῦ αἰῶνος τούτου** ἐτύφλωσεν τὰ νοήματα τῶν ἀπίστων εἰς τὸ μὴ αὐγάσαι τὸν φωτισμὸν **τοῦ εὐαγγελίου τῆς δόξης τοῦ Χριστοῦ**, ὅς ἐστιν εἰκὼν τοῦ θεοῦ (2 Cor 4:4)
among whom the god of this age has blinded the minds of those who do not believe so that the illumination of the gospel of the glory of Christ, who is the image of God, might not shine forth upon them
> ▸ The first short set of genitives, τοῦ αἰῶνος τούτου, *of this age*, modifies ὁ θεός, *God*, probably a genitive of subordination (§5.41). In the longer string of genitives each modifies the word before it and each in a different way.

1. Illumination is said to be "of the gospel," either a subjective genitive (§5.38), that is, the gospel is doing the illuminating/enlightening, or a genitive of source (§5.48), the illumination shining from the gospel.

2. Then the gospel is said to be "of the glory," which could be an attributive genitive (§5.44), the glorious gospel. Or it could be either an objective genitive (§5.38) or genitive of content (§5.45), either of which means the gospel is about the glory.

3. Finally, the glory is said to be "of Christ," which could be possessive (§5.35), it is a quality or attribute he has, or, if we take the glory as attributive (glorious gospel) then "of Christ" could be an objective genitive or genitive of content, the glorious gospel about Christ.

5.254. Prepositional Phrases

Prepositions are words placed before (prepositioned) a noun, pronoun, and certain verb forms to form a prepositional phrase. A preposition usually indicates a relationship of some sort. Spatial and temporal relations are often fundamental, which are developed into more abstract or metaphorical meanings.[279]

a. In both English and Greek such phrases are composed of the preposition and a word or cluster of words referred to as the **object of the preposition**.

> ἔστη [ἐπὶ τόπου πεδινοῦ] (Luke 6:17)
> he stood [<u>on</u> a level place]

Here ἐπί (on) is the preposition and τόπου πεδινοῦ (a level place) is its object. The preposition signals a spatial relationship and the prepositional phrase is telling us where Jesus stood.

> καὶ ὃς ἐὰν δέξηται ἓν παιδίον τοιοῦτο [ἐπὶ τῷ ὀνόματί μου], ἐμὲ δέχεται. (Matt 18:5)
> And whoever receives one such little child [<u>in</u> my name] receives me.

Here ἐπί (in) has τῷ ὀνόματί μου (my name) as its object. We have the same preposition used as in the first example, but now it does not tell us the location, but rather the grounds, reason, or motive for an action. This use, however, can be seen as an extension of the spatial sense, as in our expression "<u>on</u> the basis of" or "<u>on</u> account of."

---

279. "The prepositions express primarily notions of space, then notions of time, and finally are used in figurative relations to denote cause, agency, means, manner, etc. . . . The prepositions define the character of the verbal action and set forth the relations of an oblique case [a nonnominative case] to the predicate with greater precision than is possible for the cases without a preposition." Smyth §1637. While some scholars reject this view, Pietro Bortone provides evidence that Greek prepositions begin with spatial meanings and then develop figurative meanings that "may be regarded as metaphorical extensions of the original spatial sense." Bortone, *Greek Prepositions from Antiquity to the Present* (Oxford: Oxford University Press, 2010), 303.

b. Thus, Greek prepositions can be used in a wide variety of ways. Often the various meanings are related to the case form of the object of the preposition.[280] So it is important to pay attention to the different meanings of prepositions in relation to the case that is used for each.

c. Prepositional phrases frequently modify verbs, but may modify nouns as well.[281] In particular, when a preposition is introduced by an article it serves as a noun or adjective, but may do so without an article as well.

ἡ ἀγγελία ἣν ἠκούσατε [**ἀπ'** ἀρχῆς] (1 John 3:11)
the message that you have heard [from the beginning]

> ➤ A prepositional phrase as an adverb modifying ἠκούσατε (*you have heard*).

τοὺς προφήτας [τοὺς **πρὸ** ὑμῶν] (Matt 5:12)
the prophets [who were before you]

> ➤ A prepositional phrase with an article functioning as an adjective modifying τοὺς προφήτας (*the prophets*).

γυνὴ [**ἐκ** τῆς Σαμαρείας] (John 4:7)
a woman [of Samaria]

> ➤ A rare prepositional phrase without an article functioning as an adjective.

ἐγνώκατε [τὸν **ἀπ'** ἀρχῆς] (1 John 2:13)
you know [him who is from the beginning]

> ➤ A prepositional phrase with an article functioning as a noun, the direct object of ἐγνώκατε (*you have known*).

d. Prepositions in Compound Verbs. Prepositions are often added to the front of verbs producing a **compound verb** (§§2.37a; 4.5, 37). Sometimes the meaning of a compound verb is easy to see from the original preposition and verb. ἔρχομαι means *come* and εἰς means *into*, and the compound verb εἰσέρχομαι means *come into, enter*. The meaning of other compounds is not so easy to deduce. Indeed, often there is no difference in meaning between the compound and uncompounded forms of a verb. Thus a lexicon will be needed, at times even for compounds that seem obvious.

Frequently a compound verb is used with a prepositional phrase that repeats the preposition used in the compound. This is not a form of emphasis.

---

280. Note that the object of a preposition is never in the nominative case.
281. "All prepositions seem to have been adverbs originally and mostly adverbs of place.... Gradually the preposition-adverb was brought into closer connection either (1) with the verb..., or (2) with the noun, the preposition-adverb having freed itself from its adverbial relation to the verb." Smyth §§1636a, 1638c. See Harris, *Prepositions*, 25–28.

ἐξῆλθον ἐκ τῆς πόλεως (John 4:30)
they came <u>out of</u> the town

e. Some prepositions are never used in compound verbs. These are called **improper prepositions** and there are forty-two of them used in the New Testament.[282] The fact that a preposition is improper does not affect its meaning.

f. **Prepositional Phrases as Word Clusters.** Prepositional phrases are a very common form of word cluster. Since the object of the preposition can have quite a few modifiers itself these clusters can be large.

Διὸ μνημονεύετε ὅτι ποτὲ ὑμεῖς τὰ ἔθνη ἐν σαρκί, οἱ λεγόμενοι ἀκροβυστία [**ὑπὸ** τῆς λεγομένης περιτομῆς ἐν σαρκὶ χειροποιήτου] (Eph 2:11)
Therefore remember that formerly you, the gentiles in the flesh, who are called "uncircumcision" [<u>by</u> that which is called "circumcision" in the flesh made by hands]

> ὑπό introduces a long prepositional phrase indicating the agent who does the calling. The object of the preposition is the genitive τῆς λεγομένης περιτομῆς (*that which is called "circumcision"*). This circumcision is further modified by the prepositional phrase ἐν σαρκί (*in flesh*), and a genitive of means (§5.55), χειροποιήτου (*by hands*).

Sometimes prepositions occur in strings, with each preposition making a significant contribution to the thought.

προορίσας ἡμᾶς [**εἰς** υἱοθεσίαν] [**διὰ** Ἰησοῦ Χριστοῦ] [**εἰς** αὐτόν], [**κατὰ** τὴν εὐδοκίαν τοῦ θελήματος αὐτοῦ], [**εἰς** ἔπαινον δόξης τῆς χάριτος αὐτοῦ] ἧς ἐχαρίτωσεν ἡμᾶς [**ἐν** τῷ ἠγαπημένῳ] (Eph 1:5–6)
having predestined us [for adoption] [<u>through</u> Jesus Christ] [<u>to</u> himself] [<u>in keeping with</u> the pleasure of his will] [<u>to</u> the praise of the glory of his grace] that he has freely given us [<u>in</u> the beloved]

> This piling up of prepositions and genitives is typical of Paul's doxological style in Ephesians, making it a very rich text to read carefully.

5.255. A List of Common Prepositions

The following are the most common prepositions as well as a few of the less common.

a. The meanings listed are those that are most common, which provide a starting point for beginning to learn the prepositions. "In each Greek preposition, it seems, there is an inherent, foundational meaning that is further defined by a

---

282. For a complete list and discussion see Harris, *Prepositions*, chs. 23–24;and *AGG* §185a. Smyth §§1647, 1699–1702; and *CGCG* §31.9 also contain lists.

particular context."[283] Abbott-Smith is often particularly helpful for seeing the foundational meaning and then its extensions as used in various contexts.[284]

b. Prepositions often drop their final vowel (§1.10) or undergo other slight changes depending on the letter at the beginning of the following word (§4.37). For example, a preposition ending in π changes to φ and one ending in τ to θ before words with a rough breathing. When ἐκ is followed by a word beginning with a vowel it becomes ἐξ. The alternate forms are listed in parentheses, except for σύν whose many forms are given below in footnote 285.

One Case

Preposition	Genitive	Dative	Accusative
ἀντί (ἀνθ')	opposite, over against, instead of, for (the sake of)		
ἀπό (ἀπ', ἀφ')	off, from		
ἐκ (ἐξ)	out of, from		
πρό	before		
ἐν		in, on, at, among, by (means of)	
σύν[285]		with (association)	
ἀνά			up, each[a]
εἰς			into, to, toward

[a] "Each" represents the distributive sense that is translated in a variety of ways. For example, ἔλαβον ἀνὰ δηνάριον, *they received a denarius apiece* (Matt 20:9). χωροῦσαι ἀνὰ μετρητὰς δύο ἢ τρεῖς, *each holding 2 or 3 measures* (John 2:6).

283. Harris, *Prepositions*, 27; and see §5.254 n. 279.

284. The list of prepositions in *CGCG* §31.8 is especially helpful since it is organized in three columns for spatial, temporal, and abstract/metaphorical senses. For the New Testament, along with the lexicons, Nunn, *Short Syntax*, 28–36 provides a convenient concise list; *AGG* §§184–85 a more extensive list; and Harris, *Prepositions* is the major resource. In addition to the discussion in *CGCG*, ch. 31, Smyth's discussion of prepositions is very valuable (§§1636–1702), though the nuances in CG do not always apply in KG. See BDF §§203–40; and especially *AGG* §184 for the major differences with CG. For a more technical linguistic study see Bortone, *Greek Prepositions*, especially ch. 5, "Prepositions and Cases in Hellenistic Greek."

285. In compounds with stems beginning with a

- labial: συνπ = συμπ,   συνβ = συμβ,   συνφ = συμφ,
- velar: συνκ = συγγ,   συνγ = συγγ,   συνχ = συγχ,
- dental: συνζ = συζ,   other dentals unchanged (συντ, συνδ)
- liquid: συνλ = συλλ,   συνμ = συμμ,   συνρ = συρρ,
- also: συνψ = συμψ,   συνσ = συς.

Two Cases

Preposition	Genitive	Dative	Accusative
διά (δι')	through, by (means of)		because of
κατά (κατ', καθ')	down, against		through, according to, in keeping with, each[a]
μετά (μετ', μεθ')	with		after
ὑπέρ	over, for[b]		over, beyond
ὑπό (ὑπ', ὑφ')	by (means of)		under

[a] The distributive sense: κατ' ἐκκλησίαν, *in each church,* or *church by church* (Acts 14:23).
[b] "For" in several senses, including: on behalf of, for the sake of, instead of, because of.

Three Cases

Preposition	Genitive	Dative	Accusative
ἐπί (ἐπ', ἐφ')	on, over, near, when	on, because	over, to, toward, against, for[a]
παρά (παρ')	from (beside)	beside, with	beside, along, beyond
περί	about, concerning	around, near	about, around
πρός	from (the side of)	at, near	to, toward, regarding

[a] "For" of duration: ἐπὶ ἑπτὰ ἡμέρας, *for seven days* (Heb 11:30), and of purpose: ἐπὶ τὸ συμφέρον, *for our profit* (Heb 12:10).

5.256. Omission of Items

As in English, often in Greek some item in a phrase, clause, or sentence is omitted. Frequently the verb "to be" is lacking in the predicate position (§5.5), and a noun is missing in phrases with a genitive of relationship (§5.39). Often a missing item is obvious from the grammar or can be supplied from the context.

> οἱ δὲ λοιποὶ κρατήσαντες τοὺς δούλους αὐτοῦ ὕβρισαν καὶ ἀπέκτειναν (Matt 22:6)
> *And the others, seizing his slaves, beat and killed [them]*

> Περὶ δὲ τῆς ἡμέρας ἐκείνης ἢ τῆς ὥρας οὐδεὶς οἶδεν, οὐδὲ οἱ ἄγγελοι ἐν οὐρανῷ οὐδὲ ὁ υἱός, εἰ μὴ ὁ πατήρ. (Mark 13:32)
> *But concerning that day or hour no one knows, not even the angels in heaven nor the Son, except the Father.*

> ➤ There are three omissions here. A literal English translation works for the first two, but not the third. "But concerning that day or hour no one

knows, not even the angels in heaven [know], nor the Son [knows], [no one knows] except the Father."

WORD ORDER AND EMPHASIS

5.257. Introduction to Clause Order and Word Order

While Greek appears much less ordered than English there are actually some common patterns in the relation between clauses as well as between words within clauses. In order to read Greek it is not essential to know which order is more common. But some familiarity with the patterns of normal clause and word order enables you to recognize when emphasis is added, which in turn increases your understanding and enjoyment. While there is continuing research and debate on these matters, the following sections introduce some of the more commonly mentioned patterns and a few other forms of emphasis to get you started.[286]

a. The first sections that follow focus briefly on the order between clauses, which is largely related to the role that a subordinate clause plays in a sentence.

b. The order within clauses is more complex. Because Greek relies to a significant degree on morphological form to communicate thought, an author has more freedom to move an item earlier or later than normally expected, thereby highlighting it to some degree. The general principle is that the position of an element in a clause "is determined largely by how new and important the information which it adds to the context is."[287]

So, for example, by **fronting** an item, that is, moving it earlier than one might have done, the reader encounters that information and has it in mind as he/she

---

286. Some elements of order are clear, such as an article preceding the word it modifies. But apart from such cases, "The principles which govern word order . . . are not fully understood. However, . . . even if much remains uncertain, a number of tendencies can be observed." *CGCG* §60.3. The issue is further complicated in those ancient Greek writers who approached the ordering of communication with the sound of the syllables and words in mind much more than most modern English speakers do (§1.1c, n. 7). *CGCG* §§60.1–38 is an extensive overview for CG, and *AGG* §128 provides a concise overview for KG. Fredrick J. Long, Κοινὴ Γραμματική *Koine Greek Grammar: A Beginning-Intermediate Exegetical and Pragmatic Handbook* (Wilmore, KY: GlossaHouse, 2015) contains extensive discussion; and *Deeper*, 450, provides a clear and concise brief chart of possible emphasis within sentences. See also, Steven E. Runge, "Interpreting Constituent Order in Koine Greek," in Black and Merkle, *Linguistics*, 125–46; *DiscGram*; *Advances*, chs. 7–8; and *UEBG*, 82–85, with the resources cited there. For a detailed technical linguistic study of word order in general see Jae Jung Song, *Word Order*, Research Surveys in Linguistics (Cambridge: Cambridge University Press, 2012).

287. *CGCG* §60.20.

proceeds through the text. Similarly, if an item is moved later than expected then that information clicks into place when the reader reaches it. Even in the earlier stages of learning Greek you can begin to experience these effects by rereading a passage you have worked through, picking up each item in order as it comes to you. It is often impossible to convey these nuances in a translation, since frequently they are less intense than the English equivalent, when there even is an equivalent.

Word Order and Emphasis between Clauses

5.258. Placement of Subordinate Clauses

In general we can expect those subordinate clauses and circumstantial participles that set the scene or establish the context for what follows to come before the main clause, while those that assume and develop information in the main clause to follow it. Thus, those that usually come before the main clause include concessives and the protasis of conditions, those that usually come after include purpose, result, content, local, relative, and comparative clauses, while temporal and causal clauses are common in both positions.[288]

Such general guidelines are affected by particular constructions and the preferences of individual authors.[289] For example, in the New Testament local clauses that begin with ὅθεν always come after the main clause (15×), while those that begin with οὗ are more divided, twenty-one after and five before.[290] Comparative clauses beginning with καθώς, καθάπερ, or καθά almost always follow the main clause in the Synoptics, but in John there are nineteen before and thirteen after the main clause.[291] Some temporal conjunctions prefer one position or the other. For example, ὅτε, ὅταν, and ὡς usually come before the main clause and ἕως, ἄχρι, and μέχρις usually after.[292]

---

288. Runge, "Interpreting Constituent Order in Koine Greek," in *Linguistics*, 138–43; Young, *Intermediate*, 216; David Alan Black, *Learn to Read New Testament Greek*, 3rd ed. (Nashville: B&H Academic, 2009), 202; James H. Moulton and Nigel Turner, *A Grammar of New Testament Greek*, vol. 3, *Syntax* (Edinburgh: T&T Clark, 1963), 344–45. So also in the LXX, as noted in Muraoka, *Syntax of Septuagint Greek*, 629, though he says concessive clauses tend to follow the main clause.

289. Turner notes issues of word order in various authors of the New Testament in James H. Moulton and Nigel Turner, *A Grammar of New Testament Greek*, vol. 4, *Style* (Edinburgh: T&T Clark, 1976). For an introduction to the topic of individual style, called idiolect (> ἴδιος, α, ον, *one's own* + λεκτός, ή, όν, *spoken*), see *Advances*, ch. 6.

290. Moulton and Turner, *Syntax*, 344.

291. Moulton and Turner, *Syntax*, 345.

292. Moulton and Turner, *Syntax*, 344–45.

5.259. Discourse Significance

Such features also are significant on the level of discourse. In general, subordinate clauses and circumstantial participles before the main verb provide background information. Those coming after the main verb may provide background information or may be more in the foreground, contributing to the main thought of the clause. This is true for both narrative and nonnarrative material.[293] Such information is not necessary for reading a passage, but it adds to your appreciation of what is going on in a sentence or a passage, and is significant in exegesis.

Word Order and Emphasis within Clauses

5.260. Verb Placement

The normal or neutral order in English is subject-verb-object, while in KG Greek it is verb-subject-object.[294] Thus the verb is followed by core elements of the clause (§2.3), and then adverbial information is added, in particular through prepositional phrases.[295] Accordingly, when a subject, direct object, indirect object, or complement precedes a verb there is often some degree of focus or emphasis. So also if a prepositional phrase precedes the verb.[296]

5.261. Order with an Expressed Subject

While the position of the verb before the subject is generally the case, Stanley Porter notes that in the New Testament when a subject is expressed and not just signaled by the verbal ending, "the most common pattern . . . is for the

293. For narrative material, see Levinsohn, "Verb Forms and Grounding," 172–76. For nonnarrative, see Steven E. Runge, "The Contribution of Verb Forms, Connectives, and Dependency to Grounding Status in Nonnarrative Discourse," in *Revisited*, 261–65.

294. For example, Levinsohn, *Discourse*, 17; Black, *Learn*, 201; Young, *Intermediate*, 218, citing Bernard Comrie, *Language Universals and Linguistic Typology: Syntax and Morphology* (Chicago: University of Chicago Press, 1981), 32. *AGG* §128b notes that in CG the verb "tends to have a middle position in main clauses"—subject-verb-object or object-verb-subject—with the first item in each sequence "given special weight."

295. Runge, "Interpreting Constituent Order in Koine Greek," in *Linguistics*, 136. In this chapter he calls attention to the importance of taking into account information that can be presupposed from the context or due to the topic.

296. *Deeper*, 450. Prepositional phrases and relative clauses modifying a noun usually follow the noun.

subject to occur first."²⁹⁷ Such fronting of an expressed subject often serves "either to draw attention to the subject of discussion or to mark a shift in the topic, perhaps signaling that a new person or event is the center of focus."²⁹⁸

5.262. Genitives and Adjectival Modifiers

Genitives and adjectival modifiers, including adjectives and adjectival participles, usually come after the noun they modify. So a modifier coming before the noun it modifies is emphatic to some degree (§5.253).²⁹⁹ When there are multiple modifiers some may come before and others after the head term, with those before highlighted to some degree.³⁰⁰

5.263. Word Clusters

a. Hendiadys. Sometimes καί joins two words that together express a single complex idea (ἕν, *one*, διά, *through*, δύο, *two*). With nouns a hendiadys functions like a noun modified by an adjective or a genitive. With verbs it joins the two verbs in one complex concept. It is frequently debatable whether the two words form a hendiadys or should be understood as distinct.

> περὶ **ἐλπίδος καὶ ἀναστάσεως** νεκρῶν [ἐγὼ] κρίνομαι (Acts 23:6)
> *I am being judged with reference to the hope of the resurrection of the dead*
> ➤ Most translations interpret these nouns as forming a hendiadys, not *hope and resurrection*.

> πάντα ὅσα **προσεύχεσθε καὶ αἰτεῖσθε** (Mark 11:24)
> *all things whatsoever you ask for in prayer*
> ➤ Translations differ over whether this is a hendiadys or the two verbs are distinct, *pray and ask for*.

b. Often the words in a cluster will be together in a clause, but at other times one or more words are separated from the rest of the cluster, which signals emphasis.

> **μειζοτέραν τούτων** οὐκ ἔχω χαράν (3 John 4)
> *I have no greater joy than this*

---

297. Porter, *Idioms*, 295.
298. Porter, *Idioms*, 295–96.
299. *CGCG* §60.15; *Deeper*, 450.
300. *CGCG* §60.17.

> μειζοτέραν τούτων (*greater than these*) modifies χαράν. This modifier is emphasized by being moved forward, even before the verb.

κύριε, οὐκ εἰμὶ ἱκανὸς ἵνα **μου** ὑπὸ τὴν στέγην εἰσέλθῃς (Matt 8:8)
Lord, I am not worthy that you should come under _my_ roof

> The genitive μου is moved even before the preposition of the phrase of which it is a part, signaling the centurion's deep sense of unworthiness. Luke uses the normal order: ἵνα ὑπὸ τὴν στέγην **μου** εἰσέλθῃς (Luke 7:6).

ἀλλὰ **τὴν ἀγάπην** ἵνα γνῶτε ἣν ἔχω περισσοτέρως εἰς ὑμᾶς (2 Cor 2:4)
but that you might know _the love_ that I have abundantly for you

> The direct object of γνῶτε, τὴν ἀγάπην, is given before the ἵνα clause even starts, which is then picked up by the relative pronoun ἥν. This is another form of fronting (§5.257b).

5.264. Individual Words

a. List of Words That May Carry Emphasis. The following words may carry some degree of emphasis.[301]

1. Adverbs (for example, ἀληθῶς, εὐθύς).
2. Emphatic personal pronouns (ἐμοῦ, ἐμοί, ἐμέ, etc.), except in prepositional phrases.[302]
3. Emphatic possessive adjectives (σός, ἡμέτερος, etc.).
4. Nominative personal pronoun (ἐγώ, ἡμεῖς, σύ, ὑμεῖς, αὐτός, αὐτή, etc.).[303]
5. Intensive adverbs (οὐχί, νυνί).

b. Adjunctive, Ascensive, and Explicative καί. Most often καί is coordinating, joining two items of the same grammatical kind, for example, two nouns, two clauses, and so forth (§5.247a). When, however, καί does not occur between two grammatically similar items it is usually adding a note of inclusion, emphasis, focus, or explanation to a word or word cluster.[304]

---

301. This list is based on Black, *Learn*, 202.
302. *CGCG* §29.4.
303. *CGCG* §29.4. When used as the subject of εἰμί these pronouns are often unemphatic. Furthermore, they may be part of a particular author's style, which may mean they are not emphatic or that the author's style itself is emphatic.
304. See Funk §§621-23.2; *CGEL*, 183; BDAG, s.v. "καί," 1.c, 2.a-b, 495; Abbott-Smith, 225; *ExSyn*, 670-71, 673.

1. First, καί may function as an adjunctive (Latin, *adjunctus, united*) to bring in an additional point to the discussion or to note some other form of inclusion. This use is usually translated *and, also, too, likewise.*

   ὅστις σε ῥαπίζει εἰς τὴν δεξιὰν σιαγόνα [σου], στρέψον αὐτῷ **καὶ** τὴν ἄλλην (Matt 5:39)
   whoever strikes you on your right cheek, turn to him the other <u>also</u>

   ὑπάγετε **καὶ** ὑμεῖς εἰς τὸν ἀμπελῶνα (Matt 20:4)
   you <u>also</u> go into the vineyard

2. Second, καί may function as an ascensive (Latin, *ascensus, ascent*) to add a final or climactic point, which may be translated, *even, indeed, in fact.*

   οὐχὶ **καὶ** οἱ τελῶναι τὸ αὐτὸ ποιοῦσιν; (Matt 5:46)
   Do not <u>even</u> the revenue officers do the same thing?

   ὥστε κύριός ἐστιν ὁ υἱὸς τοῦ ἀνθρώπου **καὶ** τοῦ σαββάτου (Mark 2:28)
   so the Son of Man is lord <u>even</u> over the sabbath

3. Third, καί may signal an explanation of what has just been said, *and so, that is, namely.* This use is sometimes referred to as the epexegetical use.

   ὁ δὲ θεὸς δίδωσιν αὐτῷ σῶμα καθὼς ἠθέλησεν, **καὶ** ἑκάστῳ τῶν σπερμάτων ἴδιον σῶμα (1 Cor 15:38)
   but God gives to it a body just as he planned, <u>namely</u>, to each of the seeds its own body

Sometimes it is unclear which sense καί represents.

   ὅτι **καὶ** ἐπὶ τὰ ἔθνη ἡ δωρεὰ τοῦ ἁγίου πνεύματος ἐκκέχυται (Acts 10:45)
   because the gift of the Spirit had been poured out <u>also/even</u> on the gentiles
   ‣ Both *even* and *also* make good sense here and translations vary on which they use.

   δι’ οὗ ἐλάβομεν χάριν **καὶ** ἀποστολήν (Rom 1:5)
   through whom we received grace, <u>that is</u>, apostleship
   ‣ Here καί could be explicative, but most translations interpret it as a simple connector, *grace and apostleship.* Yet another possibility is that χάριν καὶ ἀποστολήν form a hendiadys (§5.263a), *the grace of apostleship or apostolic grace.*

   c. Particles. The term "particle" may refer broadly to words that are indeclinable, including "negatives, sequence words (conjunctions, sentence connectors, subordinators), modalizers and nuance words."[305] Such words do not have content like a noun or verb, but rather "have a **functional meaning**: they indicate how certain parts *of the text itself* relate to each other, or how the text relates to the attitudes and expectations of the speaker and the addressee."[306] Thus, conjunctions may be referred to as "connective particles." Some words function in more than one way, as the lexicons indicate. This section focuses on the nuance words.[307]

1. Greek has a number of words that add flavor and emphasis more than content. Often they have an effect like using gestures in animated speech. Note, for example, the description of γέ in BDAG (190):

"γέ (Hom.+; apolog. exc. Ar.) enclit. particle, appended to the word or words it refers to; as in Hom. it serves to 'focus the attention upon a single idea, and place it, as it were, in the limelight: differing thus from δή, which emphasizes the reality of a concept (though in certain respects the usages of the two particles are similar)' (Denniston 114).[308] In oral utterance it would be accompanied by a change in pitch of voice at certain points in the context, and a translator may use an adverb or indicate the point through word order, choice of typeface, or punctuation *at least, even, indeed,* etc."

> διά γε τὸ παρέχειν μοι κόπον τὴν χήραν ταύτην ἐκδικήσω αὐτήν (Luke 18:5)
> <u>yet</u> because this widow is inflicting me with trouble I will carry out justice for her
> > ‣ This example shows how difficult it is to convey in English the flavor of this particle as described by J. D. Denniston in the quote from BDAG.

> εἴ γε ἐπιμένετε τῇ πίστει (Col 1:23)
> *if <u>indeed</u> you remain in the faith*

2. Very often particles form combinations.

> εἰ δὲ μή γε, ῥήγνυνται οἱ ἀσκοί (Matt 9:17)
> <u>otherwise</u> the wineskins will rip apart

305. Funk §014.4.

306. *CGCG* §59.2 (emphasis original). All of *CGCG*, ch. 59 deals with particles.

307. Von Siebenthal notes that while the term particle is used very broadly by some, it is more common to use it for "different types of uninflected words with little or no lexical meaning, typically used to modify in various ways the communicative force of the text in which they occur." *AGG* §22g.

308. J. D. Denniston, *The Greek Particles*, 2nd ed., rev. K. J. Dover (London: Duckworth, 1950). Denniston's 660 page book is just on particles, focusing primarily on Homeric and CG, in which particles play a much greater role than in KG. Smyth, §§2769-3003, is very helpful; and see especially *CGCG*, ch. 59. Note also Margaret E. Thrall, *Greek Particles in the New Testament: Linguistic and Exegetical Studies*, New Testament Tools and Studies 3 (Leiden: Brill, 1962).

5.265. Double Negatives

In Greek, two negatives do not make a positive; they almost always make something more emphatically negative.[309] One common form of double negative is οὐ μή with the subjunctive (§5.139), but other tense-forms and combinations are also used.

> ἐφ᾽ ὃν **οὐδεὶς οὔπω** ἀνθρώπων ἐκάθισεν (Mark 11:2)
> *upon which no one among men has yet sat*
>
> > ‣ οὐδείς, *no one* and οὔπω, *not yet*. In English we have to change *not yet* to *yet*.

> **οὐκ** ἀποκρίνῃ **οὐδέν**; (Mark 15:4)
> *Do you not answer?*
>
> > ‣ "Do you not answer nothing" could be translated woodenly as either, "Do you not answer anything?" or "Do you answer nothing?" Either way, one of the negatives has to be changed in English, or, more smoothly, left out.

> **οὐ** δύναται ἄνθρωπος λαμβάνειν **οὐδὲ** ἓν (John 3:27)
> *A person is not able to receive anything*
>
> > ‣ Woodenly, "a person is not able to receive not even one thing." οὐδέ is often used as a conjunction, but also can serve as an adverb, as here where it combines with οὐ to modify the verb.

SENTENCE MAPPING

5.266. Sentence Mapping and Discourse Analysis

Many manuals for learning how to exegete a passage include some form of rewriting a passage to depict its flow of thought and how each word and cluster fits within the overall structure. This is a very helpful tool not only for careful exegetical analysis but also for reflection. Even when simply reading a passage a map can be helpful for sorting out difficult sentences.

In addition to mapping sentences, whole paragraphs and even documents can be mapped to help analyze the larger discourse structures. Such discourse analysis is an important part of exegesis, but is touched on in this grammar only in relation to a few details.[310]

---

309. The three exceptions in the New Testament are in Acts 4:20; 1 Cor 9:6; 12:15. BDF §431.1.

310. For an introduction to discourse analysis see Stephen H. Levinsohn, "Discourse Analysis: Galatians as a Case Study," 5, in Black and Merkle, *Linguistics*, 103–24; chs. 6–7 in *Advances*; Mathewson, *Intermediate*, 270–90; and with more detail *AGG*, 569–636. Among

5.267. A Brief Introduction to Sentence Mapping

The form of sentence mapping offered here places the core elements of each clause on a line in the order they appear in the text.[311] Also on this line are a few other elements, including conjunctions and negative particles (οὐ, μή). The other elements of a sentence are aligned or indented underneath to show their relation to these core elements.

a. There are three possible levels of detail in such maps.

Level 1 The map shows the relations between clauses in the sentences in a passage.

Level 2 The map adds the role of prepositional phrases within the clauses.

Level 3 The map highlights the role of all the elements in a sentence, for example, an adjective or a genitive would be indented under the noun it modifies.

A level 2 map is usually sufficient for showing the flow of thought in a passage, though a level 3 map can be valuable for sorting out particularly complex material.

b. The basic technique of sentence mapping is simple:

1. Keep the core elements of each clause on a single line.
2. Line up flush with each other any items that are coordinate with each other or in apposition.
3. Indent any subordinate elements or modifiers under the word they modify, with a subordinate clause being placed under the verb of the clause it modifies.
4. When a word or cluster has to be moved out of order mark its original location with ellipsis points (. . .).

c. Sample maps.

> ὁ μὴ ἀγαπῶν οὐκ ἔγνω τὸν θεόν, ὅτι ὁ θεὸς ἀγάπη ἐστίν.
> *The one who does not love does not know God, for God is love.*

1 John 4:8

Level 1 Map: Clauses Arranged

> ὁ μὴ ἀγαπῶν οὐκ ἔγνω τὸν θεόν,
> ὅτι ὁ θεὸς ἀγάπη ἐστίν.

---

the books on discourse analysis, Runge, *DiscGram*; and Levinsohn, *Discourse*, give special attention to details in the Greek.

311. The core elements are the subject, verb, direct object, indirect object, and subject complement (§2.3).

> *The one who does not love does not know God*
> > *for God is love.*

Here there are no prepositional phrases or modifiers to move. Since articles and negative particles are best kept with the words they modify, this verse has only a level 1 map.

> ἐν τούτῳ ἐφανερώθη ἡ ἀγάπη τοῦ θεοῦ ἐν ἡμῖν, ὅτι τὸν υἱὸν αὐτοῦ τὸν μονο-
> γενῆ ἀπέσταλκεν ὁ θεὸς εἰς τὸν κόσμον, ἵνα ζήσωμεν δι᾽ αὐτοῦ.
> *In this the love of God has been manifested among us, that God sent his unique son into the world, that we might live through him.*

> > > > > > 1 John 4:9

Level 1: Clauses Arranged

> ἐν τούτῳ ἐφανερώθη ἡ ἀγάπη τοῦ θεοῦ ἐν ἡμῖν,
> > ὅτι τὸν υἱὸν αὐτοῦ τὸν μονογενῆ ἀπέσταλκεν ὁ θεὸς εἰς τὸν κόσμον,
> > > > ἵνα ζήσωμεν δι᾽ αὐτοῦ.
> *In this the love of God has been manifested among us,*
> > *that God sent his unique son into the world,*
> > > *that we might live through him.*

Here the ὅτι clause is in apposition to τούτῳ and thus lined up flush with it using tab stops.

Level 2 Map: Clauses and Prepositional Phrases Arranged

> . . . ¹ἐφανερώθη ἡ ἀγάπη τοῦ θεοῦ
> > ἐν ἡμῖν,
> ¹ἐν τούτῳ
> > ὅτι τὸν υἱὸν αὐτοῦ τὸν μονογενῆ ἀπέσταλκεν ὁ θεὸς
> > > > > εἰς τὸν κόσμον,
> > > > ἵνα ζήσωμεν
> > > > > δι᾽ αὐτοῦ.
> . . . ¹*the love has been manifested*
> > *of God*   *among us,*
> > > ¹*In this*
> > > > *that God sent his unique son*
> > > > *into the world,*
> > > > *that we might live*
> > > > > *through him.*

Numbers can be used when the original location of one or more items would not be clear otherwise.

When two or more items independently modify a common word they are back indented so that each is directly under that word. So here with εἰς τὸν κόσμον and ἵνα ζήσωμεν; *into the world* and *that we might live*.

Often English and Greek maps differ. Here the genitive τοῦ θεοῦ is translated with a prepositional phrase, "of God," and thus is moved under its head term in a level 2 map in English.

Level 3 Map: Clauses, Prepositional Phrases, and Modifiers Arranged

9 . . . ¹ἐφανερώθη ἡ ἀγάπη . . . ² . . . ³
                     ²τοῦ θεοῦ

       ³ἐν ἡμῖν,
      ¹ἐν τούτῳ
       ὅτι τὸν υἱὸν . . . ⁴ . . . ⁵ἀπέσταλκεν ὁ θεὸς . . . ⁶
           ⁴αὐτοῦ   ⁶εἰς τὸν κόσμον,
          ⁵τὸν μονογενῆ
                   ἵνα ζήσωμεν
                      δι' αὐτοῦ.

. . . ¹*the love* . . . ²*has been manifested*
      ²*of God*   *among us,*
      ¹*In this*
        that God sent . . . ³ . . . ⁴*son*
                    ³*his*
                   ⁴*unique*
           into the world,
          that we might live
                through him.

For a more detailed explanation and examples of more complex maps see *Using and Enjoying Biblical Greek* and the introduction provided in two videos on the YouTube channel for that book.[312]

---

312. *UEBG*, 98–105, appendix 1. https://www.youtube.com/playlist?list=PL1T3_pk cZpPWCBfJshZ38biQkSy-_vJXB also linked on the website for the book at http://www .bakerpublishinggroup.com/books/using-and-enjoying-biblical-greek/352020/esources. See also whitacregreek.com.

Rules for Accenting

These rules for accenting expand on the introduction to accents in §1.6.

Accents were not used in written texts in CG. Scholars in Alexandria around 200 BC began sporadically marking some accents in the Homeric texts from the eighth century BC to clarify the proper pronunciation for native speakers and to help foreigners new to the language. By AD 400 the stress accent had replaced the pitch accent.

For the purposes of reading attention to accenting is not crucial apart from those few words that are distinguished by their accent listed in appendix 2.

For those interested, the following basic rules cover the main points of accenting. For discussion of further details and exceptions see Mounce, *Morphology* §28; D. A. Carson, *Greek Accents: A Student's Manual* (Grand Rapids: Baker, 1995); or John A. L. Lee, *Basics of Greek Accents: Eight Lessons with Exercises* (Grand Rapids: Zondervan, 2018).

1. The final syllable of a word is called the **ultima** (Latin, *ultimus, last*), the next to last syllable, the **penult** (Latin, *paenultimus, almost last*), and the syllable before that, the **antepenult** (Latin, *antepaenultimus, preceding the almost last*). These are the only syllables that may have an accent.

	antepenult	penult	ultima
ἄνθρωπος	ἄν-	θρω-	πος

2. Accents are placed on vowels, including diphthongs (on the second letter). Accents are affected by whether a vowel or diphthong is long or short.

    a. Long: η, ω, all diphthongs except αι and οι when they occur in an ultima in this simple form. Thus, on an ultima οι is short but οις is long, αι is short but ᾳ is long.

    b. Short: ε, ο. Also αι and οι when they occur on an ultima.

    c. May be short or long: α, ι, υ.

3. An acute may stand on any of the last three syllables of a word, but a circumflex may only stand on the ultima or penult, and the grave only stands on the ultima.

´	´	´	acute
	˜	˜	circumflex
		`	grave
antepenult	penult	ultima	

4. If the ultima is long

   a. the accent will be on the penult or ultima, not the antepenult
   b. if the penult is accented it will be an acute
   c. if the ultima is accented it may be either an acute or a circumflex.

5. If the ultima is short

   a. the antepenult may be accented
   b. a long penult will have a circumflex if it is accented
   c. the ultima will have an acute if it is accented.

6. An acute accent on the ultima changes to a grave if it is followed by another word. If it is followed by punctuation it remains an acute.

7. A noun tries to keep its accent on the syllable accented in its lexical form (persistent accent).

ἄνθρωπος: The accent begins on the antepenult and tries to stay there.
ἀνθρώπου: The genitive ending is long (§2a) so the accent cannot remain on the antepenult (§4a) and the long penult will have an acute (§4b).
ἄνθρωπον: Now the ending is short so the accent may return to the antepenult, which can only have an acute (§3).
δοῦλος: Here we have a short ultima (§2b) with the accent on a long penult (§2a), so it takes a circumflex (§5b).
δούλου: Now the ultima in long (§2a) so the accent on the penult is an acute (§4b).
δοῦλοι: Since οι is considered short when it is in the ultima, the accent on a long penult will be a circumflex.
δούλοις: Now the ultima is long (§2a) so the accent on the penult is an acute (§4b).
ζωή, ἀρχῇ: A long ultima may take either an acute or a circumflex (§4c), with nouns accented on the ultima taking an acute in the nominative and accusative, and a circumflex in the genitive and dative.[1]

---

1. Lee, *Greek Accents*, 13–14.

8. A verbs tries to move its accent to the front of the word (recessive accent).

λύω: The ultima is long so the accented penult will take an acute (§4b).
λύετε: Now the ultima is short (§2b) so the accent can move to the antepenult (§§4a, 5c).
ἐλύετε: The accent on the verb tries to recede to the front, but can only go as far as the antepenult (§3).
ἐλυόμην: The ultima is long so the accent cannot recede to the antepenult (§4a), and the accented penult will take an acute (§4b).

9. An **enclitic** leans on the word coming before it and is pronounced with it, sharing its accent.

a. If the preceding word has an acute on the antepenult or a circumflex on the penult it will add a second accent if an enclitic follows, whether the enclitic has one or two syllables.

ἄγγελος + ἐστιν → ὁ ἄγγελός ἐστιν αὐτοῦ.   *It is his angel.* (Acts 12:15)
δέησις + σου → ἡ δέησίς σου   *your petition* (Luke 1:13)
Ἑβραῖοι + εἰσιν → Ἑβραῖοί εἰσιν;   *Are they Hebrews?* (2 Cor 11:22)
γλῶσσα + μου → ἡ γλῶσσά μου   *my tongue* (Acts 2:26)

b. If the preceding word has an acute on the penult then a two syllable enclitic will add an accent on its own ultima, but a one syllable enclitic will not add an accent.

κλέπται + εἰσιν → κλέπται εἰσίν   *they are thieves* (John 10:8)
πέμψας + με → ὁ πέμψας με   *the one who sent me* (John 12:49)

c. If the preceding word is accented on the ultima that accent is unchanged when an enclitic follows. In particular, an acute is not changed to a grave.

μαθητής τις, *a certain disciple* (Acts 16:1)
τοῦ ἀδελφοῦ σου, *your brother* (Luke 6:41)

d. In a series of enclitics the first one or more are accented and the last enclitic is not.

ἰσχυρότερός μού ἐστιν (Matt 3:11): μου and ἐστιν are both enclitics.

10. A **proclitic** leans on the word coming after it and is pronounced with it, sharing its accent.

    a. Common proclitics include: ὁ, ἡ, οἱ, αἱ (definite articles), ἐν, εἰς, ἐκ (prepositions), εἰ, ὡς (conjunctions), οὐ, οὐκ, οὐχ (the negative particle).

    b. A proclitic may take an accent when followed by an enclitic.

ἔν τινι πόλει, *in a certain city* (Luke 18:2): ἐν is a proclitic and τινι is an enclitic.

    c. A proclitic at the end of a sentence is accented.

καὶ ἀπεκρίθη· οὔ. *And he answered, "No."* (John 1:21)

Words Distinguished by Their Accents and Breathing Marks

αἱ	*the* – fem.-nom.-pl. < ὁ, ἡ, τό
αἵ	*who* – fem.-nom.-pl. < ὅς, ἥ, ὅ
ἀλλά	*but*
ἄλλα	*other things* – neut.-nom./acc.-pl.-neut. < ἄλλος, ἄλλη, ἄλλο
ἄρα	*then, so* – "marker of inference based on preceding matter"[1]
ἆρα	*at all, conceivably* – "interrogative marker expecting a negative answer and connoting anxiety or impatience"[2]
αὐτή	*she* – fem.-nom.-sg. < αὐτός, αὐτή, αὐτό
αὕτη	*this* – fem.-nom.-sg. < οὗτος, αὕτη, τοῦτο
αὐταί	*they* – fem.-nom.-pl. < αὐτός, αὐτή, αὐτό
αὗται	*these* – fem.-nom.-pl. < οὗτος, αὕτη, τοῦτο
εἰ	*if*
εἶ	*you are* – pres.-ind.-act.-2-sg. < εἰμί
ἐν	*in*
ἕν	*one* – neut.-nom./acc.-sg. < εἷς, μία, ἕν
εἰς	*into*
εἷς	*one* – masc.-nom.-sg. < εἷς, μία, ἕν
ἔξω	*outside*
ἕξω	*I will have* – fut.-ind.-act.-1-sg. < ἔχω
ἡ	*the* – fem.-nom.-sg. < ὁ, ἡ, τό
ἥ	*who* – fem.-nom.-sg. < ὅς, ἥ, ὅ
ἤ	*or*
ᾗ	*to whom* – fem.-dat.-sg. < ὅς, ἥ, ὅ
ᾖ	*he/she might be* – pres.-subjn.-act.-3-sg. < εἰμί

---

1. CGEL, 52.
2. CGEL, 52.

ἦν	*he/she was* – impf.-ind.-act.-3-sg. < εἰμί
ἥν	*whom* – fem.-acc.-sg. < ὅς, ἥ, ὅ
ἧς	*of whom* – fem.-gen.-sg. < ὅς, ἥ, ὅ
ἦς	*you were* – impf.-ind.-act.-2-sg. < εἰμί
ᾖς	*you might be* – pres.-subjn.-act.-2-sg. < εἰμί
ὁ	*the* – masc.-nom.-sg. < ὁ, ἡ, τό
ὅ	*who, whom* – neut.-nom./acc.-sg. < ὅς, ἥ, ὅ³
οἱ	*the* – masc.-nom.-pl. < ὁ, ἡ, τό
οἵ	*whom* – masc.-nom.-pl. < ὅς, ἥ, ὅ
ὄν	*being* – pres.-ptc.-act.-neut.-nom./acc.-sg. < εἰμί
ὅν	*whom* – masc.-acc.-sg. < ὅς, ἥ, ὅ
οὐ	*no, not*
οὗ	*of whom* – masc./neut.-gen.-sg. < ὅς, ἥ, ὅ
πότε	*when?*
ποτέ	*when*
τίς, τί	*who?, what?*
τις, τι	*someone, something*
ὦ	*O!*
ὦ	*I might be* – pres.-subjn.-act.-1-sg. < εἰμί
ᾧ	*to whom* – masc./neut.-dat.-sg. < ὅς, ἥ, ὅ
ὤν	*being* – pres.-ptc.-act.-masc.-nom.-sg. < εἰμί
ὧν	*of whom* – masc./fem/neut.-gen.-pl. < ὅς, ἥ, ὅ

3. An interesting example: ἴδωμεν τὸ ῥῆμα τοῦτο τὸ γεγονὸς **ὃ ὁ** κύριος ἐγνώρισεν ἡμῖν. *Let us see this thing that has occurred* <u>which the</u> *Lord has made known to us* (Luke 2:15).

Common Suffixes

The study of word formation and word families is not essential for learning to read Greek, but it helps you understand better how the language works. You will often be able to figure out a basic meaning for a word you have not seen before. Such educated guessing is an important part of gaining fluency in the language, though at times a lexicon will let you know that your assumption was not correct. Some of the suffixes listed below do not always have the indicated usage, and there are other suffixes that have no particular usage. For further resources see §2.38c.

In the following list the suffix and a basic usage is listed, followed by an example and the word on which the example is based.

Noun Suffixes

-εια	an activity	ἡ προφητεία, *prophetic activity*	προφητεύω, *prophesy*
-ια	an activity	ἡ ἀδικία, *wrongdoing*	ἀδικέω, *do wrong*
-μος	an activity	ὁ βαπτισμός, *washing, baptizing*	βαπτίζω, *baptize*
-σις	an activity	ἡ κρίσις, *judging, judgment*	κρίνω, *judge*
-ευς	agent of an action	ὁ ἱππεύς, *horse rider*	ὁ ἵππος, *horse*
-της, ου, ὁ	agent of an action	ὁ βαπτιστής, *baptizer*	βαπτίζω, *baptize*
-τηρ	agent of an action	ὁ σωτήρ, *savior*	σῴζω, *save*
-μα	result of an action	τὸ βάπτισμα, *baptism*	βαπτίζω, *baptize*
-ια	quality/property	ἡ ἀγνωσία, *ignorance*	ἡ γνῶσις, *knowledge*
-συνη	quality/property	ἡ ἀγαθωσύνη, *goodness*	ἀγαθός, ή, όν, *good*
-της, τητος, ἡ	quality/property	ἡ ἁγιότης, *holiness*	ἅγιος, α, ον, *holy*
-τηριον	place	τὸ θυσιαστήριον, *altar*	θυσιάζω, *sacrifice*

Adjective Suffixes

-αιος	pertaining to	ἀρχαῖος, α, ον, *ancient*	ἡ ἀρχή, *beginning*
-ειος	pertaining to	βασιλείος, ον, *royal*	ἡ βασιλεία, *reign*
-ιος	pertaining to	οὐράνιος, ον, *heavenly*	ὁ οὐρανός, *heaven*
-ικος	pertaining to	μουσικός, ή, όν, *musical*	ἡ μουσική, *music*
-τος	(passive) state	ἀγαπητός, ή, όν, *beloved*	ἀγαπάω, *love*
-ινος	material	λίθινος, η, ον, (made of) *stone*	ὁ λίθος, *stone*
-ους	material	χρυσοῦς, ῆ, οῦν, *golden*	ὁ χρυσός, *gold*

Verb Suffixes

-αω	action or state	ἀγαπάω, *love*	ἡ ἀγάπη, *love*
-εω	action or state	τελέω, *bring to an end*	τὸ τέλος, *end*
-ευω	action or state	δουλεύω, *serve* (as a slave)	ὁ δοῦλος, *slave*
-αινω	causation or state	εὐφραίνω, *make cheerful*	εὔφρων, ον, *cheerful*
-οω	causation[1]	τελειόω, *make complete*	τέλειος, α, ον, *complete*
-υνω	causation	μεγαλύνω, *make large*	μέγας, μεγάλη, μέγα, *large*

1. See §2.36c for verbs in οω occasionally referring to consideration, that is, considering, showing, or declaring something as being the case.

Appendix 4

Paradigms for Reference

FIRST AND SECOND DECLENSION NOMINALS

App. 4.1. Core Pattern for the First and Second Declensions

	Definite article			Endings		
	Masc. sg.	Fem. sg.	Neut. sg.	Masc. sg.	Fem. sg.	Neut. sg.
Nom.	ὁ [ος]	ἡ [α]	τό [ον]	ος	η /α	ον
Gen.	τοῦ	τῆς	τοῦ	ου	ης /ας	ου
Dat.	τῷ	τῇ	τῷ	ῳ	ῃ /ᾳ	ῳ
Acc.	τόν	τήν	τό [ον]	ον	ην /αν	ον
Voc.	[ε]			ε		
	Masc. pl.	Fem. pl.	Neut. pl.	Masc. pl.	Fem. pl.	Neut. pl.
Nom.	οἱ	αἱ	τά	οι	αι	α
Gen.	τῶν	τῶν	τῶν	ων	ων	ων
Dat.	τοῖς	ταῖς	τοῖς	οις	αις	οις
Acc.	τούς	τάς	τά	ους	ας	α

App. 4.2. First Declension Nouns

	Fem. sg.	Fem. sg.	Fem. sg.	Masc. sg.	Masc. sg.	Masc. sg.	Masc. sg.
Nom.	φωνή	ἡμέρα	δόξα	προφήτης	μεσσίας	Κηφᾶς	σατανᾶς
Gen.	φωνῆς	ἡμέρας	δόξης	προφήτου	μεσσίου	Κηφᾶ	σατανᾶ
Dat.	φωνῇ	ἡμέρᾳ	δόξῃ	προφήτῃ	μεσσίᾳ	Κηφᾷ	σατανᾷ
Acc.	φωνήν	ἡμέραν	δόξαν	προφήτην	μεσσίαν	Κηφᾶν	σατανᾶν
Voc.	φωνή	ἡμέρα	δόξα	προφῆτα	μεσσία	Κηφᾶ	σατανᾶ
	Fem. pl.	Fem. pl.	Fem. pl.	Masc. pl.	Masc. pl.		
Nom./Voc.	φωναί	ἡμέραι	δόξαι	προφῆται	μεσσίαι		
Gen.	φωνῶν	ἡμερῶν	δοξῶν	προφητῶν	μεσσιῶν		
Dat.	φωναῖς	ἡμέραις	δόξαις	προφήταις	μεσσίαις		
Acc.	φωνάς	ἡμέρας	δόξας	προφήτας	μεσσίας		

App. 4.3. Second Declension Nouns

	Masc. sg.	Neut. sg.
Nom.	θεός	ἔργον
Gen.	θεοῦ	ἔργου
Dat.	θεῷ	ἔργῳ
Acc.	θεόν	ἔργον
Voc.	θεέ	ἔργον

	Masc. pl.	Neut. pl.
Nom./Voc.	θεοί	ἔργα
Gen.	θεῶν	ἔργων
Dat.	θεοῖς	ἔργοις
Acc.	θεούς	ἔργα

App. 4.4. First and Second Declension Adjectives (2-1-2)

	Masc. sg.	Fem. sg.	Neut. sg.
Nom.	ἀγαθός	ἀγαθή	ἀγαθόν
Gen.	ἀγαθοῦ	ἀγαθῆς	ἀγαθοῦ
Dat.	ἀγαθῷ	ἀγαθῇ	ἀγαθῷ
Acc.	ἀγαθόν	ἀγαθήν	ἀγαθόν
Voc.	ἀγαθέ	ἀγαθή	ἀγαθόν

	Masc. pl.	Fem. pl.	Neut. pl.
Nom./Voc.	ἀγαθοί	ἀγαθαί	ἀγαθά
Gen.	ἀγαθῶν	ἀγαθῶν	ἀγαθῶν
Dat.	ἀγαθοῖς	ἀγαθαῖς	ἀγαθοῖς
Acc.	ἀγαθούς	ἀγαθάς	ἀγαθά

	Masc. sg.	Fem. sg.	Neut. sg.
Nom.	ἄξιος	ἀξία	ἄξιον
Gen.	ἀξίου	ἀξίας	ἀξίου
Dat.	ἀξίῳ	ἀξίᾳ	ἀξίῳ
Acc.	ἄξιον	ἀξίαν	ἄξιον
Voc.	ἄξιε	ἀξία	ἄξιον

	Masc. pl.	Fem. pl.	Neut. pl.
Nom./Voc.	ἄξιοι	ἄξιαι	ἄξια
Gen.	ἀξίων	ἀξίων	ἀξίων
Dat.	ἀξίοις	ἀξίαις	ἀξίοις
Acc.	ἀξίους	ἀξίας	ἄξια

App. 4.5. First and Second Declension Adjectives (2-2)

	Masc./fem. sg.	Neut. sg.
Nom.	αἰώνιος	αἰώνιον
Gen.	αἰωνίου	αἰωνίου
Dat.	αἰωνίῳ	αἰωνίῳ
Acc.	αἰώνιον	αἰώνιον
Voc.	αἰώνιε	αἰώνιον

	Masc./fem. pl.	Neut. pl.
Nom./Voc.	αἰώνιοι	αἰώνια
Gen.	αἰωνίων	αἰωνίων
Dat.	αἰωνίοις	αἰωνίοις
Acc.	αἰωνίους	αἰώνια

App. 4.6. First and Second Declension ε Contract Adjectives

	Masc. sg.	Fem. sg.	Neut. sg.
Nom./Voc.	ἁπλοῦς	ἁπλῆ	ἁπλοῦν
Gen.	ἁπλοῦ	ἁπλῆς	ἁπλοῦ
Dat.	ἁπλῷ	ἁπλῇ	ἁπλῷ
Acc.	ἁπλοῦν	ἁπλῆν	ἁπλοῦν

	Masc. pl.	Fem. pl.	Neut. pl.
Nom./Voc.	ἁπλοῖ	ἁπλαῖ	ἁπλᾶ
Gen.	ἁπλῶν	ἁπλῶν	ἁπλῶν
Dat.	ἁπλοῖς	ἁπλαῖς	ἁπλοῖς
Acc.	ἁπλοῦς	ἁπλᾶς	ἁπλᾶ

THIRD DECLENSION NOMINALS

App. 4.7. Core Pattern for the Third Declension

	Indefinite pronoun		Endings	
	Masc./fem. sg.	Neut. sg.	Masc./fem. sg.	Neut. sg.
Nom.	τις [–]	τι [–]	ς, –	–
Gen.	τινος	τινος	ος	ος
Dat.	τινι	τινι	ι	ι
Acc.	τινα [ν]	τι [–]	α, ν	–

	Indefinite pronoun		Endings	
	Masc./fem. pl.	Neut. pl.	Masc./fem. pl.	Neut. pl.
Nom.	τινες	τινα	ες	α
Gen.	τινων	τινων	ων	ων
Dat.	τισι(ν)	τισι(ν)	σι(ν)	σι(ν)
Acc.	τινας [ες]	τινα	ας, ες	α

App. 4.8. The Square of Stops

Type	Voiceless	Voiced	Aspirate	With Sigma			
labials	π	β	φ	+ ς	=	ψ	
velars	κ	γ	χ	+ ς	=	ξ	
dentals	τ	δ, ζ	ϑ	+ ς	=	ς	

App. 4.9. Vowel Contraction

Vowel Contraction

α + ε = α	α	<	α + ε
ε + ε = ει	ει	<	ε + ε
ε + α = η	η	<	ε + α
ο + ει = οι	οι	<	ο + ει
ε + ο, ο + ε, ο + ο = ου	ου	<	ε + ο, ο + ε, or ο + ο
ο or ω + any vowel except as above = ω	ω	<	ο or ω + any vowel except as above

App. 4.10. Third Declension Lexical Form Formulas

The key to figuring out the lexical form of a 3D word is its stem ending.

	Stem Ending →	Lexical form ending
Pattern 1	π, β, or φ	ψ
	κ, γ, or χ	ξ
	τ, δ, ϑ, or ζ	ς (because the dental drops out)
Pattern 2	τ	– or ς (because τ, a dental, drops out)
Pattern 3	ρ	ηρ or ωρ
	ν	ην or ων
Pattern 4	ντ	τ, a dental, drops and the vowel before the ν lengthens

	Stem Ending →	Lexical form ending
Pattern 5	ε (often contracted)	ος, υς, ις, ευς, ης
Pattern 6	υ	υς

App. 4.11. Third Declension Noun Paradigms

	1. Masc. sg.	Masc. pl.	Fem. sg.	Fem. pl.	Fem. sg.	Fem. pl.
Nom.	κώνωψ	κώνωπες	σάρξ	σάρκες	χάρις	χάριτες
Gen.	κώνωπος	κωνώπων	σαρκός	σαρκῶν	χάριτος	χαρίτων
Dat.	κώνωπι	κώνωψι(ν)	σαρκί	σάρξι(ν)	χάριτι	χάρισι(ν)
Acc.	κώνωπα	κώνωπας	σάρκα	σάρκας	χάριτα	χάριτας (χάριν)
Voc.	κώνωψ	κώνωπες	σάρξ	σάρκες	χάρι	χάριτες

	2. Neut. sg.	Neut. pl.
Nom./Voc.	ὄνομα	ὀνόματα
Gen.	ὀνόματος	ὀνομάτων
Dat.	ὀνόματι	ὀνόμασι(ν)
Acc.	ὄνομα	ὀνόματα

	3. Masc. sg.	Masc. pl.	Fem. sg.	Fem. pl.
Nom.	πατήρ	πατέρες	εἰκών	εἰκόνες
Gen.	πατρός	πατέρων	εἰκόνος	εἰκόνων
Dat.	πατρί	πατράσι(ν)	εἰκόνι	εἰκόσι(ν)
Acc.	πατέρα	πατέρας	εἰκόνα	εἰκόνας
Voc.	πάτερ	πατέρες	εἰκών	εἰκόνες

	4. Masc. sg.	Masc. pl.
Nom./Voc.	ἄρχων	ἄρχοντες
Gen.	ἄρχοντος	ἀρχόντων
Dat.	ἄρχοντι	ἄρχουσι(ν)
Acc.	ἄρχοντα	ἄρχοντας

	5a. Neut. sg.	Neut. pl.	5b. Fem. sg.	Fem. pl.
Nom.	ἔθνος	ἔθνη	πόλις	πόλεις
Gen.	ἔθνους	ἐθνῶν	πόλεως	πόλεων
Dat.	ἔθνει	ἔθνεσι(ν)	πόλει	πόλεσι(ν)
Acc.	ἔθνος	ἔθνη	πόλιν	πόλεις
Voc.	ἔθνος	ἔθνη	πόλι	πόλεις

	5c. Masc. sg.	Masc. pl.
Nom.	βασιλεύς	βασιλεῖς
Gen.	βασιλέως	βασιλέων
Dat.	βασιλεῖ	βασιλεῦσι(ν)
Acc.	βασιλέα	βασιλεῖς
Voc.	βασιλεῦ	βασιλεῖς

	6. Masc. sg.	Masc. pl.
Nom.	ἰχθύς	ἰχθύες
Gen.	ἰχθύος	ἰχθύων
Dat.	ἰχθύϊ	ἰχθύσι(ν)
Acc.	ἰχθύν	ἰχθύας
Voc.	ἰχθύ	ἰχθύες

App. 4.12. Miscellaneous Third Declension Nouns[1]

	Fem. sg.	Neut. sg.	Neut. sg.	Neut. sg.	Neut. sg.	Masc. sg.
Nom.	θρίξ, ἡ	τέρας, τό	ὕδωρ, τό	φῶς, τό	οὖς, τό	Ἰησοῦς, ὁ
Gen.	τριχός	τέρατος	ὕδατος	φωτός	ὠτός	Ἰησοῦ
Dat.	τριχί	τέρατι	ὕδατι	φωτί	ὠτί	Ἰησοῦ
Acc.	τρίχα	τέρας	ὕδωρ	φῶς	οὖς	Ἰησοῦν
Voc.	θρίξ	τέρας	ὕδωρ	φῶς	οὖς	Ἰησοῦ

	Fem. pl.	Neut. pl.	Neut. pl.	Neut. pl.	Neut. pl.
Nom./Voc.	τρίχες	τέρατα	ὕδατα	φῶτα	ὦτα
Gen.	τριχῶν	τεράτων	ὑδάτων	φώτων	ὤτων
Dat.	θριξί(ν)	τέρασι(ν)	ὕδασι(ν)	φωσί(ν)	ὠσί(ν)
Acc.	τρίχας	τέρατα	ὕδατα	φῶτα	ὦτα

	Masc. sg.	Masc. sg.	Masc. sg.	Fem. sg.	Masc. sg.	Fem. sg.
Nom.	κύων, ὁ	ἀνήρ, ὁ	ὀδούς, ὁ	ναῦς, ἡ	νοῦς, ὁ	γυνή, ἡ
Gen.	κυνός	ἀνδρός	ὀδόντος	νεώς	νοός	γυναικός
Dat.	κυνί	ἀνδρί	ὀδόντι	νηΐ	νοΐ	γυναικί
Acc.	κύνα	ἄνδρα	ὀδόντα	ναῦν	νοῦν	γυναῖκα
Voc.	κύων	ἄνερ	ὀδόν	ναῦ	νοῦ	γύναι

---

1. For τέρας, ὕδωρ, φῶς, and οὖς see §3.24d.

	Masc. pl.	Masc. pl.	Masc. pl.	Fem. pl.	Masc. pl.	Fem. pl.
Nom./Voc.	κύνες	ἄνδρες	ὀδόντες	νῆες	νόες	γυναῖκες
Gen.	κυνῶν	ἀνδρῶν	ὀδόντων	νεῶν	νοῶν	γυναικῶν
Dat.	κυσί(ν)	ἀνδράσ(ν)	ὀδοῦσι(ν)	ναυσί(ν)	νουσί(ν)	γυναιξί(ν)
Acc.	κύνας	ἄνδρας	ὀδόντας	ναῦς	νόας	γυναῖκας

App. 4.13. Third Declension Adjectives with ντ Stems

πᾶς, πᾶσα, πᾶν

	Masc. sg.	Fem. sg.	Neut. sg.
Nom.	πᾶς	πᾶσα	πᾶν
Gen.	παντός	πάσης	παντός
Dat.	παντί	πάσῃ	παντί
Acc.	πάντα	πᾶσαν	πᾶν

	Masc. pl.	Fem. pl.	Neut. pl.
Nom.	πάντες	πᾶσαι	πάντα
Gen.	πάντων	πασῶν	πάντων
Dat.	πᾶσι(ν)	πάσαις	πᾶσι(ν)
Acc.	πάντας	πάσας	πάντα

App. 4.14. Third Declension Adjectives with υ/ε Stems

	Masc. sg.	Fem. sg.	Neut. sg.
Nom.	εὐθύς	εὐθεῖα	εὐθύ
Gen.	εὐθέως	εὐθείας	εὐθέως
Dat.	εὐθεῖ	εὐθείᾳ	εὐθεῖ
Acc.	εὐθύν	εὐθεῖαν	εὐθύ
Voc.	εὐθύ	εὐθεῖα	εὐθύ

	Masc. pl.	Fem. pl.	Neut. pl.
Nom./Voc.	εὐθεῖς	εὐθεῖαι	εὐθέα
Gen.	εὐθέων	εὐθειῶν	εὐθέων
Dat.	εὐθέσι(ν)	εὐθείαις	εὐθέσι(ν)
Acc.	εὐθεῖς	εὐθείας	εὐθέα

App. 4.15. Third Declension Adjectives with εσ/ε Stems

	Masc./fem. sg.	Neut. sg.
Nom.	ἀληθής	ἀληθές
Gen.	ἀληθοῦς	ἀληθοῦς
Dat.	ἀληθεῖ	ἀληθεῖ
Acc.	ἀληθῆ	ἀληθές
Voc.	ἀληθές	ἀληθές

	Masc./fem. sg.	Neut. pl.
Nom./Voc.	ἀληθεῖς	ἀληθῆ
Gen.	ἀληθῶν	ἀληθῶν
Dat.	ἀληθέσι(ν)	ἀληθέσι(ν)
Acc.	ἀληθεῖς	ἀληθῆ

App. 4.16. Third Declension Adjectives with ν Stems

	Masc./fem. sg.	Neut. sg.
Nom.	ἄφρων	ἄφρον
Gen.	ἄφρονος	ἄφρονος
Dat.	ἄφρονι	ἄφρονι
Acc.	ἄφρονα	ἄφρον
Voc.	ἄφρον	ἄφρον

	Masc./fem. pl.	Neut. pl.
Nom./Voc.	ἄφρονες	ἄφρονα
Gen.	ἀφρόνων	ἀφρόνων
Dat.	ἄφροσι(ν)	ἄφροσι(ν)
Acc.	ἄφρονας	ἄφρονα

App. 4.17. Mixed Adjective Patterns

	Masc. sg.	Fem. sg.	Neut. sg.	Masc. sg.	Fem. sg.	Neut. sg.
Nom.	πολύς	πολλή	πολύ	μέγας	μεγάλη	μέγα
Gen.	πολλοῦ	πολλῆς	πολλοῦ	μεγάλου	μεγάλης	μεγάλου
Dat.	πολλῷ	πολλῇ	πολλῷ	μεγάλῳ	μεγάλη	μεγάλῳ
Acc.	πολύν	πολλήν	πολύ	μέγαν	μεγάλην	μέγα
Voc.				μεγάλε	μεγάλη	μέγα

	Masc. pl.	Fem. pl.	Neut. pl.	Masc. pl.	Fem. pl.	Neut. pl.
Nom./Voc.	πολλοί	πολλαί	πολλά	μεγάλοι	μεγάλαι	μεγάλα
Gen.	πολλῶν	πολλῶν	πολλῶν	μεγάλων	μεγάλων	μεγάλων
Dat.	πολλοῖς	πολλαῖς	πολλοῖς	μεγάλοις	μεγάλαις	μεγάλοις
Acc.	πολλούς	πολλάς	πολλά	μεγάλους	μεγάλας	μεγάλα

PRONOUNS

App. 4.18. First- and Second-Person Pronouns

	1-sg.		2-sg.	
Nom.	ἐγώ	I	σύ	you
Gen.	ἐμοῦ, μου	my	σοῦ, σου	your
Dat.	ἐμοῖ, μοι	(to) me	σοῖ, σοι	(to) you
Acc.	ἐμέ, με	me	σέ, σε	you

	1-pl.		2-pl.	
Nom.	ἡμεῖς	we	ὑμεῖς	you
Gen.	ἡμῶν	our	ὑμῶν	your
Dat.	ἡμῖν	(to) us	ὑμῖν	(to) you
Acc.	ἡμᾶς	us	ὑμᾶς	you

App. 4.19. Third-Person Pronouns

	Masc. sg.		Fem. sg.		Neut. sg.	
Nom.	αὐτός	he	αὐτή	she	αὐτό	it
Gen.	αὐτοῦ	his	αὐτῆς	hers	αὐτοῦ	its
Dat.	αὐτῷ	(to) him	αὐτῇ	(to) her	αὐτῷ	(to) it
Acc.	αὐτόν	him	αὐτήν	her	αὐτό	it

	Masc. pl.		Fem. pl.		Neut. pl.	
Nom.	αὐτοί	they	αὐταί	they	αὐτά	they
Gen.	αὐτῶν	their	αὐτῶν	their	αὐτῶν	their
Dat.	αὐτοῖς	(to) them	αὐταῖς	(to) them	αὐτοῖς	(to) them
Acc.	αὐτούς	them	αὐτάς	them	αὐτά	them

App. 4.20. Demonstrative Pronouns

	Immediate (Near) Demonstratives			Remote (Far) Demonstrative		
	Masc. sg.	Fem. sg.	Neut. sg.	Masc. sg.	Fem. sg.	Neut. sg.
Nom.	οὗτος	αὕτη	τοῦτο	ἐκεῖνος	ἐκείνη	ἐκεῖνο
Gen.	τούτου	ταύτης	τούτου	ἐκείνου	ἐκείνης	ἐκείνου
Dat.	τούτῳ	ταύτῃ	τούτῳ	ἐκείνῳ	ἐκείνῃ	ἐκείνῳ
Acc.	τοῦτον	ταύτην	τοῦτο	ἐκεῖνον	ἐκείνην	ἐκεῖνο
	Masc. pl.	Fem. pl.	Neut. pl.	Masc. pl.	Fem. pl.	Neut. pl.
Nom.	οὗτοι	αὗται	ταῦτα	ἐκεῖνοι	ἐκεῖναι	ἐκεῖνα
Gen.	τούτων	τούτων	τούτων	ἐκείνων	ἐκείνων	ἐκείνων
Dat.	τούτοις	ταύταις	τούτοις	ἐκείνοις	ἐκείναις	ἐκείνοις
Acc.	τούτους	ταύτας	ταῦτα	ἐκείνους	ἐκείνας	ἐκεῖνα

App. 4.21. Relative Pronouns

	Masc. sg.	Fem. sg.	Neut. sg.	Masc. sg.	Fem. sg.	Neut. sg.
Nom.	ὅς	ἥ	ὅ	οἷος	οἵα	οἷον
Gen.	οὗ	ἧς	οὗ	οἵου	οἵας	οἵου
Dat.	ᾧ	ᾗ	ᾧ	οἵῳ	οἵᾳ	οἵῳ
Acc.	ὅν	ἥν	ὅ	οἷον	οἵαν	οἷον
	Masc. pl.	Fem. pl.	Neut. pl.	Masc. pl.	Fem. pl.	Neut. pl.
Nom.	οἵ	αἵ	ἅ	οἷοι	οἷαι	οἷα
Gen.	ὧν	ὧν	ὧν	οἵων	οἵων	οἵων
Dat.	οἷς	αἷς	οἷς	οἵοις	οἵαις	οἵοις
Acc.	οὕς	ἅς	ἅ	οἵους	οἵας	οἷα

App. 4.22. Indefinite Relative Pronouns

	Masc. sg.	Fem. sg.	Neut. sg.
Nom.	ὅστις	ἥτις	ὅτι
Gen.	οὗτινος	ἧστινος	ὅτου
Dat.	ᾧτινι	ᾗτινι	ᾧτινι
Acc.	ὅτινα	ἥτινα	ὅτι

	Masc. pl.	Fem. pl.	Neut. pl.
Nom.	οἵτινες	αἵτινες	ἅτινα
Gen.	ὧντινων	ὧντινων	ὧντινων
Dat.	οἷστισι(ν)	αἷστισι(ν)	οἷστισι(ν)
Acc.	οὕστινας	ἅστινας	ἅτινα

App. 4.23. Reflexive Pronouns

	First person (*myself*)		Second person (*yourself*)	
	Masc.	Fem.	Masc.	Fem.
Gen.	ἐμαυτοῦ	ἐμαυτῆς	σεαυτοῦ	σεαυτῆς
Dat.	ἐμαυτῷ	ἐμαυτῇ	σεαυτῷ	σεαυτῇ
Acc.	ἐμαυτόν	ἐμαυτήν	σεαυτόν	σεαυτήν

Third person (*himself/herself/itself/themselves; ourselves/yourselves*)

	Masc. sg.	Fem. sg.	Neut. sg.
Gen.	ἑαυτοῦ	ἑαυτῆς	ἑαυτοῦ
Dat.	ἑαυτῷ	ἑαυτῇ	ἑαυτῷ
Acc.	ἑαυτόν	ἑαυτήν	ἑαυτό

	Masc. pl.	Fem. pl.	Neut. pl.
Gen.	ἑαυτῶν	ἑαυτῶν	ἑαυτῶν
Dat.	ἑαυτοῖς	ἑαυταῖς	ἑαυτοῖς
Acc.	ἑαυτούς	ἑαυτάς	ἑαυτά

ADDITIONAL NOMINAL PARADIGMS

App. 4.24. εἷς, οὐδείς, μηδείς

εἷς, μία, ἕν (one)

	Masc.	Fem.	Neut.
Nom.	εἷς	μία	ἕν
Gen.	ἑνός	μιᾶς	ἑνός
Dat.	ἑνί	μιᾷ	ἑνί
Acc.	ἕνα	μίαν	ἕν

οὐδείς, οὐδεμία, οὐδέν (no one, nothing)

	Masc.	Fem.	Neut.
Nom.	οὐδείς	οὐδεμία	οὐδέν
Gen.	οὐδενός	οὐδεμιᾶς	οὐδενός
Dat.	οὐδενί	οὐδεμιᾷ	οὐδενί
Acc.	οὐδένα	οὐδεμίαν	οὐδέν

μηδείς, μηδεμία, μηδέν (no one, nothing)

	Masc.	Fem.	Neut.
Nom.	μηδείς	μηδεμία	μηδέν
Gen.	μηδενός	μηδεμιᾶς	μηδενός
Dat.	μηδενί	μηδεμιᾷ	μηδενί
Acc.	μηδένα	μηδεμίαν	μηδέν

QUICK REFERENCE CHARTS OF NOMINAL ENDINGS

The following charts in app. 4.25–27 list the basic endings from the core patterns (app. 4.1, 7) along with any alternate or modified forms these endings have in some paradigms. For zero form endings the stem ending is listed since that is what is actually seen on the end of the word.

App. 4.25. First and Second Declension

	2-masc.	1-fem. (Masc.)	2-neut.
Nom.	[ὁ] ος ους	η /α ης, ας	[τό] ον ουν
Gen.	ου	ης/ας ου	ου
Dat.	ῳ	ῃ /ᾳ	ῳ
Acc.	ον ουν	ην/αν	[τό] ον ουν
Voc.	ε		
Nom.	οι	αι	α
Gen.	ων	ων	ων
Dat.	οις	αις	οις
Acc.	ους	ας	α

App. 4.26. Third Declension

	Masc./fem.			Neut.				
Nom.	ς	ψ	ξ	–	ος	μα	ες	υ
	–	ην, ων	ηρ, ωρ					
Gen.	ος	ους	εως	ος	ους	εως		
Dat.	ι			ι				
Acc.	α, ν	η		–	ος	μα	ες	υ

Nom.	ες	εις		α	η
Gen.	ων			ων	
Dat.	σι(ν)	ψιν	ξιν	σι(ν)	
Acc.	ας			α	η
	ες	εις			

App. 4.27. Composite Chart of Nominal Endings Arranged by Paradigm

	1a	1b	1c	1d	1e	2a	2b
	Fem.	Fem.	Fem.	Masc.	Masc.	Masc.	Neut.
Nom.	η	α	α	ης	ας	ος	ον
Gen.	ης	ας	ης	ου	ου	ου	ου
Dat.	ῃ	ᾳ	ῃ	ῃ	ᾳ	ῳ	ῳ
Acc.	ην	αν	αν	ην	αν	ον	ον

Nom.	αι					οι	α
Gen.	ων					ων	ων
Dat.	αις					οις	οις
Acc.	ας					ους	α

The following chart for 3D adjectives begins with the paradigms using masculine/feminine endings then gives those using neuter endings so similar endings can be viewed together more easily.

	3 Masc./ fem.	3.1a Masc./ fem.	3.1b Masc./ fem.	3.1c Masc./ fem.	3.3 Masc./ fem.	3.4 Masc.	3.5b Fem.	3.5c Masc.	3.6 Masc./ fem.	3 Neut.	3.2 Neut.	3.5a Neut.
Stem		Square of stops	Square of stops	Square of stops	ν, ρ	ντ	ι/ε	ευ/ε	υ		ματ	ος/ε
Nom.	ς, –	ψ	ξ	ς	ην, ων ηρ, ωρ	ων	ις	ευς	υς	–	μα	ος
Gen.	ος						εως	εως		ος		ους
Dat.	ι									ι		
Acc.	α, ν									–	μα	ος
Nom.	ες						εις	εις		α		η
Gen.	ων									ων		
Dat.	σιν	ψιν	ξιν							σιν		
Acc.	ας, ες						εις	εις		α		η

	[2 - Masc.	1 Fem.	- 2] Neut.	[3 - Masc.	1 Fem.	- 3] Neut.	[3 - Masc./fem.	- 3] Neut.
Stem	contraction		contraction	υ/ε		υ/ε	εσ/ε	εσ/ε
Nom.	ους	η	ουν	υς	εια	υ	ης	ες
Gen.				εως		εως	ους	ους
Dat.								
Acc.	ουν		ουν			υ	η	ες
Nom.				εις			εις	η
Gen.								
Dat.								
Acc.				εις			εις	η

VERBALS

App. 4.28. Core Pattern for the Components of the Tense-Forms

Principal part	Tense-Form	Augment or reduplication	STEM	Tense-Form sign	Linking vowel	Endings
1st	Pres. act./MP	ε	λυ		o/ε	Primary
	Impf. act./MP		λυ		o/ε	Secondary
2nd	Fut. act./MP1		λυ	σ	o/ε	Primary
	Liquid fut. act./MP1		λμνρ	(σ)	o/ε	Primary

Principal part	Tense-Form	Augment or reduplication	STEM	Tense-Form sign	Linking vowel	Endings
3rd	1 Aor. act./MP1	ε	λυ	σ	α/ε	Secondary
	Liquid aor. act./MP1	ε	λμνρ	(σ)	α/ε	Secondary
	κ aor. act./MP1	ε	κ		α/ε	Secondary
	2 Aor. act./MP1	ε	?		ο/ε	Secondary
4th	Pf. act.	λε	λυ	κ	α/ε	Primary
	Alt. pf. act.	λε	λυ	κ	α/ε	Primary
	Plpf. act.	(ε)λε	λυ		ει	Secondary
	Alt. plpf. act.	(ε)λε	λυ		ει	Secondary
5th	Pf. MP	λε	λυ			Primary
	Fut. pf. MP	λε	λυ	σ		Primary
	Plpf. MP	(ε)λε	λυ			Secondary
6th	Aor. MP2	ε	λυ	θη		Secondary
	Alt. aor. MP2	ε	λυ	η	ο/ε	Secondary
	Fut. MP2		λυ	θησ	ο/ε	Primary
	Alt. fut. MP2		λυ	ησ		Primary

- Linking vowels: ο before μ and ν; ε elsewhere (though in the present and future indicative the ε linking vowel is ει in the singular).
- Zero endings: –α = 1 singular; –ε = 3 singular indicative or 2 singular imperative.
- Moveable ν only occurs after ε and ι (§4.3e). So ον is always an ending.

PRIMARY TENSE-FORMS IN THE INDICATIVE

App. 4.29. Core Pattern of Personal Endings for the Primary Tense-Forms

Primary Personal Endings

	Act. sg.	MP sg.
	Act. sg.	MP sg.
1.	ω, μι, –	μαι
2.	ς	σαι (= ῃ)
3.	–(ν), σι(ν)	ται

	Act. pl.	MP pl.
1.	μεν	μεθα
2.	τε	σθε
3.	ουσι(ν), ασι(ν)	νται

PRESENT PARADIGMS

App. 4.30. Present Indicative Active and Middle/Passive

(λύω)	(ἀγαπάω)	(ποιέω)	(πληρόω)
Act.	Act.3	Act.	Act.
λύω	ἀγαπῶ	ποιῶ	πληρῶ
λύεις	ἀγαπᾷς	ποιεῖς	πληροῖς
λύει	ἀγαπᾷ	ποιεῖ	πληροῖ
λύομεν	ἀγαπῶμεν	ποιοῦμεν	πληροῦμεν
λύετε	ἀγαπᾶτε	ποιεῖτε	πληροῦτε
λύουσι(ν)	ἀγαπῶσι(ν)	ποιοῦσι(ν)	πληροῦσι(ν)
MP	MP	MP	MP
λύομαι	ἀγαπῶμαι	ποιοῦμαι	πληροῦμαι
λύῃ	ἀγαπᾷ	ποιῇ	πληροῖ
λύεται	ἀγαπᾶται	ποιεῖται	πληροῦται
λυόμεθα	ἀγαπώμεθα	ποιούμεθα	πληρούμεθα
λύεσθε	ἀγαπᾶσθε	ποιεῖσθε	πληροῦσθε
λύονται	ἀγαπῶνται	ποιοῦνται	πληροῦνται

(τίθημι)	(ἵστημι)	(δίδωμι)	(δείκνυμι)	(ἀφίημι)
Act.	Act.	Act.	Act.	Act.
τίθημι	ἵστημι	δίδωμι	δείκνυμι	ἀφίημι
τίθης	ἵστης	δίδως	δείκνυς	ἀφιεῖς
τίθησι(ν)	ἵστησι(ν)	δίδωσι(ν)	δείκνυσι(ν)	ἀφίησι(ν)
τίθεμεν	ἵσταμεν	δίδομεν	δείκνυμεν	ἀφίομεν
τίθετε	ἵστατε	δίδοτε	δείκνυτε	ἀφίετε
τιθέασι(ν)	ἱστᾶσι(ν)	διδόασι(ν)	δεικνύασι(ν)	ἀφίουσι(ν)
MP	MP	MP	MP	MP
τίθεμαι	ἵσταμαι	δίδομαι	δείκνυμαι	ἀφίεμαι
τίθεσαι	ἵστασαι	δίδοσαι	δείκνυσαι	ἀφίεσαι
τίθεται	ἵσταται	δίδοται	δείκνυται	ἀφίεται
τιθέμεθα	ἱστάμεθα	διδόμεθα	δεικνύμεθα	ἀφιέμεθα
τίθεσθε	ἵστασθε	δίδοσθε	δείκνυσθε	ἀφίεσθε
τίθενται	ἵστανται	δίδονται	δείκνυνται	ἀφίενται

App. 4.31. Present Indicative of εἰμί

εἰμί	ἐσμέν
εἶ	ἐστέ
ἐστίν	εἰσί(ν)

FUTURE PARADIGMS

App. 4.32. Future Indicative Active and First Middle/Passive

			Liquid Futures	
(λύω)	(πέμπω)	(ἀγαπάω)	(μένω)	(αἴρω)
Act.	Act.	Act.	Act.	Act.
λύσω	πέμψω	ἀγαπήσω	μενῶ	ἀρῶ
λύσεις	πέμψεις	ἀγαπήσεις	μενεῖς	ἀρεῖς
λύσει	πέμψει	ἀγαπήσει	μενεῖ	ἀρεῖ
λύσομεν	πέμψομεν	ἀγαπήσομεν	μενοῦμεν	ἀροῦμεν
λύσετε	πέμψετε	ἀγαπήσετε	μενεῖτε	ἀρεῖτε
λύσουσι(ν)	πέμψουσι(ν)	ἀγαπήσουσι(ν)	μενοῦσι(ν)	ἀροῦσι(ν)
MP1	MP1	MP1	MP1	MP1
λύσομαι	πέμψομαι	ἀγαπήσομαι	μενοῦμαι	ἀροῦμαι
λύσῃ	πέμψῃ	ἀγαπήσῃ	μενῇ	ἀρῇ
λύσεται	πέμψεται	ἀγαπήσεται	μενεῖται	ἀρεῖται
λυσόμεθα	πεμψόμεθα	ἀγαπησόμεθα	μενούμεθα	ἀρούμεθα
λύσεσθε	πέμψεσθε	ἀγαπήσεσθε	μενεῖσθε	ἀρεῖσθε
λύσονται	πέμψονται	ἀγαπήσονται	μενοῦνται	ἀροῦνται

App. 4.33. Future Indicative of εἰμί

ἔσομαι	ἐσόμεθα
ἔσῃ	ἔσεσθε
ἔσται	ἔσονται

App. 4.34. Future Indicative Second Middle/Passive

(λύω)	(ἀγαπάω)	(γράφω)
λυθήσομαι	ἀγαπηθήσομαι	γραφήσομαι
λυθήσῃ	ἀγαπηθήσῃ	γραφήσῃ
λυθήσεται	ἀγαπηθήσεται	γραφήσεται
λυθησόμεθα	ἀγαπηθησόμεθα	γραφησόμεθα
λυθήσεσθε	ἀγαπηθήσεσθε	γραφήσεσθε
λυθήσονται	ἀγαπηθήσονται	γραφήσονται

PERFECT PARADIGMS

App. 4.35. Perfect Indicative Active

(λύω)	(ἀγαπάω)	(τηρέω)	(πληρόω)	(γίνομαι)
λέλυκα	ἠγάπηκα	τετήρηκα	πεπλήρωκα	γέγονα
λέλυκας	ἠγάπηκας	τετήρηκας	πεπλήρωκας	γέγονας
λέλυκε(ν)	ἠγάπηκε(ν)	τετήρηκε	πεπλήρωκε(ν)	γέγονε(ν)
λελύκαμεν	ἠγαπήκαμεν	τετηρήκαμεν	πεπληρώκαμεν	γεγόναμεν
λυλύκατε	ἠγαπήκατε	τετηρήκατε	πεπληρώκατε	γεγόνατε
λελύκασι(ν)	ἠγαπήκασι(ν)	τετηρήκασι(ν)	πεπληρώκασι(ν)	γεγόνασι(ν)

App. 4.36. Perfect Indicative Middle/Passive

(λύω)	(γράφω)	(δέχομαι)	(πείθω)
λέλυμαι	γέγραμμαι	δέδεγμαι	πέπεισμαι
λέλυσαι	γέγραψαι	δέδεξαι	πέπεισαι
λέλυται	γέγραπται	δέδεκται	πέπεισται
λελύμεθα	γεγράμμεθα	δεδέγμεθα	πεπείσμεθα
λέλυσθε	γέγραφθε	δέδεχθε	πέπεισθε
λέλυνται	γεγραμμένοι εἰσί(ν)	δεδεγμένοι εἰσί(ν)	πεπεισμένοι εἰσί(ν)

SECONDARY TENSE-FORMS IN THE INDICATIVE

App. 4.37. Core Pattern of Personal Endings for the Secondary Tense-Forms

	Act. sg.	MP sg.
1.	ν, –	μην
2.	ς	σο (= ου, ω)
3.	–(ν)	το
	Act. pl.	MP pl.
1.	μεν	μεθα
2.	τε	σθε
3.	ν, σαν	ντο

IMPERFECT PARADIGMS

App. 4.38. Imperfect Indicative

(λύω)	(γεννάω)	(ποιέω)	(φανερόω)
Act.	Act.	Act.	Act.
ἔλυον	ἐγέννων	ἐποίουν	ἐφανέρουν
ἔλυες	ἐγέννας	ἐποίεις	ἐφανέρους
ἔλυε(ν)	ἐγέννα	ἐποίει	ἐφανέρου
ἐλύομεν	ἐγεννῶμεν	ἐποιοῦμεν	ἐφανεροῦμεν
ἐλύετε	ἐγεννᾶτε	ἐποιεῖτε	ἐφανεροῦτε
ἔλυον	ἐγέννων	ἐποίουν	ἐφανέρουν
MP	MP	MP	MP
ἐλυόμην	ἐγεννώμην	ἐποιούμην	ἐφανερούμην
ἐλύου	ἐγεννῶ	ἐποιοῦ	ἐφανεροῦ
ἐλύετο	ἐγεννᾶτο	ἐποιεῖτο	ἐφανεροῦτο
ἐλυόμεθα	ἐγεννώμεθα	ἐποιούμεθα	ἐφανερούμεθα
ἐλύεσθε	ἐγεννᾶσθε	ἐποιεῖσθε	ἐφανεροῦσθε
ἐλύοντο	ἐγεννῶντο	ἐποιοῦντο	ἐφανεροῦντο

(τίθημι)	(ἵστημι)	(δίδωμι)	(δείκνυμι)
Act.	Act.	Act.	Act.
ἐτίθην	ἵστην	ἐδίδουν	ἐδείκνυν
ἐτίθεις	ἵστης	ἐδίδους	ἐδείκνυς
ἐτίθει	ἵστη	ἐδίδου	ἐδείκνυ
ἐτίθεμεν	ἵσταμεν	ἐδίδομεν	ἐδείκνυμεν
ἐτίθετε	ἵστατε	ἐδίδοτε	ἐδείκνυτε
ἐτίθεσαν	ἵστασαν	ἐδίδοσαν	ἐδείκνυσαν
MP	MP	MP	MP
ἐτιθέμην	ἱστάμην	ἐδιδόμην	ἐδεικνύμην
ἐτίθεσαι	ἵστασο	ἐδίδοσο	ἐδείκνυσο
ἐτίθετο	ἵστατο	ἐδίδοτο	ἐδείκνυτο
ἐτιθέμεθα	ἱστάμεθα	ἐδιδόμεθα	ἐδεικνύμεθα
ἐτίθεσθε	ἵστασθε	ἐδίδοσθε	ἐδείκνυσθε
ἐτίθεντο	ἵσταντο	ἐδίδοντο	ἐδείκνυντο

App. 4.39. Imperfect Indicative of εἰμί

ἤμην	ἦμεν, ἤμεθα
ἦς, ἦσθα	ἦτε
ἦν	ἦσαν

AORIST PARADIGMS

App. 4.40. First Aorist Indicative Active and First Middle/Passive

(λύω)

Act.	MP1
ἔλυσα	ἐλυσάμην
ἔλυσας	ἐλύσω
ἔλυσε(ν)	ἐλύσατο
ἐλύσαμεν	ἐλυσάμεθα
ἐλύσατε	ἐλύσασθε
ἔλυσαν	ἐλύσαντο

App. 4.41. Second Aorist Indicative Active and First Middle/Passive

(λαμβάνω)

Act.	MP1
ἔλαβον	ἐλαβόμην
ἔλαβες	ἐλάβου
ἔλαβε(ν)	ἐλάβετο
ἐλάβομεν	ἐλαβόμεθα
ἐλάβετε	ἐλάβεσθε
ἔλαβον	ἐλάβοντο

App. 4.42. Liquid Aorist Indicative Active and First Middle/Passive

(μένω)		(αἴρω)	
Act.	MP1	Act.	MP1
ἔμεινα	ἐμεινάμην	ἦρα	ἠράμην
ἔμεινας	ἐμείνω	ἦρας	ἤρω
ἔμεινε(ν)	ἐμείνατο	ἦρεν	ἤρατο
ἐμείναμεν	ἐμεινάμεθα	ἤραμεν	ἠράμεθα
ἐμείνατε	ἐμείνασθε	ἤρατε	ἤρασθε
ἔμειναν	ἐμείναντο	ἦραν	ἤραντο

App. 4.43. Root Aorist Indicative Active

(ἵστημι)	(ἀναβαίνω)	(γίνωσκω)
ἔστην	ἀνέβην	ἔγνων
ἔστης	ἀνέβης	ἔγνως
ἔστη	ἀνέβη	ἔγνω
ἔστημεν	ἀνέβημεν	ἔγνωμεν
ἔστητε	ἀνέβητε	ἔγνωτε
ἔστησαν	ἀνέβησαν	ἔγνωσαν

App. 4.44. κ Aorist Indicative Active and First Middle/Passive

(τίθημι)	(δίδωμι)	(ἀφίημι)
Act.	Act.	Act.
ἔθηκα	ἔδωκα	ἀφῆκα
ἔθηκας	ἔδωκας	ἀφῆκας
ἔθηκε(ν)	ἔδωκε(ν)	ἀφῆκε(ν)
ἐθήκαμεν	ἐδώκαμεν	ἀφήκαμεν
ἐθήκατε	ἐδώκατε	ἀφήκατε
ἔθηκαν	ἔδωκαν	ἀφῆκαν
MP1	MP1	MP1
ἐθέμην	ἐδόμην	ἀφείμην
ἔθου	ἔδου	ἀφεῖσο
ἔθετο	ἔδοτο	ἀφεῖτο
ἐθέμεθα	ἐδόμεθα	ἀφείμεθα
ἔθεσθε	ἔδοσθε	ἀφεῖσθε
ἔθεντο	ἔδοντο	ἀφεῖντο

App. 4.45. Aorist Indicative Second Middle/Passive

(πιστεύω)	(γράφω)	(αἴρω)
ἐπιστεύθην	ἐγράφην	ἤρθην
ἐπιστεύθης	ἐγράφης	ἤρθης
ἐπιστεύθη	ἐγράφη	ἤρθη
ἐπιστεύθημεν	ἐγράφημεν	ἤρθημεν
ἐπιστεύθητε	ἐγράφητε	ἤρθητε
ἐπιστεύθησαν	ἐγράφησαν	ἤρθησαν

PLUPERFECT PARADIGMS

App. 4.46. Pluperfect Indicative Active

(λύω)	(γράφω)
ἐλελύκειν	ἐγεγράφειν
ἐλελύκεις	ἐγεγράφεις
ἐλελύκει(ν)	ἐγεγράφει(ν)

(λύω)	(γράφω)
ἐλελύκειμεν	ἐγεγράφειμεν
ἐλελύκειτε	ἐγεγράφειτε
ἐλελύκεισαν	ἐγεγράφεισαν

App. 4.47. Pluperfect Indicative Middle/Passive

(λύω)
ἐλελύμην
ἐλέλυσο
ἐλέλυτο
ἐλελύμεθα
ἐλέλυσθε
ἐλέλυντο

SUBJUNCTIVE PARADIGMS

App. 4.48. Present and Aorist Active Subjunctive

Present	1 Aorist	2 Aorist
(λύω)	(λύω)	(λαμβάνω)
λύω	λύσω	λάβω
λύῃς	λύσῃς	λάβῃς
λύῃ	λύσῃ	λάβῃ
λύωμεν	λύσωμεν	λάβωμεν
λύητε	λύσητε	λάβητε
λύωσι(ν)	λύσωσι(ν)	λάβωσι(ν)

App. 4.49. Present and Aorist Middle/Passive Subjunctive

Present MP	1 Aor. MP1	2 Aor. MP1	1 Aor. MP2	2 Aor. MP2
(λύω)	(λύω)	(λαμβάνω)	(λύω)	(λαμβάνω)
λύωμαι	λύσωμαι	λάβωμαι	λυθῶ	λαβῶ
λύῃ	λύσῃ	λάβῃ	λυθῇς	λαβῇς
λύηται	λύσηται	λάβηται	λυθῇ	λαβῇ
λυώμεθα	λυσώμεθα	λαβώμεθα	λυθῶμεν	λαβῶμεν
λύησθε	λύσησθε	λάβησθε	λυθῆτε	λαβῆτε
λύωνται	λύσωνται	λάβωνται	λύθῶσι(ν)	λαβῶσι(ν)

App. 4.50. Present Subjunctive of εἰμί

ὦ   ὦμεν
ᾖς   ἦτε
ᾖ   ὦσι

App. 4.51. Subjunctive of Contract Verbs

ἀγαπάω – *Subjunctive*

Pres. act.	Pres. MP	Aor. act.	Aor. MP1	Aor. MP2
ἀγαπῶ	ἀγαπῶμαι	ἀγαπήσω	ἀγαπήσωμαι	ἀγαπηθῶ
ἀγαπᾷς	ἀγαπᾷ	ἀγαπήσῃς	ἀγαπήσῃ	ἀγαπηθῇς
ἀγαπᾷ	ἀγαπᾶται	ἀγαπήσῃ	ἀγαπήσηται	ἀγαπηθῇ
ἀγαπῶμεν	ἀγαπώμεθα	ἀγαπήσωμεν	ἀγαπησώμεθα	ἀγαπηθῶμεν
ἀγαπᾶτε	ἀγαπᾶσθε	ἀγαπήσητε	ἀγαπήσησθε	ἀγαπηθῆτε
ἀγαπῶσι(ν)	ἀγαπῶνται	ἀγαπήσωσι(ν)	ἀγαπήσωνται	ἀγαπηθῶσι(ν)

ποιέω – *Subjunctive*

Pres. act.	Pres. MP	Aor. act.	Aor. MP1	Aor. MP2
ποιῶ	ποιῶμαι	ποιήσω	ποιήσωμαι	ποιηθῶ
ποιῇς	ποιῇ	ποιήσῃς	ποιήσῃ	ποιηθῇς
ποιῇ	ποιῆται	ποιήσῃ	ποιήσηται	ποιηθῇ
ποιῶμεν	ποιώμεθα	ποιήσωμεν	ποιησώμεθα	ποιηθῶμεν
ποιῆτε	ποιῆσθε	ποιήσητε	ποιήσησθε	ποιηθῆτε
ποιῶσι(ν)	ποιῶνται	ποιήσωσι(ν)	ποιήσωνται	ποιηθῶσι(ν)

φανερόω – *Subjunctive*

Pres. act.	Pres. MP	Aor. act.	Aor. MP1	Aor. MP2
φανερῶ	φανερῶμαι	φανερώσω	φανερώσωμαι	φανερωθῶ
φανεροῖς	φανεροῖ	φανερώσῃς	φανερώσῃ	φανερωθῇς
φανεροῖ	φανερῶται	φανερώσῃ	φανερώσηται	φανερωθῇ
φανερῶμεν	φανερώμεθα	φανερώσωμεν	φανερωσώμεθα	φανερωθῶμεν
φανερῶτε	φανερῶσθε	φανερώσητε	φανερώσησθε	φανερωθῆτε
φανερῶσι(ν)	φανερῶνται	φανερώσωσι(ν)	φανερώσωνται	φανερωθῶσι(ν)

App. 4.52. Subjunctive of μι Verbs

δίδωμι – *Subjunctive*

Pres. act.	Aor. act.	Aor. act.	Pres. MP	Aor. MP1	Aor. MP2
διδῶ	δώσω	δῶ	διδῶμαι	δῶμαι	δοθῶ
διδῷς	δώσῃς	δῷς	διδῷ	δῷ	δοθῇς
διδῷ	δώσῃ	δῷ	διδῶται	δῶται	δοθῇ
διδῶμεν	δώσωμεν	δῶμεν	διδώμεθα	δώμεθα	δοθῶμεν
διδῶτε	δώσητε	δῶτε	διδῶσθε	δῶσθε	δοθῆτε
διδῶσι(ν)	δώσωσι(ν)	δῶσι(ν)	διδῶνται	δῶνται	δοθῶσι(ν)

ἵστημι – *Subjunctive*

Pres. act.	Aor. act.	Pres. MP	Aor. MP1	Aor. MP2
ἱστῶ	στήσω	ἱστῶμαι	στῶμαι	σταθῶ
ἱστῇς	στήσῃς	ἱστῇ	στῇ	σταθῇς
ἱστῇ	στήσῃ	ἱστῆται	στῆται	σταθῇ
ἱστῶμεν	στήσωμεν	ἱστώμεθα	στώμεθα	σταθῶμεν
ἱστῆτε	στήσητε	ἱστῆσθε	στῆσθε	σταθῆτε
ἱστῶσι(ν)	στήσωσι(ν)	ἱστῶνται	στῶνται	σταθῶσι(ν)

τίθημι – *Subjunctive*

Pres. act.	Aor. act.	Pres. MP	Aor. MP1	Aor. MP2
τιθῶ	θῶ	τιθῶμαι	θῶμαι	τεθῶ
τιθῇς	θῇς	τιθῇ	θῇ	τεθῇς
τιθῇ	θῇ	τιθῆται	θῆται	τεθῇ
τιθῶμεν	θῶμεν	τιθώμεθα	θώμεθα	τεθῶμεν
τιθῆτε	θῆτε	τιθῆσθε	θῆσθε	τεθῆτε
τιθῶσι(ν)	θῶσι(ν)	τιθῶνται	θῶνται	τεθῶσι(ν)

ἀφίημι – *Subjunctive*

Pres. act.	Aor. act.	Pres. MP	Aor. MP1	Aor. MP2
ἀφιῶ	ἀφῶ	ἀφιῶμαι	ἀφῶμαι	ἀφεθῶ
ἀφιῇς	ἀφῇς	ἀφιῇ	ἀφῇ	ἀφεθῇς
ἀφιῇ	ἀφῇ	ἀφιῆται	ἀφῆται	ἀφεθῇ

Pres. act.	Aor. act.	Pres. MP	Aor. MP1	Aor. MP2
ἀφιῶμεν	ἀφῶμεν	ἀφιώμεθα	ἀφώμεθα	ἀφεθῶμεν
ἀφιῆτε	ἀφῆτε	ἀφιῆσθε	ἀφῆσθε	ἀφεθῆτε
ἀφιῶσι(ν)	ἀφῶσι(ν)	ἀφιῶνται	ἀφῶνται	ἀφεθῶσι(ν)

OPTATIVE PARADIGMS

App. 4.53. Present and Aorist Optatives

Present	1 Aorist	2 Aorist
(λύω)	(λύω)	(βάλλω)
Act.	Act.	Act.
λύοιμι	λύσαιμι	βάλοιμι
λύοις	λύσαις	βάλοις
λύοι	λύσαι	βάλοι
λύοιμεν	λύσαιμεν	βάλοιμεν
λύοιτε	λύσαιτε	βάλοιτε
λύοιεν	λύσαιεν	βάλοιεν
MP	MP1	MP1
λυοίμην	λυσαίμην	βαλοίμην
λύοιο²	λύσαιο	βάλοιο
λύοιτο	λύσαιτο	βάλοιτο
λυοίμεθα	λυσαίμεθα	βαλοίμεθα
λύοισθε	λύσαισθε	βάλοισθε
λύοιντο	λύσαιντο	βάλοιντο
	MP2	MP2
	λυθείην	βαλείην
	λυθείης	βαλείης
	λυθείη	βαλείη
	λυθείημεν	βαλείημεν
	λυθείητε	βαλείητε
	λυθείησαν	βαλείησαν

2. The MP-2-sg. ending σο loses its σ when it is added to the οι in the present and second aorist, and to the σαι in the first aorist.

IMPERATIVE PARADIGMS

App. 4.54. Core Pattern for Imperatives

	Act. sg.		MP sg.
2.	-, ε, ς, ϑι, σον	2.	σο (= ου), σαι
3.	τω	3.	σϑω
	Act. pl.		MP pl.
2.	τε	2.	σϑε
3.	τωσαν	3.	σϑωσαν

App. 4.55. Present Imperative of εἰμί

ἴσϑι
ἔστω
ἔστε
ἔστωσαν

App. 4.56. Present Imperative

(λύω)	(γεννάω)	(ποιέω)	(φανερόω)
Act.	Act.	Act.	Act.
λῦε	γέννα	ποίει	φανέρου
λυέτω	γεννάτω	ποιείτω	φανερούτω
λύετε	γεννᾶτε	ποιεῖτε	φανεροῦτε
λυέτωσαν	γεννάτωσαν	ποιείτωσαν	φανερούτωσαν
MP	MP	MP	MP
λύου	γεννῶ	ποιοῦ	φανεροῦ
λυέσϑω	γεννάσϑω	ποιείσϑω	φανερούσϑω
λύεσϑε	γεννᾶσϑε	ποιεῖσϑε	φανεροῦσϑε
λυέσϑωσαν	γεννάσϑωσαν	ποιείσϑωσαν	φανερούσϑωσαν

App. 4.57. Present Imperative of Some μι Verbs

(ἵστημι)	(τίθημι)	(δίδωμι)	(ἀφίημι)
Act.	Act.	Act.	Act.
ἵστη[3]	τίθει	δίδου	ἀφίει
ἱστάτω	τιθέτω	διδότω	ἀφιέτω
ἵστατε	τίθετε	δίδοτε	ἀφίετε
ἱστάτωσαν	τεθέτωσαν	διδότωσαν	ἀφιέτωσαν
MP	MP	MP	MP
ἵστασο	τίθεσο	δίδοσο	ἀφίεσο
ἱστάσθω	τιθέσθω	διδόσθω	ἀφιέσθω
ἵστασθε	τίθεσθε	δίδοσθε	ἀφίεσθε
ἱστάσθωσαν	τιθέσθωσαν	διδόσθωσαν	ἀφιέσθωσαν

App. 4.58. Aorist and Perfect Imperatives

(λύω)	(γεννάω)	(ποιέω)	(φανερόω)
Act.	Act.	Act.	Act.
λῦσον[4]	γέννησον	ποίησον	φανέρωσον
λυσάτω	γεννησάτω	ποιησάτω	φανερωσάτω
λύσατε	γεννήσατε	ποιήσατε	φανερώσατε
λυσάτωσαν	γεννησάτωσαν	ποιησάτωσαν	φανερωσάτωσαν
MP	MP	MP	MP
λῦσαι	γέννησαι	ποίησαι	φανέρωσαι
λυσάσθω	γεννησάσθω	ποιησάσθω	φανερωσάσθω
λύσασθε	γεννήσασθε	ποιήσασθε	φανερώσασθε
λυσάσθωσαν	γεννησάσθωσαν	ποιησάσθωσαν	φανερωσάσθωσαν

2 Aorist act.	1 Aorist MP2	1 Aorist MP2	Perfect act.
(βάλλω)	(λύω)	(γράφω)	(λύω)
βάλε	λύθητι	γράφηθι	λέλυκε
βαλέτω	λυθήτω	γραφήτω	λελυκέτω
βάλετε	λύθητε	γράφητε	λελύκετε
βαλέτωσαν	λυθήτωσαν	γραφήτωσαν	λελυκέτωσαν

3. ἵστη has no ending. The η is a lengthened stem ending.

4. According to Mounce (*Morphology*, 145 n. 1), "there is no obvious reason" for the 2-sg. σον and σαι endings; and Smyth says they are "obscure in origin" (§466.1.c.); as Funk also notes (§4600.3).

2 Aorist MP

βαλοῦ

βαλέσϑω

βάλεσϑε

βαλέσϑωσαν

Perfect MP2

λέλυσο

λελύσϑω

λέλυσϑε

λελύσϑωσαν

App. 4.59. Aorist Imperative of Some μι Verbs

(ἵστημι)	(τίθημι)	(δίδωμι)	(ἀφίημι)
Act.	Act.	Act.	Act.
στῆϑι	ϑές	δός	ἄφες
στήτω	ϑέτω	δότω	ἀφέτω
στῆτε	ϑέτε	δότε	ἄφετε
στήτωσαν	ϑέτωσαν	δότωσαν	ἀφέτωσαν
MP	MP	MP	MP
στῶ	ϑοῦ	δοῦ	ἀφοῦ
στάσϑω	ϑέσϑω	δόσϑω	ἀφέσϑω
στάσϑε	ϑέσϑε	δόσϑε	ἀφέσϑε
στάσϑωσαν	ϑέσϑωσαν	δόσϑωσαν	ἀφέσϑωσαν[5]

INFINITIVE PARADIGMS

App. 4.60. Core Pattern for Infinitives

εν [ειν], ι [σαι], ναι, σϑαι

App. 4.61. Present Infinitive

	(λύω)	(γεννάω)	(ποιέω)	(φανερόω)
Act.	λύειν	γεννᾶν	ποιεῖν	φανεροῦν
MP	λύεσϑαι	γεννᾶσϑαι	ποιεῖσϑαι	φανεροῦσϑαι

5. Smyth lists this form as having the earlier ending ἀφέσϑων (§777), but neither form shows up in Perseus so you will probably never meet it. You should just focus on the regular endings for these forms.

App. 4.62. Present Infinitives of Some μι Verbs

	(ἵστημι)	(τίθημι)	(δίδωμι)	(δείκνυμι)
Act.	ἱστάναι	τιθέναι	διδόναι	δεικνύναι
MP	ἵστασθαι	τίθεσθαι	δίδοσθαι	δείκνυσθαι

Infinitive of εἰμί: εἶναι

App. 4.63. Future Infinitive

	(λύω)	(γεννάω)	(ποιέω)	(φανερόω)
Act.	λύσειν	γεννήσειν	ποιήσειν	φανερώσειν
MP1	λύσεσθαι	γεννήσεσθαι	ποιήσεσθαι	φανερώσεσθαι
MP2	λυθήσεσθαι	γεννηθήσεσθαι	ποιηθήσεσθαι	φανερωθήσεσθαι

App. 4.64. First Aorist Infinitive

	(λύω)	(γεννάω)	(ποιέω)	(φανερόω)
Act.	λῦσαι	γέννησαι	ποίησαι	φανέρωσαι
MP1	λύσασθαι	γεννήσασθαι	ποιήσασθαι	φανερώσασθαι
MP2	λυθῆναι	γεννηθῆναι	ποιηθῆναι	φανερωθῆναι

App. 4.65. Second Aorist Infinitive

	(βάλλω)	(λαμβάνω)
Act.	βαλεῖν	λαβεῖν
MP1	βαλέσθαι	λαβέσθαι
MP2	βληθῆναι	λημφθῆναι

App. 4.66. Aorist Active and Middle/Passive Infinitives of Some μι Verbs

	(ἵστημι)	(τίθημι)	(δίδωμι)	(ἀφίημι)
Act.	στῆναι	θεῖναι	δοῦναι	ἀφεῖναι
MP1	στήσασθαι	θέσθαι	δόσθαι	ἀφέσθαι
MP2	σταθῆναι	τεθῆναι	δοθῆναι	ἀφεθῆναι

App. 4.67. Perfect Infinitive

	(λύω)	(γεννάω)	(ποιέω)	(φανερόω)
Act.	λελυκέναι	γεγεννηκέναι	πεποιηκέναι	πεφανερωκέναι
MP	λελῦσθαι	γεγεννῆσθαι	πεποιῆσθαι	πεφανερῶσθαι

PARTICIPLE PARADIGMS

App. 4.68. Core Pattern for Participles

Participle Box

	Masc. sing.	Fem. sing.	Neut. sing.	Sign		Sign
Pres./2 Aor. act.	ων	ουσα	ον	οντ	MP:	ομεν
1 Aor. act.	σας	σασα	σαν	σαντ	MP1:	σαμεν
Aor. MP2	θεις	θεισα	θεν	θεντ		
Pf. act.	κως	κυια	κος	κοτ	MP:	μεν

App. 4.69. Present Active Participle

	Masc. sg.	Fem. sg.	Neut. sg.
Nom.	λύων	λύουσα	λῦον
Gen.	λύοντος	λυούσης	λύοντος
Dat.	λύοντι	λυούσῃ	λύοντι
Acc.	λύοντα	λύουσαν	λῦον

	Masc. pl.	Fem. pl.	Neut. pl.
Nom.	λύοντες	λύουσαι	λύοντα
Gen.	λυόντων	λυουσῶν	λυόντων
Dat.	λύουσι(ν)	λυούσαις	λύουσι(ν)
Acc.	λύοντας	λυούσας	λύοντα

App. 4.70. Present Participle of εἰμί

	Masc. sg.	Fem. sg.	Neut. sg.
Nom.	ὤν	οὖσα	ὄν
Gen.	ὄντος	οὔσης	ὄντος
Dat.	ὄντι	οὔσῃ	ὄντι
Acc.	ὄντα	οὖσαν	ὄν

413

	Masc. pl.	Fem. pl.	Neut. pl.
Nom.	ὄντες	οὖσαι	ὄντα
Gen.	ὄντων	οὐσῶν	ὄντων
Dat.	οὖσι(ν)	οὔσαις	οὖσι(ν)
Acc.	ὄντας	οὔσας	ὄντα

App. 4.71. Present Active Participle of Contract Verbs

		Masc.	Fem.	Neut.
α contract	Nom.-sg.	ἀγαπῶν	ἀγαπῶσα	ἀγαπῶν
ἀγαπάω	Gen.-sg.	ἀγαπῶντος	ἀγαπώσης	ἀγαπῶντος
	Dat.-pl.	ἀγαπῶσι(ν)	ἀγαπώσαις	ἀγαπῶσι(ν)
ε contract	Nom.-sg.	ποιῶν	ποιοῦσα	ποιοῦν
ποιέω	Gen.-sg.	ποιοῦντος	ποιούσης	ποιοῦντος
	Dat.-pl.	ποιοῦσι(ν)	ποιούσαις	ποιοῦσι(ν)
ο contract	Nom.-sg.	δικαιῶν	δικαιοῦσα	δικαιοῦν
δικαιόω	Gen.-sg.	δικαιοῦντος	δικαιούσης	δικαιοῦντος
	Dat.-pl.	δικαιοῦσι(ν)	δικαιούσαις	δικαιοῦσι(ν)

App. 4.72. Present Active Participle of Some μι Verbs

		Masc.	Fem.	Neut.
δείκνυμι	Nom.-sg.	δεικνύς	δεικνῦσα	δεικνύν
	Gen.-sg.	δεικνύντος	δεικνύσης	δεικνύντος
	Dat.-pl.	δεικνῦσι(ν)	δεικνύσαις	δεικνῦσι(ν)
δίδωμι	Nom.-sg.	διδούς	διδοῦσα	διδόν
	Gen.-sg.	διδόντος	διδούσης	διδόντος
	Dat.-pl.	διδοῦσι(ν)	διδούσαις	διδοῦσι(ν)
ἵστημι	Nom.-sg.	ἱστάς	ἱστᾶσα	ἱστάν
	Gen.-sg.	ἱστάντος	ἱστάσης	ἱστάντος
	Dat.-pl.	ἱστᾶσι(ν)	ἱστάσαις	ἱστᾶσι(ν)
τίθημι	Nom.-sg.	τιθείς	τιθεῖσα	τιθέν
	Gen.-sg.	τιθέντος	τιθείσης	τιθέντος
	Dat.-pl.	τιθεῖσι(ν)	τιθείσαις	τιθεῖσι(ν)

App. 4.73. Present Middle/Passive Participle

	Masc. sg.	Fem. sg.	Neut. sg.
Nom.	λυόμενος	λυομένη	λυόμενον
Gen.	λυομένου	λυομένης	λυομένου
Dat.	λυομένῳ	λυομένη	λυομένῳ
Acc.	λυόμενον	λυομένην	λυόμενον

	Masc. pl.	Fem. pl.	Neut. pl.
Nom.	λυόμενοι	λυόμεναι	λυόμενα
Gen.	λυομένων	λυομένων	λυομένων
Dat.	λυομένοις	λυομέναις	λυομένοις
Acc.	λυομένους	λυομένας	λυόμενα

App. 4.74. Present Middle/Passive Participle of Contract Verbs

		Masc.	Fem.	Neut.
α contract	Nom.-sg.	ἀγαπώμενος	ἀγαπωμένη	ἀγαπώμενον
ἀγαπάω	Gen.-sg.	ἀγαπωμένου	ἀγαπωμένης	ἀγαπωμένου
	Dat.-pl.	ἀγαπωμένοις	ἀγαπωμέναις	ἀγαπωμένοις
ε contract	Nom.-sg.	ποιούμενος	ποιουμένη	ποιούμενον
ποιέω	Gen.-sg.	ποιουμένου	ποιουμένης	ποιουμένου
	Dat.-pl.	ποιουμένοις	ποιουμέναις	ποιουμένοις
ο contract	Nom.-sg.	δικαιούμενος	δικαιουμένη	δικαιούμενον
δικαιόω	Gen.-sg.	δικαιουμένου	δικαιουμένης	δικαιουμένου
	Dat.-pl.	δικαιουμένοις	δικαιουμέναις	δικαιουμένοις

App. 4.75. Present Middle/Passive Participle of Some μι Verbs

		Masc.	Fem.	Neut.
δείκνυμι	Nom.-sg.	δεικνύμενος	δεικνυμένη	δεικνύμενον
	Gen.-sg.	δεικνυμένου	δεικνυμένης	δεικνυμένου
	Dat.-pl.	δεικνυμένοις	δεικνυμέναις	δεικνυμένοις
δίδωμι	Nom.-sg.	διδόμενος	διδομένη	διδόμενον
	Gen.-sg.	διδομένου	διδομένης	διδομένου
	Dat.-pl.	διδομένοις	διδομέναις	διδομένοις
ἵστημι	Nom.-sg.	ἱστάμενος	ἱσταμένη	ἱστάμενον
	Gen.-sg.	ἱσταμένου	ἱσταμένης	ἱσταμένου
	Dat.-pl.	ἱσταμένοις	ἱσταμέναις	ἱσταμένοις

		Masc.	Fem.	Neut.
τίθημι	Nom.-sg.	τιθέμενος	τιθεμένη	τιθέμενον
	Gen.-sg.	τιθεμένου	τιθεμένης	τιθεμένου
	Dat.-pl.	τιθεμένοις	τιθεμέναις	τιθεμένοις

App. 4.76. Future Active Participle

	Masc. sg.	Fem. sg.	Neut. sg.
Nom.	λύσων	λύσουσα	λῦσον
Gen.	λύσοντος	λυσούσης	λύσοντος
Dat.	λύσοντι	λυσούσῃ	λύσοντι
Acc.	λύσοντα	λύσουσαν	λῦσον
	Masc. pl.	Fem. pl.	Neut. pl.
Nom.	λύσοντες	λύσουσαι	λύσοντα
Gen.	λυσόντων	λυσουσῶν	λυσόντων
Dat.	λύσουσι(ν)	λυσούσαις	λύσουσι(ν)
Acc.	λύσοντας	λυσούσας	λύσοντα

App. 4.77. Future First Middle/Passive Participle

	Masc. sg.	Fem. sg.	Neut. sg.
Nom.	λυσόμενος	λυσομένη	λυσόμενον
Gen.	λυσομένου	λυσομένης	λυσομένου
Dat.	λυσομένῳ	λυσομένῃ	λυσομένῳ
Acc.	λυσόμενον	λυσομένην	λυσόμενον
	Masc. pl.	Fem. pl.	Neut. pl.
Nom.	λυσόμενοι	λυσόμεναι	λυσόμενα
Gen.	λυσομένων	λυσομένων	λυσομένων
Dat.	λυσομένοις	λυσομέναις	λυσομένοις
Acc.	λυσομένους	λυσομένας	λυσόμενα

App. 4.78. Future Second Middle/Passive Participle

	Masc. sg.	Fem. sg.	Neut. sg.
Nom.	λυθησόμενος	λυθησομένη	λυθησόμενον
Gen.	λυθησομένου	λυθησομένης	λυθησομένου
Dat.	λυθησομένῳ	λυθησομένῃ	λυθησομένῳ
Acc.	λυθησόμενον	λυθησομένην	λυθησόμενον

	Masc. pl.	Fem. pl.	Neut. pl.
Nom.	λυθησόμενοι	λυθησόμεναι	λυθησόμενα
Gen.	λυθησομένων	λυθησομένων	λυθησομένων
Dat.	λυθησομένοις	λυθησομέναις	λυθησομένοις
Acc.	λυθησομένους	λυθησομένας	λυθησόμενα

App. 4.79. First Aorist Active Participle

	Masc. sg.	Fem. sg.	Neut. sg.
Nom.	λύσας	λύσασα	λῦσαν
Gen.	λύσαντος	λυσάσης	λύσαντος
Dat.	λύσαντι	λυσάσῃ	λύσαντι
Acc.	λύσαντα	λύσασαν	λῦσαν

	Masc. pl.	Fem. pl.	Neut. pl.
Nom.	λύσαντες	λύσασαι	λύσαντα
Gen.	λυσάντων	λυσασῶν	λυσάντων
Dat.	λύσασι(ν)	λυσάσαις	λύσασι(ν)
Acc.	λύσαντας	λυσάσας	λύσαντα

App. 4.80. First Aorist Active Participle of Some μι Verbs

		Masc.	Fem.	Neut.
δείκνυμι	Nom.-sg.	δείξας	δείξασα	δείξαν
	Gen.-sg.	δείξαντος	δειξάσης	δείξαντος
	Dat.-pl.	δείξασι(ν)	δειξάσαις	δείξασι(ν)
ἵστημι	Nom.-sg.	στήσας	στήσασα	στήσαν
	Gen.-sg.	στήσαντος	στησάσης	στήσαντος
	Dat.-pl.	στήσασι(ν)	στησάσαις	στήσασι(ν)
τίθημι	Nom.-sg.	θήκας	θήκασα	θήκαν
	Gen.-sg.	θήκαντος	θηκάσης	θήκαντος
	Dat.-pl.	θήκασι(ν)	θηκάσαις	θήκασι(ν)

App. 4.81. First Aorist First Middle/Passive Participle

	Masc. sg.	Fem. sg.	Neut. sg.
Nom.	λυσάμενος	λυσαμένη	λυσάμενον
Gen.	λυσαμένου	λυσαμένης	λυσαμένου
Dat.	λυσαμένῳ	λυσαμένῃ	λυσαμένῳ
Acc.	λυσάμενον	λυσαμένην	λυσάμενον

	Masc. pl.	Fem. pl.	Neut. pl.
Nom.	λυσάμενοι	λυσάμεναι	λυσάμενα
Gen.	λυσαμένων	λυσαμένων	λυσαμένων
Dat.	λυσαμένοις	λυσαμέναις	λυσαμένοις
Acc.	λυσαμένους	λυσαμένας	λυσάμενα

App. 4.82. First Aorist First Middle/Passive Participle of Some μι Verbs

		Masc.	Fem.	Neut.
δείκνυμι	Nom.-sg.	δειξάμενος	δειξαμένη	δειξάμενον
	Gen.-sg.	δειξαμένου	δειξαμένης	δειξαμένου
	Dat.-pl.	δειξαμένοις	δειξαμέναις	δειξαμένοις
ἵστημι	Nom.-sg.	στησάμενος	στησαμένη	στησάμενον
	Gen.-sg.	στησαμένου	στησαμένης	στησαμένου
	Dat.-pl.	στησαμένοις	στησαμέναις	στησαμένοις
τίθημι	Nom.-sg.	θηκάμενος	θηκαμένη	θηκάμενον
	Gen.-sg.	θηκαμένου	θηκαμένης	θηκαμένου
	Dat.-pl.	θηκαμένοις	θηκαμέναις	θηκαμένοις

App. 4.83. First Aorist Second Middle/Passive Participle

	Masc. sg.	Fem. sg.	Neut. sg.
Nom.	λυθείς	λυθεῖσα	λυθέν
Gen.	λυθέντος	λυθείσης	λυθέντος
Dat.	λυθέντι	λυθείσῃ	λυθέντι
Acc.	λυθέντα	λυθεῖσαν	λυθέν

	Masc. pl.	Fem. pl.	Neut. pl.
Nom.	λυθέντες	λυθεῖσαι	λυθέντα
Gen.	λυθέντων	λυθεισῶν	λυθέντων
Dat.	λυθεῖσι(ν)	λυθείσαις	λυθεῖσι(ν)
Acc.	λυθέντας	λυθείσας	λυθέντα

App. 4.84. Alternate First Aorist Second Middle/Passive Participle (γράφω)

	Masc. sg.	Fem. sg.	Neut. sg.
Nom.	γραφείς	γραφεῖσα	γραφέν
Gen.	γραφέντος	γραφείσης	γραφέντος
Dat.	γραφέντι	γραφείσῃ	γραφέντι
Acc.	γραφέντα	γραφεῖσαν	γραφέν

	Masc. pl.	Fem. pl.	Neut. pl.
Nom.	γραφέντες	γραφεῖσαι	γραφέντα
Gen.	γραφέντων	γραφεισῶν	γραφέντων
Dat.	γραφεῖσι(ν)	γραφείσαις	γραφεῖσι(ν)
Acc.	γραφέντας	γραφείσας	γραφέντα

App. 4.85. Alternate First Aorist Active Participle of Some μι Verbs

		Masc.	Fem.	Neut.
δίδωμι	Nom.-sg.	δούς	δοῦσα	δόν
	Gen.-sg.	δόντος	δούσης	δόντος
	Dat.-pl.	δοῦσι(ν)	δούσαις	δοῦσι(ν)
ἵστημι	Nom.-sg.	στάς	στᾶσα	στάν
	Gen.-sg.	στάντος	στάσης	στάντος
	Dat.-pl.	στᾶσι(ν)	στάσαις	στᾶσι(ν)
τίθημι	Nom.-sg.	θείς	θεῖσα	θέν
	Gen.-sg.	θέντος	θείσης	θέντος
	Dat.-pl.	θεῖσι(ν)	θείσαις	θεῖσι(ν)

App. 4.86. Alternate First Aorist First Middle/Passive Participle of Some μι Verbs

		Masc.	Fem.	Neut.
δίδωμι	Nom.-sg.	δόμενος	δομένη	δόμενον
	Gen.-sg.	δομένου	δομένης	δομένου
	Dat.-pl.	δομένοις	δομέναις	δομένοις
ἵστημι	Nom.-sg.	στάμενος	σταμένη	στάμενον
	Gen.-sg.	σταμένου	σταμένης	σταμένου
	Dat.-pl.	σταμένοις	σταμέναις	σταμένοις
τίθημι	Nom.-sg.	θέμενος	θεμένη	θέμενον
	Gen.-sg.	θεμένου	θεμένης	θεμένου
	Dat.-pl.	θεμένοις	θεμέναις	θεμένοις

App. 4.87. Alternate First Aorist Second Middle/Passive Participle of Some μι Verbs

		Masc.	Fem.	Neut.
δείκνυμι	Nom.-sg.	δειχθείς	δειχθεῖσα	δειχθέν
	Gen.-sg.	δειχθέντος	δειχθείσης	δειχθέντος
	Dat.-pl.	δειχθεῖσι(ν)	δειχθείσαις	δειχθεῖσι(ν)
δίδωμι	Nom.-sg.	δοθείς	δοθεῖσα	δοθέν
	Gen.-sg.	δοθέντος	δοθείσης	δοθέντος
	Dat.-pl.	δοθεῖσι(ν)	δοθείσαις	δοθεῖσι(ν)
ἵστημι	Nom.-sg.	σταθείς	σταθεῖσα	σταθέν
	Gen.-sg.	σταθέντος	σταθείσης	σταθέντος
	Dat.-pl.	σταθεῖσι(ν)	σταθείσαις	σταθεῖσι(ν)
τίθημι	Nom.-sg.	τεθείς	τεθεῖσα	τεθέν
	Gen.-sg.	τεθέντος	τεθείσης	τεθέντος
	Dat.-pl.	τεθεῖσι(ν)	τεθείσαις	τεθεῖσι(ν)

App. 4.88. Second Aorist Active Participle (γίνομαι)

	Masc. sg.	Fem. sg.	Neut. sg.
Nom.	γενών	γενοῦσα	γενόν
Gen.	γενόντος	γενούσης	γενόντος
Dat.	γενόντι	γενούσῃ	γενόντι
Acc.	γενόντα	γενοῦσαν	γενόν

	Masc. pl.	Fem. pl.	Neut. pl.
Nom.	γενόντες	γενοῦσαι	γενόντα
Gen.	γενόντων	γενουσῶν	γενόντων
Dat.	γενοῦσι(ν)	γενούσαις	γενοῦσι(ν)
Acc.	γενόντας	γενούσας	γενόντα

App. 4.89. Second Aorist First Middle/Passive Participle (γίνομαι)

	Masc. sg.	Fem. sg.	Neut. sg.
Nom.	γενόμενος	γενομένη	γενόμενον
Gen.	γενομένου	γενομένης	γενομένου
Dat.	γενομένῳ	γενομένῃ	γενομένῳ
Acc.	γενόμενον	γενομένην	γενόμενον

	Masc. pl.	Fem. pl.	Neut. pl.
Nom.	γενόμενοι	γενόμεναι	γενόμενα
Gen.	γενομένων	γενομένων	γενομένων
Dat.	γενομένοις	γενομέναις	γενομένοις
Acc.	γενομένους	γενομένας	γενόμενα

App. 4.90. Second Aorist Second Middle/Passive Participle

	Masc. sg.	Fem. sg.	Neut. sg.
Nom.	γενηθείς	γενηθεῖσα	γενηθέν
Gen.	γενηθέντος	γενηθείσης	γενηθέντος
Dat.	γενηθέντι	γενηθείσῃ	γενηθέντι
Acc.	γενηθέντα	γενηθεῖσαν	γενηθέν

	Masc. pl.	Fem. pl.	Neut. pl.
Nom.	γενηθέντες	γενηθεῖσαι	γενηθέντα
Gen.	γενηθέντων	γενηθεισῶν	γενηθέντων
Dat.	γενηθεῖσι(ν)	γενηθείσαις	γενηθεῖσι(ν)
Acc.	γενηθέντας	γενηθείσας	γενηθέντα

App. 4.91. Perfect Active Participle

	Masc. sg.	Fem. sg.	Neut. sg.
Nom.	λελυκώς	λελυκυῖα	λελυκός
Gen.	λελυκότος	λελυκυίας	λελυκότος
Dat.	λελυκότι	λελυκυίᾳ	λελυκότι
Acc.	λελυκότα	λελυκυῖαν	λελυκός

	Masc. pl.	Fem. pl.	Neut. pl.
Nom.	λελυκότες	λελυκυῖαι	λελυκότα
Gen.	λελυκότων	λελυκυιῶν	λελυκότων
Dat.	λελυκόσι(ν)	λελυκυίαις	λελυκόσι(ν)
Acc.	λελυκότας	λελυκυίας	λελυκότα

App. 4.92. Perfect Active Participle of Some μι Verbs

		Masc.	Fem.	Neut.
δίδωμι	Nom.-sg.	δεδωκώς	δεδωκυῖα	δεδωκός
	Gen.-sg.	δεδωκότος	δεδωκυίας	δεδωκότος
	Dat.-pl.	δεδωκόσι(ν)	δεδωκυίαις	δεδωκόσι(ν)
ἵστημι	Nom.-sg.	ἑστηκώς	ἑστηκυῖα	ἑστηκός
	Gen.-sg.	ἑστηκότος	ἑστηκυίας	ἑστηκότος
	Dat.-pl.	ἑστηκόσι(ν)	ἑστηκυίαις	ἑστηκόσι(ν)
τίθημι	Nom.-sg.	τεθεικώς	τεθεικυῖα	τεθεικός
	Gen.-sg.	τεθεικότος	τεθεικυίας	τεθεικότος
	Dat.-pl.	τεθεικόσι(ν)	τεθεικυίαις	τεθεικόσι(ν)

App. 4.93. Alternate Perfect Active Participle of ἵστημι

		Masc.	Fem.	Neut.
ἵστημι	Nom.-sg.	ἑστώς	ἑστῶσα	ἑστός
	Gen.-sg.	ἑστῶτος	ἑστώσης	ἑστῶτος
	Dat.-pl.	ἑστῶσι(ν)	ἑστώσαις	ἑστῶσι(ν)

App. 4.94. Perfect Middle/Passive Participle

	Masc. sg.	Fem. sg.	Neut. sg.
Nom.	λελυμένος	λελυμένη	λελυμένον
Gen.	λελυμένου	λελυμένης	λελυμένου
Dat.	λελυμένῳ	λελυμένη	λελυμένῳ
Acc.	λελυμένον	λελυμένην	λελυμένον

	Masc. pl.	Fem. pl.	Neut. pl.
Nom.	λελυμένοι	λελυμέναι	λελυμένα
Gen.	λελυμένων	λελυμένων	λελυμένων
Dat.	λελυμένοις	λελυμέναις	λελυμένοις
Acc.	λελυμένους	λελυμένας	λελυμένα

App. 4.95. Perfect Middle/Passive Participle of Some μι Verbs

		Masc.	Fem.	Neut.
δίδωμι	Nom.-sg.	δεδομένος	δεδομένη	δεδομένον
	Gen.-sg.	δεδομένου	δεδομένης	δεδομένου
	Dat.-pl.	δεδομένοις	δεδομέναις	δεδομένοις
ἵστημι	Nom.-sg.	ἑστημένος	ἑστημένη	ἑστημένον
	Gen.-sg.	ἑστημένου	ἑστημένης	ἑστημένου
	Dat.-pl.	ἑστημένοις	ἑστημέναις	ἑστημένοις
τίθημι	Nom.-sg.	τεθειμένος	τεθειμένη	τεθειμένον
	Gen.-sg.	τεθειμένου	τεθειμένης	τεθειμένου
	Dat.-pl.	τεθειμένοις	τεθειμέναις	τεθειμένοις

Summary of Selected Syntax Topics

T his summary of key syntax topics provides a quick reference guide when analyzing a word or construction in a passage, as well as a convenient resource for review. The numbering of the sections in this appendix corresponds to chapter 5 (Greek Syntax). Not all sections are included here, and often the full discussion in chapter 5 will need to be consulted. Further topics are listed in the indexes.

THE DEFINITE ARTICLE

The Article as a Structure Signal

5.4. Attributive Positions

If there is an article in front of the adjective or modifier (TA) then it is modifying a noun or substantive. In the second and third positions there is often some emphasis on the modifier.

1st position:	article – adjective/modifier – noun/substantive (TAS) (*common*)
2nd position:	article – noun/substantive – article – adjective/modifier (TSTA) (*less common*)
3rd position:	noun/substantive – article – adjective/modifier (STA) (*rare*)

5.5. Predicate Position

When a noun/substantive has an article (TS) and the adjective or other modifier does not have an article (TSA, ATS), then a statement is being made.

5.6. οὗτος and ἐκεῖνος

These words use predicate position (no article before them) even though they function attributively.

5.7. αὐτός

With an article = "same." In nominative or in agreement = intensive ("self"). Neither of these = third-person pronoun.

5.8. πᾶς

With an article = "(the) whole, all." Without an article = "each, every, any, all."

Other Uses of the Article

5.9. Bracketing Force of the Article

An article and its noun/substantive may be separated from one another by one or more words that modify the noun/substantive.

5.10. Apollonius's Canon

When a noun is modified by a genitive, usually both the head term and the genitive will have an article, or they will both lack an article.

5.11. Granville Sharp's Rule (TSKS)

"When two nouns are connected by καί and the article precedes only the first noun, there is a close connection between the two" (*ExSyn*, 270). If one or both of the nouns/substantives are **impersonal, plural, or a proper name** then the grammar in itself does **not** indicate that both nouns/substantives refer to the same person or thing, though they may still do so.

5.12. The Article Used for Identification

The article points to something as specific and definite.

> a. **Monadic.** Something of which there is only one.
> b. **Anaphoric.** Referring back to the same noun earlier in the passage.
> c. **Well-known.** Something that is commonly recognized or familiar.
> d. **Par excellence.** Something viewed as the chief example of its category.
> e. **Deictic.** Like a gesture pointing to something or someone.

5.13. The Generic Article

The article can indicate the group or class to which someone/something belongs, often including some focus on the quality of that category.

5.14. The Article with Abstract Nouns

Abstract nouns refer to concepts, experiences, ideas, qualities, and feelings in contrast to people or objects that we experience by means of our five senses. The article can be used with such a noun to highlight its particular quality.

5.15. The Article as Noun Signal (Substantizer)

The article can substantize virtually any part of speech. This use occurs frequently with adjectives, participles, and prepositional phrases, but also occurs with adverbs, statements/quotes, and genitives, among others.

5.16. The Article as Adjective Signal

When the article with a prepositional phrase is in agreement with a noun, then the phrase is modifying that noun like an adjective.

5.17. The Article for a Pronoun

When followed by μέν or δέ the article serves as a pronoun. This use occurs in narratives when there is a change of subject or speaker.

5.18. The Article for a Possessive Pronoun

The context may signal that an article implies possession.

The Absence of the Definite Article

5.20. Definite

A word can lack an article and still be definite in the following cases among others (see §§5.8, 23, 24, and 77a).

- a. Monadic nouns and proper names
- b. Abstract nouns
- c. Generic nouns
- d. Objects of prepositions
- e. Ordinal numbers

5.21. Indefinite

An anarthrous noun/substantive may be indefinite, referring to a person or thing as a member of a category, but without identifying them as a specific individual.

5.22. Qualitative

An anarthrous noun/substantive may be used qualitatively, that is, with a focus on the kind of person or thing it is.

5.23. Apollonius's Corollary

A noun/substantive and its genitive modifier will often both be definite, or both be indefinite, or both be qualitative. So if one of them is itself definite without an article, then the expression can be definite even without any articles.

5.24. Colwell's Rule

When an anarthrous subject complement precedes an equative verb it is "normally qualitative, sometimes definite, and only rarely indefinite" (*ExSyn*, 262).

CASES

5.25. The Most Common Uses

	Use
Nominative	Subject
	Subject complement
Vocative	Direct address
Genitive	Description
Dative	Indirect object
	Means/instrument/agent
	Location
Accusative	Direct object

Nominative

	Use
5.26. Subject	The one acting or being acted upon
5.27. Subject complement	With an equative verb; renames, labels, or describes the subject
5.28. Direct address	The one(s) being addressed
5.29. Independent nominative	Used in titles, headings, and greetings (absolute); as a topic announced at the beginning of a sentence (hanging); as a comment within a sentence (parenthetic)
5.30. Nominative as complement with verbs used as a passive	The object of a verb in the middle used as a passive that has double accusative of object and complement in the active
5.31. Nominative for time	An adverbial expression of time

Vocative

	Use
5.32. Direct address	Identifies the one(s) being addressed

Genitive

	Use
5.34. Description	Describes the head term in a way not covered by other uses
5.35. Possession	Owner of the head term, either literally or more generally
5.36. Complement	That which completes the action of the verb
5.37. Subject of a genitive absolute	The one acting or being acted upon, with a genitive participle as the verb
5.38. Subjectival/ objectival	Identifies the subject or object of a verbal noun
5.39. Relationship	One in a family or other relationship indicated by head term
5.40. Association	A bond or connection, usually with σύν compound verbs
5.41. Subordination	The one under the authority of someone or something else
5.42. Epexegetical (explanation)	Restatement of the head term explaining or identifying it
5.43. Reference (respect)	That with reference to which something is true
5.44. Attributive/ attributed	The genitive modifies the head term like an adjective/the head term modifies the genitive like an adjective
5.45. Content	That which fills the head term, either physically or the content of a form of communication
5.46. Material	That of which the head term is composed
5.47. Partitive	A group of which the head term is a part
5.48. Source/Producer	The source or producer of the head term
5.49. Product	That which is sourced in or produced by the head term
5.50. Separation	That from which someone/something is separated or distinguished
5.51. Comparison	That with which something is compared; used with comparative adjective
5.52. Price/value	The money, price, or value of the head term
5.53. Time during which	The general time frame within which something takes place
5.54. Place	The place in which or from which something is done
5.55. Means/agent	That by which or by whom something is done
5.56. Cause/reason	The cause or reason something has happened
5.57. Purpose/goal	The goal or purpose of an action

Dative

	Use
5.59. Indirect object	That to/for which an action is done; it receives the direct object
5.60. Advantage/ disadvantage	The one to whose benefit or detriment an action is done
5.61. Possession	Ownership, either physical or often in a general sense
5.62. Relationship	Familial or social relationship
5.63. Feeling (ethical)	Personal interest expressed as emotion or personal opinion
5.64. Place/sphere	Location, either physically or in a general or metaphorical sense
5.65. Destination	Used with intransitive verbs for where the subject is going
5.66. Time When	Location in time; often the point of time at which something happens
5.67. Means/ instrument/agent	That by/with which something is done; physical or metaphorical; occasionally used for personal agency
5.68. Reference (respect)	That with reference to which something is true
5.69. Association	That which is associated with or accompanies the subject
5.70. Manner (adverbial)	Adverbial expression indicating the way in which something takes place
5.71. Cause	The reason for an action, usually an unintended reason
5.72. Complement	That which completes the action of the verb
5.73. Degree/measure	With comparative adj./adv. for the nature or degree of difference
5.74. Recipient	The one(s) who receives a letter or other form of communication

Accusative

	Use
5.75. Direct object	That which receives the action of the verb
5.76. Double accusative of person and thing	A person and thing that both receive the action of the verb
5.77. Double accusative of object and complement	The direct object and its predicate complement
5.78. Predicate	A predicate complement, used with an infinitive/participle of an equative verb
5.79. Subject of an infinitive	Accusative of respect functioning like a subject of an infinitive
5.80. Manner (adverbial)	Adverbial expression indicating the way in which something takes place
5.81. Reference (respect)	That with reference to which something is true
5.82. Extent of time/space	Duration in time or length in space
5.83. Oaths	That by which one swears an oath

PRONOUNS

5.84. A pronoun is used in place of a noun. The personal, reflexive, and reciprocal pronouns are only used as noun substitutes. Other pronouns, however, are also used to modify nouns, including the relative, demonstrative, interrogative, indefinite, and possessive pronouns.

COMPARATIVES AND SUPERLATIVES

5.85. A comparative may be used for the superlative and a superlative for a comparative. Sometimes a superlative has an elative sense, that is, it means "very."

VERBS

Aspect and Aktionsart

5.87. Verbal Aspect

Durative (Imperfective)	action viewed from within, as in process.
Aoristic (Perfective)	action viewed from without, as a whole.
Resultative (Stative)	the present situation viewed as resulting from a prior action.

5.88. Verbal *Aktionsart*

Aktionsart refers to what the author is saying about the actual nature of the action, event, or situation. It is signaled by:
   The verbal aspect of the tense-form + the meaning of the verb + the context.

Further General Verbal Details

5.91. Causative/Permissive

The subject does not do the action but causes or permits it.

5.92. Voice

   a. Variation in Voice between Tense-Forms. Verbs may be active in one tense-form and middle-only in another with no apparent change in meaning.
   b. Variation in Meaning between Voices. Verbs may have one meaning in the active and another meaning in the middle/passive.

c. **Variation in Usage between Voices.** Verbs may have an external object in the active but not in the middle/passive, corresponding in English to the transitive and intransitive senses.

5.93. Types of Subject-Affectedness in the Middle

a. **The Agent-Patient Spectrum.** The subject may be the agent doing an action which affects an object, or the subject may be the patient who is acted upon by some other agent. The middle is used when the subject is the patient, corresponding to the passive in English, but also in other ways, some of which are more agent-like and some more patient-like.

b. **Direct Reflexive.** The action comes back on the subject directly, so the subject is also the object.

c. **Indirect Reflexive.** The subject acts on an object, but is also affected by the action, usually as a beneficiary.

d. **Physical Change of Position or Location.** The subject is affected by the action as the one experiencing the change of position or location.

e. **Physical Process.** The subject undergoes an internal physical process.

f. **Mental/Emotional Process.** The subject undergoes an internal mental or emotional process.

g. **Perception.** The subject is the experiencer of a mental process which comes through the senses.

h. **Speech.** The subject speaks but is also included within the focus of the action as experiencer or beneficiary of the act of speaking.

i. **Reciprocal Action.** Two or more subjects are engaged in the same form of action in interaction with one another.

j. **Passive.** The subject is acted upon by an agent or force.

5.94. Voice in the Aorist and Future Tense-Forms

The aorist and future have two forms of the middle/passive. The first middle/passive has a σ tense-form sign and it is generally used for more agent-like senses of the middle. The second middle/passive has a ϑη or η tense-form sign. In the future the MP2 is almost always used in a passive sense, while in the aorist it is frequently used in the passive sense, but often in other middle senses as well.

Present Tense-Form

5.97. Aspect of the Present

The present has a durative aspect—action is viewed from within as in process.

Aktionsarten

5.98. Progressive	Action that is ongoing
5.99. Iterative	Action that occurs repeatedly
5.100. Customary	Action that occurs regularly, or an ongoing state
5.101. Continuative	Action that began in the past and is continuing on in the present
5.102. Instantaneous	Action that takes place at a single point in time
5.103. Gnomic	A general truth like a proverb or a statement of what generally happens
5.104. Historical (Narrative)	Action that occurs in the past
5.105. Futuristic	Action that occurs in the future
5.106. Conative (Tendential)	Action that is attempted or desired

Future Tense-Form

5.107. Aspect of the Future

It is best to view the future as having no aspect.

Aktionsarten

5.108. Predictive, Global	Future action viewed as a whole
5.109. Predictive, Punctiliar	An expectation or intention for the future
5.110. Deliberative	Reflection on what should be done, usually in questions in the first person
5.111. Imperatival	Expresses a command
5.112. Gnomic	A general truth like a proverb or a statement of what generally happens
5.113. The Future Second Middle/Passive	Usually predictive, expressing an expectation

Perfect Tense-Form

5.114. Aspect of the Perfect

The perfect has a resultative aspect—a present situation that has come about through a prior action.

5.115. Two Emphases

   a. **Intensive.** Emphasis on the present situation.
   b. **Extensive.** Emphasis on the past action/event.

5.116. Two Roles

a. Present State. A state or condition that provides a detail present in the context but that does not itself effect what follows.

b. Relevant Effects. A result of prior action that is currently relevant to the unfolding action or argument.

Imperfect Tense-Form

5.118. Aspect of the Imperfect

The imperfect has a durative aspect—action is viewed from within as in process.

Aktionsarten

5.119. Progressive	Action that is ongoing
5.120. Iterative	Action that occurs repeatedly
5.121. Ingressive	Emphasis on the beginning of an action or entrance into a state
5.122. Customary	Action that occurs regularly, or an ongoing state
5.123. Conative (Tendential)	Action that is attempted or desired

Aorist Tense-Form

5.124. Aspect of the Aorist

The aorist has, by definition, an aoristic aspect—action is viewed from without, as a whole.

Aktionsarten

5.125. Global (Constative)	Action looked at as a whole, simply saying that it happened. Sometimes this action continues up to the present and the English perfect tense should be used
5.126. Punctiliar	Action that takes place at a single point in time
5.127. Ingressive	Emphasis on the beginning of an action or entrance into a state
5.128. Culminative	The focus is on an action that has ceased now in the present
5.129. Gnomic	A general truth like a proverb or a statement of what generally happens

| 5.130. Proleptic | An action that will occur in the future viewed as if it is already completed |
| 5.131. Epistolary | A reference to the present letter, taking the point of view of the later readers |

Pluperfect Tense-Form

5.132. Aspect of the Pluperfect

The pluperfect has a resultative aspect—a present situation that has come about through a prior action.

5.133. Two Emphases

a. **Intensive.** Emphasis on the present situation.
b. **Extensive.** Emphasis on the past action/event.

5.134. Two Roles

a. **Present state.** A state or condition provides a detail present in the context.
b. **Relevant effects.** A result of prior action that was relevant to the unfolding action or discussion in the past.

5.135. The Function of Indicative Tense-Forms in Narratives

In narrative texts the aorist will often be used to move the story along, providing the framework, while the imperfect, perfect, and pluperfect indicatives, as well as periphrastic participles, fill in details. The historical present often provides background information, calls attention to narrative transitions, and/or highlights action or speech that follows.

The Subjunctive

	Sign	Simple translation
5.137. Purpose (final)	ἵνα, ὅπως	*that, so that*
5.138. Result (consecutive)	ἵνα	*that, with the result that*
5.139. Strong negation	οὐ μή	*no/not (!)*
5.140. Hortatory	First person (no other signal)	*let me, let us*
5.141. Deliberative	Question (no other signal)	*should*

	Sign	Simple translation
5.142. Indefinite relative clauses	ὅς/ὅστις + ἄν/ἐάν	*whoever, whichever*
5.143. Indefinite local and temporal clauses	οὗ, ὅπου + ἄν	*wherever*
	ὅταν, ἕως/ὡς + ἄν	*whenever*
5.144. Prohibition	μή	*no/not*
5.145. Noun clause with ἵνα	ἵνα	*that; infinitive*
5.146. Epexegetical (explanation) clause with ἵνα	ἵνα	*that; infinitive*
5.147. Appositional clause with οὗτος	οὗτος, αὕτη, τοῦτο	*that*
5.148. Content clause (indirect discourse)	ἵνα	*that; infinitive*
5.149. Future-more-likely condition	ἐάν; finite verb in apodosis	*if*
5.150. General condition	ἐάν; pres. ind. in apodosis	*if*

The Optative

5.152. Wish

The most common use of the optative is to express a wish.

5.153. Potential

The writer is pondering what could or might happen/be true, often concerning the meaning of something, the identity of someone, what should be done, or a similar idea.

The Imperative

5.154. The imperative may be used to express a command, request, permission, and suggestion.

5.155. Two Types of Commands/Requests

(1) general commands/principles or requests
(2) specific commands or requests given for particular situations.

5.157. First-Person and Third-Person Imperatives

There is no first-person imperative. A third-person imperative is often translated "let" or "should," but when the imperative is used for a command then
"must" or "is to/are to" may convey the sense better.

Major Uses of the Imperative

5.158. Command	An order for someone to do something
5.159. Request	A request addressed to God or someone considered to be a superior in some sense
5.160. Prohibition (Negative Command)	Usually with a present. May have the sense "stop"
5.161. Permission	Granting someone permission to do something
5.162. Greetings	A stereotyped expression at the beginning or conclusion of some form of communication

The Infinitive

	Sign	Simple translation
5.164. Purpose (final)		infinitive; *that, so that*
5.165. Result (consecutive)	ὥστε	*that, with the result that*
5.166. Complementary	Main verb like ἄρχομαι	infinitive
5.167. Subject		infinitive; *preparatory "it"*
5.168. Nominal uses other than as a subject		finite verb or gerund (-ing)
5.169. Content clause (indirect discourse)		infinitive; *that*
5.170. Epexegetical (explanation)		infinitive
5.171. Appositional clause with οὗτος	οὗτος, αὕτη, τοῦτο	*that*
5.172. Imperatival	Context	an imperatival form
5.173. Absolute	Context	usually a greeting
5.174. Prepositional phrases		
5.175. With a preposition for time	πρίν, πρὸ τοῦ, ἐν τῷ, μετὰ τό	*before, while, after, when*
5.176. With a preposition for cause	διὰ τό	*so that, because*
5.177. With a preposition for purpose	εἰς τό, πρὸς τό	*in order to*
5.178. With a preposition for result	εἰς τό, πρὸς τό	*with a result that*

5.179. With a preposition for content	εἰς τό	*that*; infinitive
5.180. With a preposition for explanation (epexegetical)	εἰς τό	*that*; infinitive

The Participle

5.181. The participle occurs frequently in Greek text and has a variety of uses, as outlined below.

5.182. Aspect and Time in Participles

Participles have the usual aspects related to the tense-forms. When the context suggests a participle includes reference to time it is time relative to the main verb. A present participle refers to action at the same time as the main verb and an aorist participle to action prior to the main verb.

5.183. Participles Used as Adjectives and Nouns

Usually articular.

5.184. Adjectival

Functioning like an adjective modifying a noun or other substantival.

5.185. Substantival (Noun)

Functioning like a noun.

5.186. Complementary Participles

With verbs like "begin" and "stop" whose content needs to be supplied.

5.187. The Periphrastic Use of the Participle

A form of εἰμί used with a participle to form a tense, for example, ἦσαν λύοντες, they were loosing.

5.188. List of Periphrastic Constructions

The various combinations are listed in this section.

5.189. Circumstantial (Adverbial) Use of the Participle

An adverbial clause that supplies additional information about the action or point of discussion in a main clause.

5.190. Eight Possible Nuances of the Circumstantial Participle

5.191. **Time.** ("when__," "after__").
5.192. **Cause.** ("because__").
5.193. **Condition.** ("if__").
5.194. **Concession.** ("although__").
5.195. **Means/Instrument.** ("by __").
5.196. **Manner.** ("__ly").
5.197. **Purpose.** ("in order to__").
5.198. **Result.** ("so that," "with the result that").

5.200. Genitive Absolute

Like a circumstantial participle but with a genitive participle and genitive noun or pronoun for its subject.

5.201. Attendant Circumstance

The participle functions as a finite verb in the same mood as the main verb, usually translated with and added to connect the two clauses.

5.202. Pleonastic

A rhetorical signal calling attention to the statement that follows, for example, ἀποκριθεὶς δὲ εἶπεν, And answering he/she said.

5.203. Content (Indirect Discourse)

Like a ὅτι clause providing the content after a verb referring to communication, thought, feeling, perception, and so forth.

5.204. Independent Participle

Functioning as a finite verb; a rare use.

SENTENCES AND CLAUSES

5.207. Four Basic Clause Core Types

Type 1 Subject – intransitive verb.
Type 2 Subject – equative verb – subject complement: predicate noun or adjective.
Type 3 Subject – transitive verb – direct object.
Type 4 Subject – transitive verb – direct object – indirect object.

5.210. Coordinate Clauses

Two independent clauses connected together, usually translated by *and, but,* or *or.*

Subordinate Clauses Functioning Like a Noun or Adjective

Relative Clauses

5.212. Introduction to Relative Clauses

Relative clauses often function like adjectives, but may also function like nouns.

5.214. Relative Clause as Adjective

A relative clause can modify a noun like an adjective.

5.215. Attraction of the Relative Pronoun

A relative pronoun's case may be changed to match that of the antecedent.

5.216. Reverse Attraction of the Relative Pronoun

Very occasionally the case of the antecedent may be changed to match that of the relative pronoun.

5.217. Relative Clause as Noun or Pronoun

A relative clause may function as a noun.

5.218. Relative Clause as Object of a Preposition

For example, ἐν ᾧ εὐδόκησα, in whom I am well pleased.

5.219. Indefinite Relative Clauses

Often ἄν or ἐάν will be present.

Discourse Clauses

5.220. Direct and Indirect Discourse

Direct discourse reports the actual words a person said. Indirect discourse reports the content of what a person said but not in their exact words.

Explanatory Clauses

5.227. Epexegetical (Explanation) Clauses

Clauses adding explanation usually use an infinitive or a ἵνα clause.

5.228. Appositional Clauses after οὗτος

Οὗτος may come early in a sentence and be explained by means of an infinitive, a ὅτι clause, or a ἵνα clause, functioning like a noun in apposition to οὗτος.

Subordinate Clauses Functioning Like an Adverb

5.229. Temporal Clauses

When something takes place.

5.230. Local Clauses

Where something takes place.

5.231. Indefinite Local and Temporal Clauses

Often ἄν or ἐάν will be present, sometimes as part of the conjunction, for example, ὅταν, whenever is a combination of ὅτε, when, and ἄν.

5.232. Purpose (Final) Clauses

The intended outcome of an action.

5.233. Causal Clauses

The cause or reason why something takes place.

5.234. Comparative Clauses

What something or some action is like.

5.235. Concessive Clauses

That despite which something happens or is true.

5.236. Result (Consecutive) Clauses

What happened as a result of the action of the main clause, either an intended result or an actual result whether or not it was intended.

5.237. Conditional Sentences

A sentence with two sections: "If this / then that."

Types of conditional sentences

	Signs	Assumption
5.238. Indefinite	If: εἰ + any indicative	If this is true, and the context
	Then: any finite verb	will have to indicate whether or not I think it is true.
5.239.	If: εἰ + secondary ind.	If this is true, and I don't believe
Contrary-to-fact	Then: secondary ind. + ἄν	that it is.
5.240.	If: ἐάν + subjunctive	If this is true, and I think
Future-more-likely	Then: any finite vb.	it's possible, probable, or hypothetical.
5.241.	If: εἰ + optative	If this is true, but I think it's un-
Future-less-likely	Then: various	likely to be true, or I'm just raising a hypothetical possibility.
5.242. General	If: ἐάν + subjunctive	If this is true, then this is what I
	Then: present indicative	think always happens.

5.245. Future-Most-Likely Conditions

Occasionally a future condition will be expressed with εἰ and a future indicative, rather than ἐάν and a subjunctive as in Type 3. It conveys a sense of strong emotion.

Sentence Connectors and Conjunctions

5.246. Major Sentence Connectors and Conjunctions

Some words, such as καί, ἤ, and ἀλλά, connect sentences, but also can join various other elements together. The most common words that serve primarily as sentence connectors are γάρ, οὖν, and δέ, including ὁ δέ and μέν . . . δέ.

5.248. Asyndeton

The lack of a conjunction to join a clause to what preceded it.

WORD ORDER AND EMPHASIS

Word Order and Emphasis between Clauses

5.258. Placement of Subordinate Clauses

In general we can expect subordinate clauses and circumstantial participles that set the scene or establish the context for what follows to come before the main clause, while those that assume and develop information in the main clause to follow it.

5.259. Discourse Significance

In general, subordinate clauses and circumstantial participles before the main verb provide background information. Those coming after the main verb may provide background information or may be more in the foreground, contributing to the main thought of the clause.

Word Order and Emphasis within Clauses

5.260. Verb Placement

In the New Testament the order is frequently: verb – subject – object.

5.261. Order with an Expressed Subject

When a subject is expressed it usually comes before the verb, indicating a focus on the subject, or at times a shift in topic.

5.262. Genitives and Adjectival Modifiers

These usually come after the word they modify.

5.263. Word Clusters

A word separated from its cluster may be somewhat emphasized. *Hendiadys*: two words joined to express a single idea.

5.264. Individual Words

a. Individual words that may carry emphasis
1. Adverbs (for example, ἀληθῶς, εὐθύς)
2. Emphatic personal pronouns (ἐμοῦ, ἐμοί, ἐμέ, etc.)
3. Emphatic possessive adjectives (σός, ἡμέτερος, etc.)
4. Nominative personal pronoun (ἐγώ, ἡμεῖς, σύ, ὑμεῖς, αὐτός, αὐτή, etc.)
5. Intensive adverbs (οὐχί, νυνί)

b. Adjunctive, ascensive, and explicative καί
1. Adjunctive use of καί. Adding an additional point, "and, also, too, likewise"
2. Ascensive use of καί. Adding a final/climactic point or emphasis, "even, indeed, in fact"
3. Explicative use of καί. Adding an explanation of what has just been said, "and so, that is, namely"

c. Particles. Nuance words such as γέ, "at least, even, indeed," convey emphasis, somewhat like using gestures in animated speech.

5.265. Double Negatives

Two negatives make something more emphatically negative.

SENTENCE MAPPING

5.267. Brief Introduction to Sentence Mapping

There are four basic principles to follow in sentence mapping:

1. Keep the core elements of each clause on a single line.
2. Line up flush with each other any items that are coordinate with each other or in apposition.
3. Indent any subordinate elements or modifiers under the word they modify, with a subordinate clause being placed under the verb of the main clause.
4. When a word or cluster has to be moved out of order mark its original location with ellipsis points (. . .).

Simple Overview of
English Grammar Essentials

The following simple survey of a few of the essential features of grammar may be of help to those at the outset of studying Greek who need a review of the basics. For additional help with a grammatical term an English dictionary is usually the most convenient resource; many are available online. Many websites offer more extensive help for English grammar, for example, http://grammar.about.com/.

A concise review of basic English grammar is included in H. P. V. Nunn, *Short Syntax*, 1–24. More detailed help for Greek students is provided in Kyle Greenwood, *Dictionary of English Grammar*; Samuel Lamerson, *English Grammar*; Gary Long, *Grammatical Concepts*.[1] For a sprightly written more developed discussion that is perhaps more for intermediate students see Bruce McMenomy, *Syntactical Mechanics*.[2]

The basic unit in the development of a topic is the **paragraph**. Within the paragraph the basic unit is the **sentence**. Each sentence has two parts, the **subject** and the **predicate**. "The function of every sentence, always, is to *say* something *about* something. That's all. . . . Accordingly every sentence has two fundamental parts—the what-it's-about part, which is traditionally called the *subject*, and the what-about-it part, which is traditionally called the *predicate*."[3]

Sentences are usually composed of one or more clauses, each of which has a subject and predicate. A **clause** is a cluster of words around a verb. A **verb** indi-

---

1. Kyle Greenwod, *Dictionary of English Grammar for Students of Biblical Languages* (Grand Rapids: Zondervan, 2020); Samuel Lamerson, *English Grammar to Ace New Testament Greek* (Grand Rapids: Zondervan, 2004); Gary A. Long, *Grammatical Concepts 101 for Biblical Greek: Learning Biblical Greek Grammatical Concepts through English Grammar* (Peabody, MA: Hendrickson, 2006).

2. Bruce A. McMenomy, *Syntactical Mechanics: A New Approach to English, Latin, and Greek*, new ed., Oklahoma Studies in Classical Culture 51 (Norman: University of Oklahoma Press, 2014).

3. McMenomy, *Syntactical Mechanics*, 19.

cates an action, event, condition, or state of being. A **phrase** is a cluster of words around a noun or noun substitute. A **noun** names a person, place, thing, or idea.

Thus the minimum for a clause is a **subject** and a **verb**. *The apostle arrived.* The subject does the action and the verb indicates the action.

Some sentences also have a **direct object**. *The apostle brought the gospel.* The direct object is what or whom the action directly affects.

Some sentences also have an **indirect object**. *The apostle brought the gospel to the people.* The indirect object is the one who receives the direct object, that is, the one to whom or for whom the action takes place.

Not every subject is the agent doing the action of the verb. Sometimes it receives the action. *The gospel was brought by the apostle.* When the subject does the action the verb is said to be **active**, and when the subject receives the action the verb is said to be **passive**.

Not all verbs take a direct object. *The apostle arrived.* A verb like "bring" that takes a direct object is called **transitive**, and one like "arrive" that does not is called **intransitive**. Often verbs may be either transitive or intransitive. In *The apostle stood in the marketplace* the verb is intransitive, but in *The apostle stood his staff against a wall* the verb now has a direct object, *his staff*.

Not all verbs denote action. *The apostle stood in the marketplace.* While "bring" is an **action verb**, the verb *stood* is a **stative verb**, that is, it does not indicate an action, but rather a state or condition. Some verbs may be either an action verb or a stative verb. *The apostle stood his staff against a wall.* Now *stood* refers to an action and has a direct object, *his staff*.

There are also **equative verbs** that make an assertion about the subject, usually identifying it or one of its characteristics. The verbs "to be" and "to become" are the most common equative verbs. *The apostle is joyful. The apostle became excited.* Here *joyful* and *excited* are not direct objects but rather **complements**, that is, they complete these descriptions.

No matter how long a sentence gets in Greek—and they can get much longer than sentences in modern English—the sentence can be broken down into clauses clustering around verbs. The core of the clause will consist of a verb and usually one or more of these basic elements. Everything else in the clause modifies one of these elements or relates the clause to the sentence around it.

Accordingly, each core element—the subject, verb, direct object, indirect object—can be further described. *The old apostle joyfully preached the holy gospel to the eager people.* The nouns *apostle, gospel,* and *people* are modified by the **adjectives** *old, holy,* and *eager*. The verb *preached* is modified by the **adverb** *joyfully*.

A **pronoun** can take the place of a noun, with the context usually making the reference clear. *They listened to him.*

The whole clause can be connected to the context around it by using a **conjunction**. *Therefore the apostle praised God.* The conjunction *therefore* indicates that what this clause describes is the conclusion of something that went before.

A clause may stand on its own as an **independent clause**. *The apostle praised God.* This is an independent clause, a complete sentence.

Two or more independent clauses can be joined together by a connector such as "and" or "but" to form a **compound sentence**. *The apostle preached the gospel and the people praised God.*

A clause may modify another clause, and thus be a **subordinate clause** that is **dependent** on the other clause. *The apostle praised God because the people received the gospel.* The first clause describing the apostle praising God is the **main clause** in a **complex sentence**, that is, a sentence composed of a main independent clause and one or more dependent clauses. The second clause, *because the people received the gospel*, is itself a clause, with its own verb, *received*, subject, *the people*, and direct object, *the gospel*. If the word *because* was not present then the resulting clause—*The people received the gospel*—would itself be an independent clause. But the conjunction *because* signals that this clause modifies the first clause and is thus subordinate to it and dependent on it. It is indicating why the apostle did what he did.

One clause may modify a part of another clause. A common example is the **relative clause**, which functions just like an adjective, that is, it modifies a noun or pronoun. *The apostle preached the gospel to the people who were listening eagerly.* The clause *who were listening eagerly* has its own verb, *were listening*, and an adverb, *eagerly*. The word *who* signals a relative clause that will tell us more about some element in another clause, in this case *the people*. Other relative pronouns include *which* and *that*.

A **prepositional phrase** consists of a preposition like *of, in, after, with*, and a noun or noun substitute. Such a phrase can modify either a noun or a verb. *The apostle from Jerusalem preached the gospel. From Jerusalem* describes which apostle we are talking about. *The apostle preached for four hours. For four hours* tells us how long the apostle preached.

SUMMARY: KEY TERMS

Sample sentence: *The apostle preached the gospel to the people.*

Verb	preached	the action
Subject	the apostle	who preached
Direct object	the gospel	preached what or whom
Indirect object	the people	preached to whom or for whom
Pronoun	Takes the place of a noun.	He preached it to them.
Adjective	Describes a noun.	The old apostle preached the holy gospel to the eager people.

Adverb	Describes a verb.	*The apostle preached <u>enthusiastically</u> to the people.*
Prepositional phrase	Describes a noun or a verb.	*The apostle <u>from Jerusalem</u> preached the gospel to the people.* Tells us which apostle.
		The apostle preached <u>for four hours</u>. Tells us how long he preached.

Grammatical elements such as the verb, noun, pronoun, adjective, adverb, preposition, and conjunction are referred to as the **parts of speech**.

Suggestions for Approaching a Sentence in Greek

I n order to become comfortable reading Greek it is vital that you learn to pick up the meaning in the order it comes to you in a sentence. Right from the outset of basic Greek it is best to include work on this skill. When reading/ translating a sentence cover it with a card and reveal it word by word. For each word identify its

- part of speech, that is, whether it is a noun, verb, conjunction, preposition, and so forth;
- parsing, unless of course it is a set form like a conjunction or preposition;
- use/function/contribution to the clause; and
- meaning/translation.

If much of the sentence is a puzzle, then you'll need to analyze it before being able to read it in order. Begin by identifying the words as just described and watch for how they form clusters and constructions, such as

- clauses
- prepositional phrases
- genitives modifying substantives
- articles and substantives that bracket material between them
- nouns and adjectives in agreement in gender, case, and number

You may find it helpful at times to mark up the text to highlight key signals of clauses such as punctuation, conjunctions, and finite verbs, and also to mark out clusters such as subordinate clauses, relative clauses, circumstantial participles, prepositional phrases, and genitives along with the head terms they are modifying.[1]

Once you have identified the words and clusters, work through the sentence clause by clause. Recall that the core elements within a clause are the subject,

---

1. For help with such marking and analysis see *UEBG*, 95–98, and the related video, linked at whitacregreek.com.

verb, direct object, and indirect object, though most clauses do not have all of these items (§2.3). So identify the words that have these core functions, beginning with the verb, and then sort out how the other words contribute to the clause.

Once you have sorted out the details of a sentence you are ready to read through it in order. Reread the sentence several times, trying to pick up the meaning in the Greek order. Include pronunciation of the sentence aloud at least once or twice. You may be tempted to rush on to the next sentence, but this review and pronunciation are extremely beneficial. Increasingly you will be able to sort out more and more the first time through a sentence.[2]

A major part of developing the ability to read Greek is learning not only vocabulary and the general patterns of morphology and syntax but also the idiosyncrasies of particular words, especially the irregular ones.[3] The practice of reading and rereading sentences contributes to gaining familiarity with the details of both the general patterns and the irregularities.

For an inspiring and humorous vision for learning to read through a sentence in order as recommended in this appendix see the opening section of *The Art of Reading Latin* by William Gardner Hale.[4] You will be able to follow his first pages even if you do not know Latin.

SUMMARY OF KEY POINTS FOR PUZZLING THROUGH A SENTENCE

1. Identify for each word its
   - part of speech
   - parsing
   - meaning/translation
2. Note any clusters, looking for signs such as
   - a conjunction initiating a clause
   - a preposition initiating a prepositional phrase
   - agreement in gender, case, and number
   - a genitive modifying a head term

2. See *UEBG*, 111–12.

3. See Carl Conrad, "Active, Middle, and Passive: Understanding Ancient Greek Voice," December 16, 2003, https://pages.wustl.edu/files/pages/imce/cwconrad/undancgrkvc .pdf, §6. His focus is specifically on verbs, but the same point applies to other irregularities as well.

4. William Gardner Hale, *The Art of Reading Latin: How to Teach It* (Boston: Ginn, 1888). Available online on multiple sites, including Perseus, http://www.perseus.tufts.edu/hop per/collection?collection=Perseus:collection:Greco-Roman.

3. Put the pieces together, noting the use/function/contribution to the clause of each word and cluster.
   - Work clause by clause.
   - Start with the main verb.
   - Add any other core elements that are present.
   - Add any other items, which will usually be modifiers.

Principal Parts of Common Greek Verbs

T he following list covers verbs found in the New Testament twenty-five times or more. Three reader's editions of the Greek New Testament and also the reader's edition of the LXX assume you know the words used thirty times or more, while the reader's edition for the *THGNT* assumes twenty-five times or more.[1]

In addition to principal parts used in the New Testament, those used in ancient Greek in general are included for help when you read outside the New Testament. The forms listed are from Montanari and BDAG. Some of these verbs have yet further alternatives not listed here.[2]

Forms in brackets are alternate stems you can learn in order to recognize the forms of some verbs that have significant changes or use alternate stems. See §4.67c for this approach to learning to recognize the principal parts. These forms are often actual stems, but sometimes merely a form that may be of help. Stems that undergo minor changes are not usually noted. See §§4.68–75 for many of these minor changes that follow regular patterns.[3]

1. Barbara Aland et al., eds., *The UBS Greek New Testament: A Reader's Edition*, 5th ed. (Stuttgart: Deutsche Bibelgesellschaft, 2014); Richard J. Goodrich and Albert L. Luka-szewski, eds., *A Reader's Greek New Testament*, 2nd ed. (Grand Rapids: Zondervan, 2007); Dirk Jongkind et al., eds., *The Greek New Testament: Reader's Edition*, reader's textual notes compiled by Drayton C. Brenner, James R. Covington, and Andrew Zulker (Wheaton, IL: Crossway, 2018) (This is the reader's edition of *The Greek New Testament, Produced at Tyndale House, Cambridge*); Gregory R. Lanier and William A. Ross, eds., *Septuaginta: A Reader's Edition*, 2 vols. (Peabody, MA: Hendrickson; Stuttgart: Deutsche Bibelgesellschaft, 2018); the reader's edition of the LXX assumes knowledge of words used one hundred times or more in the LXX. For LXX resources see William Ross's website: https://williamaross .com/.

2. See further the lists in Smyth, 684–722 and *CGCG* §22.9, as well as the morphological help in BDAG and LSJ.

3. For help identifying verb stems see LSJ; Smyth, 684–722; and *CGCG* §22.9.

Present	Future	Aorist (act./ MP1)	Perfect (act.)	Perfect (MP)	Aorist (MP2)
ἀγαπάω	ἀγαπήσω	ἠγάπησα	ἠγάπηκα	ἠγάπημαι	ἠγαπήθην
ἁγιάζω	ἁγιάσω	ἡγίασα	ἡγίακα	ἡγίασμαι	ἡγιάσθην
ἀγοράζω	ἀγοράσω	ἠγόρασα	ἠγόρακα	ἠγόρασμαι	ἠγοράσθην
ἄγω [ἀγαγ-]	ἄξω	ἤγαγον	ἦχα	ἦγμαι	ἤχθην
ἀδικέω	ἀδικήσω	ἠδίκησα	ἠδίκηκα	ἠδίκημαι	ἠδικήθην
αἴρω [ἀρ-]	ἀρῶ	ἦρα	ἦρκα	ἦρμαι	ἤρθην
αἰτέω	αἰτήσω	ᾔτησα	ᾔτηκα	ᾔτημαι	ᾐτήθην
ἀκολουθέω	ἀκολουθήσω	ἠκολούθησα	ἠκολούθηκα		
ἀκούω [ἀκηκο-]	ἀκούσω	ἤκουσα	ἀκήκοα	ἤκουσμαι	ἠκούσθην
ἁμαρτάνω [ἁμαρ-]	ἁμαρτήσω	ἥμαρτον ἡμάρτησα	ἡμάρτηκα	ἡμάρτημαι	ἡμαρτήθην
ἀναβαίνω [βα-, βη-]	ἀναβήσομαι	ἀνέβησα ἀνέβην	ἀναβέβηκα		
ἀναβλέπω	ἀναβλέψω	ἀνέβλεψα	ἀναβέβλεφα	ἀναβέβλεμ-μαι	ἀνεβλέφθην
ἀναγινώσκω [γνο-, γνω-] ἀναγιγνώσκω	ἀναγνώσομαι	ἀνέγνων ἀνέγνωσα	ἀνέγνωκα	ἀνέγνωσμαι	ἀνεγνώσθην
ἀνίστημι [στα-, στη-]	ἀναστήσω	ἀνέστησα ἀνέστην	ἀνέστηκα	ἀνέσταμαι	ἀνεστάθην
ἀνοίγω [ἀνεῳγ-]	ἀνοίξω	ἀνέῳξα ἤνοιξα	ἀνέῳγα	ἀνέῳγμαι	ἀνεῴχθην ἠνεῴχθην
ἀπαγγέλλω	ἀπαγγελῶ	ἀπήγγειλα	ἀπήγγελκα	ἀπήγγελμαι	ἀπηγγέλθην
ἀπέρχομαι [ἐλευ-, ἐλθ-]	ἀπελεύσομαι	ἀπῆλθον	ἀπελήλυθα		
ἀποδίδωμι [δο-, δω-]	ἀποδώσω	ἀπέδωκα	ἀποδέδωκα	ἀποδέδομαι	ἀπεδόθην
ἀποθνῄσκω [θαν-]	ἀποθανοῦμαι	ἀπέθανον	ἀποτέθνηκα		
ἀποκαλύπτω	ἀποκαλύψω	ἀπεκάλυψα	ἀποκεκάλυφα	ἀποκεκάλυμ-μαι	ἀπεκαλύφθην
ἀποκρίνω	ἀποκρινῶ	ἀπέκρινα		ἀποκέκριμαι	ἀπεκρίθην
ἀποκτείνω	ἀποκτενῶ	ἀπέκτεινα	ἀπέκτονα		ἀπεκτάνθην
ἀπόλλυμι [λε-]	ἀπολέσω ἀπολῶ	ἀπώλεσα	ἀπολώλεκα ἀπόλωλα		ἀπωλέσθην
ἀπολύω	ἀπολύσω	ἀπέλυσα	ἀπολέλυκα	ἀπολέλυμαι	ἀπελύθην

Present	Future	Aorist (act./ MP₁)	Perfect (act.)	Perfect (MP)	Aorist (MP2)
ἀποστέλλω	ἀποστελῶ	ἀπέστειλα	ἀπέσταλκα	ἀπέσταλμαι	ἀπεστάλην
ἅπτω	ἅψω	ἧψα		ἧμμαι	ἥφθην
ἀρνέομαι	ἀρνήσομαι	ἠρνησάμην		ἤρνημαι	ἠρνήθην
ἄρχω	ἄρξω	ἦρξα	ἦρχα	ἦργμαι	ἤρχθην
ἀσθενέω	ἀσθενήσω	ἠσθένησα	ἠσθένηκα		
ἀσπάζομαι	ἀσπάσομαι	ἠσπασάμην		ἤσπασμαι	
ἀφίημι [ἡ-, ἑ-]	ἀφήσω	ἀφῆκα	ἀφεῖκα	ἀφεῖμαι	ἀφέθην
βάλλω [βαλ-, βλη-]	βαλῶ	ἔβαλον	βέβληκα	βέβλημαι	ἐβλήθην
βαπτίζω	βαπτίσω	ἐβάπτισα	βεβάπτικα	βεβάπτισμαι	ἐβαπτίσθην
βαστάζω	βαστάσω	ἐβάστασα	βεβάστακα	βεβάσταγμαι	ἐβαστάχθην
βλασφημέω	βλασφημήσω	ἐβλασφήμησα	βεβλασφήμηκα	βεβλασφήμημαι	ἐβλασφημήθην
βλέπω	βλέψω	ἔβλεψα	βέβλεφα	βέβλεμμαι	ἐβλέφθην
βούλομαι	βουλήσομαι			βεβούλημαι	ἐβουλήθην
γαμέω	γαμήσω	ἐγάμησα ἔγημα	γεγάμηκα	γεγάμμαι	ἐγαμήθην
γεννάω	γεννήσω	ἐγέννησα	γεγέννηκα	γεγέννημαι	ἐγεννήθην
γίνομαι [γεν-, γον-] γίγνομαι	γενήσομαι	ἐγενόμην	γέγονα	γεγένημαι	ἐγενήθην
γινώσκω [γνο-, γνω-] γιγνώσκω	γνώσομαι	ἔγνων	ἔγνωκα	ἔγνωσμαι	ἐγνώσθην
γνωρίζω	γνωρίσω	ἐγνώρισα	ἐγνώρικα	ἐγνώρισμαι	ἐγνωρίσθην
γράφω	γράψω	ἔγραψα	γέγραφα	γεγράμμαι	ἐγράφην
δεῖ[a] Impf., ἔδει	δεήσει				
δείκνυμι [δεικ-]	δείξω	ἔδειξα	δέδειχα	δέδειγμαι	ἐδείχθην
δέχομαι	δέξομαι	ἐδεξάμην			ἐδέχθην
δέω	δεήσω	ἐδέησα	δεδέηκα	δεδέημαι	ἐδεήθην
διακονέω	διακονήσω	διηκόνησα	δεδιακόνηκα	δεδιακόνημαι	ἐδιακονήθην
διδάσκω	διδάξω	ἐδίδαξα	δεδίδαχα	δεδίδαγμαι	ἐδιδάχθην
δίδωμι [δο-, δω-]	δώσω	ἔδωκα	δέδωκα	δέδομαι	ἐδόθην

Present	Future	Aorist (act./MP1)	Perfect (act.)	Perfect (MP)	Aorist (MP2)
διέρχομαι [ἐλευ-, ἐλθ-]	διελεύσομαι	διῆλθον	διελήλυθα		
δικαιόω	δικαιώσω	ἐδικαίωσα	δεδικαίωκα	δεδικαίωμαι	ἐδικαιώθην
διώκω	διώξω	ἐδίωξα	δεδίωχα	δεδίωγμαι	ἐδιώχθην
δοκέω	δόξω δοξήσω	ἔδοξα ἐδόκησα	δεδόκηκα	δέδογμαι δεδόκημαι	ἐδοκήθην
δοξάζω	δοξάσω	ἐδόξασα	δεδόξακα	δεδόξασμαι	ἐδοξάσθην
δουλεύω	δουλεύσω	ἐδούλευσα	δεδούλευκα		ἐδουλεύθην
δύναμαι	δυνήσομαι	ἐδυνησάμην		δεδύνημαι	ἐδυνήθην
ἐγγίζω	ἐγγιῶ	ἤγγισα	ἤγγικα		ἠγγίσθην
ἐγείρω	ἐγερῶ	ἤγειρα	ἐγήγερκα	ἐγήγερμαι	ἠγέρθην
εἶδον [ἰδ-] see εἴδω					
εἴδω[b]	εἰδήσω	εἶδον	οἶδα		
εἰμί [ἐ-] Impf., ἤμην	ἔσομαι				
εἶπον (see λέγω)					
εἴρω (see λέγω)					
εἰσέρχομαι [ἐλευ-, ἐλθ-]	εἰσελεύσομαι	εἰσῆλθον	εἰσελήλυθα		
ἐκβάλλω [βαλ-, βλ-]	ἐκβαλῶ	ἐξέβαλον	ἐκβέβληκα	ἐκβέβλημαι	ἐξεβλήθην
ἐκπορεύω	ἐκπορεύσω	ἐκεπόρευσα		ἐκπεπόρευμαι	ἐκεπορεύθην
ἐκχέω [χυ-]	ἐκχεῶ	ἐξέχεα	ἐκκέχυκα	ἐκκέχυμαι	ἐξεχύθην
ἐλεέω	ἐλεήσω	ἠλέησα	ἠλέηκα	ἠλέημαι	ἠλεήθην
ἐλπίζω	ἐλπίσω	ἤλπισα	ἤλπικα	ἤλπισμαι	ἠλπίσθην
ἐνδύω	ἐνδύσω	ἐνέδυσα	ἐνδέδυκα	ἐνδέδυμαι	ἐνεδύθην
ἐξέρχομαι [ἐλευ-, ἐλθ-]	ἐξελεύσομαι	ἐξῆλθον ἐξῆλθα	ἐξελήλυθα		
ἔξεστιν[c]	ἔξεσται				
ἐπερωτάω	ἐπερωτήσω	ἐπηρώτησα	ἐπηρώτηκα	ἐπηρώτημαι	ἐπηρωτήθην
ἐπιγινώσκω [γνο-, γνω-] ἐπιγιγνώσκω	ἐπιγνώσομαι	ἐπέγνων	ἐπέγνωκα	ἐπέγνωσμαι	ἐπεγνώσθην

Present	Future	Aorist (act./ MP1)	Perfect (act.)	Perfect (MP)	Aorist (MP2)
ἐπικαλέω	ἐπικαλέσω ἐπικαλῶ	ἐπεκάλεσα ἐπεκάλησα	ἐπικέκληκα	ἐπικέκλημαι	ἐπεκλήθην
ἐπιστρέφω	ἐπιστρέψω	ἐπέστειψα			ἐπεστράφην
ἐπιτίθημι [θε-, θη-, θει-, τε-]	ἐπιθήσω	ἐπέθηκα ἐπέθην	ἐπιτέθεικα	ἐπιτέθειμαι	ἐπετέθην
ἐπιτιμάω	ἐπιτιμήσω	ἐπετίμησα	ἐπιτετίμηκα	ἐπιτετίμημαι	ἐπετιμήθην
ἐργάζομαι	ἐργάσομαι ἐργῶμαι	εἰργασάμην		εἴργασμαι	εἰργάσθην
ἔρχομαι [ἐλευ-, ἐλθ-]	ἐλεύσομαι	ἦλθον	ἐλήλυθα		
ἐρωτάω	ἐρωτήσω	ἠρώτησα	ἠρώτηκα	ἠρώτημαι	ἠρωτήθην
ἐσθίω [φαγ-]	φάγομαι	ἔφαγον			
ἑτοιμάζω	ἑτοιμάσω	ἡτοίμασα	ἡτοίμακα	ἡτοίμασμαι	ἡτοιμάσθην
εὐαγγελίζω	εὐαγγελιῶ	εὐηγγέλισα		εὐηγγέλισμαι	εὐηγγελίσθην
εὐλογέω	εὐλογήσω	ηὐλόγησα εὐλόγησα	ηὐλόγηκα εὐλόγηκα	ηὐλόγημαι εὐλόγημαι	ηὐλογήθην εὐλογήθην
εὑρίσκω [εὑρ-]	εὑρήσω	εὗρον	εὕρηκα	(εὕρημαι)	εὑρέθην
εὐχαριστέω	εὐχαριστήσω	εὐχαρίστησα ηὐχαρίστησα	εὐχαρίστηκα	ηὐχαρίστημαι	εὐχαριστήθην ηὐχαριστήθην
ἔχω [σχ-]	ἕξω	ἔσχον	ἔσχηκα	ἔσχημαι	ἐσχέθην
ζάω/ζῶ	ζήσω	ἔζησα	ἔζηκα		
ζητέω	ζητήσω	ἐζήτησα	ἐζήτηκα	ἐζήτημαι	ἐζητήθην
ἡγέομαι	ἡγήσομαι	ἡγησάμην		ἥγημαι	ἡγήθην
ἥκω	ἥξω	ἧξα	ἧκα		
θαυμάζω	θαυμάσω	ἐθαύμασα	τεθαύμακα		ἐθαυμάσθην
θέλω earlier = ἐθέλω	θελήσω ἐθελήσω	ἐθέλησα ἠθέλησα	τεθέληκα ἠθέληκα	τεθέλημαι	ἐθελήθην
θεραπεύω	θεραπεύσω	ἐθεράπευσα	τεθεράπευκα	τεθεράπευμαι	ἐθεραπεύθην
θεωρέω	θεωρήσω	ἐθεώρησα	τεθεώρηκα	τεθεώρημαι	ἐθεωρήθην
ἰάομαι	ἰάσομαι	ἰασάμην		ἴαμαι	ἰάθην
ἴδε, ἰδού[d]					
ἵστημι [στα-, στη-]	στήσω	ἔστησα ἔστην	ἕστηκα	ἕσταμαι	ἐστάθην
ἰσχύω	ἰσχύσω	ἴσχυσα	ἴσχυκα		ἰσχύθην

Present	Future	Aorist (act./ MP1)	Perfect (act.)	Perfect (MP)	Aorist (MP2)
καθαρίζω	καθαριῶ καθαρίσω	ἐκαθάρισα	κεκαθάρικα	κεκαθάρισμαι	ἐκαθαρίσθην
κάθημαι	καθήσομαι				
καθίζω	καθίσω καθιῶ	ἐκάθισα	κεκάθικα		ἐκαθέσθην
καλέω [κλη-]	καλέσω καλῶ	ἐκάλεσα ἐκάλησα	κέκληκα	κέκλημαι	ἐκλήθην
καταβαίνω [βα-, βη-]	καταβήσω	κατέβην	καταβέβηκα		
καταργέω	καταργήσω	κατήργησα	κατήργηκα	κατήργημαι	κατηργήθην
κατοικέω	κατοικήσω	κατῴκησα	κατῴκηκα	κατῴκημαι	κατῳκήθην
καυχάομαι	καυχήσομαι	ἐκαυχησάμην		κεκαύχημαι	ἐκαυχήθην
κελεύω	κελεύσω	ἐκέλευσα	κεκέλευκα	κεκέλευσμαι	ἐκελεύσθην
κηρύσσω [κηρυγ-]	κηρύξω	ἐκήρυξα	κεκήρυχα	κεκήρυγμαι	ἐκηρύχθην
κλαίω	κλαύσω κλάσω	ἔκλασα	κέκλακα	κέκλασμαι	ἐκλάσθην
κράζω	κράξω	ἔκραξα ἐκέκραξα ἔκραγον	κέκραγα		
κρατέω	κρατήσω	ἐκράτησα	κεκράτηκα	κεκράτημαι	ἐκρατήθην
κρίνω	κρινῶ	ἔκρινα	κέκρικα	κέκριμαι	ἐκρίθην
λαλέω	λαλήσω	ἐλάλησα	λελάληκα	λελάλημαι	ἐλαλήθην
λαμβάνω [λαβ-]	λήμψομαι	ἔλαβον	εἴληφα	εἴλημμαι	ἐλήμφθην ἐλήφθην
λέγω [ἐρ-, εἰπ-]	ἐρῶ[e]	εἶπον[f]	εἴρηκα[e]	εἴρημαι[e]	ἐρρέθην[e]
λογίζομαι	λογιοῦμαι	ἐλογισάμην		λελόγισμαι	ἐλογίσθην
λυπέω	λυπήσω	ἐλύπησα	λελύπηκα	λελύπημαι	ἐλυπήθην
λύω	λύσω	ἔλυσα	λέλυκα	λέλυμαι	ἐλύθην
μανθάνω [μαθ-]	μαθήσω	ἔμαθον	μεμάθηκα		
μαρτυρέω	μαρτυρήσω	ἐμαρτύρησα	μεμαρτύρηκα	μεμαρτύρη-μαι	ἐμαρτυρήθην
μέλλω	μελλήσω	ἐμέλλησα ἠμέλλησα			
μένω	μενῶ	ἔμεινα	μεμένηκα		

Present	Future	Aorist (act./ MP1)	Perfect (act.)	Perfect (MP)	Aorist (MP2)
μετανοέω	μετανοήσω	μετενόησα	μετανενόηκα	μετανενόημαι	μετενοήθην
μισέω	μισήσω	ἐμίσησα	μεμίσηκα	μεμίσημαι	ἐμισήθην
νικάω	νικήσω	ἐνίκησα	νενίκηκα	νενίκημαι	ἐνικήθην
οἶδα [εἰδ-] see εἴδω	εἰδήσω	ἤδειν[g]			
οἰκοδομέω	οἰκοδομήσω	ᾠκοδόμησα	ᾠκοδόμηκα	ᾠκοδόμημαι	ᾠκοδομήθην
ὀμνύω [ὀμο-] ὄμνυμι	ὀμόσω	ὤμοσα	ὀμώμοκα	ὀμώμοσμαι	ὠμόσθην
ὁμολογέω	ὁμολογήσω	ὡμολόγησα	ὡμολόγηκα	ὡμολόγημαι	ὡμολογήθην
ὁράω [ὀπ-, ἰδ-]	ὄψομαι	εἶδον[h]	ἑώρακα ἑόρακα		ὤφθην
ὀφείλω	ὀφειλήσω	ὠφείλησα ὤφειλα			
παραγγέλλω	παραγγελῶ	παρήγγειλα	παρήγγελκα	παρήγγελμαι	παρηγγέλθην
παραγίνομαι [γεν-, γον-] παραγίγνομαι	παραγενή- σομαι	παρεγενόμην	παραγέγονα	παραγεγένη- μαι	παρεγενήθην
παραδίδωμι [δο-, δω-]	παραδώσω	παρέδωκα	παραδέδωκα	παραδέδομαι	παρεδόθην
παρακαλέω [κλη-]	παρακαλέσω παρακαλῶ	παρεκάλεσα	παρακέκληκα	παρακέκλη- μαι	παρεκλήθην
παραλαμ- βάνω [λαβ-]	παραλήμψο- μαι	παρέλαβον	παρείληφα	παρείλημμαι	παρελήφθην
παρέρχομαι [ἐλευ-, ἐλθ-]	παρελεύσο- μαι	παρῆλθον	παρελήλυθα		
παρίστημι [στα-, στη-] παριστάνω	παραστήσω	παρέστησα παρέστην	παρέστηκα	παρέσταμαι	παρεστάθην
πάσχω [παθ-, πονθ-]	πείσομαι	ἔπαθον	πέπονθα		
πείθω [ποιθ-]	πείσω	ἔπεισα	πέποιθα	πέπεισμαι	ἐπείσθην
πειράζω	πειράσω	ἐπείρασα	πεπείρακα	πεπείρασμαι	ἐπειράσθην
πέμπω [πομφ-]	πέμψω	ἔπεμψα	πέπομφα	πέπεμμαι	ἐπέμφθην
περιπατέω	περιπατήσω	περιεπάτησα ἐπεριπάτησα	περιπεπάτηκα	περιπεπάτη- μαι	
περισσεύω	περισσεύσω	ἐπερίσσευσα			ἐπερισσεύθην

Present	Future	Aorist (act./ MP₁)	Perfect (act.)	Perfect (MP)	Aorist (MP₂)
πίνω [πι-, πο-]	πίομαι	ἔπιον	πέπωκα	πέπομαι	ἐπόθην
πίπτω [πετ-]	πεσοῦμαι	ἔπεσον	πέπτωκα		
πιστεύω	πιστεύσω	ἐπίστευσα	πεπίστευκα	πεπίστευμαι	ἐπιστεύθην
πλανάω	πλανήσω	ἐπλάνησα	πεπλάνηκα	πεπλάνημαι	ἐπλανήθην
πληρόω	πληρώσω	ἐπλήρωσα	πεπλήρωκα	πεπλήρωμαι	ἐπληρώθην
ποιέω	ποιήσω	ἐποίησα	πεποίηκα	πεποίημαι	ἐποιήθην
πορεύω	πορεύσω	ἐπόρευσα		πεπόρευμαι	ἐπορεύθην
πράσσω [πραγ-]	πράξω	ἔπραξα	πέπραγα πέπραχα	πέπραγμαι	ἐπράχθην
προσέρχομαι [ἐλευ-, ἐλθ-]	προσελεύ-σομαι	προσῆλθον	προσελήλυθα		
προσεύχομαι	προσεύξομαι	προσηυξάμην		προσηῦγμαι	
προσκαλέω [κλη-]	προσκαλέ-σομαι	προσεκάλεσα	προσκέκληκα	προσκέκλη-μαι	προσεκλήθην
προσκυνέω	προσκυνήσω	προσεκύνησα			
προσφέρω [οἰ-, ἐνεκ-]	προσοίσω	προσήνεγκα	προσενήνοχα	προσενήνεγ-μαι	προσηνέχθην
προφητεύω	προφητεύσω	ἐπροφήτευσα	πεπροφήτευκα	πεπροφήτευ-μαι	ἐπροφη-τεύθην
σκανδαλίζω	σκανδαλίσω	ἐσκανδάλισα		ἐσκανδάλι-σμαι	ἐσκανδαλί-σθην
σπείρω [σπαρ-]	σπερῶ	ἔσπειρα ἐσπάρην	ἔσπαρκα	ἔσπαρμαι	ἐσπάρην
σταυρόω	σταυρώσω	ἐσταύρωσα	ἐσταύρωκα	ἐσταύρωμαι	ἐσταυρώθην
συνάγω [ἀγαγ-]	συνάξω	συνήγαγον συνῆξα	συνῆχα	συνῆγμαι	συνήχθην
συνέρχομαι [ἐλευ-, ἐλθ-]	συνελεύσομαι	συνῆλθον	συνελήλυθα		
συνίημι συνίω	συνήσω	συνῆκα	συνεῖκα		
σῴζω	σώσω	ἔσωσα	σέσωκα	σέσωσμαι	ἐσώθην
τελέω	τελέσω	ἐτέλεσα	τετέλεκα	τετέλεσμαι	ἐτελέσθην
τηρέω	τηρήσω	ἐτήρησα	τετήρηκα	τετήρημαι	ἐτηρήθην
τίθημι [θε-, θη-, θει-, τε-]	θήσω	ἔθηκα	τέθεικα	τέθειμαι	ἐτέθην

Present	Future	Aorist (act./MP1)	Perfect (act.)	Perfect (MP)	Aorist (MP2)
ὑπάγω [ἀγαγ-]	ὑπάξω	ὑπήγαγον	ὑπῆχα	ὑπῆγμαι	ὑπήχθην
ὑπάρχω	ὑπάρξω	ὑπῆρξα		ὑπῆργμαι	ὑπήρχθην
ὑποστρέφω	ὑποστρέψω	ὑπέστρεψα	ὑπέστροφα	ὑπέστραμμαι	ὑπεστράφην
ὑποτάσσω [ταγ-]	ὑποτάξω	ὑπέταξα	ὑποτέταχα	ὑποτέταγμαι	ὑπετάχθην ὑπετάγην
φαίνω	φανῶ	ἔφανα	πέφηνα	πέφασμαι	ἐφάνην, fut. = φανήσομαι
φανερόω	φανερώσω	ἐφανέρωσα	πεφανέρωκα	πεφανέρωμαι	ἐφανερώθην
φέρω [οἰ-, ἐνεκ-]	οἴσω	ἤνεγκα	ἐνήνοχα		ἠνέχθην
φεύγω	φεύξομαι	ἔφυγον	πέφυγα	πέφυγμαι	ἐφεύχθην
φημί	φήσω	ἔφησα ἔφην			
φιλέω	φιλήσω	ἐφίλησα	πεφίληκα	πεφίλημαι	ἐφιλήθην
φοβέω	φοβήσω	ἐφόβησα	πεφόβηκα	πεφόβημαι	ἐφοβήθην
φρονέω	φρονήσω	ἐφρόνησα	πεφρόνηκα		
φυλάσσω [φυλακ-]	φυλάξω	ἐφύλαξα	πεφύλακα πεφύλαχα	πεφύλαγμαι	ἐφυλάχθην
φωνέω	φωνήσω	ἐφώνησα	πεφώνηκα	πεφώνημαι	ἐφωνήθην
χαίρω	χαρήσω	ἐχαίρησα	κεχάρηκα	κεχάρημαι	ἐχάρην

[a] δεῖ is the pres.-ind.-act.-3-sg. < δέω, *lack, need*. It is listed separately in lexicons because it has a distinct usage as an impersonal verb. Another word spelled δέω, *bind*, is listed in New Testament lexicons as δέομαι since the active is not used in the New Testament.

[b] εἴδω, from ϝιδ- (compare Latin *video*), means *see* in most tense-forms, but in the perfect it means *know*.[4] Some New Testament lexicons list εἶδον under ὁράω since it functions like the aorist of ὁράω, but BDAG and *CGEL* list εἶδον as a separate word. See note h below. New Testament lexicons list οἶδα as a separate word, since this perfect form functions as a present, and εἴδω is not listed because it is not used in the New Testament. See Montanari, 597–98; BDAG, 279, 693. See further §4.75c.

[c] ἔξεστιν is the pres.-ind.-act.-3-sg. < ἔξειμι, *be, exist*. It is listed separately in New Testament lexicons since it functions as an impersonal verb, and ἔξειμι is not used in the New Testament.

[d] ἴδε and ἰδού are 2-sg. aorist imperatives < εἶδον. Lexicons list them separately since

4. For the digamma (ϝ) see §4.75a.

they have become set expressions, used for both singular and plural. The acute accent on ἰδού is in contrast to the normal circumflex on the MP-2-sg. ἰδοῦ.

ᵉ ἐρῶ and the other three forms marked ᵉ are included under λέγω for convenience since they function as these tense-forms for the same meaning as λέγω and are listed under λέγω in some lexicons. They are actually forms of εἴρω and are listed as such in *CGEL* and Montanari. BDAG includes them under εἶπον.

ᶠ εἶπον is included as the aorist of λέγω for convenience, since it has that function and is listed this way in some lexicons. It is listed in BDAG, *CGEL*, and Montanari as a separate verb with only this form.

ᵍ ᾔδειν is a pluperfect but serves as an aorist, in keeping with οἶδα, a perfect form that serves as a present. See note b above.

ʰ εἶδον is included as the aorist of ὁράω for convenience, since it has that function and is listed this way in some lexicons. See note b above.

Glossary of Grammatical Terms

Active voice	The subject is the agent, the one doing the action, experiencing the state, or being described.
Adjective	A word giving information about a noun or pronoun.
Adverb	A word giving information about the meaning of a verb.
Agreement	Words sharing the same gender, case, and number.
Aktionsart	The kind of action conveyed by a verb through its aspect, the meaning of the verb, and signals in the context.
Alpha copulative	an α added to the front of a word signaling union or likeness, like "con-."
Alpha privative	an α added to the front of a word signaling the opposite meaning, like "a-" and "un-."
Anaphoric	A word or expression that refers back to something earlier in a text.
Antecedent	The word a relative pronoun refers to.
Aorist tense-form	A tense-form expressing aoristic aspect. In the indicative it is usually used for past time.
Aoristic aspect	A viewpoint from outside the verbal idea, seeing it as a whole.
Apposition	A nominal added to explain another nominal. Both have the same referent, the same syntactical relation to the rest of the clause, and are in agreement.
Aspect	The point of view or perspective a writer takes toward an action, event, or state as signaled by a verb's tense-form.
Atelic verb	A verb whose meaning does not inherently include the idea of completion of the action. For example, "I love."
Augment	Prefix on indicative verbs in the secondary tenses signaling past time.
Case	The form a nominal takes that signals its function in a clause.

467

Cataphoric	A word or expression that refers forward in a text.
Clause	A cluster of words that has a verb at its core.
Complement	A nominative, genitive, or dative that completes the meaning of a verb. Analogous to an accusative direct object.
Conjunction	A word joining words, clauses, or sentences.
Consecutive clause	Another name for a result clause.
Crasis	The joining of two words, for example, κἀγώ from καί + ἐγώ.
Declension	One of three general patterns of noun and adjective paradigms.
Dentals	The letters τ, δ, ϑ, which drop when a σ is added. ζ acts the same way.
Diaeresis	Two dots over the second vowel when two vowels are together but pronounced separately, not as a diphthong.
Diphthong	Two vowels together pronounced with a single sound.
Durative aspect	A viewpoint from within the verbal idea, seeing it as in process.
Elision	Omission of letters, marked with a single quotation mark: '.
Enclitic	A word that shares its accent with the preceding word.
Equative verb	A verb not referring to an action but making an assertion about the subject. The main equative verbs are εἰμί, γίνομαι, and ὑπάρχω.
Epexegetical	A word or construction that offers an explanation.
Final clause	Another name for a purpose clause.
Finite verb	A verb that has voice, person, and number. All verbal forms are finite except infinitives and participles.
Fronting	Placing a word or expression earlier than usual in a clause or sentence.
Future tense-form	A tense-form without an aspect, used for future time.
Gender	Masculine, feminine, and neuter. This grammatical gender often does not correspond with natural gender.
Gloss	A translation of a Greek word. "God" for ϑεός.
Grammar	The study of the inflections of words (morphology) and their functions and relations within sentences (syntax).
Gutturals	The letters γ, κ, χ, which become ξ when a σ is added. Also called palatals and velars.
Head term	A word modified by another word such as the noun modified by a genitive.
Hendiadys	Two words joined by καί to express a single complex idea.
Idiolect	An individual's style of speech and language.

Imperative mood	A verb form used for expressing a command, request, or suggestion.
Imperfect tense-form	A tense-form expressing durative aspect.
Indeclinable	A word that does not change its form.
Indicative mood	A verb form used for expressing a statement or question. The time frame is primarily conveyed with the indicative mood.
Inflection	Changes in the form of a word according to its function.
Intransitive verb	A verb that does not take a direct object.
Labials	The letters π, β, φ, which become ψ when a σ is added.
Lemma	The form a word takes when listed in a lexicon.
Lexeme	A basic word and its range of meanings apart from its inflected forms.
Linking vowel	A vowel used to join a verbal ending to a verb's stem. Also called a connecting vowel or thematic vowel.
Liquids	The letters λ, μ, ν, ρ, which cause the σ of the tense-form signs in the future and first aorist to drop. Technically, μ and ν are nasals.
Middle-only	A verb that prefers the middle and lacks an active form. It is used as a middle, but is translated with an active.
Middle voice	The subject is affected by the action of the verb.
Mood	The kind of expression being communicated as signaled by the verb's form, such as statements, questions, commands, conjectures, wishes.
Morpheme	A component of a word that has grammatical significance, such as a personal ending on a verb or the ending on a noun or adjective signaling gender, case, and number.
Morphology	The study of the inflectional patterns of words.
Nominal	The parts of speech that include nouns, pronouns, and adjectives.
Noun	A word for a person, place, or thing.
Number	Singular or plural. In CG there was also dual form used for a pair.
Object of a preposition	The noun or other substantive that joins with a preposition to form a prepositional phrase.
Optative mood	A verb form primarily used for expressing a wish.
Palatals	The letters γ, κ, χ, which become ξ when a σ is added. Also called gutturals and velars.
Paradigm	A specific inflectional pattern of a nominal or verbal.
Participle	A verbal adjective that may also function substantively and adverbially.
Passive voice	The subject is the patient, the one being acted on.

Pattern	In this book "pattern" often refers to one of the twelve core morphological patterns, some of which are also paradigms.
Perfect tense-form	A tense-form expressing resultative aspect. In the indicative it may focus on the present situation, the past event, or often both.
Periphrastic	A roundabout way of saying something. For example, the use of εἰμί and a participle to form a tense-form.
Person	First person (I, we), second person (you), third person (he/she/it, they).
Phrase	A cluster of words that does not have a verb at its core either explicitly or implicitly.
Pluperfect tense-form	A tense-form expressing resultative aspect. In the indicative it may focus on a past point of reference, the prior event, or both.
Postpositive	A particle that cannot come first in its clause.
Predicate complement	The complement with an equative verb that is describing the subject. Also referred to as a subject complement.
Preposition	A word joined with a substantive (the object of the preposition) to form a phrase that functions as an adverb, or, less often, an adjective.
Present tense-form	A tense-form expressing durative aspect. In the indicative it is usually used for present time.
Primary tense-forms	The present, future, and perfect tense-forms.
Proclitic	A word that shares its accent with the following word.
Pronoun	A word that takes the place of a noun already known from the context.
Reduplication	The doubled consonant with an ε or a lengthened vowel on a perfect or pluperfect tense-form. Also the doubled consonant with an ι on some μι verbs in the present and imperfect tense-forms.
Resultative aspect	A viewpoint from within a current situation in which an action/state has come about through a prior action or event.
Root	The underlying core of a word that is shared in common among various parts of speech within a word family.
Secondary tense-forms	The imperfect, aorist, and pluperfect tense-forms. These tense-forms are augmented in the indicative.
Semantic	Related to the expression of meaning in a language.
Semantic range	A word's range of meanings.
Stem	A word's root along with any additional elements that form the word's part of speech.
Subject complement	The complement with an equative verb that is describing the subject. Also referred to as a predicate complement, or predicate noun/adjective.

Subjunctive mood	A verb form used to express something that is possible, probable, or uncertain rather than definite.
Substantive	A part of speech functioning as a noun.
Syllabic augment	When an ε is added to a stem as an augment, thereby adding a syllable.
Syntax	The ways words join together to form phrases, clauses, and sentences.
Telic verb	A verb whose meaning inherently includes the idea of completion of the action. For example, "I close."
Tense-aspect stem	A verb stem with any additions or changes that signal its tense-form.
Tense-form	The forms verbs take to express different aspects and, in the indicative, different time frames.
Transitive verb	A verb that takes a direct object.
Transliteration	Representation of a Greek word in English letters. For example, "theos" for θεός.
Velars	The letters γ, κ, χ, which become ξ when a σ is added. Also called gutturals and palatals.
Vowel gradation	A shift in vowels or in the length of a vowel within the forms of a word.
Zero form	A blank ending on a nominal or verbal.

Bibliography

Aland, Barbara, Kurt Aland, Johannes Karavidopoulos, Carlo M. Martini, Bruce Metzger, Barclay Newman, and Florian Voss, eds. *The UBS Greek New Testament: A Reader's Edition.* 5th ed. Stuttgart: Deutsche Bibelgesellschaft, 2014.

Allan, Rutger J. *The Middle Voice in Ancient Greek: A Study in Polysemy.* Amsterdam Studies in Classical Philology 11. Amsterdam: Gieben, 2003.

Allen, W. Sidney. *Vox Graeca: The Pronunciation of Classical Greek.* 3rd ed. Cambridge: Cambridge University Press, 1987.

Arndt, William F., Walter Bauer, and F. Wilbur Gingrich. *A Greek-English Lexicon of the New Testament and Other Early Christian Literature.* Chicago: University of Chicago Press, 1957.

Aubrey, Michael G. "The Greek Perfect Tense-Form: Understanding Its Usage and Meaning." Pages 55–82 in *Linguistics and New Testament Greek: Key Issues in the Current Debate.* Edited by David Alan Black and Benjamin L. Merkle. Grand Rapids: Baker Academic, 2020.

———. "Greek Prohibitions." Pages 486–538 in *The Greek Verb Revisited: A Fresh Approach for Biblical Exegesis.* Edited by Steven E. Runge and Christopher J. Fresch. Bellingham, WA: Lexham Press, 2016.

Aubrey, Rachel. "Motivated Categories, Middle Voice, and Passive Morphology." Pages 563–625 in *The Greek Verb Revisited: A Fresh Approach for Biblical Exegesis.* Edited by Steven E. Runge and Christopher J. Fresch. Bellingham, WA: Lexham Press, 2016.

Bakker, Egbert J. *A Companion to the Ancient Greek Language.* Oxford: Blackwell, 2010.

Baugh, Steven M. *Ephesians.* Evangelical Exegetical Commentary. Bellingham, WA: Lexham Press, 2016.

———. "Greek Periods in the Book of Hebrews." *Novum Testamentum* 60 (2018): 24–44.

———. "Hyperbaton and Greek Literary Style in Hebrews." *Novum Testamentum* 59 (2017): 194–213.

———. *Introduction to Greek Tense Form Choice in the Non-Indicative Moods.* Self-published, 2009. Available as a pdf (https://dailydoseofgreek.com/wp-content/uploads/sites/2/2015/09/GreekTenseFormChoice-Baugh.pdf); and

print (http://www.lulu.com/shop/sm-baugh/introduction-to-greek-tense
-form-choice/paperback/product-4631581.html).

Beekes, Robert. *Etymological Dictionary of Greek.* 2 vols. Leiden Indo-European Etymological Dictionary Series 10. Leiden: Brill, 2010.

Biblehub. https://biblehub.com.Biblical Language Center. https://www.biblicallan
guagecenter.com/.

Black, David Alan. *Learn to Read New Testament Greek.* 3rd ed. Nashville: B&H Academic, 2009.

Boler, Michael. *Introduction to Classical and New Testament Greek: A Unified Approach.*
Washington, DC: Catholic Education Press, 2020.

Bortone, Pietro. *Greek Prepositions from Antiquity to the Present.* Oxford: Oxford University Press, 2010.

Burton, Ernest De Witt. *Syntax of the Moods and Tenses in New Testament Greek.* 3rd
ed. Edinburgh: T&T Clark, 1898. https://archive.org/details/syntaxmoodsandt
00burtgoog.

Buth, Randall. https://www.biblicallanguagecenter.com/.

———. "Participles as Pragmatic Choice: Where Semantics Meets Pragmatics." Pages
273–306 in *The Greek Verb Revisited: A Fresh Approach for Biblical Exegesis.* Edited by Steven E. Runge and Christopher J. Fresch. Bellingham, WA: Lexham
Press, 2016.

———. "The Role of Pronunciation in New Testament Greek Studies." Pages 169–94
in *Linguistics and New Testament Greek: Key Issues in the Current Debate.* Edited
by David Alan Black and Benjamin L. Merkle. Grand Rapids: Baker Academic, 2020.

———. "Ἡ Κοινὴ Προφορά Koiné Pronunciation: Notes on the Pronunciation System of Koiné Greek." https://www.biblicallanguagecenter.com/koine-greek
-pronunciation/; http://www.biblicallanguagecenter.com/wp-content/up
loads/2012/08/Koine-Pronunciation-2012.pdf.

Campbell, Constantine R. "Aspect and Tense in New Testament Greek." Pages 37–53
in *Linguistics and New Testament Greek: Key Issues in the Current Debate.* Edited
by David Alan Black and Benjamin L. Merkle. Grand Rapids: Baker Academic, 2020.

———. *Basics of Verbal Aspect in Biblical Greek.* Grand Rapids: Zondervan, 2008.

Caragounis, Chrys C. *The Development of Greek and the New Testament: Morphology, Syntax, Phonology, and Textual Transmission.* Grand Rapids: Baker Academic, 2006.

Carson, D. A. *Greek Accents: A Student's Manual.* Grand Rapids: Baker, 1985.

Clarke, Michael. "Semantics and Vocabulary." Pages 120–33 in *A Companion to the
Ancient Greek Language.* Edited by Egbert J. Bakker. Oxford: Blackwell, 2010.

Coderch, Juan. *Greek Grammar: A New Grammar; Greek Grammar Taught and Explained,
with Examples.* CreateSpace, 2012.

Comrie, Bernard. *Language Universals and Linguistic Typology: Syntax and Morphology.*
Chicago: University of Chicago Press, 1981.

Conrad, Carl. "Active, Middle, and Passive: Understanding Ancient Greek Voice."

December 16, 2003. https://pages.wustl.edu/files/pages/imce/cwconrad/un dancgrkvc.pdf.

Daily Dose of Greek. http://dailydoseofgreek.com/.

Decker, Rodney J. *Reading Koine Greek: An Introduction and Integrated Workbook.* Grand Rapids: Baker Academic, 2014.

Denniston, J. D. *The Greek Particles.* 2nd ed. Revised by K. J. Dover. London: Duckworth, 1950.

Dooley, Robert A., and Stephen H. Levinsohn. *Analyzing Discourse: A Manual of Basic Concepts.* Dallas: SIL International, 2001.

Duolingo. https://www.duolingo.com/.

Ellis, Nicholas J. "Aspect-Prominence, Morpho-Syntax, and a Cognitive-Linguistic Framework for the Greek Verb." Pages 122–60 in *The Greek Verb Revisited: A Fresh Approach for Biblical Exegesis.* Edited by Steven E. Runge and Christopher J. Fresch. Bellingham, WA: Lexham Press, 2016.

Fanning, Buist M. *Verbal Aspect in New Testament Greek.* Oxford Theological Monographs. Oxford: Clarendon, 1990.

Fresch, Christopher J. "Typology, Polysemy, and Prototypes: Situating Nonpast Aorist Indicatives." Pages 379–415 in *The Greek Verb Revisited: A Fresh Approach for Biblical Exegesis.* Edited by Steven E. Runge and Christopher J. Fresch. Bellingham, WA: Lexham Press, 2016.

Friberg, Timothy, Barbara Friberg, and Neva F. Miller. *Analytical Lexicon of the Greek New Testament.* Grand Rapids: Baker Academic, 2000.

Funk, Robert W. "Appendix II: Nominal System Catalogue." https://westarinstitute .org/wp-content/uploads/Appendix-2-Catalog-of-the-Nominal-System.pdf.

———. "Appendix III: Verbal System Catalogue." https://westarinstitute.org/wp -content/uploads/Appendix-3-Verbal-System-Catalogue.pdf.

Gentry, Peter J. "The Function of the Augment in Hellenistic Greek." Pages 353–78 in *The Greek Verb Revisited: A Fresh Approach for Biblical Exegesis.* Edited by Steven E. Runge and Christopher J. Fresch. Bellingham, WA: Lexham Press, 2016.

George, Coulter H. "Jewish and Christian Greek." Pages 267–80 in *A Companion to the Ancient Greek Language.* Edited by Egbert J. Bakker. Oxford: Blackwell, 2010.

Gibson, Jeffrey. *The Disciples' Prayer: The Prayer Jesus Taught in Its Historical Setting.* Minneapolis: Fortress, 2015.

Goodrich, Richard J., and Albert L. Lukaszewski, eds. *A Reader's Greek New Testament.* 2nd ed. Grand Rapids: Zondervan, 2007.

Greenwood, Kyle. *Dictionary of English Grammar for Students of Biblical Languages.* Grand Rapids: Zondervan, 2020.

Hadley, James, and Frederic Forest De Allen. *A Greek Grammar for Schools and Colleges.* New York: D. Appleton and Company, 1885.

Hale, William Gardner. *The Art of Reading Latin: How to Teach It.* Boston: Ginn, 1887. https://archive.org/details/artofreadinglatioohale.

Harris, Murray J. *Prepositions and Theology in the Greek New Testament.* Grand Rapids: Zondervan, 2012.

Harvey, John D. *Listening to the Text: Oral Patterning in Paul's Letters*. Evangelical Theological Society Studies Series. Grand Rapids: Baker, 1998.

Horrocks, Geoffrey. *Greek: A History of the Language and Its Speakers*. 2nd ed. Chichester: Wiley, 2014.

Jongkind, Dirk, Peter J. Williams, Peter M. Head, and Patrick James, eds. *The Greek New Testament: Reader's Edition*. Reader's textual notes compiled by Drayton C. Brenner, James R. Covington, and Andrew Zulker. Wheaton, IL: Crossway, 2018. This is the reader's edition of *The Greek New Testament, Produced at Tyndale House, Cambridge*.

Kemmer, Suzanne. *The Middle Voice*. Typological Studies in Language 23. Amsterdam: Benjamins, 1993.

Kühner, Raphael. *Grammar of the Greek Language: Principally from the German of Kühner*. Translated by William Edward Jelf. 2 vols. New York: Appleton, 1852.

Lakoff, George, and Mark Johnson. *Metaphors We Live By*. Chicago: University of Chicago Press, 2003.

Lamerson, Samuel. *English Grammar to Ace New Testament Greek*. Grand Rapids: Zondervan, 2004.

Lanier, Gregory R., and William A. Ross, eds. *Septuaginta: A Reader's Edition*. 2 vols. Peabody, MA: Hendrickson; Stuttgart: Deutsche Bibelgesellschaft, 2018.

Lee, John A. L. Basics of Greek Accents: Eight Lessons with Exercises. Grand Rapids: Zondervan, 2018.

———. "Etymological Follies: Three Recent Lexicons of the New Testament." *Novum Testamentum* 55 (2013): 383–403.

———. *A History of New Testament Lexicography*. Studies in Biblical Greek 8. New York: Lang, 2003.

Lee, Margaret Ellen, and Bernard Brandon Scott. *Sound Mapping the New Testament*. Salem, OR: Polebridge, 2009.

Levinsohn, Stephen H. "Discourse Analysis: Galatians as a Case Study." Pages 103–24 in *Linguistics and New Testament Greek: Key Issues in the Current Debate*. Edited by David Alan Black and Benjamin L. Merkle. Grand Rapids: Baker Academic, 2020.

———. *Discourse Features of New Testament Greek: A Coursebook on the Information Structure of New Testament Greek*. 2nd ed. Dallas: SIL International, 2000.

Lewis, C. S. *Studies in Words*. 2nd ed. Cambridge: Cambridge University Press, 1967.

Long, Fredrick J. Κοινὴ Γραμματικῇ *Koine Greek Grammar: A Beginning-Intermediate Exegetical and Pragmatic Handbook*. Wilmore, KY: GlossaHouse, 2015.

Long, Gary A. *Grammatical Concepts 101 for Biblical Greek: Learning Biblical Greek Grammatical Concepts through English Grammar*. Peabody, MA: Hendrickson, 2006.

Louw, Johannes E., and Eugene A. Nida. *Greek-English Lexicon of the New Testament: Based on Semantic Domains*. 2 vols. 2nd ed. New York: United Bible Societies, 1989.

Mango Languages. https://www.mangolanguages.com.

Mastronarde, Donald J. *Introduction to Attic Greek*. 2nd ed. Berkeley: University of California Press, 2013.

Mathewson, David L., and Elodie Ballantine Emig. *Intermediate Greek Grammar: Syntax for Students of the New Testament.* Grand Rapids: Baker Academic, 2016.

Mayor, Joseph B. *The Epistle of St. James: The Greek Text with Introduction, Notes, and Comments.* 2nd ed. 1897. Repr., Grand Rapids: Baker, 1978.

McMenomy, Bruce A. *Syntactical Mechanics: A New Approach to English, Latin, and Greek.* New edition. Oklahoma Studies in Classical Culture 51. Norman: University of Oklahoma Press, 2014.

Metzger, Bruce M. *Lexical Aids for Students of New Testament Greek.* 3rd ed. Grand Rapids: Baker Academic, 1998.

Miller, Neva F. "A Theory of Deponent Verbs." Pages 423–30, Appendix 2, in *Analytical Lexicon of the Greek New Testament.* Edited by Barbara Friberg, Timothy Friberg, and Neva F. Miller. Grand Rapids: Baker, 2000.

Morwood, James, and John Taylor, eds. *The Pocket Oxford Classical Greek Dictionary.* Oxford: Oxford University Press, 2002.

Moulton, James Hope. *A Grammar of New Testament Greek.* Vol. 1, *Prolegomena.* 3rd ed. Edinburgh: T&T Clark, 1908.

Moulton, James Hope, and Wilbert Francis Howard. *A Grammar of New Testament Greek.* Vol. 2, *Accidence and Word-formation with an Appendix on Semitisms in the New Testament.* Edinburgh: T&T Clark, 1929.

Moulton, James Hope, and Nigel Turner. *A Grammar of New Testament Greek.* Vol. 3, *Syntax.* Edinburgh: T&T Clark, 1963.

———. *A Grammar of New Testament Greek.* Vol. 4, *Style.* Edinburgh: T&T Clark, 1976.

Mounce, William D. *The Morphology of Biblical Greek.* Grand Rapids: Zondervan, 1994.

Mueller, Hans-Friedrich. *Greek 101: Learning an Ancient Language.* Great Courses. Chantilly, VA: Teaching Company, 2016.

Muraoka, T. *A Syntax of Septuagint Greek.* Leuven: Peeters, 2016.

The NET Bible. Biblical Studies Press, 2006. https://netbible.org/bible/Matthew+1.

Newman, Barclay M. *A Concise Greek-English Dictionary of the New Testament.* Rev. ed. Stuttgart: Deutsche Bibelgesellschaft, 2010.

Nunn, H. P. V. *A Short Syntax of New Testament Greek.* 5th ed. Cambridge: Cambridge University Press, 1938. https://archive.org/details/shortsyntaxofnewoohpvn/page/n5/mode/2up.

Pennington, Jonathan T. "The Greek Middle Voice." Pages 83–102 in *Linguistics and New Testament Greek: Key Issues in the Current Debate.* Edited by David Alan Black and Benjamin L. Merkle. Grand Rapids: Baker Academic, 2020.

Perschbacher, Wesley J. *New Testament Greek Syntax: An Illustrated Manual.* Chicago: Moody Press, 1995.

Perseus Digital Library. http://www.perseus.tufts.edu/hopper/collection?collection=Perseus:collection:Greco-Roman.

Porter, Stanley E. *Idioms of the Greek New Testament.* Biblical Languages: Greek 2. Sheffield: Sheffield Academic, 1992.

———. *Verbal Aspect in the Greek of the New Testament, with Reference to Tense and Mood.* Studies in Biblical Greek 1. New York: Lang, 1989.

Robar, Elizabeth. "The Historical Present in NT Greek: An Exercise in Interpreting

Matthew." Pages 329–52 in *The Greek Verb Revisited: A Fresh Approach for Biblical Exegesis*. Edited by Steven E. Runge and Christopher J. Fresch. Bellingham, WA: Lexham Press, 2016.

Robertson, A. T. *A Grammar of the Greek New Testament in the Light of Historical Research*. 4th ed. Nashville: Broadman, 1934.

Robinson, Thomas A. *Mastering New Testament Greek: Essential Tools for Students*. Grand Rapids: Baker Academic, 2007.

Runge, Steven E. "The Contribution of Verb Forms, Connectives, and Dependency to Grounding Status in Nonnarrative Discourse." Pages 221–72 in *The Greek Verb Revisited: A Fresh Approach for Biblical Exegesis*. Edited by Steven E. Runge and Christopher J. Fresch. Bellingham, WA: Lexham Press, 2016.

———. "Interpreting Constituent Order in Koine Greek." Pages 125–46 in *Linguistics and New Testament Greek: Key Issues in the Current Debate*. Edited by David Alan Black and Benjamin L. Merkle. Grand Rapids: Baker Academic, 2020.

Song, Jae Jung. *Word Order*. Research Surveys in Linguistics. Cambridge: Cambridge University Press, 2012.

Spicq, Ceslaus. *Theological Lexicon of the New Testament*. Translated by James D. Ernest. 3 vols. Peabody, MA: Hendrickson, 1994.

Stagg, Frank. "The Abused Aorist." *Journal of Biblical Literature* 91 (1972): 222–31.

Taylor, Bernard A. "Deponency and Greek Lexicography." Pages 167–76 in *Biblical Greek Language and Lexicography: Essays in Honor of Frederick W. Danker*. Edited by Bernard A. Taylor, John A. L. Lee, Peter R. Burton, and Richard E. Whitaker. Grand Rapids: Eerdmans, 2004.

Thrall, Margaret E. *Greek Particles in the New Testament: Linguistic and Exegetical Studies*. New Testament Tools and Studies 3. Leiden: Brill, 1962.

Tripp, Kristopher D. *RAW Greek Dictionary: By Root and Prefix*. Self-published e-book, 2013.

Van Voorst, Robert E. *Building Your New Testament Greek Vocabulary*. 3rd ed. Resources for Biblical Study 40. Atlanta: Society of Biblical Literature, 1999.

Wallace, Daniel B. *Granville Sharp's Canon and Its Kin: Semantics and Significance*. Studies in Biblical Greek 14. New York: Lang, 2009.

Whitacre, Rodney A. *John*. IVP New Testament Commentary 4. Downers Grove, IL: InterVarsity Press, 1999.

———. Videos for *Using and Enjoying Biblical Greek*. https://www.youtube.com/playlist?list=PL1T3_pkcZpPWCBfJshZ38biQkSy-_vJXB.

Young, Richard. *Intermediate New Testament Greek: A Linguistic and Exegetical Approach*. Nashville: Broadman & Holman, 1994.

Zerwick, Maximilian, SJ. *Biblical Greek: Illustrated by Examples*. Rome: Biblical Institute Press, 1963.

Zerwick, Maximilian, and Mary Grosvenor. *An Analysis of the Greek New Testament*. 5th ed. Subsidia Biblica 39. Rome: Biblical Institute Press, 2010.

Index of Subjects

Greek letters and words are alphabetized according to their English transliteration.

Index of Scripture

Index of Greek Words